HUMAN LEARNING

Thomas Hardy Leahey
Virginia Commonwealth University

Richard Jackson Harris
Kansas State University

Prentice-Hall, Inc. Englewood Cliffs, New Jersey 07632

Library of Congress Cataloging in Publication Data

LEAHEY, THOMAS HARDY.
  Human learning.

  Includes bibliographies and index.
  1. Learning, Psychology of. 2. Learning—
Physiological aspects. 3. Human behavior. 4. Cog-
nition. 1. Harris, Richard Jackson. II. Title.
BF318.L37 1985   153.1   84-13381
ISBN 0-13-445164-3

Editorial/production supervision and
  interior design: Dee A. Josephson
Cover design: Ben Santora
Manufacturing buyer: Ron Chapman/Barbara Kittle

Printed in the United States of America

10 9 8 7 6 5 4 3 2 1

ISBN 0-13-445164-3   01

Prentice-Hall International, Inc., *London*
Prentice-Hall of Australia Pty. Limited, *Sydney*
Editora Prentice-Hall do Brasil, Ltda., *Rio de Janeiro*
Prentice-Hall Canada Inc., *Toronto*
Prentice-Hall of India Private Limited, *New Delhi*
Prentice-Hall of Japan, Inc., *Tokyo*
Prentice-Hall of Southeast Asia Pte. Ltd., *Singapore*
Whitehall Books Limited, *Wellington, New Zealand*

To William F. Brewer
mentor, friend and teacher,
and a truly scholarly cognitive psychologist

He modeled for us not only a scholar's quest for knowledge through
research, but also a scholar's commitment and excitement in
communicating this knowledge in the classroom.

CONTENTS

v

PREFACE

Until World War II, and for some years after it, the psychology of learning was the heart of psychology. Since then, so many new fields have been born or have grown—social psychology, developmental psychology, consumer psychology, clinical psychology, counseling psychology—that psychology no longer has a single vital center, but many. At the same time, the cognitive revolt against the behaviorist learning theory of the 1930's, 40's and 50's seemed to topple the study of learning and replace it with the study of cognition. Today, the psychology of learning as a distinct, identifiable field scarcely exists in the shifting boundaries of our protean discipline.

Still, the concept of learning involves change, and almost all psychologists study change: the clinician or counselor wants to change the client's behavior; the social psychologist to understand attitude change; the developmental psychologist, how children, adolescents, adults, and the elderly change. Broadly understood, then, while learning is no longer at the heart of psychology, it may be found throughout, and its study remains an important one for every psychologist.

We wrote this book with a broad treatment of learning in mind. You will read about learning in animals and in humans, in children and in adults, in advertising and in science, and in the individual and in the species. Our focus throughout is on human learning—how people change their behavior, understand their world, and adapt to changing circumstances.

We bring to our task a similarity of background, but a divergence in interests. We were both trained in cognitive psychology at the University of Illinois at Urbana-Champaign in the early 1970's, Thomas Leahey specializing in cognitive development and reasoning, Richard Harris in psycholinguistics. We each owe an intellectual debt to William F. Brewer, our mentor and teacher, an unorthodox cognitive psychologist who taught us to see technical questions against larger backgrounds, and to connect apparently distant ideas. Thomas Leahey's interests turned to the history and philosophy of psychology (*A History of Psychology*, 1980; *Psychology's Occult Doubles*, 1983) and to sociobiology. Richard Harris's continued in psycholinguistics, but moved into applied (*Information Processing Research in Advertising*, 1983) as well as basic research.

Many debts are incurred in writing a book. THL benefited from discussions with colleagues Don Forsyth, Bob Hamm, and Joe Porter, and with Grace Leahey, who also read and edited his chapters (1–4, 10–12, and the Reasoning section of 9). RJH appreciated the helpful comments of Tony Dubitsky, Charles Thompson, and Mário Perini, as well as students on whom early drafts of chapters 5–9 were inflicted as class assignments.

We both found useful the thoughtful reviews of prepublication reviewers:

Randall Engle, University of South Carolina
Howard R. Pollio, University of Tennessee
Michael L. Epstein, Rider College
Chizuko Izawa, Tulane University
Joel S. Freund, University of Arkansas
Robert E. Prytula, Middle Tennessee State University
Janet M. Leonard, Siena College
George A. Cicala, University of Delaware

The support of Psychology Editor John Isley and his staff at Prentice-Hall was also encouraging and appreciated.

What was once our personal property and our private thoughts are now set down and fixed in print. We hope to aid your own learning about psychology, and to interest and excite you about studying how you and your fellow humans learn.

HUMAN
LEARNING

CHAPTER ONE
LEARNING AND PSYCHOLOGY

THE SCIENCE OF LEARNING

So much has been written about the psychology of learning that no text can pretend to cover it all. Learning has been a central topic of psychology for most of its hundred years, and learning is involved in every field of study.

Development: How do children learn to be adults?
Social psychology: How are sex roles learned?
Personality: What part of personality is learned?
Abnormal psychology: How do people learn pathological behavior patterns, and how can we help people unlearn them?
Perception: How do we learn to see the world as we do?
Linguistics: How is language learned?
Psychopharmacology: How do drugs affect learning?
Physiological psychology: How is the nervous system changed by learning?
Applied psychology: How can we teach children more effectively? How can we improve industrial efficiency and manage business more productively?

So it is no surprise that the psychology of learning is like an old and growing volcano, spewing forth technical reports, articles, books, and symposia at an alarming rate. Our problem is to wade through the volcanic ash and hardening magma to pick out the most important features of the volcano of learning. To help us choose among the pile of works, we need some principles.

We will use two sorts of principles. One is borrowed from the field of philosophy of science, where recent students of science have proposed some useful ideas for getting at the nature of scientific practice and progress. From the profusion of studies, we will use these ideas to unravel the main threads of development in the psychology of learning.

The second organizing principle focuses our attention on three major problems with which psychologists of learning have wrestled. Naturally, the questions addressed in the field number far more than three, but these three have done more than all others to shape the field and are, moreover, as yet unresolved, perhaps even unresolvable.

In this chapter we will also briefly discuss ideas about learning that held sway before psychology was officially begun in 1879. Psychologists do not pluck ideas out of thin air as a magician plucks coins, and pre–1879 notions about learning have been a fertile and continuing source of psychological ideas.

Paradigms and Research Programs

Most people think scientists are diligent beachcombers on the sands of reality. They go about, without any particular hypothesis or theory in mind, picking up interesting facts here and there. After a while, the scientists sit down with their piles of facts and try to discover a law that will explain all the facts. If a fact does not fit, a proposed law is known to be incorrect. Eventually, some bright scientist comes up with an adequate law, other scientists accept it, and beachcombing begins on a new beach of facts. Eventually, as law is added to law, a comprehensive picture of reality takes shape. Presumably at some point everything will be known, and scientists will have to look for new jobs.

But psychologists, of all people, should suspect this notion. Scientists are people, and people have interests and commitments that mean they are never free of ideas and hypotheses. Scientists are people who live in a particular culture, and in a particular segment of that culture, in the community of science. Psychologists know that cultures and communities deeply determine the way a person thinks, sees, and behaves, and they should know that this can be no less true of scientists than for other people. In the last two decades historians and philosophers of science have confirmed these suspicions and have offered alternative accounts of science that we can use to organize our discussion of learning.

The hidden preconceptions of scientists and the important role of the scientific community have been studied by Thomas Kuhn (1970). Kuhn argues that during long stretches of **normal science,** young scientists are effectively taught a set of theories and methods called a **paradigm.** The paradigm tells a young scientist what the world is generally like, indicates unanswered scientific questions, and provides acceptable methods for answering them. The paradigm is an unconsciously held world view that lets the scientists work on specific questions rather than wander aimlessly in a muddle of questions too deep for science to solve, questions such as, "Do we have immortal souls or are we just environmentally determined machines?" Such questions, so far at least, cannot be answered by science to the satisfaction of the religious, or by religion to the satisfaction of the scientific. Such questions, therefore, would clutter up the scientist's mind if they were not unconsciously answered by the paradigm.

Armed with a paradigm, then, scientists conduct research, or practice normal science, what Kuhn calls **puzzle solving.** Just as a jigsaw puzzle solver assumes the picture on the box is an accurate guide to solving the puzzle, so the normal scientist assumes the general accuracy of what he or she has learned, that is, of the paradigm. Naturally, a paradigm can be only a general picture of the way things work. The goal of science is to fill in the missing details. Moreover, since scientists do not work alone they come to a puzzle already partly done, and they join a group of scientists working on one part of that puzzle. Still, the scientist's job is like that of a puzzle solver—to find just the right piece that will fit in with what is already known and add a bit of detail to the emerging picture. Scientists are not free to do anything they want, and by and large cannot tell everyone that they have got everything all wrong. Bringing forward puzzle pieces that do not fit in will make their colleagues dismiss them as cranks, or even as frauds. Odd pieces will be dismissed as a piece from a long-distant part of the puzzle, or from a pseudopuzzle that exists only in one's mind.

To Kuhn, then, normal science is a cautious extension into the unknown from a solid base of the known. Each new piece of research must be designed to extend what is known one step further, to provide a new detail to the paradigm. Normal science, however, does undergo periods of crisis, or of extraordinary science, that may lead to scientific revolutions. Frequently in the history of science the scientific community *did* have it all wrong. Scientists found themselves with a paradigm increasingly inconsistent with new research findings. Under these circumstances wild ideas may be tolerated. Eventually a new paradigm is put forward, one that successfully deals with the problematic details. If so, a revolution will take place in which scientists will adopt a new paradigm. Normal science then resumes, although the top of the puzzle box is different, for now the puzzles to be solved are different.

While Kuhn's ideas are controversial (Shapere, 1964; Scheffler, 1967; Toulmin, 1972), he shows that science cannot be practiced like beachcombing, without a paradigm. Imagine trying to solve a large and intricate puzzle with no box top to go by. Without an idea of the subject of the puzzle, all you have is a meaningless assemblage of oddly shaped bits of colored cardboard. With a box top, each piece has meaning—this is a bit of Napolean's hat, of his left foot—and can be fitted into the picture eventually. Working carefully from one part to another, you ignore a few strange pieces, confident that as you get to the end they too will find their proper places, even if at the moment you have no idea where they should go. Science must work in this way if it hopes to progress.

A related but more specific perspective on scientific research is offered by Imre Lakatos (1970). Instead of looking at a scientific field as a whole, Lakatos focuses on individual *research programs* that may be pursued by as small a scientific group as one. A research program investigates a limited problem developing over time.

At its center is a set of general ideas, rather like Kuhn's paradigm, that are very rarely questioned. Lakatos calls this the **"hard core"** of the research program. An example from a research program in learning might be, "All learning results from reinforcement." These general statements raise questions that may be addressed by specific hypotheses. What happens if reinforcement amount is varied? If the time between response and reinforcement is varied? If we reinforce only some, but not all, of the responses? Each of these questions may generate several hypotheses that can be tested in the laboratory. Taking the last question, one might propose that partial reinforcement will weaken a response compared to continuous reinforcement and do an experiment comparing the two kinds of reinforcement.

Lakatos calls the specific hypotheses that grow out of the hard core the **protective belt.** This seems an odd name until we reflect on what happens when a hypothesis proves false—as they usually do. For example, the hypothesis that partial reinforcement weakens a response would be proven wrong (see Chapter 4). But scientists would not abandon their hard-core belief that all learning involves reinforcement. Instead, they would retain that belief and change the specific hypothesis to "partial reinforcement strengthens a response," a hypothesis that in turn would spin off yet more specific hypotheses about why this is the case. In any event, the hypothesis about the weakening effect of partial reinforcement *protected* the hard-core belief that all learning involves reinforcement.

As a research program develops, hard-core theory changes little if at all, while the protective belt of hypotheses is continually adjusted as new information arrives. The trick for the practicing scientist who is looking for a puzzle to solve is always to devise a hypothesis that is consistent with both available data and the accepted hard-core theory of one's discipline.

The psychology of learning has been organized under several paradigms and pursued by several research programs. Therefore we can use Kuhn's and Lakatos' concepts to penetrate to the core of theories of learning, to illuminate how research on learning is organized, and to pick out essential lines of development. As a first illustration of the method, we will examine the first experimental research on learning.

A Case Study: Ebbinghaus on Memory

In 1879 Hermann Ebbinghaus began to use himself as the only subject in the first experimental investigations of learning and memory. As the pioneer in the psychology of learning, Ebbinghaus gives us a chance to observe the formation and early stages of a research program.

Although he does not say so explicitly it is clear that the hard core of Ebbinghaus' program was built on **associationism.** By the nineteenth century, most philosophical psychologists thought of the mind as a sort of tinkertoy arrangement. Your mind is full of ideas: "Horse," "boy," "telephone," "Ebbinghaus," and so on. Associationists believe that these ideas are connected to one another by a kind of mental thread—Ebbinghaus' term—that is, an *association.*

Everyone with even a passing acquaintance with psychology has heard of *free-association tests:* "Say the first word that comes to your mind when I say _____." Likely free associates would be boy–girl, horse–rider, telephone–call, Ebbinghaus–memory. According to the associationists, when you learn something you learn an idea (for example, the idea of "associationism") and tie it, or associate it, to other ideas you already have. Thus, you learn to associate, for a multiple-choice test perhaps, "associationism" with "Ebbinghaus" and "mental thread." Pushing this theory as far as it can go, associationists argue that mind and behavior are just collections of ideas or responses linked by association, and that the basic problem of the psychology of learning is finding out how people learn to associate ideas.

Ebbinghaus was the first person to use experiments to find out how ideas and associations are learned. His most important achievement was thinking of an experimental procedure to substitute for philosophical speculation. According to Kuhn, an important part of a paradigm is the **shared exemplar,** a concrete model of a good experiment. The shared exemplar is important because it poses puzzles to the experimenter by offering specific independent variables to manipulate and specific dependent variables to measure. It shows a scientist how to manipulate which parts of the reality he or she sees through the paradigm.

Ebbinghaus saw that in starting out in a new field, as memory then was, he would have to simplify the problem to be solved. Most of our learning is both complex and haphazard. You sit down in your chemistry class and listen to the lecture. The material you must learn is complicated; you do not have time to ask yourself, "How am I learning this?" So a simple, controllable bit of learning is needed for scientific study.

How and what you learn will also be affected by irrelevant influences such as time of day, interest in chemistry, and the attractive student in the next row. To avoid such complications, Ebbinghaus simplified the material to be learned and introduced experimental control.

To simplify the material, Ebbinghaus invented the **nonsense syllable,** constructed by placing a vowel between two consonants: TOB, SAB, GEN, and so on. They were easy to make up and produced a large amount of learnable material. Being meaningless, they simplified the process of learning to sheer memorization, ruling out such factors as motivation, interest, and relevance to what has already been learned. Ebbinghaus believed they would reveal the processes of learning, retention, and forgetting, unclouded by any other mental processes. We may also suggest that they resemble the associationists' **simple ideas,** the basic tinkertoy nodes of the mind.

To impose experimental control, Ebbinghaus would compose lists of syllables to be presented to himself at a constant rate of speed, and at consistent times of the day. The whole procedure was easily quantifiable:

Ebbinghaus could measure how long it took him to learn or relearn lists of syllables as he changed independent variables. He hoped to hit on scientific laws that govern the process of learning and, thus, to transform at least part of psychology from a branch of philosophy into a branch of experimental science. Having in place a hard core, or paradigm—the theory of associationism and the experimental setup of learning lists of syllables—Ebbinghaus could ask the specific, testable questions of normal science.

One of the most obvious facts about memory is that the longer ago we learned something, the harder it is to remember. On the basis of personal experience we can say no more than that—hardly a scientific statement. But Ebbinghaus' experimental approach made it possible to frame the question more precisely and receive a quantitative answer. In a series of experiments, Ebbinghaus learned by heart eight lists of 13 nonsense syllables each; later, after differing amounts of time (20 minutes, 1 hour, 8.8 hours, 1 day, 2 days, 6 days, or 31 days), he learned them by heart again. Consequently, Ebbinghaus could ask precisely, in terms of difficulty of relearning: How much of a list of nonsense syllables is forgotten at a given time?

Figure 1–1 illustrates the results of Ebbinghaus' experiments; it shows the percent of material forgotten as a function of hours after initial learning. Most forgetting takes place quickly. Only an hour after learning, more than 55 percent of the nonsense syllables have been forgotten, while the additional loss past 8.8 hours is only 14 percent after 31 days. Common sense told us only that we forget over time. Ebbinghaus showed exactly how

FIGURE 1–1   Ebbinghaus Curve of Forgetting. (Based on Ebbinghaus 1885, p. 76.)

After 6 days (144 hrs.) — 74.6% forgotten
After 31 days (744 hrs.) — 78.9% forgotten

PERCENT FORGOTTEN

HOURS AFTER INITIAL MEMORIZATION

forgetting takes place, rapidly at first and then more slowly; moreover, he managed to quantify the rate of forgetting.

Ebbinghaus' invention of the nonsense syllable learning experiment also enabled him to investigate precisely other common sense hypotheses. He asked, What is the effect of amount of material on learning? He quantified amount as nonsense syllable list-length, and obtained quantitative results showing (not surprisingly) that the longer the list the longer it takes to learn. He compared learning a list of nonsense syllables to learning a stanza of poetry from Byron's *Don Juan,* and found that learning the poem was easier, notwithstanding the fact that the poem contained many more syllables than the lists. This demonstrates that the more organized material is, the easier it is to learn. Nonsense syllables are meaningless and the list has no structure; poetry is made of meaningful words put together with controlled structure of grammar, meter, and rhyme. This discovery of Ebbinghaus', and his finding that the number of syllables he could hold in his mind at one time was seven, are important to memory researchers today. Ebbinghaus also showed that the more a list is repeated, the better it is remembered after one day. — more an action repeated, · · ·

Ebbinghaus could also use his experimental method to scientifically answer questions raised by philosophical associationists. So, for example, philosophers had argued over whether, if three ideas *a*, *b*, and *c* are presented in a series one at a time, will *a* and *c* be associated, or if only *a* and *b* and *b* and *c* will be associated. Ebbinghaus experimented on this heretofore speculative question. He learned lists, scrambled them in various ways, and then relearned them. He found relearning was always easier despite the scrambling. He concluded from this that syllables do get associated not only with their immediate successors but also with their remoter fellow list members, although the farther apart two syllables are, the weaker the association is. His conclusion follows, because if only adjacent pairs were associated, then learning *a*, *b*, *c*, *d*, *e*, and *f* will not make it easier a day later to learn *a*, *c*, *e*, *d*, *b*, *f*, since none of the new pairs is the same.

The important thing about Ebbinghaus' research is not his results, although they are by and large sound, but the way he established a scientific research program to enquire into human learning. Its paradigm, or hard core, consisted of a set of theoretical ideas taken from associationism, plus an innovative experimental procedure that allowed Ebbinghaus to formulate precise, quantifiable versions of the associationists' speculations. The paradigm raised specific questions that posed researchable puzzles: What happens if we vary list length? If we vary the time after initial learning? Change the number of list presentations? These puzzles could be given quantitative answers.

Ebbinghaus' lonely labors show us the essential features of a research program in its early days. A theoretical structure is wedded to a well-defined method, and the offspring are puzzles that find precise answers. Ebbinghaus' program was continued by others, and up until the 1960s it was the most important tool in investigating human memory. Our brief

look at Ebbinghaus' pioneering work previews our discussions of later research programs in learning.

BASIC CONCEPTUAL ISSUES

The methodology of paradigms and research programs will help us observe the central lines of development of different schools of thought in the
psychology of learning. We also need to identify the central issues that have
concerned scientists studying learning, which will help us selectively organize the great mass of studies in the field. We will next consider three major
issues that have shaped the scientific study of human learning.

Learning and Cognition

The most basic question in psychology concerns its subject matter: Do
psychologists study the mind or behavior? Until the twentieth century,
philosophical psychologists and early scientific psychologists agreed that
psychology was the study of human, and sometimes animal, mental life.

However, the mind proved to be difficult to study scientifically. A
person's mind is private, unobservable by anyone else, and only partially
observable by its owner, who cannot observe the unconscious. Only two
methods are open to the student of mental life: **Introspection,** studying either one's own mind or the reports of introspection done by others, and
inference from behavior to underlying mental processes. Both methods
were used by early psychologists to paint a picture of the conscious and unconscious mind.

But in the early twentieth century it appeared to many young psychologists that the mind was not a fit subject for scientific investigation. Precisely because it is not public, not out in the open the way a scientist's chemical reactions are, they thought that the mind, if it exists at all, is forever
beyond the ken of science. There are no *mental* facts, for they are
unobservable, but there are *behavioral* facts that are public. Behavior, unlike mind, contended these behaviorists, is the proper subject matter for
scientific psychology.

From the early twentieth century to the 1960s, behaviorism dominated the psychology of learning. Instead of relying on introspective reports, the behaviorists measured quantifiable behavioral responses that
they related to observable, manipulable factors in the environment.
Ebbinghaus' own work, though published in 1885, is a good example of the
behaviorist approach. He manipulated identifiable features of his experimental environment, such as list length, number of presentations, and time
since learning, and observed the effect on a controllable behavior, such as
number of trials required to learn or relearn a list of nonsense syllables.

In its turn, however, behaviorism became unsatisfactory to younger
psychologists in the late 1950s and 1960s. Behaviorism seemed to leave important questions unanswered. For example, it is clear that "blind Venetian" and "Venetian blind" mean very different things, even though the

two phrases are composed of the same words. "They are cooking apples" is another such ambivalent statement—either people are cooking apples on the stove, or someone is pointing out a pile of apples suitable for cooking. Clearly, more than a dictionary knowledge of meanings is needed to understand language. Under the influence of the linguist Noam Chomsky (1957, 1959), many psychologists became convinced that, at least in the case of language, studying only measurable stimuli, such as "blind" and "Venetian," could not yield an adequate knowledge of psycholinguistics. Instead, the mind would have to be reintroduced in order to explain how people go beyond given information to create their responses. So, the mind imposes certain grammatical rules to combine the words "blind" and "Venetian," or "cooking" and "apples" and different rules produce different meanings. This new group of psychologists who proposed to study the mind were called **cognitive psychologists.**

In the psychology of learning, disagreement between behaviorists and cognitive psychologists has been heated. Working within different paradigms, these two groups have carried on highly dissimilar research programs. In Part II we will examine the approaches and results of the behaviorist and cognitive schools.

Learning and Biology

Every student of psychology is familiar with the nature–nurture issue: How much of human nature is genetically determined and how much is due to learning? This issue impinges on the psychology of learning. Traditionally, most psychologists, especially those in the field of learning, have espoused an *empiricist* answer to this question: At birth, the human being is a "blank slate," or piece of unformed clay, ready to be written on or shaped by the environment. Learning psychologists have generally minimized the effects of genetic constraints on human nature.

The other approach to this question is *nativist:* Much of what a person is or becomes is innate, determined by one's genes rather than by the environment. This position has been held by some philosophers going back to Plato, and by some biological students of animal behavior, most notably by the ethologists. Few psychologists, however, have supported nativism.

But recent years have seen the rapid growth of an aggressive group of biologists called sociobiologists (Wilson, 1975). Sociobiologists claim to have shown that "learned" behaviors that appear to be social in origin, such as altruism, are in fact programmed into the genes by natural selection. Although their primary work has been with animal species, such as E. O. Wilson's insects, sociobiologists have extended their approach speculatively to human beings (Wilson, 1979).

While the nature–nurture issue is perhaps psychology's oldest question, the aggressive claims of sociobiologists that all behavior is genetically rooted has sparked enormous controversy. At a meeting of the American Association for the Advancement of Science, a protestor dumped a bucket of water on Wilson's head! In Part III we will examine the claims and counterclaims in this area, focusing on the most significant human sociobiological phenomenon—language acquisition.

Learning and Development

Two kinds of psychologists study behavioral change. The psychologist of learning, whether behaviorist or cognitive, usually studies short-term change in the laboratory. She or he asks subjects to learn something, observes how they learn it, measures how well they learn it, and that is the end. Ebbinghaus extended the range of his memory results to at most 31 days.

The developmental psychologist, on the other hand, studies long-term changes that take place in people as they grow up, mature, and die; most research has concentrated on childhood and adolescence. The developmental psychologist, then, measures slow change over years and even decades.

Inevitably, a question arises. Excluding physical maturation and decay, are the long-term changes observed by the developmental psychologists anything more than the product of many short-term learning events no different from what the learning psychologists study in the laboratory? The learning psychologists say that given enough time, small learning events add up to large behavioral changes; they argue that the only difference between a five-year-old and a ten-year-old is that the ten-year-old has learned a lot more. According to the learning psychologists, development, aside from physical growth, is just a matter of learning, of being shaped by one's environment.

On the other hand, some developmental psychologists, most notably Jean Piaget (1971b), maintain that, although learning is a factor in behavior, it alone is insufficient to explain cognitive development. The four-year-old thinks that when you pour water from one glass into a taller, narrower one you have created more water. The eight-year-old correctly realizes that the amount of water stays the same. This and similar changes occur for all children, but no one *teaches* them the right answer. No one even realized that young children had such odd beliefs until Piaget revealed them. So Piaget contends that large steps in cognitive development come about because of autonomous forces within the child that push it from the primitive, prelogical thinking of the four-year-old to the deductive, rational thought of the adult. For Piaget, the environment does not simply shape the growing child and teach it; the child autonomously reaches out to the world to make sense of it, and this reaching out is guided by internal, unlearned processes.

In Chapter 12 we will look into both learning and developmental approaches to cognitive development, and link both with biological bases of learning.

THE HISTORY OF LEARNING

Learning and the Mind: Philosophy

Learning is a basic problem of human life; so, naturally, wondering about how we learn dates back centuries before scientific psychology began. Greek philosophers in the fifth century B.C. initiated a continuous series of speculations about learning and memory that still provides the basis for contemporary psychological concepts. The part of philosophy that interests us here is **epistemology**: What do I know about reality? How do I get knowledge? How can I be certain my knowledge is true?

One early view expresses what is accepted by many people as common sense. This is the **copy theory**, propounded by Alcmaeon (sixth century B.C.), Empedocles (fifth century B.C.), and Democritus (circa 420 B.C.). The copy theory says that when I sense an object my mind forms a copy of it that it then stores away in memory. So I have knowledge of things via their copies, and learning is the process of experiencing the world and building up in the mind an internal copy of the world.

While this theory seems reasonable, straightforward, and appealing, it has one fatal flaw, at least to philosphers. The problem is, "How do I know that my mental images of objects are *accurate* copies?" We know that perception is a complex physical process, and it is quite probable that as information moves from sensory receptors into the brain it is altered in some way. We are all familiar with visual illusions that fool us into thinking something is true when it is not; we have all heard of hallucinations and mirages, when a person sees something that is not there; and we all dream, experiencing complex stories that are completely unreal. So it is altogether possible and, as we shall see, probable, that our mental world is not a copy of the outside world, so that learning is never completely accurate.

Psychologically speaking, this may not be very important. Whether people see and learn accurately or not, it is our job as scientists to describe and explain what they do. But philosophers are concerned with larger issues. They worry that if the copy theory is wrong, it means we can never attain certain knowledge, and that the resulting doubt will spread to scientific knowledge, because scientific description and explanation themselves depend on scientists' observations. If these observations are inaccurate—so is science!

So philosophers after Democritus, who first noticed the flaw in the copy theory, have tried to overcome this difficulty, and their answers have shaped later psychological investigations into learning. Two broad traditions developed in ancient Greece that still continue today. One tradition, called **rationalism,** renounces the copy theory altogether and says that real learning has little to do with simply experiencing the world as a passive observer. The other tradition, called **empiricism,** sticks with some form of the copy theory, considering it, however flawed, the only plausible account of learning.

Rationalists, beginning with Plato (427–347 B.C.), having found the copy theory hopelessly flawed, concluded that we simply cannot have knowledge of the world of the senses. Instead, rationalists argued, there is a higher, invisible reality not present to the senses, and is attainable only through *reason* (hence the name rationalism) and mystic contemplation. Given this disdain for the empirical world of science, and distrust of perception and learning, it is no wonder that rationalism has had little appeal for psychologists and little direct influence on the psychology of learning. It has, however, influenced some of our basic, underlying presuppositions about the mind.

Rationalists turned away from sense perception and observation of the external world to look inside the person for the true source of knowledge. In doing so they created two ideas that have strongly influenced psychologists concerned with learning. First, by denying that a person just passively records sense impressions, rationalists made the mind autonomous. For rationalists, the mind actively seeks knowledge and self-perfection; it is not merely shaped by the environment it copies, as empiricists believe. The rationalists' commitment to autonomous internal forces of mental growth and perfection remains today in those psychologists, such as Jean Piaget, who believe that learning alone is insufficient to explain all of human development.

The other underlying presupposition that grew out of the rationalists' decision to look inside people rather than outside for knowledge is **nativism,** the contention that some of what we know is innate, inborn, or, in modern terms, written in the genes. Rationalists argue that there are some concepts we could not have derived from experience; for example, even an untutored person will concede that if $A = B$ and $B = C$, then $A = C$. According to the rationalists, there are "clear and distinct" untaught truths, especially those of mathematics. If these ideas did not come from experience, they must have been implanted by God or have evolved in the genes. The rationalist commitment to nativism remains today in those psychologists, such as Chomsky, who believe in important innate mechanisms that limit or direct external learning.

Empiricists are more matter-of-fact than rationalists. Despite the difficulties of the copy theory, empiricists continue to insist that human knowledge comes from the senses. Plato's own student Aristotle (384–322 B.C.) was the major empiricist of the Greek age. According to Aristotle, knowledge results from repeated experience of similar objects. As you meet many cats you eventually build up in your mind a general concept of "cat." You abstract from particular cats—Siamese, Persian, alley—the essential and defining features that all cats share and that distinguish them from similar creatures such as dogs. Your entire knowledge of the world, then, is a set of abstract concepts derived from your concrete, particular experiences in the world of sense perceptions, in what William James called "the blooming, buzzing confusion" of the external world as perceived by the human senses.

In addition to knowledge, Aristotle also distinguished memory, as many cognitive psychologists do today. Not only do you possess a concept of "cat," but you also have recorded memories of individual cats you have met, and you can usually recall these memories, reexperiencing the cats in your mind. Thus, in Aristotle's view two kinds of learning take place together: Your experiences are recorded in memory, and they also provide information that leads to the formation of abstract concepts.

Aristotle's picture of the mind contains different departments, or *faculties,* that serve particular functions in learning. Figure 1–2 shows these in an information-processing flowchart similar to more contemporary ones we will study later. There are the five *special senses* that detect different kinds of information in the environment. These are assembled together in

The Special Senses

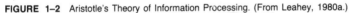

FIGURE 1–2 Aristotle's Theory of Information Processing. (From Leahey, 1980a.)

conscious experience by *common sense*, the sense common to all experiences—no relation to today's meaning. Then the information is recorded briefly by imagination and permanently by memory. At the same time information is worked over by the *active mind*, and the resulting abstract concepts are stored in the *passive mind*.

Despite its quaint terminology, Aristotle's account of learning is reasonable, intuitively appealing, and similar in many ways to the accounts of contemporary information-processing psychologists. Nevertheless, the incorporation of Platonism into early Christianity, and the loss of Aristotle's works with the fall of Rome, meant that Plato's less scientific views dominated epistemological thinking for the centuries of the Middle Ages.

Alongside theoretical speculations about memory, the Greeks developed the practical side of memory. Before the invention of writing, a good memory was vitally important, especially to public speakers. Thus, there arose an art of memory—the development of mnemonic devices—as well as a nascent science of memory. Box 1–1 discusses one ancient mnemonic device still effective today. In Chapter 6 we will look at some current ideas on how to improve memory.

The revival of Aristotle's empiricism began with William of Ockham (1300?–?1349) who repeated Aristotle's insistence that knowledge is derived from sense experience, memory, and abstraction. But it was not until the time of John Locke (1632–1704) that modern empiricism began its rapid climb to dominance in English-speaking philosophy.

Locke rejected innate ideas and introduced his famous *tabula rasa* or "blank slate" image of the mind. Like Aristotle, Locke believed the mind possessed faculties at birth but was devoid of content or ideas. The mind is

BOX 1-1   *THE ART OF MEMORY*

Plato rebuked the discoverer of writing. "This invention will produce forgetfulness . . . because [its users] will not practice their memory. Their trust in writing, produced by external characters that are not part of them, will discourage the use of their own memory within them."

Moderns are amazed at the memory feats of the ancients. Seneca, a Roman teacher of rhetoric, could repeat 2000 names in the order in which he had just heard them!

Frances Yates, in *The Art of Memory* (1966), explains how memory was cultivated until printing appeared in the Renaissance. The key to the system was construction of a vivid mental place, such as Dante's Hell or, for the lucky, Heaven (Figure 1-3), with memorable parts such as the sufferings of heretics, infidels, and gluttons. Then when you wanted to learn something new, such as a list of names, you would associate each name through an image, such as Harold is a heretic, to each place. To recall, you "walked through" your mental place and let the images return, bringing their associates with them. People in the Middle Ages acquired the art from the ancients and added a moral twist: Using Hell and Heaven as memory places made you dwell on the afterlife. In the Renaissance, as memory became less useful in a writing society, the art of memory got caught up in a mystical, magical, secret, religious system, and it eventually aided the birth of science.

a blank slate at birth and experience fills it with ideas, which are the basis of human knowledge. Locke also formally introduced the concept of association of ideas, which had been only briefly sketched by Plato and Aristotle.

Later empiricists purified Locke's empiricism, eliminating innate mental faculties and substituting association for them. This process culminated with David Hume (1711–1776), who revealed the fatal flaw in the copy theory, but concluded that we would just have to live with it. Hume argued that both perception and association can be in error, but that since both are how the mind really works, we have to live with the knowledge that we can never know anything with certainty.

At the same time, the school of thought known as **associationism** developed, beginning with the philosopher-physician David Hartley (1705–1757). Associationism developed a protoscientific theory of learning and memory. Its advocates developed "laws" of association, saying for example that two ideas, *a* and *b*, will be associated when they occur at about the same time, and that the strength of the association would depend on how closely in time *a* and *b* were paired, and how often the pairing occurred. We have already seen how associationism became scientific research on memory through Ebbinghaus' studies, and since then associationism has remained, in one form or another, an important component of psychological theories of learning.

One last philosophical influence on the psychology of learning needs to be mentioned. As we said, the philosophers who were interested in epistemology—in how we learn what we know—always stopped at the point

FIGURE 1–3 Hell and Heaven as Artificial Memory. From Cosmas Rossellius, *Thesaurus Artificiosae Memoriae*, Venice 1579 (p. 122) (From Yates, 1966).

when a concept was formed. They took little if any interest in how the concept was used, that is, in behavior. In epistemology, what we know remains cut off from what we do.

This situation began to change with René Descartes (1596–1650). Philosophically, Descartes was a rationalist who distrusted the senses and believed in innate ideas. But he was also a leading figure in the scientific revolution, and he wrote about humans and animals as natural creatures. Descartes said animals were just machines that responded reflexively to stimuli—the beginning of the stimulus → response doctrine of behaviorism, the idea that every behavior is a response (R) to some stimulus (S). The human brain and body were machines, too, and Descartes proposed that most human behavior could be explained as mechanically reflexive. But Descartes also held that humans possess souls capable of intervening (via the pineal gland) in the mechanics of nerve operation, making us fundamentally different from animals. Unlike animals, humans have thinking souls, possess free will, and are morally responsible.

Descartes' concept of behavior as a sequence of mechanical reflexes was developed by later French *mechanists,* most notoriously Julien Offroy de la Mettrie (1709–1751). In Descartes' scientific discussion of the mind he attributed so much to the action of nerves, brain, and muscle, and made the intervention of the soul so difficult, that it was easy for la Mettrie and others to dismiss the soul entirely, and say that not only are animals machines but that human beings are machines also. The modern psychology of learning is deeply indebted to the tradition of mechanism, as modern psychologists sometimes acknowledge (Skinner, 1931). To assume that humans are not free is necessary to scientific psychology, just as chemists must assume chemicals are not free to do what they like. The essential similarity of humans and animals justifies experimenting on animals in the laboratory and applying the results to human beings—impossible if one allows for any sort of free will or intervening soul. The view that human beings are machines also makes it possible to try to create computer models of memory and behavior that will think and act like people.

As the mechanistic view developed, it became naturally linked to associationism. In the eighteenth and nineteenth centuries brain scientists concluded that the nervous system was indeed an input-output reflex device. Input arrives at the brain via the sensory nerves and gets linked through synapses with outgoing motor nerves that terminate in muscle movements. David Hartley and Alexander Bain (1818–1903) integrated this sensory-motor concept of the nervous system and brain with associationism (Young, 1970). The idea that the brain worked by linking up incoming and outgoing impulses meshed nicely with the view that the mind works by associating incoming ideas and outgoing actions. Hartley and Bain took the natural step of explaining association as the result of sensory-motor linkages in the brain, thus completing the mechanization of mind and behavior begun by Descartes. The integration of mind and brain into a general associative psychology set the stage for empirical, scientific psychologies of learning.

Learning and Consciousness: Early Psychology

Learning has become such an important part of Anglo-American psychology that students are surprised to learn that the European founders of psychology had little to say about it. For them, psychology was the study of human consciousness, and learning entered into their work only insofar as they studied how ideas in consciousness get associated. Much of their work was almost epistemological—determining how ideas get into consciousness, but neglecting their expression in behavior.

Wilhelm Wundt (1832–1920), the acknowledged founder of psychology, considered the problem of learning beyond the reach of the laboratory. For him, memory and cognition were "higher mental processes" functioning so deeply in the mind that superficial control of sensory stimuli and measurement of motor responses that can be imposed by an experimenter cannot penetrate to them. We now know that Wundt was wrong—Ebbinghaus quickly showed that—but Wundt did have an important insight about memory, one only recently recovered by cognitive psychologists. It is altogether too easy to think, as Ebbinghaus did, that memory is the recovery of accurate copies of experiences. But Wundt believed that memory is really a process of reconstruction based on a few clear details.

Some of today's most exciting research in memory (defects of eyewitness testimony, for example) has supported, without knowing it, Wundt's insight. As it turns out, eyewitnesses do not remember what they actually saw, but rather what they are led to believe they saw.

Both those who followed Wundt and those who rebelled against him had equally little influence on the psychology of learning. Some, like his English student E. B. Titchener, neglected learning altogether. Others, most notably the Würzburg school, defied Wundt by studying thinking and memory in the laboratory. Their findings, however, were so advanced for their time that they were forgotten until the 1970s. Gestalt psychologists also did pioneering work in memory, thinking, and creativity, but their theory, despite its fame and clever demonstrations, remained outside the mainstream of research on learning.

Learning and the Unconscious: Freud

As children all of us played with a "magic slate"; you draw with a wooden or plastic stylus on a sheet of clear plastic that covers a thinner sheet of gray plastic overlaying a black, wax-like slate. As you draw, lines appear on the gray film, and when you are done you "erase" the lines by pulling up both plastic sheets. In this humble toy, then called a "mystic writing pad," Sigmund Freud (1925) found a model for learning and memory.

The stylus may be thought of as analogous to incoming sensory stimulations, which register, or write, on consciousness, represented by the thin gray film. Consciousness always reflects the here-and-now, what you are immediately experiencing, and it is constantly being "erased" as each new experience replaces the previous experience. But if we lift the plastic sheets and carefully examine the black tablet, we find faintly impressed on it the very lines we just "erased." So the black tablet is a permanent memory that records all the ideas placed in consciousness by experience. With this model Freud independently hit on an important distinction made by cognitive psychologists, namely, that there are two kinds of memory—a temporary one, roughly equivalent to consciousness, that holds information for our immediate use, and a permanent one, holding lasting impressions of what we have learned.

In his writings, Freud (1895, 1896, 1900) describes memory in terms that strikingly anticipate another major theory of memory, the "levels of processing" approach (see Chapters 7 and 8). Figure 1–4 schematically sets out Freud's ideas. Information enters the mind through the conscious **perceptual system,** equivalent to the gray film of the "magic slate." The perceptual system registers but does not store this information, which passes in turn to the unconscious **memory system,** where it lays down a series of traces. According to Freud, memories do not just leave a single impression; rather, they leave at least three traces, each of a distinct aspect of the experience. Ultimately, information stirs us to action as it enters the preconscious* **motor system,** which effects actual behavior. Freud's notion that

---

*Preconscious ideas are those that, while not immediately conscious, can easily become so. The conscious and the preconscious together form the rational ego.

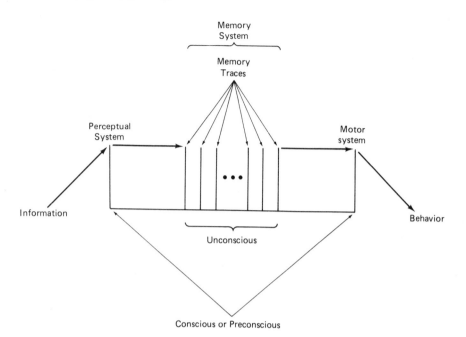

FIGURE 1–4 Freud's Description of the Memory System. Adapted from THE INTERPRETATION OF DREAMS by Sigmund Freud, ed. and trans. by James Strachey. ©1956 by Basic Books, Inc., Publishers. Reprinted by permission of the publisher.

learning leaves not one but several kinds of memory traces is remarkably modern.

Because we think of Freud as a clinical psychologist, his ideas of cognitive psychology are usually neglected (but see Pribram & Gill, 1976). Despite the fact that Freud wrote little about memory per se, memory looms important in psychoanalysis because, as Breuer and Freud (1895) wrote, hysterics suffer from "reminiscences," unconscious memories expressed as a neurotic symptom. Hence, Freud had to propose a theory of memory that would not only show how experiences leave lasting influences for good or ill as we grow up, but would also show how the unconscious record of past experience turns up in symptoms and dreams (Freud, 1900), which the example of the "mystic slate" achieved.

Learning and Adaptation: Evolution

Until the nineteenth century the problems of understanding learning and memory remained with philosophers, especially the associationists. Despite some occasional attempts by physicians to explain memory in terms of brain function (Thorndike 1923–1958), biological ideas had almost no influence on the psychology of learning. Nor was this changed by Bain's integration of associationism and the sensory-motor concept of the brain and nervous system. All Bain did was provide a plausible neurophysiological account of the process of association, something he got from the philosophers.

In the nineteenth century, however, theories of evolution were applied to psychology, and the outcome made learning the central problem of psychology that it is today.

Theories of evolution—whether Lamarck's purposive evolution based on the striving of animals for perfection, or Darwin's theory of natural selection—maintain that today's living creatures, including humans, are heirs to millennia of shaping by the environment and to our ancestor's responses to that environment. This central conception of evolution raises for psychology two questions, the **species question** and the **individual question** (Leahey, 1980a).

The species question asks: If each species of animal has evolved over millions of years to fit a particular environment, what effect does its unique genetic heritage have on its behavior? In other words, evolutionary theory invites us to investigate species-specific behaviors, to understand how each species has been shaped by evolution in its own way, and how species differ from one another. Applied to the psychology of learning, the species question would establish research programs designed to find out how the genes—the products of evolution—shape, constrain, and direct the learning and memory of different species. The species question was raised, but only briefly pursued, by Charles Darwin himself in his study of how animals and people express emotion through nonverbal channels (Darwin, 1872).

The individual question uses evolution as a metaphor for a single animal's adaptation to its environment. Just as a species has been shaped over time into its present form by centuries of adapting to the environment, so we may regard an individual animal as shaped into its present behavioral form by a lifetime of adapting to its environment. And what else is an individual adapting to the environment doing but learning? A research program organized around the individual question will not focus on how different species come to adapt each to its own environmental niche. Instead, the individual question will focus on the individual organism as it learns about its environment, learns to cope with environmental demands, exploits its resources—in short, as the individual, like a species, adapts.

The fundamental character of the psychology of learning, at least through the 1960s, has been determined by pursuit of the individual question in an associationistic framework first articulated by Herbert Spencer (1820–1903). Spencer (1855) accepted associationism and its integration with the sensory-motor conception of the brain. Learning, in this view, was the acquiring of correct connections between incoming stimuli and outgoing responses—what philosophers had called making associations. This plausible view of how *individuals* learn was extrapolated by Spencer to explain how *species* acquire instincts: In the long lifetime of a species some stimulus-response (S-R) connections have been so well learned by so many of its members that they become innate reflexes, that is, instincts.

As Spencer presented his evolutionary psychology, the species question reduces to the individual question. At all times and places species learn the same way, by making associations, S-R connections in the brain. Spencer's view implies that the psychology of learning may be pursued by intensive study of how a few individual organisms learn. Once we understand, for instance, how a rat learns to make S-R connections, we will automatically know how other species learn, since all species learn in the same way. The only species-difference in learning ability will be quantitative: Species with larger brains can make *more* S-R connections than can species with smaller brains, but the process of learning is the same in rat, pigeon, dog, and human being.

Furthermore, Spencer's paradigm implies that learning is best investigated in the laboratory, with its tight controls, which means that field studies would be unncesssary. Since all learning is association, according to Spencer, it makes no difference whether we study the kinds of assocations a rat makes in the wild—for example, associating the taste of tainted water and its sickening effect—or the kind of associations only a laboratory could provide—for example, between the sound of a buzzer and delivery of food in a Skinner box's food magazine.

Evolution rapidly changed psychology from a sort of experimental philosophy of consciousness into a branch of biology concerned with how the individual learns to adapt to its environment. The psychology of learning—the study of the adaptive process—soon became the core area of experimental psychology. Specifically, Spencer's broad paradigm became the foundation for the research programs of behaviorism's laboratory-based studies of how a few species (mostly rats and pigeons) learned arbitrary S-R connections, with these findings extrapolated to human learning, often with no modification or independent research.

Behaviorism's pursuit of the individual question within an associationistic framework went largely unchallenged into the 1960s. But, as we shall see in Part III, the species question has been reopened.

Having arrived at Spencer's rationale for the modern psychology of learning, we are now prepared to enter the psychology of learning proper. We will begin with the research spawned by Spencer's ideas.

SUGGESTED READINGS

The application of the philosophy of science to psychology, and to the history of learning is discussed in greater detail in Thomas Leahey's *A History of Psychology* (Prentice-Hall, 1980), Chapter 1. Ebbinghaus' contributions to psychology and the verbal learning tradition that followed him have been recently described by Charles Cofer, "Human Learning and Memory," a chapter in Eliot Hearst (Ed.) *The First Century of Experimental Psychology* (Hillsdale, N. J.: Lawrence Erlbaum, 1979).

CHAPTER TWO
FUNDAMENTALS OF CONDITIONING

INTRODUCTION

The study of human learning today encompasses two fields that arose separately and somewhat in conflict. The first area is the traditional field of human learning narrowly defined, and is largely the application to human beings of learning principles derived from research on animals. The second area is cognitive psychology, whose beginnings go back only to the late 1940s. Cognitive psychologists are interested in higher mental processes, including attention, memory, and thinking.

In this book we present a variety of approaches to how human beings change over time, so we do not restrict the term **learning** to simple animal principles, but include cognition, too. We will, therefore, use the term **conditioning** to apply to the simple processes of classical and operant "learning"—the subject of Chapters 2–4. Chapters 5–9 will present the work of cognitive psychologists, and will range broadly from attention to scientific reasoning.

Learning and Conditioning: Behavioral Psychology

Beginning with John Watson in 1913, behaviorists committed themselves to studying only what they could observe as psychologists, namely, human behavior. They rejected the study of the mind as inherently unscientific, although they disagreed about whether minds exist. Methodological behaviorists such as Hull, Tolman, and Guthrie argued that although minds exist they cannot be brought to public view, and so are outside the scope of scientific method. Radical behaviorists such as Skinner go further and deny that minds exist at all; they argue that our belief that we have minds is just operantly conditioned verbal behavior.

Regardless of this difference, behaviorists have built their different theories of learning primarily on studies of animal behavior, and they have moved on to study or theorize about human conditioning. Believing that there are few important differences in how different species learn, behaviorists have done with animals what cannot be ethically done with humans—studied them under totally controlled and sometimes painful conditions. From their animal work (which is why we call them animal-based theorists), they have extrapolated to the human case, sometimes doing actual conditioning studies with human subjects, sometimes just speculating about human behavior.

Chapter 2 describes the basic processes of conditioning elucidated by behavioral psychologists: classical conditioning and operant conditioning. Chapter 3 will present several old, but important, theories of learning based on conditioning principles, namely, the theories of Guthrie, Hull, and Tolman. Chapter 4 will consider the more extreme and still-living alternative of radical behaviorism that sees humans as mindless creatures whose behavior is shaped by their environment and nothing else. While in this section some attention must necessarily be paid to studies of animal learning, we will wherever possible focus on human subjects.

We intuitively distinguish involuntary reflexes and voluntary acts. A reflex is an immediate response to some stimulus over which we have little if any control. Next time the doctor taps your knee, just try to stop the knee jerk before it happens! We possess many reflexes, many of which we never even think about: Our pupils enlarge in the dark, get smaller in sunlight; if someone brushes a finger against our bare feet, our toes contract (in babies they spread out); if wind suddenly blows in our face, we blink. Emotional responses often are reflexive: In grade school, when the local bully hit us we felt afraid; going to the dentist makes us feel queasy; erotic stimuli arouse us. While we may stand up to the bully, see the dentist, and not attend pornographic films, our basic emotional reactions usually remain, showing them to be deeply rooted reflexes.

Over against reflexes we set voluntary behavior: We choose to fight (or run away from) the bully; we choose to see (or avoid seeing) the dentist; we choose to attend (or not attend) pornographic films. To common sense, these two kinds of behavior are quite different. Reflexes have to do with extremely simple muscle-responses and gut feelings, while volumtary behavior concerns how we choose to live our lives. We make different kinds of moral and legal judgments about reflexes and voluntary acts. We do not blame soldiers for being afraid of battle, but we punish them severely for running away. We may exonerate the criminal whom we judge insane—He "had to do it." He "couldn't help himself!"

From the beginning, the psychology of learning has maintained the same distinction, speaking of two types of learning and conditioning. Historically, the two forms of learning were brought into the laboratory at the close of the nineteenth century by two widely separated scientists. But the basic strategy behind each research program was the same: Isolate a simple form of learning that is subject to experimental control and map out its parameters and limits in animal subjects.

In each case the hope was that by breaking down complex learned behaviors into simpler parts—something more easily achieved with animals than with humans—the elementary processes of learning would be revealed. After the parts were understood, later psychologists would be able to put the pieces back together, so to speak, and explain complex, perhaps uniquely, human behavior as an assemblage of simpler parts with animal foundations.

CLASSICAL CONDITIONING

Pavlov's Research Program

The scientific study of reflexes began in Russia with a serendipitous discovery by Ivan Petrovich Pavlov (1849–1936). Pavlov was a brilliant physiologist, whose study of the digestive system won him a Nobel Prize in 1904. In the course of that work, part of which involved surgically bringing the opening of the salivary gland to the outside of a dog's skin and watching the secretion of saliva when food was presented, Pavlov noticed a curious thing. After being used as a subject for some time, a dog would not only salivate when food was presented, but would also salivate to previously neutral stimuli—the sight of the experimenter who fed it, for example. Pavlov saw that not only are there innate reflexes (put food in a dog's mouth and it salivates) but there are also learned reflexes (the dog salivates at the sight of food or at the sight of the experimenter). The learned reflexes Pavlov originally called **psychical** (as opposed to biological) reflexes, and he soon came to focus his research on them, abandoning the term "psychical" and bringing both unlearned and learned reflexes into the province of physiology.

Pavlov's basic conceptions, the hard core of his research program, came from the founder of Russian physiology, I.M. Sechenov (1829–1905), mixed with associationism. Sechenov (1863) espoused an extreme form of the sensory-motor conception of the nervous system. All behavior is reflex behavior to some external stimulus. As we have seen, the sensory-motor view of the brain meshes with associationism, for learning can be thought of as acquiring new reflexes by association of stimulus and response.

Of course Pavlov's novelty did not lie in accepting these commonplace views. Pavlov's achievement was harnessing them to a particular experimental setting, as Ebbinghaus also did. Pavlov saw that his "psychical secretions" were the outcome of associative learning; the food, which already elicited salivation, being associated with the experimenter, who came to

FIGURE 2–1   Diagram Illustrating Experimentation on the Dog (From Pavlov, 1928, p. 271)

elicit salivation. As an experimental physiologist, Pavlov knew how to put careful controls on his happenstance discovery, and to create a rigorous experimental paradigm. Pavlov went to great lengths to control the experimental conditions, building a special laboratory which, to ensure exclusion of uncontrolled stimuli, had thick glass windows, specially separated rooms, a foundation embedded in sand, and a straw-filled moat! The dogs were kept in a harness (see Fig. 2–1), and from another room the experimenter could control stimulus presentations and count the drops of saliva produced in the dog's mouth. When Pavlov's experimental setup allowed complete control of the animal's environment and produced an objective quantitative measure of learning, his brilliant research program could begin. Between associationism and the reflex model of the brain, many investigations were opened using Pavlov's new objective method.

Before considering these experiments, however, we must develop some Pavlovian terminology. A stimulus that biologically elicits a reflex (food placed in the mouth, a puff of air at the eye) does so reliably and unconditionally, and so is called an **unconditional stimulus,** abbreviated US. The biologically elicited reflex is, therefore, an **unconditional response,** or UR. A stimulus that through pairing with a US comes to elicit a response usually almost identical with the UR is called a **conditional* stimulus,** for its ability to elicit the UR is *conditional* on pairing with the US and other conditions elucidated by Pavlov; it is abbreviated CS. The reflex elic-

---

*Although time has sanctioned the mistranslation of the Russian word *ooslovny* as condition*ed*, the proper translation should always have been condition*al*, which expresses Pavlov's idea much more clearly. In any case, US and CS have become the regular tokens for unconditioned and conditioned stimuli.

ited by a CS is a **conditional response,** or CR. Finally, the US is often called a **reinforcer,** since its pairing with the CS strengthens (reinforces) the power of the CS to elicit the CR.

Relations between CS and US   One of the primary laws of associationism is **contiguity,** which says that two ideas will get associated if they occur in the mind at the same time. Translated into Pavlov's hypothetical brain-theory, it says that stimuli set up centers of activity in the cerebrum, and that centers regularly activated together will become linked, so that when one center is activated, the other will be, too. Given Pavlov's experimental paradigm, the law of contiguity may be readily investigated by controlling when we present CS and US in relation to each other. Pavlov employed two US's—food, which elicited salivation as part of digestion, and mild acid, which elicited salivation as a defensive reflex. He used many CS's—the clicking of a metronome, musical tones, odors, the sound of bubbling water, though he did not use the famous bell. We will here assume the US is food (appetitive conditioning) and the CS is a musical note, or tone.

From the law of contiguity we might expect exact *simultaneous* presentation of US and CS to be most effective. Oddly enough, such pairings produce no conditioning (except in special circumstances [Rescorla, 1980]), as also happens when the US is presented, however briefly, before the CS begins (*backward conditioning*). Instead, the CS must begin slightly *before* the US and overlap with it. If the CS begins and ends before the US, it is called *trace conditioning,* which is extremely difficult to establish. The fact that CS and US must overlap to create a CR supports the law of contiguity, but the finding that the onset of the CS must precede the US suggests that CS's become effective only if they act as informational signals to the organism (Pavlov, 1927). This informational value of CS's has come to be stressed in the most recent theory of classical conditioning.

One other kind of CS-US arrangement was investigated by Pavlov. Suppose the CS starts well before the US is presented, perhaps 30 seconds before, and overlaps US onset. This is called *delay conditioning*; it is like the standard procedure except that the CS begins far before the US. In this case a CR gets established, but it changes as CS-US pairings proceed. At first, the dog begins to salivate as soon as the CS begins, but as trials continue, the salivation does not begin until a little before the US is scheduled to arrive. This finding suggested to Pavlov (1927) that time itself could act as a CS. The tone alone no longer was the CS eliciting the salivation CR, but it was the *compound stimulus* of tone *plus* a certain passage of time.

Other compound stimuli were investigated by Pavlov. He found you could condition two or more CS's at the same time, for example, pairing a light and a tone with food. An old law of association was *vividness*: A given idea will get mostly associated with concurrent vivid ideas, rather than with weak ones. Pavlov's work bore this out. If the two CS's were about equal in intensity, and if they were presented alone, after conditioning, each would elicit the CR. But if one were stronger than the other, a bright light and a dim tone, for instance, only the more vivid stimulus became a CS. This phenomenon, when one CS of a compound is much more powerful than the others, is called *overshadowing*.

Excitation and inhibition   The conditioning of a distinct positive response, such as salivation, Pavlov (1927) called conditioning of **excitation**. The US naturally excites the brain center controlling the UR, and, after several pairings, so does the CS. Pavlov also believed that the action of CR's could be **inhibited** as well as excited.

If we return to delay conditioning we see inhibition in action. After many CS-US pairings, the CR occurred only near the end of the CS interval, near the anticipated time of the US. Why then did the earlier CR's to the start of the CS disappear? Was the first part of the tone simply disconnected, disassociated from the CR? Pavlov thought not. He believed that the early part of the tone actively *inhibited* the CR from taking place. As evidence, Pavlov pointed to *disinhibition*: If, during the early stages of the CS, before any CR would occur, a wholly new stimulus is introduced, such as a light flash, the CR would occur. Now if the CR had simply been disconnected from the early CS, the light would not cause salivation, any more than it would outside the laboratory. But the unexpected appearance of salivation when the light flashed during the CS indicated to Pavlov that the light interfered with the cortical process, specifically, inhibition, thus releasing the suppressed CR to the tone.

Pavlov (1927) distinguished several kinds of inhibition, the most important of which is *extinction*. What happens if we present an established CS alone, without further reinforcement? The CR occurs for a while, slowly weakens, and finally falls to zero: No saliva appears when the tone is sounded. It seems plausible to say here that the CS has been disassociated from the CR, even that the CS is no longer a CS but a neutral stimulus, and there is no CR—the reflex has literally extinguished.

But further investigation reveals that the CS-CR association is still present, only inhibited by the extinction procedure. In the first place, if we simply put the animal aside for some time, even as little as 20 minutes, and present the CS again, salivation appears. The conditional reflex has spontaneously recovered. This indicates that the reflex was not unlearned by extinction, but was actively inhibited; it also indicates that inhibition is a temporary state, abating with time.

Another kind of evidence also supports Pavlov's argument. Suppose we continue extinction well beyond the point at which zero salivation occurs, presenting the CS over and over. If extinction were simply unlearning the conditional reflex, additional unreinforced pairings would have no effect: Once a CS has become a neutral stimulus, it makes no sense to say it has become "more neutral" still. Instead, Pavlov found that the longer extinction continued past zero, the longer it took for the CR to spontaneously recover, indicating that additional reinforced pairings deepened and so prolonged the inhibition of the CR.

Higher order conditioning   What happens when we take an established CS (CS$_1$) and pair it with a new, neutral stimulus? Will the new stimulus become a CS eliciting a CR of salivation? Pavlov found that in the right conditions it could, and called it a *secondary conditional reflex*; the building of a new CS on old CS's is called **higher order conditioning.** If CS$_2$ is presented before, and not overlapping with CS_1, then CS_2 will come to elicit a CR. On the other hand, if CS_1 and CS_2 overlap, *conditional inhibition* occurs. The dog will salivate to CS_1 alone, but will not salivate to CS_1 and CS_2. CS_1 has been reinforced, and so a CR remains until extinction occurs, but the compound stimulus $CS_1 + CS_2$ has never been reinforced, and so the CS_1-CR reflex is inhibited by the presence of CS_2.

How far can higher order conditioning be pushed? Can we build CS_3 on CS_2 and CS_4 on CS_3? Pavlov found that in alimentary conditioning he could go no further than secondary conditioning, and with defensive conditioning he could go no further than third-order conditioning. Pavlov's finding has not been overturned.

Generalization and discrimination   Another law of association is *similarity*: Similar ideas are easily associated. Pavlov found that CR's occur not just to the trained CS, but to similar stimuli, too. Suppose we have trained a dog to salivate to a tone of 1000 cycles per second, and then present tones near or far from 1000 cycles, either above or below. We find that the CR occurs to the related tones, and that the closer the new tone is to the original CS, the greater the CR; the farther away, the less the CR. The extension of a CR to stimuli similar to the CS is called **generalization,** and the gradual weakening of the CR as the test stimuli increasingly differ from the CS is called the *generalization gradient*. Pavlov experimented with many different kinds of CS's and replicated the same finding over many stimulus dimensions.

On the other hand, we can set excitation and inhibition against one another to produce **stimulus discrimination**. Suppose we condition salivation to a CS (CS +) of a luminous circle presented on a screen before the dog's eyes (Pavlov, 1927). If we then present ellipses varying from near-circular to extremely elliptical, we find a generalization gradient. However, right after presenting the CS, we repeatedly present an extreme ellipse alone and never reinforce it. Inhibition will build up to the ellipse (CS−). We have created stimulus discrimination. The animal responds to CS+, and does not respond to CS−.

Knowing about generalization, we can now ask the following question. Suppose we continue the discrimination procedure while making successive CS−'s more and more circular? The generalization gradients of excitation and inhibition will begin to clash: CS−, being like a circle, will to some degree elicit salivation, while as an ellipse it will elicit inhibition; CS+, being similar to an ellipse, will to some degree elicit inhibition, while as a circle it will elicit salivation. As CS− increasingly resembles CS+, the antagonistic tendencies will agonizingly clash. Pushed far enough, Pavlov's dog "presented all the symptoms of acute neurosis." It squealed, it wiggled, it tore at the apparatus and barked violently. All conditioning vanished and had to be started over, with the same results (Pavlov, 1927, p. 291). These results indicated to Pavlov that psychopathology is learned by conditioning and should be "undoable" by new conditioning. Many of his later papers were an extension of his point of view to abnormal psychology and psychotherapy (Pavlov, 1941).

While our brief survey has not exhausted all of Pavlov's research, it has presented the fundamental procedures, findings, and terminology of classical conditioning, many of which also apply to operant conditioning. We have also seen how a firm conception of the theoretical problems in an area, given to Pavlov by associationism and the reflex conception of the brain, plus a well-defined and controllable exemplar of research, discovered in Pavlov's "psychical reflexes," led to the beautiful development of a research program. The hard core and the exemplar together defined the problems to be investigated and provided the means for devising specific, concrete experiments with clear-cut results. Pavlov could ask and answer a whole host of questions, working his way systematically through all the variations defined by his central conceptions of mind and brain and by his research procedure.

Extension of the exemplar to humans   Pavlov was a physiologist, and he conducted his experiments in order to learn about how the brain worked. For Pavlov, the behavioral data he collected was of interest only insofar as it illuminated the functions of the cerebral hemispheres; conditioning was, for Pavlov, *evidence* of underlying nerve processes that could not be directly studied, only inferred. But at the time Pavlov's work became known to American psychologists (Yerkes & Morgulis, 1909) the rebellion against introspection was well under way, and behaviorism was about to be born.

Behaviorists eagerly adopted Pavlov's objective method—here was sound experimental procedure yielding quantitative results with no nonsense about consciousness and introspection. But the behaviorists' interests were altogether different from Pavlov's. They were interested in finding regularity in behavior, and Pavlov's method let them do that. But they did not care at all about supposed brain-functions. They were *behavior-theorists*, not physiologists, questing after knowledge of adaptive behavior, not after the inferred secrets of brain function. They therefore took classical conditioning as a fact, and Pavlov's technique as a proven method, and went on from there, for which Pavlov himself (Pavlov, 1941) reproved them.

The behaviorists, even when they experimented on animals, really aimed at explaining human behavior. It is no surprise, therefore, that it was American psychologists, not Pavlov, who applied his method to human beings. But it should be remembered that it was the method which had become a model shared by the behaviorist community, that they took from Pavlov. Pavlov's physiological theorizing they left alone. Behaviorists, like Pavlov, were in the associative tradition. However, they looked directly at the connection of stimulus and response, neglecting underlying neural mechanisms. In a sense, then, despite his substantial contribution to the movement, Pavlov cannot be considered a behaviorist.

The most famous application of Pavlov's method to a human being was carried out by the founder of behaviorism himself, John B. Watson (1878–1958). He worked with Rosalie Rayner, his lover who was soon to be his second wife (Watson and Rayner, 1920). For the surrounding scandal, see Cohen, 1979. We remarked earlier that reflexive learning was important to the emotions. Pavlov himself did not investigate this side of classical conditioning, preferring to stick to the quantifiable salivary reflex. Watson, however, wanted to unravel human emotional life, and used classical conditioning to do so.

Watson (1930) argued that all human behavior was reflexive, and his studies with Rayner were designed to support his thesis. Watson and Rayner stated that in newborns there are a few emotional UR's (fear, rage, and love) elicited by a few US's (noise, frustration, patting, and rocking). The complex emotional patterns of the adult or older child, such as fearing the I.R.S., raging at the Ayatollah, loving one's spouse, had to be learned, specifically through classical conditioning—they were CR's and CS's. Emotional CR's Watson and Rayner called *CER*'s, **conditioned emotional reactions.**

To demonstrate this, Watson and Rayner secured a nine-month-old baby, "Albert B.," as a subject, and investigated the CER of fear. First, they determined for a wide range of stimuli that Albert was not afraid of them, that is, that they elicited no fear UR or CER. Then they found a reliable elicitor (US) of fear, striking a hammer on a steel bar. Albert would check his breathing, start, and finally cry.

At 11 months, Albert was presented with a tame white rat he was known to approach. This time, when he touched the rat, the US was applied—the bar was struck. After a total of seven pairings (spaced over a week), the rat was presented alone and proved to be a CS: "The instant the rat was shown the baby began to cry. Almost instantly he turned sharply to the left, fell over on the left side, raised himself on all fours and began to crawl away . . . rapidly . . ." (Watson & Rayner, 1920, p. 5, italics deleted). A CER had been established.

Five days later, Albert's CER was tested for generalization. Albert still showed fear to the rat, considerable fear to a rabbit and a fur coat, less to a dog, Watson's hair, a Santa Claus mask, and cotton balls, and none at all to his blocks. Moreover, there was less fear to the same stimuli in a very different setting. So generalization of the CER was shown. Watson did, however, have to keep "freshening up" the CR with new reinforcement. Even without freshening, the CER lasted at least a month, when Albert was removed from the hospital where his mother worked as a wet nurse, and the tests ended.

Contrary to popular belief (Harris, 1979), Watson and Rayner never undid their conditioning. It is to be hoped that the CER weakened completely. Watson and Rayner had intended to "cure" Albert, however, and they list three of the later important techniques of behavior modification they would have used: implosion (extinction), counter-conditioning (pair the CS with a pleasant US), and modeling.

Watson and Rayner demonstrated classical conditioning in a young human being—although doubts about the validity of their results have recently been expressed (Samelson, 1980). Many other studies on children and adults also were carried out, but the Watson–Rayner study exemplifies the others, and is one of the most widely cited works in all of psychology.

Classical Conditioning Today

Despite Watson's protestations that there was only one kind of learning, the interests of most American psychologists shifted from classical conditioning to instrumental, or operant, learning. Classical conditioning work continued, nevertheless, since it was one of the two shared exemplars of behaviorism (see Kimble, 1961, and Prokasy, 1965, for reviews). However, no fundamental questions arose until the 1960s, when three important issues surfaced. First, questions of species' constraints on what could be learned were discovered, contrary to Pavlov and others (see Chapter 4). Second, the distinction of the two kinds of learning was questioned. The third fundamental question arose because it became apparent that there was a cognitive aspect to conditioning that was more important than simple US-CS contiguity. We have hinted at this before when we observed that *exact* contiguity between US and CS produced no conditioning, and that the CS had to "signal" the onset of the US by slightly preceding it. A simple experiment underscores the importance of the CS being a signal. Rescorla (1968) paired neutral CS's with foot-shock US's to condition fear in rats. But in addition to the US-CS pairings, the rats received shocks at random intervals as well. The CS-US contiguity was present, for the CS always occurred with a US, but no conditioned fear was learned. The random shocks robbed the CS of its informational or predictive value: Although CS and US were paired, the extra shocks meant the CS was useless to the rats as a signal for expecting shocks, and so the rats showed no fear of it.

Another experimental finding, the *blocking* of conditioning (Kamin, 1968, 1969), also reveals the importance of CS signaling. Rats were shocked (US) while a noise sounded (CS), and conditioned fear resulted. Then, for a number of trials an additional CS (a light) was added, and the rats continued to receive shocks to the two CS's. However, despite contiguity of the light CS with the shock US, no fear was conditioned to the light. The new CS added no information to the old, so no learning occurred.

These and other findings have moved theorists of classical conditioning to incorporate cognitive elements into their theories. The most influential theory is that of Rescorla (Rescorla, 1975, 1978; Rescorla & Wagner, 1972), who in the spirit of Tolman (see Chapter 3) views conditioning as learning the regularities of events in one's environment, not as establishing S-R reflexes. Adaptive behavior then flows from what the animal knows about the world, instead of being blind responses to triggering stimuli.

Mackintosh (1978) takes a different cognitive stance, considering conditioning a matter of learning what to attend to or ignore in the environment. A CS that does not predict a US is ignored; one that does predict is attended to and controls behavior. Finally, Wagner (1978) has brought the complex information processing model of human beings (see Chapters 6 and 7) to bear on the problem of blocking in rats. While traditional behaviorists proposed animal-based theories of human learning, their modern descendents are proposing human-based theories of animal memory!

Rescorla (1975) has also chastised traditionalists for narrowly looking at CR's that resembled the original UR, as Pavlov did, ignoring other behavioral changes that accompanied learning. Seeing this opens up a new perspective on learning. Consider this long-standing puzzle in human (and some animal) classical conditioning. If you shock someone, this aversive stimulus causes the person's heart rate to go up. Now pair the shock with a CS, a tone, for example. The conditioning that takes place is paradoxical: After some pairings the tone elicits not heart rate acceleration, but rather *deceleration*. The CR is the *opposite* of the UR! (See Obrist, Sutterer, & Howard, 1972.) This becomes explicable only with a new perspective on learning that moves away from the reflexive orientation, and even has interesting implications for understanding drug addiction, as explained in Box 2–1.

BOX 2–1*

Understanding classical conditioning as an adaptive process has led to an intriguing hypothesis about drug addiction: that it is a primarily *learned* phenomenon. This hypothesis is based on the observation that in conditioning with a drug as the US, the acquired CR is the opposite of the UR. This makes adaptive sense, because the CS acts as a signal warning of imminent drug delivery (the US), and the body prepares itself by altering its physiology (the CR) in directions opposite to the effects of the drug (the UR). As a result, over trials, the actual effect of the drug becomes weaker and weaker. The adaptive process of learning is shown in Figure 2–2.

Now consider a person taking heroin. Initially, the drug creates a pleasurable high. However, certain stimuli regularly precede drug use—most immediately the sight of the hypodermic, but also the user's regular haunts and friends. These stimuli come to act as CS's, signaling drug delivery, and a preparatory CR appears and strengthens over time. So increasing doses are needed to experience any high at all, as the net drug effect diminishes; the addict—for such he or she has become—may overdose in time. Moreover, the CR is the opposite of the UR—the wretched craving of the addict for more heroin, making life miserable without the drug.

If this hypothesis is correct, then certain implications for drug rehabilitation become apparent. For example, in animal studies, drug tolerance has been extinguished by presenting the cues (CS's) that formerly signaled drug delivery, without administering the drug (US). So perhaps the best way to treat drug addicts is in their home community, where familiar places and people may be experienced without heroin. Removing addicts to a remote treatment center may be ineffective, as their eventual return home will return them to CS's that will elicit an unextinguished CR, and a probable return to the heroin habit.

*See Siegel, S. The role of conditioning in drug tolerance and addiction. In J. D. Keehn (Ed.), *Psychopathology in animals: Research and clinical implications.* New York: Academic Press, 1979.

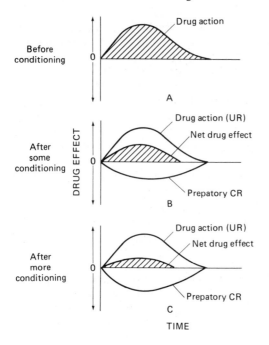

FIGURE 2-2 Time course of the net drug effect (shaded area) resulting from the interactions between the pharmacological unconditional response (UR) and the compensatory conditional response (CR) during successive stages in conditioning. From K. Hollis, Pavlovian conditioning of signal-centered action patterns and autonomic behavior: A biological analysis of function. In J. Rosenblatt et al. (Eds.) *Advances in the study of behavior* (Vol. 12). New York: Academic Press, 1982.

As Schwartz (1978) points out, learning, to be advantageous to the organism, must be adaptive. Now, it is not very adaptive to elevate your heart rate just before a stimulus will occur that in turn will elevate it even more. The functional and adaptive thing to do would be to lower heart rate when the CS signal occurs, to minimize the impact of the shock on your system.

Thus, it seems that even in classical conditioning, more than blind, stupid reflexive learning takes place: Organisms, especially human ones, learn about the world from their experience, and what they learn provides the basis for adaptive action.

Adaptive activity has always been the central focus of our second kind of learning, trial-and-error, instrumental, or operant conditioning.

OPERANT CONDITIONING

Thorndike's Research Program

Just a few years before Pavlov discovered his "psychical reflexes," an American psychologist named Edward Lee Thorndike (1874–1949) began his own experimental researches into what he called **trial-and-error learn-**

ing. Today, this other kind of learning is usually called *instrumental* or *operant learning*, because instead of being completely passive, like Pavlov's harnessed dogs, organisms in this kind of experiment must *operate* on the environment in some way to get rewarded.

While Thorndike also was influenced by associationism, his research program was quite different from Pavlov's. To begin with, Thorndike was a psychologist, not a physiologist, and was consequently interested in behavior change itself instead of in the light thrown by learning on cerebral functioning. Moreover, the intellectual tradition out of which Thorndike came was American functionalism, not physiological, Russian reflexology. The functionalists were interested in the individual Darwinian question: How does the organism's mind adapt it to the demands of its environment? Finally, the specific context in which Thorndike worked was Anglo-American comparative or, as it was called then, animal psychology.

Animal psychologists wanted to be able to establish the relative mental abilities of different animal species. The work began with Darwin's friend George Romanes (1848–1894) and his 1882 book *Animal Intelligence*. Romanes employed what has come to be called the *anecdotal method*. He collected stories (anecdotes) about the behavior of animals, often pets, in different situations. He then sifted through the stories and attempted to reconstruct the mental processes of the animals involved, aiming at a relative assessment of the intelligence of each species.

But Thorndike (1911) was highly critical of the anecdotal method. It tended, he believed, to overestimate the abilities of animals. One tends to notice only when animals are being clever, not when they are being ordinary or even stupid; in the case of pets, the tendency to see only the best will be especially marked. Worse, the anecdotal method, with its attendant reconstruction of the animal's thought processes, was easily given to anthropomorphism. If we watch an animal solving a problem, we tend to put ourselves in its place and project onto the animal the thoughts we would have while doing the same thing. Thorndike observed, as had Pavlov, that experimentation was needed to gather conservative, objective scientific data about this area of psychology.

But Pavlov was a physiologist studying the reflexes of the brain, and Thorndike was a functionalist psychologist studying the adaptation of individual organisms to their environment. Thus, their methodologies diverged sharply. Pavlov's research exemplar was admirably suited to studying nervous reflexes: Start with a US that already elicits a reflex and pair it with a CS to create a new, learned reflex. What Thorndike needed was an environment, more controlled than a pet-owner's back yard, that could present a set problem to an animal. In short, he needed to invent a controlled but challenging environment to which a subject would have to adapt. He hit on a solution with his famous *puzzle-boxes*.

Less well established than the famous Pavlov, Thorndike, a graduate student at Harvard, set up his laboratory in William James' basement. Soon, fortune smiled, however, and he did most of his work at Columbia University. Thorndike constructed a number of puzzle-boxes (see Figure 2–3) in which he placed one of his subjects, a kitten or a dog (he also experi-

FIGURE 2-3 One of Thorndike's Puzzle Boxes. (From Thorndike, 1911, p. 30)

mented with chicks placed in a maze). As you can see, the puzzle-box is a sort of cage so constructed that the door can be opened by the animal from the inside, providing it learns to make a correct response. Thorndike designed many variations of his boxes, but most required the animal to pull on a string dangling in the box, which in turn ran over a pulley and opened the door, releasing the animal, who was then fed before being placed back in the box. Thorndike wanted to know exactly how the subject learns the correct response. He described what happens:

> The cat that is clawing all over the box in her impulsive struggle will probably claw the string or loop or button so as to open the door. And gradually all the other nonsuccessful impulses will be stamped out and the particular impulse leading to the successful act will be stamped in by the resulting pleasure, until, after many trials, the cat will, when put in the box, immediately claw the button or loop in a definite way. (Thorndike, 1911, p. 36)

Thorndike conceived his study as one of association-formation, and interpreted his animals' behaviors in terms of associationism:

> Starting, then, with its store of instinctive impulses, the cat hits upon the successful movement, and gradually associates it with the sense-impression of the interior of the box until the connection is perfect, so that it performs the act as soon as confronted with the sense-impression. (Thorndike, 1911, p. 38)

The phrase *trial-and-error,* or perhaps more exactly *trial-and-success,* learning aptly describes what these animals did in the puzzle-boxes. Placed inside, they try out (or, as Skinner called it later, *emit*) a variety of familiar behaviors. In cats, it was likely to try squeezing through the bars, clawing at the cage, sticking its paws between the bars. Eventually, the cat is likely to scratch at the loop of string and so pull on it, finding its efforts rewarded:

The door opens and it escapes, only to be caught by Thorndike and placed back in the box. As these events are repeated, the useless behaviors die away, or extinguish, and the correct behavior is done soon after entering the cage; the cat has learned the correct response needed to escape.

Thorndike's description of his cats' struggles meshes with our own intuitions of how we learn our own nonreflexive, voluntary behaviors. Confronted by a new situation, we try out a number of reactions. Eventually, we hit on a behavior that works (unless we give up). Later, when we meet the situation again, or one like it, we know what to do. In short, both Thorndike's cats and people slowly *adapt* to the environment. This kind of learning is not reflexive. Pavlov could initially *make* his dogs salivate by presenting the US, but there is no stimulus that Thorndike could have presented that would have forced the cats, zombie-like, to walk over to and pull the dangling cord leading to escape. In a sense, a US forces a subject to make the correct, reinforced response; the dog salivates and is fed. In trial-and-error learning, however, we must await for the correct response to occur, and then pounce on it with reinforcement. This is the most obvious laboratory difference between reflexive learning and operant learning.

Thorndike began his research program seeking to understand how the mind adapts an organism to its environment. He ended up, however, seeing learning as a far simpler affair, probably not involving mind at all. He showed that animals, or at least cats, dogs, and chicks, do not learn by imitation, nor do they reason and have memory. Instead, he found himself driven to the conclusion that although association is real enough, what is associated is not ideas at all, but simply situations (S) and responses (R). Learning, Thorndike concluded, consisted only in changing the degree of control a certain stimulus exerts over a given response, by either rewarding or punishing the connection. Thorndike states this in his famous **law of effect,** the basic law of all operant learning:

> The Law of Effect is that: Of several responses made to the same situation, those which are accompanied or closely followed by satisfaction to the animal will, other things being equal, be more firmly connected with the situation, so that, when it recurs, they will be more likely to recur; those which are accompanied or closely followed by discomfort to the animal will, other things being equal, have their connections with that situation weakened, so that, when it recurs, they will be less likely to occur. The greater the satisfaction or discomfort, the greater the strengthening or weakening of the bond. (Thorndike, 1911, p. 244)

As Thorndike moved into his first love, education, he extended his S-R psychology to human beings (Thorndike, 1928), but it was never as influential as Clark Hull's S-R psychology (see Chapter 3). In doing so, Thorndike also anticipated some of the problems that would lead cognitive psychologists away from behaviorism and back to the ideas Thorndike himself rejected.

The specifics of Thorndike's shared exemplar, the puzzle-box, also had a limited influence. Although the puzzle-box exerted more experimental control than the natural environment of the anecdotalists, it really did not give the experimenter much to manipulate besides the intricacy of the release mechanism. Therefore, later behaviorists used other specific experimental arrangements, first the maze and then, the triumphant exemplar of operant learning, the Skinner box. Despite their differences, the spirit of each device remains Thorndikian—provide a controlled environment in which an animal is rewarded for the specific response you want the animal to learn.

Pavlov and Thorndike, between them, laid the experimental foundations of behavioral psychology. Each provided a first experimental technique for investigating the laws of association in animals, reasoning that in this way the laws could be clearly worked out for later application to complex human behavior. Each elucidated important fundamental laws and phenomena of learning; Thorndike the law of effect, and Pavlov the phenomena of extinction, spontaneous recovery, generalization, discrimination, and inhibition, that by and large apply to operant conditioning as well as classical conditioning (Hearst, 1975).

Since instrumental learning in one form or another became the subject of most behavioral investigations—even in parapsychology (see Box 2–2)—we do not need a section here on operant learning today because we will be looking at that in Chapter 4. But one current controversy does belong here, for it challenges our intuitive notion, shared by most learning psychologists, that there are two kinds of learning.

BOX 2–2   *LEARNING ESP?*

Parapsychology's card-guessing experiments are familiar: One subject, a sender, goes through a set of specially designed playing cards, one at time, while another subject, a receiver, tries to guess what each card is. If ESP is present, then the receiver will make more correct guesses than we would expect on the basis of random guessing.

In these experiments the receiver isn't told whether each guess is a hit or a miss. The parapsychologist Charles Tart (1975) has pointed out that these experiments are therefore just like extinction experiments in operant learning. The subject makes a response, and even if it is correct, it is never reinforced; just as a cat in a Thorndike puzzle-box would stop pulling the string if it never opened the door. Tart says we see the same thing in the notorious *decline effect* in card-guessing experiments: Gifted subjects start off well but *always* lapse to chance toward the end of the experiment.

Tart came up with a sort of ESP Skinner box, in which receivers guess a hidden target and find out if they're right (reinforcement) or wrong. Starting with gifted subjects, Tart found he could maintain their guessing, although no subject actually improved performance. Whether or not there's anything to ESP, it is surprising it took so long to apply operant methods to it. And even then, Tart's results are disappointing. Either you have ESP or you don't; and you can lose it (extinction), but you cannot learn it.

Two Kinds of Learning or One?

Although we have found the distinction between operant and classical conditioning to be intuitive and comfortable, and have seen how different kinds of research programs develop out of each one, current research has shown that the two kinds of conditioning are more similar than we thought. Psychologists now are feeling uneasy over the simple picture they formerly accepted.

We can most easily approach the new confused situation through a simple thought experiment. Suppose I subject you to a typical classical conditioning procedure involving the eyeblink reflex. Holding your head fixed in a stand, I sound a tone and mechanically puff air into your face. If I do this a few times, I find that when I sound the tone you blink your eye. We can analyze this as an experiment in classical conditioning. We start with an unconditional reflex between a US (puff of air) and a UR (eyeblink), and pair the US with a neutral CS (the tone), finding that you acquire a CR (eyeblink). This appears a straightforward example of Pavlovian conditioning.

But is it? Suppose instead of the above procedure I had told you, "When the tone sounds, you'll shortly find your eye puffed at with air." In all likelihood, to avoid the unpleasant air in your eye, you would blink voluntarily when you heard the tone. The following US would not elicit the reflex, the eye already being closed. So there need be no US-CS pairing at all for "conditioning" to occur, since eyeblinks are voluntary as well as reflexive behaviors.

If we return to the original experiment, then, we find it can be analyzed as operant conditioning. You find the air puff aversive and close your eye for the "reward" of ending your pain. The law of effect seems to operate—you learn to blink your eye for the "satisfaction" of ending the uncomfortable blast of air. Such ambiguity between what is classical and what is operant learning has grown since the 1970s.

While a number of criteria have been advanced to separate classical and instrumental learning (see Hearst, 1975, for a review), two of these, one substantive and one procedural, have been most frequently defended. Substantively, it has been proposed that different *kinds of responses,* mediated by different nervous systems, are conditionable only by one kind of procedure or the other. Thus, classical conditioning applies only to the glandular and smooth muscle responses of the autonomic nervous system, while operant conditioning applies only to the striated muscle, and "skeletal" responses of the somatic nervous system.

But eyelid movement is a "skeletal" response, and it is best conditioned by classical procedures. On the other hand, operant control of autonomic processes has proved possible, and indeed has become famous as "biofeedback." People have learned to modulate their heart rate, blood pressure, and brain alpha waves simply by being hooked up to devices that tell them if their heart rate is high or low, blood pressure high or low, or alpha wave production high or low. People do not necessarily learn direct control over these "involuntary" responses, however, using instead little tricks that lead to the rewarded bodily change. Hence, one might alter one's heart rate by indulging in sexual fantasies, or salivate by thinking of food. In these cases, an operant behavior has been learned that happens to lead to a change in a "classical" response. Consequently, animals have been given curare, which suppresses all skeletal activity, and then have been rewarded for changes in smooth-muscle activity. Rats have been taught, to mention only their most spectacular achievements, to control the dilation of blood vessels in each ear and to regulate the amount of urine produced by their kidneys! (Miller, 1969).

Thus, it seems we cannot distinguish operant and classical learning on the basis of the responses each produces. This conclusion is strengthened by remembering that sometimes in classical conditioning the CR is the opposite of the UR. This leaves us with the procedural distinction. In classical conditioning the experimenter presents US and CS together, quite independent of, and indeed before, any response occurs. In operant conditioning, on the other hand, the reward follows and, more importantly, is *contingent on* some response—the reward is given only when the desired response occurs (the cat must pull the string to escape).

But as Hearst (1975) points out, even this simple procedural distinction is often blurred in practice. Skinner has studied what he calls "superstitious behavior" (see Chapter 4). Food is delivered at regular intervals to a pigeon walking around in a chamber. What happens is that each reward strengthens the behavior occurring when it's delivered, and after a few rewards, the pigeon is behaving very oddly indeed, trying to do all the behaviors it has been "rewarded" for. However, the food delivery did not actually depend on what the pigeon did, any more than food delivery depended on what Pavlov's dog did. Nevertheless, Skinner regards superstitious behavior as an example of operant, not classical, conditioning. Is he right?

How muddy the waters have become is shown by considering that operant and Pavlovian conditioning always go on at the same time—to further confuse the issue. After pressing a bar to get food in a Skinner box, the animal eats food (US) in the box (CS) and so we should not be surprised to find that the animal begins to salivate when we put the creature in the box for a new day of training. Similarly, a dog, classically conditioned to salivate to the sound of a metronome, would, if simply released in the room, run to the machine, jump up to it, and wag its tail—all operant behaviors (Hearst, 1975).

The interaction of Pavlovian and classical conditioning is powerfully demonstrated in auto-shaping (Brown & Jenkins, 1968), which we will look at again in Chapter 4. Here, a pigeon is put in a Skinner box with a key that can be lighted up. Then we simply put food in the cup and light the key at the same time. We find that after some pairings of US (food) and CS (light), the pigeon will peck the key when it's lighted even though it does not have to in order to get fed. The behavior of pigeons during auto-shaping is just like that of pigeons being taught to peck a key in order to be rewarded with food. So, we find operant behavior controlled by simple, "classical" US-CS pairings. Auto-shaped key-pecks even violate the law of effect, as a variation on this experiment shows. If the pigeon's pecking at the key is made to block delivery of food, while not pecking would produce food, the pigeon pecks the key anyway! This is called *negative auto-maintenance*. In addition to blurring the line between operant and classical learning, such studies also reveal biological constraints on learning, which we will consider in Chapter 4. This area of operant Pavlovian interactions has become an intensive focus of research (Davis & Hurwitz, 1977).

Of course, as the psychophysicist S.S. Stevens has remarked, just because the exact borderline between night and day may be hard to pinpoint does not mean we should not distinguish them, and similarly the distinction between classical and instrumental conditioning may be defended as useful if a little fuzzy.

In any event, the rise of cognitive theories of learning and memory may make the issue moot. Cognitive theories say that what any organism, human or animal, learns is useful information about its environment, information that tells it how to act. But cognitive theories do not care much about how the information gets into the organism, whether by US-CS pairings or response-reward pairings. Concentrating on the stored information will lead psychologists away from drawing a hard and fast line between kinds of learning, be they one, two, or many.

DO HUMANS CONDITION?

Asking whether humans condition may be surprising, since we have already discussed some studies of human conditioning, but William Brewer (1974) has suggested that the picture is not so simple. Obviously, if we reward people for some activity, or pair US's and CS's, their behavior will change. But as scientists, we want to know *why* behavior changes, not just record that it does.

From the time of Thorndike, most behaviorists have believed in the *automatic action of reinforcers*. As Thorndike put it, reward and punishment simply stamp in or stamp out the responses they follow. A subject does not have to be aware of the connection between one's behavior and its consequences, or of the regular pairing of US and CS, for conditioning to occur. The action of reinforcers was held to be direct and automatic, unmediated by consciousness or thought (Postman and Sassenrath, 1961), which behaviorists were trying to throw out of psychology anyway. In the behaviorist view, then, the mental state of a person is simply irrelevant to behavior, which is instead the outcome of stimuli and reinforcers in one's environment (Skinner, 1954).

On the other hand, cognitive psychologists like Brewer contend that when a subject learns something, or "conditions," what really happens is that the subject figures out what's going on in the experiment and then acts appropriately. In the cognitive view, then, what changes during a person's "conditioning" is his or her conscious mental state, with behavior changing because the subject has "solved" the experiment. Therefore, it should be possible to create and extinguish CR's and operant responses by directly manipulating subjects' mental states, without actually doing any conditioning. Or it should be possible to fool people about what's really going on in an experiment so that they do not condition despite manipulation of stimuli or reinforcers, or learn associations other than those of CS and US, or response and reward. In general, the cognitive hypothesis maintains that beliefs about the environment are more important in regulating behavior than the actual environment.

Brewer (1974) reviewed over 200 studies done by others that tested the automatic action of the reinforcers view against the cognitive view. To illustrate the findings on this dispute we will just look at the results from two traditional areas of learning, one autonomic, or classical, and the other operant.

Autonomic Conditioning

As an example of classical conditioning of an autonomic response, we will consider conditioning the galvanic skin response (GSR). When you are frightened or aroused, you sweat, changing the ability of your skin to conduct electricity; lie detectors use this fact to detect the bodily arousal that should accompany the stress of lying. Electric shock produces the GSR response, and we can pair a tone (CS) with the shock (US) to condition a conditional GSR. Many such studies have been carried out.

What if we simply tell subjects that when they hear the tone they will be shocked, without ever doing it? The result is that subjects acquire a conditional GSR. On the other hand, already conditioned subjects who are told the shocks will no longer follow the CS show immediate extinction, at least in those subjects who believe us; however, many don't. Studies that follow the usual conditioning procedures and then ask the subjects if they figured out the CS-US connection found that only those who had figured out the connection displayed any conditioning.

More sophisticated experiments fool the subject about what is going on. For example, in one experiment subjects heard a repeated series of five tones, the last of which was either high or low. The high tone was accompanied by shock; the low tone was not. From Pavlov's work, we would expect this to condition a GSR to the high tone, but not to the low tone. After they heard each series of tones, the subjects had to say which of the last four tones was most like the first. Finally, half the subjects were told they were just in a sensory discrimination experiment, and were not told about the shock–last-tone relation. Although *all* subjects in fact received US-CS pairings, *only* those who had been told about the last-tone–shock connection acquired a conditional GSR.

Motor Conditioning

As an example of motor response learning, we will select finger-withdrawal conditioning. In this kind of experiment, subjects rest their fingers, palm down, on an electrode. A tone is sounded and the subject is shocked. Subjects soon learn to avoid the shock.

Behaviorists take nothing for granted, and one investigator showed that people will lift their finger when instructed to do so to avoid shock, even if they never get shocked. Similar experiments were done with eyeblink conditioning, except that *five* studies had to be done to convince behaviorists that subjects can blink when told to! Like the GSR studies, telling the subjects the shocks will stop produces immediate extinction, and only subjects who are aware of the shock-tone relation do condition.

Subjects in finger-withdrawal conditioning have also been fooled by instructions. After we condition subjects by ordinary means, suppose we turn their hand over and present the tone? Will they withdraw their finger, making the opposite motor response from what they had learned, or will they move their finger in the same way as before, pressing their finger into the electrode? By and large, about 75 percent of subjects make the new flexion response that gets their finger off the electrode, 5 percent press their fingers into the electrode, and 20 percent make no response.

With this established finding in mind, let us consider an experiment in which subjects' beliefs are manipulated. One group is put through the above procedure. Another group receives the same conditioning, but is told that what they are expected to learn is a particular muscle movement— withdrawing the finger up, with palm down. Finally, the last group is conditioned, but in the second half of the experiment they are lied to about the location of the electrode, so that in trying to avoid the shock they will actually be pressing their finger into the electrode. The first, or standard, group produced the usual results just described. In the group told they were learning a simple muscle reflex, only about one-third gave responses away from the electrode in the second part of the experiment when they turned their hands over. The third group gave *all* their responses into the electrode. We see here that what subjects think the experimenter wants them to do is generally more powerful than actually getting shocked.

Conclusion

These are only a few of the studies Brewer (1974) reviews to challenge the view that human beings condition automatically without the intervention of mental processes. Exactly if and when people condition without awareness is an open issue. Some experiments have been done to support Brewer's position (Solanto & Katkin, 1979). Others support the finding that only aware subjects learn, but interpret this as an outcome, not a cause of physiological learning (Maltzman, 1977, 1979; Pendery & Maltzman, 1977; Maltzman, Raskin, & Wolff, 1979); still others have attempted to assimilate Brewer's challenging findings into standard behavior theories (Galizio, 1979). Despite Brewer's review, advertisers believe people condition—and even believe in the old stimulus–substitution theory of conditioning; see Box 2–3.

In conclusion, it is interesting to observe that the studies Brewer reviews, almost all of which support the cognitive position, go back as early as 1919 and were produced in all the following decades up into the 1970s, right through the dominance of behavioral theories in the field of learning. This shows the power of paradigms: If research programs are going well, then occasional results that appear contrary to the program's hard core (that is, the automatic action of reinforcers) are either quietly ignored,

BOX 2-3   *PAVLOV ON MADISON AVENUE**

Joel S. Dubow, communication's research manager at the Coca-Cola Company says "We nominate Pavlov as the father of modern advertising. Pavlov took a neutral object and, by associating it with a meaningful object, made it a symbol of something else; he imbued it with imagery, he gave it added value. That is what we try to do in modern advertising."

Whether Coke's "Pavlovian" advertising techniques work or not, they cannot work the way Mr. Dubow thinks. In the first place, as we've just learned, it is unlikely that humans classically condition at all; Brewer's (1974) view is now the consensus (Fox, 1983). Even Mr. Dubow's own description of conditioning is cognitive and unbehavioristic; he is not really describing conditioning at all, even if he thinks he is.

Moreover, Mr. Dubow is still clinging to the outmoded stimulus-substitution theory of classical conditioning, which explained conditioning as a process in which the CS comes to be a substitute for the US. But as we discussed earlier, the stimulus-substitution theory has been replaced by the cognitive theory of the CS coming to be a signal preparing the learner to adapt to the coming US. So a "neutral object" in an advertisement will not become a "symbol" of a "meaningful object" through classical conditioning.

As we will see in several later chapters, advertisers often use psychological methods and themes in producing an ad campaign. In the present case, the method is not properly understood and the theory is out of date. Again, we do not mean Coke's ads are ineffective, only that like so many psychological phenomena, they don't work the way we used to think.

*See John Koten, Marketing: Coca-Cola turns to Pavlov. *Wall Street Journal*, Thursday, January 19, 1984, p. 33.

called interesting phenomena to be shelved for later study, or explained away. Only when an alternative view emerges, as cognitive theory emerged in the 1960s to rival behavior theory, do the old anomalies appear significant. Not until the 1970s did anyone assemble the separate pieces into a picture disquieting to traditionalists.

SUGGESTED READINGS

Biographies of the major figures in this chapter are available. *Pavlov*: B. P. Babkin, *Pavlov* (Chicago: University of Chicago Press, 1949); *Watson*: David Cohen, *J. B. Watson* (London: Routledge & Kegan Paul, 1979); *Thorndike*: G. Joncich, *The Sane Positivist* (Middletown, Conn.: Wesleyan University Press, 1968). Broader treatments of all three figures as well as early behaviorism can be found in T.H. Leahey, *A History of Psychology* (Englewood Cliffs, N. J.: Prentice-Hall, 1980).

CHAPTER THREE

ANIMAL-BASED THEORY I: FORMAL BEHAVIORISM

Having reviewed the fundamental research that began the behavioral psychology of learning, we will now turn to the theoreticians who built their ideas on Pavlov's and Thorndike's work. The 1930s and 1940s were known as "The Golden Age of Theory" in American psychology. During that time, behaviorism was the dominant school of psychology, and learning was the core of psychology. The field of learning was contested by the three theoreticians that are the subject of this chapter: Edwin R. Guthrie (1886–1959), Clark L. Hull (1884–1952), and Edward Chace Tolman (1886–1959). Their critic and most influential successor, B. F. Skinner, will be treated in the following chapter.

Don Dulany (see Leahey, 1980a) has also called the period 1930–1950 the era of formal behaviorism, because each of the major theories was proposed as a relatively formal theory cast in the mold of the day's dominant philosophy of science, namely, logical positivism. Of the three leading contestants, Hull's theory was by far the most formal, while Guthrie's was the least formal, and Tolman's was somewhere in the middle. So strong was the desire for rigorous theorizing in the manner of physics—at least as psychologists took it to be (Leahey, 1980b)—that both Guthrie's (Voeks, 1950) and Tolman's (MacCorquodale & Meehl, 1954) theories were brought up to Hull's standards of formalization by other psychologists.

None of the three theories discussed in this chapter has survived in anything like its original form, having been subject to a general decline of interest (Koch, 1951) and to scathing criticism by Skinner (1950) and others (Estes, Koch, MacCorquodale, Meehl, Mueller, Schoenfeld, & Verplanck, 1954). The influence of each has been more subterranean, raising important issues and spawning related theories. They also kept alive certain points of view that would have been lost if the psychology of learning had been dominated by a single paradigm. We will therefore focus only on the general orientation of each theory, citing references for the student who wishes more detail.

STRICT ASSOCIATIONISM:

The Theoretical Program of E. R. Guthrie

Guthrie did relatively little research, producing a primarily theoretical program, which was the least influential of the big-three theories of the Golden Age. Guthrie was not nearly as systematic as Hull, or even Tolman. But his theory did raise several important issues. Certain theoretical and empirical problems are endemic to the psychology of learning, and Guthrie forcefully drew attention to three that are still extant today.

Two kinds of learning or one?   We have already examined some recent evidence casting doubt on the instrumental conditioning–classical conditioning dichotomy. Already in the 1930s Guthrie's theory was based on the premise that there is only one kind of learning (Guthrie, 1940). The single learning process Guthrie recognized was the forming of simple associations between stimuli and movements. These associations are not to be identified with either classical or operant conditioning, but were held by Guthrie to underlie both.

Guthrie believed in strict association by immediate simultaneous contiguity. That is, in a learning situation you learn a connection between whatever stimuli are present at a given moment and the behaviors that are occurring at the same time. As Guthrie put it, "Stimuli which are acting at the time of a response tend on their recurrence to evoke that response" (Guthrie, 1933, p. 365). This is his one fundamental law of learning, superseding Pavlov's cortical account of classical conditioning and Thorndike's law of effect in instrumental learning. Guthrie always sought the simplest theory possible, and he believed that bare association by contiguity could account for all learning.

Applying this idea to classical conditioning, Guthrie had to face Pavlov's showing that simultaneous presentation of US and CS resulted in little or no conditioning. The best arrangement Pavlov found was for the CS to precede and overlap the US. This appears inconsistent with Guthrie's insistence on simultaneous association.

But Guthrie had an ingenious explanation, subsequently invoked by other psychologists who in other situations needed to fill gaps between S's and R's. As Guthrie (1930, 1952) saw it, every stimulus, even an apparently neutral CS, provokes some response or series of responses. Sound a tone and a dog may flex an ear to listen, shift his posture, or turn his head. All these responses in turn produce stimuli, which themselves produce responses, which produce stimuli, etc. . . . So any stimulus, even a CS, initiates a chain of R—S—R—S . . . connections. Thus, when Pavlov sounded a tone, the CS created in the dog certain movements, which in turn produced stimuli present when the US subsequently occurred, and it is these *movement-produced stimuli* that get conditioned to the CR. So the real CS in Pavlov's experiment is not the CS he administered, but the stimuli it evoked, and simultaneously present when salivation occurs.

Guthrie's reasoning also gave a clever account of generalization. Generalization appears to be inconsistent with Guthrie's associationism: If a dog has learned to salivate to a 1000-cycle-per-second tone, why does it also salivate to a 900-cycle-per-second tone? The 900 Hz (Hertz) tone was never coupled with salivating, and so under Guthrie's theory ought not be associated with salivating. But Guthrie argued that listening to a 900-Hz tone was quite like listening to a 1000-Hz tone, and therefore elicited many of the same movement-produced stimuli; it is these identical movement-produced stimuli that elicit the "generalized CR" (Guthrie, 1952).

Having briefly reviewed Guthrie's analysis of classical conditioning, we will turn to Thorndike's puzzle-boxes, with which Guthrie was quite familiar. They had been the object of his one extensive piece of research (Guthrie & Horton, 1946; also fully reported in Guthrie, 1952). Guthrie was very tough on the law of effect and the terms *reward* and *punishment* (Guthrie, 1934). The law of effect seemed to him to be unscientific, for it let one thing (the reward or punishment) affect another thing that had already occurred. This appears to be backward causation, since we say the reward strengthens a *past event,* the response. Guthrie thought causes had to precede effects. Reward and punishment were, Guthrie believed, unscientific "moral" terms used by people in power to describe the effects they wish to have on another's behavior; Guthrie preferred to find out objectively what kinds of stimuli have what kinds of effects.

Now, remember a cat struggling to escape from a puzzle-box. At some point the cat bumps into or claws at a vertical lever (in Guthrie's boxes) that opens the door and allows the cat to escape. Thorndike saw here the effect of reward (escape) on behavior (the cat learns to work the lever to get out). Guthrie's view was quite different. The box is a distinct stimulus-situation in which responses are occurring, and by Guthrie's law of learning each time a response occurs it gets conditioned to the box-stimuli. Moreover, as each response occurs it *replaces* the S-R bond between the previous response and the box-stimuli. At some point the cat makes a response that operates the lever; say it rubs against the lever with its left shoulder. The door flies open, and the cat flies out.

Thus, the *last response* to occur in the presence of and, therefore, be conditioned to, the box stimuli was rubbing the lever with the left shoulder; after that the cat left the box, so no *new* responses could occur that would get conditioned to the box stimuli, and so replace the lever-rubbing response. When the cat is placed back in the box, the stimuli conditioned to the rub-lever-with-shoulder response elicits that response and the cat escapes once more. In Guthrie's (1934, 1939) account, the lever-rub is not stamped in by reward at all. Escape simply ensures that no new responses will occur in the box that would get conditioned to the box-stimuli, breaking the bond with lever-rubbing.

We find, then, that Guthrie was able to interpret plausibly both classical and instrumental conditioning as the outcome of a single process of constantly associating current responses with current stimuli. His single-process theory failed to carry the day, however, succumbing to the traditional distinction of "reflexive" and "voluntary" learning. But we have seen how that distinction is itself in danger of dissolving and being replaced by a new one-process view in which the organism learns relations between environmental stimuli (for example, Rescorla, 1975). Modern one-process theorists have not adopted Guthrie's theory, but they owe him something for having kept the issue alive for many years.

Gradual, or one-trial learning?   Careful study of Guthrie's description of puzzle-box learning reveals another startling feature of his theory, namely that learning takes place all at once, on one trial (Guthrie, 1939). The cat rubs the lever, bonding together S and R, and escapes—the S-R bond is complete; all that subsequent escapes do is to continue to ensure that no new *R* gets conditioned to the box stimuli.

Guthrie's position seems outrageously absurd. Anyone who has learned to hit a golf ball, pitch a baseball, drive a car, or type knows that it took a long time—often unbearably long—to master. It appears ridiculous to say we learned these things all at once.

But Guthrie would reply that these are complex activities. In the jargon of his era, Guthrie was a militantly *molecular* theorist, claiming that a psychologist should not study whole acts. A psychologist who studies swinging a golf club was called *molar*. Instead, a molecular psychologist studied specific muscle movements such as all the muscle activity taking place when swinging a golf club. In Guthrie's theory, then, it is not an act that gets conditioned to stimuli but whatever movements are happening in their presence. To state what the cat learned in Guthrie's puzzle-box was not to push the lever, or even to rub the lever with the left shoulder, but it learned those *exact* muscle movements that were going on when the door opened, and that associative conditioning took place on one trial.

Objecting that it takes a long time to learn to drive a golf ball is not a tenable objection, for golfing is a complex series of muscle movements, not just one response, and each movement must be learned and linked properly into the chain of movements we call "driving a golf ball." Moreover, our movements keep conditioning to new stimuli, since the second tee isn't exactly like the first. (Maybe this is why golfers hit better at a driving range than on the course, since the stimulus situation is always the same at the range, and why we are told to keep our eye on the ball, since at least the ball looks much the same from "trial-to-trial"—and golfers certainly find it a trial!) In Guthrie's scheme of things, essentially, we learn particular muscle-responses on one trial, but it may take many trials to learn and coordinate all the muscle responses that assemble together into a complex act.

To give any empirical support to Guthrie's theory, it is obvious the researcher cannot study a complex act. Guthrie himself tried to do so in his puzzle-box studies (Guthrie, 1952). He and his colleagues photographed cats at the moment they activated the lever and escaped. They found that a cat's subsequent responses varied only a little from trial to trial, indicating that it had learned, and retained, the first trial's movements.

But an even more precise study was carried out by Virginia Voeks (1954) on a simple human reflexive movement, the eyeblink. Specifically, Voeks compared Guthrie's theory to that of Hull, who held the common sense view (mathematically expressed) that learning a habit, however simple, is a gradual affair, each reinforcement adding a little bit to the strength of the habit. Previous studies had supported Hull. If 20 subjects are put through a conditioned eyeblink experiment and we plot trial-by-trial the total number of eyeblinks given to the CS on each trial, we find that total rises slowly and finally levels off.

Adopting Guthrie's molecular strategy, however, Voeks argued that group data are misleading. Suppose one-trial learning does occur. Then, on each trial a given subject either learns or does not learn. One subject may learn on the first trial, another on the third; three may learn on the fourth trial and so on. Adding their responses together we would see "evidence" of gradual learning: trial 1, 1 blink; trial 2, 1 blink; trial 3, 2 blinks; trial 4, 5 blinks, and so on. Each subject would learn to blink on a given trial, and blink on every subsequent trial (all or none learning). However, since as we go from trial to trial *more* subjects condition (and blink ever after), the total number of blinks rises slowly and gradually, seeming to show gradual learning. Voeks looked at the behavior of each subject in her study and found that for most of them, once the blink CR occurred it occurred on every trial thereafter, just as Guthrie's theory predicted. But when she pooled the data, "gradual learning" appeared, an illusion created by adding up everyone's responses.

Despite her acute reasoning and novel treatment of learning data, Voeks' experiment did not convince psychologists of the correctness of Guthrie's theory. But it did at least teach them the perils of mistaking group results for individual learning processes. Since psychologists want to understand individual learning, Voek's study stands as a permanent reminder to pay attention to what individual subjects do. Later, when we study thinking and problem solving we will see Voek's work still giving lessons to cognitive psychologists.

Forgetting: Decay or interference?   Psychologists of learning and memory must study not only how responses are learned and material acquired, but also how responses are lost and previously remembered material forgotten. We have already seen Pavlov addressing the problem of unlearning or forgetting in his studies of extinction. He suggested that CR's that no longer occur are still present, only inhibited, to reoccur when the inhibition lifts. Pavlov's theory of inhibition somewhat resembles Freud's theory of repression, which claims that when we "forget" something we have really only forced it into the unconscious so that we do not have to think about it, as when a boy represses his Oedipal wish to kill his father. In both inhibition and repression, things are not forgotten; they are suppressed. Thorndike, on the other hand, maintained in his law of effect that punishment weakens S-R connections, eventually stamping them out. In Thorndike's view things can be unlearned or forgotten, not just repressed. The effect of punishment is still controversial, and we will come to it again in the next chapter.

Guthrie's (1930) view was different from any of these. In the puzzle-box, for instance, Guthrie claimed that reward, that is, escape, works because it prevents new responses from occurring to the stimuli present when the crucial response was made and conditioned. Guthrie argued from his standpoint of strict associationism that old responses, or S-R connections, get lost not because of inhibition or punishment, but by being *replaced* by new responses to the same situation, creating new S-R connections. So if we don't let the puzzle-box door open when the cat presses the lever as it has learned to, new responses will occur in the presence of the puzzle-box stimuli, replacing the old learned S-R connection. If we let the cat escape after making some new responses, say, rearing on its hind legs, that response will be associated with the puzzle-box stimuli and will recur on the next trial.

Guthrie's argument anticipates a modern issue in the cognitive theory of memory: Do we forget things simply because memories weaken over time (decay theory) or because new learning overlays old learning, making it harder to recall the old material (interference theory)? Guthrie's theory is an interference theory because he did not think S-R bonds, once acquired, naturally weaken with age, but are instead broken by new learning. We will return to this issue in its cognitive form in Chapters 5–6.

Guthrie's Legacy

Of the three major theories of the Golden Age, Guthrie's theory was the least elaborated and the least influential. The amount of research done to support it was small compared to Hull's or Tolman's theories, and it was criticized for its looseness, informality, and lack of systemic rigor (Mueller & Schoenfeld, 1954).

Two other illustrative difficulties deserve mention. First, Guthrie's account of reinforcement as something that protects the most recent response from being unlearned is implausible. It seems to work for the the puzzle-box, where escape indeed releases the animal. But so would a trap door opening under the cat when it pushed the lever; but surely, when placed back in the box, pushing the lever is the last thing the cat would do (Hilgard & Bower, 1975). The second problem concerns Guthrie's molecularism. Consider the experiments on finger withdrawal conditioning (Chapter 2). Subjects first learned to lift their finger to avoid shock. When they turned their hands over they did not repeat the same muscle movement, as Guthrie would have expected, but instead made the opposite movement, curling their finger toward the palm (Wickens, 1938). This shows that people learn such acts as "get finger away from shock," not simple muscle movements such as "flex finger extensor muscle."

Despite these problems, and the recently discovered fact that he tripped over the cat (Box 3–1), we have seen several areas in which Guthrie's theory offered novel analyses of problems in learning, and raised issues that might otherwise have been ignored. His theory also gave rise to a sophisticated and highly technical theory of learning called *stimulus sampling theory* (beginning with Estes, 1950). Stimulus sampling theory attempts to quantify the way in which stimulus elements in a situation get conditioned to responses when accompanied by reinforcement. Guthrie's beliefs in association by contiguity, in all-or-none one-trial learning, and in forgetting as interference, are given elegant formulation in Estes' work (see Robbins, 1980, for a review). Even if it did not really develop a research program, Guthrie's theory was provocative and different.

BOX 3–1   *HOW GUTHRIE TRIPPED OVER THE CAT**

As mentioned in the text, Guthrie's major experiment was a modification of Thorndike's work with puzzle-boxes. Cats were placed in a box that had a tall, thin rod projecting from the floor, and if the cat rubbed against the rod the door of the box opened allowing the animal to escape. The results of the experiment were offered as support for Guthrie's views. The rubbing behavior was stereotyped, occurring in the same form on trial after trial, indicating first-trial learning (since no subsequent modification of behavior occurred), and indicating learning without reward.

However, like all behaviorists, Guthrie ignored the species-specific behavior of his subject. Cats—great, small, and domestic—share a common form of greeting behavior. The tail is raised, the back is arched, and the animal rubs against the greeted cat as it walks by. Should the target animal be far away, the greeter displaces the greeting on to some convenient object such as a tree. Domestic cats typically regard people as conspecifics (i.e., fellow cats) and, as any cat owner knows, perform the greeting on human legs, or on door posts or furniture.

In his research on cats, Guthrie, along with as many as eight other people, observed the cat's behavior in full view of the cat. Recently, Bruce Moore and Susan Stuttard have shown that Guthrie tripped over this part of feline nature. Guthrie's results were an artifact of the situation and the cat's innate greeting response. Moore and Stuttard reproduced Guthrie's experiment except that bar-rubbing opened no doors and whether a person was present or not was varied. They found that when a person was present, the bar was rubbed; when absent, the bar was not rubbed. And the rubbing was quite stereotyped, as we would expect of a genetically programmed behavior.

It was typical of behaviorists to ignore animal nature and to believe that any behavior an animal manifested, aside from a few reflexes, must have been learned. They disagreed about how learning worked, but not its power and ubiquity. We will see in Chapter 4 that not only did Guthrie trip over the cat, but that Hull, Tolman, and Skinner tripped over their rats and pigeons.

*Read Bruce Moore and Susan Studdard, "Professor Guthrie and *Felis domesticus,* or: Tripping Over the Cat." *Science,* 1979, *205,* 1031–1033.

LOGICAL BEHAVIORISM

The Research Program of Clark L. Hull

Guthrie's theory was simple and he never worked it out in systematic detail; Hull's theory was fearsomely complex and systematically stated as a network of axioms, corollaries, and theorems expressed in mathematical and logical form. Where Guthrie seemed content with qualitative interpretations of learning, Hull aimed at exact quantification carried out to many decimal places. The student who opens Hull's *A Behavior System* (1952) finds this as early as page 6:

$$D = D' \times \xi$$

where

$$D' = 37.824 \times 10 - 27.496 \; 1h + 4.001$$

and

$$\xi = 1 \text{-}0.00001045h^{2.4826}$$

The student is likely to give up all hope of learning about learning. But all Hull states here is that one's motivational state, or drive *D*, is a component of three factors: D′, which increases the longer you go without food; h, which is hours of food deprivation; and ξ (the Greek letter *eta*), representing the slow weakening effect of starvation. Hull has just dressed up the commonplace notion—that motivation increases until you get too weak to move—with logico-mathematical clothes. Fortunately for today's student, Hull's quantitative clothes have been the least durable part of his program. Neo–Hullians quickly put on more informal dress (Chapter 12).

Don E. Dulany (see Leahey, 1980a) has called Hull's school **logical behaviorism.** While all the behaviorists of the Golden Age aspired to systematic formal theory, only Hull achieved it, and he set the standard for others to emulate. More particularly, Hull believed that a good scientific theory should be stated as a set of logically expressed axioms from which observable consequences, that it, predictions, could be deduced. In his view, the scientist then constructed an experiment to test the predictions, and should they fail, the theory would have to be changed.

For example, one of the fundamental postulates of Hull's system as set forth in 1943 was

$$sE_R = {}_sH_R \times D$$

What this says is that the tendency to make a given response, *reaction potential* or sE_R, is a function of motivation, *drive* or *D*, multiplied by how well the response has been learned, *habit strength* or $_sH_R$. Hull's proposed axiom is based on common sense, for it says you will only give a response if you have learned it as a habit ($_sH_R$ is positive) and are motivated to give the response (*D* is positive). Should you either not know what to do ($_sH_R$ is *0*) or not be motivated (*D* is *0*), you will not respond ($_sE_R$ is *0*).

Testing the axiom is relatively straightforward, at least if we do not try to put exact numbers on the theoretical terms. As our response we might choose pressing a bar in a Skinner box to get food, and as our measure of the strength of the response ($_sE_R$) we can use how quickly the bar is pressed after our subject, a rat, is released into the box, assuming quite reasonably that the more quickly the bar is pressed the stronger is the response tendency; $_sE_R$ is our dependent variable, and we can manipulate our independent variables $_sH_R$ and *D* to see if they affect $_sE_R$ in the right way.

To manipulate *D* we simply compare well-fed animals (*D* is zero) to animals of moderate drive strength (for example, 12 hours without food) and animals of high drive strength (24 hours without food). We cross the drive factor with $_sH_R$. Contrary to Guthrie, Hull believed that learning, the acquisition of habits, is a gradual affair, and he expressed this by saying that habit strength grows slowly to a limit as an organism's responses are reinforced. More precisely, $_sH_R$ is a positive function of the number of reinforced responses. So we manipulate $_sH_R$ by having some rats never learn the bar-press response ($_sH_R$ is zero), some learn it moderately well (50 reinforced presses) and some very well (100 reinforced presses).

We can infer from the equation that those animals who have no motivation (*D* is zero) will not respond no matter how well they have learned the bar press; neither will animals respond who have not learned the response ($_sH_R$ is zero) regardless of their drive state. Other groups will respond to the bar with varying degrees of swiftness, with the fastest responding (highest $_sE_R$) coming from the group that combines the longest food deprivation with the best-learned habit. Experiments along these general lines were carried out (Hull, et al., 1947), although they were aimed at actually quantifying Hull's theoretical terms.

Hull's system was open to change. For example, it doesn't take research—though research was done—to see that other important factors should determine reaction strength besides drive and habit strength. Surely you, or any organism, will work harder for a large reward than for a small one, and will react more strongly to powerful than to weak stimuli. These considerations were duly incorporated into Hull's revised system (Hull, 1952) as *incentive motivation* (*K*) and *stimulus-intensity dynamism* (*V*), respectively. The revised equation constituting reaction potential became

$$_sE_R = D \times V \times K \times {}_sH_R$$

Logical behaviorism evolved as a research program through the 1930s and 1940s as Hull modified his theory in the light of new data and theoretical reflection. Nevertheless, as Kuhn and Lakatos would suggest, certain paradigmatic ideas formed the hard core of Hull's program; the formal postulates were the protective belt open to, and receiving, change. To begin with, Hull's theory was an S-R theory. He believed there was only one kind of learning (Hull, 1937), in which responses are attached to controlling stimuli. For Hull, every response had its eliciting stimulus, however hard to find. When it was impossible to find an external stimulus for some response, Hull (1930b, 1931) argued there had to be internal, covert stimuli controlling it. Hull's search for nonobservable stimuli to control otherwise inexplicable responses shows that the basic S-R formula was a hard core idea not to be abandoned.

Not only did every response have to have a stimulus, but Hull also believed only stimuli could control behavior. Motivation presents a problem here: How can food deprivation, in which nothing actually happens to an organism, act as a stimulus? Hull (1930b, 1931) supposed that food deprivation, or any other motivation-producing circumstance, created internal stimuli, such as hunger pangs, that could be associated with responses leading to reduction of the drive. In fact, Hull believed that all learning depended on drive reduction—that is, he accepted the law of effect. This belief led to controversies with Tolman's informational psychology (see below), and apparent refutation when electrical stimulation of the brain was discovered (Box 3–2).

You may have wondered why some of Hull's theoretical terms are bracketed by S and R ($_sH_R$, and $_sE_R$) and others are not (D, V, K). Hull used in his thinking about learning something called *intervening variables,* a characteristic of formal as opposed to radical behaviorism. An actual observed response is a *dependent variable,* because we assume that its occurrence depends on environmental conditions. The conditions that affect behavior are called *independent variables,* because we can manipulate them independently of the organism. Hull believed that when learning takes place something inside the organism changes, linking up stimulus and response. These changes are *intervening variables,* because they intervene between the independent and dependent variables, that is, between stimulus and response, and so we have $_sE_R$ and $_sH_R$. D, V, and K are not intervening variables; they refer directly to something outside the organism—how many hours we have not fed it, how strong a CS or US is, how large a reward is. Use of intervening variables sets Hull and Tolman off quite sharply from B.F. Skinner. Hull and Tolman, whatever their other differences, tried to infer what happens inside an organism when it learns; Skinner sees in this an invitation to myth-making.

The final feature of the hard core of Hull's program is his commitment to *continuity theory* in learning. Guthrie argued that learning always occurs all at once, on one trial. Opposed to Guthrie's all-or-none view was Hull's belief that habit strength grows a little bit at a time, continuously as rewards are given, until learning is complete. Hullians regarded results like Guthrie's and Horton's, and Voeks' as unrepresentative of learning in general.

These, along with a commitment to logical theory, are the central ideas in the hard core of Hull's research program. Surrounding them were the explicit postulates and defined theoretical terms that were always open to change. New terms such as V and K could be added, old ones could be redefined, and postulates could be revised, as when Hull's student Spence altered $_sE_R = D \times V \times K \times _sH_R$ to $_sE_R = (D+K) \times V \times _sH_R$. But un-

BOX 3–2   *REINFORCEMENT WITHOUT REWARD?*

In Hull's theory of learning, acquisition of a habit depended on reduction of a motivational drive, a position Tolman effectively attacked in his latent learning experiments. In 1954 a new kind of reinforcer was discovered that could powerfully change behavior without reward or long-term benefit to the learner—electrical stimulation of the brain (Olds & Milner, 1954; Olds, 1960). Electrodes could be planted in certain areas of the brain, and rats would work hard for stimulation of their brains; they would drive themselves to exhaustion, ignoring hunger and thirst, just to get a jolt from the electrode; stimulation to certain other areas is aversive.

More limited studies have been done with human patients undergoing brain surgery (Delgado, 1976). These patients report feelings of intense pleasure, sometimes sexual, when the "pleasure centers" of the brain are stimulated. Cases of chronic pain and some forms of epilepsy have been treated by long-term implantation of electrodes (Delgado, 1976; Sem-Jacobsen, 1976). If rat behavior and human self-report may be integrated, we find that sheer pleasure—completely divorced from any biological imperative—is quite reinforcing on its own.

Besides its theoretical interest, electrical stimulation of the brain raises serious ethical issues because it holds out the threat, or promise, of physical *control* of the mind (Delgado, 1969). While its advocates, such as Delgado, see in physical mind-control the promise of a "psychocivilized society," most people fear it as a threat. Long-term electrode implanting was nightmarishly portrayed in Michael Crichton's novel *The Terminal Man,* later made into a popular movie.

In our increasingly technological age, when computers have become pocket-size, citizens must weigh the good and evil of electrical stimulation of the brain. It may cure epilepsy and relieve chronic pain, but could it lead to routine implants, first in criminals, who might be aversively shocked for criminal acts or even thoughts, then in the retarded, to promote learning efficiency, and perhaps finally in anyone who rubs the authorities the wrong way?

disturbed by all these changes were logical behaviorism's commitment to S-R theory, continuity, intervening variables, and the drive-reduction theory of learning.

The Habit-Family Hierarchy

Perhaps because it appeared in Hull's writing very early (Hull, 1930a) and so was not inextricable from the later axiomatic theory, his **habit-family hierarchy** proved to be a flexible and durable concept of widespread application. While the formal system generated much animal research, the habit-family hierarchy has been a useful tool to behaviorists concerned with human learning.

The idea is really quite simple, and is inherent in any S-R psychology. Recall what a cat does when placed in a puzzle-box by Thorndike. The situation calls forth many responses: The cat reaches through the slats, claws at the walls, pushes its head against the door, and eventually pulls the string and escapes. In trial-and-error learning a single stimulus situation calls forth a series of responses, one at a time, until the correct one is executed and reinforced. Adopting S-R terminology, we can say that the situation elicits several responses, but each S-R connection is of a different strength. We may note this

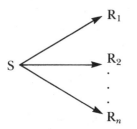

and call it a *divergent habit-family hierarchy*. There is a family of habits diverging from a single stimulus arranged in a hierarchy of strengths.

What happens in trial-and-error learning is this (Hull, 1930a, 1934). A situation calls forth a hierarchy of responses, and the one with the strongest $_sH_R$ occurs first. If the response is not reinforced, the S-R bond, that is, the habit strength, weakens. When it weakens enough, it becomes weaker than the next habit in the hierarchy, which now is tried out. If it fails, too, it will weaken until the third response takes over. The trial-and-error process continues until the incorrect responses are extinguished and the correct response occurs and is reinforced. Subsequent reinforcements strengthen the response until it is the strongest response in a remade habit-family hierarchy. Hull's reasoning provides a neat scheme for accounting for trial-and-error learning.

Just as one stimulus may elicit many responses, so many stimuli may tend to elicit the same response in a *convergent* hierarchy:

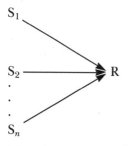

The phenomenon of stimulus generalization can be thought of as a convergent hierarchy: Many related stimuli evoke a CR with differing strengths. All learning involves convergent mechanisms embracing at least two distinct stimuli: stimuli from the external environment, and internally produced drive stimuli.

Finally, we can have *compound* habit-family hierarchies:

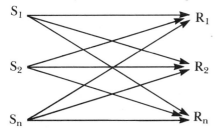

Habit-family hierarchies are flexible, and Hull used them to give speculative S-R accounts of mysterious mentalistic ideas such as knowledge, purpose, and direction of behavior (Hull, 1930b, 1931). However, it was left to Irving Maltzman (1955) to extend Hull's account to human thinking, and to carry out supporting research (Maltzman & Morrisett, 1952, 1953a, 1953b) on the topic of anagram solution set learning.

Almost everyone has played with anagrams at one time or another: You are given the letters of a scrambled word and try to rearrange the letters to recover the original word. Anagrams provide cheap and simple problems that psychologists can pose to research subjects, studying mental *set*; it is one of the oldest ideas in experimental psychology, dating back to the Würzburg psychologists around the turn of the century. They found that problem-solving behavior is not random, but has a definite direction. In the case of anagrams you can see a set at work when a subject solves a series of anagrams all scrambled in the same order. After doing a few, the subject no longer tries different letter combinations, but immediately applies the correct unscrambling order. The subject has acquired a disposition, or set, to solve the problem in a given way. Sets can be useful or they can be detrimental as when they make us persistently apply old solutions to new and different problems. This danger can be seen, for example, in generals who are "still fighting the last war," sending cavalry up against tanks, as the leaders of the valiant Poles did in World War II. A mental set can be a deadly problem.

Mental sets appear to challenge behaviorism because they show that problem solving need not always involve trial and error, but may have a definite direction. Maltzman, however, argued that sets are just mental habits. We may analyze the solution of one anagram as a trial-and-error process analagous to figuring out a puzzle-box. We are given the letters N-O-P-D-S and we try out different letter-orders until we get PONDS, the successful R finally rising to the top of our habit-family hierarchy to the stimulus N-O-P-D-S.

Maltzman accounted for "mental" set in the Hullian framework by treating anagrams having the same solution as a class of stimuli that can be conditioned to a class of responses. In the above anagram, N-O-P-D-S, the letters of the target word PONDS were placed in the order 32145. After doing several 32145 anagrams, you could do the next one right away—you would have acquired the response-set for unscrambling 32145 anagrams. In S-R notation we might write the set as a habit:

$$S_{\overline{32145}} \rightarrow R_{(321)45}$$

where S_{32145} represents the class of 32145 anagrams and $R_{(321)45}$ represents the response of unscrambling them into the right order by reversing the first three letters.

Of course, other sets could be learned. Suppose all the target words were closely related in meaning, for example, RIVER, BROOK, CREEK, FOGGY—all (wet) nature words. Even if the scrambling order were different for each anagram, knowing it was a nature word would facilitate solving it, that is, it would be a set:

$$S_{nature} \longrightarrow R_{nature}$$

Suppose that in a series of anagrams both sets were present: PONDS is a nature target word and its anagram N-O-P-D-S is in 32145 order. In this case, according to Hullian theory, *both* sets, as habits, should be acquired, setting up a convergent habit-family hierarchy:

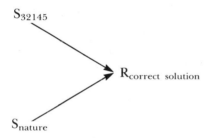

$$S_{32145}$$

$$R_{correct\ solution}$$

$$S_{nature}$$

In Hullian theory, two $_sH_R$'s converging on the same terminal R will *summate,* so that the strength of the compound R will be greater than either S-R habit alone. In terms of anagram solving, the letters N-O-P-D-S will be more readily solved if it has been preceded by a series of anagrams containing both nature and 32145 (order) sets than by either of these sets alone.

Hullian habits can also interact subtractively. If you learn a set of anagrams havings two sets converging on one solution, you acquire the summation of two $_sH_R$'s. If, however, you move on to anagrams having only one of the sets, the number of solutions should decrease, as one habit is no longer operable.

Maltzman and Morrisett (1953a) tested these predictions as well as some others we will pass over. In the *learning* phase of the experiment, ten subjects ($N = 70$) in seven different groups learned 20 five-letter anagrams that embodied the *nature set (N)*, the order set 32145 (*O*), or both (*ON*). Then in the test phase subjects solved 15 anagrams that had two solutions each, one adhering to the learned set, the other not. For example, L-D-I-E-F can be unscrambled as FIELD, a nature word, or FILED, not a na-

TABLE 3–1   Mean set solutions in the test phase in the anagram problem-solving experiment of Maltzman and Morrisett (1953a)

O-O	N-N	ON-ON	ON-O	ON-N
73.3	55.3	87.3	61.3	63.3

ture word. K-A-B-E-R can be unscrambled BAKER, if you follow the 32145 order, or BREAK or BRAKE, if you use another order. Finally, E-I-F-L-D, is a compound set anagram, since the 32145 order unscrambled yields FIELD, while the other solution is FILED.

To illustrate the principles discussed here, the important groups are *O-O* and *N-N*, the control groups involving only one set in both learning and test phases; *ON-ON*, the group that learns and is tested on the compound sets; and *ON-N* and *ON-O*, groups in which the compound habit is learned, and then one habit becomes inapplicable in the test phase. The mean percent of set solutions in the test phase for each group is shown in Table 3–1.

We see that in a general way the Hullian predictions have been borne out. The compound habit group shows more set solutions than any other group, as we expected from the convergent hierarchy set up during training. And in those groups where a habit learned during training can be applied in the test phase, there is a drop in number of set solutions, to be expected from the removal of one of the converging habits acquired during the learning phase.

On the other hand, there are some inconsistent results. Removal of one $_sH_R$ from a converging hierarchy leaves a single habit, either $S_N{\rightarrow}R_N$ or $S_O{\rightarrow}R_O$, but the *ON-N* group has more set solutions than the *N-N* group, and the *ON-O* group has fewer set solutions than *O-O* group. This is surprising since in both cases the remaining habit in training is identical to the one habit acquired by the control groups, leading us to expect that both control and experimental groups should give the same number of set solutions on the test phase.

However, these difficulties are quantitative only, the general predictions having been confirmed. Results like this were typical of later logical behaviorist research, especially in human learning. The theory could explain broad aspects of learning but failed in the quantitative predictions so important to Hull. Consequently, neo-Hullians gradually abandoned Hull's obsession with mathematical precision and they used Hull's theory more informally, as Maltzman did. This retreat from quantification was especially great in those psychologists of learning, Maltzman among them, who applied Hull's approach to human problems.

The Legacy of Logical Behaviorism

Not long after Hull's death in 1952, his theory was subjected to some severe criticism. It was argued that Hull's predictions could not really be logically derived from his theory (Cotton, 1955), that it could not account for certain maze-learning experiments with rats that suggested they could reason (Deutsch, 1956), and that Hull's theory was just too simple to explain human behavior (Ginsberg, 1954). The most scathing and influential critique was that of Koch (1954), who showed that Hull's formal system was a logical mess; that he did not practice what he preached, for example, ignoring contrary data available while writing his postulates; and that his quantificational program was ill-conceived and doomed from the start. For Koch, Hull's usefulness lay in his failure, demonstrating the impossibility of Hull's heroic, or foolhardy, system-building.

In any case, the stream of influence from Hull's theory divided after World War II. Those of his students, colleagues, and admirers who wanted to study human learning, such as Maltzman, largely abandoned the formal and quantificational aspects of logical behaviorism, while retaining a commitment to the hard core of Hull's program. The hypotheses in the neo-Hullian protective belt were stated rather informally, and in this respect they merged into a mass of eclectic behaviorists dominating American psychology in the 1950s. They also augmented the S-R formula by elaborating the idea of central, covert mediating responses, S-r-s-R, to handle certain special problems of human learning, which we will review in Chapter 12.

Hull's major student, Kenneth Spence, continued to study animal learning, and his influence has been long lasting. While moving away from Hull's excessive quantification, Spence remained a powerful spokesperson for a psychology based on logical positivism (see Spence, 1944, 1956). Since our topic is human learning, we will pass over the important contributions of Spence and his students to animal learning. The interested student can get a good discussion of their work in Hilgard and Bower (1975). We will move on to Hull's formidable rival, a devilishly clever experimenter and charming writer named E. C. Tolman.

COGNITIVE BEHAVIORISM

The Research Program of E. C. Tolman

Tolman (1959) himself tells us that both his system and his research were based on hunch and common sense. His research program was not guided by formal deductions from postulates like Hull's, or by a single law of learning, like Guthrie's. Rather, it appears that in designing an experiment Tolman asked himself what *he* would do in the rat's position as opposed to what a Hullian or Guthrian rat would do. Tolman was gratified to learn that rats were generally as common-sensical as he was. Especially in reading his occasional attempts to formalize his theory (see Tolman, 1932, 1938, 1959), one senses that technical formulae and a playful, occasionally bizarre vocabulary ("means-ends-readiness," "sign-gestalt-expectation") are being used to express straightforward common sense.

In Tolman's case, therefore, formal statements of his theory are even less important than in Hull's case. Central to Tolman's theory are two ideas that, more than anyone else, he kept alive during the behaviorist era: **purpose** and **cognition**.

Tolman always maintained that behavior and learning are a "getting toward" or a "getting away." That is, behavior is purposive; it is oriented toward a goal, be it securing something good or avoiding something bad. In Tolman's view no psychology could dispense with reference to purposes, and in common sense we tend to agree with him.

But purposes were viewed askance by other important behaviorists, who thought "purpose" to be too vague and mentalistic for scientific psychology. Instead, Guthrie, Watson, and even Hull sought a more mechanistic account of behavior. Guthrie wanted to understand learning as the acquisition of *muscle-movements,* such as twitching a finger, not as the learning of purposeful acts, such as removing a finger from the source of an electrical shock. In the old-fashioned jargon, Guthrie was a molecular theorist, believing that scientific psychology studied movements, not acts.

Tolman was the supreme molar theorist because of his commitment to purpose. Since behavior for Tolman was guided by goals, the proper level of analysis is of the acts that lead to the goal, not of the muscle twitches that happen to be involved at the moment. So, for example, a rat that has learned to walk through a maze could also swim through it when it was filled with water, even though the muscle responses were different in each case (MacFarlane, 1930). Moreover, simply pulling a rat through a maze in a basket can result in learning, even though no R's have occurred to be reinforced and learned (McNamara, Long, & Wike, 1956). These results support Tolman's contention that the proper study of psychologists is an organism's goals and the acts it can mobilize to reach them.

The molecular-mechanistic versus molar-purposive issue is profound and important, involving much more than interpreting rat maze-learning behavior. Consider a game of tennis. In a molecular-mechanistic account all that happens is a series of physical events: A ball is propelled through different trajectories because of the muscle movements two organisms use to strike the ball. The psychologist could only talk about the fluctuating strengths of $_sE_R$'s under changing stimulus conditions. The psychologist could *not* talk about strategies for winning, and could not even account for the end of the match except to say that when the ball fell on the outside of a certain line the behavior exchange ended. But of course we, and Tolman, reject such a view. Tolman would talk about a player's purpose—winning—and we could discuss a player's game as a set of meaningful acts aimed at the goal of winning. A purposive, molar account respects the human world of meaning and purpose; a molecular-mechanistic account reduces them to muscular twitches and glandular secretions. Nor is this issue dead with Guthrie, Tolman, and Hull. It is very much alive in debates over Skinner's theory, cognitive science, and sociobiology.

The other notion central to Tolman's program was *cognition.* Tolman believed that an organism learns *about* its environment; it doesn't just learn to react to it. In the last chapter we questioned if human beings really condition, or if their behavior is determined by thinking. Tolman (1932, p. 330) wrote in a similar vein that a conditioned response will occur only if an organism "believes" that the old response-reinforcement contingencies hold. Subsequently, Seward and Levy (1949) demonstrated in animals the kind of "instant extinction" Tolman's theory predicts, which we also found in Brewer's review of human research.

Seward and Levy trained rats to run from a start box down an alleyway to a goal box containing food. Then they simply placed the rat in the goal box several times without feeding it. The rats, "knowing" that food was no longer in the goal box, now generally did not run down the alley when placed in the start box. As others had shown with humans, Seward and Levy showed that extinction in animals can occur even without the occurrence of nonreinforced R's. This is contrary to Hull's theory, in which $_sH_R$ must be lowered by nonreinforcement of a response, but is expected by Tolman's cognitive theory.

Nor were beliefs the only cognitive processes Tolman attributed to rats. His associate I. Krechevsky (later David Krech) showed that rats seemed to act on hypotheses. Krechevsky (1932) found that in certain kinds of mazes rats would systematically try different modes of behavior. Thus, a rat might try all right turns, then all left turns, then alternating left and right, as if it were formulating hypotheses and then trying them out, rather than engaging in a random trial-and-error process (see also Tolman, 1948).

Tolman's cognitive emphasis led him to reject the law of effect. S-R reinforcement theories like Thorndike's and Hull's say that what causes learning to occur, or be "stamped in," is pleasure or pain-avoidance. Rather, Tolman stressed the cognitive role of reinforcement as a signal to the organism.

Tolman, Hall, and Bretnall (1932) offered a disproof of the law of effect, in which introductory psychology students learned a punchboard maze. In front of them was placed a board with many sets of pairs of holes. The subjects inserted a metal stylus into one of each pair of holes, one of which was "correct," the other "incorrect," and they had to pass through the maze by repeatedly inserting the stylus in sequential pairs of holes until they did it once without choosing a "wrong" hole.

For our purposes, the important groups are as follows:

Bell-right—when the subject inserted the stylus into the *correct* hole of each pair, an electrical circuit closed and rang a bell.

Bell-wrong—when the subject inserted the stylus into the *incorrect* hole of each pair the bell rang.

Bell-right-shock—when the subject chose the *correct* hole, not only did the bell ring, but the subject also received a painful electric shock through the stylus.

Bell-wrong-shock—when the subject chose the *incorrect* hole, not only did the bell ring, but the subject was shocked.

The results were that the *bell-right* group made the fewest errors followed very closely by the *bell-right-shock* group. Many more errors were made by the *bell-wrong* group, and many more still by the *bell-wrong-shock* group.

Let us first discuss the effects of the bell. The bell is a supposedly neutral stimulus of no reinforcing value, yet it acted to "emphasize," in Tolman's words, whatever response it followed. So, regardless of shock, both *bell-wrong* groups learned more slowly than the *bell-right* groups. As Tolman put it, the bell exerted a "baleful fascination" on his subjects, who had some trouble learning to choose the hole that did *not* ring the bell.

Turning to the shock, we find that it acted contrary to the law of effect. Subjects in the *bell-right-shock* group were learning to *receive* shocks, not avoid them, as suggested by the law of effect. Indeed, their rate of learning was not significantly different from the *bell-right* group. On the other hand, the *bell-wrong-shock* group was learning to avoid shocks, since for them every error resulted in a shock. But the shock did not make them learn faster; in fact, they were the slowest of all the groups. The shock seemed to act as an emphasizer that impeded learning rather than helped it. Tolman's result was not a fluke, because more recent research, following the advent of cognitive psychology, has shown consistently that the information value of reinforcers is more important than their supposed reward or punishment value (see Estes, 1972).

Thus, we see that contrary to his colleagues, Tolman placed purpose and cognition at the center of his research program, distinguishing himself from the S-R psychologists who studied learning in terms of muscle movements and habits learned by reward and punishment. But nothing sets Tolman's cognitive view off more clearly from S-R views than the contrast between his cognitive maps and their habit-family hierarchies.

Cognitive Maps vs. Habit-Family Hierarchies

Tolman's theory was well summed up in his paper "Cognitive Maps in Rats and Men" (1948). In it, Tolman contrasted the S-R view, in which learning consists in establishing S-R connections by reward and breaking them by punishment, with his own view in which organisms selectively take in information from the environment and work it over into a map of their world. It is this cognitive map that controls behavior for Tolman, not blind reactions to external and internal stimuli.

The most famous kind of research that addresses this question, as well as the role of reinforcement in learning, is research on **latent learning** (see reviews by Thistlethwaite, 1951; MacCorquadale & Meehl, 1954). The classic experiments were Blodgett's (1929) and Tolman's and Honzik's (1930). In these experiments some rats learned to negotiate a maze for food reward in the goal box, while others simply wandered around the maze for several trials before food was introduced in the goal box. According to reinforcement theory, learning will not take place without reward—the first group of rats should learn because they are rewarded for learning, and the second group should not begin to learn until reinforcement begins. According to Tolman, even the rats just wandering the maze are learning about their environment—building up a *cognitive map*—even though that learning may not be apparent. Since the food box is not yet a goal, the wandering rats will not head right to it like the rewarded rats.

An S-R reinforcement theory predicts for this experiment that the always rewarded group will learn the maze in some number of trials, for example 12; the wandering group will only *begin* to learn when food is introduced, for example, on the eleventh try, and should take 12 trials beyond that to master the maze. Tolman's theory maintains that after ten trips through the maze even the nonrewarded rats will have learned its layout, and when food is introduced on trial 11 they will do just as well as the rewarded group, their "latent learning" being immediately transformed by purpose into goal-directed performance. Most of the many experiments designed to test latent learning supported Tolman's prediction.

After enough tinkering, Hull's theory was adjusted to "predict" latent learning, but such tinkering has the appearance of defensive rationalization. Tolman's theory is the simpler and more appealing, and he had other research designed to challenge the fundamental S-R idea of the habit-family hierarchy.

We have seen how Hull's habit-family hierarchy is able to give a plausible account of some kinds of trial-and-error learning. Tolman, however, was able to design experiments in which the hierarchy leads to predictions contrary to intelligent common sense, and thus to Tolman's cognitive-map theory. One of the simpler experiments is shown in Figure 3–1, where a maze used by Tolman and Honzik (Tolman, 1933) is schematically shown.

By suitable placing of blockades, we can force rats to run from start through the different paths to the goal, where they are fed. The crucial choice-point is just down the path from the start box, where the rat must choose path 1, path 2, or path 3. According to Hull, after learning, the

FIGURE 3–1 Tolman-Honzik Maze.

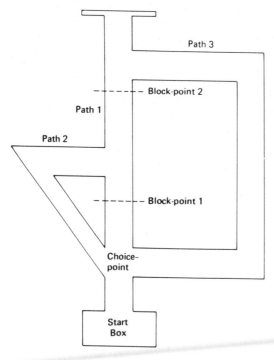

stimuli at the choice-point evoke a divergent hierarchy (shown below) such that path 1 is preferred to path 2, which is preferred to path 3.

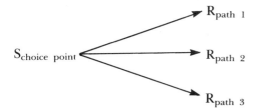

This is quite reasonable, since rats, like people, won't work any harder than they have to for a given reward. We can also justify it on more technical Hullian grounds because Hull's is an S-R chaining theory. Running down a maze path is, in Hull's theory, a chain of responses ultimately rewarded by the terminal reinforced response. The longer the behavior chain, the weaker is its first link. Therefore, since the chain of response links is longest along path 3, the initial turn-right response will be weaker than the turn-left or straight-ahead response. Similarly, the turn-left response will be weaker than the straight-ahead response.

After the rats have learned the three paths, we introduce a barrier at block-point 1. What will a Hullian rat do after bumping its nose on the barrier? It will retreat to the choice-point and execute the next habit in its hierarchy, running, successfully as it turns out, down path 2. Now suppose, instead of blocking at point 1, we block at point 2. The Hullian rat will retreat to the choice-point and again execute its second strongest habit, running down path 2, only to be thwarted again. S-R path 2 now being eliminated, it will return to the choice-point and finally and successfully run down path 3.

But a Tolman rat would behave differently. What it learned to begin with was a map of the environment, rather like Figure 3–1 itself. Now you, and the rat, can see on the diagram that if there is a barrier at choice-point 2, then there is no point in taking path 2, since only path 3 will get you to the goal box. Therefore, the Tolman rat will return to the choice-point and immediately choose path 3. Of course when the block is at point 1, the Tolman rat will choose the shorter path 2, being just as common-sensically lazy as the rest of us.

Unsurprisingly, Tolman's research found most rats to be Tolman rats, and so did most outside research. This kind of finding is powerful evidence that the S-R connection formula and its associated habit-family are hard put to account for all learning by animals or humans. It appears that psychologists will have to look for cognitive maps in the brains of learning organisms (see Box 3–3).

The Legacy of Cognitive Behaviorism

Tolman was a resourceful and clever experimenter, able to challenge effectively S-R psychologies with uncomfortable data. But his own theory was never set out in a systematic enough way for others to use it as well as

BOX 3–3   *COGNITIVE MAPS IN THE BRAIN?*

The hippocampus is not a college for large, semiaquatic African mammals, but is a distinct structure in human and mammalian brains (see Figure 3–2). Two physiological psychologists have recently claimed that the hippocampus is where Tolman's cognitive maps are to be found (O'Keefe & Nadel, 1974, 1978, 1979). They offer two kinds of evidence to support their views. First, a rat with lesions in its hippocampus loses the ability to learn about places and the desire to explore its environment, although its ability to learn S-R tasks, such as bar-pressing, remains unimpaired, or even enhanced. As O'Keefe and Nadel (1974, p. 750) put it, "In short, they behave like Hullian animals." Second, O'Keefe and Nadel have mapped the cells of the hippocampus, finding, among other things, "place cells," which fire whenever a rat enters a particular place, regardless of the reason it is there, and "place-mismatch cells," which fire when a rat enters a familiar place but fails to find what it expected, such as food.

The work of O'Keefe and Nadel is widely admired, but is not without its critics (see the comment section of O'Keefe & Nadel, 1979). However, should their hypothesis be accepted, it will provide the most striking possible support for Tolman's intuitive concept of the cognitive map.

FIGURE 3–2

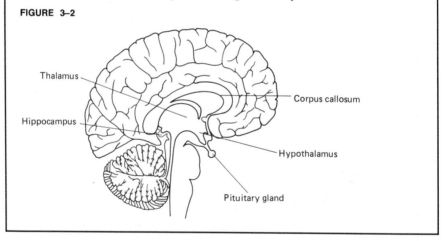

he did. As he conceded in 1959, his research program was really guided by his own common sense and his own hunches, and these do not travel well to even the closest associates. He seems to have had more fun than most psychologists of learning (Tolman, 1959), but his influence is hard to trace, and turns up in unlikely places (see Box 3–4). When a psychologist, all too rarely, follows common sense, is he doing it on his own or following Tolman? Tolman did not have the kind of neo-Tolmanians who followed him the way neo-Hullians followed Hull.

Nevertheless, Tolman did keep open a line of theorizing that without him would perhaps have vanished. He upheld a cognitive account of learn-

BOX 3-4   *SUBJECTIVE MENTAL MAPS*

> While Tolman was interested in cognitive maps as an objective guide to one's environment, Peter Gould and Rodney White (1974) have shown that human's cognitive maps reveal important subjective and social facts about our relationship to our environment. For example, one may ask people to draw maps of their city. Results for three classes of Los Angelenos graphically portray the lives led by whites, blacks, and Hispanics (see Figure 3-3).
>
>   In their book *Mental Maps*, Gould and White extensively explored the inner geography of our cognitive maps. They discovered interesting facts about where people want to live, patterns of geographic learning and ignorance, and the effects of class and other social factors on one's perception of the world.

ing while most psychologists were S-R connectionists. So even though his direct influence on them has not been great, cognitively oriented psychologists such as Rescorla and the human-information-processing psychologists pay homage to Tolman as their precursor.

THE LEGACY OF FORMAL BEHAVIORISM

Guthrie, Hull, and Tolman, each in his own way, influenced the psychology of learning. But the overall impact of the Golden Age of Theory is harder to make out. For our purposes (see Leahey, 1980a, for a broader view) two influences are paramount.

First, the grand battle of the theorists convinced one psychologist that theories were useless at best, positive burdens at worst. B. F. Skinner (1950) argued that psychology did not really need theories at all, and he proposed his atheoretical approach instead. His radical behaviorism has been so successful that today Skinner is Mr. Behaviorist, and radical behaviorism is the only behaviorism. The radical behaviorist approach to learning will occupy the next chapter.

On the other hand, many psychologists considered the grand theories to be dinosaurs, impressive but unwieldy, which should be replaced by newer ways of theorizing. Two new theories did evolve to replace the formal dinosaurs. Many psychologists simply reduced the scope of their theorizing, occupying themselves with relatively specific kinds of animal and human behavior. These mini-theorists, often called *modelers,* proposed small theories in their particular problem areas and refused to think about the laws of all mammalian behavior. This method of constructing theoretical models of specific behaviors has been characteristic both of much of learning theory in the 1950s and the information-processing psychology of the 1960s and 1970s.

Other psychologists were reluctant to abandon the broad claims of the big learning theories, especially those psychologists concerned with social learning and clinical intervention. They wanted some scientific base for

FIGURE 3-3   a. Los Angeles perceived through the eyes of upper middle class whites in Westwood
b. Los Angeles through the eyes of black residents in Avalon. From Gould and White (1974)
c. Los Angeles through eyes of Spanish-speaking residents in Boyle Heights

b. Los Angeles through the eyes of black residents in Avalon

c. Los Angeles through the eyes of Spanish-speaking residents in Boyle Heights thinking about aggression, moral learning, and psychotherapy, but saw that the fine details of the grand theories, especially Hull's, were simply unworkable. So they "liberalized" the theory, which meant including new concepts to help deal with human learning, and giving up mathematical precision for informal theorizing about significant problems. This *informal behaviorism* we will discuss in Chapter 12.

SUGGESTED READINGS

Broad views of the Golden Age of Theory may be had from T. Leahey, *A History of Psychology* (Prentice-Hall, 1980), and from Sigmund Koch (ed.) *Psychology: A Study of a Science* (New York: McGraw-Hill, 1959). Volume 2 of Koch's work contain the theories presented here, plus others, and are reviewed by the participants themselves.

CHAPTER FOUR

ANIMAL-BASED THEORY II: RADICAL BEHAVIORISM

The thinkers of the Golden Age of theory wore themselves out disputing the field of learning. Then a new voice arose calling for an end to theories. B. F. Skinner (1950) argued that theories, while they might be fun, got in the way of the real job of the psychology of learning—collecting hard facts about behavior change. Skinner would heartily agree with the character in many detective stories who challenges the sleuth by saying, "But this is mere theory. What we need are facts."

RADICAL BEHAVIORISM

Skinner (1974) distinguishes his research program, the experimental analysis of behavior, from the philosophy of mind and science that justify and are justified by his empirical findings. Skinner's philosophy is **radical behaviorism.** Like the behaviorism of Guthrie, Hull, or Tolman, it takes behavior as psychology's subject matter. Radical behaviorism, however, goes much further than formal behaviorism in the implications it draws from this idea. In fact, Skinner's central idea is so simple, yet so challenging to common sense, that it is difficult to grasp.

Every day, each of us tries to explain the behavior of people we know or of public figures. We ask, "Why did Bill break up with Susan?" "Why did that Congressman take a bribe?" We generally try to explain these things by appealing to causes *inside* the person. So we might say that Bill "felt threatened" by Susan's academic excellence; or that the Congressman is "greedy." We do not *see* Bill's insecurity or the Congressman's greed, but we infer it from their behavior and then use it to explain their actions.

In a more sophisticated way, most psychologists, including the formal behaviorists, do the same thing. Tolman did not see little maps in the rats' brains. Rather, he inferred them from their maze-running behavior, and then explained their maze-running as based on having acquired maps. Hull, similarly, did not see little $_sH_R$'s and D's in rats; he inferred them from what he did to the rats—reinforcements for $_sH_R$ and food deprivation for D—and then explained their behavior as an outcome of the joint action of $_sH_R$ and D, namely $_sE_R = {}_sH_R \times D$. Within both common sense and the scientific study of learning, people try to explain behavior in terms of internal causes or purposes.

It is precisely this that Skinner's radical behaviorism repudiates. According to Skinner, "greed," "cognitive map," and "$_sH_R$" are equally unscientific and mythical. We do not *observe* any of these things. Instead, we *infer* them from behavior, thus leaving the realm of facts—behavior—for the realm of fiction—mental or hypothetical concepts.

Skinner insists on sticking to what we can observe, describing behavior precisely and scientifically, and refraining from unnecessary inferences. Why do we say, "Congressman X is greedy"? Because we see him or her take bribes. Skinner says we should forget about "greed"—a mythical mental concept—and just say, "Congressman X tends to take bribes," which precisely describes such behavior and makes no inference past the facts. Similarly, a Hullian would say, "$_sH_R$ is high" because a rat has received 500 reinforcements. Skinner says that inventing $_sH_R$ is needless—just say, "This rat has received 500 reinforcements." A Tolmanian would say, "This rat has a cognitive map," because the rodent chose the smart route in the Tolman-Honzik maze. Skinner says that inventing the cognitive map is needless. Just say, "This rat chose route 3 over route 2 in the Tolman-Honzik maze."

Skinner's philosophy of radical behaviorism is that the causes of behavior and learning lie entirely in the environment rather than in the organism itself. Observable behavior is a lawful function of environmental changes, and the job of the psychologist is to understand that function without inventing mental or other hypothetical entities to intervene between environment and behavior. Skinner hopes to do for psychology what Newton did for physics. Before Newton, many people believed angels pushed the planets around their orbits; Newton's laws of motion showed the angels to be unnecessary and therefore probably mythical. Before Skinner, people believed the mind controls behavior; Skinner hopes to show the mind to be a myth.

Radical behaviorism says that behavior is a lawful function of environmental variables. This belief dictates a research program aimed at discovering such functional relationships or natural laws. That program is the experimental analysis of behavior.

THE EXPERIMENTAL ANALYSIS OF BEHAVIOR

The Shared Exemplar

Prior to Skinner's initial work (Skinner, 1938) the most popular experimental setting in learning research was the maze, whether a simple straight alley or a replica of the complex, royal Hampton Court maze in England. Skinner, however, believed that maze learning was not a representative behavior. Most notably, maze learning requires the imposition of separate learning trials: The rat is placed in the start box, navigates the maze, is picked up, and replaced in the start box. But real-life behavior—which is what psychologists of learning ultimately want to understand—is not chopped up into discrete and separate trials. One bit of action leads immediately to another as long as we are awake. So Skinner looked for an experimental arrangement that would keep the virtues of experimenting—control and precise manipulability of the environment—without artificially segmenting the free flow of behavior.

In his desire to achieve the most general account of behavior possible, Skinner made another important decision, namely, to study the acquisition of an *arbitrary* behavior. Skinner saw that many of the responses studied by other psychologists, such as Pavlov's salivation or Watson's conditioned fear, raised the possibility that whatever laws emerged from research on these or similar responses would be valid only for such responses and could not be generalized to other behaviors. Skinner believed that if he studied an arbitrary behavior, one not tied to a specific reinforcer or eliciting circumstance, any discovered regularities in its acquisition would be of general validity.

Putting these requirements together we see that Skinner desired a methodology that would be rigorously experimental, that would produce results of wide generality, without interfering with the natural flow of behavior. What he hit upon has become famous as the "Skinner box," although he prefers to call it "an experimental space," and it quickly eclipsed all competitors as the favored methodology in animal learning research, even among psychologists who are not radical behaviorists.

There are two main kinds of Skinner boxes, one for rats, Skinner's original subjects, and one for pigeons, his favorite subjects in later years. Both boxes are usually made of clear plastic on three walls, some with a shock grid on the floor, and are just large enough to hold the subject comfortably and allow it to move around. The fourth wall contains a magazine that can dispense food or water to a feeding cup, a speaker, a light or lights for discriminative stimuli, and the manipulandum that the subject must operate to get food or water. The manipulandum for the rat is a horizonal lever sticking out of the wall; for pigeons it is a lighted key or keys set into the wall. Operation of the manipulandum activates recording devices and the food or water magazine. Figure 4–1 shows the chamber for a rat (4–1a) and for a pigeon (4–1b).

With one exception, these boxes meet Skinner's requirements. Once

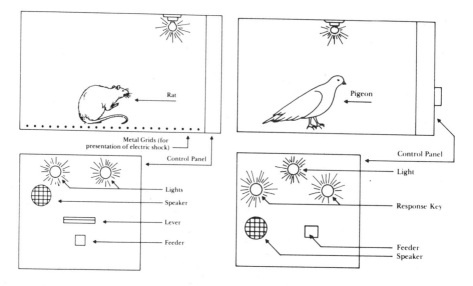

a. The Rat-Conditioning Chamber. *Diagram of a standard conditioning chamber for rats (a) and a rat's-eye view of the control panel housed in the chamber (b).*

b. The Pigeon-Conditioning Chamber. *Diagram of a standard conditioning chamber for pigeons (c), and a bird's-eye view of the control panel housed in the chamber (d).*

FIGURE 4–1 The Skinner Box (Reproduced from *Psychology of Learning and Behavior* by Barry Schwartz by permission of W. W. Norton & Company, Inc. Copyright ©1978 by W. W. Norton & Company Inc.)

placed in the box, animals move about freely and need not be handled until an experiment is over, so that separate trials are not imposed. For the rat, bar-pressing is an arbitrary behavior unlikely to occur in the wild and, therefore, unlikely to be closely tied with a special set of circumstances. In the case of the pigeon, pecking a lighted key appears to be an arbitrary behavior, but it really is not, because pecking is how wild pigeons get their food and drink. Consequently, to get a more arbitrary behavior in a new type of Skinner box, pigeons must work a foot-treadle for reinforcement. But just as Guthrie's difficulties with the cat's greeting response, this shortcoming of the key-peck did not become apparent for more than 20 years.

In addition to meeting Skinner's theoretical requirements, Skinner boxes have practical virtues. Bar-presses and key-pecks are easily defined and counted, allowing precise quantification of behavioral laws. A good dependent variable—response rate—is easily calculated and graphed, directly revealing the impact of experimental manipulations. Finally, data collection can be automated, removing much of the drudgery from research. Because there are no experimental trials, the experimenter need not be present after putting the animal in its box. The control panel can be linked to simple computers that record and plot each response and control discriminative stimuli and reinforcement delivery. Unlike their counterparts in human research, Skinnerians can start an experiment on Friday afternoon and return Monday to a laboratory full of data already collected. Skinner's shared exemplar has also provided the inspiration for various human applications. These range from teaching machines to behavior therapy. One application—biofeedback—for a while seemed to open a technological Western doorway to *satori*. See Box 4–1.

BOX 4–1   *BIOFEEDBACK*

In Chapter 2 we learned how Neal Miller's demonstration of the operant conditioning of autonomic functions helped undermine the distinction between operant and classical conditioning. Not long after, psychologists applied similar techniques to human beings, and in 1969 coined the term **biofeedback** to name the learned, voluntary control of bodily states. In biofeedback learning, subjects are hooked to a device that signals when a certain bodily process is being altered. By using these signals the subjects learn to produce the change at will.

While "biofeedback" designates the learned control of any ordinarily involuntary physiological state or activity (Blanchard & Epstein, 1978; Yates, 1980), the most famous example is the control of one of the brain's four known brain waves, the *alpha* wave. Because of concurrent popular interest in "altered states of consciousness," and because early reports of subjects in the learned alpha state resembled reports of mystic meditation, alpha-wave feedback became famous. Demonstrations were given on television talk shows, and alpha-wave biofeedback devices were advertised in the back of *Psychology Today*, a popular journal where alpha-wave biofeedback made its first splash in 1968.

Unfortunately for its enthusiasts—in California there was for a time a Church of the Holy Alpha—early claims that subjects in alpha biofeedback experiments were learning to alter, and presumably raise, their consciousness have not panned out. There is good evidence that what subjects learn to do in such experiments is just to unfocus their eyes—which hardly seems a likely path to enlightenment. Moreover, what a subject expects to happen has proven to be a powerful determiner of alpha-wave production, sometimes overriding effects of actual feedback about being in the alpha state.

Biofeedback training has been applied to many clinical problems, from alcoholism to sexual dysfunctions, from dental hygiene to blindness (Yates, 1980). Nevertheless, the effectiveness of such applications has been questioned, and why biofeedback works, if it does, remains completely mysterious (Yates, 1980). In a debate familiar to students of learning, it is still unclear whether the biofeedback signal that subjects use to monitor the bodily function they are trying to control is an operant reinforcer (Black, Cott, & Pavloski, 1977) or an informational signal (Lazarus, 1977). Until these controversies are resolved, anyone contemplating biofeedback training or investing over a hundred dollars in an alpha-wave signaler should proceed with caution, reading, for example, *A Biofeedback Primer* (Blanchard & Epstein, 1978) which, while positive, is not over-enthusiastic.

The Contingencies of Reinforcement

Skinner believes that in order to describe scientifically the acquisition, retention, and loss of a piece of behavior one must be able to specify three things: the response itself, the setting in which the response is most likely to occur, and the reinforcer responsible for acquisition and maintainence of the response. These three things Skinner (1969) calls the **contingencies of reinforcement.**

The response

Two kinds of learning   Skinner has always been one of the most influential advocates of the view that there are two kinds of learning corresponding to two kinds of responses, *respondents* and *operants*. Respondent behavior was studied by Pavlov. A respondent is a response that is unconditionally *elicited* by some particular stimulus, a US. Operant behavior was studied by Thorndike. An operant is a response that simply occurs for no observable reason; as Skinner explains, an operant is a response that is simply emitted, not reflexively elicited. An operant *operates on* the environment, and the result of the operation—reinforcement, punishment, or nothing—determines whether the response will become more or less likely to occur.

While we have seen some psychologists of learning challenge the two-process theory, it has always been a part of Skinner's program.

Defining the operant   Because behavior is observable, it seems at first glance easy to define a particular operant behavior. But this ease is altogether illusory, and Skinner has been careful to avoid the pitfalls into which other behaviorists have stumbled.

The major pitfall of behaviorism has been defining responses as particular movements, as Guthrie and Hull did. It is tempting to define the operant a rat learns in a Skinner box as a paw push of the lever, that is, as a particular movement made by the rat.

But doing this leads to serious difficulties that may be best illustrated with respect to language, an important topic to Skinner. In the first place, the same physical response can have wildly different meanings. For example, the response "Fire!" means very different things when shouted by a patron in a theater and when shouted by the captain of a firing squad. It would be totally misleading to define an operant as the movements producing the sound "fire." In the second place, several physically different responses may mean the same thing. For example, "George Washington," "The first President of the U. S.," "The father of his country," and "The man on the one-dollar bill" all designate the same person.

One of the important criticisms of behaviorism has always been that in reducing action to mere physical movement, the meaning and significance of behavior is lost. Tolman tried to get around this difficulty by leaving purpose in animals, ascribing the significance of behavior to the purpose behind it, be that purpose avoiding a finger shock in Wickens' (1938) experiment, or getting fed at the end of a maze.

But Skinner thought purposes too mentalistic because we cannot see them or describe them directly. So in his characteristic way Skinner moved the meaning and significance of behavior out of the organism's invisible mind and into its visible environment. Skinner, therefore, defines an operant in terms of the setting in which it occurs and in terms of the reinforcer that maintains it.

We can illustrate this definition first with the Skinner box situation and then apply it to human language. We could teach a hungry and thirsty rat to press one bar for water and another for food. While the movements involved in pressing each bar might be identical, Skinner would identify two different operants, each controlled by its consequence, or reinforcer. Here is a laboratory analogue to the case of "Fire!" For the firing squad or the audience the shout creates different reactions and different consequences for the speaker, and so, despite the similarity of the vocal movements and sounds, we may identify two different operants. In our human example, of course, the operants are distinguished by setting as well as by consequences.

On the other hand, in a standard Skinner box the rat could press the lever in many ways—with the right paw, left paw, both paws; with the nose, by biting it and pushing down, etc. But all these movements achieve the same end, namely, depressing the lever and closing an electrical switch that delivers food. Therefore, since the setting and the consequence of all these movements are the same, we identify only *one* operant, lever-pressing, or even switch-closure. As Schwartz (1978) points out, an operant exists only for the experimenter, not for the learner. The learner may do many things, but the Skinnerian counts only one thing—switch-closure. Applying this example to language, Skinner would identify only one operant in the various phrases that designate George Washington. Each phrase is different, but the discriminative stimulus for each is the same.

Skinner, then, defines an operant not as a single behavior, but rather as a *class of behaviors,* all controlled by the same setting and consequences, that is, by the same contingencies of reinforcement.

Shaping   Precisely because operants are emitted and not elicited, there is no way we can make them occur. If we put a naive rat in a Skinner box we might have to wait days before it pressed the lever and got reinforced. Similarly, if parents waited until their child said, "Mother, I am thirsty and would like some juice," before responding, they would have a long and fuss-filled wait. Both experimenters and parents, therefore, resort to *shaping*, to leading the organism to make the correct response.

The basic idea behind shaping is the law of effect—an animal will be more likely to do that for which it has just been rewarded. We place our naive rat in the Skinner box. It wanders around the cage, and when it goes into the end near the bar we press a button and food is delivered in the tray. As a result, the rat will spend more time near the control panel. Next we require a little more. At some point while hanging around the control panel the rat will align itself facing the bar. We reinforce it. Soon the rat is facing the bar most of the time. So we require a little more, that the rat touch the bar before we reinforce it. Now that we have gotten it to touch the bar, the rat is likely to press it sometime, and the *terminal response* of bar-pressing will have been acquired.

Shaping, therefore, is the gradual molding of diffuse behavior into a well-defined operant. Just as the sculptor shapes clay, so the experiementer shapes the behavior of animals into the form he or she wants it to take. Similarly, parents respond to imperfect "ma-ma's" and badly pronounced "juice's" when their children are two, but successively require better responses as the childen get older. Thus, the parent, albeit not always successfully, tries to shape a fussing baby into a civilized adult.

Having discussed operant responses, we will turn now to the environmental factors that control emission of operants, the **setting** and the **reinforcer.**

The setting

Both common sense and psychologists of learning agree that behavior is controlled by its setting. We act very differently with friends, with parents, with professors or deans, in the gym, in bed, or in the army. Beginning with Pavlov, psychologists have studied the controlling effect of the situation as *the stimulus control of behavior.* We have already studied how Pavlov discovered and elaborated on stimulus generalization—the tendency of a response learned in one setting to occur in similar ones—and stimulus discrimination—the capacity of an organism to respond to one stimulus but not to another.

These processes also apply to operant behaviors. An operant trained to one discriminative stimulus, for example a 1000-Hz tone, will generalize to tones close to 1000 Hz, the rate of response declining as new tones depart from 1000 Hz. We can create a *discriminated operant* by reinforcing a lever-press in the presence of a 1000-Hz tone, but withholding reinforcement to a 2000-Hz tone. Soon the animal will use the lever only when the 1000-Hz tone is sounding.

The fact that generalization and discrimination apply to the wider field of instrumental behavior, as well as to classical responses, gives radical behaviorists the hope that even complex behaviors, not obviously under stimulus control, can be explained if only the search is conducted thoroughly enough. So, for example, much of child development might be explained as the outcome of generalization and discrimination. Children must learn to act appropriately in certain settings (parents are fond of saying things like, "This is the dining room, not a gymnasium!") and this is discrimination learning. At the same time children must apply what they learn in school to new situations—being able to add not just 2 + 2 but also 432 + 182—and this is generalization.

In discussing Pavlov's study of discrimination learning we spoke of discrimination as setting the processes of inhibition and generalization against one another. So a nonreinforced CS becomes an active inhibitor of the response, while the reinforced CS becomes an elicitor. This is also normally the case in operant conditioning. A discriminative stimulus that signals reinforcement (S⁺) increases response rate, while a nonreinforced discriminative stimulus (S⁻) reduces the rate.

However, it has proved possible in operant conditioning to create discriminations in which the subject almost never responds to S⁻, so that it never acquires negative, inhibitory properties, remaining a truly neutral stimulus. This technique is called *fading* (Terrace, 1963a, 1963b).

Terrace first trained pigeons to peck a red key to obtain reinforcement; the red key became a S⁺. Then he turned the light on the key off for 1 second. Pigeons generally do not peck dark keys, so they resumed responding when the light came back on. Then Terrace gradually increased the duration of the dark interval to 30 seconds. The change was so gradual that the pigeons rarely pecked the darkened key. Thus, an errorless discrimination was established between the red S⁺ and the dark S⁻. Then Terrace *faded* in a new S⁻ by very dimly illuminating the key during its darkened interval with a green light. Since the key was still mostly dark, it remained an S⁻, not being pecked. Very gradually Terrace again increased the green illumination until it was just as bright as the red S⁺. Nevertheless, the green key became an S⁻, and a new discrimination was established between green and red, with few if any errors being made.

In his second experiment, Terrace showed that the fading procedure was much more efficient than the usual method of discrimination learning, which may involve hundreds or even thousands of keypecks to S⁻ and various emotional reactions of rage and frustration.

However learning takes place, it is through the process of discrimination and generalization, in the radical behaviorists' view, that the setting comes to exert control over behavior. Learning involves not only the acquisition of a new response, but also learning when that response will be reinforced and when it will not be—discrimination—and learning to transfer the new response to similar situations—generalization.

The reinforcer

Kinds of reinforcement.   A **reinforcer** is anything that strengthens the behavior that leads to it. More technically, a reinforcement is any event that increases the probability, that is, raises the response rate, of the operant upon which it is contingent. Between them, the setting and the reinforcer determine what behavior will occur when.

There are two types of reinforcement, **positive reinforcement** and **negative reinforcement.** Positive reinforcement corresponds to what common sense calls *reward.* Positive reinforcement is an event that, when it follows an operant response, increases the likelihood that that response will recur. Obvious examples of positive reinforcers are food, water, sex, and money, although, as we will discover shortly, almost anything an organism does can be a positive reinforcer.

Negative reinforcement is an event whose *termination,* when it occurs following an operant response, increases the likelihood that the response will recur. A negative reinforcer is typically a noxious stimulus that an animal will learn to avoid. So, for example, if a rat is placed in a box divided into two compartments by a low wall and is shocked in one compartment, and jumps the wall into the safe compartment, we can say that the jump was *negatively reinforced* by the termination of shock. Obviously, the rat will quickly learn to jump the barrier whenever placed in the electrified compartment. An example of everyday negative reinforcement is nagging—your mother nags at you to clean up your room until you do so, and then she stops her nagging, hoping you will keep your room clean. Torture may also be regarded as negative reinforcement—"Tell us what we want to know and then we will stop!"

One of the two most common confusions in all psychology (the other being confusing schizophrenia with multiple personality disorder) is to identify negative reinforcement with punishment. This happens because "negative reinforcement" sounds like the opposite of "positive reinforcement," as punishment is the opposite of reward, and because the stimuli used to engender negative reinforcement are frequently the same used in punishment.

But punishment is not a reinforcer at all, since its aim is the *reduction* of the frequency of some behavior. Punishment may be defined as an event, following an operant response, that reduces (or attempts to reduce) the likelihood of that response being repeated. The difference between negative reinforcement and punishment may be painfully illustrated by the Inquisition (Le Roy Ladurie, 1978). If a heretic is put on the rack as a consequence of being a heretic, this is punishment, for the pain follows the offensive behavior and aims to reduce it. If, on the other hand, the heretic is put on the rack to obtain the names of other heretics, this is negative reinforcement. For the pain will cease when the desired behavior occurs, and the Inquisitor hopes it will lead to further confessions.

To our list of behavior controllers—positive reinforcement, negative reinforcement, and punishment—we may add *extinction*. Extinction (already familiar from Pavlov's research) like punishment aims at the reduction of some response rate, but it does this by withdrawing previously available reinforcement.

Which means of controlling behavior works best is controversial, even among behaviorists. Punishment is the traditional favorite among governments and parents alike. Typically, the citizen or child is allowed to emit behaviors except for a few that are punished. Negative reinforcement is also popular, whether as parental nagging or as government harassment.

Positive reinforcement mostly occurs in praise, raises, and government contracts, but in a day when most raises depend on union threats and the cost of living, it is unclear if they are really rewards for any individual's behavior. Extinction—simply ignoring an unpleasant behavior until it goes away—is probably the least-used technique.

Skinner himself has been a consistent opponent of punishment as a behavior controller. In the first place, Skinner maintains that punishment is generally ineffective. It does not really "unlearn" behavior; it just temporarily suppresses it. The high recidivism rates of American convicts may support his view. In the second place (and this shortcoming applies to negative reinforcement as well), aversive stimuli create unfortunate emotional side effects. Punishment or its threat produces anger, hostility, and anxiety, even in animals. Since happiness consists in getting what you want, Skinner advocates thoroughgoing and careful use of positive reinforcement by parents and by society. People can be shaped into acceptable behaviors by proper application of rewards, and, as a direct consequence, they will be made happy by receiving rewards.

However, there have always been those who dispute Skinner's negative evaluation of punishment (for example, Solomon, 1964). They argue that punishment can be effective, but that it is generally badly used. For instance, it is well established that delaying the consequences of an act, whether reward or punishment, attenuates the reinforcing or punishing effects and does little to strengthen or weaken the behavior. But in most human cases punishment is long delayed, as when a mother waits for father to get home to spank his naughty boy. And, of course, criminals do not go to jail until months, even years, after their crimes were committed.

Likewise, to be effective, punishment must be reasonably severe— which rarely happens to children. Finally, punishment is most effective if alternative, rewarded behaviors are available, but all too often neither children nor criminals are taught such alternatives.

Ultimately, the choice of whether or not parents and society should use punishment depends on ethics as much as on science. Can we in good conscience eliminate the legal system that creates the delay between crime and incarceration? If imprisonment is too weak to be an effective punishment do we return to whips, to the severing of noses and ears? Capital "punishment" is, of course, not punishment at all since it does not reduce the strength of the operant that led to the crime, except in the sense that it reduces all operant strengths to zero. "That'll learn him!" is a silly statement to make about someone who is dead.

Similarly, we must ask how much pain are we willing to inflict on a child to get it to behave? While Skinner's critics may be technically right about the effectiveness of punishment, Skinner is probably right about punishment as it is actually used and as we may morally use it.

Primary and secondary reinforcement   In Chapter 2 we discussed higher order classical conditioning, in which an established CS can be paired with a neutral CS until the new CS elicits the same response as the established CS. The same phenomenon occurs in operant conditioning, where it creates a secondary, or conditioned, reinforcer.

A primary reinforcer, like a US, is a reinforcer whose reinforcement value is biologically established. Food is a US in classical conditioning and a primary reinforcer in operant conditioning. We can create new reinforcers by pairing a neutral stimulus with a primary reinforcer, whether as a CS in classical conditioning or as an S^+ in operant conditioning. The new stimulus then acquires reinforcing powers. We can use it to reward and establish some new behavior. Of course, primary reinforcement must sometimes be forthcoming, otherwise the secondary reinforcer would lose its value through extinction.

Since it is obvious that most human behavior is neither taught nor maintained by primary reinforcement, the concept of secondary reinforcement is of special importance in accounting for human learning. Parents, teachers, and employers do not run around popping food into the mouths of those who please them, but they do dispense praise, gold stars, and bonuses. Behaviorists treat all these as secondary reinforcers, assuming, even when they cannot prove it, that these acquired their reinforcing properties through higher order conditioning.

Relativity of reinforcement A student of Skinner's, David Premack (1959, 1962, 1965a), offers an interesting extension of the notion of secondary reinforcement. He proposes what has come to be called the principle of **relativity of reinforcers.**

The basic idea is simple and commonsensical. A person or other animal engages in many activities and does some more frequently than others. So activity A is more frequent than activity B, which is more frequent than C, and so on: $A > B > C > D$ ... Premack says simply that any activity higher on the scale can be used to reinforce any activity lower on the scale. Eating is more common than lever-pressing in a naive rat, and so we can use the opportunity to eat to reinforce bar-pressing. A child may prefer playing baseball to reading, and so we can use access to baseball as a reinforcer for reading.

Premack's suggestion is useful in two ways. First, it reminds us of individual differences. At least in people, what is reinforcing for one person may not be reinforcing for another. A shy, introverted child may read more than play baseball, and a teacher concerned with the child's loneliness may make access to books contingent on playing with other children.

Second, Premack's principle offers concrete guidance to the behavior modifier. It points out that for any given low-level behavior you wish to strengthen there must be many potential reinforcers, and it tells how to locate and use them.

Theoretically, Premack's idea suggests that the distinction between primary and secondary reinforcement is too simple. Instead of two categories of reinforcers there is a continuum, from the most powerful and general, such as food and water, to the weakest and most idiosyncratic. In any event, the relativity of reinforcers helps extend the behaviorists' analysis of human behavior by showing how reinforcers are everywhere in behavior, not just in objects, and that what is in one context a behavior to be reinforced by a stronger one, may in another context become itself a reinforcer.

Patterns of reinforcement

The patterns of reinforcement effect Because he (Skinner, 1959) wanted to economize on the costs of feeding his experimental subjects, Skinner (1938) made an interesting discovery, one that was made independently by Humphreys (1939). Instead of reinforcing every bar-press his subject made, Skinner reinforced only some of the responses. In the developed jargon of learning psychology, Skinner shifted from *continuous reinforcement,* in which every response is reinforced; to *partial reinforcement,* in which only some of the responses are reinforced on one schedule or another.

Skinner found that when an animal was on a partial reinforcement schedule it took longer for a learned bar-press response to extinguish than if it had been on a continuous reinforcement schedule. Particularly in the light of Hullian theory, this finding appeared paradoxical. Suppose we compare two hypothetical rats, both of which have made 500 bar-presses, but one rat has been continuously reinforced while the other has been only partially reinforced, receiving one reinforcement every ten presses. Since habit strength grows with the number of reinforcements, we would expect the continually reinforced rat, who has received 500 reinforcers, to have a stronger, more resistant habit than the partially reinforced rat, who has received only 50 reinforcements. The opposite, however, is the case.

This greater resistance of partially reinforced responses is called the **partial reinforcement effect,** and it is a reliable and robust phenomenon. Practically, it has proved to be of great value to behavior modifiers, because it provides a reliable means of strengthening a behavior and preparing it for the real world, where people get less attention than in an institution, be it a school, a prison, or a mental hospital. The partial reinforcement effect indicates that positive learned behaviors should transfer to the real world if they are at least occasionally reinforced.

Of course, the effect has its drawbacks. If a child learns to whine and fuss to get things from its parents, and the parents decide to ignore the behavior to get it to go away, then they will have to possess great fortitude and resistance to aversive stimuli. For, if they give in occasionally, they put their child on a partial reinforcement schedule and will wind up with more persistent whining than if they simply indulged the child for a while when it was an infant and then stopped cold.

Theoretically, the partial reinforcement effect has proven quite controversial. Two main theories have been offered to explain it. The first one, the discrimination theory, says that it is easy for a continuously reinforced animal to tell when extinction begins, because the shift from continuous reinforcement to no reinforcement is abrupt and obvious. But to a partially reinforced animal the onset of extinction is much less obvious, and so, instead of quickly giving up responding, it keeps pressing the bar for no reward, hoping that the food will reappear—a familiar response, evident, for example, in gamblers playing the slot machines.

The second theory, the expectancy theory, says that when an animal expects a reinforcement but it does not occur, this event is frustrating and aversive. In a sense, failure to get an expected reward is punishing. Now the partially reinforced animal has learned to live with this kind of frustration, but the continuously reinforced animal, having never experienced nonreward, has not. Consequently, when extinction begins, the punishing effect of nonreward is much greater for the continuously reinforced animal, and it quickly stops responding, while the partially reinforced animal, feeling less punished, will continue the response longer.

In the field of animal learning these theories have been developed in much greater detail than given here, by Capaldi (1966, 1971), for the discrimination theory and by Amsel (1958, 1962, 1967) for the expectancy theory.

Schedules of reinforcement

Once the idea of partial reinforcement was in hand, it opened up a new research program. It became possible to manipulate systematically the schedule on which reinforcement was delivered to the learning organism and to observe the effect of each schedule on the response rate. Such a program occasioned Skinner's most massive empirical work (Ferster & Skinner, 1957) and has remained a prime focus of research among radical behaviorists ever since. While the number of schedules investigated by Ferster and Skinner is quite large, and new ones have been invented since, there are four basic schedules of reinforcement— **fixed ratio, variable ratio, fixed interval,** and **variable interval.**

Fixed ratio   In a ratio schedule, delivery of reinforcement depends on the number of times the learner makes the response. In a fixed ratio (FR) schedule, there is a fixed number of responses that must be made before the reward will be forthcoming. Continuous reinforcement is an FR1 schedule, because there is a fixed ratio of one reinforcer per response. In an FR5 schedule only every fifth response is reinforced, while in FR8 every eighth response is reinforced, and so on.

Variable ratio   In a variable ratio schedule, it is still the number of responses that determines delivery of reinforcement, but in this case the ratio changes from reinforcement to reinforcement. So, for example, reinforcement might be delivered after the fifth response, then the second, then the tenth, twelfth, third, and so on. In some cases the ratios may go through a regular cycle; for example, reinforcing the third response, then the tenth, then the fifth, then the seventh, and then back to the third, the tenth, and so forth. Or the variable ratio may be *random,* with the number of required responses varying unpredictably.

Fixed interval   In an interval schedule, delivery of reinforcement depends on the passage of time. After a reinforced response, some interval of time passes during which reinforcement is unavailable; after the interval is over, the next response is reinforced which begins the nonreinforcement interval again. In a fixed interval schedule, the nonreinforcement period is the same every time. For example, a FI30″ schedule would impose a 30-second interval of nonreinforcement, while a FI2′ schedule would impose a two-minute wait, and so on.

Variable interval   By now you should be able to guess what this is. A variable interval schedule is an interval schedule in which the period of nonreinforcement is different after each reinforced response.

Ratio schedules typically produce higher rates of responding than interval schedules. Variable schedules produce a steadier rate of response than fixed schedules. This is because fixed schedules produce what is called the *post-reinforcement pause:* After reinforcement the animal does not respond at all for a while, then begins to respond slowly, and finally more quickly. Such acceleration is especially pronounced in FI schedules, when the animal may be be responding quite frantically at the time of reinforcement.

Schedules of reinforcement sometimes have unforseen effects on other behaviors apparently unrelated to the operant under study. These *adjunctive behaviors* have been studied extensively in the last decade, and have even been proposed as a third kind of learned behavior; see Box 4–2.

BOX 4–2.   *IS THERE A THIRD KIND OF LEARNING:?**

Research on the effects of schedules of reinforcement has turned up some puzzling findings, leading John Falk (1971, 1981) to propose a third class of behavior distinct from both operant and respondent behavior—*adjunctive behavior.* Adjunctive behaviors occur during intermittent food reinforcement and are often referred to as *schedule-induced behaviors.* The prototypical adjunctive behavior about which the most is known is *schedule-induced polydipsia.* When rats are reduced to abut 80 percent of their free-feeding body weights and allowed to earn food by bar-pressing on a variable-interval one-minute reinforcement schedule, a very curious phenomenon occurs when water is made available at the same time. Falk (1961) found that rats which weighed about 200 grams would consume an average of 92.5 ml of water during a three-hour test session (normal free-feeding water intake for a 24-hour period in the home cage would be 20–30 ml). This excessive drinking does not occur if the food pellets are simply given to the rats in one big "meal" at the beginning of the 3-hour test session (that is, a mass feeding). Thus, the intermittent food schedule "induces" this excessive drinking (polydipsia). Unlike operant behavior, such as bar-pressing for food, adjunctive behaviors occur primarily during the postpellet period of the interpellet interval. Yet, they are not elicited as an unconditioned response to eating, as several sessions are required before the schedule-induced polydipsia emerges. Thus, schedule-induced polydipsia cannot be classified as a respondent behavior. Unconditioned responses (UCR) such as an eye blink are elicited the very first time that the unconditioned stimulus (UCS), a puff of air, is presented.

In addition to polydipsia, a number of other behaviors seem to be induced by intermittent food reinforcement schedules. These include behaviors such as aggression, escape, pica (eating of inedible substances), air-licking, grooming, and wheel-running. Moreover, the species generality of adjunctive behaviors has been extended from rats to mice, guinea pigs, hamsters, pigeons, rhesus monkey, chimpanzees, and even humans. For example, Fallon, Allen, and Butler (1979) have shown that eating, drinking, grooming, and movement can be induced in humans during intermittent reinforcement schedules. Thus, there is ample evidence that adjunctive behaviors exist, and a number of the behavioral parameters (such as body weight, reinforcement schedule, and so forth) have been determined for the optimal production of the adjunctive behavior. There is, however, some controversy over whether adjunctive behaviors should be classified as a form of learning distinct from respondent and operant learning.

One approach to resolving this controversy has been to study the similarities or differences between adjunctive, operant, and respondent behaviors. For example, the phenomenon of stimulus generalization has long been known to exist for both respondent and operant behaviors. Recently, stimulus generalization as also been demonstrated with schedule-induced polydipsia, which is supposed to be an adjunctive behavior (Hamm, Porter, & Kaempf, 1981). Another phenomenon common to both respondent and operant behaviors is that of behavioral contrast. Porter and Allen (1977) demonstrated that behavioral contrast occurs with schedule-induced polydipsia when access to the water is limited during one component of a multiple reinforcement schedule. When similar behavioral phenomena can be demonstrated in supposedly different types of learning, the basis for the distinction between these different "types" of learning becomes questionable. Thus, it may be that adjunctive, operant, and respondent behaviors reflect the procedural differences used to produce and study those behaviors rather than actually being distinct types of learning that have different underlying control processes.

*This box was prepared by Dr. Joseph H. Porter, see C. L. Wetherington, "Is Adjunctive Behavior a Third Class of Behavior?" *Neuroscience and Biobehavioral Review*, 1981, 6, 329–350.

Humans and schedules of reinforcement   When we think of applying schedules of reinforcement to interpreting human behavior there are only two obvious examples. Workers who are paid on a piece-work basis, in which the amount of pay depends on the number of items built, may be on a fixed ratio schedule—a certain number of pieces yields a fixed return. Slot machines are a more obvious analogue, right down to the response of lever-pressing. These machines pay off at random, on a variable schedule, and produce steady, persistent responding that is highly resistant to extinction.

Other interpretations of natural human schedules are more dubious. Is a person who gets paid every Friday on a fixed-interval schedule, as appears at first glance? Probably not. In the case of animals, the reinforcement, on whatever schedule, reinforces the immediately preceding response. This would make the paycheck reinforce the behavior of going to the payroll office and picking up the check. If people behaved exactly like animals, we would hang around the payroll office all Friday, periodically asking if the check had arrived, and never going to work. In any case, there is growing evidence from the laboratory that people are not very sensitive to actual schedules of reinforcement.

There is a body of data (for example, Baron, Kaufman, & Stauber, 1969) that shows that

1   Human subjects on a given schedule of reinforcement do not exhibit the characteristic behavior associated with that schedule unless they are instructed as to the schedule in effect.

2   Instructions induce behavior appropriate to the described schedule even when subjects receive no reinforcement.

3   Instructions induce behavior appropriate to the described schedule, even if some *other* schedule is really in effect.

An example shows the difficulty of directly applying operant learning laws to human behavior, even in the laboratory. Weiner (1970) explored the effects of certain kinds of instructions on extinction following partial reinforcement. Subjects sat alone in a room and pressed a key that operated a digital counter on an FR3 schedule: Three presses yielded a one-digit advance on the counter. Subjects were told that at the end of the session they would receive as many pennies as there were digits on the counter. The five subjects in the first of three groups were told that 700 pennies were the most they could earn. The five subjects in the second group were told they could earn 999 pennies. The five subjects in the last group were given no instructions about how much they could earn. In all cases the objective situation was the same—after the counter got to 700, extinction was begun and lasted for two hours.

The results were that the first group extinguished quite quickly, two subjects making no response after 700, and the others very few responses past 700. Subjects in the second group persisted longer, but completely extinguished after a while. Subjects in the third group showed little, if any, slowing of their response rates during extinction. Weiner comes to the stunning (at least for a behaviorist) conclusion that his study (and many others done by radical behaviorists) shows that people can follow instructions!

These studies further support Brewer's (1974) argument that human behavior is determined less by the objective manipulations to which experimenters subject their subjects than by what the subjects believe is happening. This means that objective schedules of reinforcement may not be very useful to our understanding of human learning. In fact, some animal researchers (Jenkins, 1970, for example) have suggested that, because of their inapplicability to the natural environment and the complexity of long-term schedules of reinforcement, exhaustive study of animal learning under various schedules of reinforcement is a waste of time.

Conclusion

For Skinner, complete analysis of the contingencies of reinforcement completely exhausts what a psychologist should say about a piece of behavior. Skinner sometimes calls this approach *functional analysis,* because it aims at uncovering lawful functional relationships that hold between behavior and its environmental determinants.

The response itself is the *dependent variable,* usually quantified by measuring the rate of response. The things in the environment the experimenter manipulates—discriminative stimuli; kind, quality, and quantity of

reinforcer; schedule of reinforcement; and hours of reinforcer deprivation—are the *independent variables* of which the dependent variable is a
function. The research program dictated by Skinner's framework is clear:
Exert total control over the learner's environment by controlling all the independent variables, and then systematically manipulate the independent
variables, observing the consequent changes in behavior, the dependent
variable. Properly done, functional and causal laws linking the dependent
variable to its antecedent independent variables will emerge. Given this
clarity and simplicity, it is no wonder that the experimental analysis of behavior is the best contemporary example of normal science in psychology.

In the perspective of radical behaviorism, the organism, animal or human, is reduced to a *locus of variables* (Skinner, 1969). A person is no more
than a place where independent variables come together and interact to
determine the dependent variable—behavior. In radical behaviorism there
is no need to look inside the organism for the causes of behavior; they lie in
the environment, in the independent variables. Even physiological explanations of behavior may be ignored, for, however the nervous system
works, the facts of behavior remain, and Skinner insists we can hunt for the
laws of behavior without worrying about why, physiologically, they are
true.

Another important way of looking at radical behaviorism and the experimental analysis of behavior is by comparing them to Darwin's theory of
natural selection, as Skinner often does (Skinner, 1969). Darwinian theory
states that species' offspring are variants on their parents—new combinations of genes and mutations of genes—each quite different from the
other. Out of this variation nature selects some favorable traits and rejects
harmful ones; animals with the good traits live while those with the bad
traits die. Finally, the successful variants grow up and pass their successful
traits on to their offspring. Variation, selection, and retention are the three
processes of evolution.

Skinner views individual learning the same way. An organism emits
many different behaviors (variation). Some of these are reinforced; others
are not reinforced or are even punished (selection). Reinforced behaviors
are learned (retention). Darwin's theory of natural selection eliminated the
need for God or any other supernatural principle to give direction and
purpose to evolution, by reducing evolution to blind variation, natural selection, and genetic retention. In the same way, Skinner hopes to eliminate
the need for a mind or inner purpose to account for learning, by reducing
learning to blind emission of operant behaviors, selection by reinforcement, and retention of learned behaviors.

EXTENSION TO HUMANS

Especially since World War II, Skinner's major preoccupation has been extending the results of his animal research and his philosophy of radical behaviorism to human behavior. Two problems in particular have occupied
him: understanding language and scientifically designing cultures.

Verbal Behavior

As a would-be writer (Skinner, 1976), Skinner has a keen interest in language. He worked for years on the problem of language, and his operant analysis was finally published in 1957 as *Verbal Behavior.* He treats language as a complex set of operant responses shaped by a child's parents, teachers, and peers, being brought under the control of stimulus and reinforcement. This is in strong contrast to the traditional, Cartesian account of language as a unique human possession that sets people—who have free souls—apart from merely mechanical animals.

Skinner's book is lengthy, complex, and full of novel terminology. (The interested student may consult a simpler and more recent version by Stephen Winokur, 1976.) To both illustrate the approach and show one of its difficulties, we will briefly consider one operant class distinguished by Skinner, the *tact,* which has nothing to do with polite public behavior.

What Skinner calls a tact we might intuitively call a naming response; it deals with the ancient philosophical problem of universal concept terms (see Leahey, 1980). The problem is this: How does a child learn to categorize correctly the objects in its world as cats, dogs, toys, cars, and so forth? As every parent knows, it takes a long time for children to label correctly what they see. One child known to the author had a pet gerbil, and at the age of two the youngster called all furry animals, even big dogs, "Gerbil!"

Skinner views such class names—or universal terms as opposed to the individuals that make up the class—as *discriminated operants.* Applying contingencies analysis, let us select one operant, the class-name, or *tact,* "cat." The discriminative stimulus controlling emission of "cat" is, of course, some cat the child sees. Stimulus generalization comes into play, for since all cats resemble each other, learning to label a few cats "Cat!" will generalize to new cats. The reinforcement control is through praise for correct responses of "cat" to cats, and corrections of incorrect responses of "cat" to other animals. In this way, shaping takes place, and soon the child will say "cat" only to cats.

This is Skinner's whole analysis; he does not bring in mental images of cats, or "the idea of the cat," or "the concept of the cat," or any other unobservable mental entity. For Skinner, a class-label, a tact, is no more that a type of verbal operant that refers to its controlling stimulus. It makes con*tact* with the environment, hence its name.

While Skinner's analysis of class names, or tacts, is unusual, it has some plausibility. Its difficulties emerge when we try "tacting" our own behavior. Skinner faces up to the difficulty of accounting for utterances such as, "I am looking for my glasses." This utterence has elements of the tact about it for it names the object of my search. But the object is not present to control my speech, and Skinner cannot allow that I have an image of my glasses to which I am referring. Instead Skinner (1957) maintains that the stimulus control of the verbal operant, "I am looking for my glasses," is the observation of my searching behavior. The meaning of the statement does not derive from any idea in my mind, but instead means, "When I have behaved in this way in the past, I have found my glasses and have then stopped behaving this way." Simply put, according to Skinner when you ask me what I am doing, I observe my own behavior, see myself rummaging around in my desk, and am moved to say as a result of my observations, "I am looking for my glasses."

As an otherwise sympathetic observer (Malcolm, 1964) has observed, Skinner's description of such sentences is "weird." If you asked me what I am doing and I uttered the real meaning of "I am looking for my glasses," namely, "Well, since I'm rummaging around in my desk, I must be looking for my glasses," you would think that I was either joking or behaving like a radical behaviorist who takes his theory too seriously—or perhaps an alien who had read only Skinner's works as preparation for visiting Earth.

On the empirical front, difficulties have arisen in showing that speech is under operant control. Beginning in the mid-1950s, various researchers (Greenspoon, 1955; Verplanck, 1955) tried to show that verbal behavior follows the laws of reinforcement and extinction. In Verplanck's study, for example, undergraduate student experimenters modified subjects' opinion-giving statements. The experimenters talked to subjects and were only to agree, disagree, or keep silent when opinions were given, refraining from nodding, smiling, asking questions, and so forth. They talked to their subjects for 30 minutes, which was divided into learning phases, when they agreed with opinions, and extinction phases, when they kept silent (in some groups) or disagreed (in other groups). The results were that the frequency of emission of opinions rose when they were reinforced and fell when they were extinguished.

However, Azrin, Holz, Ulrich, and Goldiamond (1961) showed that Verplanck's data were suspect. In the course of replicating Verplanck's study (as a class exercise), they discovered that many of the experimenters had violated the procedures; for example, by participating in the conversation through nods, smiles, and questions, or had been unable to finish the study because the subjects quit during extinction.

Using undergraduate classes, they replicated Verplanck again, except that one class was told what Verplanck told his student-experimenters—that agreement increases verbal operant rate and disagreement depresses it—while the other class was told just the *opposite*. Each class reported data confirming what it was told to expect. Covert questioning by a student who the class members did not know was working for Azrin et al. showed that most of the students had simply made up their data, while nearly all the rest cheated during the experimental sessions.

Finally, four professional experimenters, well-drilled in animal behavior shaping and scientifically aware of the importance of negative results (one suspects they were Azrin, Holz, Ulrich, and Goldiamond themselves), tried to condition 12 subjects. None could complete an experimental session of 30 minutes because each of the 12 subjects got up and left the room before ten minutes were up. As we discovered before, we again find great difficulties in extending the theories and methods of behaviorism to human beings.

Scientific Design of Cultures

During World War II, Skinner (1960) worked on a bizarre project, building a pigeon-guided missile! He designed a missile that contained pigeons in the warhead; their pecking at an image of their target operated flaps on the missile and guided it home. While the kamikaze pigeons performed well in dry runs, the Navy found the project a bit laughable, and Skinner lost his funding. It is ironic that the same military problem— guiding weapons to their targets—helped produce computers and the information-processing psychology that is radical behaviorism's main rival today. But at the time Skinner was most impressed by the degree of behavioral control he had established over the pigeons. In the aftermath of his project's failure he wrote a novel, *Walden II* (1948b), which reveals his postwar obsession, the idea of constructing a scientifically managed society. *Walden II* describes Skinner's fictional utopia, while other works (for example, Skinner, 1972) argue that this utopia can actually be attained through behavioral technology.

Through these works the same ideas run like distinct threads. Skinner maintains that existing societies are badly managed, mainly because we believe in myths such as free will. People are no freer than pigeons, Skinner asserts, and to deny that our behavior is controlled is to deny scientific truth. Instead, Skinner asks us to accept that we are just as mechanical as pigeons and rats, and apply the established laws of learning to ourselves. If we do this, Skinner concludes, society will be much better managed, and everyone will be happy under the control of positive reinforcement.

Walden II and Skinner's vision of a remade Western culture are the fruits of his psychology of learning; he maintains that what we have learned in the laboratory of behavior should be applied to the problems of society in the same way that we apply what we have learned from physics and chemistry. While no one has seriously tried to remake Western society along Skinnerian lines, applying behavior modification to social and individual problems has been tried in many settings.

TRENDS IN OPERANT THEORY

Escape and Avoidance Learning

We may begin here by recalling J. B. Watson's demonstration of classically conditioned fear in his unfortunate subject Little Albert. We say that not only did Albert exhibit fear when he saw the rat—the rat CS having acquired the fear-arousing properties of the loud clanging of the bar, the UCS—but he also attempted to get away from the rat. That is, he tried to *escape* from the now fear-producing stimulus. Moreover, he would, of course, try to *avoid* the rat. Doubtless he would not go places where he would be likely to see the rat, and if he caught signs of a rat's presence he would get away.

Now the motor behaviors of escape and avoidance are operant responses, and so we need to ask how they are acquired and how they are reinforced.

The usual laboratory experiment for studying escape and avoidance learning involves a shuttlebox. A shuttlebox is a container separated into two compartments by a divider that the subject, typically a dog, can jump over. One compartment is the "shock" side equipped with an electrified floor; the other compartment is the nonelectrified "safe" side. Escape learning takes place when we place the dog in the electrified side and turn on the shock. The dog will act fearful and distressed, and after a number of such trials will learn to jump the barrier to the safe side. After the response is learned, the length of time between shock onset and the escape response shortens until the jump is made as soon as shock begins. If we provide a discriminative stimulus, or *cue*, that signals that shock is about to begin, the animal will learn to avoid the shock by jumping when the signal occurs. At first the dog simply *escaped* shock; now it has learned to *avoid* it just as Little Albert learned to escape and then avoid the white rat.

The most influential account of escape and avoidance learning was the *two-process theory* advocated by neo-Hullians. This theory holds that first classical and then operant conditioning are involved in escape and avoidance learning. First, a classically conditioned CER of fear is acquired to stimuli predicting onset of shock, specifically the shock signal. As a result, a learned or secondary drive is set up, in which the CS comes to elicit fear just as shock does. Both escape and avoidance are acquired and maintained by negative reinforcement. Jumping the barrier to the safe side terminates shock in the case of escape, or conditioned fear in the case of avoidance.

The two-process theory is a simple and direct application of standard conditioning principles to a new situation. Much of its appeal to applied behavior analysts derives from its easy extension to a class of human neuroses, namely, the phobias. Fear, whether of punishment or loss of love, is a socialization tool employed by most parents, and it seems plausible to root adult phobias in childhood escape and avoidance situations. We may imagine the 40-year-old Little Albert presenting himself for psychotherapy because of his irrational fear of rats and white furry objects. In this way, Freud's insight that adult behavior is determined by childhood experience is retained, while the unconscious is demystified and replaced by simple conditioning.

A more direct therapy than psychoanalysis' "talking cure" is also suggested by the two-process analysis of escape and avoidance learning. What happens when we simply prevent the animal from jumping to the safe side, perhaps by raising the barrier, and present the avoidance signal but not follow it with shock? We observe extinction: The CS occurs but no US follows, and the avoidance response disappears, even when we lower the barrier and the response can be made in later trials.

Such "therapy" is not only effective but also appears to be an extension and confirmation of learning principles, showing how fear is learned and unlearned according to the laws of conditioning. However, things are not so simple. A bit of reflection shows that every avoidance trial is an extinction trial, because if the subject avoids the shock by jumping when the CS is presented, there is a CS not followed by the US, and extinction should occur. But it is almost invariably the case that an avoidance response once learned will occur on every trial for as long as the experimenter has the patience to go on. We know, of course, that phobias once established rarely go away by themselves.

This and some other problems with the two-process theory have led to something we have come to expect by now, the introduction of a cognitive theory of avoidance learning (Seligman & Johnston, 1973). Like the two-process theory, the cognitive theory says that the first step in avoidance learning is classical conditioning. The shock elicits fear and muscle responses that eventually lead to escape. However, once the animal figures out the contingencies operating in the shuttle box, Tolman-like *expectancies* develop. The dog comes to expect that it will be shocked when the signal comes on and, more importantly, it expects that it can avoid shock by jumping the barrier. According to the cognitive theory, an expectancy is confirmed and strengthened whenever it proves true, as it does every time the animal makes a successful avoidance response, for it does indeed not get shocked. Nonshock, which ought to extinguish an operant response, confirms a cognitive expectancy; naturally, extinction of the jumping response, under the control of the expectancy, does not extinguish. Blocking the avoidance response without delivering shock quickly disconforms the expectancy, and so the animal quits jumping. Seligman and Johnston have shown that paying attention to a subject's beliefs provides a more satisfactory account of escape and avoidance learning than does a theory that ignores them.

Contingency, Contiguity, and the Law of Effect

Despite his reference to the *contingencies* of reinforcement, Skinner, in fact, attributes the power of the law of effect to simple *contiguity* between a response and the reinforcement, or nonreinforcement, that follows it. That Skinner relies on contiguity can be seen best in his concept of *superstitious behavior* (Skinner, 1948; Schwartz, 1978). In inducing superstitious behavior the experimenter randomly delivers reinforcement to a subject (Skinner used pigeons), which is not actually dependent on the behavior taking place at the moment of reward. *Whatever* the animal is doing would then be "reinforced" at that moment. What Skinner found was that his pigeons would acquire and persist in giving those behaviors that had been followed by reinforcement. For example, a pigeon might happen to be turning around when food was delivered, and would tend to repeat this response in the future, performing an action, turning around, that has no obvious rational connection to food gathering. This action might look like a superstitious ritual to an observer who did not know about the initial reinforcement the pigeon had received for turning around.

So, simply because of the contiguity between an irrelevant response and reinforcement, the response has been learned and will be repeated. Skinner believes human superstitions are acquired in the same way. A black cat crosses your path and a minute later you trip and fall. It is easy to attribute your pain to "bad luck" and the causally irrelevant black cat. (This explanation, however, fails to take into account the extremely long life of superstitions in popular culture. Many people, for example, do not like to walk under ladders, although they have never had a bucket of paint fall on their heads when walking under a ladder.) Not only superstitions but also human depression may result from reinforcements that cannot be controlled. See Box 4–3.

BOX 4–3   *LEARNED HELPLESSNESS: CONTIGUITY VS. CONTINGENCY*

One of the most dramatic findings to emerge from the controversy between the contiguity and contingency accounts of reinforcement is the phenomenon of *learned helplessness* (Seligman, 1975; Maier & Seligman, 1976). Two dogs are placed in harnesses and subjected to identical periodic electrical shocks. One dog can terminate the shock by pressing a lever in front of its nose; the other dog, his yoked companion, has no control over the shock. When the first dog receives a shock, the second one does too. When the first dog stops the shock by pressing the lever, the shock stops for the second dog too. Both dogs receive identical patterns of shock and nonshock. The only difference is that the first dog can control its shocks, and naturally learns to do so, while the second dog is a helpless victim—what does the animal learn?

What the second dog learns is revealed in the second phase of the experiment when each animal must learn to jump a barrier to avoid receiving a shock. The first canine, like any normal dog that had never before been exposed to shock, quickly learns to jump the hurdle and avoids being shocked. The second dog, however, who was helpless during the first phase of the experiment, remains helpless even now when action could relieve its suffering. The creature whines and yelps, but after a while it becomes totally passive, simply accepting the shocks without complaint or any attempt to avoid them. It has *learned* to be *helpless*. A pious observer might even say that the second dog has acquired the resignation to the will of God, or of the gods, that most religions try to teach.

How does this dreary finding reflect on the contiguity-contingency debate? Remember that the two dogs received exactly the *same* pattern of shock and nonshock in phase 1. A contiguity view of learning would say that the first dog learned to press the lever because it was followed by negative reinforcement while the second dog learned "superstitiously" to act passive in the face of shock. A contingency analysis would say that the first dog learned that what it did made a difference—that it could avoid shock through effective action, learning that appropriately transferred to the hurdle-jumping phase of the experiment. But the second dog learned literally to be helpless—that there was no connection between what it did and shock, that there was no point even in wasting its energy whining and yelping—and so remained helpless even in the new situation of phase 2.

To test these hypotheses Maier (1970) repeated the original experiment, except that this time the first dog learned to be master of its fate by standing rigidly still to terminate the shock. The creature's companion remained helpless as in the standard experiment. Now, if the first dog learned simply, "Stand still to avoid shock," we would expect it to stand still in the hurdle-jumping phase of the experiment. But these dogs did not act passively—they learned to jump the hurdle—while the yoked dogs were again rendered helpless. So it appears that reinforcement works because of contingency between action and reward, not just because reward happens to follow a behavior. Organisms can tell when their activities affect their lives and when they do not.

The concept of learned helplessness has received wide clinical application. For example, one of the oddest aspects of neurosis is the "neurotic paradox." Neurotics often know something is wrong in their lives but seem helpless to change it. It is not implausible to suggest that a neurotic's helplessness has somehow been learned in a way similar to a dog's learned helplessness.

Whether or not this theory of Skinner's can be applied directly to human superstitions, it may not even be quite true of pigeons. Staddon and Simmelhag (1971) replicated Skinner's study but recorded the pigeon's behavior more fully. Delivering food every 12 seconds regardless of what the pigeon was doing, they found in part what Skinner had found: that each pigeon would acquire some idiosyncratic "superstitious" behavior such as circling or flapping its wings. However, each of these idiosyncratic behaviors ended with the same behavior—pecking, a normal, nonsuperstitious behavior for hungry pigeons. The pecking might be in the food tray or on the floor, but *every* pigeon acquired a peck response. Following a reinforcement, the "superstitious" behavior recurred, followed by a peck. Furthermore, when the pigeons were subsequently put on an FI12″ schedule for pecking a key, the *frequency* of pecking did not change, only its location— the pigeons now pecked the key—and the "superstitious" behavior remained.

Contiguity alone cannot explain these results, because the behavior closest in time to reinforcement, namely, pecking, was the *same* in all pigeons, even though to begin with food was delivered when the pigeons were not pecking. There appears to be a close connection between certain activities and reinforcement; in pigeons, pecking is naturally closely connected to food-gathering, and even when pecking is not related to food reward, the pigeons peck anyway in any situation where food is available. Nor did an actual contingency of reinforcement (the FI12″ schedule) *strengthen* the pecking response; it only shifted its location. Staddon and Simmelhag (1971) therefore distinguished *terminal behaviors,* those naturally and closely connected with reinforcement and controlled by the law of effect, from *interim behaviors* engaged in between terminal behaviors, which also appear when reinforcement is not available.

Staddon and Simmelhag (see also Staddon, 1975, 1977) also revised Skinner's Darwinian analysis of learning. Skinner leaves the reason for the emission of operants quite mysterious; they simply occur and may be reinforced or not. Staddon and Simmelhag, however, distinguish principles of behavioral *variation* from principles of behavioral *selection.* Principles of variation determine the range of behaviors an organism can do in a given situation. Situations constrain and determine behavior. None of Thorndike's cats rolled over and purred in the puzzle-box; they all engaged in behaviors likely to produce escape. So the setting of conditioning determines what kinds of responses will occur. The principles of behavioral

selection boil down to reinforcement: delivery of a US in classical conditioning or of reinforcement in operant conditioning.

The principles of behavioral variation say that in a given situation certain behaviors are likely to occur; from this range reinforcement selects
one, because of the contingent relation between response and reinforcement. In this perspective reinforcement does not strenghthen or teach a
novel behavior; it merely selects from a repetoire of already present behaviors whose rate of emission in a given situation is controlled by the principles of variation—the response that will work now. What happens is not so
much that the selected behavior is strengthened as that the unselected behaviors desist.

Staddon's and Simmelhag's arguments are only a modification and
extension of Skinner's radical behaviorism. They do not violate the hard
core of radical behaviorism by introducing hypothetical entities inside
learning organisms, nor do they extend much beyond careful description.
All they have done is to reformulate the relation between response and reinforcement, playing down the role of contiguity. They have examined
more thoroughly than Skinner the reasons why behaviors get emitted in
the first place, and they have separated these reasons from the effect of
reinforcement. They also recognized the role of genetic constraints in
learning by separating terminal and interim behaviors, and by recognizing
genetic factors in the principles of variation. Staddon's and Simmelhag's
work is altogether an impressive extension and revision of the paradigm of
radical behaviorism, but it is work in the protective belt and in no way repudiates the hard core of Skinner's program.

More radical challenges come from those animal behaviorists who
want to incorporate cognitive constructs, such as short-term memory, into
accounts of animal learning. Such theorists have become numerous in recent years. (for symposia see Medin, Roberts, & Davis, 1976; Hulse, Fowler,
& Honig, 1978.) They have occasioned controversy in the pages of the radical behaviorists' journals (for example, Shimp, 1976, on the side of memory; reply by Branch, 1977, defending radical behaviorism). Nevertheless,
the same journals have published papers that quietly and without fanfare
use information-processing terminology (Wasserman, Nelson, & Larew,
1980). Since the animal behaviorists by and large simply appropriate cognitive apparatus from the human information-processing psychologists we
will study in later chapters, we need not describe their proposals here. But
it is an important trend to be noted, one that is deeply threatening to the
hard core of radical behaviorism.

Constraints on Learning

Another important trend in operant psychology has been the investigation of biological constraints on what and how an animal learns. Much of
the impetus to research and theory in the area comes from ethology and
sociobiology (see Chapter 10).

While they stress the contributions of the genes, ethologists and
sociobiologists have not been blind to the roles that learning and imitation

play in molding behavior. For example, Wilson (1975) discusses what amounts to transmission of a cultural tradition among members of a troop of Japanese macaques living on Koshima Island. Scientists studying the troop began scattering sweet potatoes on the island's beaches, and the macaques extended their normal forest habitat to the beach. A young female monkey, Imo, invented potato-washing, dipping the potato in the water with one hand and wiping off the sand with the other. Beginning with other young monkeys potato-washing spread throughout the troop until only the oldest, most conservative macaques continued to resist the innovation. Imo—whom Wilson calls "the monkey genius"—also invented another clever technique. Researchers also scattered wheat on the beach, and the monkeys had to pick up each kernel with their fingers. But Imo discovered how to pick up whole handfuls of sand and wheat and throw them on the water, scooping up and eating the wheat that remained floating when the sand sank. Again, Imo's tradition spread throughout the troop starting with her age-mates. Intimate contact with the water changed the macaque's whole way of life in unforeseen ways. Young macaques began to splash and play in the water, learned to swim and dive for edible seaweed. One adventuresome young macaque swam to another island! Learning, exploration, and imitation can play very important roles in determining behavior, as this preculture of the macaques demonstrates. The capacity to learn possesses an important survival value—and is therefore probably innate—in providing flexible behaviors that can be adapted to rapid environmental change. Genetic change—evolution—is a slow process requiring many generations, but extensive cultural change may be complete in a single generation.

Nevertheless, ethologists and sociobiologists insist that learning is constrained by evolution. A nice illustration of how ecology shapes what an animal learns is found in three species of gull. One species nests on open flat ground in close groups, and as a result are able to recognize fine differences between their eggs' size and speckling and the eggs of others that might make their way into their nests. It would reduce fitness to hatch a stranger's egg, and so the gull's powers of visual learning and discrimination are well developed.

Herring gulls, however, nest rather farther apart, so that eggs are unlikely to get mixed up, and herring gulls are poor at recognizing their own eggs. They will even sit on a large, black fake egg in preference to their own small, speckled one. But chicks can run around and get mixed up with one another after birth, so that herring gulls are excellent at learning what their own chicks look like and at recognizing strange chicks.

Finally, kittiwake gulls nest in niches on the faces of cliffs so that neither eggs nor chicks are likely to get mixed up, and the kittiwakes show no sign of recognizing their own eggs or offspring, and may happily tend large, black cormorant chicks substituted for their small white ones (Gould and Gould, 1981; Tinbergen, 1951/1972).

The lesson here is not that some gull species are smarter than others. On the contrary, the gulls suggest that a single dimension of intelligence or ability to learn is not very useful. Although unable to recognize their eggs, herring gulls clearly can learn fine visual discriminations as they must to recognize their own chicks. What biology does is direct the gull's learning in certain ways. Ecologically, it makes sense for herring gulls to learn what their chicks look like but not what their eggs look like, and evolution—the ultimate determiner of behavior—has shaped the herring gull's visual learning appropriately.

The view of biology as shaping and constraining learning is, however, contrary to the received tradition among learning theorists who have generally pursued the goal of a **general process learning theory.**

General process learning theory   Whatever other issues separated them, the noted learning psychologists believed that there were only one or two kinds of learning, and that the laws of learning were the same for all species. As Skinner (1961, p. 118) put it, "Pigeon, rat, monkey, which is which? It doesn't matter." The only recognized constraints on what an animal could learn were peripheral: Obviously a dog cannot flap its legs and fly, and a person cannot discriminate a 30,000-Hertz tone from a 32,000-Hertz tone, being unable to hear either one. But apart from that, it was widely held that any stimulus an animal could perceive could be associated by conditioning to any response the animal could make (Seligman & Hager, 1972).

The assumption that learning theory was general and not species-specific was particularly important because the real aim of the learning theorists was to explain human behavior, even though they based their ideas on research on animal learning. Such an indirect research program can be justified only if what Skinner wrote in his *Verbal Behavior* (1957) is true:

> The basic processes and relations which give verbal behavior its special characteristics are now fairly well understood. Much of the experimental work responsible for this advance has been carried out on other species, but the results have proved to be surprisingly free of species restrictions. Recent work has shown that the methods can be extended to human behavior without serious modification. (Skinner, 1957, p.3)

However, our review of sociobiology suggests that Skinner's statement of faith in general-process learning theory is seriously mistaken. We will see how behavior from altruism to sex is tuned—often very precisely—by evolutionary pressures to fit organisms into their environmental niches. The ability to learn is an adaptive trait, but clearly it benefits each kind of organism to learn some kinds of things rather than others; it pays the herring gull more to learn how its chicks look than learning how its eggs look. Beginning in 1961 (Breland & Breland, 1961/1972) it gradually became clear to learning psychologists that general-process learning theory was at best a distant hope. (Increasing lines of evidence have emerged, as reviewed by: Bolles, 1975; Domjon, 1980; Garcia, McGowan, & Green, 1972; Rozin & Kalat, 1971, 1972; Shettleworth, 1972; and in Hinde & Stevenson-Hinde, 1973, and Seligman & Hager, 1972.)

Without stressing it, we have already touched upon some constraints on learning in earlier chapters. The fact that rats can learn mazes without reinforcement (latent learning) demonstrates that since rats live in underground burrows they are genetically predisposed to learn spatial layouts (Shettleworth, 1972). Autoshaping may be viewed not just as classical instead of operant conditioning, but as revealing an innate connection between food and pecking. Staddon and Simmelhag's principles of variation implicitly appeal to biology to provide constraints on the kind of behaviors an animal will emit under a given circumstance. But the severest blow to the hopes of general-process learning theory was the "message from Garcia" (Rozin, 1977).

The message from Garcia   John Garcia, for a time a student in Tolman's old laboratory, studied, with a variety of associates, aversion learning based on food. During the course of his research, Garcia discovered phenomena anomalous to the general-process program. Rats allowed to drink a novel-tasting fluid (saccharin-flavored water), and made sick hours later by drug injection or X-irradiation, learned to avoid drinking the flavored water. This violated the usual law of classical conditioning, which holds that the US-CS interval must be very short—about .5 seconds—for learning to occur. Moreover, the aversion was always to the most *recent* novel substance, since rats who drank saccharin water, then familiar tap water, and then got sick, avoided only the saccharin water.

The selectivity of the taste-sickness association is strengthened by further experiments. Rats would learn to avoid foods on the basis of its taste, not its appearance (Domjon, 1980). In an elegant two-factor experiment, Garcia, Clarke, and Hankins (1973) let rats drink saccharin water while they heard a click, were shocked, or were later made ill (see Figure 4–2). The rats learned specifically to associate sweetness with illness and the click with shock. Sickened rats avoided only the food and did not try to run away from the click. Shocked rats tried to avoid the click but drank the sweet water. The obvious conclusion is that sick rats conclude: "It must have been

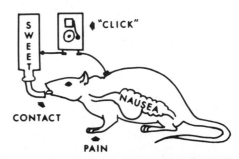

FIGURE 4–2 The cue to consequence paradigm, a fourfold experimental design where two cues, taste or auditory stimuli, are paired with two consequences, illness or pain. Learning is more probable in the cells indicated, and the conditioned responses are qualitatively distinct. (From Garcia, Clarke, & Hankins, 1973).

	CONSEQUENCES	
	NAUSEA	**PAIN**
SWEET	ACQUIRES AVERSION	DOES NOT
"CLICK"	DOES NOT	LEARNS DEFENSE

something I ate," and attribute the cause of their distress to the newest food they ate rather than exterior cues or to familiar foods (Domjon, 1980). That this process is genetic is supported by findings that the same phenomena occur in newborn rat pups (Domjon, 1980).

These particular dispositions to learn are well adapted to the rat's ecology (Shettleworth, 1972). Wild rats are omnivores who sample small amounts of new foods and avoid those that make them ill. Long before Garcia, rodent-control experts knew that rats easily become bait-shy, outwitting their hunters. Under these conditions it could be an ill-adapted rat indeed who drank tainted water, later got ill under a bush and learned to avoid the bush (the immediate CS), while returning to drink the water. Evolution has produced rats who adaptively associate taste with illness and external cues with external threats.

Different ecologies produce different food aversions. Wild rats are nocturnal feeders with poor vision, so taste, not food appearance, is their best cue to avoid poison. Quail, on the other hand, are diurnal (daytime) feeders with excellent vision, and they can easily and directly associate a new food's appearance with later illness (Wilcoxon, Dragoin, & Kral, 1971). On the other hand, bluejays, like rats, are scavengers and learn as rats do, in a two-step process: Taste (CS) is averted by illness (US) and then visual cues (CS) are avoided by the aversive taste (US). We must conclude that animals' ecological niches and consequent evolutionary pressures direct the ways animals learn even simple associations (Shettleworth, 1972; Wilson, 1975).

Garcia's findings, although now recognized as prize-winning classics, were greeted by the learning community with skepticism, hostility, and rejection (retold by Rozin, 1977; Garcia, 1981; Lubek & Apfelbaum, 1981). Seligman and Hager (1972) report that one reader of Garcia's first paper in the area—written after Garcia's long and distinguished career as a psychologist—said publicly, "Those findings are no more likely than birdshit in a cuckoo clock."

Nevertheless, Garcia's findings were replicated, and many new instances of constraints on learning emerged, far too many to be reviewed here (see the review papers and symposia cited earlier). One other finding does deserve brief mention: Bolles' (1971) work on the familiar topic of avoidance learning. Bolles argued (as does Hineline, 1981) that the traditional two-step theory of avoidance learning is incorrect. Noting that rats can be easily conditioned to run, jump, or freeze to avoid shock, but not to bar-press, Bolles argues that avoidance learning is a matter of selecting from an array of *species-specific defense mechanisms* (SSDR's), an analysis reminiscent of Staddon and Simmelhag (1971). Threat, whether from a predator or shock, sets up a "flight or fight" reaction, eliciting one or more specific, genetically programmed reactions. In the wild, it is adaptive for a threatened animal to freeze (to avoid being seen), to flee (and escape), or to stand and fight, and evolution has programmed these innate responses; nothing like lever pressing, however, has ever been adaptive for a rat. So in the laboratory a shocked rat (and most animals) will try to jump off the grid, run away from the shock, or, if another rat is present, fight it; it will almost never learn to bar-press. So avoidance learning is a process of threat → SSDR's occur → reinforcement (escape) selects the SSDR. We do not need to postulate a derived fear drive to a shock-cueing CS.

After all the evidence on constraints on learning has piled up, psychologists remain uncertain what to make of it. Most students of learning want to abandon entirely the search for general laws of learning, while a few others want to continue the search, but at the level of the neuron. Learning theory having collapsed (Fox, 1983), new directions to take remain obscure. If any consensus is emerging it is that while scientists may be able to give some general account of animal learning they will have to acknowledge and work within a broader biological context that recognizes evolution as an important determiner of behavior in each species (Gould & Gould, 1981). Some attempts at a new learning-biology synthesis have been offered (Plotkin & Odling-Smee, 1979; Rozin, 1976; Johnston, 1981, is particularly useful reference, because the appended commentary by other researchers reveals the full range of contemporary opinion). In any event, it seems unlikely that any psychologist will be able ever again to blandly assert the extendability of findings from rats to other lower animals, much less to human beings.

SUGGESTED READINGS

The best single introduction to the ideas of B. F. Skinner is his *Science and Human Behavior* (MacMillan, 1953) where he discusses his scientific work, the experimental analysis of behavior, and his extension of radical behaviorism to humans and human society. A more recent and highly controversial statement of his radical restructuring of human self-understanding and its social implications is *Beyond Freedom and Dignity* (Bantam, 1972). Both are available in paperback.

CHAPTER FIVE

MEMORY AND INFORMATION PROCESSING I: PERCEPTUAL AND SHORT-TERM MEMORY PROCESSES

INTRODUCTION

During W.W.II scientists actually built a device that earlier generations had dreamed of: a digital computer. After the war, as computer science was declassified and the modern computer age began, psychologists found in computers and computer programming a new conceptual basis for psychology. Computers accept information, store and process that information, make decisions, and generate output. In short, computers seemed to think.

It became attractive to view humans and computers alike as information-processing devices studied by psychologists on the one hand and computer scientists on the other. The marriage of cognitive psychologists (who regard humans as information processors taking in information through the senses, processing it and storing it in memory, and making decisions and behaving as a result) and computer scientists, counseled by philosophers of mind, has so far been a happy one, creating a new field called **cognitive science,** the study of computational devices both of wire and steel and of nerve and tissue.

It is very common to distinguish cognitive psychology from behavioral psychology, but we believe things are not so simple. Clearly, cognitive psychology and radical behaviorism are quite different, since Skinner does not tolerate the postulation of any inner psychological agencies, whether it be Freud's ego or a cognitive psychologist's long-term memory. However, both Tolman and Hull postulated inferred entities that controlled behavior, cognitive maps, and mediating responses; Neo-Hullians have proved eager to embrace cognitive concepts in studying human development (Chapter 12), and we have already found some animal behaviorists talking in cognitive terms.

What cognitive psychology has primarily done is to create an entirely new vocabulary for discussing learning. Stimulus becomes input; behavior, output; response mediators, levels of information processing. This new vocabulary is so different, in fact, that many colleges and universities have separate courses with separate texts in Learning and Cognitive Psychology. However, the basic question of cognitive psychology is the same as human learning, namely, How does the environment modify the behavior of people? While the specific answers cognitive psychologists give are different from behaviorists', their quest is the same.

In this section we will present the cognitive view of learning beginning with the simplest and best understood information processes, then moving to the deeper, harder to study and less well-known ones. Chapter 5 opens the section by discussing early information processing—what happens to stimuli (input) as they are registered and prepared for storage. In Chapter 6 the subject is long-term memory, the processes and representations involved in storing, maintaining, and retrieving learned information. Chapter 7 takes up the topic of language, perhaps humans' most important cognitive tool. Chapter 8 concerns comprehension, the understanding of complex linguistic information. Finally, Chapter 9 surveys work on thinking, including reasoning, problem solving, and scientific thinking, the traditional higher mental processes.

The first time that one of the authors (RJH) taught a psychology course in the area of human learning or cognition, the course happened to be called "The Psychology of Thinking." Somehow it was very amusing to friends to hear that someone was actually teaching a course on thinking. The usual response was a chuckle, if not a guffaw, and a comment like, "Well, I sure could use a course in that myself." However, neither that course nor this book is a collection of practical problem-solving pointers on how to think better. Still, if you leave this semester with a better understanding of how your mind works, you will probably be able to put that knowledge to use in improving your own thinking.

The next few chapters look at many different aspects of information processing. Most human experiences, whether studying for a test, sizing up a new acquaintance at a party, or listening to a commercial on television, involve processing information. It is difficult to separate perception, memory, comprehension, language, problem solving, and decision making. Thus, our discussion of each problem will necessarily have frequent allusion to other topics. The chapter begins with an overview of the information-processing system as viewed by most contemporary cognitive psychologists. Following that, we shall examine several topics in memory in this chapter and the next. In Chapter 7 we will look at language in some detail and in Chapter 8 at comprehension, which will tie many of the themes of the preceding three chapters together. Finally, in Chapter 9 we will examine problem solving, reasoning, and decision making. In all cases, both applications in our daily lives and theoretical conceptual principles will be stressed.

AN OVERVIEW
OF THE INFORMATION PROCESSING SYSTEM

Before examining the various processes that occur when we take in and interpret information, it is useful to have some general understanding of the information-processing system. Figure 5–1 schematically illustrates a general conceptual view of the most characteristic way that contemporary cognitive psychologists view the information-processing system. Much of this conceptualization is traceable to the model of Atkinson and Shiffrin (1968), who developed an extensive description of such a model. What is presented below is very much in the tradition of Atkinson and Shiffrin, without necessarily adhering to all the details and assumptions of their theory.

Generally, with some important exceptions to be discussed later, processing proceeds from left to right in Figure 5–1. Environmental input comes into sensory memory, which holds information for a very short time (about 0.5 to 1.0 seconds in the visual system), just long enough for us to select what to attend to for further processing. Our sensory memory contains everything impinging on our senses, including not only voices we hear and colors we see, but also background noises we "tune out," that is, those we do not send on for further processing.

Attention and pattern recognition occur to help identify and select information for further processing. Though we will discuss these processes in more detail later in the chapter, one important paradox should be introduced here. Although we said earlier that information is generally processed left to right in Figure 5–1, sometimes the processes of attention and pattern recognition must draw on material "farther along" in the information-processing chain, specifically, knowledge from long-term memory. For example, we choose to attend to one conversation rather than another at a party because the material being discussed in one interests us more than that being discussed in the other. To make this decision about attention, we must draw on information already in long-term memory. Such anecdotal examples and experimental evidence pointing in the same direction have been used to argue against Atkinson-Shiffrin-type models, sometimes labeled "multistore" models because of their postulation of three different memory stores (see Figure 5–1). For now, however, we will ignore this anomaly in our left-to-right linear processing of information, but we will return to this important theoretical issue near the end of Chapter 6.

Material in short-term memory includes everything we are thinking about right now. This material comes from two basic sources: the external environment (new sensory information) and previously learned informa-

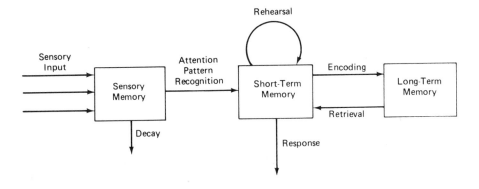

FIGURE 5–1   Overview of Information-Processing System

tion retrieved from long-term memory. Both types of information interact in short-term memory in ways discussed at length later in the book. To give a brief informal example, suppose you are introduced to someone new, Laura, whom you have never seen before. That is new information coming in through your senses through sensory memory to short-term memory. However, let us suppose, as frequently happens, that Laura reminds you very much of someone else you already know, Jane. Thus, information about Jane is retrieved from long-term memory to mingle in short-term memory with new information about Laura. Sometimes the information about the two people may become very confused, with some important ramifications we shall explore later.

Material may be retained in short-term memory only a very short time (some experiments suggest 15 to 30 seconds), unless it continues to be processed in some way. This could occur by repeating (rehearsing) the material over to yourself, as when you look up a phone number and repeat it to yourself while you dial the phone. It could also be retained in short-term memory indefinitely by continuing to think about it for some reason, for example, when solving a problem. If we make a response (verbal or behavioral), it must be from short-term memory, not sensory memory, which is too short-lived and unprocessed, and not long-term memory, which is not in immediate consciousness.

If we want to remember something for the future, we generally seek to encode it somehow into long-term memory. If it is thus encoded successfully, we can forget about it for the moment, knowing we can retrieve it later when we need it. If it is not encoded and we do not continue to process it in short-term memory, it is quickly and permanently forgotten. For example, in the case of the phone number, we rehearse it only long enough to dial the phone. The importance of encoding in memory can hardly be overstated. Most popular books on how to improve one's memory are really about how to encode information more efficiently. If material is encoded well, it can more likely be readily retrieved. On the other hand, if it is not encoded accurately or at all, even the best retrieval strategies are probably doomed to failure. Encoding and its sister set of processes, retrieval, are both places where memory can go wrong. This topic, too, will be explored in more detail in later chapters.

A consistent and recurring issue in information processing is the juxtaposition of *top-down* (conceptually-driven) and *bottom-up* (data-driven) processes. Bottom-up processes refer to the processing of the actual environmental stimuli with the course and character of that processing determined only by the nature of those stimuli (data) themselves. Although such "pure processing" is perhaps the lay person's view of how we perceive and comprehend information, it almost never occurs in the real world or even in the laboratory. This is so because we typically have top-down (conceptually-driven) processing going on simultaneously. Such processing involves expectations about what the data will hold, based on our past experiences and knowledge in long-term memory. Such expectations inevitably color our interpretation of those data and prevent us from doing purely data-driven processing. We will see examples of simultaneous top-down and bottom-up processes occurring at several different levels of information processing throughout the next few chapters.

An important distinction to make when discussing cognitive processes is differentiating *serial* and *parallel* processes. Processes done serially are performed sequentially, one after the other, while those done in parallel are performed simultaneously, or are at least partially overlapping in time. For example, if you scan a list of words to see if the letter *T* occurs in any of them and then scan the list again to see if the letter *P* occurs, you are performing the two scanning processes serially. If you scan the list once, looking for either a *T* or a *P,* you may likely be performing the operations in parallel.

While the difference between serial and parallel processing is often neither as easy to identify nor as conceptually distinct as the above example might suggest, it is a useful distinction to make in studying the covert processes of cognition. It is often possible to infer whether processes must have occurred serially or in parallel, especially through the use of reaction-time methodology, which is discussed later.

At this point we will begin examining each of the separate memory stores and sets of processes that occur as we comprehend and remember information. In general, the coverage of topics in the next two chapters will proceed from left to right as in Figure 5–1.

SENSORY MEMORY

The most immediately perceptual store of memory is **sensory memory,** also sometimes called the *sensory registers* or *sensory information store.* Its function is merely to hold information very briefly, just long enough for it to be selectively attended to and identified for further processing in short-term memory. The material in sensory memory is completely unorganized and is basically a perceptual copy of objects and events in the world. Material decays very rapidly from sensory memory (about 0.5 to 1.0 seconds for vision and 3.0 to 4.0 seconds for hearing), unless it is selected for further processing. Although we generally are not conscious of information while it is in sensory memory, you can informally demonstrate its existence by quickly waving your arm from side to side in front of your face. You continue to see a very faint copy or shadow of your arm for a fraction of a second after it has sped by. This is the "icon," or visual sensory memory representation.

Although information in sensory memory is not generally open to introspection, its existence was convincingly demonstrated many years ago in a clever experiment by George Sperling (1960). When an array of 12 letters (three rows of four each) was flashed on a screen for 50 milliseconds (one-twentieth of a second), subjects were barely aware of their presence yet could consistently report three to four letters accurately. While this result appeared to reflect the actual processing capacity, Sperling demonstrated that many more letters had in fact entered sensory memory. To do so, Sperling used a high-, middle-, or low-pitched tone to indicate to the subject to report only the top, middle, or bottom line of the array. Using this "partial-report" method, subjects could report about 75 percent of the letters correctly, as opposed to half that many when the whole-report ("repeat all the letters") method was used. This suggests, then, that the limits of sensory memory are temporal, not visual, and that considerable information is there, but decays very rapidly, faster than the time it takes to report it. In the case of the visual system, decay from sensory memory is essentially complete in one second or less.

In another study, Sperling (1960) showed that the accuracy of recall of the letters decreased substantially if the tone signaling which line to recall was delayed even for a fraction of a second. In fact, if it is delayed as much as a second, the number of letters recalled was down to the equivalent of four out of twelve, the number reported under the whole-report procedure.

The Sperling effect was replicated in a study using the auditory system, with one important difference (Darwin, Turvey, & Crowder, 1972). The auditory sensory memory, or *echo*, lasts for several seconds, with recall under partial report being superior to that under whole report for up to four seconds. At least in theory, there must be a sensory memory for other senses beside vision and hearing, though these have not really received much examination.

The fact that information decays so rapidly from sensory memory is actually an adaptive feature of our information-processing system, since we might experience double images in the visual system or confusing echoes in the auditory system if everything we had perceived in the last few seconds remained in our sensory memory. There are, in fact, a fortunate (or unfortunate, depending on your point of view) few people who have icons that persist for very long periods of time and can be recalled at will. This is called *eidetic imagery* (or somtimes photographic memory) and is a truly remarkable ability. See Box 5–1 for the story of one person with this ability.

BOX 5–1   *EIDETIC IMAGERY*

There are a small number of children, and a much smaller number of adults, who possess an unusual ability to maintain visual images for much longer periods of time than most of us are able to. This is called "eidetic imagery" (or sometmes, less precisely, "photographic memory"). It may be viewed as the ability to retain icons from sensory memory far longer than the usual second or so that they last. One of the most striking "eidetikers" ever studied is "Elizabeth," a very exceptional woman studied by Charles Stromeyer (1970; Stromeyer & Psotka, 1970). Elizabeth was a very intelligent young artist and teacher at Harvard. She could mentally project an exact image of a picture onto the canvas or any other surface she was looking at. She could also retrieve images of pages of textbooks she had read and copy them in writing from memory. In an effort to determine the limits of her eidetic abilities, Stromeyer tested Elizabeth with computer-generated random-dot stereograms. A normal person can look through a stereoscope at a pair of stereograms, a different one with each eye; the machine allows the eyes to fuse the two patterns and thus see some figure emerge from the combination. Elizabeth, however, could do this without the stereoscope! She looked at a 10,000-dot pattern for one minute with one eye. Then she looked at another pattern with the other eye and superimposed the eidetic image retained from the first pattern over the second pattern, thus causing the figure to emerge.

In later studies Elizabeth showed other amazing eidetic feats, including retaining an eidetic image of a million-dot pattern for at least four hours and a kinetic image of ten seconds from a Laurel and Hardy movie one week later. For some reason we do not understand, eidetic imagery is much more common in children than adults (Haber, 1979). Why it disappears with development remains a mystery.

ATTENTION

The purpose of sensory memory is to hold information just long enough for some of it to be selected for further processing in short-term memory. For this to occur, it must be attended to and we must start to recognize patterns. It is to these processes that we now turn, in examining how material is selected from sensory memory for further processing. Let's begin by examining **attention.**

General Issues

Attention is another one of those many psychological topics that everyone has intuitions about, but no one knows exactly how to define precisely. Although discussed by William James (1890) and even earlier by the German introspectionists, it was long ignored in the behaviorist era as being too mentalistic and unobservable to be worthy of study in scientific psychology. In the 1950s and 1960s, however, there arose a resurgence of interest in studying attention, primarily by several British researchers, notably Donald Broadbent (1958); Anne Treisman (1964); and Colin Cherry (1953). Since then, and especially in the last ten years, the problem has received intense study, though many unanswered questions remain.

One of the most fundamental issues in studying attention involves a basic paradox common in information processing. While attention seems to be an early process in the sequence of processing information (that is, we must attend to something before it can be processed too deeply), the variables affecting how we choose what we attend to sometimes require extensive processing before that "early" decision is made. How to resolve this tension between the top-down and bottom-up processes is both a continuing theme and conflict within this area of cognitive psychology.

To return to our earlier example, suppose that you are at a party and suddenly turn your head to begin attending to a new conversation because you've just heard your name spoken in that conversation. Even though you were not consciously attending to it, you must have been unconsciously processing meaningful elements of that unattended conversation to some degree, in order to be able to recognize your own name. The top-down process of drawing on knowledge from long-term memory, specifically the knowledge of what your name is, has interacted with the bottom-up processes of understanding the words spoken by the other people in the conversation.

Generally, attention has been conceptualized in two ways. First of all, it has often been considered as a state of concentrating on something. In this tradition, William James (1890) called attention the "focalization of consciousness." As a state, it has some similarities to other psychological states such as emotions like anxiety or happiness, which are not directly observable, but rather must be inferred from behavior.

An alternative, though not necessarily totally inconsistent, way to conceptualize attention is as processing capacity, which can be allocated in a variety of ways to different stimuli and activities (see Kahneman, 1973). The concept of time-sharing is useful here. A finite amount of capacity (attention) exists that may be allocated or time-shared among the various stimuli and activities demanding attention. It is as if you had 12 cookies to give to 12 children. They could all be given to one especially hungry child, distributed two each to six children, or one each to all 12 children.

Selectivity in Attention

How we select activities to attend to and how we determine how many stimuli we can process simultaneously depends on a variety of factors. First of all, the number of sources is important. It is harder to pay attention to five people talking than it is to one. Secondly, the similarity of sources is important. For example, some people find that they can study well with instrumental music in the background, but not with vocal music. The latter, being verbal, is similar enough to reading to interfere, while purely instrumental music is not. To develop the example a bit further, if you are solving algebra problems rather than reading, you may be able to work them to vocal music, since here there is only one linguistic stimulus. One of the most highly interfering, and thus extremely difficult, tasks known is the "shadowing" task used in many laboratory experiments studying attention. This requires you to "shadow" or repeat a message as it comes into your ear through earphones. Because the content of the message you shadow and the words you speak are identical, this is a very difficult thing to do, though practice improves performance considerably. The task can be made even more difficult by giving you delayed auditory feedback (DAF), which involves hearing in one ear the recording of what you just spoke a few seconds earlier, all the while repeating the message heard in the other ear. In this case, the DAF message is in your own voice, thus increasing the similarity of sources and making the task more difficult.

The complexity of sources or tasks is another important variable. It is much easier to pay attention to several simple stimuli or simultaneously perform more than one simple task than it is if the stimuli or tasks are complex. For example, you may be able to read *TV Guide,* watch *Dallas,* and talk to your roommate about dinner simultaneously, but watching a complex documentary on television or reading your psychology textbook would each require all your attention for that single activity. Some people, especially children, have trouble selecting a single source to attend to. See Box 5–2 for a discussion of a disorder of selective attention.

Automaticity

Unpredictable sources tend to capture our attention, while highly predictable ones do not require it. Sometimes very predictable stimuli are not really noticed until they stop; for example, a whirring heater or air-conditioner or a continuing conversation goes unnoticed until it stops, at which time everyone's attention immediately is drawn to it. In this case the cessation of the stimulus is the unpredictable and, thus, attention-capturing

BOX 5–2 *ATTENTION DEFICIT DISORDER*

According to the American Psychiatric Association (1980), about three percent of preadolescent children in the United States, about 90 percent of them boys, suffer from Attention Deficit Disorder, a condition that makes selective attention very difficult because the child is unable to "turn-off " the irrelevant messages. The condition may or may not occur with associated hyperactivity. Although it is not correlated with intelligence, the children often perform poorly in school, because they are easily distracted and do not listen well, due to their inability to focus their attention on one activity to the exclusion of others. Sometimes children may lose major symptoms of this disorder as they grow older, though sometimes they persist. Drug therapy using Ritalin has been shown to help many children, probably by stimulating part of the brain involved in controlling attention; in addition, behavior modification, sometimes in combination with drug therapy, is sometimes useful (Gittelman-Klein, Klein, Abikoff, Katz, Gloisten, & Kates, 1976).

event. Gradual habituation occurs to continual, highly predictable stimuli; that is, we gradually allocate less and less attention to it until we may not even be consciously aware of its presence.

Perhaps the most important variable in determining the allocation of attention is the degree of **automaticity.** Shiffrin and Schneider (1977) and others have made the distinction between automatic and controlled (or deliberate) processes. *Automatic* processes do not require much allocation of attention and can be executed in parallel with other cognitive processes or activities. For example, we can often drive and carry on a conversation simultaneously because little if any attention must be allocated to the motor activity. If, however, unusually demanding conditions arise while driving, we may have to cease the conversation to devote full attention to the driving activity, which now becomes a *controlled,* no longer automatic, process. Controlled processes must generally be executed serially because they require so much attention, while automatic processes may be executed in parallel.

As a controlled task becomes habitual, it becomes greatly overlearned and eventually may become automatic. Amateur or professional musicians may recall the first thrill of realizing that their hands moved to the right piano keys or guitar frets without conscious attention to the finger movement. Another good illustration of automatic versus deliberate processes comes in the area of sports. A skilled basketball player is not consciously worrying about placement of the feet at most times, whereas a beginner might be very preoccupied with such considerations and not able to devote much attention to larger considerations such as overall game strategy. Much of the process of learning skills like sports or musical performance may be seen as increasing the automaticity of more and more of the specific motor and cognitive skills involved. Box 5–3 further explores the information processing involved in skill learning.

Apparently the limits of what tasks can become automatic are less than we might think. For example, Spelke, Hirst, and Neisser (1976) trained subjects for several weeks in the formidable job of taking dictation and reading an unrelated story aloud simultaneously. While these are both tasks that normally are highly controlled, with several weeks of intensive practice the subjects acquired a high enough degree of automaticity to carry them out simultaneously with little apparent interference. This suggests that attentional limits in the area of automaticity may be due more to limited practice than any inherent cognitive limits on such processing. Our minds may be capable of a lot more than we suspect, given sufficient practice of the right kind.

Models of Attention

The earliest contemporary psychological model of attention was Broadbent's (1958) filter model. This proposed that there are different information "channels" coming through our senses into our information-processing system. The "filter" selects one of these channels for further processing and tunes the other out. The basis for this selection was thought to be perceptual, often based on gross physical characteristics, such as over-

BOX 5–3　*DECLARATIVE VERSUS PROCEDURAL KNOWLEDGE*

A useful distinction may be made between declarative and procedural knowledge (Anderson, 1976, 1980). Declarative knowledge ("knowing that") consists of information, which typically can be communicated verbally. Most studies of memory and cognition over the years have been studying declarative knowledge. On the other hand, procedural knowledge ("knowing how") is a skill. It is often, though not necessarily, motor in character: typing, riding a bicycle, driving a car, dribbling a basketball, or playing a piano. Procedural knowledge, especially that which is involved in motor skills, is not readily expressible verbally. If you don't find yourself convinced of this, try to write a description of how to ride a bicycle.

Procedural knowledge may be entirely internal, such as our knowledge of how to apply linguistic rules in speaking or our knowledge of how to use certain strategies in decision making or problem solving. Such knowledge is often applied implicitly without our being able to verbalize the rule we are using. For example, the four-year-old child, if not the adult, may be unaware consciously of the set of linguistic rules that tell whether to add /d/, /t/, or /əd/ sound to form a past tense in English. Try for yourself to verbalize the rule that tells when to add each of the three sounds. Even if you cannot articulate the rule, you can probably apply it correctly; for example, to make past-tense forms of the nonsense verbs *gurge, gurch,* and *gurt.*

Anderson (1980) distinguished three stages of skill learning. While these are probably not clearly serial and separable in all cases, the taxonomy is useful in understanding the general process better. First is the *cognitive* stage, which involves an internal, probably declarative, representation of what the learner must do. For instance, when you memorize the steps in starting a car, shooting a basketball, or conjugating a verb, you are forming a mental representation of this appropriate procedural knowledge, even though the knowledge at that point may be declarative, in that you are learning specific information.

The second stage is the *associative* stage, where the declarative knowledge is translated into procedural knowledge. Errors made in learning in the cognitive stage are detected and eliminated, and connections among the elements required for successful performance are strengthened.

Finally, the *autonomous* stage occurs, in gradual evolution from the associative stage. Here the procedure becomes faster and more automatic. The less attention that must be allocated to the task, the more automatic it becomes.

all voice quality or loudness. While this model has much intuitive appeal (we speak of "tuning someone out"), there are numerous anecdotal and experimental counter-examples, showing that we do in fact perceive some, though usually very limited, information from the unattended channels. A simple example would be when we suddenly "perk up our ears" and start attending to another conversation at a party when we hear our name or some other very salient stimulus spoken. This suggests that we must be monitoring the unattended source at some level rather than totally filtering it out. To account for such cases, Anne Treisman (1964) modified Broadbent's filter model. Instead of a filter, she proposed an attenuator that "turns down" the unattended channels, somewhat as we would turn down a television set to the point that we would perceive something especially interesting but otherwise would not attend to it. This still leaves unexplained what determines when something is important enough to be perceived from an unattended channel.

Later models have been proposed (Shiffrin & Schneider, 1977; Schneider & Shiffrin, 1977) though none has been demonstrated to be completely adequate. Generally, our attentional capacity is very limited, but there is also ample evidence that we can "monitor" other sources at some level while not allocating much attention, or even conscious awareness, to it. Just how we do this and how much is processed by such monitoring is not yet well understood.

PATTERN RECOGNITION

Besides attending to a stimulus, we must start to analyze and identify it in order to begin processing it in short-term memory. Pattern recognition is a basic problem in perception and human information processing. It concerns the question of how we recognize environmental stimuli as exemplars of concepts we already have in our memory. This is part of the more general set of processes of attaching meaning to information that we process.

Pattern recognition is a very general phenomenon, cutting across all sensory modalities, including everything from how we recognize a certain letter we read as a *T* or understand someone's speech as containing the sound /p/ to how we recognize Rover as a dog or recognize a certain social interchange as one of that class of events of "getting dumped" in a dating relationship.

There are three general classes of models of pattern recognition: template matching, prototypes, and feature analysis. Which class of models one chooses carries implications both for processes used in the pattern-recognition process and for the form of the representation of information in long-term memory.

Template Matching

In many ways the **template-matching** model is the most straightforward and intuitively appealing of the three classes of models. This approach says that we store mental copies of environmental stimuli in our memory, and that pattern recognition proceeds by matching up the external stimuli with these stored mental copies. This model postulates something like police fingerprint files, where a suspect's fingerprints are checked with a computer file of other prints until a match is recognized. Another example of a template-matching system is a bank's method of identifying and matching checks by matching the characters printed in the corner of the check with those stored in its memory. In both cases the stored template is an exact match with the stimulus.

In spite of the practicality of such a system for fingerprints and check processing, template matching fails as a model of human pattern recognition. For one reason, we would have to have an enormously large number of templates to match up with every possible stimulus, including all the possible variations on a basic theme.

Figure 5–2 shows several possible variations of even a trivially simple stimulus like the letter *X*. An *X* that was slightly larger, smaller, tilted, elongated, flattened, or stylized would not match one's stored template of an *X*. Even modifying the theory to include some preprocessing operations to reduce, enlarge, or rotate the retinal image before comparing it to the stored template cannot adequately deal with the variety of stimuli that are still recognized as members of the same class. For example, how do we recognize as members of the class "dog" such breeds as German shepherds, chihuahuas, fox terriers, collies, and any other number of canines, while at the same time recognizing that physically similar wolves, coyotes, and cats belong to other categories?

Frequently it is very small features that distinguish the different categories, while much grosser physical differences occur across members of the same category. For example, a tiny mark differentiates and *O* from a *Q*, while a cursive *Q* (*2*), though also a *Q*, looks much less like a *Q* than a *O* does.

Moreover, sometimes we recognize an instance of a category even when we have never seen that particular stimulus before; for example, a mongrel is still recognized as a dog even if we've never seen that particular type of dog before. Clearly, some more abstract type of model than template matching is required to account for pattern recognition.

Prototypes

The **prototype** model of pattern recognition says that what is stored is not an exact copy of each stimulus, but rather an abstracted general instance. This prototype represents no particular object in that class, but con-

FIGURE 5–2　Examples of Stimuli Recognized as "X"

tains key features present in all or most instances. The pattern-recognition process recognizes a match if enough of the properties of the stimulus match the properties of the prototype. Memory about particular instances of subclasses may be stored as the prototype plus information about variations and special features; this would be a much more parsimonious and economical system than storing separate templates for each example.

A prototype theory has intuitive appeal and support in that we often seem to have truly general ideas about what a dog, a criminal, or a party is like, without necessarily storing information about any particular instance. Still, defining exactly what is contained and is not contained in the prototype is difficult and far from obvious. Recent work in schema theory (see Chapter 8) is a promising approach to describing prototypes.

Feature Analysis

The third class of theories of pattern recognition is **feature analysis.** With this type of theory, the input is analyzed into specific perceptual attributes called *features.* After such analysis, the resultant list of features is examined for a possible match to the concept identified by that particular list of features.

Such a model has both intuitive and experimental support. Many concepts and classes of stimuli are defined, at least in part, by distinctive features. For example, a break in a certain place in the circle distinguishes a *C* from an *O*, resonance in the throat differentiates an /s/ from a /z/sound, and such features as warm-bloodedness and the presence of feathers distinguish birds from reptiles. Because features may be combined in so many possible ways, feature-analysis models get around the problem of the template-matching model having to store such a large number of templates. Although feature-analysis models are sometimes criticized for not clearly specifying how all those features are organized and structured, there are obviously many possibilities for combination. Further, features have the advantage of greater specificity than prototypes.

There is also evidence supporting feature analysis from physiological studies, going back to the pioneering studies of Hubel and Wiesel (1962, 1968) of single-cell recording of neurons in the eye and visual cortex of cats and monkeys. There are cells at various places in the visual pathways and in several layers of the visual cortex in the occipital lobe of the brain that fire in response to very specific types of stimuli that are well characterized by features. For example, one cell might fire in response to a vertical line, another only to a moving vertical line, and another to a moving small, dark, round object. It would appear that certain combinations of features are the triggering stimulus for certain neurons to fire. The brain's analysis of the firing patterns of all these neurons then recognizes the object.

Gestalt Principles of Organization

Besides the identification of features and the use of prototypes, there are also a number of more holistic principles that operate in pattern recognition and perception more generally. These are often called **Gestalt prin-**

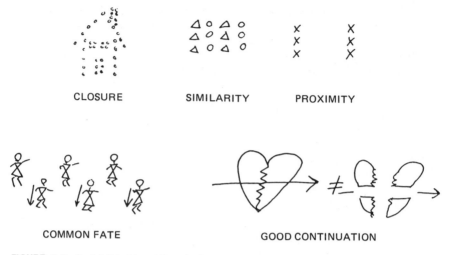

FIGURE 5–3   Gestalt Principles of Organization

ciples, from the untranslatable German word meaning something like "configuration" or "whole." These principles include *closure, similarity, proximity, good continuation,* and *common fate,* and they are illustrated in Figure 5–3. Closure involves a mental "filling in the blanks" to complete some sort of unit. Looking at a follow-the-dots picture and seeing the figure illustrates this principle. Our minds tend to impose organization and interpretation on all incoming input; this is one way of doing so.

The principles of similarity and proximity involve perceiving elements that are similar in character or close together in space or time as belonging to a unit. For example, what do you see between the following parentheses? (XXXOOO) If you said something like "three X's and three O's" you were probably grouping the three similar elements in proximity with one another into a unit.

Good continuation involves the perception of a line or other element as continuing through an intersecting line; see Figure 5–3. The straight line is perceived as continuing across the curved lines rather than as turning the corner and becoming the curved line, though both interpretations are equally consistent with the retinal image.

These principles applied to movement occur in the principle of common fate, where elements that move in similar patterns are perceived as a unit. This is a very important principle in choreography, employed in dance or marching bands. If every other person in a line of marchers or dancers steps forward at the same time, they are perceived as one group, while those who stay behind are perceived as a separate group.

Whatever emerges as an eventual definitive model of pattern recognition must somehow incorporate such holistic principles, as well as very fine-tuned analytical processes like feature analysis.

Speech Perception

Now that we have examined the basic problem of pattern recognition and looked at the major theoretical explanations, let's examine in detail one of the most important but also most complex problems in pattern recognition—how we understand speech. Before beginning, we must first have a little background knowledge of the nature of speech sounds. Then we will examine how these sounds are perceived. Finally, we will examine the rules specifying how phonemes are to be combined and the role of suprasegmental cues like intonation and stress in the speech-perception process.

On an intuitive level any word or sentence may be analyzed into a chain of discrete sounds called *phonemes,* the smallest acoustic units of language that can make a meaningful psychological difference in that language. For example, the word *bit* is made up of three phonemes. By substituting the first phoneme /p/ for /b/, the meaning of the resulting sequence of three phonemes is changed; *pit* instead of *bit.* (Note: letters between slashes represent the phonemes, not the written letters.) Incidentally there is not always exactly one phoneme in the pronunciation for each letter in the spelling. For example, *date* only has three phonemes, and the sounds spelled *th* or *sh* in English typically are in fact only one phoneme. Since writing is a representational system imposed on speech, it is the phonemes, not the letters, that we must consider in examining speech perception.

Perception of phonemes   Although with a little practice you may be able to sit down and identify the sequence of phonemes in any sample of coherent speech, there is, perhaps surprisingly, no machine that can do this nearly as well as people. This is because the same phoneme is not always perceived for a particular sequence of acoustic sounds. For example, the physical sound is not identical every time the phoneme /b/ is understood. If such were the case, it would be a relatively simple matter for the brain to perceive the sound and record the information, which it would then immediately identify as a particular phoneme /b/, perhaps using a template-matching theory discussed earlier. A sequence of sounds like this could thus be identified and eventually be put together into words.

There are several reasons why speech perception cannot possibly occur in this way, however. One reason is that the acoustic speech stimulus changes depending on the pitch, intensity, and voice quality of the speaker. A four-year-old girl, a gruff old man, and an operatic soprano are not emitting the same physical stimulus for the sound that anyone hearing any of them interprets as the phoneme /m/. Similarly, we can usually understand different dialects of English quite readily even though the actual sequence of phonemes may be quite different. For example, in standard American English the word *water* is pronounced [WAH-der], whereas in standard British English it is more like [WAU-tuh]. Even with three out of the four phonemes altered, these sounds are still clearly identifiable by most people on either side of the Atlantic as the word *water*, especially if it occurs in an appropriate meaningful context.

Although computer scientists have so far been unable to program a machine to analyze and interpret reliably a wide range of phonemes from real speech, human listeners can do so quickly and easily. Spoken speech can be followed as fast as 400 words per minute, about 30 phonemes per second. This is quicker than the fastest rate that we can pick out individual sounds in any other sequence of sounds; thirty separate sounds per second of most anything else except natural language is perceived only as "white noise," that is, like static on the radio.

Other evidence also indicates that the sequence of phonemes heard in a word or syllable is not a succession of physically separate sounds. Single phonemes can be spliced from spoken speech by cutting a tape where the boundaries between the phonemes appear to be. Such detached "phonemes" are only identified about 80 percent as accurately as the same phonemes in either normal spoken language or in a group of phonemes that are pronounceable but do not make an identifiable word (*bup, jiz*). This suggests that part of how we identify the phoneme /p/ comes not only from the part of sound clearly identified as the phoneme /p/, but also from the surrounding vowels and the transitions between phonemes.

Another series of speech-splicing experiments have produced even more surprising and compelling evidence. Take the syllable /pee/ and splice it to separate the part of the tape containing the /p/ and that containing the /ee/. If the /p/ part of the tape is then spliced to a recording of the vowel /oo/, the resulting string is understood as /poo/. So far, so good. However, if the same cutting /p/ from /pee/ is spliced to /ah/, the resulting syllable is consistently heard as /kah/ (Schatz, 1954). Even more surprising are results indicating that nothing may be perceived as something! For example, the word *slit* was recorded and then 75 milliseconds of time, less than a tenth of a second, spliced in between the /s/ and the /l/ phoneme. The resulting word perceived was *split*, that is, the pause was heard as /p/ (Liberman, Harris, Eimas, Lisker, & Bastian, 1961)! Similarly, a 75-millisecond pause inserted after the /s/ in *sore* caused the word to be heard as *store* (Bastian, Eimas, & Liberman, 1961). Typically, taking recorded speech and cutting it into pieces and splicing the phonemes back together in a different but meaningful order does not produce intelligible speech, but only gibberish or, at best, misperceived phonemes such as the *split*-for-*slit* example above.

How then do we explain how we understand speech at all, given that phonemes are perceived as other phonemes, pauses are perceived as phonemes, and so on? The fact is there is no generally accepted theory of speech perception that produces the "right answer" to this question, and scientists from several disciplines are busily working on this very difficult question. However, we can identify certain kinds of acoustic cues that are definitely involved in understanding language.

One type of physical cue is the particular sound that always occurs in a sequence of sounds heard as a given phoneme. Although this type of cue is the exception and not the rule, there are nevertheless some such invariant cues, especially for certain consonants called *fricatives* (/s/, /z/, /f/, and /v/), which always have some kind of rush of air out of the mouth, slightly different for each consonant, but always the same for that particular consonant.

A more typically but far more complex type of cue occurs in the transition from consonant to vowel, precisely the type of information that is obliterated by cutting a tape of *pah* into /*p*/ and /*a*/. On an electronic recording of the frequencies and intensities of your speech (speech spectrogram), it is impossible to identify definitively a point where a consonant ends and the following vowel begins. One critical variable in determining what consonant is heard is called *voice onset time,* the amount of time between the stopping of the flow of air from the lungs in a consonant such as /*p*/ or /*b*/ and the resonance of the air in the mouth which is heard as the succeeding vowel. For example, much of the acoustic difference between /*b*/ and /*p*/ is that the voice onset time is only 0.001 second following /*b*/, but is 0.058 seconds following /*p*/. This difference in time causes one sequence of sounds to be heard as containing a /*b*/ and the other a /*p*/.

In normal speech the difference in voice onset time may be even less, but there we have contextual cues to help identify the words. Although the research is controversial and difficult to interpret, there is even some evidence that newborns may be able to discriminate between the sounds /*b*/and /*p*/, suggesting that infants can identify the differences in voice onset time (Eimas, Siqueland, Jusczyk, & Vigorito, 1971). The ability to hear such a subtle discrimination may be a part of the innate perceptual system for language processing present in all of us.

One often overlooked way that spoken language is more complex than written language is that there are no clear physical boundaries among words or phrases comparable to the spaces between words or sentences in writing. Although there are sometimes clear pauses between phonemes, such pauses do not necessarily occur at word boundaries more often than at other places in normal rapid speech. If this is not convincing, consider yourself listening to someone speaking a foreign language you do not understand. Can you pick out the word boundaries? In comprehension, there are segmentation ambiguities that occur precisely because such acoustic cues of spacing are absent; these ambiguities may be bases for humor. Consider the symbol below.

This is a *round tuit,* which you give to someone who always says they'll do such-and-such "as soon as I get a round tuit!" Similarly, there is the case of the little girl who named her cross-eyed teddy bear "Gladly." When questioned by her parents about this unusual name, she replied that she named it after the animal they sang about in church: "Gladly, the cross-eyed bear."

Finally, as a young child, the author (RJH) once felt left out of the Pledge of Allegiance to the American flag, because his sister, whose nickname was Widget (for reasons long since obscure) was mentioned in it ("...and to the republic for Widget stands...").

Every language uses a different subset of all the possible phonemes available. While there is surely a high degree of overlap, an examination of any two languages will show that each contains certain sounds that do not occur in the other and thus are especially difficult for speakers of the other language to learn. People have been aware of such differences since ancient times and have even used them to their own advantages. For example, *Judges* 12:5–6 in the Old Testament relates the following story:

> And when any of the fugitives of Ephraim said, "Let me go over," the men of Gilead said to him, "Are you an Ephraimite?" When he said, "No," they said to him, "Then say *shibboleth*, and he said *sibboleth*, for he could not pronounce it right [because the /sh/ phoneme did not exist in the Ephraimite language]; then they seized him and slew him at the fords of the Jordan.

Sometimes whole sets of sounds may be present in one language but absent in another. For example, French, Polish, and Portuguese have nasal vowels that do not occur in English, German, Spanish, or Italian. German, Dutch, Welsh, Polish, and some Scottish dialects of English have one or more fricative consonants spoken far back in the throat (for example, the last phoneme of *loch* or *Bach*). Some languages, including Arabic, cockney English, and many American Indian languages, contain consonants that involve stopping or constricting the air stream very far back in the throat. American English does in fact contain a related sound, the phoneme spelled by *t* in words like *carton* and *mountain*. This is not a /t/ or /d/ in most American dialects, though in British English it is pronounced /t/.

Phonological rules   Besides the knowledge of phonemes themselves, we also have knowledge of the phonological rules of our language; these are the implicit directions that tell how to combine these phonemes into possible words in that language. Such knowledge is very important in speech perception. Sometimes certain phonemes are permitted, but only in certain places and under certain conditions. For example, the final consonant in *sing* (which is not /n/ or /g/ or a combination of them) is very common in English at the end of a syllable, but never occurs at the beginning of one; in fact, it is very difficult for an English-speaker to pronounce in such a position, though some languages allow it; for example, *Ngo* and *Nguyen* are common names in Vietnamese. Similarly, the sound spelled by *s* in *measure* and *ge* in *rouge* cannot begin a word in English, except possibly for loan words from other languages, though it very commonly begins French words. Moreover, English contains a constraint that the schwa /ə/ sound, the vowel spelled by *e* in *women*, *ai* in *curtain*, *o* in *lemon*, and so forth, may occur only in unstressed syllables. Some languages—Arabic or French—allow it in stressed syllables, and the resulting sequence, even if it contains only phonemes that occur in English, sounds very unlike English, simply because of the stressed schwa vowel. Still another example involves consonant blends. English allows only certain consonants to follow /s/. Thus /st/, /sk/, and /sp/ are allowed but not /sd/, /sg/ or /sb/, although the latter three are pronounceable and occur frequently in Italian.

Suprasegmentals Besides phonemes and phonological rules for combining them, there is a whole class of additional and very important sound cues in language, the **suprasegmental** (prosodic) factors such as *stress, pitch, pause,* and *intonation.* The most important suprasegmental in English is *stress,* which often can make the meaningful difference between two words. For example, IN-sult and PER-mit are nouns, while in-SULT and per-MIT are verbs; the phonemes are the same in both cases, but each member of the pair stresses a different syllable. Differential stress in a sentence can also distinguish between an adjective-noun combination and a proper name. Consider the spoken sentence RON LIVES IN THE WHITE HOUSE. If *house* is stressed it may be the place next door, while if *white* is stressed it is most likely 1600 Pennsylvania Avenue, and Ron is President Ronald Reagan.

Compared to many languages, English has a high degree of differential stress, with clear primary and secondary stress on syllables in all words of two or more syllables. Where these stresses occur is determined by some fairly regular, though highly complex, rules. This is a very difficult aspect of English for speakers of languages such as French or Japanese, where differential stress is much less marked. Similarly, it is a reason that makes song lyrics, which depend heavily on differential stress, difficult to translate from a heavily stressed language to a lightly stressed one, or vice versa. It also is one reason that an otherwise fluent speaker of a second language may appear to have "an accent" if, for example, a Parisian speaks English with the comparatively even stress of French. For a more detailed discussion of different "rhythms" of different languages, see Box 5–4.

Another suprasegmental cue is *pitch,* or *tone.* While in English and most other modern European languages it makes no difference within a given syllable what pitch is used, in many so-called tonal languages such as Chinese, Vietnamese, and many American Indian Languages, pitch can distinguish one word from another! For example, in the northern dialect of Vietnamese, there are six distinct tones, that is, six different pitch patterns with which a given syllable may be spoken. For example, the word *ba* may mean "three," "to hug," "grandmother," "bane," "dregs," or "haphazardly," depending on the pitch with which it is spoken. It is small wonder that such languages pose difficulties for the English speaker to learn!

Pitch is important in English, however, insofar as it combines with stress to produce characteristic *intonation* patterns, which are used to indicate the speech act (statement, question, exclamation) of an utterance. For example, statements in English typically have an intonation pattern of the highest pitch toward the end of the sentence, but then falling at the very end. On the other hand, yes-no questions end with a rising intonation, with the highest pitch near the end. Intonation patterns carry such strong information that even a declarative sentence becomes a question if spoken with a rising intonation: *This is a good job?*

BOX 5–4   *STRESS-TIMED VERSUS SYLLABLE-TIMED LANGUAGES*

You may have noticed that different languages appear to have characteristic overall rhythms. English, for example, is a *stress-timed* language, whereby the time between two heavily stressed syllables is about the same, regardless of how many unstressed syllables intervene. For example, in the sentences below, all would typically be spoken with heavy stress on *John's* and the first syllable of *banker,* with the same amount of time in between in all four cases:

> *John's a banker.*
> *John's not a banker.*
> *John's not a rich banker.*
> *John's not a very rich banker.*

In English, unstressed syllables tend to be reduced to schwa /ə/, but only if they are unstressed. In the sentence *Sue went to the store,* the vowel in the preposition *to* is normally pronounced /ə/, even though we would say the vowel in the word *to* spoken alone as /o͞o/. Speakers of languages that do not use schwa, such as Spanish or Portuguese, often mispronounce English by speaking "too precisely," that is, not reducing the unstressed vowels to schwa. This is one factor that makes them appear to have a "foreign accent."

In constrast to stress-timed languages such as English or Portuguese are the *syllable-timed* languages like Spanish, French, or Turkish. In these there are an approximately constant number of syllables per unit of time, regardless of the stress. Such languages often have relatively less differential stress than do the stress-timed languages—though differential stress does still exist—and more precise pronunciation of every sound. To speakers of languages like English, a syllable-timed language often sounds very regular, staccato, and mechanical. Speaking Spanish with a stress-timed rhythm and reducing lighly stressed vowels to schwa is a giveaway of an American accent.

In addition, stress is important in that any word receiving particularly heavy stress is interpreted as being emphasized in some way, which can radically alter the meaning of the sentence. Stressing different words implies different sorts of contrasts, as in the following example.

a   Drive to the *park* (not downtown).
b   *Drive* to the park (don't walk).

Another suprasegmental cue is *pause.* Although we have already discussed the voice onset time difference between phonemes, pause may also be important between syllables. For example, depending on whether the long pause comes before or after the /t/, a particular sequence of sounds may be heard as *night rate* or *nitrate.*

To fully appreciate the contributions of suprasegmental cues to the understanding of language, consider an example of how an appropriate intonation pattern can suggest meaning even when the phonemes are in-

BOX 5–5   *CUR HAZE SEEM USE SICK*

"Omen Do Wrench"

Oak if my you womb
Were dew buff hello roman
Do tyranny ankle hope lay,
Wears hell dumb absurd
Add as courage inward
Andrew's geyser knock loud do walled hay.

"Gin Goo Belts"

Gin goo belts, gin goo belts
Gin goo wall dew weigh
Owe it phone add his two rye
Donna won norse soapings lay.

The fact that these chains of unrelated words can sound like meaningful song lyrics, even when the phonemes are not quite "correct," suggests the powerful contribution of suprasegmental cues, specifically intonation, in speech perception.

---

correct. If Box 5–5 is read as what it appears to be, i.e., a list of unrelated words, it will in no way make sense. However, if read, or better, *sung,* with a certain intonation pattern, it is recognized as two familiar songs.

Any adequate theory of comprehension will have to include how we perceive phonemes and suprasegmental cues in speech. The pattern recognition process involves the recognition of sounds, but much more than that. Speech perception remains one of the most complicated puzzles facing psychologists.

Now that we have completed our look at attention and pattern recognition, those processes that occur to select information in sensory memory for further processing, let's look at short-term memory, where some further processing occurs.

SHORT-TERM MEMORY

After some material has been selected for further processing, it comes to the memory store that is variously called *short-term memory, short-term store, working memory, immediate memory, active memory,* or *primary memory.* Each of these labels highlights a different aspect of this limited-capacity memory store. It contains all the information that we are thinking about and "working on" right now; hence the term *working memory.* In this sense it is our current consciousness, where information is held just enough for a decision to be made on further processing, especially encoding for long-term memory storage. All the information that we are thinking about right now includes both information activated from long-term memory and new stimulus information entering through perceptual senses and sensory memory; hence the term *active memory*.

Material in short-term memory does not stay in this state of activation very long unless it is continually being used in some way; hence the term *short-term memory* (or *store*), which emphasizes this transient character. Of course, if material is actively attended to, rehearsed, or otherwise thought about, it can remain in short-term memory indefinitely. For example, if you look up a number in the phone book and hold it in your working memory by repeating it to yourself while you walk across the room to dial the phone, that will hold the numbers there. Presumably you could rehearse the number for hours on end and thus keep it in short-term memory all that time, though why you would want to do that is unclear.

Limited Capacity and Rapid Decay

One of the most important aspects of short-term memroy is its **limited capacity**. There is only so much that we can think about at one time. Measuring exactly what this amount is is more difficult than you might expect, however. As we have already seen, there are clearly attentional limits on what we can process. George Miller (1956) showed many years ago that the so-called memory span was about 7 ± 2 numbers in a digit-span task; that is, you hear a list of numbers read and immediately afterward must repeat them. It is probably no coincidence that local phone numbers are exactly seven digits long; anything more would be much more difficult to remember for a few seconds without encoding.

The metaphor is often used of a series of slots (called the *rehearsal buffer*) in short-term memory. As new material is processed and/or old material retrieved from long-term memory, these slots are filled one-by-one until there is no remaining space in the rehearsal buffer. Once this happens, in order for new material to be added to short-term memory, something currently there must be "bumped," either through forgetting or encoding and transfer to long-term memory, out of immediate consciousness. This metaphor reflects the intuitive feeling we often have that our mind is so full that there is no room for even one more piece of information without something already there being pushed out.

If information is not attended to or processed in some way, it decays from short-term memory in 15 to 30 seconds, a phenomenon first demonstrated by Brown (1958) and Peterson and Peterson (1959), in milestone short-term memory studies. Subjects were presented with a consonant trigram (for example, NKX), followed by a retention interval of 3 to 18 seconds, after which they were to recall the letters. While this task is trivially easy if one is allowed to rehearse during this interval, the experimenters tried to prevent this from occurring by having the subjects spend the retention interval counting backwards by threes from a given three-digit number. This task was intended to keep them from rehearsing the letters, thus measuring the curve of "pure decay" in short-term memory. They found that, while recall was about 80 percent correct at a three-second interval, it had dropped to between 10 percent and 15 percent by 18 seconds. They concluded from this that the decay function of material in short-term memory falls very sharply. Although it might at first sound unfortunate, this rapid-decay property is actually very adaptive; it keeps our mind from becoming cluttered with unnecessary information we have already finished thinking about.

While Miller's so-called "magical number" of 7±2 "bits" of information has generally been demonstrated as the memory span for a wide variety of materials, there is a tremendous amount of variation of what can be put into each of those seven bits. For example, we can hold seven numbers in our short-term memory, but also seven words, seven pictures, or sometimes even seven sentences. In fact, the bits may be made considerably larger through the processes of *chunking,* by which we combine pieces of information together to allow them to take up less space in working memory. For example, you might chunk the words *rabbit, hat,* and *hamburger* from three bits into one by encoding them as one coherent image of a rabbit wearing a baseball cap and chomping on a Big Mac. Similarly, you might chunk the 16 letters TWAFDRAIDSERASOB into the five units TWA, FDR, AIDS, ERA, and SOB. The issue of chunking is discussed further in the discussion of mnemonics in Chapter 6.

Rehearsal

Another important process that occurs in short-term memory is **rehearsal,** the temporary activation or recycling of information through memory. Rehearsal may be of two sorts, either *maintenance* or *elaborative* rehearsal. Maintenance rehearsal merely holds information in short-term memory long enough for it to be acted upon in some way. For instance, when you look up a phone number, it may serve your needs adequately to repeat it over to yourself while you dial the phone; you make no effort to encode it into long-term memory. Often in such cases a brief maintenance in short-term memory is all that is required by the situation, since you do not anticipate needing to recall the information at a later time.

In fact, it is very difficult to prevent people from rehearsing or to accurately assess rehearsal efforts. The Brown-Peterson task of having people count backward by threes has been frequently used in short-term memory studies. While this is fairly effective in diverting attention and effort to the counting rather than the rehearsal, there is still some evidence that people often may manage to slip in a few rehearsals during the counting task. Although other tasks have been developed that may be somewhat more effective at preventing rehearsal, for example, auditory signal detection (Reitman, 1971, 1974; Shiffrin, 1973), it is very difficult, if not impossible, to be absolutely sure that someone is not rehearsing.

Rehearsal has been used to explain the primacy effect of the so-called *serial position curve* (Figure 5–4), that is, relatively good memory for the first few items in a list of things to remember. Early items in the list have received more rehearsal, both because they have had more time to be prac-

FIGURE 5-4 Serial Position Curve

ticed and because when they were presented there was relatively little information competing for the limited resources available for rehearsal. The recency part of serial position curve—relatively good memory for the last few items in the list—is explained by the fact that the last items are still in short-term memory simply because they have not yet had time to decay. Very often studies examining long-term memory will have a brief interfering task immediately after presentation of the to-be-remembered material and before the response task; this exists purely to insure that none of the material will remain in short-term memory and thus that anything retained must have been encoded into long-term memory and been retrieved from there during recall.

In contrast to maintenance rehearsal, elaborative rehearsal helps transfer information to long-term memory. Rather than merely repeat the to-be-remembered information, elaborative rehearsal relates it to other concepts already in long-term memory and develops new associations among those concepts. An example would be learning the concept of *reinforcement* by relating it to concepts already learned (e.g., response, contingency, operant conditioning, punishment, behavior) and by generating examples of its application, such as animal training or child rearing. Elaborative rehearsal is very helpful in learning class material for exams. It is also helpful for your teachers, as illustrated in Box 5–6, which discusses learning the names of students in a class.

Finally, either maintenance or elaborative rehearsal often serves another function that is very useful but has not been investigated thoroughly. To describe that function, we first have to point out that a lot of rehearsal done all at once (the equivalent of cramming) improves memory for the information studied. However, studies have shown that the rate at which memory for that information deteriorates is the same as for more poorly

BOX 5–6   *LEARNING NAMES OF STUDENTS IN A CLASS*

At the beginning of every semester a teacher is faced with the task of learning the names of all the new students. Employing maintenance and elaborative rehearsal and other techniques from memory research, I (RJH) am now able to learn the names of almost all the students in my classes (up to 40 or so per class) during the first three or four class meetings. Below are some "secrets" of the trade.

1   Collect information on each student the first day (address, phone, major, year in school, interests, hometown, career goals) on index cards.
2   Rehearse names from these cards frequently, at least before and after each class, until names are learned. This ensures your familiarity with the names and starts you associating the names with the other information, which serves to elaborate the memory network around that name.
3   Call the roll the first few classes until names are learned. Go through slowly to concentrate on associating the name and the face.
4   During the first few classes, maintain good eye contact and think about making the faces familiar. Once the faces and the names are both familiar independently, associating the two is much easier.
5   Elaborate the concept of each student by associating the name or face with information collected on the card the first day or actions observed in class.
    a   Notice the place where the student generally sits in the room.
    b   Notice the general physical appearance, especially very salient physical characteristics or those that strongly remind you of someone else you know.
    c   Take note of unusual names or cases where a student uses a middle name or nickname. Such information can serve to distinguish that student from others.
    d   Remember comments made in class, especially insofar as they relate to information given on the card the first day; for example, mentioning a two-year-old child in class discussion and writing "learning how to toilet train a child" as an interest on the card.
    e   Remember behavior in class, as it might be reflected in information on the card. For example, Fred might mention "girls" as an interest and Cheryl might mention "Fred." Two people in the class might not be able to keep their eyes off each other the first day; thus, you have learned who Fred and Cheryl are.
    f   Look for similarities of the students to people you know; try to remember possible prior contacts with the student. ("I remember seeing her in the animal lab last semester.")
    g   Use mnemonic techniques to associate the face with the name or other information, for example, "Cutie Katie Keeney," "Save a seat for David Sweet" (because he's always late), "Lefty Hefty" for a left-handed fellow named John Hefty. If you've already associated together all the information about the student, all it takes is linking one piece of that information to the physical appearance.
    h   Once the rich network of information about the student is learned, in addition to having observed him or her a couple of class periods,

> it is fairly easy to make some connection between these visual and informational domains.
>
> 6 Use every possible opportunity to connect these two knowledge domains.
>
>   a Call the roll as long as necessary and concentrate on the face while rehearsing the name.
>
>   b Take advantage of individual contacts (students talking to you individually after class) and watch the names as students hand in papers.

learned information. The poorly-learned material is forgotten sooner (because it starts out as a weaker memory), but the rate of forgetting is the same as for the better-learned material "crammed" in a very short amount of time.

By contrast, consider rehearsal of an event in our lives. Whenever we think about something that has happened to us, we are rehearsing that event. If the event was interesting, the rehearsal will be frequent and spread over time. Each time we rehearse the event, we refresh, or reinstate, the memory for that event. Because the rehearsal is spread over time, that rehearsal should slow the rate of forgetting for that event. Such slowing of forgetting through frequent rehearsal has been demonstrated in studies of memory for naturally occurring events (Thompson, 1982).

Encoding

Although material in short-term memory has not been as extensively processed as has most encoded material in long-term memory, it has been partially analyzed and interpreted with a variety of encoding involved. Acoustic or phonetic encoding is very common in short-term memory, and for a long time psychologists thought that was the only (or at least the predominant) method of encoding. While we now know this is not completely true, acoustic encoding is still a very important form of memory representation in short-term memory. Evidence of its importance is documented by studies that show, for example, the letters *C* and *T* are more likely to be confused in short-term memory than *C* and *O*, even when they are presented visually. Such results suggest that subjects are recoding the visual symbols to acoustic representations, thus explaining why the similar-sounding *C* and *T* are more easily confused than the different-sounding (though visually similar) *C* and *O*.

In spite of the great importance of acoustic encoding, there is ample evidence of visual and especially semantic encoding in short-term memory as well. For example, the Stroop color-word task requires one to name the color ink in which names of colors are written (for instance, the word GREEN written in blue ink). When you try to name the colors, the meanings of the words interfere, because it is hard not to semantically encode information in short-term memory, even when we consciously try to ignore such information as totally irrelevant to the task at hand. Another example of semantic encoding in short term memory is shown in the way we semantically cluster words in a free-recall task; for example, remembering all the animal words together, the clothing words together, and the food words together, when animal, clothing, and food words had been all mixed together in the acquisition list.

Box 5–7 presents an extended application of short-term memory encoding to musical performance.

BOX 5–7   *SHORT-TERM MEMORY AND MUSICAL SIGHT-READING*

An interesting application of information-processing research to musical performance was made by Thomas Wolf (1976), who is both a cognitive psychologist and a professional flutist. He particularly examined the skill of sight-reading, the act of reading music and immediately performing it. Like oral reading, this skill makes heavy use of short-term memory, since the notes of music must be held in short-term memory for a few seconds before they are played on the piano (or on the flute, or sung, or whatever). This is a very different use of memory from that of the musician who memorizes the whole piece and performs from rote memory. In his study of professional pianists, Wolf found that most of them were either excellent sight readers or excellent memorizers, but seldom highly skilled at both. Either technique could lead to excellent performance, but for entirely different reasons: Either the short-term or long-term memory store (but not both) was highly developed.

Wolf identified several factors involved in sight-reading ability. During sight-reading the information on the written music is chunked into units in short-term memory. The skilled musician can draw on his or her knowledge of music theory as well as all of one's performance experience to chunk those visual stimuli into larger and more useful units; for example, coding all the notes in both clefs for a whole measure as one chunk, whereas the less accomplished musician might have to code every note, every key signature, and every tempo indicator as a separate chunk.

This offers a scientific argument for the importance of studying music theory, at least for its usefulness in sight-reading. Wolf's subjects reported that there were vast differences in difficulty of sight-reading different types of music, with the most predictable genres of music being the easiest and the least predictable the most difficult. For example, baroque chamber music is quite easy, because there is so much similarity in the different parts of a given piece and the constraints on composition at the time were so great that the predictability is much greater than, say, atonal twentieth-century music, which follows many fewer "rules." Thus, the latter is far more difficult to sight-read because the chunks of information in short-term memory must be much smaller. There is also a lot less redundancy involved in the modern music.

Wolf illustrates this point with a highly compelling anecdote about the discovery of a misprinted note in a Brahms capriccio (opus 76, no. 2). One of Wolf's pianist subjects reported that a student of his, upon arriving at a certain *C#* major chord, played a *G* instead of the *G#* that would normally occur in a *C#* major triad. When her startled teacher stopped her, the student replied that that was what was written on the page, which was true. In later checking other editions of the piece, it was found that they all had the same "misprint," assuming Brahms must have really meant a *G#* rather than a *G* in that *C#* major chord. Apparently few, if indeed anyone, had ever caught his error before, since everyone had apparently been playing the chord with the predictable *G#* instead of the written *G*-natural. This suggests that in sight-reading, we don't really read everything, but rather read some of the input and construct the rest drawing on knowledge from long-term memory, perhaps in the forms of schemata (see Chapter 8).

Forgetting

The explanations offered for forgetting from short-term memory generally cluster around two general phenomena. On the one hand, forgetting is said to occur due to the decay of the memory trace over time. This type of explanation uses the notion of the strength of a memory trace. In this view, a strong memory trace is more likely to be retrieved than a weak memory trace. Thus, forgetting results from the weakening of a memory trace over time. This type of explanation would be very appealing if we were to find that the underlying physiological correlate of short-term memory is some sort of transient change whereby a neuron or set of neurons is temporarily altered in some way and then takes some time to restore to its initial state. Up to now, however, there is no evidence for any such physiological process occurring.

The other class of explanations uses the concept of interference. Material is forgotten because other material that is similar is some way interferes by replacing or distorting it. Interference may be *retroactive*, which means it occurs after the original learning. For example, if you are meeting people at a party and first are introduced to Marilyn Smith and soon after Marylou Schmidt, you may call Marilyn "Marylou" because of retroactive interference. If you did the reverse, that is, called Marylou "Marilyn," that would be *proactive* interference, because the interfering material came first and hindered the learning of something else later. There is much experimental evidence that both types of interference occur.

As frequently is the case in psychology, there is probably some truth to both the decay and interference explanations. While interference can be demonstrated fairly easily, it is difficult in principle to design an experiment to once and for all definitively test the two predictions. This is because any test of decay involves allowing time for the decay to occur. However, it is difficult to be sure that no interfering activity is occurring during that time. No matter what you ask the subject to think about, there is no assurance that whatever is going through his or her mind is not in some way interfering with the material to be tested.

CONCLUSION

We have now completed our examination of the perceptual and short-term memory aspects of information processing. In the next chapter we shall turn to long-term memory, and the encoding and retrieval processes involved with it.

Even though long-term memory is probably the sort of memory that you primarily think of when someone talks about remembering, it is not the only important component of information processing. All of the prior steps we have discussed in this chapter must occur before material is ever encoded in long-term memory, much less retrieved from there. Material must be attended to and patterns recognized and it must be passed onto short-term memory for initial processing. If it "survives" all these hurdles, it may pass on to more permanent memory.

Conceptualizing short-term memory and long-term memory as qualitatively separate memory stores, as represented in Figure 5–1 and Atkinson and Shiffrin (1968), is not the only possible framework for conceptualizing memory, however. After we have examined long-term memory in the next chapter, we shall return to the examination of some alternative theoretical frameworks.

SUGGESTED READINGS

For the student interested in the conceptual foundations of cognitive science, we recommend the following. Begin with Jerry Fodor, "The Mind-Body Problem" (*Scientific American,* January 1981, *244*(1), 114–123). Then move on to D. R. Hofstadter and D. C. Dennett (Eds.), *The Mind's Eye* (New York: Basic Books, 1981). While Hofstadter and Dennett are supporters of cognitive science, they reprint one of the major critiques of the information-processing view, including John Searle's "Minds, Brains, and Programs" (originally in *Behavioral and Brain Sciences,* 1981, *3*). Fodor also discusses shortcomings of the new view.

For additional information on perceptual and short-term memory processes, see Lindsay and Norman's *Human Information Processing* (1977), a highly readable and comprehensive text, although it is regrettably highly biased toward the authors' own research and theorizing. Some excellent textbooks in cognitive psychology include Anderson (1980), Howard (1983), Moates and Schumacher (1980), Matlin (1983), and Reynolds and Flagg (1983). All include chapters on these topics. For a more rigorous treatment in the context of a Kuhnian paradigm analysis, see Lachman, Lachman, and Butterfield (1979).

Speech perception is frequently given cursory treatment in these texts, which tend to concentrate more on visual pattern recognition. In fact, it is quite difficult to find a readable introduction to speech perception. This is one reason that this chapter has developed this topic fairly extensively.

CHAPTER SIX

MEMORY AND INFORMATION PROCESSING II: LONG-TERM MEMORY

In discussing short-term memory, we have already begun to consider aspects of long-term memory, especially in processes of encoding material for storage in long-term memory. In this chapter we will continue to examine this more permanent store of memory. In doing so, there are many facets to consider: encoding and retrieval processes relating long- to short-term memory, the structure of information in long-term memory, and processes for searching through that information structure. Such issues will be examined here. Not only is it difficult to consider long-term memory totally apart from short-term, but it is also difficult to consider it in isolation from other issues and problems in language and cognition. Thus, we will continue to mention attention, pattern recognition, and short-term memory. Toward the end of the chapter we will look at alternative conceptualizations of the whole memory system and a detailed application of memory principles to the problem of eyewitness identification.

EPISODIC AND SEMANTIC MEMORY

Endel Tulving (1972) first made a useful distinction of **episodic** versus **semantic memory** in long-term storage. While semantic memory is all the general information that we have ("stored knowledge" is another term often used) in our long-term memories, episodic memory is information about particular personal memories associated with the time and place that we learned that information. For example, remembering that you had a fried egg and toast for breakfast this morning while you crammed for your Abnormal Psychology exam is episodic memory; remembering that people frequently have eggs for breakfast and that eggs come from chickens is semantic memory. Remembering that Bismarck is the capital of North Dakota is semantic memory; remembering that you first learned this on a cold, snowy December day when your fifth-grade teacher made you stay after school and write "Bismarck is the capital of North Dakota" 50 times is episodic memory. Your "autobiographical memory" of particular experiences that have happened to you is episodic memory; your storehouse of general information ("mental encyclopedia") is semantic memory.

Episodic and semantic memories may be related. For example, one result of traveling can be to accumulate episodic memories to relate to previously learned semantic memories. For example, before the author (RJH) ever visited Brazil, I knew that Rio de Janeiro was a large coastal city in a beautiful setting where rugged mountains meet the Atlantic Ocean and Guanabara Bay. I also knew that popular tourist spots there included Copacabana Beach, the cable car ride up Mt. Sugarloaf, and the Christ statue on Mt. Corcovado. Now, however, my semantic memory of that information is supplemented by episodic information of the wave that knocked me in the surf at Copacabana, the lunch I had with my friends at the halfway stop on Sugarloaf, and the cold wind blowing at the top of Corcovado as we savored the magnificent view of Rio on that early spring afternoon.

Tulving argued that most memory research up to 1972 tested episodic memory, specific information learned at a particular time, that is, in a memory experiment (such as, "Was this word on the list or wasn't it?"). Also important, Tulving said, was semantic memory, all the knowledge that we have and can retrieve at will, even though we don't remember exactly when and where we learned it. In the years since Tulving drew this distinction, cognitive psychologists have increasingly turned to studying semantic memory, though episodic memory is still widely researched as well.

One of the major aims of the research in semantic memory since Tulving's landmark paper has been the attempt to discover the structure of the knowledge in semantic memory. In exactly what form is that information stored? How is it organized? How do we search through it when we try to retrieve information from long-term memory? It probably will not surprise you to learn that a definitive answer to these questions has not emerged, though we have learned quite a bit. It is helpful to look briefly at some types of structures that have been posited for semantic memory and some of their implications.

Networks Models of Semantic Memory

One general class of models is the network models (see Anderson, 1976; Collins & Loftus, 1975; Collins & Quillian, 1969; Anderson & Bower, 1973). These models posit the existence of concept-like "nodes," which are connected to each other in various ways, depending on the particular model. Probably the best-known, though now quite obsolete, model is the earliest one (Collins & Quillian, 1969). They posited a branching network of subordinate and superordinate nodes (concepts) hierarchically arranged. Information about the various nodes is stored as attributes at each node. Each attribute applies to that node but also to all those nodes below it in the hierarchy. For example, such information as "has feathers" and "is two-legged" is stored at the node "bird" and thus does not need to be stored at each of the many specific bird nodes subordinate to "bird."

More recent network models have focused on specifying the character of the relationships between the various nodes and have also explored different types of organization other than hierarchical. Most of these recent models take the structure of language (to be covered in Chapter 7) more seriously. Thus, we will defer further discussion until later.

One advantage of network models, or indeed of most models of semantic memory, is that they allow for individual differences. Each person's hierarchy of information may be slightly different, or perhaps substantially so. For example, the typical urban American, especially from the East or West Coast, may divide the superordinate class "farm animals" into subordinate classes like horses, cows, pigs, sheep, and chickens, with no further differentiation within each subordinate class.

On the other hand, the farmer or rancher would require further subdivisions; a class "livestock" could be divided into dairy and beef cattle, beef cattle could be divided into Angus, Herefords, Charolais, and Simmentals, subclasses that would have little meaning or use to the New York apartment dweller. See Box 6–1 for a further example.

The failure to subcategorize concepts within one's semantic memory can have some important social and political consequences when certain types of semantic memory organizations are characteristic of whole cul-

BOX 6–1 *ESKIMO WORDS FOR SNOW*

One Eskimo dialect (Knauth, 1972) has at least five words for snow:

> *qali*—snow on trees
> *api*—snow on the ground
> *pukak*—bottom layer of api; home for many animals in winter
> *siquotaoq*—crusty snow whose top layer has thawed and refrozen; dangerous for animals
> *upsik*—hard-packed, wind-driven snow of open spaces such as lakes

While most non-skier Americans probably never thought deeply about the conceptual differences among these different kinds of snow, they would naturally be important for the Eskimo, for whom, for example, the dangerous *siqotoaq* may threaten the Eskimo's animals in a way that *api* or *upsik* would not.

tures. For example, North Americans' failure to distinguish subordinate classes of Moslems (Sunni and Shi'ite) makes it difficult for them to fully understand the dynamics behind certain Middle Eastern conflicts, such as the Iran-Iraq war of the early 1980s and neighboring countries' diverse reactions to the Iranian Revolution of 1979 and its aftermath.

Latin Americans consistently resent the North American's failure to develop subordinate categories of "Latin America" to recognize the tremendous social, cultural, and political differences that exist there (Brazil is a Portuguese-speaking, industrialized, multiethnic society; Peru and Bolivia are largely Indian and rural; Argentina prides itself on being the most European country in America, with the possible exception of Canada). Though both countries are in Central America, Costa Rica is an ethnically Spanish, highly literate, and stable democratic society, while nearby Guatemala is largely Indian, poor, and feudal, having seldom ever known democracy.

Feature Comparison Model of Semantic Memory

An alternative conception of the structure of semantic memory was proposed by Smith, Shoben, and Rips (1974; see also Smith, 1978). Instead of claiming that concepts were stored in hierarchies of networks, Smith et al. (1974) proposed that each concept contains lists of features, corresponding to its common attributes (for example, a bird has feathers, can fly, has two legs, is warm-blooded). These features are of two types: **defining** and **characteristic**. *Defining* features are those that absolutely must be present for the example to be a member of that concept. For example, a bird *must* have feathers; otherwise it isn't a bird. *Characteristic* features, on the other hand, are attributes that are typically, but not necessarily, present. For instance, birds typically can fly, but there are exceptions (penguins and ostriches can not). In fact, characteristic features are much more numerous than defining features when considering real-world concepts. (See the discussion of fuzzy sets in Chapter 7.)

Smith et al. (1974) proposed different sorts of processes in verifying the truth of a sentence. Specifically, they proposed a two-stage process. Look at the following example:

(1)   A canary is a bird.
(2)   A chicken is a bird.
(3)   A bat is a bird.
(4)   A table is a bird.

If a subject sees (1), for example, he or she retrieves the concepts "canary" and "bird" and begins comparing both the defining and characteristic features to determine if there is a sufficient match to respond "true." In this case subjects would quickly find such a match and could immediately reply "true." Similarly, for (4), there is such a clear mismatch between "table" and "bird" that the subject can quickly respond "false."

The other two cases are more complex, however. With either (2) or (3) the subject will probably find an intermediate degree of matching on defining and characteristic features. In such cases, that is, when the match is intermediate, a second stage of processing must be initiated, namely, a comparison on the basis of the defining features only. Thus, one would compare only on the attributes that a bird *must have,* not those it usually has but may not. After this second stage of comparison, (2) could be answered "true" and (3) could be answered "false."

Even though "bat" and "bird" share many characteristic features (can fly, are small), when compared on defining features only, the match is poor. The model proposed by Smith et al. (1974) nicely explains the so-called "typicality" effect, where it takes longer to verify the truth of category membership of less typical instances ("goose" as opposed to "robin"). This is a robust and consistent finding that had always posed problems for the simple network model of Collins and Quillian.

Feature-comparison also has its drawbacks, however, most notably the criticism that it does not deal seriously enough with the question of the organization of all the features. Positing collections of features all through semantic memory could be very uneconomical if they are not organized in some way. See Smith (1978) for a review of semantic memory models.

The theory-building and methodology involved in studying semantic memory offer excellent object lessons on the use of reaction-time methodology to infer unobservable structures and processes. By observing that it takes longer to respond to sentence (2) than sentence (1) in our example, we can infer what kind of a memory structure is likely being traversed during those times. One must always be cautious, naturally, in concluding that one's theory is the only possible explanation consistent with the observed reaction times. Let us turn now to some dependent measures for studying memory, namely, ways we can measure it.

WAYS OF MEASURING MEMORY

How do we measure memory? What kinds of dependent variables can be used to make inferences about structure and process in long-term memory?

When we test someone's memory, there are a great variety of measures that we may use. Many of them fall into two general categories: **recall** and **recognition**. Though both have been developed and widely used in studying episodic memory, they have some applications to semantic memory as well. Both recall and recognition have several variations, but the overall distinction has proven a useful one. The basic difference is that in recall, one must both generate the response *and* recognize that it is correct, while in recognition memory the response is already generated and all we are asked to do is judge whether or not it is the correct response.

Recall

Recall may either be **free recall** or some form of **cued recall**. In total free recall we are given no cues or hints to help us remember the desired information. An extreme form of this might be a history test question that asks: "Tell all that you know about World War II." Perhaps more realistically, an attorney might ask a witness, "Tell me what you remember about the night of the murder." Because there are no potentially biasing cues present, recalled information is less subject to distortion than more structured memory tasks. Unfortunately, there is a tradeoff, in that there is also less total accurate information remembered. Thus, quality is high but quantity is low (Lipton, 1977).

In contrast, cued recall is generally easier, since there is some sort of cue present to aid retrieval, but the cue may bias the reconstruction of the response. Any kind of memory situation where someone gives us a "hint" is a cued-recall task. Cued recall has been studied extensively in the psychological literature using paired-associate learning tasks and various forms of completion tasks. In "real life," an actor learning lines for a play is practicing a form of cued recall task, where each preceding line (and perhaps movement, sound effects, etc., associated with it) acts as the cue for the next line.

Recognition

In contrast to recall measures, **recognition memory** presents some pregenerated stimulus for the person to judge whether or not it is accurate. Like recall, there are two general kinds of recognition. The first kind, often called *yes-no* or *old-new recognition,* presents some item and asks you to indicate, "Yes, I remember that" or "No, I don't remember it." There are two important factors involved in this type of recognition memory. Most obviously, there is the *strength* parameter, that is, how strong the memory ("trace") of the information is. Generally, a strong memory is going to be recognized more accurately than a weaker memory.

However, strength is not the only relevant dimension in such a situation. There is also a *criterion,* that is, how sure you have to be in order to say, "Yes, that's it." Upon examining a recognition-memory item and your own memory trace of that information, a decision must be made. If there is a strong and obvious match or mismatch, the decision is easy, but how about the middle ground? For example, if you are looking at a suspect and asked to indicate whether he was the man who mugged you or not, how sure do you have to be before you say "yes," given that your fragmentary memories at least somewhat match the characteristics of the suspect in front of you?

If a "yes" decision meant sending a suspect to life in prison, you might set a more stringent criterion than you would in a more trivial situation with a memory of equivalent strength and match to the recognition-memory item.

Besides yes-no recognition, we also have *forced-choice recognition* memory, perhaps best exemplified by the multiple-choice test, where you must choose one answer from among several but where one, and only one, is correct. The difficulty of forced-choice recognition memory may be greatly altered depending on the nature of the distractors, the wrong answers in which the correct item is embedded. Consider the relative difficulty of the two multiple-choice test items below:

(5)   The capital of Upper Volta is
  a.   Los Angeles, b. Mexico City, c. Tokyo, d. Ouagadougou
  e.   All of the above.
(6)   The capital of Mali is
  a.   Timbuktu, b. Bamako, c. Niamey, d. Abidjan, e. Conakry.

One could easily answer (5) correctly with no knowledge whatsoever of Upper Volta, while (6) could be difficult even for someone quite knowledgeable about West Africa. (Incidentally, the answers to (5) and (6) are *d*. and *b*., respectively.)

Reaction Time

A very different, and currently popular, dependent measure in memory and cognition experiments is **reaction time** (RT). This measure has the advantage of being a concrete and quantitative measure of very covert and unobservable cognitive *processes* of thought. This is in contrast to recall or recognition, which measures only the remembered *products* of thought processes. The general logic of RT, going back to Donders (1868), is that a longer time reflects either more complex processes or a greater number of processes than a shorter time reflects. To understand further how RT is used, an example will be discussed in detail, with emphasis on the logic behind this measure.

Consider a situation like those discussed previously (1 through 4), where the subjects are asked to verify a sentence as being true or false and their time to do so is measured. Usually such sentences are very simple, and the reaction times themselves short, often measured in milliseconds. Suppose we find, for example, that it takes significantly longer to answer true to (2) than to (1), and significantly longer to answer false to (3) than to (4). Researchers studying semantic memory concluded that the relatively longer times to verify (2) and (3) were obtained because those statements were more difficult than (1) and (4), requiring a more extensive search of features stored in semantic memory about the two concepts in each statement. This can be a window to view the otherwise unobservable cognitive processes of searching one's knowledge structure in memory. It can be used as a way of inferring what the structure of one's memory is like. Such logic was employed extensively in the research used to support and build the network models of semantic memory discussed earlier in the chapter.

ENCODING AND RETRIEVAL

Although we have mentioned encoding quite a bit so far, we have not discussed much how **encoding and retrieval** are so intimately related, especially insofar as the way the methods of encoding can affect the ease of retrieval. The next section will examine encoding, specifically from the perspective of its implications for retrieval. The first part will deal with encoding strategies called *mnemonics*; next we will look at one type of encoding (imagery) in detail; finally, we will examine contextual variables in encoding and retrieval.

Mnemonics

As mentioned earlier, probably the most promising way to work on improving your memory is by improving your encoding strategies. One, though by no means the only, way to do this is to use **mnemonics,** strategies for more efficient encoding. Mnemonics are the products of conscious decisions to organize and chunk information into larger and more meaningful units for the purpose of remembering it better. For a long time in psychology (the S-R era, specifically) mnemonics occupied a much maligned position of being considered somewhat devious and underhanded "tricks" for remembering, if one had to stoop to using less-than-pure methods of learning. Happily, mnemonics are now recognized as frequently useful and eminently respectable strategies.

Let us examine some types of mnemonics to better understand what they do and how they work. Sometimes they may add an additional memory code to the original code, allowing two, instead of one, avenues of retrieval. For example, if you make up a little song to help you remember something, this gives you two possible ways to retrieve that information later—either remember the words, or remember the tune and use that to retrieve or reconstruct the words. This is why advertising jingles ("You deserve a break today . . .") are so durable in memory.

Mnemonics are perhaps at their most useful when they impose meaning on a rote series of items that otherwise would have little or no meaning. For instance it may seem arbitrary whether to set the clocks ahead or behind in the spring and fall, but if you remember that maxim "spring ahead and fall behind," the direction seems less capricious because it has been linked meaningfully (through the use of the second meanings of *spring* and *fall*) to the season to which it belongs.

To take another similar example, suppose you want to remember the words spelled with "ei" that are exceptions to the "I before E except after C" rule of English spelling. You could memorize a list of words, or you could make a meaningful sentence out of them, thus chunking them all together in one (more or less) coherent semantic unit (for example, "*Either* the *weird sheik* will *inveigle* his *weighty neighbor* on the *heights* or *neither* of them will *feign seizures* in *their leisure* time"). Mnemonics may also be used to remember spelling of those few troublesome words that continually elude us ("The Double-C Double-M Motel gives good accommodations" to remind us that "accommodation" has two *C*'s, two *M*'s, and an *O* after the *M*'s). Try to make the mnemonic as meaningful as possible and as closely related as possible to all aspects of the to-be-remembered information.

Series of numbers may also be learned using mnemonics (remember 539–4079 because the *5* people born in 19*39* were *40* years old in 19*79*. A long sequence of numbers can be memorized by creating a sentence where each successive word has the exact number of letters as the next number in the sequence (for instance, remembering that the value of *e*, the base of the natural logarithms, equals 2.718281828 with the sentence, "It enables a dumbbell to memorize a quantity of numerals"). To recall the value of *e*, simply retrieve the sentence and count the number of letters in each successive word. It is, of course, recommended that you construct mnemonic sentences with words that you know how to spell!

There are more elaborate mnemonic systems. The *method of loci* has been around since ancient times, reported in Cicero's *De Oratore* to have been used by the Greek poet Simonides (Yates, 1966). This involves learning a list of items by associating them in sequence with different positions in some very familiar spatial network. For example, you might remember a shopping list by associating milk with your front door (a milk carton hanging on the doorknob); eggs with the sidewalk (eggs rolling up the walk toward your house); coffee with the street corner (coffee flowing into the sewer at the intersection), and so on. To retrieve the information, simply retrace your familiar route and "pick up" the images left there earlier.

The *pegword system* involves learning a system of associations in advance and then using these to "peg" items to be learned on. One popular system involves the associations 1 = bun, 2 = shoe, 3 = tree, 4 = door, 5 = hive, 6 = sticks, 7 = heaven, 8 = gate, 9 = line, 10 = hen. Notice that these are made easier to learn initially because of the auxiliary code of rhyme. To use the pegword system, associate the first item to be learned with a bun, the second with a shoe, and so on. To retrieve, simply count through the numbers and retrieve the associated images. The same pegword associations, once learned, may be reused any number of times.

A highly developed use of mnemonics can have valuable practical benefits and is not limited to people with exceptional ability. A Boulder, Colorado, waiter and college student, John Conrad, developed his own mnemonic system for remembering customers' dinner orders, associating the entree with the person's face and afterward associating the side dishes and salads they had ordered (Singular, 1982). He perfected this system up to the point where he could take orders from a party of 19 without writing anything down and without making any errors. His extraordinary skill captured the attention of his customers and helped him win lucrative tips. His co-workers were so impressed that they asked him to teach them his system, as did University of Colorado psychologists interested in studying memory. These studies revealed Conrad to be highly organized and systematic; intellectually, he was probably only average. Some even more extraordinary memory feats are discussed in Box 6–2.

Why do mnemonics work?   On the surface, mnemonics might appear to make learning more difficult, since usually some additional information must be learned beyond what one is trying to master (the pegword associations, the sentence chunking, the *ei*-words). However, if done well, learning this extra information can actually make learning the target information easier, because it increases the meaningfulness of the information. The more meaning something has for you, the easier it is to remember it.

Mnemonics are not very helpful in learning material that is already meaningful, but they are quite useful in learning arbitrary, verbatim infor-

BOX 6–2   *AMAZING FEATS OF MEMORY*

While most psychological research on memory has been done on "normal" people, usually college students, there are occasional reports of outstanding memory feats by other individuals. Neisser (1982) excerpts and comments on several of these reports. While it is often difficult to draw general conclusions from such anecdotal evidence, the tantalizing fact remains that these astounding memory feats are possible, at least in some people in some circumstances. At the very least they provide important counter-examples that any theory of memory cannot totally ignore.

While many professional musicians have exceptional memories, astounding even among these was Arturo Toscanini (Marek, 1975). Maestro Toscanini apparently had rote-memorized every note of every instrumental part for around 250 symphonic works and about 100 operas. He could apply this knowledge in a most impressive fashion. One anecdote reports a bassoonist discovering just before a performance that the lowest note on his instrument was broken. Upon hearing this, Toscanini thought for a moment and replied that there was no problem, since that note did not occur anywhere in the repertoire of that evening's concert! He could also, at will, sit down and correctly write from memory any instrumental part from a huge collection of works.

Some preliterate societies have oral traditions that often place a high value on an extensive memory for past history of the community or the nation. This can be seen, for example, in the *griots*, the oral historians of the West African forest societies (D'Azevedo, 1962; Haley, 1976), such as that discovered by American writer Alex Haley searching in the early 1970s for his roots in Africa. With our easy access to reading and recorded written history, it is hard to imagine the high value placed on such oral memory; thus, the memory feats of these oral historians seem entirely amazing. With the motivation and circumstances of their situation, however, such feats may have been within the reach of many.

One of the most astounding memory feats was Stratton's (1917) reporting of the Jews called "Shass Pollaks," who memorized all of the thousands of pages of the Babylonian Talmud. They not only could recite each page from memory but could also tell exactly what word was in any given position on any given page.

mation where elements are not particularly associated with other elements or where a specific and arbitrary order must be learned.

Mnemonics take advantage of our natural information-processing tendency to impose structure and organization on material that we process. It is natural, not exceptional, to try to make meaningful something that does not have much meaning. The more links we can establish between the material we are trying to learn and information already in our long-term memory, the more potential avenues we have to retrieve the information when we need it. This same principle applies to your studies, in that it is easier to learn and remember information if you have made connections of that information with knowledge already in your memory. If you find it difficult to make such connections, it will probably be difficult to remember that information.

Many, though by no means all, mnemonics make use of visual imagery in one way or another. This draws on our naturally large capacity for picture memory. Visual images tend to be among the easiest units of information to remember. They also have the advantage of allowing us to combine elements within an image. For example, the logo for a product to use on basement walls to seal out water once used a seal (animal) splashing in water under the label "water seal." This combines one aspect of the function of the product (water) with its specific function (sealing) plus an additional meaning (the animal seal) of the same sound. Such information-processing principles are known and used by advertisers. See Alesandrini (1983) for a complete discussion of the use of imagery in advertising strategy. Box 6–3 develops an application of imagery mnemonics to second-language vocabulary learning.

The next section of the chapter examines imagery in more depth. Imagery is a commonly used type of memory code and is also of considerable theoretical importance in cognitive psychology.

Imagery

Analogue and analytic representations   The form of the information stored in long-term memory may be either **analogue** or **analytic** (abstract) representations. An analogue representation physically resembles what it represents in some important way. Such similarities may be very thorough and detailed or contain only one or two superficial similarities. One clear example of an analogue representation is a map, which physically resem-

---

BOX 6–3   *APPLICATION OF MNEMONICS TO SECOND-LANGUAGE LEARNING*

Atkinson (1975; Atkinson & Raugh, 1975) has developed a key-word method for second-language vocabulary learning, frequently a process of tedious rote memory for language students. The idea in the key word method is to provide a key word relating the pronunciation of a word with its English translation. An image is then constructed using the key word and the English equivalent of the to-be-learned word. For example, to learn the Spanish word "pato" (duck), one might use the key word "pot" and image a duck with a pot on its head. Thus, one could remember "pato" by thinking of a duck, remembering the image, retrieving "pot" from the image, and associating "pot" with "pato." An experimental group using this method was shown to be superior to a control group in a vocabulary test six weeks after learning. In fact, it was so successful that it was implemented in Russian classes at Stanford University. Computers are programmed to present the word, its translation, and the key word. The student then forms his or her own image.

bles the territory it represents in the comparable locations of places, while remaining very different in other ways, such as size, color, and amount of detail.

Other examples of analogue representations include physical models, graphs, drawings, and thermometers. Such representations may have partially analytic characteristics, as when a map shows rainfall amounts or population densities in terms of different colors to represent different quantities. Assignment of these colors to different rainfall amounts is largely arbitrary and bears little physical resemblance to those amounts of rainfall.

In contrast to analogue representations are *analytic* representations, which are totally abstract and arbitrary, with the representation bearing no physical resemblance to its referent at all. Probably the most complex and pervasive analytic representational system is language, which is entirely analytic, with the possible exception of onomatopoeic words like "meow" and "ding dong." A dog has no more relation to the word "dog," "chien," "perro," "cachorro," or "Hund" than to "truck" or "idea." Other examples of analytic codes include mathematics, formal logic, musical notation, computer languages, and propositions (to be discussed in Chapter 7).

Language will be discussed in more detail in the next chapter and will not be further considered here. Rather, let us now turn to examining one of the most important types of analogue mental representations, namely imagery.

What is imagery?   Imagery has been discussed by philosophers for centuries and was a major area of inquiry among the nineteenth-century German introspectionists (see Chapter 1), the earliest experimental psychologists. However, because of its mentalistic character, imagery fell out of favor during the behaviorist era and was only "rediscovered" in the 1960s. It has been a very active area of research ever since, with some major theoretical papers on the subject appearing each year, along with dozens of reports of empirical studies (see Block, 1981; Kieras, 1978; Shepard, 1978, for reviews).

Although imagery is most often discussed in terms of *visual* examples, it is not exclusively a visual phenomenon. Imagery, in fact, occurs in all the sense modalities. *Auditory* imagery is clearly illustrated by one's mental response to the request "think of the sound a cow makes" or "think of the first few notes of Beethoven's *Fifth Symphony*." *Olfactory* imagery occurs when we image the smell of a Thanksgiving turkey cooking in the oven; this may be followed by *taste* imagery imagining how it would subsequently taste. When we imagine how velvet would feel on the skin or imagine the touch of another person in an anticipated sexual encounter, we use *tactile* imagery. *Kinesthetic* imagery is even involved in some forms of relaxation training, where people are taught to put their bodies in a relaxed state and become sensitive to (among other cues) kinesthetic feedback from muscles that may be tense or relaxed (for example, "Imagine how your lungs feel as you breathe all the tension from your stomach to your lungs and then exhale it from your body"). It can even be used in psychotherapy (see Box 6–4).

BOX 6–4   *MENTAL IMAGERY AS A ROUTE TO SELF-FORGIVENESS*

"Imagine yourself sitting in a balcony of a theatre. You are watching a play unfold down on the stage. The characters consist of yourself as a child and your family. The plot focuses on some incident where you became angry and were punished for this behavior. Watch what the parents did, how you as a child reacted, and how your siblings responded. Watch the play through to its natural conclusion."

"Next, imagine that child (yourself) alone on the stage after the performance is over. The child feels bad after the incident in the drama. Imagine yourself now, as an adult going up to that child and showing love, acceptance, and forgiveness. Show this in whatever way you feel more appropriate and comfortable; continue to imagine this act occurring." (adapted from J. Sward, personal communication.)

The preceding guided imagery exercise was used to help an adult client come to terms with childhood memories and self-criticism.

Imagery is often discussed in terms of the metaphor "pictures in the head." Such a metaphor is useful in certain ways but may be misleading in others, even within the visual modality. Imagery, unlike pictures, is very dynamic and constructive with a high degree of plasticity. We can image moving objects, changing events, and things and situations we have never actually seen or experienced. The mental imagery of our minds has a richer store of special effects than directors Steven Spielberg or George Lucas will ever create in their motion pictures.

In a very general sense, imagery is a major reason that we can remember the past and anticipate the future. Some sort of imagery code is almost certainly at the base of the earliest instances of memory in children, such as when an infant moves an arm to indicate "bye-bye" to an adult. Upon doing this act, the child's mind must contain some mental representation of an adult making such a motion to indicate that he or she was leaving.

Indeed, a child's conception of time must rely on imagery in conceptualizing the past and future, as well as imagining hypothetical present events. Perhaps the earliest concrete evidence of this is the demonstration of the attainment of object permanence by a child of ten months. If a child sees a toy covered up with a blanket and immediately removes the blanket to reach the toy, that child must have had some representation, probably an image, of that toy in mind after it had been covered. If that had not occurred, the child would have presumably stopped looking for the toy or, indeed, doing any other behavior that reflected a memory of the missing toy. This is, in fact, the way that infants six months or younger behave.

Imagery can be used in problem solving as a means of assessing and testing out possible solutions and restructurings of a problem (see Chapter 9). This occurs in ill-defined real-world problems such as trying to figure out how to rearrange the furniture in your living room to increase the available seating in a reasonable conversational pattern. It is certainly easier to rearrange the furniture through visual imagery first before doing so in reality. Similarly, it is easier to decide what meal to prepare for a dinner party if you have visually imagined the appearance of the dish, and used the senses of taste and smell to imagine those properties.

Imagery may be useful in problem solving in a variety of ways beyond such purposive imagining. Shepard (1978) reports several examples of scientific and literary discoveries made through the use of visual imagery. For example, the German chemist Kekule frequently used the visual imagery of "dancing atoms" linking together to form molecules. In one such reverie the atoms united to form a ring, which Kekule immediately recognized as the long elusive structure of benzene, a discovery that became central to all organic chemistry.

Imagery can be used to perform different types of operations. Perhaps one of the most studied of such operations is mental rotation of figures such as letters and three-dimensional block patterns studied with reaction-time methodology by Roger Shepard and his colleagues (Cooper & Shepard, 1973; Shepard & Feng, 1972; Shepard & Metzler, 1971). For example, in one study subjects saw a picture of some sort of three-dimensional block pattern and were asked to judge if one pattern was a rotation of the first pattern or not (Shepard & Metzler, 1971). The time it took to identify a match correctly was a linear function of the number of degrees of rotation separating the two figures. Researchers argued from this result that subjects were mentally rotating the first figure until they produced a match with the second figure.

Imagery is quite frequently used as a means of encoding information for transfer to long-term memory. Some types of information are more amenable to imagery encoding than others. University of Western Ontario psychologist Allan Paivio (1971, 1975; Begg & Paivio, 1969; Paivio & Begg, 1981) has proposed the *dual-coding* theory to account for why concrete information is typically remembered better than abstract information. For example, in a serial-learning task, subjects remember words like *chicken, piano,* or *truck* better than equally frequent but abstract words like *liberty, idea,* or *happiness.* The same effect has been demonstrated with sentences (Begg & Paivio, 1969). Paivio postulates that concrete words have a readily available imagery code that abstract words lack. Therefore abstract words must be encoded as the words themselves, or perhaps as abstract propositions. Concrete words may be encoded in these ways as well, but they also have an additional memory code available to them, namely, visual imagery. This accounts for their greater memorability. Although abstract words could conceivably be encoded by visual imagery, and no doubt are on occasion, it is a considerably less efficient code than it is for the concrete words.

Imagery often is useful in comprehension of language, especially to help conceptualize and understand something as it is being processed. One type of input where imagery may be especially important is the comprehension of metaphorical language. If you hear, for example, "The reporters torpedoed difficult questions at the President" or "Bill is an octopus on a date," part of the process of interpreting metaphors might involve the use of imagery in a creative and even surrealistic fusion of the two semantic domains of the tenor and vehicle of the metaphor. For example, one might picture, upon hearing "Bill is an octopus on a date," a man with several arms with suckers on them wrapped around a woman. For further discussion of this issue see Harris, Lahey, and Marsalek (1980) and Riechmann and Coste (1980).

Cognitive maps   One way that we all use imagery on a daily basis is in our use of **cognitive maps** (or mental maps). We have image representations of places that we are familiar with and use these to find our way around or tell someone else how to get somewhere. Like much of what we have discovered in dealing with imagery, however, these cognitive maps are not merely internalized aerial photographs of the environment remembered. In an early milestone book on cognitive maps, Lynch (1960) identified several elements of one's mental maps. *Paths* are channels along which people move (streets, walkways, railroads). *Edges* are linear elements other than paths (shores, boundaries of neighborhoods). *Districts* are areas having some common identifiable character (parks, neighborhoods). *Nodes* are important focal areas, such as junctions, path crossings, or plazas. *Landmarks* are points of reference like towers, signs, or buildings.

The general axes of orientation are important in cognitive maps. While the most common type of axis is a type of grid system (city blocks, NSEW directions, and so forth), some geographical areas, especially coastal and mountainous regions, use different axes. For example, in areas near large bodies of water, people often figure mental maps in terms of distance away from the shore. This may be especially confusing if that body of water has an unexpected orientation in that area. For instance, the normally north-south Pacific coast runs roughly east-west between Santa Barbara and Los Angeles. In mountainous areas, a perpendicular grid system is useless, because the paths are consistently curving. Someone moving from hilly Boston or Pittsburgh to the flat and perpendicular American Midwest at first has a difficult time thinking and speaking in terms like north, south, east, and west. Similarly, a Midwesterner has difficulty understanding directions like, "Follow the highway for three miles, then bear to the right and follow the road a ways down the hollow, till you get to a little past the red barn, where you veer to the left . . . ."

Another important characteristic of cognitive maps is their mobile quality; they are not purely static images. When Linde and Labov (1975) asked New Yorkers to describe the layout of their apartments, 97 percent of them gave a "tour," including the information in the form of "mobile vectors" such as, "you keep walking straight ahead, turn right at the kitchen," or "go from the bathroom into the bedroom." Very few used a static "aerial view" cognitive map.

Like most memory representations, cognitive maps include *inferred* and *constructed* information as well as information mentally reproduced. We draw on stored knowledge about what typical rooms, cities, or countrysides are like. We assume that the room has four straight walls, a ceiling, and at least one door unless we are told otherwise. This knowledge may occasionally be misleading if the environment in question is an unusual one. For example, most people would answer that Reno, Nevada, is east of Los Angeles, although in fact it is west. However, we draw on our schematic information (see Chapter 8) that Nevada is east of California. Although this is generally true, not everything in Nevada is east of everything in California.

We may acquire our initial cognitive map information from one of two sources: maps or navigation (Thorndyke & Hayes-Roth, 1982). Information acquired from maps is survey knowledge and is very similar to the map itself, including shapes, locations of objects, and easily estimated straight-line distances. In contrast, knowledge acquired from navigation, that is, actual experience traveling through that environment, is more procedural (see Box 5–3). We remember specific routes with associated landmarks, but the information is organized around the routes we travel. In many ways knowledge from navigation is probably stronger and more useful than knowledge from maps, but it is much harder to acquire.

Now that we have examined some types of long-term memory codes and some processes of encoding, let us look a bit more broadly at the *context* of encoding, which often is a major determinant of what is remembered.

Contextual Variables in Encoding and Retrieval

Memory and cognition research has frequently been curiously silent about contextual, especially social-personality, variables. However, this situation is rapidly changing; several recent books and papers have looked at encoding more broadly and even tried to integrate personality and social variables like attitude, empathy, and mood into existing theories of cognition (Bower, 1981; Hastie, 1983; Nisbett & Ross, 1980; Wyer & Carlston, 1979).

Encoding specificity   One important basic construct pointed out some years ago by Thomson and Tulving (1970) and Tulving and Thomson (1973) is **encoding specificity**. This principle says that the probability of recall at test time depends on the similarity of the context of encoding at study and the context of retrieval at test time. To illustrate this, if you hear the list of words "January, March, June, July, September, October, December, Mary, Alice, Joanne, Linda, Cathy, Ann" and are then asked for the seven girls' names, you may find it difficult to find all seven. The word "June" at study appeared in the context of months and was probably encoded that way, not as a girl's name, which was the context at retrieval. Similarly, Anderson and Ortony (1975) gave subjects the sentence: "The container held the apples" or "The container held the cola." They found that "basket" was an effective cue for the former but not for the latter, and "bottle" exactly the reverse. Unlike the "June" example, container does not have two separate meanings here, but is vague as to the type of container. Thus, the material held therein serves to encode the information about the container as more like either a basket or a bottle, and it is easier to recall in the same context.

State-dependent learning   Encoding specificity is related to the concept of *state-dependent learning*, which derives from the literature on the effects of drugs. Information learned in one state of mind (such as while intoxicated) is less accessible for retrieval while one is in other states of mind. Thus, it may be easier to recognize someone when you are drunk if you originally met that person while in a similar state of inebriation, though this does not, of course, mean that memory is enhanced by alcohol. In fact, it is depressed overall; state-dependent learning merely suggests that it may not be as far depressed when intoxicated again as during subsequent sober moments.

The same logic is invoked in forensic hypnosis, when witnesses are hypnotized and put into a mental state more similar to that which they were in when they observed the critical crime. The hope is that, in this similar state, they will remember information about the crime that had been unretrievable in mental states very different from that in which the crime occurred. Similarly, the fact that memory deteriorates under stress may be due in part to the stress-inducing environment at retrieval being very different from the relaxed conditions at encoding (Jones, 1979).

In an extension of the state-dependent learning research to personality variables, Bower (1981) has demonstrated *mood-dependent learning*. For example, happy subjects remembered words learned in another happy moment better than words learned in a sad moment, while the reverse was true for subjects in a sad mood. When recalling childhood events, people tended to remember more happy moments when they were in a happy mood and more sad ones when they were in a sad mood. In still another study, subjects read a story with a happy and a sad character. They identified more with the character that matched their own mood; the next day, when in a neutral mood, they recalled more information about that character than about the other one.

Several studies of memory have used diaries to examine the effect of the pleasantness or unpleasantness of recorded personal events on recall for those events. In those studies, no attempt was made to manipulate the subjects' mood during recall. Under those "neutral" conditions, events with high affect (that is, very pleasant or very unpleasant events) were recalled better than events with neutral affect (Thompson, 1982; Thomson, 1930). Interestingly, the effect of the pleasantness of the event is different when subjects attempt to recall the date (rather than the content) of the event. Pleasant events are dated much more accurately than unpleasant events, with neutral events in between (Thompson, 1982). Thompson speculated that we are much more likely to deliberately associate a date with a pleasant event than with an unpleasant one—and he referred to the result as "the red-letter-day effect."

Bower argued that emotions, as well as information, are coded in memory. During retrieval, one's memory network is entered at the point of the event being remembered but also at the point of emotion. Activation (discussed later in the chapter) spreads outward from both points. When the activation spreading from both points meets, it comes together to make a strongly activated memory that is then recalled. The whole area of the

BOX 6–5   *JOHN DEAN'S WATERGATE MEMORY*

In an interesting and insightful application of memory research, Neisser (1981) studied former Nixon presidential counselor John Dean's memory for Watergate conversations by comparing his courtroom testimony about these conversations with the actual transcripts of the conversations as covertly taped by President Nixon. This offered an unusual opportunity to test the accuracy of verbatim recall in a natural setting, in that there was a tape recording of the original conversation made without the subject's knowledge. Neisser found that, as laboratory studies have shown, verbatim memory was very poor. However, he also found, unlike laboratory studies, that "gist" memory was not all that good either. Neisser, however, argued that Dean's memory was in fact quite good at a still more abstract level, that he "captures the 'tenor,' though not the gist, of what went on" (Neisser, 1982, p. 150). Distortions tended to be in the direction of details and intrusions from other conversations. They also were somewhat distorted by "ego needs" of Dean himself; memory errors tended to somewhat enhance his own importance in the conversations. Nonetheless, Neisser concludes that overall Dean captured the "theme and spirit" of the Watergate conversations quite well. This abstract level of memory is a topic that has not yet been explored much in research.

role of emotions in memory is just beginning to be studied in cognitive psychology. Later findings could have important ramifications for counseling and clinical psychology, especially for the process of developing tools for helping clients to remember long-forgotten events and their associated affect. The retrieval of such memories could be very instrumental in helping someone work through personal problems. Box 6–5 discusses a case study of one person's memory for highly emotion-laden events.

FORGETTING

Through our examination of encoding and retrieval, we have implicitly considered **forgetting,** since the failure to either encode or to retrieve effectively will naturally lead to forgetting. In this section, however, we will focus more specifically on forgetting from long-term memory. There are several possible reasons why we may forget something that we had apparently learned previously.

Failure to Encode

One major reason for forgetting is that the material was never encoded properly to begin with. While we may have used the material in short-term memory, there was perhaps not enough elaborative rehearsal or active rehearsal strategies to transfer it to long-term memory. This may occur, for example, when you fail to remember information on a test because you never encoded it when studying, that is, never learned it to begin with.

Retrieval Failure

Sometimes the forgetting is due not to failure to encode but rather from failure to access the material in long-term memory. A book that is in the library but misplaced on the wrong shelf is nearly impossible to find, unless one stumbles upon it serendipitously. So it is sometimes with "lost" memories.

Issues discussed earlier in regard to encoding specificity are very important here. It is easier to retrieve information if the context at retrieval is similar to that which was present at encoding. Again we see that effective encoding is the best way to ensure effective retrieval.

The selection of an appropriate retrieval cue is critical to the retrieval process. What is an effective retrieval cue for one person might be ineffective to another person trying to retrieve the same information. For example, if you try to remember all the states of the United States and all the provinces of Canada that begin with the letter *M*, there are many possible retrieval cues you could use. If you have good visual memory and imagery ability, you might imagine a map of North America and start scanning east to west (or whatever direction) for states and provinces starting with *M*. Another retrieval cue might be to imagine combinations of letters (MA . . . ME . . . etc.), which may form official abbreviations. Still another approach would be to retrieve a previously learned alphabetical list. Other strategies include retrieving by regions (New England, Rocky Mountains, Prairie provinces). One sports-minded student even reported retrieving the names by recalling different collegiate athletic conferences! Whatever strategy one uses, failure to retrieve the eight states and one province starting with *M* would not necessarily mean that those names had not been learned, only that they could not be retrieved.

The Freudian defense mechanism of *repression* would explain retrieval failure by saying that some threatening event was unconsciously expelled from our consciousness because of its anxiety-evoking nature. We cannot access this memory because of the defensive barriers that have been erected to prevent it from becoming conscious. Therapy, especially in the psychoanalytic tradition, tries to break down the barriers to allow retrieval of the repressed memory, in order to start the healing process.

Decay and Interference

The *decay-interference* issue, discussed in the section on short-term memory in the last chapter, is also relevant to long-term memory. As with short-term memory, there is ample demonstration of forgetting due to interference (both proactive and retroactive), but it is far more difficult to demonstrate unequivocally the existence of decay. Clearly, we remember less with the passage of more time; whether this is due purely to decay, that is, the passage of time, is much less clear.

Over the last few decades the prevailing view has been that anything we have ever learned is still in our long-term memory somewhere and that forgetting occurs because of retrieval failure: We can't find the information, much like the library book that is in the library but on the wrong shelf and thus is never found.

Much of the evidence for this permanence of memory has come from case studies from the brain stimulation neurosurgery by Wilder Penfield (1969; Penfield & Roberts, 1959). Penfield reported some very dramatic case studies of neurosurgical patients who, when under local anesthesia with their brain electrically stimulated during the course of neurosurgery, reported long-forgotten memories from early childhood. In an important recent paper reexamining Penfield's findings, along with other arguments from hypnosis and psychoanalysis, Loftus and Loftus (1980) concluded that this permanence hypothesis is a severe overinterpretation of some case-study data, which may in fact have been reflecting reconstruction, based on other memories, rather than actual retrieval.

Amnesia

Perhaps the most dramatic form of forgetting occurs in **amnesia,** which usually occurs as a result of some traumatic incident. For this reason, most of the evidence concerning amnesia is in the form of medical case studies, rather than controlled experimentation, so general conclusions must be considered somewhat tentative. We don't even know yet how many different problems are subsumed under the label "amnesia."

One type of amnesia is *retrograde amnesia,* the forgetting of events immediately prior to the trauma. For example, if you are in a car accident, you may find, even after your complete recovery, that you are unable to remember anything about what happened immediately prior to the impact of the crash. Retrograde amnesia frequently occurs in response to electroconvulsive therapy and the administration of certain drugs. There is even recent evidence to suggest that it may occur, at least to a small degree, in response to mentally, as opposed to physically, shocking events, such as suddenly seeing a very gory scene in a film (Loftus & Burns, 1982). Exactly what occurs physiologically in retrograde amnesia is not entirely understood. It has frequently been suggested that the trauma temporarily jars electrical activity in the brain, thus preventing "consolidation," the physiological events underlying the psychological process of rehearsal, encoding, and transfer of information from short-term to long-term memory.

There are, however, other competing explanations for the phenomenon, such as that the trauma is an extreme form of distraction that hinders association of new information to related information already in memory, or that amnesia is due to a retrieval deficit perhaps due to an inability to utilize retrieval cues effectively.

Another type of amnesia is *anterograde amnesia,* where the person forgets events occurring after the trauma. This occurs, for example, in patients with Korsakoff's syndrome, a severe psychosis associated with chronic severe alcoholism. Such anterograde amnesia is often not total, and speculation exists that that problem may be primarily one of retrieval failure and/or a difficulty in encoding new information from short-term to long-term memory. Amnesia is a humbling reminder that, in spite of all the research and advances in the study of memory and cognition over the last 30 years, there is a tremendous amount that we don't know yet, especially in the area of understanding the physiological processes involved in memory. In a careful review of the research and theory on amnesia, Hirst (1982, p. 455) admits that "the study of amnesia is in its infancy."

ALTERNATIVE CONCEPTUALIZATIONS OF MEMORY

Now that we have examined the basic phenomena of memory, it is time to step back and take another broad look at memory. Although we have largely been assuming an Atkinson-Shiffrin type of multistore model, as described at the beginning of the last chapter (see Figure 5–1), there is considerable evidence that such a qualitative separation of short- and long-term memory may not be warranted. While no other approach has been so completely developed or widely accepted, there are other frameworks for conceptualizing memory, the best-known being the levels-of-processing approach, which we now will examine.

The Levels (Depth) Metaphor

Craik and Lockhart (1972; see also Craik & Tulving, 1975) proposed an alternative metaphor for conceptualizing memory. Instead of discrete memory stores like short-term and long-term memory, they proposed that memory involves different **levels of processing,** with trace persistence being a function of how deeply the analysis has proceeded. For example, processing speech only to the point of understanding what language the speaker is using or how loud or soft the speech is would be a very shallow level of processing, while understanding the content in great depth, including all its implications and nuances, would be a very deep level. Memory is thus viewed as the natural residues of both the transient products of sensory analyses and the much more durable traces of semantic (meaningful) processing.

Familiar memory phenomena may be reinterpreted using a levels-of-processing framework. For example, forgetting due to what might otherwise be described as a failure to transfer from short-term to long-term memory occurs because the analysis during comprehension has not proceeded to a sufficiently deep level. Rehearsal or continued attention to the material is reconceptualized as recirculation of the material, which may occur at any level by continued attention to the analysis at that particular level.

The well-documented superiority of intentional over incidental learning (we remember something better if we try to remember it than if we see it accidently for other reasons) is reinterpreted by saying that in intentional learning we have processed the material to a deeper level and it is this, rather than an intention to remember as such, that accounts for the better performance. If subjects can be induced to process material deeply, even though they are not expecting a memory test, incidental recall is much improved. This finding suggested that depth of processing, not the intention to remember, is the critical factor.

Some of the strongest evidence for a multistore approach to memory has come from the physiological domain. It is often argued that short-term-memory processes are primarily electrical, perhaps in the form of reverberating circuits of neuronal firings, while long-term memory involves structural biochemical changes. For this reason it is more permanent, while short-term memory is ephemeral. This, however, is probably an oversimplification (see Lewis, 1979; Loftus & Loftus, 1980).

As insightful as it has been, there are some criticisms of the levels-of-processing approach (Baddeley, 1978), many of them centering around the vagueness of its constructs. See Craik (1979) for a summary of this debate.

One major criticism is that there is no independent measure of depth of processing. In most studies using this framework, two tasks are chosen intuitively as differing in depth of processing. It is also sometimes defined by what is remembered better. Shallow processes are usually done faster than deeper ones, but there may be some exceptions; for example, deciding if the word "rabbit" fits the CVCCVC pattern by most definitions would be shallow processing, since it is totally nonsemantic, but it is not trivially easy. Lockhart and Craik (1978) in a sense admit this problem but defend the approach by saying that levels-of-processing was intended to be a framework, not a theory, and that it can still have heuristic (discovery) value even without the independent measure of depth. As a parallel, they argue that the concept of reinforcement has been useful in psychology, even though there is no independent measure of its effectiveness beyond its operational definition of increasing the probability of the response recurrence.

A related concern comes from the fact that, especially within semantic processing, there is no real consensus on what constitutes deep versus shallow processing. For example, people very readily draw inferences from all that they hear or read (see Chapter 8; see also Harris, 1981; Harris & Monaco, 1978). In a sense this would seem like a deep level of processing; however, to stop people from drawing such inferences requires considerable effort to invoke a metalinguistic monitor to stop such natural processes from occurring. Is such a monitor relatively deep or shallow processing? The answer is not clear. Perhaps depth of processing is not a linear dimension.

There is also evidence that under some conditions we remember information from so-called shallow processing very well, such as the way people remember certain kinds of thematically irrelevant comments verbatim, such as jokes and offhand comments in a lecture or conversation (see Keenan, MacWhinney, & Mayhew, 1977; Kintsch & Bates, 1977; MacWhinney, Keenan, & Reinke, 1982).

In spite of its definitional and precision problems, the metaphor of levels of processing continues to be very influential in offering an alternative way to think about memory from the traditional multistore model. There are, however, other possible metaphors that we can use to describe our memories.

Domains of Processing

Baddeley (1982) has suggested replacing the concept of levels of processing with the more abstract concept of **domains of processing**. A domain is a whole area of memory with extensive links and connections. Processing need not proceed linearly through the domains, nor are there necessary implications about the durability of the memory traces left from the processing. This concept is promising, as developed and applied by Baddeley (1982), but it remains to be tested further to assess its eventual usefulness to the theory of memory.

Spreading Activation

Another useful metaphor for looking at memory is the notion of **spreading activation** (Collins & Loftus, 1975). Instead of speaking of two separate memory stores, with information retrieved from long-term to short-term memory, we may say that this information is *activated* or brought into a state of activation. When we enter our memory to search for information, this activation spreads from the node of entry to related concepts stored close by. The more nodes there are in that area, the more diffuse the activation and probably the longer the time required to retrieve the information. Such activation may or may not be a conscious process. In fact, the concept of spreading activation may eventually be useful in describing other areas in psychology. For example, psychoanalysis may be viewed as an attempt to activate previously dormant concepts and relations among those concepts in the patient's mind.

The concept of activation has important implications for structural aspects of memory discussed early in the chapter. How the activation spreads through memory from the entry point will be determined in part by the structure of that particular individual's memory. Instead of positing separate short- and long-term memory stores, activation theorists often argue that what we are thinking about at the moment are the highly activated concepts, while nonactivated concepts remain in (long-term) memory until needed and activated. In a sense it reconceptualizes the old concept of consciousness as a continuum with measurable consequences.

The use of different models and metaphors to describe memory can each be helpful and lend insight in different ways, even if none of them is totally "correct." Over the years memory has been described using all sorts of metaphors; some others are discussed in Box 6–6.

To complete our discussion of long-term-memory, we turn now to a detailed examination of one practical application of many of the memory phenomena we have studied in the last two chapters—eyewitness memory.

BOX 6–6   *MEMORY METAPHORS*

The way we talk about something may actually affect the way we conceptualize it. Roediger (1980) offers a fascinating and important survey of the metaphors used to discuss memory. Like most basically abstract and unobservable concepts, memory is typically described in concrete, though metaphorical, terms. In examining these metaphors, Roediger concludes that the majority of them have been some sort of spatial metaphor, usually combined with some action of searching through this space. While the most popular and prevalent of these spatial search metaphors is probably the computer metaphor, there have been many others as well, including the wax tablet, rooms in a house, switchboard, workbench, acid bath, dictionary, push-down stack, conveyor belt, subway map, leaky bucket, and even a cow's stomach!

While the spatial-search metaphors predominate, they are not the only metaphors used to discuss memory. For example, all the network models of semantic memory use a more structural metaphor, and there are several more dynamic metaphors, such as construction, levels of processing, and signal detection.

Though metaphors are certainly often insightful, perhaps even essential, to discuss such an abstract concept as memory, it is also good to examine them critically, for they can guide our thinking into excessively rigid modes of conceptualizing. For example, Roediger warns against thinking of memory so much as spatial storage and search that we do not take seriously enough its other characteristics not included in or consistent with this particular metaphor. Craik and Lockhart's levels of processing or Collins and Loftus' spreading activation are two examples of popular alternative metaphors to spatial storage and search conceptualizations. However, each of these (and indeed any metaphor) has its dangers and limits.

EYEWITNESS MEMORY

The popular viewpoint seems to be that eyewitness testimony is nearly infallible. To say that there is an eyewitness to a crime is considered practically the equivalent of saying the whole event was recorded on videotape. Many television stations title their local news broadcasts "Eyewitness News." If they knew the psychological research on eyewitness memory, they might have had some second thoughts about that name. This section applies some of the principles of memory discussed above to the problem of eyewitness memory. While this problem was considered in psychology as far back as Hugo Münsterberg's (1908) book, *On the Witness Stand,* it has only been rediscovered in the last decade (Clifford & Lloyd-Bostock, 1983; Loftus 1979; Wells & Loftus, 1983; Yarmey, 1979).

Eyewitness identification may be considered a recognition memory problem with four possible outcomes. Someone could be guilty and be correctly recognized as guilty. Someone could be innocent and be correctly not recognized. As well as these two correct recognitions, there are two types of errors, analogous to the two types of errors in statistical inference, where one falsely rejects a true null hypothesis or fails to reject a false null hypothesis (Type I and Type II). Someone could be guilty but not be recognized; therefore, the guilty party might go free. On the other hand, the person could be innocent but falsely recognized as guilty (false alarm). Part of the philosophy of the legal system of many democratic countries is the desire to minimize the false alarm type of error, assuming that it is better to set an occasional guilty person free than to risk punishing someone who is innocent.

What Is Eyewitness Memory Like?

Many factors can affect eyewitness memory for a criminal act (Buckhout, 1974). One major factor is the delay between the crime and the identification. Frequently, an identification lineup is days, if not weeks or months, after the crime, allowing much opportunity for decay and retroactive interference to occur in memory.

Secondly, there are many situational factors that would frequently contribute to the event's not being deeply processed at the time of occurrence. For example, most crimes that are observed happen very quickly and are totally unexpected. There is little time to reorient one's attention; by the time one has done so, the criminal is often gone and the crime is over, as in a car wreck or purse snatching. In one mock assault study (Buckhout, 1974), subjects estimated that the event they had witnessed had taken 2.5 times as long as it in fact had (81 seconds versus 34 seconds). Typically, the observer has no previous knowledge of the criminal and thus can make no quick recognition or relate to other information in long-term memory. Moreover, crimes often occur in settings with poor lighting (at night, in the shadows) with a poor angle for viewing the event.

Third, several factors about the observer contribute to less-than-perfect memory for eyewitness events. Often the observer is under extreme stress, especially if one feels in any personal danger, which is often the case when witnessing a crime in progress. One's own prejudices enter in the way we process information; we are more likely to recognize an assailant as a member of another racial group than our own. Additionally, many otherwise upstanding and conscientious citizens develop some strong motivation to be heroes, to prove themselves right, to ensure that someone is convicted, or to be important. Such motivations can do strange things to one's information processing.

A number of creative and clever studies have demonstrated that eyewitness memory is frequently very poor. For example, Buckhout (1974) and his colleagues had 141 students in a class witness a staged assault on the professor; seven weeks later students looked at a lineup of six photos. Sixty percent (including the professor who was attacked) chose the wrong man!

Twenty-five percent chose one innocent bystander, who happened to have the misfortune to be sitting in the front of the class that day. This is not unlike a pretrial questioning situation where a witness may have previously seen a suspect being led in and thus be more likely to recognize the suspect later, without realizing that the previous encounter had occurred a few minutes earlier in the police station rather than last week at the scene of the crime.

One of the authors (RJH) regularly stages a mock theft in front of his introductory psychology lecture class and obtains similar results. In this case the class members choose the "thief" from a lineup about five minutes after the "perpetrator" has stolen the teacher's watch at the front of the class and had run out the door. Every semester a large proportion (30 percent to 80 percent, depending on how well the "theft" is orchestrated that semester) identify the wrong person, frequently incorrectly identifying someone wearing the same coat as the "thief." This occurs almost immediately after the crime; how much worse would the result be at a more realistic interval?

People place great faith in eyewitness testimony in spite of its demonstrated fallibility. For example, Elizabeth Loftus presented the same evidence in a simulated robbery-murder case to three groups of subjects. In two of the groups some of the evidence was presented as having come from an eyewitness, though in one of those two groups additional evidence was presented discrediting the eyewitness by showing his vision was too poor to have possibly recognized anyone at that distance. While in the control (no eyewitness) group, only 18 percent of the subject-jurors voted to convict, 72 percent of the eyewitness group did. Most surprising, however, was the eyewitness-discredited group, where 68 percent voted to convict, suggesting that the mere fact there was an eyewitness carried more weight than expert testimony discrediting it.

Expert testimony of a different nature may, however, be useful. In a later study, Loftus (1980a) did show that expert testimony about the general fallibility of eyewitness testimony led to fewer verdicts of conviction by juror-subjects (see also Hosch, Beck, & McIntyre, 1980; Wells, Lindsay, & Tousignant, 1980). There is considerable debate among psychologists and legal scholars today about the usefulness and advisability of whether psychologists should testify about the fallibility of eyewitness memory. See McCloskey and Egeth (1983) and the two brief reply papers following their article for further discussion of this issue.

In what may prove to be a landmark state court decision, *Kansas* vs *Warren* (1981, Vol. 230, #52,753) ordered a new trial in a case where the court had not allowed the expert testimony of Elizabeth Loftus warning of the fallibility of eyewitness testimony. While not insisting that the expert be heard, the court ordered a new trial for the defendant because the instructions given the jury did not specifically enough discuss the fallibility of eyewitness testimony. This is apparently the first far-reaching decision recognizing the necessity of the jury's being informed of the imperfect character of eyewitness memory.

While eyewitnesses can often be discredited, either through specific cross-examination or through general expert testimony about the fallibility of such testimony, most eyewitnesses to crimes never enter a courtroom and are never cross-examined, because a large majority of criminal cases are settled by plea bargaining. The mere presence of an eyewitness carries a lot of weight in arranging such pleas.

The Question Matters

In a careful study of several important variables in eyewitness memory, Lipton (1977) showed subjects a film of a robbery and shooting in a park and questioned them either immediately afterward or one week later. He was interested in the effects of time and type of question on both accuracy and quantity of information. First, in terms of delay, he found a slight (4.3 percent) decrease in accuracy in the group tested one week later but a much greater decrease (18 percent) in the quantity recalled. It made no difference whether the testimony was in written or oral form.

In terms of types of questions, Lipton used several varieties, ranging from very open-ended questions to highly structured (multiple-choice) questions. He also varied the bias of some of the structured questions in a positive or negative direction. Results generally showed that accuracy and quantity were inversely related. The most open-ended questions elicited the most accurate information, but the smallest quantity of it. On the other hand, multiple-choice questions elicited more information, but it was less accurate. Biased questions elicited more information than neutral questions but that information was highly subject to reconstructive bias. In conclusion, the style of questioning has enormous impact on how much an eyewitness remembers and how accurate those memories are. Such effects are applicable even beyond the problem of eyewitness memory (see Box 6–7).

Over the past decade, Elizabeth Loftus and her associates at the University of Washington have conducted an important research program in eyewitness memory. Many of her findings and conclusions, as well as reviews of the work of others, are contained in her book *Eyewitness Testimony* (Loftus, 1979). Her most typical method has been to show subjects a film of some incident such as a crime or auto accident and then question them afterward about their recollection of the incident. She has demonstrated tremendous biasing effects of the wording of the question on eyewitness memory. For example, asking subjects what happened when the car "came to the yield sign" when in fact it was a stop sign increased the number of subjects who later falsely remembered that there had been a yield sign (Loftus, Miller, & Burns, 1978).

Sometimes such an alteration may be even more subtle yet still have strong effects. For example, Loftus and Palmer (1974) asked subjects either

(7) Did you see the broken headlight? or
(8) Did you see a broken headlight?

after they had viewed a film of an auto accident in which there was no broken headlight. Twice as many subjects questioned with (7) responded "yes"

BOX 6–7 *BEING AN EYEWITNESS TO YOURSELF*

The subject of how the form of a question influences one's memory has ramifications beyond the eyewitness memory problem. The wording that a doctor or counselor would use to question a person about his or her physical or psychological condition could greatly affect their responses and even their self-perception. This may be an even greater problem here than with eyewitness testimony, since what is being remembered is often very subjective and ambiguous to begin with, for example, one's feelings or reactions to others. Consider how differently you might answer each question in each pair below:

1 Do you feel threatened by your boss?
   Don't you feel threatened by your boss?
2 Do you occasionally have sinus trouble?
   Do you frequently have sinus trouble?
3 Are you often very anxious when talking in front of a group?
   Are you often unable to cope when talking in front of a group?

In such cases, as with eyewitness memory, the form of the question can structure our response and even alter our comprehension and memory of our own state of mind or body. This application awaits careful laboratory study.

as those questioned with (8). While (8) is a neutral question, (7) actually says something like, "There was a broken headlight; did you see it?", and it perhaps carries an implication that one is unobservant if one did not see it.

Such biasing effects of questions can permanently alter the character of eyewitness memory. In the same set of studies, Loftus and Palmer questioned subjects with either

(9) About how fast were the cars going when they smashed into each other?

or the same sentence with "smashed" replaced by "hit." The speed estimates were faster by subjects questioned with "smashed" than those questioned with "hit" (41 mph versus 34 mph), though, interestingly enough, both were significant overestimates.

One week later, subjects were asked if they had seen any broken glass in the film (there was none); more "smashed" subjects falsely reported that they had seen it than did "hit" subjects. Apparently broken glass is very consistent with one's knowledge about what happens when cars smash into each other. The wording of the question thus helps guide reconstruction through the activation and retrieval of relevant knowledge from long-term memory. Slightly different knowledge is activated to remember an accident of "smashing" than one with "hitting."

Loftus has also demonstrated that such reconstructive biases can affect the verdict that jurors arrive at as well as the information they remember. Kasprzyk, Montano, and Loftus (1975) had subjects read excerpts from a trial about an ambiguous waterfront incident. The lawyer's questions were either neutral, (10) or biased, (11). Almost twice as many subjects in the biased group voted to convict (41 percent versus 22 percent).

(10) How much of the incident did you see?
(11) How much of the fight did you see?

There can also be biasing effects from testimony by the witnesses. For example, in simulated-courtroom studies (Harris, 1978; Harris, Teske, & Ginns, 1975) a witness either stated something directly (12) or merely implied it (13). In both cases subjects remembered that the witness had stated the information

(12) I walked away without taking any money.
(13) I was able to walk away without taking any money.

unequivocally. Lawyers and juries should be aware of such information-processing tendencies.

Conclusion

What may we conclude from this examination of eyewitness memory? Should we completely reject it as inherently unreliable? Probably not. It is not necessarily inaccurate and sometimes may be about all that a case is based on. However, all parties involved must bear in mind that eyewitness memory is highly subject to distortion by reconstructive errors, stemming both from a failure to encode the event accurately at the time it occurred or from the distortion introduced in the questioning process by the wording of the questions. Courtroom procedural rules rather tightly prescribe the sort of questions that may or may not be asked of a witness on the stand, and many, though not all, of the blatantly biasing questions would not be allowed. Control of pretrial questioning, however, is much less regulated, and this is as far as most eyewitnesses ever get. Even those who do come to trial have already been through the potentially distorting influence of the pretrial questioning.

In an article in the *University of Pennsylvania Law Review* Levine and Tapp (1973, p. 1130) very aptly describe our minds as eyewitnesses:

> The mind is not a mirror which reflects the external world, but an organism with its own needs, values, and capacities—its own vision of "reality" through which the outside world is interpreted.

Indeed, this is an excellent statement about information processing and memory in general.

MEMORY AS CONSTRUCTION AND RECONSTRUCTION

Throughout this chapter and the last, we have examined questions in the psychology of information processing. The major byproduct of information processing is memory. Whenever we process any information more than extremely superficially, we are necessarily encoding it, though usually to a less-than-perfect degree. Encoding involves processes of *constructing* a memory representation, that is, we build something in our memory to represent that information we have been thinking about. Such construction may be very conscious and deliberate, as in the use of mnemonics, or it may be completely unconscious and accidental, as in the impression you take away of someone you meet in a social encounter when you are not even aware of forming a judgment. When you have cause to think about that information again, you retrieve the relevant information from long-term memory and set about to *reconstruct* the original input ("Let's see, what were the freedoms guaranteed in the Bill of Rights?" "What does Mary Jones look like and what did she tell me when I saw her last week?"). In this process of reconstruction, we have the remains, perhaps very fragmentary, of our original constructed memory representation, plus all the information that we have added to it through subsequent experiences and during the processes of reconstruction.

This reconstructive character of memory was discussed at length by pioneering British psychologist Sir Frederick Bartlett (1932) in his book *Remembering,* but it was not studied widely in American psychology until the last decade or two. More recently, the emphasis has shifted some to *construction* (see Spiro, 1980) and its implications for memory.

The ideas of construction and reconstruction in memory have many actual and potential applications, some of which will be discussed later in this book. Look at Box 6–8 for a brief account of the way an actor constructs a memory for a character being portrayed on the stage and then uses this constructed memory to cover a forgotten line during a performance.

Before we can deal further with construction and reconstruction, we need to examine our most abstract and analytic representational system—language—in more detail. Particularly in our society, so much of our information comes to us in the form of language that we must understand something of its structure and character. This will be the focus of the next chapter, after which we will return to the questions of construction and reconstruction, viewed through the eyes of schema theory, a promising contemporary approach to information processing.

SUGGESTED READINGS

A very thorough but readable nontextbook introduction to memory is Elizabeth Loftus (1980b), *Memory,* a book the author (RJH) once gave his engineer

BOX 6–8 *INFORMATION PROCESSING IN THE THEATER*

The information-processing system as outlined in this chapter and the last may be useful in understanding the job of an actor in creating a character. Learning the lines and actions for a part is basically a paired-associate learning task, a real-world analogue of the laboratory paired-associate learning task. In fact, many actors learn their lines by taping the other actors' lines and leaving blank spots on the tape for them to say their lines in practice.

More abstract but more significant, however, is the issue of an actor creating a character on stage. Learning the lines of the dialogue, though certainly not trivial, is one of the most superficial parts of an actor's preparation for a role. He or she must also "create the character" and learn to think and react as that character does. What this really involves is a creation of second short- and long-term memory stores, this time for the character instead of oneself.

Some directors go so far as to ask their actors to write a biography of their character, building up a long-term memory of events and influences that could have happened prior to the raising of the curtain on Act 1.

By constructing such a mind of the character, not only can the actor come across more convincingly in the role, but unforeseen circumstances can be handled much more adeptly, thus obeying every director's cardinal maxim of "stay in character." For example, if the roof of the theater suddenly starts leaking at center stage one night, an actress could respond from her own short-term memory by asking, "What's going on here? This isn't supposed to happen!" Or she could respond in the character of the part she is playing by observing, "It looks like the kids let the tub run over again."

Of course this response would only be appropriate in certain contexts; the line above would sound pretty bizarre if the setting of the play were a ranch-style house or the family contained no children. Such a parallel memory store also allows the actor to cover for missed or bungled lines of oneself or others. As long as the actor responds from the short-term store of the character and not that of the actor, the audience will probably never know there was a missed line.

To a lesser extent this principle of creating a character, specifically the short- and long-term memory of the character, is useful to a teacher (Harris, 1977b). A teacher can create a character that he or she feels would be the most effective teacher. This character would have a lot of characteristics of the person but probably some that were not characteristic at all. For example, a rather shy teacher might create a teacher character that was somewhat less shy, figuring that a high degree of shyness would diminish one's effectiveness as a teacher. Keeping this "teacher persona" in mind, the teacher could respond from the short-term memory of this created teacher character instead of his or her own when approached by a student and thus be a more successful teacher.

father for Christmas to help him understand what the author studies in psychology. He greatly enjoyed it.

For a more rigorous experimental approach, there are several good paperback texts on memory, including Howe (1983), Zechmeister and Nyberg (1982), Klatzky (1980), Wingfield and Byrnes (1981), and Seamon (1980). Memory is also extensively treated in all the cognition texts mentioned at the end of Chapter 5.

Neisser's *Memory Observed* (1982) is a fascinating and highly readable anthology of papers about memory in natural settings. For an extended case study of one highly exceptional individual, see Alexander Luria's *The Mind of a Mnemonist* (1968).

People interested in further reading on eyewitness memory might consult Elizabeth Loftus' *Eyewitness Testimony* (1979), or A. D. Yarmey's *The Psychology of Eyewitness Testimony* (1979).

CHAPTER SEVEN
LANGUAGE

As highly evolved as we humans are compared to other species, we tend to rely heavily on language, our most abstract representational system. Thus, this chapter will deal with language, though we shall see in the next chapter that many of the principles of language comprehension also operate in the comprehension of nonlinguistic information. When people say that they "know" a language, what is it that they know? In fact, it is many types of information, including elements such as sounds, letters, words, meanings, and sentences, and grammatical constituents and rules for combining these elements. Generally, the information that we know when we know a language may be grouped into four general categories, or components: the **phonological** (sound) component, the **semantic** (meaning) component, the **syntactic** (structural) component, and the **pragmatic** (contextual) component. Each of these components includes both elements of information and rules about how those elements may and may not be combined and used together. In this chapter we will look at each of these components. Finally, we shall discuss the psychology of reading and writing.

PHONOLOGY

The **phonological** (sound) component of language includes 1) the perceived speech sounds, phonemes, and the suprasegmental cues in speech and 2) the implicit phonological rules for how these sounds may be combined. This component of language was discussed in Chapter 5, as an example of complex pattern recognition. Thus, we will not discuss it further here, except to note that any adequate theory of comprehension will have to include how we perceive phonemes and suprasegmental cues in speech and how we use phonological rules. However, the phonological component is only one of four components that any such comprehension theory must consider. It is the other three that we will now examine.

SEMANTICS

A second component of language is meaning, or **semantics.** In a sense this facet of language is central, since if there were no meaning to be communicated or understood, there would be little reason for any structure, sounds, or context. Because it is so difficult to isolate and identify, however, meaning is in many ways the most difficult aspect of language to study.

Word Meaning

One major concern in semantics is the meaning of individual words. Every word has come to have a particular meaning. Many, if not most, words may have more than one completely distinct meaning (river *bank* versus money *bank*). In fact, however, ambiguity is more potential than real in the normal usage of language. For example, the context would typically make it perfectly clear which sense of *bank* was intended. Occasionally, of course, genuine confusion does result because of the ambiguity of some word, and such ambiguity can be the source of humor. Often the so-called punch line of a joke is the information that the earlier, and normally most likely, interpretation of some word or words was, in fact, incorrect, as in (1):

(1)   The bells were peeling; in fact, the whole church needed painting badly.

Presupposition The semantics of even single words that are not ambiguous can be quite complex. For instance, there are many verbs that carry as part of their meaning a *presupposition* about whether the speaker believes some other piece of information to be true (Kiparsky & Kiparsky, 1970; Harris, 1974). A presupposition is something that the speaker assumes to be true; it is a necessary precondition to a statement being either true or false. For example,

(2)   Janice regretted that Elaine had left.

This presupposes that the speaker of sentence (2) believes the information in the subordinate clause, namely, that Elaine had left, to be true. Indeed, if Elaine has not left, (2) would not be either true or false; it would just be strange. Consider the weirdness of (3) and (4), that follow. While both (3) and (4) suggest that

(3)   Eric knew the unicorns were real.

(4)   Eric was sure that unicorns were real.

Eric is a little weird for believing that unicorns were real, (3) suggests as well that the speaker is also a little weird and holds the same strange belief. (A possible exception would be if heavy unnatural stress were laid on *knew* to make it sound ironic, but that possibility will be ignored at present.)

Sometimes what a word asserts directly versus what it presupposes can be the basis of the difference of two contrasting words. For example, *accuse* presupposes that the act in question is considered bad by the speaker while it asserts that a particular person was responsible. In contrast, the otherwise similar verb *criticize* presupposes that a particular person is responsible and asserts that the act was bad (Fillmore, 1971). If a presupposition is violated, absurdity (as opposed to falsehood) results.

(5)   Bill accused Jim of rescuing the little girl.

(6)   Bill criticized Betty Crocker for shooting Abraham Lincoln.

While (5) presupposes that the act is bad, it seems odd that the speaker would think it bad to rescue a little girl; thus, a presupposition of *accuse* appears to be violated. In (6), the presupposition of responsibility appears to be violated, since Betty Crocker did not shoot Abraham Lincoln, and it seems highly unlikely anyone would believe she did.

Fuzzy sets   When examined closely, even what at first appear to be very clearly defined semantic concepts or classes become "fuzzy," or difficult to define precisely. A good example is *furniture.* What constitutes a piece of furniture? Most would agree that objects like beds, couches, chairs, tables, and dressers are furniture, but how about grandfather clocks, end tables, card tables, ping-pong tables, wastebaskets, rugs, footstools, floor lamps, table lamps, vases, pillows, flower pots, plant stands, built-in bookshelves, pianos, cellos, music stands, typewriters, coasters, trunks, and picture frames? Is the class furniture defined by size (for example, a grandfather clock is a piece of furniture, but an alarm clock isn't), by position (all things that sit on the floor are pieces of furniture while those that sit on tables or hang on walls aren't), or by object class (plants and flower pots are not furniture, even if a six-foot plant sits in a two-foot diameter pot on the floor)? Everyone has his or her own conceptions of what is and is not furniture, and each definition may be slightly different from all the others. For this reason we say that furniture is a *fuzzy set.* Fuzzy sets are very common, being the rule rather than the exception.

A similar example involves differentiating between a *glass,* a *cup,* and a *mug.* People typically classify based on physical attributes, such as cups having handles and sitting on saucers (but then what about paper and styrofoam cups—why aren't they glasses?). If mugs also have handles but are thicker and don't take saucers, then is there a certain thickness after which a cup becomes a mug? If a glass can be of many shapes (tumblers, wine glasses, shot glasses, juice glasses) but must have no handle and be made of either plastic or glass, then why is an object the same size, shape, and thickness but made of paper a cup instead of a glass? One final complication: Does what we call a drinking vessel in part depend on what drink is in it? If a paper cup is filled with cola or beer, is it still a cup of cola or a cup of beer, or has it become a glass (or perhaps a glass of cola in a cup!)?

If we have coffee in a large, transparent glass vessel with no handle or saucer, is it still a glass? Clearly glasses, cups, and mugs, like furniture, are all fuzzy sets, but, surprisingly, we are usually able to comprehend and converse about them with little confusion. In fact, we can construct categories whenever we need them; such categories may sometimes contain objectively very disparate items; for example, ways to make friends (Barsalou, 1983).

The fuzzy set issue is not a purely academic one, but manifests itself in some serious social problems. For example, physicians and legal scholars are discovering that the concept *death* is a very fuzzy set. Such issues as euthanasia, organ transplants, and reviving someone after a brief heart stoppage underline the importance of defining death more precisely. Similarly, the abortion debate issue can be posed as: When does personhood begin? If a first-trimester fetus is in fact a person, then aborting it is murder; if it is not, then the abortion is merely a surgical procedure. *Person* is a fuzzy set in that an egg and sperm are not persons, but a baby at birth is; just where in between does the entity enter the class *person*?

Negation   One semantically interesting type of word is a *negation* (*not, no one, never, none,* and so forth). This may be expressed by a directly negative word, like *not,* or by negative prefixes (*un-, dis-, im-, in-*), or even by certain words that have an inherent negation in their meaning (*abolish, subtract, lose, refrain from, forget, fail, prevent*). Most psychological research has found that, other things being equal, a negative sentence is typically more difficult to comprehend or remember than a corresponding affirmative sentence. However, this may depend considerably on the context. Negatives are often used to deny something and tend to be reasonable only if such a denial is plausible (Wason, 1965; Johnson-Laird & Tridgell, 1972). Thus, sentence (7) below seems a reasonable negation because someone could easily assert that a bat was a bird, but (8), though a true statement, is somewhat bizarre in that it is hard to imagine the need to ever assert it; who would ever think a table *was* a bird?

(7)   A bat is not a bird.
(8)   A table is not a bird.

Sometimes a negation can be ambiguous as to exactly what it is negating, that is, its *scope*. Example (9) is ambiguous in that Dolly may have done

(9)   Dolly did not turn on the microphone.

something else to the microphone, Dolly may have turned on something else, or somebody else may have turned on the microphone. Some languages, like German, could more easily clarify just what was being negated by placement of the negative particle *not* (German: *nicht*). In English we usually have to depend on the context to clarify it, although we can more narrowly specify the scope using a more formal style in the following examples.

(10) It wasn't Dolly who turned on the microphone.
(11) It wasn't the microphone that Dolly turned on.
(12) What Dolly did to the microphone was not to turn it on.

Context A curious fact about the meaning of certain words is that their meaning is partly determined by surrounding words or even by nonverbal context. One type of word for which this is true are *quantifiers,* words like *many, few,* and *several.* For example, consider (13) and (14).

(13) Many people earned over $10,000 last year.
(14) Many people were killed by tornadoes last year.

How many people would have to have earned over $10,000 to make (13) true, and how many would have to have died in tornadoes to make (14) true? For most people, "many" killed by tornadoes is not nearly as many as "many" earning over $10,000. Thus, *many* has meaning only in relation to what it is modifying and what the person using it expected; it means "many" relative to what might be expected. Hence, something as "purely linguistic" as word meaning can, in fact, be defined in part by psychological factors.

Another type of context-dependent word meaning involves *deictic* words, that is, words that take on their meaning only by relating to a context. For example, demonstrative adjectives such as *this, that, these,* and *those* mean nothing more than *the* unless there is a near or far context to point to in order to discriminate, for example, *these* people from *those* people. Consider the silliness of sitting in an office and saying (15), unless there happen to be pictures of ostriches there or real birds outside the window.

(15) These ostriches are pretty.

Other examples of deictic words include *here* and *there,* verb tense, time adverbs and verbs like *come* and *go* and *bring* and *take.* For instance, whether one uses *come* or *go* depends on where he or she is in relation to the movement described. If one is in Kansas, one can say (16) but typically not (17), while a speaker in Washington could say (17) but not (16), in describing the same Presidential visit.

(16) The President came to Kansas.
(17) The President went to Kansas.

People remember, or misremember, deictic words as having been spoken from the rememberer's own perspective (Brewer & Harris, 1974).

Sometimes one language will have one word to cover two different ideas, while another language will have two separate words. For example, in American English the word *rent* can refer either to what the landlord or the tenant does in a rental transaction, while in a sales transaction we distinguish between *buy* and *sell*. In German, however, there are two corresponding words for the two senses of rent (*mieten* and *vermieten*), as exists in British English (*let* and *rent*). English has one word, *know*, which can mean either to know a piece of information or to be acquainted with someone. French, Spanish, Portuguese, and German have two separate verbs for these two senses of *know* (*savoir-connaître*, *saber-conocer*, *saber-conhecer*, and *wissen-kennen*, respectively). On the other hand, Romance languages have one verb (*faire, hacer, fazer*) which means both *make* and *do* in English. Translation across languages, and even across dialects, can be fraught with peril. See Boxes 7–1 and 7–2 for further discussion of this issue.

BOX 7–1   *EMBARRASSMENTS IN TRANSLATION*

North Americans are notorious around the world for being scandalously inept in languages other than English. While most educated people in a majority of countries study two or more languages, with North Americans this seems to be the exception. There are excellent arguments, however, for having knowledge of languages other than our own. For example, in international business some embarrassing and costly gaffes have been made due to such ignorance.

General Motors did not understand for a while why its popular Chevrolet Nova was not selling in Puerto Rico. When someone finally pointed out that *Nova* in Spanish means "it doesn't go (run)," the name was changed to "Caribe" and sales improved. For similar reasons, AMC's Matador did not do well in Latin America, but then an imported car named "Killer" or "Murderer" probably wouldn't sell too well in the United States!

The company that is now the Exxon Corporation made some preliminary plans several years ago to change the firm name to "Enco," short for "Energy Company." While this sounded very appropriate in English, in Japanese the word "enco" means "flat tire," hardly a good name for a company of service stations. Thus, that name was dropped too.

A certain brand of toothpaste did not sell well in Buenos Aires, quite possibly because "Colgate" in Argentinian Spanish means "go hang yourself!" A type of Brazilian bank account was recently marketed under its Portuguese acronym PIS, which would not market well to North America. Some other foreign products that did not sell well in North America include Calpis (a Japanese soft drink pronounced "cow-piss"), Pfanni (a German dumpling mix), and Superglans (a Dutch carwax). (Aman, 1982).

BOX 7–2   *SUBTLE TRANSLATION DIFFERENCES*

Sometimes the same word can mean something slightly, or considerably, different in another dialect or language. Consider, for example, the many differences between British and American English. For example, what Americans call "cookies" and "apartments" the English call "biscuits" and "flats." If you talk about your "pants" in London, you may receive a few titters, since the word refers only to underwear in Britain; "trousers" are what you wear over your underwear. "Chips" in Chicago are "crisps" in London, while "chips" in Britain are "french fries" on the other side of the Atlantic. If a woman says "I'm easy," it means "I don't care" in Britain, but something else altogether in America.

There are differences in connotations as well. For example, the word "toilet" means approximately the same on both sides of the Atlantic, but whereas it is the standard word for public bathrooms in Britain, in America it has slightly crude connotations, and terms like "restroom" or "comfort station" are favored.

The outskirts of large cities in Brazil have facilities called "motels," which look somewhat like American buildings of the same name and where you can rent rooms overnight. However, the resemblance in terms of purpose is superficial. Brazilian motels are explicitly for clandestine sexual encounters between people not married to each other; travelers seeking only overnight lodging stay in similar-looking places called hotels.

So far we have considered the semantic aspect of language only in regard to the meaning of single words. In fact, another important fact of the semantic component of language is the meaning of a sentence or utterance as a whole. This may be referred to as its *propositional meaning,* and it will be considered more carefully after a look at syntax.

SYNTAX

The third aspect of language is **syntax,** or structure. This involves rules for describing how words, or, more precisely, abstract grammatical constituents like subjects, predicates, noun phrases, and other elements may be put together to form an acceptable sentence in a given language.

Syntax, as the linguist and psychologist deal with it, is descriptive; it attempts to identify rules actually used in real language. It is not intended to be normative or prescriptive, that is, what we *should* do. Contrary to what might be your memories of eighth-grade English class, the interest in psychology is not on coercing people to say *isn't* instead of *ain't* or *brought* instead of *brung.* The scientist studying language is interested in how people actually talk, not how someone thinks they *should* talk.

Surface and Deep Structure

Language may be looked at as having structure on different levels. Most superficially, of course, it is a sequence of successive words, each following the other. Since such a view of syntax does not tell us very much about overall rules of how words in English may be put together or, indeed, even how they have been put together in a particular sentence, this level will not be considered further.

Any sentence may be broken down into grammatical constituents, or structural units, such as noun phrase, verb phrase, and modifier. Such an analysis of a sentence is its *surface structure*. For example, the surface structure of (18) is noun phrase–verb phrase–predicate complement–infinitive.

(18) Henry is easy to please.

A very large number of different words could be plugged into each of these "slots," but they would have to conform to the type of word allowed there. For example, the word *the* could not be inserted in the predicate complement position, nor the word *friendly* in the noun phrase position. The sentence diagramming you learned back in junior high and the grammar drills you labored through studying a foreign language were basically surface structure exercises, training you to identify the surface syntactic constituents of the language. Syntactic knowledge is in some sense implicit in a school child, since he or she would have to possess it to be able to speak intelligibly at all, but this knowlege is certainly not at a conscious level. To come to such a level, it must be carefully, even laboriously, taught as in those junior high grammar drills.

Surface structure is not the only possible level of analysis, however. There is a deeper level, pointed out by the linguist Noam Chomsky (1957, 1965a), called the *deep*, or sometimes the *underlying*, structure. Let's go back to (19) and make a companion to it so we have (18) and (19).

(19) Henry is eager to please.

Both of these have the identical surface structure, explained above. They do, of course, contain one word different from the other, and that changes the meaning somewhat, but it is structure, not meaning, which is of concern here. Although the two sentences have identical surface structures, there is something very different about them syntactically, specifically the relation of the noun phrase *Henry* to the verb *please*. In (19) *Henry* is the deep-structure subject of *please*, while in (18) *Henry* is the deep-structure object. In one case he is doing the pleasing; in the other he is being pleased. We might say that *Henry* is the agent or actor in (19) and the acted-upon in (18) (cf. Fillmore, 1968). Nowhere in the surface structure of noun phrase–verb phrase–predicate complement–infinitive is this important distinction captured.

Even though you may have never before thought about differences like the contrast between the syntax of (18) and (19), you must have in some sense "known" that knowledge in order to be able to speak and understand such sentences correctly, that is, to know whether Henry was pleasing or being pleased. This also has ramifications for language acquisition in children. If part of what children must know about a language involves deep-structure relationships, there is no way they could learn that purely by imitating surface structures of parents.

The importance of deep-structure relationships can be further illustrated with an additional example (20), which has one surface structure (noun phrase–verb–predicate adjective–infinitive), but two possible deep structures, depending on whether the chicken is the deep-structure subject or object of *eat*.

(20)   The chicken is ready to eat.

On the other hand, there are cases where one deep structure may have different alternative surface structures, such as the active and passive versions of the same idea (21) and (22). Here the same deep structure can be realized into either of two surface structures.

(21)   Robin Hood rescued the princess.
(22)   The princess was rescued by Robin Hood.

Linguistic studies of syntax, especially those of Noam Chomsky and his followers studying *transformational grammar,* have identified many grammatical rules called *transformations* that move constituents of sentences around in different orders and add or delete elements. Examples of some transformations would be the rules that change an active sentence to a passive one, move an adverb to the front of the sentence, change a redundant noun to a pronoun, delete a repetitious word, or turn a statement into a question.

The Given-New Contract

Although Chomsky and other linguists focused mainly on describing the structural knowledge we must have to know a language, syntax is also very important psychologically in helping us understand language we hear and read every day. While syntax is not the meaning as such, it helps to *signal* the meaning and thus help us interpret a given sentence. To take a simple example, the definite article *the* signals that a noun phrase is beginning and one can reasonably expect the next word to be either a noun or a modifying adjective preceding a noun.

Syntax can signal more than just the part of speech that is to follow, however. It can also tell us what information the hearer already knows and what information is new in that sentence. For example, consider (23) and (24).

(23)   The ugly toad is on the mushroom.
(24)   The toad on the mushroom is ugly.

Both contain the same information, even the same words, but somehow there is a difference. A particular piece of information (that the toad is ugly) is in a different syntactic structure in each sentence. As (23) would normally be used, the hearer and the speaker are both aware of some toad that is ugly (given information) and the speaker is telling the hearer that the toad is on the mushroom (new information). In (24), however, the speaker and hearer know that there is a toad on the mushroom and the new information says that it is ugly.

Part of the unwritten conventions of language is that we have an implicit agreement to put given information in certain syntactic structures of a sentence, for example, in adjectives or prepositional phrases modifying the subject of a sentence, and new information in other forms—in adjectives or phrases following the verb. This allows the listener to pick out what the new information is and link it up with given information already in our memory and repeated in the given part of the sentence. (Clark, 1977; Clark & Haviland, 1977; Haviland & Clark, 1974).

The *given-new* distinction may be further illustrated by looking at appropriate and inappropriate denials of (23) and (24). For example, (25) would be an appropriate denial of (24), but a very strange response to (23), while the reverse is true for (26).

(25) No, it's a pretty toad.
(26) No, it's on the lily pad.

Style

Another manifestation of differences in syntax occurs in the matter of **style**. Certain placements of words and phrases indicate a more formal style than others. Subtle stylistic differences are some of the cues that tip off a teacher that a student paper is plagiarized, because its style is a little too formal to be a typical student composition. Moreover, in formal speaking and writing, people tend to use more complex syntax, involving a greater number of subordinate clauses. In more colloquial speech, shorter, choppier sentences are the rule, if indeed speech is composed of grammatically well-formed sentences at all, which it often is not.

Sometimes the use of an uncommon syntactic transformation is the surest indication of awkward or archaic style. For example, in modern English to transform a declarative (27) into a yes-no question requires the addition of a form of the verb *do* (28).

(27) Anne likes broccoli.
(28) Does Anne like broccoli?
(29) Likes Anne broccoli?
(30) Think you that the king is mad?

However, in Elizabethan English you could simply invert the subject and verb (29), a form of question common in the time of Shakespeare (30), but no longer used. It is in part the many uses of unfamiliar syntax that makes Shakespeare and his contemporaries difficult for the modern reader. Unfortunately, sometimes contemporary language is also very difficult to understand because of its style. See Box 7–3 for a discussion of a judge's instructions to the jury.

BOX 7–3. INSTRUCTIONS TO THE JURY

A current area of considerable concern in forensic psychology is the language in the judge's instructions to the jury prior to deliberation. Some historical background is helpful here. The custom of the judge instructing the jury arose from the need to inform the jurors and help them apply the law to the case at hand. In the late nineteenth and early twentieth centuries, U. S. state statutes started requiring the courts to reduce all instructions by the judge to writing; this had the effect of a formalization of the instructions and a stratification resulting from their being read verbatim for each such trial. These verbatim instructions were adhered to precisely because these were the instructions that had been upheld on appeal. Any judge who deviated and used another set of instructions ran the risk of having that decision later overturned on a technicality. Now most state and federal courts have those so-called *pattern instructions* available for most crimes. Since they are used for all trials for a particular crime, they are, not surprisingly, broad and abstract and do not allow very well for integration of the specifics of the trial. The instructions seldom use examples, for fear of biasing the jury.

While the use of pattern instructions makes excellent sense from a legal point of view, from an information-processing perspective, the wisdom is considerably more questionable. The legal community generally assumes that the instructions are adequately comprehended; to a cognitive psychologist, this is an empirical question that has not been answered, or often even asked. Frequently the jurors are not allowed to ask any clarifying questions, for fear that the answer given them might in some way bias them in a way that is unfair to one of the parties of the trial or that risks a reversal in the appeals process.

Another problem is that instructions are typically given to a jury *after* they have heard the evidence, just before deliberation begins. Cognitive psychologists would stress the importance of instructions in comprehending the information as it is initially processed and encoded, not after the fact when it must be retrieved and reconstructed. Thus, we have, in pattern instructions and their use, a practical problem of information processing, but one that has not been considered much from that perspective.

In a very interesting and important cognitive study of a judge's instructions to the jury, the lawyer-linguist researcher couple Robert and Veda Charrow (1979) set out to provide some empirical evidence of juror failure to comprehend pattern instructions and to identify some particular linguistic constructions that posed problems. They asked prospective jurors to paraphrase 14 standard civil instructions from the California state judicial system for a highway accident case.

Their results showed that over 60 percent of the ideas in the instructions were either paraphrased inaccurately or completely forgotten. Although ideas from long and short sentences were remembered equally well, certain types of syntactic constructions cause a lot of comprehension difficulty. These included passive constructions, certain prepositional phrases, especially those containing the stylistically awkward expression "as to," and sentences with two or more negations in them. Other constructions causing difficulties included sentences with discontinuous constituents, such as (1).

(1)   A proximate cause is a cause which in natural and continuous sequence produces an injury.

The phrase "which produces an injury" is broken up with another phrase, thus making it more difficult to assign a subject of "produces." Another type of phrase that proved difficult was the deletion of optional relative pronouns, as in " . . . questions and facts submitted to you . . . ." In English we can optionally delete the "which are" from this phrase. However, this is often at the cost of some clarity.

Charrow and Charrow examined the claim we sometimes hear that legal language is necessarily complex because the legal concepts are so complex. They did not find support for this, in that jurors' difficulty with the instructions stemmed not from the inherent difficulty of the concepts themselves, but rather from the way the concepts were stated. Every concept was much more understandable if phrased in a way more consistent with our natural language comprehension strategies.

Propositional Structure

At a level more abstract (or deep, if you will) than even the deep structure is the structure of the ideas in the sentence. This is when the division between syntax and semantics becomes murky. Although cognitive psychologists differ as to exactly how to describe and measure these idea-units, most agree that meaningful discourse is composed of semantic units called **propositions.** An example of how a sentence could be broken up into propositions would be (31). The sentence (31) contains five separate simple propositions; we might remember some of these and forget others at some time after hearing the sentence.

(31) The brave young Snoopy withstood the cat's sharp blows.
   (a)   Snoopy was brave.
   (b)   Snoopy was young.
   (c)   The blows were sharp.
   (d)   The blows came from the cat.
   (e)   Snoopy withstood the blows.

As you can see, the propositional level of analysis really involves semantic factors (meaning), as well as syntactic ones. In fact, many psychologists and linguists (Fillmore, 1968; Norman & Rumelhart, 1975; Kintsch, 1974) question the usefulness of talking about a deep-structure level of syntax, preferring to consider the level more abstract than the surface structure as entirely semantic. Arguments for and against these approaches need not concern us here. It is worth noting, however, that when syntax and semantics are carefully considered in their appropriate abstractness, it typically becomes very difficult to separate them completely, as illustrated by our sample propositional analysis (31).

In describing propositions, it is easier to say what they are not than what they are. First of all, they are not analogical, that is, they bear no physical relationship to the referent they represent. They are highly abstract, a fact worth keeping constantly in mind upon seeing graphic or schematic representations of them, which necessarily must represent them as words (see Kintsch, 1974) or some combination of words and graphic representations (Anderson, 1980).

Propositions have several important characteristics. First of all, they are primarily semantically based, that is, a representation of the meaning, although some versions of propositional theory do also contain some structure. Unlike sentences, they are not ambiguous and do not contain the surface structure at all. A proposition coding the idea of John kissing Mary could have had its stimulus source in any one of several spoken or written sentences ("John kissed Mary," "Mary was kissed by John,") or in an observation of the event of John kissing Mary. Propositions are not dependent on the form of the input, nor are they typically good avenues to retrieving that exact surface information.

Propositions have some kind of internal organization and, as such, contain both units and relations. Units could be abstract entities like *agent, object,* or *instrument,* while relations could be the identity relationship (A is B), possession, or relationships like *acts upon* or *object of.* The internal organization of propositions may be reflected in its different components. For example, an action *hit* may contain elements of agent, object, and instrument, any of which could appear as the surface structure subject of the sentence (for example, "the boy hit the ball," "the ball was hit by the boy," "the bat hit the ball").

Unlike images or some kind of units or concepts alone, propositions often have a truth value (in the case of a statement about something, asserting either a stative relation or an action) or demand a response, in the case of a question or imperative. An image or concept cannot be true or false or demand a response; it is merely a representation. On the other hand, a proposition asserts something, which may in reality be true or false, or requests a response, which may or may not be complied with.

Propositions have developed as a very useful construct in studying linguistic information processing. Memory studies of prose are typically scored for the number of propositions recalled, rather than number of words or sentences. Theoretical models of propositional learning continue to be developed and doubtless will have increasing impact on the study of information processing in the future.

PRAGMATICS

The final of the four major aspects of language is its use in a context, or **pragmatics.** Every instance of language is used within some context, even if that context is a total lack of context, a highly unusual situation in the real world. In most cases the contextual appropriateness is assumed; you simply would not say (32) while sitting in class.

(32) My, what a fierce rhinoceros that is!

Occasionally, however, the context lends meaning where it otherwise would not exist at all, as in the case of the deictic words and quantifiers discussed earlier. Other times the context may radically alter the meaning, perhaps totally changing the "speech act" function of the utterance; for example, irony and sarcasm (33), turning a question into a command (34), indicating a metaphorical intent by the speaker (35).

(33) My, what a beautiful day!
      (Context: in a blizzard)
(34) John, are you able to reach the cookies?
      (Context: a hungry speaker out of reach of the cookies and John within reach of them)
(35) The troops marched on into battle for two hours.
      (Context: a harried baby sitter explaining children's rambunctious behavior to their parents upon the latter's return)

Sometimes when scientists study language they easily forget about its typical use in conversation, a continuing dialogue and interplay between two or more people. A conversation may be looked at as a type of game, consisting of a sequence of exchanges involving rule-governed processes (Weiner & Goodenough, 1977). Speakers make different "moves" with their remarks. These moves may be directly dealing with the subject being discussed, or moves that add nothing new to the subject but indicate information about whether the speaker wants to change or to keep the current topic. For example, if in a conversation between two people there is a sequence of two so-called *passing moves,* like *okay, uhhmm,* and *all right,* spoken with falling intonation (not as a question), that usually signals a change in the topic being discussed, as desired by both speakers. Even the way that we address each other can indicate our relative social status or amount of identification with that person (Box 7–4). Sometimes even the choice of a language we use has social or political implications (see Box 7–5).

There are implicit rules that we all follow in conversation whether we realize it or not (Grice, 1975). One is to give enough information, but not

BOX 7–4   *FORMAL AND FAMILIAR FORMS OF LANGUAGE*

There are different ways that we address other people to indicate our relationship to them. Many languages have two forms of the second-person pronouns (French *tu-vous*, Spanish *tú-usted*, German *du-Sie*), one to be used with close friends and family members and one to be used with other adults. Modern English only captures such differences through the choice of the use of a first name or a title and last name. However, English once did have a familiar second-person pronoun, *thou*, which has now fallen into disuse. Thus, we lose certain distinctions in modern English. For example, in Shakespeare's *Two Gentlemen of Verona* two friends, Proteus and Valentine, address each other with *thou* until one takes the other's girl friend. The indignant friend then begins addressing his former buddy with *you*, a clear mark of distance to Elizabethan playgoers, but a signal likely to be missed by today's audiences.

Whether we use the formal or familiar form of address with another person may depend on how we perceive our relationship on one of two relevant dimensions. The first is power. A person in a position of greater power addresses a person of lesser power with the familiar form, but receives the formal in return. This power may take many forms: teacher-student, parent-child, employer-employee, and so forth.

The second dimension is solidarity, that is, the degree of perceived commonality and shared experience. If this dimension is operating, members of a group with something in common address each other with the familiar form, but address others outside the group with a formal form. These may be members of a family, a class, an office, or whatever. In the modern world, there is a gradual tendency for solidarity to assume more importance in determining forms of address and power to assume somewhat less importance, but both are still important. If they come into conflict, the participants must resolve what forms to use; for example, should all workers in an office address each other with the familiar form or should the bosses expect to be addressed with the formal form?

Formal and familiar forms are subject to dialectal differences. In Spanish, for example, Venezuelan and some Caribbean dialects use *tú* for everyone, regardless of power or solidarity relationships (like the English *you*). On the other hand, European Spanish has, as well as *tú* and *usted,* a special familiar-plural pronoun (*vosotros*), which is not used in Latin America. Even among English-speakers, the British are likely to use titles and last names longer in a relationship than Americans do. Such cultural differences often lead to Americans' perceptions of the British as formal and aloof and Britons' perception of Americans as pushy and impudent.

too much. If a four-year-old asks where he or she came from a response of "Go away" would be too little information, but a 10,000-word treatise on genetics would be too much. (Perhaps the best answer would be "Kansas City.") Certain conventional expressions carry strong expectations of just how much information to respond with. If someone asks "How are you?"

BOX 7–5 *SOCIAL IMPLICATIONS OF BILINGUALISM*

In spite of the strongly monolingual character of some major nations such as the United States, Japan, Brazil, and Great Britain, bilingualism is actually the rule rather than the exception in most areas of the world. The degree and character of bilingualism varies substantially, however.

Bilingualism is difficult to measure. It is seldom the case that an individual is exactly equivalent in fluency in all aspects in two languages. For example, many people around the world can read English, which they have studied as an academic language, but they often have almost no facility in speaking or in oral comprehension. Others have a conversational facility in a language, but cannot read or write it. Although some elaborate scales have been developed for measuring bilingualism, they have shown no better predictive validity than a simple questionnaire about one's language experience.

Although some nations like Switzerland have been happily multilingual for centuries, language can be a divisive force in a country. A major example is Canada, which is officially bilingual, but with a predominance of largely monolingual English-speakers. Predominantly French-speaking Quebec province has passed blatantly anti–English laws, and the French influence at the national level is widely resented, especially in western Canada. Similarly, Belgium has had a long history of competition of the Flemish-speaking Flemings and the French-speaking Walloons of the north and south of the country, respectively. Unlike the situation in Canada, however, the Flemings and the Walloons have usually kept closer to a numerical and power balance.

Sometimes a second language may be a source of regional consciousness and political difficulties, especially in cases where speakers perceive that a language is in danger of dying altogether. For example, in Wales there has been a great revival of Welsh over the last two decades. The old Celtic tongue is the first language of a sizable minority (10–20 percent) of Welsh, especially in northern Wales, and the whole country has recently seen the introduction of bilingual signs and increased broadcast programming in Welsh. Although its sister tongue Irish Gaelic is seldom spoken as a first language today, it is sometimes studied by Irish Republican Army prisoners jailed in Northern Ireland; thus it has become a political symbol.

Very frequent in many communities is a situation called *diglossia,* where there is a high-status formal language and a lower-status everyday language, with most people bilingual. This is very typical of immigrant communities of the first or second generation in immigrant societies like the United States, Canada, Brazil, and Australia; typically, in such situations, the original language is lost as the younger generations adopt the host country's language as its vernacular.

Sometimes the diglossia continues for many generations, especially in colonial settings. In colonial Africa, for example, residents learned English, French or Portuguese as the high-status language, but continued to speak their indigenous languages at home. Diglossia has existed relatively unchanged for four centuries in parts of South America, where the everyday language is Quechua or Aymará in much of Peru and Bolivia and Guarani in most of Paraguay, but where many, if not most, people know Spanish as well. (Baetens Beardsmore, 1982; Grosjean, 1982) that person really does not want a detailed medical report, and such a response would typically not be appreciated, if even tolerated. Another implicit rule of conversation involves telling the truth, and assuming others are too, unless we have some compelling reason to suspect otherwise, or unless we recognize from the context that some sort of nonliteral conventional use of language is intended.

A speaker can communicate more in a conversation than merely the propositional content. He or she can also communicate information about the speaker's intentions, beliefs, and relations with the listener (Keenan, MacWhinney, & Mayhew, 1977). For example, in response to an idea suggested by another person, you might say (36) or (37).

(36) Another one of your ridiculous schemes!

(37) That's a good possibility, though we might want to consider some other factors also.

While the responses are similar in that the speaker is expressing disagreement with the idea, (36) expresses a very different attitude from (37) and would probably lead the conversation in a different direction.

Pragmatic considerations also help to determine if a statement is meant to be taken in some unusual, nonconventional fashion. For example, a statement exactly the opposite of what is appropriate for the context is often the object of *irony*. Thus, if someone says (38) on a cold day after it has snowed all night, he or she is interpreted as being ironic, not psychotic. (Though interestingly enough, if someone labelled mentally ill made the same statement in the same situation, it might be labelled psychotic and not ironic!)

(38) Can you open the window?

Sometimes ironic statements may be used to communicate intentions and opinions of the speaker that have nothing at all to do with its surface, deep, or propositional structure. For example, if a student comes in and says her term paper fell in the mud and washed down a sewer on the way to class, the teacher could respond (39).

(39) Yes, and I just got trampled by 15 purple elephants in the hall.

This statement has nothing whatever to do with elephants or hallways, but rather communicates to the student that the speaker does not believe the explanation of what happened to the term paper.

When is a question not a question? When the context tells you it is a command. For example, suppose I am teaching a class where the room is getting very stuffy and I turn to one of the students near the window and say (38). In terms of surface structure, deep structure, and propositional content, that utterance is a question calling for a yes or no answer. However, either a simple *yes* or *no* in the context above would be interpreted as an inappropriate, perhaps even a highly discourteous, response. The context here has told us that what initially appears to be a question is, in fact, an imperative, just as surely as if I had said (40).

(40) Please open the window.

Of course, in some other context such as my questioning an ailing student about how well he is gaining back his strength in his recently broken arm, such a question could indeed be a yes-no question. Sometimes the context of such expressions can even turn a negative into an affirmative and vice versa. For example, consider the same context as above and someone uttering (41) or (42).

(41) Why not open the window?
(42) Why open the window?

The negative (41) is really an affirmative imperative (*Do open the window*) and the affirmative (42) a negative imperative (*Do not open the window*)! Such is the power of pragmatics.

Along the same line, an apparent question can actually be a statement.

(43) Haven't I been good to you?
(44) Can any group compare to the Beatles?

In many contexts (43), which is an apparent negative question, is, in fact, an affirmative statement (*I have been good to you*) while (44), which is an apparent affirmative question, is a negative declarative (*No group can compare to the Beatles*).

Now that we have examined the phonological, semantic, syntactic, and pragmatic components of language, let us apply these concepts by examining two of the major functions of language—reading and writing.

READING AND WRITING

Writing Systems

Although writing is a newer invention than speech, it is hardly a recent phenomenon, with writing systems going back at least as far as 5000 B.C. in Mesopotamia, Egypt, and the Indus and Yangtze valleys.

There are generally three different types of writing systems: **logographic, syllabic,** and **alphabetic,** roughly based on whether one written symbol corresponds to a word, a syllable, or a sound. While English and most other languages you are familiar with are alphabetic, it is worth taking a brief look at logographic and syllabic writing systems, because our information-processing systems must also be capable of reading in those systems.

A logographic system has one symbol to stand for a word. This is the only type of writing system where one symbol represents a semantic unit.

Chinese is the most important example of a logographic system. Compared to a syllabic or alphabetic system, logographic writing has a very large number of symbols (about 50,000 in Chinese, although only about 1000 account for about 90 percent of Chinese writing). Obviously the stage of learning to read where one learns the symbols is much more complex in Chinese than in English, although the former is easier in the sense that there is no spelling-sound correlation that must be learned. Another interesting property of logographic systems is illustrated by the fact that all of China, the world's most populous country, uses the same written language of logographic symbols, which are comprehensible anywhere. However, there are many spoken languages and dialects (as many as 1800, according to one source) that are mutually incomprehensible, in spite of the fact that they all use the same written system.

Although the written form of English and other European languages is alphabetic, logographic symbols are not totally outside the realm of our experience. For example, symbols like $+$, $-$, $<$, $>$, $=$, %, &, *, and ™, are logographic symbols and translate directly to meaning, even though in their spoken version, $+$ (for example) might be "plus" in one "dialect," "and" in another, and "added to" in a third.

A syllabic writing system, of which Japanese is the most important example, uses one symbol to stand for a syllable. Although Japanese also uses many logographs borrowed from Chinese and also sometimes transliterations into the Latin alphabet, we shall not consider these borrowed systems further. The Japanese syllabic writing system has about 100 consonant-vowel syllables, which are combined into words.

Alphabetic systems, of which the Latin, Cyrillic, Greek, Arabic, Hebrew, and most Indian scripts are examples, have roughly one symbol per sound, although there are many systematic and idiosyncratic exceptions to this rule, such as the many ways of spelling the sound /e/ in English or final consonants not being pronounced in French. An alphabetic symbol has no meaning on its own and is useful only for the way it can combine with other symbols to form words. There have been 200 to 300 alphabets in the world, about half of them in India. The widely used "Latin" alphabet that we use was originally an adaptation of Greek, which evolved out of ancient Phoenician writing.

There are some significant variations in alphabetic systems. For example, biblical Hebrew represented only the consonants in symbols; vowels were interpreted in as one read. Modern Hebrew, and also Arabic to a large extent, indicates vowels in writing, but usually only as marks above or below the consonants.

Although writing has been around for thousands of years, widespread literacy has not, and for most of human history reading and writing have been the province of the very few. Early Greek and Latin manuscripts were written without spaces between the words; around the eleventh century this innovation developed in Latin manuscripts. The modern book has its origins in the wooden wax-coated tablets of ancient Greece and Rome. Although paper was known to the ancient Chinese, it was only introduced into Europe by the Arabs in the eighth century and was little used before the twelfth or thirteenth century. With the development of printing in the Renaissance, forms of writing tended to become more standardized, with the most convenient forms gaining ascendancy and acceptance and other forms falling from use. Since that time, spelling has become more standardized and the rate of change in language has decreased. With this background in mind, let us turn the psychological processes involved in reading and writing.

Eye Movements in Reading

Studies of eye movements have shown that when people read, their eyes move in short jumps and hops, called *saccades*. Most people have a nearly constant rate of saccadic movement, about 3 to 4 movements per second. What differentiates the good from the poor reader or the scanner from the studier is how much information is contained in each saccade. There is occasional backward eye movement, though most of it is forward.

Essential Prereading Skills

Before a child can begin to read, he or she must have certain cognitive abilities that adults would take for granted. For example, children have to be able to perceive speech and begin to understand the idea of segmentation in speech and have some rudimentary understanding that there is a correspondence between that string of spoken sounds and the written symbols on the page.

Graphic discrimination is also important. Many preschoolers start scribbling at age two or earlier. They soon progress to drawing, which does not necessarily closely resemble what it purports to represent, but to the child it does represent something. Children aged three to five frequently start copying letters and often do so spontaneously if verbal models are available in the parents. Children must also be able to discriminate writing from pictures before they can begin to read. Even most three-year-olds are able to distinguish writing from nonwriting in sorting tasks (Lavine, 1972). This occurred for children both in Ithaca, New York, and rural Yucatan in Mexico. Written language has several characteristics that pictorial stimuli do not. For one, language is linear, usually left-to-right but occasionally vertical. Further, the units are nonrepetitive and not too systematic in appearance; in fact, if most adults could see (45) or (46), they would quite likely describe them as something other than writing, simply because the repetitiveness is too great to be considered language.

(45)   OOOOOOOOOOOOOOOOOOOOOOOOOOOOOOOOOOOOOOO
(46)   OXOXOXOXOXOXOXOXOXOXOXOXOXOXOXOXOXOXOXOX

Children also learn that words have different numbers of letters, not always five, or two, or whatever. Older preschoolers may start to identify and discriminate certain features of letters that are critical features differentiating similar letters.

Graphic discrimination is good even in preliterate kindergarteners.

For example, given a matching task like *G-CQDGO* or *b-hdbfk*, kindergar-teners can correctly identify with about 80 percent to 90 percent accuracy which of the five letters is identical with the first (Calfee, Chapman, & Venezky, 1972). Most of the errors youngsters do make are mirror-image transforms (mistaking *d* for *b*, for example). Accuracy with a *bigram* matching task (CQ-OQ OC QC CQ CO) drops to about 40 percent for the same group, with most errors being mirror-image transforms (QC for CQ).

When children actually do begin to learn to read, there is some con-troversy today about how to teach members of various minorities. See Box 7–6.

Perception in Reading

Like so much other information processing, reading is a constructive process, not a simple mechanical transmission of written symbols to the mind. As we read, we process information from beyond the immediate fo-cus of our eyes. There is even a measure of how far the eye is ahead of the mouth in oral reading; this is called the *eye-voice span*. Better readers have a longer eye-voice span, and all readers have a longer eye-voice span for easier, as compared to more difficult, prose.

We know from the speed that we read that we could not possibly be processing each individual letter. We know that some letters, and some fea-tures of letters, are more important than others. Kolers (1972) has done a series of so-called *mutilated word* studies where prose is degraded in various ways and given to subjects to read. Such studies have shown the consonants are more important than vowels, that is, it is easier to construct the missing vowels than missing consonants. Similarly, letters extending above or below the line tend to carry more information than those doing neither. Further,

BOX 7–6   *BILINGUAL AND BIDIALECTAL EDUCATION*

A major controversy in education is the question of whether it is desirable to teach minority children to read in their own dialect or language or in the pre-vailing language and dialect of the society, that is, the so-called "standard" language. This is a complex issue with some strong proponents, especially among minorities, on both sides of the issue. In the U. S. the debate usually centers on Black English dialect or Spanish for the Hispanic population. On the one hand, members of these communities argue that teaching in the ma-jority tongue puts the minority child at a disadvantage, because he or she is not as familiar with that type of speech, and, more seriously, that the very process denies the worth of their own dialect or language, thus relegating it and its speakers to an "inferior" status. On the opposite side, equally vocal spokespersons of the same minority groups argue that to teach the children in anything other than the "standard" language is to deny them forever the tools to "get ahead" in that society, which, for better or worse, will continue to use the majority tongue and require it from those who aspire to rise to higher socioeconomic wrungs of the social ladder. The debate continues.

the top halves of letters seem to be more important than the bottom halves, as evidenced from the relative difficulty of reading a text degraded by removing either the top or bottom half of the letters. Eye-fixation studies reveal that eye fixations generally fall to the left of the center of words, suggesting that we are more likely to perceive the first parts of words and construct the last part than the reverse, at least in English.

There is much debate today over the exact relationship between listening and reading. Foss and Hakes (1978) identify three hypotheses that help to clarify this relationship. The *subvocalization* hypothesis argues that, as we read, we are converting the written symbols to subvocal speech. There is limited evidence for such a process sometimes in some people, in that there are occasional movements in the larynx or even the lips that accompany silent reading. In cases where this occurs, evidence suggests that suppressing such activity interferes with comprehension.

However, there is ample evidence that subvocalization does not regularly or necessarily occur, even though it has been observed on occasion. We can read much faster than we could possibly be subvocalizing everything, with comprehension occurring much more rapidly than can the motor response of vocalizing.

In sharp contrast to subvocalization is the *direct access* hypothesis, which says that we go directly from the written symbols to some sort of mental dictionary, with no intermediate step of using a phonological representation. While this is the process that probably occurs regularly in reading logographic languages, as well as logographic symbols (such as $, + , or =), direct access is not a very efficient method for alphabetic languages; each word would have to be a separate logogram and there would be no perceptual way to use the spelling-sound correspondence that exists in such languages. Individuals use the direct-access process in varying degrees. For example, adults who first learned to read using the "whole-word," as opposed to the phonics, method are more likely to use direct access when reading. Thus, they do fine on identifying familiar words, but they have a more difficult time than the phonics people in reading new words, because they have fewer skills for "sounding them out."

The third hypothesis, *phonological recoding*, argues that written symbols are converted to some sort of underlying sound representation, but not so completely as in subvocalization. Although phonological recoding is probably not absolutely essential, there is ample evidence that it frequently occurs in reading alphabetical writing.

When people proofread, it is more difficult to catch "silent" letters that are incorrect or omitted than it is to catch letters that do represent some sound (Corcoran, 1967; Gough & Cosky, 1977). Similarly, if an incorrect letter would make a sound identical to what the correct letter would make, it is more difficult to catch in proofreading. For example, if someone had intended to write "WORK," it is easiest to catch the error "WXRK," which is unpronounceable in English, hardest to catch "WERK," which is pronounced identically to the correct version, and of intermediate difficulty to catch "WARK," which is pronounceable, but with a different pronunciation from that of the correct version. If direct access occurred with no involvement of the phonological representation, such differences should not occur. Incidentally, the studies obtaining these differences have controlled for physical similarity of the letters and thus have been able to rule that out as the critical factor.

The reading process has been studied extensively in psychology using the tachistoscope (or t-scope), a machine that can present visual stimuli at very fast durations, even a small fraction of a second. Several t-scope studies have shown the importance of phonological recoding in reading. For example, on exposures of 30 to 250 milliseconds, pronounceable nonwords (KIV) can be perceived on shorter duration than nonpronounceable nonwords (QKU). While this is perhaps not too surprising, this difference occurs even when the unpronounceable nonword is highly meaningful and the pronounceable nonword is not; for example, BIM can be perceived faster than IBM (Gibson, Bishop, Schiff, & Smith, 1964). This argues strongly for the importance of phonological recoding as primary over semantic interpretation, at least at this early perceptual stage.

Another type of evidence for phonological recoding comes from reaction-time studies of classification tasks. For instance, in classifying strings of letters as words or nonwords, the reaction time measured can be a useful yardstick. For certain nonwords, the unpronounceable "SAGM" can be detected as a nonword faster than the pronounceable "MELP," which can in turn be detected faster than "BRANE," which is also pronounceable but, unlike "MELP," has the sound identical to an English word (Rubenstein, Lewis, & Rubenstein, 1971). In classifying pairs of words as words or nonwords, rhyming sets like "set-wet," "handle-candle," and "bribe-tribe" are classified as words faster than sets like "few-sew," "lemon-demon," or "mint-pint," (Meyer, Schvaneveldt, & Ruddy, 1974). Since the direct-access hypothesis would predict no such difference, this again suggests that phonological recoding occurs.

There is also ample evidence for the use of higher-order units in reading. For example, letters can actually be perceived faster in the context of a word than they can by themselves (Reicher, 1969; Wheeler, 1970). For example, if a t-scope flashes one of the following six arrays (47),

(47) a   N
      b   R
      c   BANK
      d   BARK
      e   ZANK
      f   ZARK

followed by a marker where the N or R had been, subjects can correctly report the letter after shorter t-scope exposures if the letter occurred in the context of a word (c-d) or pronounceable nonword (d-f) than if it had occurred by itself (a–b). While this may seem counterintuitive, since the word array contains four times as much stimulus information as the single-letter array, apparently we do not process each letter as a separate unit. There is something more "cognitively economical" about the pronounceable string in contrast to the individual letter.

In conclusion, then, reading may be viewed as a continual set of processes of constructing and testing hypotheses at several difference levels: letter identification, sentence construction, and overall gist. As we have seen in every facet of information processing, top-down and bottom-up processes interact as we actively construct interpretations. Exactly what processes we use will also depend on the purpose and situation in any given instance (see Box 7–7). Reading aloud is very different from spontaneous speech (see Box 7–8).

BOX 7–7   *CONTROL OF READING RATE*

One important way that we control our reading habits is controlling the speed and strategies used in our reading (Anderson, 1980). Surprisingly, many college students and people in general do not do this and thus they try to read novels, textbooks, newspapers, and scientific articles in exactly the same way. Predictably, this often leads to frustration. Sometimes scanning or skimming is sufficient. Scanning (about 10,000 words per minute) is adequate when you need to search for a specific piece of information in a larger text, and that is all you care about; for example, scanning an article to see if there is any mention of Pavlov. There is no need to retain or even process any semantic information except the word "Pavlov." Skimming (about 800 to 1500 words per minute) is used to extract the basic gist of a text without catching details. This would not be an adequate method of reading your psychology text initially, but it might be a useful technique for the very final review before an exam. Many "speed-reading" courses really focus on teaching scanning and skimming. Insofar as you could learn to use these skills in ways you have not before, they might be useful. However, to believe you could learn to do all your reading at 10,000 (or even 1000) words per minute and retain everything is naive.

Control of reading rate and purpose is very helpful in professional reading. For instance, many journal articles in my field come across my desk, far more than I have time to read even superficially. However, I can scan or skim them (or parts of them), depending on my purpose, and file them away (literally and figuratively) for future reference. If I am interested in seeing if an article deals with pragmatic inferences, I could scan it for the appearance of that term. If I am interested in the procedural details of the study, because I am designing a similar one, I might read part of the method section very carefully and slowly, but scan or skim the rest of the article. Such strategies are necessary skills for a teacher or researcher to gain in order to keep on top of one's field professionally.

BOX 7–8   *WHY LECTURERS WHO READ ARE BORING*

Why is it always so boring to listen to someone read something aloud, even if it is very well read, where it is much more interesting to hear someone speak spontaneously, even if that speech is more halting and imperfect? Why does it bother us if actors in a play sound like they are reading their lines, rather than speaking them spontaneously? How can we tell the difference, anyway?

There are several ways that oral reading and spontaneous speech systematically differ. Oral reading is generally slower than speech, with speed increasing with the degree of informality. Oral reading contains very few false starts or "filled pauses" (such place-holding interjections as *uh, well,* and *um*), while spontaneous speech contains many of both, especially in more informal speech. On the other hand, breathing pauses (places where we stop to breathe) occur almost entirely at major syntactic constituent boundaries in oral reading, but in many different places in spontaneous speech. If someone's breathing pauses are entirely at major syntactic boundaries, that is a strong clue that the person is reading directly from a text, where the constituents are already formed and available to allow for breathing in between.

Oral reading includes many words from one's "passive vocabulary," that is, words that we comprehend but do not ourselves use in speech. Each of us has a large passive vocabulary that we do not use in speaking, even in formal situations.

Oral reading uses relatively flat intonation, while spontaneous speaking shows more variation in pitch and stress, the greater variety being one reason it is more interesting to listen to than oral reading. Enunciation is usually better in oral reading, however; often it is so good that it sounds unnatural.

If you need something to do during the next boring oral presentation you must listen to, try analyzing the language for the characteristics just described.

The Process of Writing

Let us now turn to the other major process involving written language, namely, its production. Writing is a critical problem in cognitive psychology, but it has been surprisingly ignored until very recently. Although its oral analogue—speech production—has also been somewhat neglected, writing has been even more so. There is, happily, some evidence that this omission is being corrected (see Frederiksen & Dominic, 1981; Gregg & Steinberg, 1980; Martlew, 1983).

Writing as a psychological process may be considered to have three stages: prewriting, drafting, and editing.

Prewriting   The prewriting stage (also called rehearsing, composing, or planning) deals with the generation, organization, and evaluation of ideas before any text is actually put on paper. This is sometimes conceptualized as the "internal dialogue" in the mind of the writer.

Prewriting may involve conscious problem-solving procedures with oneself or others (brainstorming, outlining, notetaking). It may be that exercises to improve one's observational and perceptual skills may be useful in prewriting. People's perception of and memory for very common objects that are seen frequently, but may not be directly attended to often (for example, the design on a coin), is surprisingly poor (Nickerson & Adams, 1979). A parallel recommendation is developed in detail by Edwards (1979) in regard to learning to draw.

During the prewriting stage it is necessary always to keep in mind the audience for whom one is writing. Just as we talk very differently to different people on different occasions, so we should write differently for a research paper and a personal letter. Not surprisingly, the prewriting stage is often sadly neglected in the teaching of writing. Many times students are expected to begin immediately to produce prose out of nothing on the blank paper in front of them, with those who cannot easily do so being made to feel inadequate.

Drafting   The second stage of the writing process is drafting, or composition. This involves the actual generation of text, usually in prefinal draft form. The ideas generated and organized in the prewriting stage are here clothed in a surface structure of words and sentences. There are great individual differences in specific strategies for producing this prose. Sometimes it may even be produced initially in parallel with prewriting activities. For example, as I write the prose in this book, I am initially generating ideas while I write the first draft of these sentences into my word processor. The crucial point is not so much whether or not one does prewriting and drafting serially or in parallel, but rather that both are done in some satisfactory way.

Revising   The third stage of writing is the revising, or editing, stage. This is where preliminary drafts are read through and revised to be suitable for the final version of the writing. Several aspects of writing must be monitored during this stage (Anderson, 1980). First of all, does it make sense? Are the ideas expressed good ones, containing truth and no contradictions? Is the writing well organized? In revising, one checks for overall coherence, including whether one's organization decided on in the drafting stage is in fact effective. Thirdly, one examines the draft for so-called connective tissue, that is, appropriate transitions between sections, statements of relationships, overview and summary statements, and headings. This aspect of composition is one of the most sorely neglected in college students' writing, and it is something that could be easily remedied, or at least vastly improved, with a more careful editing job.

Finally, the prose is edited and revised for elements of style, grammar, spelling, and usage. Verbose prose is condensed, inappropriate vocabulary is changed, and spelling and punctuation are corrected. Unfortunately, many students progress through our entire educational system thinking that writing is largely this most superficial aspect of the editing stage. Thus, they are often paralyzed from producing ideas because they are not sure how to spell or use commas. Such matters, while not unimportant, may be best handled at a much later stage than generation of ideas. Thinking you cannot write because you can't spell well is something like assuming you cannot build a house because you don't know how to lay carpet. There's a lot that can be done before the carpet is laid, just as there's much that can be done in writing before the final spelling is checked. Just as carpet-laying could be subcontracted, so can an editor (often in the form of a friend or colleague) check your writing for mechanical and technical correctness.

Types of Writing

Britton and his colleagues (Britton, Burgess, Martin, Macleod, & Rosen, 1975) have argued that there are three general categories of writing, although they are not mutually exclusive categories. **Transactional** writing is writing to accomplish something; to inform, persuade, or instruct someone. This can be subdivided into two major subtypes of *informative* and *conative*, basically differentiated by whether there is a behavioral (for example, imperative to change behavior or persuasion to change attitude) change intended or merely an addition to the reader's memory (informative).

The second category, **expressive** writing, has as its major purpose to express the consciousness of the writer. Expressive writing is typically less structured than transactional writing and may be most clearly exemplified by the personal journal where thoughts are expressed for the purpose of expressing them, the writer, perhaps, never even intending or desiring anyone else to read them.

BOX 7–9   *USING JOURNAL WRITING TO TEACH PSYCHOLOGY*

One of the authors (RJH) has used journal writing as a means of teaching psychology. In his introductory psychology classes, students are assigned to keep a personal journal with a minimum of one entry per week, to be turned in and responded to, but not graded. Students are encouraged to apply course concepts to their own lives and experience, but are allowed to write anything they want. Either the instructor or the teaching assistant in charge of the student's weekly recitation section reads and responds in the journals, emphasizing affirming, reassuring, and nonjudgmental responses, as well as answering specific content questions asked. Students responded quite favorably to this experience and felt it had not only helped them understand themselves and the course material better, but also allowed them some opportunity for self-expression. Journals of different sorts have also been successfully applied to upper-level psychology classes. The cognitive processing that is required during writing ensures both a deeper processing of class information and more connections of the new information with knowledge already in long-term memory. Both will help improve memory for the class information. See Harris (1982) for further details.

The third type of writing is **poetic,** which is writing for its own sake, or more specifically, for the aesthetic quality of the language itself. This could include much poetry, but also song lyrics, puns, quips, and other verbal humor. Clearly, a given piece of writing could be more than one of the three types Britton and his colleagues describe, but the taxonomy is a useful one to highlight the major emphasis. One interesting application of this taxonomy was the finding from content-analysis studies of writing assigned in elementary and secondary schools, that the bulk (80 percent to 95 percent) of school writing was transactional, with very little being expressive or poetic. Writing can be used to teach in all areas of the curriculum at all levels of education. Box 7–9 explores its use in teaching psychology.

Now that we have examined language in some detail, it is time to return to information processing and memory and examine the processes of comprehension.

SUGGESTED READINGS

There are several good textbooks on psycholinguistics available for the reader wishing to pursue topics of this chapter in more detail. Glucksberg and Danks' *Experimental Psycholinguistics* (1975), and Kess' *Psycholinguistics: Introductory Perspectives* (1976) are fairly brief but good introductory surveys of the area, with the former being more research oriented and the latter more sociocultural. More thorough texts on psycholinguistics, with emphasis on research findings, are Clark and Clark's *Psychology and Language* (1977), and Foss and Hakes' *Psycholinguistics* (1978). Somewhat more recent, though treating the authors' dual-coding theory far too heavily, is Paivio and Begg's *Psychology of Language* (1981).

The reader interested in further detail on Chomsky's transformational grammar could turn to Chomsky's original writings, though these are very difficult. Far easier is John Lyons' paperback *Noam Chomsky* (1970), which, the title notwithstanding, is a highly readable explanation of Chomsky's theory, not a biography.

The best comprehensive text on the psychology of reading is *The Psychology of Reading* by Gibson and Levin (1975). Although there is as yet relatively little on the psychology of writing, the papers in the volumes edited by Whiteman (1981), Gregg and Steinberg (1980), and Frederiksen and Dominic (1981) offer the best insight into current thinking on writing.

For an extraordinarily interesting yet comprehensive review of research on bilingualism, see François Grosjean's *Life with Two Languages* (1982).

CHAPTER EIGHT
COMPREHENSION

A common way of thinking about comprehension has been to view the mind as some sort of organic tape recorder, ready to make perfect, or nearly perfect, copies of everything it sees and hears. Something is thought to be understood if that perfect copy is made and is considered to have been not understood, or perhaps forgotten, if no such copy exists. *Meaning* is considered to be an inherent property of the stimulus. Just as a word has letters, or an object has color, so does each word or object contain meaning. Thus, meaning has been most often considered a property of the stimulus.

This chapter will take a somewhat different and more dynamic approach to comprehension, considering meaning not as a property of the stimulus, but rather as an emergent property of the interaction of the stimulus and the mind of the comprehender. Meaning only arises as someone constructs an interpretation of some stimulus, and the meaning that one individual constructs will be somewhat different from what every other person comprehends from that same stimulus. Such a perspective may be termed *interactionist,* in that it stresses the dynamic interaction of the active mind of the comprehender and the external stimulus. In this sense it is different both from a behaviorist position, which stresses the environment, and a nativist position, which claims that the mind develops naturally independent of external stimuli.

This chapter first examines the comprehension of connected discourse, drawing on our study of language in Chapter 7. We then proceed to looking at schema theory, one of the "hottest" new approaches to comprehension. It offers the opportunity to relate language information processing to nonlinguistic processing. Next we will examine the theory and applications of inference-drawing in comprehension. Finally, we shall explore one application in detail, that of misleading advertising, as a practical problem where information-processing psychology, especially themes discussed in this chapter, can make a significant impact.

THE ROLE OF THEME

In the last chapter we examined the four components of language; now it is time to put these components together and examine connected discourse. Normal comprehension involves parallel processing of linguistic information on the phonological, semantic, syntactic, and pragmatic levels. As well as being guided by the data-driven processes of the language itself, comprehension is also simultaneously guided by the conceptually driven processes of forming hypotheses based on our expectations, prior knowledge, and contextual clues predicting what the speaker (or writer) will be saying.

The Construction of Memory Representations

Just as we can not discuss memory totally apart from comprehension, it is impossible to discuss comprehension too long without considering memory. What we remember from prose is largely determined by how we understood it to begin with.

Many studies reveal that information in several separate but thematically related sentences is integrated into a single memory representation during the comprehension process. Later it is often difficult to remember the exact input sentences in subsequent memory tasks (see Bransford & Franks, 1971). For example you may hear (1), but remember that you heard (2). The propositional representation in memory would be identical

(1)   a.   The house was in the valley.
      b.   The house was little.
      c.   The valley was green.
      d.   The house burned down.
(2)   The little house in the green valley burned down.

whether one had heard (1) or (2). Most research has indicated that, after the meaning is comprehended, the surface structure and exact words are forgotten. There are, however, some cases where verbatim memory can be substantial (Alba & Hasher, 1983; Keenan et al., 1977; Kintsch & Bates, 1977), especially in situations outside the laboratory.

Theme as an Organizing Top-down Force

One of the most important conceptually driven factors in comprehension is the overall **theme** of the material. A comprehender's expectation of what the passage is about can serve as a guiding force in understanding the material.

The overall theme of a passage can markedly affect most every aspect of comprehension. It is very difficult to understand or remember much from prose such as (3) or (4), which may at first appear to have no theme (Bransford & Johnson, 1972; Dooling & Mullet, 1973; Johnson, Doll, Bransford, & Lapinski, 1974).

> (3) The haystack was important because the cloth ripped.
> (4) With hocked gems financing him, our hero bravely defied all scornful laughter that tried to prevent his scheme. "Your eyes deceive," he had said, "an egg, not a table, typifies this unexplored planet." Now three sturdy sisters sought proof, forging along through calm vastness, yet more often over turbulent peaks and valleys. Days become weeks as many doubters spread fearful rumors about the edge. At last from nowhere welcome winged creatures appeared signifying momentous success.
>
> (Dooling & Lachman, 1971, p. 217)

This effect was also demonstrated pictorially with cartoons (Bower, Karlin, & Dueck, 1975; Bransford & McCarrell, 1974). Subjects who knew that (3) was about a parachute jump and (4) about Christopher Columbus discovering America understood the passages much better and remembered more. Supporting information is remembered better if it is relevant to the overall theme (Bransford & Johnson, 1973; Kozminsky, 1977) or to prior world knowledge (Morris, Stein, & Bransford, 1979); new, but thematically consistent, material is often falsely recognized as having been previously presented (Kennedy, 1973; Sulin & Dooling, 1974).

Prior Knowledge and Point of View

The comprehension of something is dependent on one's *prior knowledge* of the general semantic domain which is the topic of the prose. For example, subjects with a high degree of knowledge of baseball remembered more than "low-knowledge" subjects from a summary of a baseball inning. These "high-knowledge" subjects were better able to integrate the new information with a goal structure in their stored knowledge of the game of baseball (Chiesi, Spilich, & Voss, 1979; Spilich, Vesonder, Chiesi, & Voss, 1979). Teachers would do well to remember that some students have trouble comprehending and remembering assigned reading because they have very little knowledge structure already in memory with which to relate it.

The amount of prior knowledge available can also determine how much attention or cognitive capacity must be allocated to the comprehension process (Britton & Tesser, 1982). For example, a particular array of chess pieces will require an expert to allocate more cognitive capacity to the task of deciding the next move than a novice would have to use, because of the much greater amount of knowledge possessed by the expert and activated during the comprehension and decision process.

As another example, a speaker of one language will have different knowledge from a speaker of another language and thus will comprehend a slightly, or perhaps substantially, different meaning from even the most careful and precise translation (Carrell, 1983).

Prior knowledge can also come in the form of a *point of view*, which then helps organize information thematically as it is comprehended. As an example, Pichert and Anderson (1977) and Anderson and Pichert (1978) gave subjects a story to read about two boys playing in a house. One group was told to read the story from the point of view of a burglar considering robbing the place; these subjects tended to remember details about valuable objects, isolation from surrounding houses, and other such details of relevance to a potential burglar. The other group of subjects read the story from the point of view of a real estate agent; these subjects remembered details such as size and number of rooms, condition of the house, and quality of the yard.

In discussing voters' reactions to campaign advertising of candidates George McGovern and Richard Nixon in the 1972 American Presidential election, Patterson and McClure (1976) note strikingly different reactions to the same political advertisement, depending on one's political point of view (5). Depending on the voter's political outlook, a very different

(5) a. McGovern had his coat off and his tie was hanging down. It was so re-laxed, and he seemed to be really concerned with those workers. (McGovern supporter)

  b. McGovern is trying hard to look like one of the boys. You know, roll up the shirt sleeves and loosen the tie. It's just too much for me to take. (Nixon supporter)

meaning of the same ad was constructed by the two voters in response to the same McGovern TV spot.

SCHEMA THEORY

An important recent development in cognitive psychology has been the growth of **schema theory** (Alba & Hasher, 1983; Brewer & Nakamura, 1984; Casson, 1983; Rumelhart, 1980). A fundamental assumption of such an approach is that spoken or written text does not in itself carry meaning; rather, it provides directions for listeners or readers on how to use their own stored knowledge to retrieve and construct the meaning (Adams & Collins, 1979). The goal of schema theory is thus to specify the interface between the comprehender and the text. This involves both data-driven and conceptually-driven processes, with knowledge and input interacting at all levels in the process of reading or listening: word and letter level, syntactic, semantic, and interpretive levels. The original notion of a schema dates back to the cognitive psychologist Sir Frederick Bartlett (1932), the physiologist Sir Henry Head (1920), and more indirectly back to the philosopher Immanuel Kant (1781), who argued that concepts only had meaning insofar as they could relate to knowledge the individual already possessed.

What Is a Schema?

A *schema* (plural: schemata) is a very subjective and ill-defined concept, but a central one in contemporary cognitive psychology. Somewhat informally, it may be defined as "a unit of organized knowledge about events, situations, or objects" (Moates & Schumacher, 1980, p. 33) or, more technically, "a data structure for representing generic concepts in memory" (Rumelhart, 1980, p. 34). As such, a schema guides both information acceptance and information retrieval; it affects how we process new information and how we retrieve old information from memory. While the very concept of a schema emphasizes top-down processing, it may be activated either in the context of top-down or bottom-up processing. To illustrate, we may activate and retrieve our knowledge schemata about California either in anticipation of meeting a man we know is from San Diego (top-down) or upon hearing someone say "Joe is from San Diego."

Rumelhart (1980), in an excellent theoretical paper on schemata, described them in terms of four metaphors. First, schemata are like *plays*, which are written with characters, actions, settings, and so forth. However, this information is merely a skeleton for the *instantiation* that will occur when that play is actually produced with particular actors by a particular direction on a particular set. Each different production of the same play might be strikingly different, even though the playwright's text would ensure some similarity. The same is true for schemata in each instantiation.

Secondly, schemata are like *theories* in that they guide the construction of an interpretation and become the basis for predictions that are tested and then confirmed or rejected.

Thirdly, schemata are like *procedures*, for example, computer programs; that is, an organization of activities with structural relationships among these activities and other entities. This is especially characteristic of the type of schema called a *script* (discussed below). Finally, a schema is like a *parser*; it breaks down, organizes, and interprets incoming data.

Schemata and Encoding

Although there is a lot of variability about the way that the term schema is used, Alba and Hasher (1983) suggest that most schema theorists would agree with four basic principles of how schemata become involved in the encoding process: selection, abstraction, interpretation, and integration.

Selection   The principle of *selection* refers to the fact that, of all the information in a given event or message, only some of it will beome incorporated into the memory representation that is constructed. Two factors are relevant in determining the selection of information for encoding. One is simply whether or not an appropriate schema already exists in memory. If no relevant schema is available, both comprehension and memory will be very poor (Bransford & Johnson, 1972; Dooling & Mullet, 1973). Further, if some people have more information available than others, such as a rich network of schemata, they will comprehend and remember more than those with less knowledge, as demonstrated in the baseball studies by Voss and his colleagues.

A second reason that the appropriate schema might not be available would be that it may not be activated from long-term memory, even though it may exist there. For example, a particular schema may be activated by external circumstances, as in the Pichert-Anderson studies where subjects were told to read a story from the point of view of either a realtor or a burglar. The phenomenon of encoding specificity may be reinterpreted as ensuring that the same schemata are available at retrieval that occurred at encoding. When the context has set the theme, this allows you to identify some information as more important—highly related to overall theme. Such information will tend to be processed more deeply and remembered better. Information that appears to be irrelevant or easily reconstructible will likely be forgotten. The accuracy of later recall will largely be a function of both how well the initial information was selected and how accurately it was later reconstructed.

There is some controversy in the research literature about whether the schema information must be present at encoding or whether its introduction at retrieval will suffice to direct memory. Generally, effects have been stronger with schematic information presented at encoding, but its presentation at retrieval has sometimes also been helpful (Alba & Hasher, 1983).

Abstraction   The second principle of encoding is *abstraction,* by which details tend to be lost in a reduction of information into main points, with the schema indicating relative importance of different pieces of information. In this process a lot of detail is lost, which is typical of lengthy recall protocols. Still, however, there is some evidence that sometimes specific information is remembered verbatim.

Interpretation   The third principle, *interpretation,* results from the elaboration during or just after encoding. One major characteristic of schemata is that they have slots or variables where specific information is "filled in" when the schema is instantiated, that is, when it is used to accept or retrieve information about a particular instance, such as using our schema about a California lifestyle to infer how Joe, from San Diego, must spend his time. When we make such inferences, we often are necessarily interpreting beyond the information given. The issue of inference-drawing will be discussed in more detail later in this chapter.

Integration   The fourth principle of encoding through schemata is *integration,* by which information is combined into relatively holistic representations. Inferences are drawn to relate previously unrelated information. Even the schemata themselves may be integrated, embedded within each other, thus allowing for a hierarchical structure of schematic information. For example, while we have a schema for "face," that it contains two eyes, a nose and a mouth, we also have subschemata for eyes, noses, and mouths, all subsumed under the most global schema "face." While integration is a principle that operates in everyone, there is some evidence that elderly people integrate information to an even greater degree than younger adults (Woodruff, 1983). This could be reflected in the fact that more senior professors frequently write a lot of theoretical, integrative writing, while their younger colleagues frequently are more active in carrying out specific experiments.

The range of schemata   Clearly, the notion of schema is a very general one, and schemata may be of a great variety. They may be general packets of knowledge about a particular subject area, such as what faces are like, what information is relevant to a realtor, or what the game of baseball is like. It may be a very specific schema, such as what a capital *A* looks like, or very general schemata, such as various literary genres; for instance, what to expect from a mystery story, Western, or television soap opera.

Information may be organized around a motivational schema, that is, a perceived overriding purpose or goal of a character (see Owens, Bower, & Black, 1979). It may even be information about oneself, perhaps akin to the traditional personality concept of self (Rogers, 1981; Greenwald, 1981; Markus, 1980); see Box 8–1 for further discussion of this aspect. Finally, a schema may be information about particular actions or classes of actions. It

BOX 8–1   *SOME IMPLICATIONS OF YOUR PERSONAL SCHEMA*

Perhaps the richest and most complex schema in our memory is our knowledge and memory about ourselves. That schema is referred to as the personal schema or self-schema. It contains all of the information about ourselves, including our values, our motivations, and those things that have happened to us that we consider personal events.

We have noted that schemata guide and direct both the encoding and retrieval of information from our memory. Our personal schema, then, has some very important implications for how we interpret what happens to us and for what we remember about our lives. To give just one example, our personal schema is much more rich and complex than our schema for anyone else. As a schema becomes more rich and complex, it should be easier to encode and retrieve information. Thus, we should remember events that we view as "our events" better than events that we view as "someone else's events"—even when those events are of equal importance to us. In a recent study, Thompson (1983) showed that is exactly what happens. He had some students record events (that were public and not embarrassing) for themselves and events for their roommates for a three-week period. The roommates didn't know these events were being recorded. One month after the recording period, both the recorders and the roommates were tested for their memory of the events. In spite of the fact that the recorders selected the events, wrote the description of the events, and knew they were going to be tested for their memory of those events, the roommates remembered the events recorded for them better than the recorders did, impressive testimony to the effectiveness of the personal schema in facilitating memory.

is on this type of action schema, called a script, that we next focus our attention.

Scripts

Schemata about activities or processes are called **scripts**. They have all the properties of schemata already discussed, but are specifically concerned with actions (Abelson, 1981; Bower, Black, & Turner, 1979; Schank & Abelson, 1977). We have many scripts in our long-term memory for a variety of familiar activities, which may be looked at as complex "action-concepts." A good example is Bower, Black, & Turner's (1979) restaurant script, which contains information about what it's like to go to a restaurant. (see Table 8–1). For example, there are certain roles to be filled (customer, waiter or waitress, cashier), certain "props" (silverware, food, dishes, check, napkins), and certain activities (sitting down, ordering, eating, paying the bill). Not every specific use—instantiation—of this script would provide specific information to fill in all these variables. Still, we would infer that there were dishes, a waiter or waitress, that the customer paid the bill, and so forth, even though we may not have been told specifically that these activities occurred.

The way a script operates can perhaps best be illustrated by examining what happens when the stimulus/input information does not fit the apparently appropriate script very well. One especially interesting example of how a script is applied, especially when the incoming data do not precisely "fit," comes from Bransford (1978, pp. 184). Assuming that you have a script for eating in a restaurant that is roughly similar to the one most Americans have, how might you process the following story you read or hear someone tell you?

> Jim went to the restaurant and asked to be seated in the gallery. He was told that there would be a one-hour wait. Forty minutes later, the applause for his song indicated that he could proceed with the preparation. Twenty guests had ordered his favorite, a cheese soufflé. Jim enjoyed the customers in the main dining area. After two hours, he ordered the specialty of the house— roast pheasant under glass. It was incredible to enjoy such exquisite cuisine and yet still have fifteen dollars. He would surely come back soon.

While all the words make sense in this story, for most people there is a problem. It does not fit the restaurant script that we most naturally retrieve and try to use to process the story. Specifically, it violates information about roles; the customer appears to be entertaining and cooking as well as eating, roles that are generally separate in this script.

Suppose, however, that a new type of restaurant begins and introduces a new restaurant "subscript" into your memory, specifically the following (Bransford, 1978, pp. 186–187):

> Assume that Jim went to a very special type of restaurant. The owner allows people who can cook at least one special meal to compete for the honor of preparing their specialty for other customers who desire it. Those who wish to compete sit in the gallery rather than the main dining room (although a

TABLE 8–1   Theoretical Restaurant Script[a]

Roles:	Customer Waiter/Waitress	Cashier Host/Hostess

Props:			
	Table	Check	Plates
	Menu	Money	Silverware
	Food	Tip	Napkins

Entry Conditions:	Customer has money Customer hungry Restaurant is open
Results:	Restaurant has more money Customer has less money Customer is not hungry

Scene 1:	Entering
	   Customer enters restaurant
	   Customer (or Host/Hostess) decides on table
	   Customer goes to table
	   Customer sits down

Scene 2:	Ordering
	   Customer receives menu
	   Customer looks at menu
	   Customer orders food

Scene 3:	Eating
	   Waiter/Waitress brings food to customer
	   Customer eats food

Scene 4:	Exiting
	   Waiter/Waitress gives check to customer
	   Customer pays cashier
	   Customer leaves tip
	   Customer leaves restautrant

[a]This is a general script. Each scene could be made more specific. This is a script for a general-service, family-type North American restaurant. Script would vary somewhat for fast-food restaurant, nightclub, bar, or for restaurants in other cultures (see Box 8–2).

Source: Adapted from G. H. Bower, J. B., Black, and T. J. Turner. Scripts in memory for text. *Cognitive Psychology*, 1979, *11*, 177–220. Reprinted by permission of Academic Press and the author.

central stage is accessible to both). The competition centers on the competitor's entertaining the crowd, by singing, for example, or dancing or playing an instrument. The approval of the crowd is a prerequisite for allowing the person to announce his or her cooking specialty. The rest of the crowd then has the option of ordering it, and the person receives a certain amount of money for each meal prepared. After doing the cooking and serving the meal to the customers, the person can then order from the regular restaurant menu and pay for it out of the money received for cooking. In general, this arrangement benefits the manager as well as the person. The manager obtains relatively inexpensive entertainment, and the person is usually able to make more than enough to pay for an excellent meal.

Now go back and reread the original story; with this new script it may make more sense!

Schemata and scripts are useful concepts beyond the confines of traditional cognitive psychology. To illustrate, social schemata can be very important in processing information about people in social situations (Taylor & Crocker, 1981), sex-role stereotyping (Bem, 1981), or responses to mass media (Janis, 1980). It has potential in understanding cultural differences (Casson, 1983; Harris & Lee, 1983). See Box 8–2 for further discussion of this application.

The Narrative Schema

One especially important and generalizable example of a schema in Western culture is the **narrative** (story) **schema** identified by Kintsch (1977). The basic unit of the narrative schema is the *episode,* which consists of three parts, the *exposition, complication,* and *resolution.* The exposition introduces the characters and setting. The complication occurs when those characters encounter some problem that presents a barrier that must be overcome. Finally, the resolution is the process of overcoming the complication and wrapping up the story.

One major difference between children's and adults' stories is that children's stories more clearly identify the parts of the narrative schema and follow it more closely, whereas adult stories, while still following the same schema, may require the reader to use more inference processes to make use of the schema. For example, fairy tales may start out, "Once upon a time there was . . . ," a very blatant signal that expository material is to follow. In contrast, an adult story might actually begin talking about the problem (complication) and only gradually complete the exposition later. Whereas an adult can make the appropriate inferences to instantiate the schema, the child will have trouble doing so and thus will not fully comprehend (and probably will quickly lose interest in) the story. On the other hand, a children's story will be uninteresting and unchallenging to an adult, because relatively little cognitive effort is required in comprehension; the surface form of the story fits the narrative schema so perfectly that it becomes too predictable. Beyond literature, the narrative schema has many applications in other domains of our experience; watching television, for example (see Box 8–3).

Episodes may have different sorts of structure beyond a simple exposition-complication-resolution format. For example, the complication of a story may contain an entire episode embedded within the larger episode, much as a subordinate clause might be embedded as the subject of a sentence (*What I want to do is to leave*). Another example might be the resolution containing two additional episodes embedded as the last part of the

BOX 8–2 *CULTURAL KNOWLEDGE AS SCRIPTS*

People frequently speak of having to "learn the culture" when they move to another country, or perhaps even a different part of their own country. This knowledge may be conceptualized as scripts about activities in that culture and how to do them. Many times the scripts will be similar to ones we already have from our own culture, but with a few differences in roles, activities, or conditions. Before proceeding further, read the following paragraph:

Nelson and Sonia sat down at a table on the sidewalk. They were both starving, since it was already almost eleven o'clock. After looking at the menu full of delicious choices, they decided on the lasagna, which they knew to be excellent at that restaurant. It seemed to be an unusually large crowd for such a late hour. Sonia commented that she thought the outside of the building had been repainted since their last meal there some months before. After the waiter had brought the plates, Nelson saw their friends Marcia and Rita a few tables away. He immediately went over and gave the two women a friendly kiss. They had not seen each other for several weeks. As they saw the waiter on his way with their food, Nelson and Sonia returned to their table, just in time to help themselves to some lasagna from the platter. Tasting it, Nelson added some more olive oil and then pronounced it delicious. Sonia thought it had a little too much ham, but she also enjoyed it. The lasagna had been a good choice. Some ragged children came to their table selling roses, but they told them no and turned away. Finally, the waiter chased them away altogether. What a delicious meal, and for a very reasonable cost too. The conversation was also very pleasant. Upon paying the check, Nelson had to break a large bill, but the restaurant changed it easily, and the waiter brought the change to the table. Nelson and Sonia left the restaurant satisfied and happy. They would have to do this more often.

If you live in the United States or Canada, you probably noticed a few details as being strange in this story. However, if you live in Brazil, you probably notice that it perfectly fit your script of what a restaurant is like. When I (RJH) lived and taught in Brazil and regularly ate at restaurants, I had to learn variations on the restaurant script, such as the fact that you must ask for the check before it is brought, food is always brought on serving dishes to be served by the customers onto individual plates, and that you always pay the waiter and never the cashier. Certain activities, like poor children wandering from table to table selling roses or peanuts, occur frequently in Brazil, but would be very unlikely to occur in North America. Such knowledge of "learning the culture" that an immigrant or long-term visitor must acquire as part of becoming "at home" in the new culture may be characterized as scripts or schemata (Harris & Lee, 1983).

BOX 8–3 *THE NARRATIVE SCHEMA ON TELEVISION*

The narrative schema occurs in modern Western society in many manifestations, one of which is in television and other mass entertainment media. Obviously, many television dramas are built around the narrative schema; first there is an introduction of the characters and situation (some of this may be assumed in cases of a series where viewers may be very familiar with the characters already); this is followed by some complication or problem, finally culminating with a resolution of that problem. This is the basic pattern of television dramas and situation comedies, as well as children's stories, fables, and so forth. Sometimes a narrative schema may be intentionally incomplete in order to draw us back to the program. An example would be when a soap opera concludes at the end of the complication, the viewer must tune in the next day to discover the resolution. Our tendency to use the narrative schema is so strong that we are drawn back the next day to complete instantiating the schema.

Beyond television fiction, the narrative schema also applies to a sizeable number of broadcast commercials, as well as print advertising. Frequently the format of ads is one of "problem solving," that is, there is an exposition (Mary is about to do her wash), followed by a complication (her children's clothes are too stained for her detergent to clean), and a resolution (spray on some Scream Spot Remover to get out those tough stains). Such ads have basically the same format as a story where there is a villain who is overcome by a hero, except in this case the villain is usually dirt, stains, inferior taste, or excessive work, and the hero is almost always the product being sold. An advertiser can more easily communicate the message about the product by drawing on this readily available story structure, the narrative schema.

larger episode. In this way the narrative schema offers a sort of syntax for discourse, offering a structural analysis for connected prose, not unlike syntactic analyses of sentences discussed in the last chapter.

INFERENCE-DRAWING IN COMPREHENSION

Basic Processes

One function of a schema is to guide the **drawing of inferences** from the passage. It is a natural process to draw inferences beyond the material actually presented (Clark, 1977; Harris, 1981; Harris & Monaco, 1978). Exactly what inferences will be drawn by a given individual is in part a function of what schemata are initially activated during comprehension. If the reader activates schemata about robberies in response to hearing Pichert and Anderson's story described earlier, very different inferences will be drawn than if the schemata about selling homes are activated. This inferred material has been totally integrated in the constructed memory representations with the information stated directly (Brewer, 1977; Harris, 1974; Harris & Monaco, 1978; Johnson, Bransford, & Solomon, 1973; Loftus & Palmer, 1974; Marschark & Paivio, 1977; Masson, 1979; Spiro, 1980).

The inferences drawn during comprehension fulfill two general functions (Warren, Nicholas, & Trabasso, 1979). On the one hand, they make connections between information in the new material and between this new information and knowledge already in memory. This allows for the integration of new material in memory representations of previously learned information and also helps to provide some organization and structure to the information. Secondly, inferences fill in empty "slots" in the overall structure. To illustrate, if a strongly implied instrument of some action is not explicitly mentioned (*Ed hit the nail*), it may be inferred and added to the memory representation (*Ed used a hammer*), just as if it had appeared explicitly (Corbett & Dosher, 1978; Johnson, Bransford, & Solomon, 1973; McKoon & Ratliff, 1981; Singer, 1979, 1981). Although a natural and integral part of the comprehension process, inferences may be drawn even more frequently in response to inadequately developed prose in an attempt to fill the many open slots to make an otherwise elliptical passage comprehensible (Glenn, 1978). The study of inferences drawn in comprehension has been a major recent emphasis in cognitive psychology.

If there is no value for a given variable in the particular instance at hand, then a *default* inference is used to fill in the most typical value which is contained in the stored schema. For example, if we hear "the hungry python caught the mouse," we use our knowledge of pythons and hunger to make the default inference that the snake subsequently consumed the mouse. Such information was not stated in the stimulus input; rather, it was filled in by using a default inference and inferring that, with no evidence to the contrary, the catching was followed by eating. If we had heard "the hungry little girl caught the mouse," a different schema would have been activated. This "small-child" schema would not contain the default inference that, no information to the contrary, little children who catch mice subsequently eat them. Though default inferences are clearly a part of the information-accepting function of schemata, the comprehended information is then stored in memory and remembered as interpreted, which may be inaccurate. For example, in the example above, if a person were subsequently questioned about the fate of the mouse, he or she would probably remember and respond that the mouse had been eaten. In this sense, memory is a by-product of the interpretation during the comprehension process, as it is the residue left after the schemata have done their job of interpreting the new information or reconstructing old information during an attempt to remember.

In some sense, knowledge that we have in any situation is always incomplete and must be "filled in" using inferences (Harris & Monaco, 1978; Harris, 1981). As Collins, Warnock, Aiello, and Miller (1975, p. 414; see also Gentner & Collins, 1981) have said, "People can often extract what they do not know explicitly from some forms of implicit knowledge by plausible, but uncertain inferences." Even very incomplete (or total lack of) knowledge about something can be the basis for an inference, as in answering a question like (6).

(6)   Is Malawi a major oil-exporting country?

Upon finding information (or lack thereof) about Malawi in one's memory, one may find no information about oil. Thus, one may infer that, since there was nothing about that in memory, then probably Malawi is not a major oil-exporting country, since that information would probably be in one's memory if it were true.

Inferences in Social Cognition

Such inference processes operate more broadly than just in language comprehension settings. For example, we process social information by observing social behaviors and then drawing inferences about those behaviors (Hastie, 1983).

One of the most common types of such social inferences made is that of inferring a causal relationship of events. Owens et al. (1979) conducted a causal attribution study about how the inference of a motive for behavior can guide the inferences drawn from a person's actions. Subjects read a story about Jack or Nancy (same story except for names) doing a series of routine actions such as fixing a meal, attending a class, visiting a doctor. Some subjects (the "context subjects") received initial information describing a context that provided a motive for later behavior (Nancy just discovering she was pregnant). On a free-recall task 30 minutes later, the context subjects recalled more episodes and in better order than subjects not receiving the context. They also made more intrusions representing distortions to fit the inferred motive schema (remembering "usual medical procedures" as "pregnancy tests"). Owens et al. (1979) concluded that the knowledge of a motive helps integrate episodes into a coherent whole in comprehension.

This tendency to infer causes of observed events is the reason that we so frequently interpret correlated events as causally related. You may remember back to your introductory psychology class where you learned about correlational relationships. At that time you were warned not to assume correlated events are causally related. While it may be obvious that the number of deaths in Bangladesh is not causally related to the consumption of ice cream in Chicago (both are *correlated,* presumably due to seasonal weather patterns in the Northern Hemisphere), it may be more difficult to realize that someone's death after taking an experimental drug may not necessarily be due to the drug.

Many cognitively oriented social psychologists are studying impression formation using memory measures and focusing on cognitive inference processes (Cantor & Mischel, 1977; Hamilton, Katz, & Leirer, 1980; Hastie, 1983; Hastie & Kumar, 1979; Lingle, Geva, Ostrom, Leippe, & Baumgardner, 1979; Rothbart, Evans, & Fulero, 1979; Rothbart, Fulero,

Jensen, Howard, & Birrell, 1978; Snyder & Uranowitz, 1978; Woll, Weeks, Fraps, Pendergrass, & Vanderplas, 1980; Woll & Yopp, 1978). The focus of these studies is on how information is combined to form an impression of a person. Though a social process, it is one of information processing as well.

One area where impression formation takes on considerable practical significance is the case where jurors form impressions of witnesses in a courtroom trial. O'Barr (1982; see also Conley, O'Barr, & Lind, 1978; and Erickson, Lind, Johnson, & O'Barr, 1978) has shown that the speech style of a witness may imply much about his or her character, and this, in turn, affects what is encoded into a juror's memory, which later influences a verdict decision. If the speech style implies a relatively "powerless" position, jurors comprehend the witness' message differently than if that witness is inferred to be "powerful," even if the content of the testimony is the same. Similarly, one's accent and its perceived status can influence the outcome of a medical diagnosis (Fielding & Evered, 1980).

In another interesting piece of research, Arkes and Harkness (1980) demonstrated the use of inference in diagnostic procedures. Speech pathology students were given 12 symptons, eight of which were related to Down's syndrome. After the first four related symptoms were presented, subjects were asked to diagnose the hypothetical patient. In a memory test 12 days later, subjects who had diagnosed the case as Down's syndrome were less able to correctly reject new symptoms related to Down's syndrome than were subjects not making that diagnosis. In other words, the diagnosis had acted as a schema for organizing information and directing inference-drawing during comprehension and for directing reconstruction during retrieval.

Thus, inference processes are general cognitive processes that operate naturally in the comprehension of written and spoken language, social interactions, and any situation where information processing occurs. Comprehension involves constructing meanings through the interaction of stimulus information and stored memory representations (knowledge). During these interaction processes, inferences are drawn.

Sometimes what we read does not tie in well to our natural inference-drawing processes; thus, we perceive that text to be different or poorly written. Box 8–4 discusses the case of so-called legalese and what really makes it so difficult psychologically. Issues of language comprehensibility have some far-reaching legal and policy-making effects, as explored in Box 8–5. See Charrow (1982) for further discussion of these issues.

Misleading Advertising

One area where natural inference-drawing processes of language comprehension can lead us to cognitive and even economic difficulty is the realm of advertising, especially ads that may be misleading or deceptive. It is to this problem that we now turn. Each of us sees on the average over 22,000 television commercials per year (Liebert, 1979), plus many more

BOX 8–4   *THE MISCOMPREHENSION OF LEGAL LANGUAGE*

Over the last decade or so we have heard repeated complaints of official language being too complex and incomprehensible to the average person. In 1977, U.S. President Jimmy Carter signed an executive order directing federal government agencies to simplify the language used in official documents. Since that time there have been increasing amounts of legislation directing insurance companies, government bureaus, and lawyers to write documents in everyday language that everyone can understand. There is even an organization, the Document Design Center, that publishes a newsletter and coordinates communication among researchers studying the problem of clarifying language.

The issue is basically one of information processing, that is, how people comprehend or fail to comprehend this information in such legal writing. If people are not understanding it, how could that document be written to better communicate its message?

Before examining what is wrong with legal language in terms of information processing, it is helpful to look at its purpose. Very often the attacks on so-called *legalese* are strident and poorly thought out, reflecting little understanding of the original purpose of such language. The overriding priority of legal language is conveying information, which is a higher value than aesthetic quality, brevity, or anything else. The language must be explicit, both technically and legally precise, leaving minimal room for the reader to draw inferences other than those clearly intended by the writer. In this sense it is markedly different from artistic writing such as literature, poetry, or even humor, where the reader's imagination is heavily drawn upon. Although the defense of legal language is often made in a defensive manner itself, in a sort of siege mentality by lawyers fending off their many critics, there is a valid point to their argument and this must be kept in mind. If the information priority is sacrificed, any additional clarity or aesthetic pleasingness is worthless.

Georgetown University linguist Roger Shuy (pronounced "shy") has studied the language of insurance policies to find out exactly what it is that makes such language difficult to comprehend. His results are not always entirely what we might expect or what many of the "legalese" critics would have us believe (Shuy, 1981; Shuy & Larkin, 1978).

Shuy explored some popular misconceptions about legal language. The first myth is that simplicity is equivalent to clarity. Greatly simplified language may in fact be quite ambiguous and unclear. Consider examples (1) and (2).

(1)   The center fielder dropped the ball. The base runner ran home. A run was scored.

(2)   After the center fielder dropped the ball, the base runner ran home, scoring a run.

While (1) is clearly simpler than (2), it is so skeletal as to be ambiguous. Clearly, such simplification would not be helpful in legal language. Very imprecise vocabulary and overly simplified syntax are often unable to express the subtleties and nuances of meaning and the relationships of ideas that we have come to expect.

The second misconception about legal language is in a sense the opposite from the first. Contrary to what many people believe, total explicitness is not always the most comprehensible; for example, (3).

(3)   John hit the baseball with the baseball bat. After it was hit, the baseball went out to right field in the air. The right fielder caught the baseball in right field. Then the batter who had hit the ball was out because the right fielder had caught it in the right field with his glove.

Shuy makes several recommendations for making legal language more comprehensible. The first is the most general and the most important: Make better use of the natural strategies and expectations that we all bring to the language-comprehension process. To illustrate, we are used to having given information signaled with the definite article "the"; if a contract replaces "the" with "such," this makes the given-new strategy harder to apply.

Like (3), much of the insurance contract language examined by Shuy was extremely repetitive, so much so that it was unnatural and thus did not make maximum use of our natural language-comprehension strategies. For example, legal language uses fewer pronouns relative to nouns than does ordinary language. While presumably this is done in order to reduce any possible ambiguity of figuring out who the pronouns refer to, it violates natural conversational rules and thus leads the reader to wonder why these are being violated.

Other types of constructions overused by legal language are passive verbs and the use of nominalized constructions instead of verbs. For example, contracts often use words like "as of the date of signing by the owner" instead of "when the owner signs it" or "at the time of receipt at the home office" instead of "at the time the home office receives it." The more natural way to say such ideas is often the active voice with an active verb. If such constructions can be employed with no accompanying loss in clarity, then it is desirable to do so.

Although passives and nominals frequently have the problem described above, sometimes they may actually be the clearest way to say something, especially in cases where the actor (agent) is unknown or of little importance; consider (4) and (5). In this case the passive (4) is the most direct and clear way to state the idea.

(4)   The race begins when the starting gun is fired.
(5)   The race begins when someone fires the starting gun.

print and radio ads. The language of advertising raises some interesting information-processing issues (Geis, 1982).

One of these is the question of what constitutes deceptive or misleading advertising. The Federal Trade Commission (FTC), the agency of the federal government charged with overseeing advertising practice, defines "false advertising" in its statutes as advertising that is "misleading in a material respect." While this is not a very complete definition, it does contain

BOX 8–5   *THE IMPORTANCE OF READABILITY*

Educators have developed readability scales that are used to measure the reading level (difficulty) of textbooks and other prose (see Kintsch & Vipond, 1979). Georgia psychologists Blumenfeld, Blumenfeld, and Terrell (1978) applied one of these readability scales to the U. S. federal documents explaining the Medicare program to senior citizens, whose average reading level was slightly less than the average high school sophomore. They found that the documents, which are the simplest in a series, required the equivalent of a college sophomore reading level, the same required to understand the King James Version of the Bible!

In the 1970's a landmark case (*Rogers et al.* vs. *U.S. Steel*) entered the courts. This was a class action suit filed on behalf of 600 black steelworkers of a Homestead, Pennsylvania, steel mill alleging discrimination in hiring. The crucial issue was the wording of a waiver from further compensation; the plaintiffs had signed this waiver as a condition to receiving an earlier settlement from the company. Some critical testimony came from linguists and educators who claimed that the readability level of the waiver document was considerably above the level of the plaintiffs. The issue is important because if it is eventually held on judicial appeal that someone is legally bound to ensure the readability of his or her document for whoever needs to sign it, this forces a new attention to readability.

one interesting and important feature. "In a material respect" means, roughly, in any way which makes a difference. Thus, the door is left open for defining inappropriate advertising by the *effect* it has on the consumer, rather than by the *intent* of the advertiser.

While we will use the term *deceptive,* we will not be referring to the intent of the advertiser. Deceptive advertising so defined places the burden on the plaintiff to prove an intent to defraud on the part of the advertiser, something very difficult to prove legally. In any sense, fraud is a legal, not a psychological, question. Thus, we will use the terms "deceptive" and "misleading" to mean advertising that somehow communicates something to the consumer that is not true. This is a psychological question, since it deals with how the person understands the ad.

Truth and falsity in ads   The FTC term "false advertising" is unfortunate in that truth or falsity is not an appropriate criterion for defining deceptive advertising. An ad may be either true or false in terms of its content and either deceptive or nondeceptive in terms of its effect on the consumer. Two of these possibilities are very straightforward. If an ad is true and nondeceptive, it states something clearly and directly, and that information is true; this is how we might hope most ads are. On the other hand, a false deceptive ad is one that states an out-and-out falsehood, for example, "this product costs $1.49," when in fact it costs $3.98. This type of ad is not very common because it is both blatantly illegal and counterproductive in terms of business good will.

More interesting are the other two alternatives, the true deceptive and the false nondeceptive ads. First of all, the latter: False ads are not necessarily misleading. For example, to claim that "our cookies are made by elves" is literally false, but unlikely to mislead anyone, since few would believe that statement literally. This type of claim is fairly common, especially in animated television commercials ("a white tornado in every can"). Another type of false nondeceptive ad would be some of the so-called mock-ups—photographic displays for print or television ads. Because of practicalities of studio photography, certain conventions are often in some such ads (see Box 8–6).

Content in an ad may be either *factual* or *evaluative* (Holbrook, 1978; Shimp, 1979, 1983). Factual content is tangible, objective, and easily verifiable or falsifiable, often dealing with physical attributes of the product or quantitative dimensions like price. Evaluative content, on the other hand, is much more ambiguous since it involves subjective statements and judgments, claims of nonverifiable psychological benefits, and generally evaluative statements about how wonderful the product is. That latter type of statement is called "puffery" and has been roundly attacked by Ivan Preston (1975; 1977; Rotfeld & Preston, 1981) as being misleading, in spite of being difficult to prove unequivocally false. Puffery and similar types of claims are frequent in the fourth category of ad—the true misleading (deceptive) message.

BOX 8–6   *ADVERTISING MOCK-UPS: FALSE—YES, DECEPTIVE—MAYBE*

That cool and sweet ice cream on television might really be mashed potatoes (because ice cream melts too fast under hot studio lights), or that foaming head on that nice cold beer in the magazine might in fact be shampoo (because suds last longer for photographers than beer heads). Sometimes such acceptable conventions may border on the deceptive. For example, there was a case several years ago where a soup company was censured for putting marbles in the bottom of the soup bowl during photography (Preston, 1975). While the company argued that this was necessary to buoy up the solid ingredients and keep them all from sinking unseen to the bottom of the bowl while the photographers readied their cameras and lights, the courts ruled that this constituted a misleading implication that the soup contained more solid ingredients than it in fact did. In another famous case, a shaving cream manufacturer used grains of sand on Plexiglas for a mock-up purporting to be a razor shaving sandpaper with its product. While the razor in fact would shave fine sandpaper, fine sandpaper looks like flat paper when photographed. However, if coarse sandpaper was used, the razor wouldn't shave it; hence, the sand grains on Plexiglas solution. Do you consider such a mock-up deceptive?

True-but-misleading ads   The fourth type of advertising claim is in many ways the most potentially damaging of all. This is the statement that is misleading without really being false, because it is either an evaluative statement or a factual statement that implies something beyond itself. There are several types of language constructions which, though true themselves, may imply something else that is not true. (Harris, Dubitsky, & Bruno, 1983; Schrank, 1977).

First are claims that contain a hedge word or phrase that seriously weakens the force of a claim; see examples (6) through (10).

(6) Lavium Pills *may help* relieve tension (then again, they may not).

(7) Spring Fluoride *fights* cavities (but it may fight and lose).

(8) This detergent leaves dishes *virtually* spotless (whatever "virtually" means).

(9) The shampoo *helps control* dandruff *symptoms with regular use.* (What is regular use? Does controlling the symptoms mean controlling the condition? Is helping to control sufficient to control?)

(10) *Nobody can promise you a good return on* your investment, but try us and someday you too *may* be a millionaire (or you may not, and this is no promise anyway).

In all of these cases there is a word or phrase that severely qualifies the basic claim that is made. As such, the statement would be difficult, if not impossible, to prove false. However, if the hedge is not totally understood or remembered, the hearer might receive a much more positive idea of the product.

A second type of true but potentially deceptive claim is the *deleted comparative.* Whenever an adjective or adverb is modified by "more" or an "-er" suffix, it involves a comparison with something else. What this basis for comparison is may or may not be stated, and if it is not, it may or may not be obvious to the inferring reader or listener. Sometimes in ads the basis of the comparison is not stated, and the strength of the claim would vary considerably depending on what that claim was. For example, consider (11).

(11) Snarfo makes you healthier.

If there is anything at all (cyanide capsules?) that is worse to take than Snarfo, then (11) is not false. However, if the consumer infers that Snarfo is being compared to its competitors in the marketplace, the claim is a considerably different one.

A few years ago there was a case where an auto manufacturer claimed that its car was "700 percent quieter." When the FTC asked the manufacturer to produce the research evidence to back up its claim, it produced a study showing that the car was 700 percent quieter on the inside of the car than on the outside! Was that the basis of comparison that you inferred when you first read the claim? If you hear that a car "goes farther on a tank of gas," do you infer that it has better mileage than its competitors (which ones?) or that it has a larger gas tank?

A third category of true but potentially misleading claims are the *jux-taposed imperatives:* (12) and (13). In these cases two imperatives are stated successively. Though no causal relationship of the two is stated, as we have already seen above, it is very easy to infer such a relationship.

(12) Get a beautiful tan this summer. Use Bronzoline.

(13) Help your son get better grades. Buy him an Addo calculator.

Advertising copy frequently makes use of juxtaposed imperatives to imply a causal relationship, taking advantage of this natural information-processing tendency.

Another way to imply something beyond what is stated is to ask a negative question; for example, (14). Inserting the word "not" into a yes-no question (15) in English changes the question by implying that the questioner believes the answer to be "yes," thus implying that to the respondent. Although a lawyer in most cases would not be allowed to ask (16) in the courtroom, advertisers are perfectly free to ask (14).

(14) Isn't quality the most important thing to consider in buying aspirin?

(15) Is quality the most important thing to consider in buying aspirin?

(16) Weren't you in the victim's apartment on the night of the murder?

Another type of true but potentially deceptive claim involves the citing of statistical or other scientific research information. Any evidence of "science" tends to give an ad a greater aura of authority and prestige, but such statistics may often be a very slippery way to imply something very different than what the claim directly states.

One way this may be done is reporting results of a survey only by the absolute number or by the percent, but not both: (17) and (18). Similarly, the number of respondents reporting may be mentioned with no consideration of the number questioned (19). Sometimes the competition in a comparative ad may be inadequately or inappropriately specified (20).

(17) 75 percent of dentists recommended Fizzle Toothpaste (75 percent of how many? Four?)

(18) 5000 doctors recommended Cashprin Aspirin. (5000 out of how many?)

(19) 2000 satisfied customers responding to our survey favored . . . (How many were questioned and didn't respond?)

(20) Czar Scrubitoff Oven Cleaner has 40 percent more cleaning power than another popular brand. (What is cleaning power?) (What was popular about the other brand?)

Results may be reported in piecemeal fashion, with specific comparisons drawn comparing one's product to different competitors, but each on a different dimension. The overall set of comparisons may imply something far beyond what is stated directly. For example, one might infer from (21) that the car was larger on all interior dimensions than any of its competitors, while that is not at all what is stated.

(21)   The Wallaby Medalist has more rear seat headroom than a Chevette, more leg room than a Ford Escort, a larger trunk than a Toyota Tercel, and more hip room than a Honda Civic.

Sometimes something negative may be implied about the competition without stating it directly, as in examples (22) through (25). All of the statements are unquestionably true, but the implications they carry are considerably more questionable.

(22)   Tipsi-Cola has no cancer-causing artificial sweetener. (But maybe the competition does?)

(23)   S & M Schlock will accompany you to an audit if the IRS questions a tax return we prepare. (Any tax preparer must by law do so.)

(24)   Wouldn't it be terrible to be stuck somewhere with some of those traveler's checks that don't give refunds easily? (But all do give refunds.)

(25)   Slurpo Mushroom Soup—there's no asbestos in our mushrooms! (But beware the other brands.)

Demonstrating deception psychologically   So far we have discussed several types of advertising claims that may imply more than they state directly and thus possibly imply a falsehood while remaining themselves true. The psychological question remains to be answered, however. Do people in fact infer the (perhaps false) implications going beyond what is said? Yes, they do, as we have demonstrated in a research project summarized in Harris, Dubitsky, and Bruno (1983).

The general methodology was to present subjects with a list of about 20 audiotaped commercials 30 seconds long each and later test their memory for the claims put forth in the ads. The crucial test comes from the fact that half of the subjects heard a given commercial state a claim directly (26), while the other half heard the same commercial imply the same claim (27). All subjects later rated the truth of the critical claim (28).

(26)   Do you have tired, aching feet at the end of a long day? You should be wearing the Moon Shoe, with its revolutionary new cushion sole. Be kind to your sore feet. *Moon Shoes will relieve tired, aching feet.*

(27)   Do you have tired, aching feet at the end of a long day? You should be wearing the Moon Shoe, with its revolutionary new cushion sole. Be kind to your sore feet. *Moon Shoes are just right for you.*

(28)   Moon Shoes make your tired, aching feet feel better.

In the baseline condition, subjects make the inferences and believe the claims very strongly regardless of which ad they heard; thus, it does not matter whether the claim is stated directly or merely implied (Harris, 1977a).

Later extensions of this work tried to train subjects not to draw such unwarranted inferences from radio ads (Bruno & Harris, 1980; Harris, Dubitsky, & Thompson, 1979; Harris, Dubitsky, Connizzo, Letcher, & Ellerman, 1981). This is difficult to do and, although some progress was

BOX 8–7   *OTHER COGNITIVE PROCESSES IN ADVERTISING*

Besides the issue of deception in advertising, there are other problems of information processing of ads that are amenable to study using the methods of modern experimental psychology. Some of these issues include how we make purchase decisions, how visual and auditory information interact in television advertising, how repeated presentations of ads affect memory, and how imagery is evoked in comprehending ads. Numerous other issues abound as well.

There are three different classes of dependent measures used in psychological research on advertising (Shimp, 1983). *Cognitive* measures involve how we interpret the ads. *Attitudinal* measures assess our attitudes or feelings about the product. *Behavioral* measures determine how our behavior changes, with primary focus on buying behavior. The latter is, of course, the "bottom line" in advertising research, but it is also the most difficult of the three types of measures to implement. Clearly, we need more of that type of research, but there are many possibilities for information-processing studies of advertising (see Harris, 1983, for a collection of readings on this topic). Preston (1975, 1977, 1980) has argued that behavioral evidence from research is becoming gradually more acceptable and even sought out among Federal Trade Commissioners when formulating a ruling on a deceptive advertising case.

---

achieved through small group interactive training, it is very difficult to stop this general information-processing activity from occurring. The most effective training required subjects themselves to generate alternative interpretations besides the obvious implied claim.

Deceptive advertising is not the only advertising issue where information-processing psychology can be of use. See Box 8–7.

CONCLUSION

At the beginning of this chapter we introduced the interactionist perspective on meaning, whereby the meaning is not a property of the stimulus, but rather is something that, emerges from the interaction of the stimulus and the active mind and memory of the hearer/reader. In comprehension, the sounds (listening) or letters (reading) are perceived and recognized and then constructed into words. These words are then decoded to meanings, using information in the mental dictionary and the syntactic structure of the words. In constructing the meaning of a whole sequence of words, one retrieves knowledge schemata from memory and draws inferences based on such knowledge, taking into account pragmatic considerations surrounding the utterance or text. Information of several sorts (phonetic, lexical, syntactic, pragmatic) is processed in parallel during the comprehension process as the meaning is constructed. In this way comprehension involves top-down and bottom-up processing and is a multifaceted set of processes, not an all-or-none operation.

SUGGESTED READINGS

The material in this chapter is usually discussed very briefly in chapters on memory or language in cognition texts.

Schema theory is only now starting to receive serious treatment in textbooks. For good integrative discussions of the topic, see the articles by Rumelhart (1980), Alba and Hasher (1983), and Brewer and Nakamura (1984).

A highly readable, entertaining, and fact-filled discussion of deceptive advertising, especially in regard to puffery, is Ivan Preston's (1975) *The Great American Blow-up: Puffery in Advertising and Selling.* Michael Geis' (1982) *The Language of Television Advertising* looks at advertising language a bit more generally. Both are highly critical of advertising.

CHAPTER NINE
THINKING

A panel of psychologists has interviewed and administered personality tests to 30 engineers and 70 lawyers, all successful in their respective fields. On the basis of this information, thumbnail descriptions of the 30 engineers and 70 lawyers have been written. You will find below three descriptions, chosen at random from the 100 available descriptions. For each description, please indicate, on a scale from 0 to 100, what you think the probability is that the person described is an engineer. (Adapted from Kahneman & Tversky, 1973, p. 241).

1   Dick is a 30-year-old man. He is married with no children. A man of high ability and high motivation, he promises to be quite successful in his field. He is well liked by his colleagues. (p. 242)
Probability Dick is one of the 30 engineers out of the 100 people _____?

2   Jack is a 45-year-old man. He is married and has four children. He is generally conservative, careful, and ambitious. He shows no interest in political and social issues and spends most of his free time on his many hobbies, which include home carpentry, sailing, and mathematical puzzles. (p. 241)
Probability that Jack is one of the 30 engineers out of the 100 people _____?

3   No information provided on Fred.
Probability that Fred is one of the 30 engineers out of the 100 people _____?

If you are like the subjects studied by Daniel Kahneman and Amos Tversky, you guessed that the probability that Dick is an engineer is about

50 percent, that Jack is an engineer is about 95 percent, and that Fred is an engineer is about 30 percent.

Only one of these estimates—the last one—is correct. Another group of subjects was told that the initial group of 100 contained 70 engineers and 30 lawyers, and their estimates were identical to yours, except for Fred, who was considered now 70 percent likely to be an engineer. Again, only the estimate concerning Fred is correct.

This chapter will examine thinking, the cognitive processes that bring together all the others in order to accomplish something, such as solve a problem, make a judgment, or conduct scientific research. The results of this experiment and others we will describe in this chapter suggest that people are not as skilled at thinking as they could be or even as skilled as they think they are.

In the above example, we obviously understand that if a person is chosen at random from a group of 30 engineers and 70 lawyers, he or she is much more likely to be a lawyer than an engineer, and so we estimate the chances that Fred is an engineer, correctly, at 30/100, or 30 percent. But as soon as we are given a personality description, we forget all about the objective probabilities. The description of Dick is worthless—it could describe any professional person—doctor, lawyer, engineer, politician, scientist, or professor. There is no reason to think Dick is an engineer rather than a lawyer, and so we set down an estimate of 50 percent—equally likely to be a lawyer or an engineer—quite forgetting the population distribution of 30 engineers and 70 lawyers. We ought to treat Dick like Fred and estimate 30 percent, but few of us do.

With Jack we go even further astray. His profile fits the stereotype of the engineer we have in long-term memory, and we jump to the conclusion that he *must* be an engineer, again ignoring the objective probabilities. Even if the engineer stereotype is true—which it very likely is not—we should not ignore the fact that there are only 30 engineers in the group to begin with, so that *any* randomly sampled profile will probably be a lawyer's. The finding that both groups of subjects—whether told there were 30 of 100 engineers or 70 of 100 engineers—gave the *same* estimate that Jack is an engineer shows that the subjects just ignored the objective probabilities and followed their intuitive personality theory.

We will find that, as this example illustrates, human thinking is an imperfect process, a much more hit-and-miss affair than most of us would care to suppose. We ignore relevant information, rely too much on stereotypes and personal experience, jump to conclusions, resist challenging facts, and even have trouble reasoning according to the rules of logic.

In this chapter we will examine several areas in the psychological study of thinking, including problem solving, reasoning (inductive, deductive, and scientific), and decision making.

PROBLEM SOLVING

When we talk about problem solving, we are considering a very broad topic, which could in some sense include most of the material in this chapter. J. Richard Hayes (1978), a prominent researcher in problem solving, has defined a problem as the "gap that separates us from the present state and the goal state." Obviously, this includes a wide variety of situations. Although problem solving has most often been studied by psychologists using little puzzles of some sort (anagrams, cryptarithmetic, or hobbits-orcs problems), the principles of problem solving have broad application beyond puzzles and games to the many problems we face in our daily lives. Our discussion of problem solving will take this broad approach.

The topic of problem solving has been studied in several traditions in psychology. The Gestalt psychologists examined it a generation ago, with emphasis on holistic aspects like restructuring the problem and combining elements in new ways. The behaviorist tradition studied problem solving from the perspective of analyzing it into simple processes of learning responses to stimuli and achieving the solution incrementally (see Chapter 3) Finally, the computer-influenced information-processing tradition has dominated recent research, which has been active especially since Newell and Simon's (1972) landmark book, *Human Problem Solving*. It is generally this information-processing approach that is taken in this section, since that best represents current thinking on the topic. We will, however, bring in insights from other traditions as well.

Understanding the Problem

The entire problem situation may be subdivided into (a) **understanding** the problem, and (b) **solving** the problem. Contrary to what might be your first impression, understanding the problem is far from trivial. Many of the barriers to solving a problem stem not from inappropriate strategies in solving but rather from inappropriate conceptualizations of what the problem is all about.

Considering a problem as a sequence of continually changing states from the start to the finish, there are several aspects to understanding the problem. The initial situation (start state) must be understood. What are the "givens" at the start of the problem? These *givens* would include a full description of the context of the problem and all of the parameters under which one must operate in solving the problem. This would include, among other information, a description of the *operators* (moves) available for changing the state of the problem. For example, a description of all the allowable moves of each piece in chess would completely define the operators for that game. In contrast to puzzles and games, many real-world problems do not have the operators so well defined. To illustrate, it may take a depressed person several sessions of counseling just to identify available operators he or she might have to use in order to change that person's life situation and attitude.

Another important aspect of understanding the problem is defining the *goal state*, the situation where you want to end up. While this is sometimes very clear, such as in games or many puzzles, often it is ill-defined; this lack of specificity of the goal state becomes part of the difficulty of the problem. For example, if a student has difficulty concentrating in school and feels lethargic and apathetic, he or she may not have a clear goal state for that problem. It is hard to make much progress toward a goal if you do not know what that goal is. Merely knowing that you want to change from the start state is not sufficient. Problem solving must be goal-directed, even though that goal may not always be achieved.

When we construct representations of problems as we understand them, we do so in our short-term memory and draw heavily on information in our long-term memory, including schemata and scripts (discussed in Chapter 8). The extent and character of our knowledge about that problem area will naturally affect how we understand the problem. For example, if you have considerable mechanical knowledge, you are probably better able to describe the givens and recognize available operators that you have at your disposal to solve the problem of your car dying at the side of the road. A person with little mechanical knowledge could not describe the problem nearly so completely.

Solving the Problem

The actual solution of the problem may be viewed as searching through the "problem space" for a "solution path," a path connecting the start state and the goal state. There may be one or several solution paths; usually the discovery of one good solution path is sufficient. Very often there is a huge number of solution paths for a given problem. For example, a 40-move chess game has around 10^{20} solution paths! Ridding yourself of depression has some unknown number of solution paths.

Algorithms and heuristics   Procedures used in solving problems may be either algorithms or heuristics. **Algorithms** are strategies guaranteed to produce a solution, while **heuristics** involve using hunches, good guesses, practical knowledge, and experience.

Algorithms are most useful for well-defined, highly structured problems. For example, we have a division algorithm for solving long-division problems. It is guaranteed to work and in this case is eminently usable. Very often no algorithm exists (for example, you are shy and want to be more popular socially) or the algorithm is so cumbersome that it would make no real sense to use it. For instance, anagrams could be solved by the algorithm of rearranging the letters in all the possible permutations, assuming there is a solution. However, the number of such permutations is huge; the eight-letter anagram THREAGUD has 40,320 possible rearrangements of its eight letters! To start writing these out would be pretty futile. Instead, we draw on our knowledge of English spelling rules to eliminate a large majority of those 40,320 possibilities (words that start out RG or GD need not be considered). Thus, we use heuristics, in this case drawing on our knowledge of the English language. In such a case, heuristics are much more efficient strategies than the available algorithm, though the latter might work better in a computer program.

Sometimes the distinction is made between *well-defined* and *ill-defined* problems. Well-defined problems typically have a clear goal state and often clearly defined operators, such as most games. On the other hand, ill-defined problems are much less structured, and part of the task of the problem solver is to structure the problem. Well-defined problems are often, though not always, amenable to algorithmic solutions, whereas ill-defined problems almost never are. Most of the real problems we face in our jobs and personal lives are ill-defined, at least to a large degree.

Subgoaling   A good general strategy in problem solving is subgoaling, that is, dividing a problem into subproblems to be worked on one at a time. Very often an entire problem can seem forbidding ("I don't know where to begin") and subgoaling can help. For example, I can start writing this book by first making an overall outline, then an outline of a particular chapter, then write a part of the chapter, and so on. Sometimes a counselor can help a client with a personal problem to subgoal that problem; divide the problem of excessive shyness into subproblems of heightened anxiety, a poor self-image, and a lack of social skills in conversation. It is easier to work on each of these one at a time than it is to work generally on being less shy.

If you have a problem of feeling uptight from having too many responsibilities, you could subgoal the problem into particular tasks and work on each separately (your psychology lab due Friday, the chemistry exam Monday, showing your little sister around campus next Saturday). You might also identify particular aspects of your personality to reevaluate (you accept responsibilities too quickly, perhaps from an excessive desire to please others). Such subgoaling can often help move the person off the unproductive dead center of feeling totally immobilized and defeated by the problem ("Where do I begin?").

Restructuring   Sometimes it may be necessary to restructure the problem in order to solve it. It was this aspect of problem solving that was studied by the Gestalt psychologists, who were interested in holistic approaches to thought. For example, consider the following conversation between a waiter (W) and a customer (C):

C: FUNEX?
W: SVFX.
C: NEM?
W: SVFM2.
C: DUFT?
W: ST2.
C: LFMNXNT.

The problem is: What was the customer ordering? As long as you do not structure this problem correctly, it is impossible to solve. For example, you may experience *functional fixedness* of being able to think of the letters only as letters spelling words (or perhaps as initials or cryptograms). You have to think of the letters in a new way in order to discover the solution. The inability to see objects in a novel way is a common barrier in problem solution. Restructuring may be necessary to remove the functional fixedness. Such restructuring frequently comes in a moment of insight. There has been a long debate in the psychology of problem solving over whether problem solving occurs incrementally as a result of *trial-and-error* or suddenly in a moment of *insight* (the "aha experience," as the Gestalt psychologists called it). This turned out in many ways to be a false issue, since support for each process was obtained, depending on what task was used. Insight has qualities of dramatic suddenness, at least in terms of conscious experience. It also tends to produce a novel solution that is a complete one, at least to a major subpart of the problem. Sometimes it occurs after a period of incubation, when one goes off and does not work on the problem after a period of intense work on it. Why insight sometimes comes (though certainly not always) after a period of incubation is a matter of some debate. Explanations typically range from arguments that the brain is rested and able to think more productively to claiming that the functional fixedness established in the earlier period of work on the problem has weakened after the rest and thus the problem solver is able to see the problem in a new way. Box 9–1 gives some additional problems where you may experience functional fixedness and need some insight to restructure the problem. The answers to those problems and the answer to what the customer ordered in the preceding example can be found in Box 9–9, at the end of the chapter.

Expertise What makes an expert an expert? Some people are obviously much more adept at solving a given kind of problem than other people are. In large part this is due to the greater amount of knowledge about that problem area in their long-term memory. This rich knowledge base allows many more possibilities for reconceptualizing the problem. The Dutch psychologist A. D. DeGroot (1965) studied chess masters and chess novices to determine just how they differed. He found that while they did not differ in the number of moves they considered on a given turn, the experts considered much better moves than the novices, that is, they were able to use their knowledge of chess and heuristics drawn therefrom to eliminate poor moves from their consideration and only examine the promising ones. The masters had much better memory for chess positions

---

BOX 9–1 *OTHER EXAMPLES OF PROBLEMS REQUIRING RESTRUCTURING*

> A   In days of old, two knights were competing for the hand of the king's daughter. The king, being an ingenious old man, decided to settle the competition in a unique type of horse race. The two knights would be required to race against each other on horseback, but with the unusual stipulation that whosever horse crossed the finish line *last* would be the winner and would get to marry the daughter. How could the knights make sure that this race wouldn't be the slowest race in history?
>
> B   In Italy during World War II, American soldiers found standing on the ground small wooden billboards about two feet high. They looked like Figure 9-1. What was the purpose of these boards?
>
> C   What is the only English four-letter word ending in *-eny*?
>
> D   Given the circle in Figure 9-2, with radius 2, find the length of line *C*.

FIGURE 9–1

FIGURE 9–2

and tended to chunk many pieces together in memory; they would remember not merely one piece and its location but a whole array of pieces and their relationship to each other stored in a unit.

Next we will examine a type of problem solving of a more specific and structured sort, *reasoning*.

REASONING

An important component of thinking is **reasoning,** the process of drawing warranted conclusions from evidence or from given premises. There are two kinds of reasoning recognized by philosophers and mathematicians: *inductive* reasoning and *deductive* reasoning. Inductive reasoning involves drawing a general conclusion from a set of data; deductive reasoning involves drawing a conclusion from a given set of initial statements, or premises. We will look at the psychology of these logics in turn, and then consider *scientific reasoning*, which involves both deduction and induction at once.

Inductive Reasoning

If we consider it to be a cognitive process and not a matter of habit-formation, anagram solution set learning may be regarded as a form of inductive reasoning, because we learn a general rule based on a series of specific instances. Let us now consider the Maltzmann and Morrisett experiment described in Chapter 3 from a cognitive standpoint (Leahey, 1979).

Recall that Maltzmann regarded anagram set learning as acquiring S-R habits; he explained the superior number of set solutions given by subjects in compound anagram groups as due to the learning by each subject of two habits converging on a single solution in a convergent habit-family hierarchy. But we also learned from Voeks' Guthrean analysis of learning curves that Hullian theory often mistakes group learning effects for changes in an individual learner. Voeks demonstrated that, while group learning curves apparently showed incremental change in habit strength, in each person learning took place all at once.

Similarly, a cognitive analysis of anagram set learning as a kind of inductive reasoning suggests that people try to figure out some general *rule* for solving the anagrams. If subjects are exposed to a series of nature anagrams, they may learn a rule such as "look for a nature word." Subjects exposed to a series of 32145 anagrams will likely learn a rule such as "reverse the first three letters." If exposed to a series of 32145 anagrams with a nature-word solution, subjects could learn either rule, or perhaps both. Thus, there would be more set solutions in the last group, not because each subject acquired two habits, but because there were two rules that could lead to the (same) set solution; and with more rules available to learn, more subjects would pick up one set or the other.

When subjects are asked how they solve anagrams, the vast majority report looking for a rule that applies to all the cases, showing a strong preference for reordering rules rather than semantic ones (Leahey, 1979). Moreover, in a group for whom a series of test anagrams were constructed such that Hullian theory predicted the presence of antagonistic habits and a reduction of set solutions due to negative summation of habits, there was, in fact, an *increase* in set solutions, as predicted by a cognitive theory of greater hypothesis availability (Leahey, 1979).

In these anagram-learning experiments, people displayed reasonably good inductive reasoning skills, detecting cues that suggested some general rule for solving future anagrams. However, another induction problem—familiar to anyone who has taken an intelligence test or college-entrance exam—detected an important flaw in people's inductive ability.

Three numbers, 2, 4, 6, were shown to a subject, who was told they conformed to a simple relational rule, and the subject's task was to discover the rule by generating successive triads of numbers. After generating a triad, the subject (who kept a written list of hypotheses) was told whether the triad fit the rule or not. The subject was instructed to announce the rule when he or she was "highly confident" it was correct. Again, the subject found out if the rule was correct, and if it was not, the subject continued. The following protocol is representative of the results obtained (Wason & Johnson-Laird, 1972, p. 209):

No. 2   Four incorrect announcements. Female. Psychology undergraduate.

Instances		*Hypotheses*
2 4 6 (+)	(Given)	
8 10 12 (+)		Two added each time.
14 16 18 (+)		Even numbers in order of magnitude.
20 22 24 (+)		Same reason.
1 3 5 (+)		Two added to preceding number.

Announcement: *The rule is that by starting with any number two is added each time to form the next number.* (Incorrect)

Instances	*Hypotheses*
2 6 10 (+)	The middle number is the arithmetic mean of the other two.
1 50 99 (+)	Same reason.

Announcement: *The rule is that the middle number is the arithmetic mean of the other two.* (Incorrect)

3 10 17 (+)	Same number, seven, added each time.
0 3 6 (+)	Three added each time.

Announcement: *The rule is that the difference between two numbers next to each other is the same.* (Incorrect)

12 8 4 (−)	The same number is subtracted each time to form the next number.

Announcement: *The rule is adding a number, always the same one, to form the next number.* (Incorrect)

1 4 9 (+)	Any three numbers in order of magnitude.

Announcement: *The rule is any three numbers in order of magnitude.*

The real rule is extremely simple and broad, so that many more specific rules generate triads consistent with it. The only way to solve the problem, unless one stumbles on the right answer immediately, as many children—unused to the usual subtleties of such number series problems—do, is to test one's hypothesis by attempting to *falsify* it by generating triads inconsistent with one's hypothesis.

But this is what Subject 2 (along with most subjects) conspicuously failed to do. Instead, subjects set out to *verify* their hypothesis by generating triads consistent with their rule. But since many rules are consistent with the true rule, a subject can spend quite some time receiving "confirmations" of an incorrect hypothesis. One's mistakes can be discovered much more quickly by seeking falsification rather than verification.

The effect of a piece of single, vivid, confirming evidence can be found in social reasoning. Some politicians have exploited our willingness to believe a compelling anecdote and our resistance to falsifying statistics, tendencies demonstrated in an experiment reported by Nisbett and Ross (1980). Three groups of subjects filled out questionnaires evaluating their attitudes toward welfare recipients. Control subjects were then given correct statistics about people on welfare, including, for example, that the median stay on welfare is two years and that only 10 percent of welfare recipients remain on the rolls for as long as four years. These subjects—who believed initially that the average stay was ten years—were unaffected by the figures, expressing the same generally negative attitudes on a second questionnaire.

Two groups of experimental subjects read a description of a welfare mother that the experimenters had adapted from the *New Yorker* magazine. As described by Nisbett and Ross (1980, p. 57),

> The description painted a vivid picture of social pathology. The central figure was an obese, friendly, emotional, and irresponsible Puerto Rican woman who had been on welfare for many years. Middle-aged now, she had lived with a succession of "husbands," typically also unemployed, and had borne children by each of them. Her home was a nightmare of dirty and dilapidated

plastic furniture bought on time at outrageous prices, filthy kitchen appliances, and cockroaches walking about in the daylight. Her children showed little promise of rising above their origins. They attended school off and on and had begun to run afoul of the law in their early teens, with the other children now thoroughly enmeshed in a life of heroin, numbers-running, and welfare.

The experimental subjects were then given information making the woman's case seem either (falsely) typical, or (correctly) atypical.

In one condition, the woman's very long stay on welfare was characterized as *typical*: "The average length of time on welfare for recipients between the ages of 40 and 55 is 15 years. Furthermore, 90 percent of these people are on the welfare rolls for at least eight years." In the second condition, the woman's length of time on welfare was made to seem atypically high: "The average length of time on welfare for recipients between the ages of 40 and 55 is two years. Furthermore, 90 percent of these people are off the welfare rolls by the end of four years." (Nisbett & Ross, 1980, p. 86)

The effect of the single, vivid case that confirmed entrenched stereotypes (social schemata—see Chapter 8) was dramatic. Whereas the control subjects had stubbornly persisted in beliefs falsified by statistics, the experimental subjects reported *increased* negative attitudes toward welfare recipients on the second form, regardless of whether they had been led to believe the case was typical or not. So not only do we have stereotypes about engineers and "welfare queens," these stereotypes also resist change, and are strengthened by isolated, "confirming" instances. Nor does presenting fair, balanced discussions reflecting both sides of controversial issues help people on each side to understand each other better. See Box 9–2.

Induction is merely learning from experience. What the above experiments seem to show is that we learn from experience in a haphazard, highly selective fashion. Once we form a belief we are loath to give it up, and grasp eagerly for any confirming evidence, no matter how isolated and unusual. Sometimes induction is short-circuited altogether, and real pathology sets in. In Wason's and Johnson-Laird's "2, 4, 6" experiment,

One subject broke down completely. Our assistant, Martin Katzman, entered the room and informed us, quite politely, that the subject, whom he was testing, was "behaving like a lunatic." And, indeed, he was certainly behaving in a strange way. On the one hand, he would not allow the experimenter to persuade him to break off the task, because "he could do wonderful things with numbers," and on the other hand, he constantly engaged in self-recriminations. What was more disconcerting, however, was that he was apparently unable to stand up, and had to be carried bodily down the stairs, and taken to the Harvard Health Center. (Wason & Johnson-Laird, 1972, p. 235)

Deductive Reasoning

Inductive reasoning has no rules, and as the philosopher David Hume showed two centuries ago, no inductive generalization is ever certain, because tomorrow's experience may prove it wrong. For certainty and

BOX 9–2 *POLARIZING OPINIONS THROUGH BALANCED DISCUSSIONS*

Nisbett and Ross (1980) describe a study seeming to show that "fair" presentations of both sides of an issue—what every news reporter aims at—is likely to strengthen preexisting opinions, not create an atmosphere of tolerance.

Undergraduates who on a survey reported themselves strongly for or against capital punishment read two articles describing studies either supporting or refuting the deterrent effect of execution. Half the subjects read the confirming study first; half read the falsifying one first. Subjects filled out an attitude questionnaire on capital punishment after reading their first article, and after the second.

As we have come to expect, subjects displayed strong confirmation bias, judging the study that supported them as sound and valid, and dismissing the disconfirming study as sloppy and poorly conducted. Reading a confirming study strengthened their original opinion; reading a disconfirming study had little impact.

The inevitable consequence of these tendencies was polarization of opinion after reading both articles, that is, the "fair," "balanced," total presentation. Since disconfirming evidence had no effect and confirming evidence a strengthening effect, subjects had stronger opinions about capital punishment at the end of the study than at the beginning.

The disturbing conclusion is that presentations of both sides of an issue do not reduce differences between holders of opposing opinions, but widen them. People are not swayed by the balance of the evidence but tend to pick and choose, believing only what conforms to their views and rejecting what does not, all the while growing ever surer that they are correct and that those who differ with them must be fools.*

*Read Lord, C. , Ross, C. , & Lepper, M. R. "Biased Assimilation and Attitude Polarization: The Effects of Prior Theories on Subsequently Considered Evidence." *Journal of Personality and Social Psychology*, 1979, *37*, 2089–2109.

proof we must go to deductive reasoning, where we can deduce conclusions from given propositions in accordance with formal rules, and show that the conclusions must follow from the premises.

For example, if I assert the premise (4)

(4)   If a person is 21, then he or she may drink wine

and then am given the information in (5),

(5)   Fred is 21

then I may validly deduce the conclusion (6):

(6)   Fred may drink wine.

An important thing to bear in mind about deductive reasoning is that following the rules of logic guarantees only that the conclusion is valid, that is, that it really does follow logically from the given premises; there is no guarantee that the conclusion is true: The premises may be false. So the argument—(7), (8), (9)—is just as valid as (4), (5), (6), even though it is absurd:

(7)   If Julius Caesar is President, then horses are purple.

(8)   Julius Caesar is President.

(9)   Therefore, horses are purple.

Although deductive logic cannot assure us that our conclusions are true, it is still an essential component in reasoning. For when we reason, we assemble what we know about a problem; in logical terms, we establish a set of premises from which we make inferences. It is important that we reason logically; otherwise, we still may fall into error even with the truest of premises.

Of the various kinds of deductive logic and types of logical rules, we will consider here just one, *reasoning with material implication (if . . . then* statements), an important kind of reasoning intensively investigated by several teams of researchers over the last two decades. Sample problems from their experiments are given in Boxes 9–3 and 9–4; the correct answers are found in Box 9–5. Please read these boxes and do the problems before going on to read about the research results.

BOX 9–3   *PETER WASON'S FOUR-CARD PROBLEM*

The cards in Figure 9–3 have information on both sides. On one side of a card is a letter, and on the other side is a number.

FIGURE 9–3

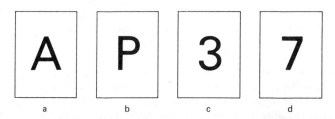

Here is a rule: **If a card has an "A" on one side, then it has a "3" on the other side.**

·Select those cards that you definitely need to turn over to determine whether or not the cards are violating the rule.*

*Instructions from Cox & Griggs, 1982.

BOX 9–4   *RICHARD GRIGGS' DRINKING AGE PROBLEM*

On this task imagine you are a police officer on duty. It is your job to ensure that people conform to certain rules. The cards in Figure 9-4 have information about four people sitting at a table. On one side of a card is a person's age and on the other side of the card is what a person is drinking. Here is a rule:

If a person is drinking beer, then the person must be over 19. Select those cards that you definitely need to turn over to determine whether or not the people are violating the rule.*

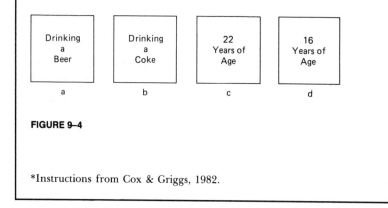

FIGURE 9–4

*Instructions from Cox & Griggs, 1982.

BOX 9–5   *ANSWERS TO THE PROBLEMS IN BOXES 9–3 and 9–4*

The correct answer in each case is to turn over only cards *a* and *d;* if you are like most American subjects you almost certainly got Box 9–3 incorrect, and probably got Box 9–4 correct. Remember that you are told to *falsify*—not *verify*—the rule. Turning over a card *a* can do this, since in 9–3 if (say) a 2 is on the other side, the rule is violated, and in 9–4 if the other side says, "Fourteen years of age," the rule is violated. Turning over card *b* can *not* falsify the rule, because it does not satisfy the "if . . . " part of the rule, called the *antecedent.* So no matter what is on the other side, the rule stands unviolated. Card *c* is similarly unhelpful: In 9–4 it does not matter what the 22-year-old is drinking; he can't be violating the drinking law. Similarly, in 9–3 it doesn't matter what is on the other side of the 3; the rule cannot be violated. Finally, card *d* can violate the rule: If the 16-year-old is drinking beer, the rule is violated; if there is an *A* on the other side of the card in 9–3, the rule is violated.

While the two problems differ in content, they both have the same logical structure, and should therefore have the same answer. The formal justification for the correct choices comes from the *truth table* (as logicians call it) for implication, which specifies the conditions under which an implication statement, of whatever content, is to be judged true or false. In logic, an *if . . . then* statement may be represented as $p \supset q$: If p, then q, which has the following truth table:

p	p⊃q	q
T	T	T
T	F	F
F	T	T
F	T	F

That is, the proposition $p \supset q$ (for example, if there is an *A* on the front (*p*), then (⊃) there is a *3* on the back (*q*) is *false* when *p* is true (the card has an *A* on front) and *q* is false (there is a 2 on the other side). Otherwise, the proposition is true.

In the two tasks, only cards *a* and *d* can falsify the rule, because only they can give the combination in line 2 of the truth table. Similarly, only two kinds of inferences may be drawn from an implicative proposition. One is called *modus ponens:*

(1) $p \supset q$
(2)   *p* is true
(3)   therefore, *q* is true.

This is a valid inference, because assuming the premise is true, as one must do in deductive reasoning, if we know that *p* is true, *q* must be true also.

The other valid conclusion is *modus tollens:*

(1) $p \supset q$
(4)   *q* is false (not-q, or $\sim q$)
(5)   therefore, *p* is false (not-p, or $\sim p$).

In *modus tollens* we reason by falsification. Again, assuming the rule is true, given that *q* is false, it must be the case that *p* is false.

There are two fallacious forms of reasoning with implication, *denial of the antecedent* and *affirmation of the consequent*. In denial of the antecedent, a person reasons incorrectly:

(1) $p \supset q$
(6) $\sim p$
(7)   therefore, $\sim q$.

The truth table shows this to be a fallacy, since if *p* is false, the rule is always true.

In affirmation of the consequent, one reasons incorrectly

(1) $p \supset q$
(8)   *q*
(9)   therefore, *p*.

Again, inspection of the truth table shows that when *q* is true, the whole rule is true.

This basic problem, expecially in its original, abstract form (Box 9–3), is especially difficult. Researchers in both Great Britain and America have shown that only about 10 percent of subjects make the correct choices when the problem is presented as in Box 9–3. The most common error is to choose cards *a* and *c* (see Evans, 1982, for a review). Similarly, when subjects are given an abstract rule and asked to draw inferences from it in combination with propositions forming the argument patterns discussed in Box 9–5, they show poor command of logical implication, typically doing *modus ponens* correctly, while rejecting the validity of *modus tollens,* and making the invalid inferences denial of the antecedent and especially affirmation of the consequent (Evans, 1982; Leahey, 1977a, 1977b, 1980b; Leahey & Wagman, 1974). Such erroneous reasoning has proved most difficult to modify (Wason and Johnson-Laird, 1972; Leahey & Wagman, 1974; Leahey, 1977a).

When the problem has been presented in a verbal form, as in Box 9–4, the results have been exceedingly varied. Early results (summarized in Wason & Johnson-Laird, 1972) showed that verbal formulations produced superior performance, even in subjects who could not do the abstract version, suggesting that people understood the logic of implication but just could not bring it to bear on abstract material.

However, these findings could not always be replicated (see Leahey, 1977b), and further research by Richard Griggs and his colleagues (Griggs & Cox, 1982; Cox & Griggs, 1982) and E. Golding (1981) showed why. The verbal formulation yielded improved performance only when the rule and its manner of testing were already familiar to the subjects. So, for example, the drinking age problem (Box 9–4) facilitated performance among American undergraduates familiar—naturally—with alcoholic beverage rules, even though the same subjects did badly with the abstract problem and with concrete versions involving British postal rules or travel between British cities, problems on which British students had done well.

Such results have been explained in several ways, each of which suggests that people do not reason as logically as they suppose, when they reason at all. One factor is the familiar tendency of people to verify a rule, rather than attempt to falsify it, leading them to choose cards *a* and *c, p* and *q,* hoping to find verifying cases, *q* and *p,* respectively, on the other sides (Wason & Johnson-Laird, 1972). Evans (1982) has proposed a dual-process theory, claiming that people possess nonrational Type 1 cognitive processes (akin to Freud's primary process) and rational, logical, verbal, Type 2 processes. When a task is especially difficult, as in the abstract four-card problem, Type 2 processes fail and are short-circuited, replaced by the simpler strategies drawn from Type 1 processes; in short, the subjects are not reasoning at all. On top of this subjects do not realize what has happened, and they rationalize their irrational choices by drawing on Type 2 reasoning (Evans & Wason, 1976). Evans' proposal finds support in some interesting recent research (reported in Evans, 1982) showing that subjects reason more logically with their left brain hemisphere than with their right hemisphere, indicating that Type 2 reasoning is controlled by the verbal-rational left hemisphere, while the shortcut strategies of Type 1 processing take place in the right hemisphere, relatively cut off from left-hemisphere verbal report.

On the other hand, Griggs (for example, Griggs & Cox, in press) has argued that people are not reasoning logically with the verbal material on which they appear to do better. Griggs proposed that superior performance on the concrete tasks is due not to better application of logical abilities, but to sheer familiarity. Specifically, on the familiar, concrete problems people do not figure out—that is, reason out—the correct answers, they already know them from experience and just have to recall them. Florida undergraduates know all about drinking age rules, and can recall the conditions that violate such rules, but do badly on unfamiliar problems concerning British postage and rail travel.

In other words, people seem hardly to reason at all. In abstract tasks, demands are so great that logic is short-circuited and simplified, if nonlogical, strategies are substituted. On familiar tasks, subjects just remember the correct answer; they do not reaon logically to a correct conclusion. It appears that only when people can activate what Griggs calls the "detective set strategy"—looking for rule-breaking instances—that logical reasoning occurs at all. And the results reviewed so far indicate that trying to be wrong is something people rarely do.

The conditional reasoning framework is implicit in many situations beyond those where there is an explicit "If . . . then" rule. Box 9–6 gives an example of how advertisers can capitalize on the less-than-logical ways that we reason. The use of implicit conditional reasoning framework is very common in persuasive discourse such as advertising and political rhetoric.

Scientific Reasoning

In practice, inductive and deductive reasoning are rarely practiced alone. In the induction problems we studied, people must draw a generalization from experience, that is, they must use induction, but then they must test the hypothesis by deducing from it predictions about future experience. Similarly, in the four-card problems, subjects had to deduce what would falsify the given premise, and evaluate it against potential evidence.

Such interweaving of induction and deduction, prediction and proof, is at the center of science. Moreover, since science prides itself on being rational, logical, and orderly, we should examine scientific reasoning in light of our findings that people are less rational, logical, and orderly than we usually suppose.

Scientists as reasoners   To start, let us ask if scientists, trained in the rigors of disciplinary methodology, are any better at reasoning than the lay people psychologists study. Kern, Mirals, and Hinshaw (1983) suggest the answer is "not much." They administered several logical problems to university scientists in three fields, including the Wason four-card problem, the results from which are shown in Table 9–1. While the physicists did better than the biologists and psychologists, no group did really well, and

BOX 9–6   *CONDITIONAL REASONING IN ADVERTISING.*

Sometimes the conditional reasoning paradigm is implicitly contained in advertising even when it may not be overtly stated. Consider a claim like "Panacea Capsules relieve headaches." This may be reworded thus: "If you take Panacea Capsules, they will relieve your headache," to put it into the "if p, then q" form. Consider the four possible logical arguments. Suppose you take Panacea Capsules (p); you could then conclude that they would relieve your headache (q); this is the *modus ponens* argument. As a second argument, consider that you have a headache that is not relieved (not-q); you could conclude that you must not have taken Panacea Capsules (not-p). So far both of these arguments have been logically valid (*modus ponens* and *modus tollens*).

Now let us consider the other two possible arguments; first the case where you did not take Panacea Capsules (not-p). Like subjects in the reasoning studies discussed earlier, you might conclude not-q, that is, that your headache wouldn't be relieved. This is the logically invalid but very frequent fallacy of denying the antecedent, but it may be very useful to advertisers if the consumers make this implied but invalid deduction—that if you don't take their product, you won't get the relief you need.

The last of the four possible arguments is the case where you did experience relief from your headache (q). Though you may be tempted to conclude p, that you must have taken Panacea Capsules, this, too, is invalid (affirming the consequent fallacy) but potentially useful to advertisers.

Thus, advertisers can draw on natural information-processing tendencies to encourage you to deduce more information than they actually state.

TABLE 9–1   **Percent of Scientists Giving Correct Responses on the Wason Four-Card Problem, Abstract Version**[a]

	FIELD			
	BIOLOGISTS	PHYSICISTS	PSYCHOLOGISTS	TRAINED[b] IN LOGIC
Correctly Identified Cards b and c as Irrelevant	8%	21%	13%	12%
Correctly Chose Cards a and d as Falsifying	13%	25%	17%	16%

[a]Table constructed from data reported by Kern, Mirals, and Hinshaw, 1980.

[b]There were too few subjects trained in logic to break down by discipline, and their data are not included in the other cells.

performance overall was only marginally better than college-student subjects, even among those scientists with some training in logic.

Mahoney and DeMonbreun (1978) presented Wason's 2, 4, 6 problem to two groups of university scientists (physicists and psychologists) and to a group of conservative Protestant ministers. The results, summarized in Table 9–2, were essentially similar to Wason's findings with college students. Only a minority of subjects adopted a strategy of hypothesis falsification, and very few triads, in fact, resulted in disconfirmation. Many subjects—especially the scientists—retested previously refuted hypotheses. The only reliable differences between the scientists and the ministers revealed that the latter more closely fit the conventional image of scientists. The ministers generated lots of triads—that is, collected a lot of data—before advancing an hypothesis, while the scientists based hypotheses on small samples, and seemed to stick to them longer.

One might object that these experiments fail to impugn scientists' reasoning skills since they involve unusual, difficult, and abstract material. Perhaps they would do better on problems in their field, where expertise and methodological sophistication could be brought to bear.

However, the work of Chapman and Chapman (1967, 1969; reported by Nisbett & Ross, 1980), showed scientists committing the same sorts of errors as lay people. The Chapmans studied clinical psychologists' faith in two projective personality tests, the Draw-A-Person (DAP) test, and the Rorschach Inkblot Test. Repeated empirical studies have shown the DAP

TABLE 9–2   The Relative Performance of Psychologists, Physical Scientists, and Ministers on the Wason 2, 4, 6, Problem[a]

	GROUP PERFORMANCE		
VARIABLE	PSYCHOLOGISTS	PHYSICAL SCIENTISTS	MINISTERS
Percent who announced the correct hypothesis	47	27	40
Percent who disconfirmed	40	40	33
Percent of trials that were disconfirmatory	9	12	19
Average number of hypotheses generated	3.07	3.33	2.00
Average number of triads generated	7.53	7.60	8.33
Average ratio of triads generated to hypotheses	3.03	2.01	6.22
Average number of triads generated before first hypothesis	1.93	1.07	5.40
Latency in seconds to first hypothesis	35.4	37.7	132.9
Percentage who reconfirmed a previously falsified hypothesis	93	93	53

[a]Adapted from Mahoney and DeMonbreun, Cognitive Therapy & Research, Psychology of Scientist, 1978, 1, 229–238

to be unreliable and invalid, and the Rorschach to be of limited validity. Nevertheless, many practicing clinicians put great faith in the DAP and in discredited forms of Rorschach interpretation. The Chapmans' research indicates that the clinicians' continued faith in the tests is based on well-entrenched "folk" beliefs that resist falsification, and, like the welfare-mother stereotypes, find enough random "confirmations" in their clinical practice to allegedly justify it. For example, the clinicians believe (falsely) that paranoia is expressed in the way a person draws eyes, either under- or over-emphasizing them. The Chapmans found that psychologically naive subjects also believed (falsely) that paranoids would draw emphasized or de-emphasized eyes. Clinical psychologists, then, despite their years of training, are just like anyone else in resisting falsification of their ideas, looking for confirmation, and being swayed by the immediate concrete, isolated, confirming instance against masses of statistical findings.

Perhaps most disturbing is the persistence of incorrect beliefs in areas in which scientists are specifically trained. One folk-belief is the "gambler's fallacy." Suppose we take a coin known to be fair—to have a 50 percent chance of turning up heads or tails (T)—and flip the following sequence: T, T, T, T, T, T, T, T, T; what is the probability the next flip will be heads? Most people commit the gambler's fallacy and think heads is more likely to turn up than 0.50, the correct answer; they think the coin is "due" to turn up heads. To see the fallacy, just realize that nothing has altered the molecular structure of the coin—it's the same coin it was at the start—and, given that it is a fair coin, the probability of heads is still 0.50 on each flip.

Tversky and Kahneman (1981) discovered that the gambler's fallacy persisted among psychologists, who are all trained in statistics and should therefore have been disabused of the mistake. Nevertheless, when questioned on a number of statistical problems, psychologists showed themselves prone to the gambler's fallacy. Most of the problems were too technical to describe here, but one was not. It read:

> The mean IQ of the population of eighth graders in a city is known to be 100. You have selected a random sample of 50 children for a study of educational achievements. The first child tested has an IQ of 150. What do you expect the mean IQ to be for the whole sample? (Tversky & Kahneman, 1981, p. 269)

The correct answer is 101. A score of 150 is *extremely* unlikely: Fewer than .07 percent (that's not 7 percent but 7 *one-hundredths* of a percent) of Americans have an IQ of 150 or more. In order to counterbalance the score of 150 you would have to have in the sample an IQ of 50, which is most unlikely to happen; as a result, the whole sample of 30 will likely be a bit unrepresentatively high. Nevertheless, most psychologists, like most people, thought the sample IQ would be 100, because, like the gambler waiting for the coin to turn heads, they thought the 150 would *inevitably* be balanced by a 50. But any given sample hardly ever exactly mirrors the population as a whole—that's why political polls are so unreliable and must be repeated many times.

It seems, then, that scientific sophistication just lets scientists make sophisticated mistakes.

The layman as scientist   Experiments by Doherty, Mynatt, Tweney, and Schiavo (1981), and Mynatt, Doherty, and Tweney (1981) asked student-subjects to pretend to be scientists (archaeologists or physicists), and then placed them in simulated research environments that required the subjects to formulate and test scientific hypotheses. In the physics experiment, some subjects were given indoctrination concerning falsification as the optimum scientific strategy. Regardless of instructions, however, subjects shared a strong tendency to confirm rather than disconfirm their hypotheses, persisted in repeating disconfirmed hypotheses, and especially in the archaeology experiment, were poor at choosing data that could prove *or* disprove their hypotheses.

In social situations—where we conduct "experiments" to find out about strangers—confirmation bias is so strong that it creates self-fulfilling hypotheses. Snyder, Tanke, and Berscheid (1977; reported by Nisbett & Ross, 1980) had male subjects talk over an intercom with an unseen female they had been led to believe was either attractive or unattractive. Another group of subjects listened to tapes made of the female's side of the conversation only and—without seeing her or knowing what the first subject had been told about her appearance—rated her attractiveness. Evidently, the questions and probes used by the conversing males had elicited verbal evidence of attractiveness or unattractiveness, because the second group of males followed the first group's hypotheses. If the women had been labeled "attractive," her verbal behavior made her seem attractive, even to the blind raters in the second part of the experiment. The reverse held for "unattractive" women. So the hypothesis led to questions that created confirming behavior from the questionee, creating a self-fulfilling circle of hypothesis and "evidence."

Conclusion   By now you may want to ask with a reader of Nisbett & Ross (1980): "If we're so dumb, how come we made it to the moon?" One answer—not Nisbett's and Ross'—is that rationality should not be equated with logic (Toulmin, 1972), and that disconfirmation is not really the best way to do science.

Science does work; its success is established. Yet the major result of work in history and philosophy of science over the past few decades has been that scientists are not logical automata; the work we have surveyed in this chapter already supports such a conclusion. Moreover, it seems wise to argue (see Kuhn, 1970) that science succeeds not *despite* its deviations from falsificationist logic but *because* of them (Leahey & Leahey, 1983). In the Mynatt et al. (1981) simulated physics experiment the subject who performed best quickly formulated a partially correct hypothesis and then stuck to it, using disconfirmations to gradually modify the wrong parts. The results described by Mahoney and DeMonbreun suggest that real scientists do likewise.

Ian Mitroff (1981) studied the very scientists who took us to the moon, and his results (dare we say it?) confirm the view that these "good" scientists were illogical. Project scientists singled out three of their colleagues as especially stubborn in defending their ideas, stubborn to the point of infuriating pig-headedness. Yet these same scientists were rated as the three most creative, most brilliant scientists in an already gifted group. Less stubborn, speculative scientists, who cautiously generalized from large amounts of data, were rated as impartial but dull and unimaginative. Speaking of the brilliant but tenacious three, a colleague said:

> The commitment of these guys to their ideas, while absolutely infuriating at times, can be a very good thing too. One should never give up an idea too soon in science—any idea, no matter how outrageous it may be and no matter how beaten down it seems by all the best evidence at the time. I've seen too many totally disproven ideas come back to haunt us. I've learned by now that you never completely prove or disprove anything; you just make it more or less probable with the best of what means you've got at the time. It's true that these guys are a perpetual thorn in the side of the profession and for that reason a perpetual challenge to it too. Their value probably outweighs their disadvantages although I've wondered many times if we might not be better off without them. Each time I reluctantly conclude no. We need them around. They perpetually shake things up with their wild ideas although they drive you mad with the stick-to-itiveness that they have for their ideas. (Mitroff, 1981, pp. 173–174)

The real key to scientific success is not the individual reasoning—logical or not—of the individual scientist, but the collective reasoning—even wisdom—of the scientific community. Scientists function as a group, a tightly knit community, and while each one is often wrong, it is out of the clash of commitments and confirmation biases toward competing viewpoints that success comes. One moon scientist put it this way:

> Scientist A—Commitment, even extreme commitment such as bias, has a role to play in science and it can serve science well. Part of the business (of science) is to sift the evidence and to come to the right conclusions, and to do this you must have people who argue for both sides of the evidence. This is the only way in which we can straighten the situation out. I wouldn't like scientists to be without bias, since a lot of the sides of the argument would never be presented. We must be emotionally committed to the things we do energetically. No one is able to do anything with liberal energy if there is no emotion connected with it. (Mitroff, 1981, pp. 171–172)

For discussion of how reinforcement (see Chapter 4) can affect reasoning, read Box 9–7.

DECISION MAKING

Although a large part of problem solving and reasoning discussed above involves making decisions, there has been a branch of information-processing psychology that has concentrated on studying how people make choices. Much of this work is in a highly mathematical tradition, going back to the seventeenth-century statistician Jacques Bernoulli (1654–1705), who

BOX 9–7 *REASONING AND REINFORCEMENT*

What happens if we reinforce people for solving problems? Behavior theory would predict improvement in their success at problem solving. However, there is evidence that reward actually undermines cognitive abilities by diminishing their intrinsic attractiveness; it turns fun into work (Lepper & Greene, 1978). Moreover, an elegant series of experiments by Schwartz (1982) demonstrates that reward not only undermines intrinsic motivation, but actually damages thinking, almost turning if off.

Schwartz adapted a pigeon experiment for use with undergraduate students. Subjects sat at a display panel containing a 5-by-5 matrix of electric lamps with the top left light illuminated. There was also a response console with two levers, one for each hand, and a digital counter that showed how many reinforcements—later translated into money—they had received. A certain sequence of lever presses was rewarded. When the left lever was pressed the light went out on the display panel and the one below it was lighted. When the right lever was pressed, the light was extinguished and the one to the right was lighted. The rewarded sequence of lever presses brought the light from the upper left corner to the lower right corner; the subject, however, was told nothing about the display panel.

In the first experiment, the rewarded sequence was any series of presses such that each lever was pressed exactly four times. However, as Figure 9–5 shows, subjects quickly fell into a stereotyped sequence of responses. Moreover, as did subjects in Wason's 2, 4, 6 task, subjects believed their sequence—equivalent to a hypothesis in Wason's problem—to be the only correct one. That is, each subject confused a sequence *sufficient* to get a reward—the one he or she had used—with the sequence *necessary* to get the reward, which could be *any* sequence of four presses to each key.

Subsequent experiments explored the factors affecting behavioral stereotypy. Schwartz found that partial reinforcement schedules also induce stereotypy, although extinction increases variability. When subjects are instructed to look for a rule they show less stereotypy, although it appears after they've learned the rule. Subjects looking for a rule were quite confused by partial reinforcement; they refused to believe rewards were being given on a probabilistic basis, and this interfered with rule-finding. When subjects who had been through the procedure without being told the rule were now told to find a rule in a new experiment, they did very poorly when compared to naive subjects who only did the rule-finding problem. Of the four experienced subjects, only one learned the new rule while all four of the naive subjects did. Even reinforcement of changing response sequences interfered with rule learning in a second task.

In the critical experiment, naive and experienced subjects were again compared, with four groups defined within naive and experienced subjects: One-fourth were reinforced for correct response sequences as before; one-fourth were reinforced only for rule-finding; one-fourth were reinforced for correct sequences *and* were paid a bonus for finding the rule; and the remaining one-fourth received neither reinforcement nor bonuses. All subjects had to solve four problems of varying difficulty, in the same order.

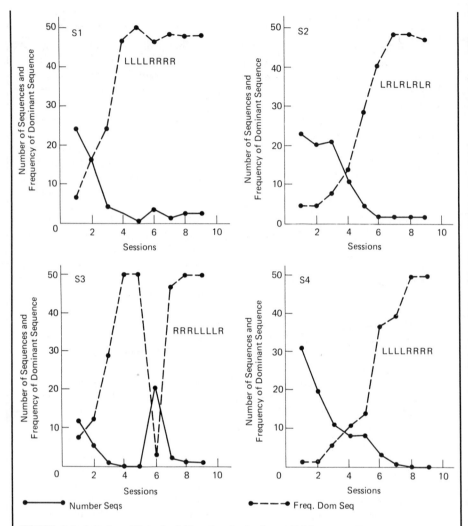

FIGURE 9–5 Induction of Behavioral Stereotypy by Contingent Reinforcement. Number of different sequences (dashed lines) and frequency of the dominant sequence (solid lines) in each 50-trial
block (session) for each subject. (Each subject's dominant sequence is indicated in the appropriate panel. L = left; R = right.)
From B. Schwartz, Reinforcement-induced behavioral stereotyping: How not to teach people
to discover rules. *Journal of Experimental Psychology: General,* 1982, *111.* Reprinted by permission of American Psychological Association.

Figure 9–6 shows some of the results. Naive subjects performed equally
well under all reinforcement and bonus conditions. Experienced subjects uniformly performed more poorly than naive subjects, especially when they were
receiving reinforcement for correct sequences of key presses. The specific
deficit induced by reinforcement is revealed in Figure 9–6b where we see that

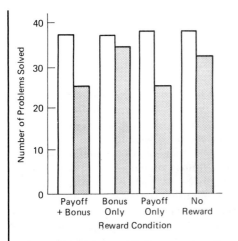

(a) Number of problems solved per group (*n* = 10) under the four different reinforcement conditions identified on the x-axis. (Data are presented separately for naive and pretrained subjects.)

(b) Number of trials per hypothesis under the four different reward conditions. (Data are presented separately for naive and pretrained subjects. Each bar represents the mean of 10 subjects × 4 problems

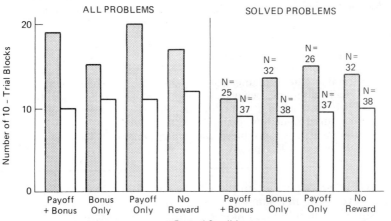

(c) Mean number of 10-trial blocks required per group (*n* −10) under the four different reinforcement conditions identified on the x-axis (Data are presented separately for naive and pretrained groups. Data on the left are from all problems and all subjects. Data on the right are from only those problems that were solved. The number above each bar indicates how many solved problems contributed to the bar [maximum = 40])

 Pretrained   ☐ Naive

FIGURE 9–6   Effects of Experience, Reinforcement, and Rule-Finding Bonus on Problem-Solving Ability
From B. Schwartz, Reinforcement-induced behavioral stereotyping: How not to teach people to discover rules. *Journal of Experimental Psychology: General,* 1982, *111.* Reprinted by permission of American Psychological Association.

reinforced experienced subjects tried out many fewer hypotheses per block of 50 trials than other subjects. Schwartz suggests that reinforcement induces a passive approach to problems, that pretraining and reinforcement "switches off their active intelligence" (Schwartz, 1982, p. 41). Finally, we should note that reinforcement is both damaging and unnecessary; naive subjects who received no payoffs at all did just as well as subjects receiving both reward and rule-finding bonuses.

Schwartz worries—and we should join him—about the effect of behavior modification programs in schools. These programs typically involve reinforcing particular desirable behaviors, and are in widespread use. But if Schwartz's findings are correct, the reinforcement techniques are unnecessary and dangerous. Reinforcement for particular behaviors seems to undermine intrinsic motivation, to short-circuit human problem-solving skills, and to strengthen the confirmation bias already so entrenched. If we want creative scientists, we had better be careful about using reward systems in school.

Finally, Schwartz's research underlines an important and perennial problem of psychology as a science. Unlike the ideas of physicists, psychologists' ideas can affect their subjects' behavior. Society adopts psychological concepts—"Freudian slip" is a household word, and *behavior modification* is used in prisons, hospitals, schools, and workplaces—and so psychology changes the way people behave. In this way, psychological theories can produce self-fulfilling data by changing human nature. As Schwartz puts it:

> It may be that as more components of the natural environment are subjected to modification by applied reinforcement theory, and more components of human behavior are thus controlled by reinforcement contingencies, a point will be reached at which virtually all human behavior will look like operant behavior. If this point is reached, it will tell us not that reinforcement theory has captured something general and essential about human nature, but that it has produced something general in human nature. (Schwartz, 1982, p. 58)

studied probabilities in simple choice situations. Ever since, people have been developing mathematical models of probabilistic decision making, often studying simple tasks like gambling or coin-tossing.

Gambling has been around for thousands of years. There is archaeological evidence of ancient dice in Egyptian tombs from 3000 B.C. The Old Testament speaks of casting lots (Joshua 18:10; Proverbs 16:33), with the results interpreted as the will of God. Ancient Greek amphorae (large jars) show Ajax and Achilles shooting dice.

When we talk about decision making, we can do so in either a **normative** (prescriptive) or **descriptive** sense. That is, we can talk about how people *should* make decisions (normative) or how they actually *do* make decisions (descriptive). While the psychologist's approach to the problem is most often descriptive, nuances of the normative approach creep in frequently, particularly in discussions of particular mathematical models of decision making, which are largely beyond the scope of this book. In recent years the emphasis has been increasingly on a more descriptive approach to decision making, which will be the emphasis in the brief treatment of decision making that follows.

Rationality

When we discuss decision making (or problem solving or reasoning, for that matter), the assumption is usually made that our decisions, if not all of our thought processes, are **rational.** We like to think that thought is rational, but, after all, what is rationality? This can perhaps best be approached by examining several principles of rational thought (Lee, 1971). First of all, a rational decision is one that is made *from a set of alternatives* that one has identified and been able to make some choice among. Part of making a good decision is first identifying all the reasonable alternatives to choose from initially. If a highly desirable or likely choice is not even considered, then the final choice may not be the best one.

A rational decision follows the principle of *transitivity*. For example, if, on a given afternoon, you would choose to play tennis rather than golf and choose golf rather than jogging, then you should also choose tennis over jogging, given that choice.

A rational decision is intended to maximize *utility* for the person. Utility is an important concept in decision making; it is the value to a person of a particular consequence. Utility is a psychological, subjective concept. It is related, but not identical, to the concept of *value*. An outcome of the same value may have two different utilities to two different people. For example, bending down to pick up a dollar bill off the sidewalk has the same value to anyone ($1); however, it would have a much greater utility to a poor vagrant than to a millionaire. The higher utility in the one case might lead to the vagrant's deciding to pick it up, while the millionaire might walk on by.

A rational decision is one that has been made based on the relevant, but not the irrelevant, information available to the person. Whenever we make a decision, we consider some information that is relevant, or *diagnostic,* while we ignore (or at least *think* we ignore) other information that is irrelevant (or nondiagnostic). As we shall see later, ignoring nondiagnostic information is not as easy as you might think.

Box 9–8 uses the concept of utility to analyze and use diagnostic information to come to a decision about a personal course of action. You may find this approach useful in your own life.

When we make any kind of decision, the diagnostic information is combined in various ways. Some researchers in decision making focus their studies on what information is combined and how it is combined. Norman Anderson (1981) uses the term **cognitive algebra** to refer to the mathematical laws that describe how we integrate various pieces of information together to come up with a decision. For example, if Nancy was trying to decide whether to go out with Kevin, she might have an impression of his personality and his appearance. For purposes of research, we could have

BOX 9–8 *MULTIATTRIBUTE UTILITY (MAU) ANALYSIS.*

This is a technique for analyzing a decision with several possible outcomes and several attributes on which to consider each outcome. It also uses the concept of subjective utility.

To understand the MAU approach, let's take a sample problem. Suppose you are trying to decide on what car to purchase. The following discussion will explain the technique through the use of this example. In reality, of course, the development of the example would be different for each individual.

1   The first step is to define the different alternatives (outcomes). Be sure to consider all the alternatives that would be real possibilities. For this example, suppose the cars listed across the top of the table below were the appropriate alternatives, determined through comparative shopping.

2   Next, identify the relevant attributes for making your decision. As with the alternatives, be sure not to leave out an important attribute. These are the criteria on which you expect to make your decision.

3   Third, assign utility values to each alternative X attribute combination on a 9-point evaluation scale, where 1 = bad and 9 = good. These are the values that attribute on that alternative has to you. For example, on the attribute of age, a 1984 Nissan rates a higher utility than an older car, though it rates more poorly on initial cost, because it is more expensive. (Remember that 9 is good and 1 is bad; this is not a cost scale!)

4   Fourth, assign weight values to each attribute based on that attribute's importance to you. *The weights must sum to 100.* In the example below, we chose to weight initial cost and gas mileage much higher than style. The weights, of course, reflect your personal attitudes and values.

5   Next, multiply each utility by the weight value for that attribute. These products appear in the table below.

6   Add the totals of these products for each alternative.

7   Compare the totals for each alternative. The alternative with the highest total should be your best choice. In the example below, that is the 1984 Nissan Sentra.

8   Now try the MAU approach for a decision you face in your own life.

ALTERNATIVES: Utilities/Weighted Utilities for Each Case

ATTRIBUTES	1984 NISSAN SENTRA	1982 OLDS OMEGA	1978 FORD MUSTANG	1976 PLYMOUTH FURY	WEIGHT
Age	8/160	5/100	3/60	3/60	20
Initial cost	2/70	4/140	7/245	8/280	35
Mileage	9/360	5/200	4/160	2/80	40
Style	4/20	5/25	7/35	1/5	5
Sum	610	465	500	425	100

Nancy quantify these impressions. She could combine these two pieces of information according to an additive (or perhaps an averaging) model if she considered both personality and appearance more or less equally (though this could be changed by introducing weighting factors into the model; for example, weight personality 75 percent and appearance 25 percent).

On the other hand, she could combine the pieces of information multiplicatively. In this case, if Kevin scored high on both personality and appearance, Nancy's total impression of him would be much better than if he were merely moderately high on both. On the other hand, if he was very low on either measure, that would pull her overall impression of him way down, even if he was very high on the second measure (great looks but a zero personality). A multiplicative model fits well with the intuitive notion that someone with personality = 0 is still 0, even if extremely attractive.

Estimating Likelihoods of Occurrence

Some events have objective probabilities of occurrence. For example, the probability of throwing a six on any given toss of a fair die is 1/6. The probability of drawing the six of clubs from a deck of 52 cards is 1/52. The probability as we estimate it is called **subjective probability,** which may or may not be equal, or even close to, the objective probability. Gambling casinos make a lot of money on patrons by using the "gambler's fallacy" discussed earlier in the chapter; the patrons' subjective probabilities of winning are much greater than the objective probabilities that they will do so. Feelings of being "on a streak" or "my luck's got to change" are merely subjective, not objective, probabilities. Many times there are no objective probabilities, and we must rely on subjective estimates. Many real-world decisions are like this. For example, there is no objective probability of how likely you are to watch the *Tonight Show* next Tuesday.

The Availability Heuristic

It has become increasingly obvious in the study of the psychology of decision making that people do not reason totally as the mathematical laws would predict (Kahneman, Slovic, & Tversky, 1982), just as they do not reason according to laws of formal logic. Rather, they frequently use **heuristics,** or practical strategies, for decision making. Some psychologists at Decision Research in Eugene, Oregon, have studied some of these heuristics extensively, both in the laboratory and the "real world."

One heuristic very widely used is *availability* (Tversky & Kahneman, 1973; Kahneman & Tversky, 1982). In such cases we estimate the likelihood or frequency of occurrence of some event based on the ease with which instances or associations can be brought to mind. Certainly, we always make decisions by retrieving appropriate schemata from long-term memory, but if we interpret our own experience and examples as being more typical than they really are, then we are being biased by the availability heuristic.

For example, when people were asked to say if the letter K is more likely to appear in the first or third position in a five-letter word in English, about two-thirds of the subjects responded "first," although, in fact, it is much more common in the third position. It is easier to generate examples of words starting with K than those with K in the middle, however. Consider how much easier it is to solve a crossword when we know only the first letter (K– – – –) than when we know only a letter in the middle (– –K– –).

The availability heuristic occurs widely beyond the laboratory in a great variety of significant situations. Recently there have been efforts to study its use in interpersonal situations where we draw on availability to make decisions about people in a social context (Ross & Sicoly, 1979; Taylor, 1982). Some of the most available schemata we draw on to interpret the actions of other people often tend to be stereotypes or otherwise inaccurate or biased information. Better understanding of our thought processes in such situations may eventually help us to reduce our dependence upon stereotyped ideas in the perception of others.

Looking at availability more generally, we tend to underestimate the probability of even a very likely event if it has never occurred before, because there is not a readily available instance to use in constructing a scenario. A current and controversial issue in the American Great Plains concerns the rapid depletion of the water table in the once-abundant groundwater of the Ogallala Aquifer that underlies much of the western Great Plains. Scientists warn that unless agriculture reduces its rate of groundwater pumping (primarily through heavy irrigation to nourish thirsty but profitable crops like corn), this rich agricultural region could revert to a desert in the next half century. Though this is a highly probable event if policies do not change, many find the scenario hard to imagine, just as Americans found a projected gasoline scarcity difficult to imagine before 1973. Once the event occurs, however, people may err and overestimate the probability of its recurrence, such as people who would move from an area after a very unusual flood that occurred once but would (mathematically) probably not recur in their lifetime. Another example of a perhaps not unlikely but never-before-happened event that people do not take very seriously is the feared excessive accumulation of carbon dioxide in the Earth's atmosphere due to pollution, leading to a calamitous rise in the earth's temperature.

Frequently the mere mention in the media of an occurrence of an event can serve to introduce an available scenario that increases our subjective probability estimations of the likelihood of its occurrence. When Slovic, Fischhoff, & Lichtenstein (1982) studied subjects' perceptions of the likelihood of different causes of death, they found that certain catastrophes were consistently overestimated and others consistently underestimated, and the difference was not particularly related to overall actual frequency (objective probability). For example, people overestimated the likelihood of dying from botulism, tornadoes, floods, venomous bites or stings, and car accidents. A death from such causes is likely to make the front page of the evening news. On the other hand, subjects consistently underestimated the probability of dying from asthma, emphysema, diabetes, strokes, and tuberculosis. Some kinds of cancer were overestimated and other kinds underestimated, with differences likely related to media coverage.

Sometimes the communications media alter our subjective probabilities in a helpful way. For example, when young drivers are shown gory films of auto accident victims, they may revise upward their probabilities of having such an accident themselves and thus drive more carefully. In such a case it might actually be better to overestimate mathematically the likelihood of that event occurring. Thus, the normatively "best" estimate would not be the "best" choice for one's health, just as the most "logical" scientific reasoning discussed above was not always the "best."

Another way that the availability heuristic manifests itself is in what has sometimes been called *illusory correlation*. People may infer that a causative relationship exists simply because a correlated event with some face validity as a causal agent exists. For example, suppose a hurricane with 100-mph winds is headed for Miami. The government seeds the cloud with silver iodide crystals. Following this, the hurricane gains force to 120-mph winds, slams into Miami Beach, and demolishes several large hotels. The owners try to sue the government for "causing" the destruction by cloud-seeding. Who is to say, however, that the hurricane might not have been even worse had the seeding not occurred, or indeed that it had any effect at all? Perhaps the seeding was the cause, but perhaps also the availability heuristic intervened and mentally assigned a convenient cause for a terrible event that people want very much to explain, to keep within the bounds of their rational model of the world.

A similar example may be seen in medical malpractice cases. A man has surgery; his condition deteriorates. Was the deterioration due to the surgery or not? Often courts are called on to make a very difficult decision, in part involving questions of how we process information, particularly our inferring of causal relationships.

The Anchoring Adjustment Heuristic

Another heuristic is the **anchoring-adjustment heuristic** (Slovic & Lichtenstein, 1971; Tversky & Kahneman, 1974). In these cases we make some initial estimate (*first impression*) and later revise that estimate upward or downward according to new information. However, the bias enters in that we often do not adjust the initial estimate (*anchor*) sufficiently and thus are overly biased by our original estimation. Personality studies show that we often are unduly biased by our first impression of a person. For example, a negative first impression may require many later positive encounters to balance the overall impression. Students sometimes complain that a teacher makes up his or her mind about them early in the semester and labels the student from that point on. For example, students may feel that poor performance on the first exam in a class may forever brand them as "stupid" in that teacher's eyes, even if later test performance is notably better. If the teacher is, in fact, thinking this way, the anchoring-adjustment heuristic is operating. The schema of that person in the teacher's mind would have been formed initially from highly negative information. It thus becomes the prototype from which change must be made.

Another type of example of anchoring-adjustment biases comes from cost and duration estimates for construction projects. For example, it is known that cost overruns and delays are quite frequent in building construction. When project costs are figured, they are initially figured at current cost levels and assuming that construction will proceed as planned. That overall figure is then revised upward to account for projected inflation, allowances for strikes, delivery delays, and other factors. Often, however, this revision is not sufficient; that is, there is too much reliance on the initial estimate.

Hindsight

Another heuristic is **hindsight** or "creeping determinism," as studied extensively by Baruch Fischhoff (1975, 1977; Fischhoff & Beyth, 1975). Fischhoff demonstrated experimentally that people are overly biased by hindsight; that is, how an event came out. When asked to make an estimate of probability of some event occurring from the point of view of someone answering *before* the event occurred, people are unable to ignore their knowledge of the outcome, even when specifically warned to do so. Again, the mind's tendency to impose order, structure, and interpretation on events reorganizes information in ways that can distort it.

After an unfortunate event occurs, people often look back and say, "We should have seen that coming." People retrospectively said the Japanese attack on Pearl Harbor in 1941 was predictable. In another type of example, a prisoner on parole commits another crime; people will say the parole officer should have foreseen that. Often people in responsible positions receive the blame after such events occur. No doubt sometimes they are at fault and, indeed, the event should have been anticipated. On the other hand, it is also highly likely that the hindsight bias in information processing is operating in some of these cases, and the unfortunate event really may not have been predictable before it happened.

Slovic and Fischhoff (1977) have demonstrated that hindsight operates in interpreting psychological research. For example, we overestimate the likelihood of replicating preliminary results. One disturbing theme found by these researchers has been the way mathematicians and scientists are almost as vulnerable as anyone else to distorted thinking through use of judgment heuristics (cf. results of scientific reasoning studies discussed above).

CONCLUSION

As you can see from this chapter, the study of thinking encompasses a wide range of problems and issues, as do your own processes of thinking. There is no comprehensive theory or even theoretical framework that can claim to

BOX 9–9 *ANSWERS TO PROBLEMS IN CHAPTER 9*

To find out what the customer ordered, simply *read the letters*, preferably with a certain intonation pattern:

C: Have you any eggs?
W: Yes, we have eggs.
C: Any ham?
W: Yes, we have ham too.
C: Do you have tea?
W: Yes, tea too.
C: I'll have ham and eggs and tea.

Answers to Questions in Box 9–1.

A: The knights trade horses.
B: TO/TIE/MULES/TO (The O is the hole.)
C: deny
D: $c = 2$ (c must be equivalent to the other diagonal of the rectangle, which is also a radius of the circle.)

describe or explain all types of thinking, nor is there likely to be such a theory in the near future. Still, cognitive psychology has managed to shed many important insights on these complex and often mysterious thought processes, processes that caused Shakespeare to write (long before the emergence of cognitive research!) the following description of people:

How noble in reason, how infinite in faculties . . .
In apprehension how like a god . . .
The beauty of the world, the paragon of animals.

SUGGESTED READINGS

The topics in this chapter, especially decision making, frequently receive cursory treatment or are totally ignored in cognitive psychology textbooks, which focus on memory and more basic information processing. However, Anderson (1980) has good chapters on problem solving and deductive reasoning and a chapter on "inductive reasoning," which includes some information on decision making. An integrative approach to problem solving and reasoning appears in Mayer (1983). Wason and Johnson-Laird (1972) remains a classic review of reasoning research up to that point.

James Adams' *Conceptual Blockbusting* (1976) and Barry Anderson's *The Complete Thinker* (1980) attempt to apply problem-solving research to one's daily life. Beyth-Marom and Lichtenstein's *An Elementary Approach to Thinking under Uncertainty* (1984) does the same for the judgmental biases in decision making.

CHAPTER TEN
LEARNING AND SOCIOBIOLOGY

INTRODUCTION

Learning and Biology

Without doubt, the single oldest issue in psychology is the nature-nurture, or nativism-empiricism debate. Plato was the first nativist, believing that human knowledge was an innate potential awaiting release by appropriate childhood experience. His pupil Aristotle, on the other hand, was the first empiricist, though not always a consistent one. He argued that gaining knowledge was essentially a matter of learning: the child, at birth devoid of any kind of knowledge, observed the world as it grew up, and gradually formed general ideas based on experience. Since ancient Greece, nativism and empiricism have confronted one another in the ideas of philosphers, theologians, biologists and psychologists. Occasionally the confrontations have become bitter clashes; now is such a time.

Resolving the nature-nurture issue has deep and serious consequences not only for the psychology of learning but for human society as well. Obviously—or so it seems—what is learned is not innate, and what is innate is not learned. Traditionally, psychologists have assumed, quite in accord with American tradition (Hogan & Schroeder, 1981), that there is no inherent human nature, that people are quite malleable and are shaped into what they are by society. This attitude is an important reason why the psychology of learning has been the central topic in modern psychology.

Learning psychologists have typically downplayed the role of the genes in constraining and directing the learning process.

For society, too, the issue is an important one. Literature abounds with engineered Utopias that reshape human behavior. Recent history is littered with failed attempts to construct a New Man—Marxist or communitarian—by engineering the society that raises him. The Khmer Rouge in Cambodia nearly drove their people to extinction in their bloody effort to reshape human nature. Our own society is built on the assumption that differences between people—especially between groups—are learned social differences not rooted in an essential human nature.

But more and more, learning psychologists are recognizing that biology can direct or even override learning, and some biologists are asserting that there *is* a human nature. The old controversy turns nasty again.

Related to the problem of nature versus nurture is the problem of development versus learning. Learning is about change. The most dramatic and important change each of us undergoes is growing up: changing from an infant into an adult. Everyone recognizes two broad forces behind human development, *maturation* and *learning*. Some developmental change is just physical maturation—growing taller, walking, puberty—about which the environment has little to do. Children start walking at about the same age all over the world quite independently of whether they had been carried around on cradle boards as infant Indians or whether each clumsy step was cheered by doting middle-class parents.

On the other hand, some development is equally clearly just a matter of learning. The American teenager learns to drive on the right side of the road, the British teenager on the left; neither is natural; each is equally arbitrary. Learning here includes both social and nonsocial learning, including learning that fire is hot and (perhaps) that stealing is wrong.

But are maturation and learning all there are? Some psychologists, including both behaviorists and cognitive scientists, believe this to be the case, no matter whether learning is conceived as simple conditioning or as cognitive learning. In other words, excluding maturation, only those processes that operate in short-term learning or memory experiments in the laboratory are operating in development. Behavioral and cognitive development is simply the cumulative result of thousands of hours of small learning events; development *is* learning.

Conversely, many developmental psychologists believe that there are specific developmental forces beyond maturation and learning. The processes of learning revealed in laboratory experiments are not, in their view, sufficient to explain all the great changes that occur between infancy and adulthood. While disagreeing on specific points, developmental theorists argue that development possesses a direction and autonomy deriving from inner processes of change, and not explicable in terms of environmental shaping alone.

It is important to bear in mind that the debate between learning and development is not the same as the nurture-versus-nature debate. Both groups recognize biological maturation as a force in human development, though of course each scientist has particular views on how important it is.

The debate focuses primarily on whether development is a wholly externally driven learning process, or whether it is at least in part the expression of inner, teleological directive processes.

Again, resolution of this issue is not simply an academic matter. For different child-rearing and educational strategies follow from each viewpoint. If the learning view is correct, then parents and teachers must be active, directive educators, constantly seeing to it that the right kinds of experiences, rewards, and punishments are given to the child to mold him or her into a mature and worthwhile adult. On the other hand, if development is inner directed and follows an unfolding logic of its own, then parents and teachers need only provide a rich environment and then step back, letting spontaneous development occur at a natural pace. Directive teaching would be viewed as ineffective at best, and at worst as a harmful intrusion on natural growth. Naturally, advocates of the learning view might in turn accuse developmentalists of neglect that, while benign, is nonetheless dangerous.

This part of the book will explore the nature-nurture and development-learning problems in three chapters. In Chapter 10 we will examine the exciting new field of sociobiology, the study of the biological basis of animal and human social behavior. Humans' most important social behavior is language, and is taken up in Chapter 11, where we will examine the biology, development, and learning of language. Chapter 11 raises the theme of development by considering how children acquire language, and then Chapter 12 pursues the learning-development-biology theme more generally.

The Emergence of Sociobiology

On February 15, 1978, Harvard entomologist Edward O. Wilson was about to address a symposium of the American Association for the Advancement of Science. Suddenly, about a dozen demonstrators rose up and, proclaiming Wilson's ideas "all wet," dumped a bucket of water over his head, and finally marched out chanting slogans linking Wilson with racism, sexism, facism, and Nazism. In the letters pages of *The New York Review of Books,* some of Wilson's fellow scientists—including colleagues at Harvard—accused him of providing "a genetic justification for the status quo and of existing privileges for certain groups according to class, race, or sex" (Allen et al., 1975/1978; reply by Wilson, 1975b/1978). What had Wilson done to bring all this down on his head?

He had published *Sociobiology* (1975a). *Sociobiology* was a text defining a new field of the same name, namely, the study of the biological basis of social behavior from the simplest orders to human beings. Its content was not new; it synthesized and named an already developing discipline dating back to the early 1970s, with roots in the still older disciplines of ethology and behavior genetics. Nor was Wilson the first synthesizer; Robert Hinde had synthesized ethology and comparative psychology in his book *Animal Behavior* (1966, 1970). The ruckus around Wilson's *Sociobiology* centered on his last chapter extending sociobiology from animals to human beings; not only did he suggest that there was an irreducibly biological human nature, but he also made sweeping claims that sociobiology would "cannibalize" the social sciences and provide a new biological ethics. Social scientists, including psychologists, found Wilson challenging both their basic assumptions about learning and their right to independent existence as scientists (a theme carried further by Rosenberg, 1980). This explains why there was so much excitement and consternation about a long, technical, university press book.

In the present chapter we will examine the basics of sociobiology, give some examples of the sociobiological approach to behavior, and look at how sociobiological thinking may be extended to human behavior.

BASIC PRINCIPLES OF SOCIOBIOLOGY[1]

Darwinian Evolution

The central paradigm of modern biology is the neo-Darwinian theory of evolution, and at root sociobiology is no more than the extension of evolutionary thinking from physical traits and simple behaviors such as reflexes to complex social behaviors including altruism, mating, and child rearing. The central theorem of sociobiology is: "When any behavior under study reflects some component of genotype, animals should behave so as to maximize their inclusive fitness." (Barash, 1977). That is, since social behavior may help or hinder the survival of any animal and its offspring, social behavior is very likely to have a genetic basis (be part of the genotype), and be subject to Darwinian rules of natural selection.

Although everyone has heard of Darwin and Darwin's theory, it is so misunderstood that a review of its basics is called for. The first thing we associate with Darwin is something he did not discover, and which was well on its way to acceptance before Darwin published his *Origin of Species* in 1859. It is the idea of *descent*—the notion that present living forms are the altered descendants of long-extinct predecessors down millions of years of change. What Darwin contributed was a workable *mechanism* for explaining why species should change; why some should go extinct, some remain stable for millenia, and still others undergo alteration toward their present form. Integrated with Mendelian genetics, this Neo-Darwinian theory is the most widely accepted account of the mechanism of evolutionary change, and forms the foundation of sociobiology.

The basic Darwinian concept was best stated by its co-discoverer, Alfred Russel Wallace:

> The life of wild animals is a struggle for existence. The full exertion of all their faculties and all their energies is required to preserve their own existence and provide for that of their infant offspring. The possibility of

---

[1]In order to avoid cluttering the text with repetitive references, only direct citations will be made. What follows draws on the following works: Alcock (1979); Barash (1977, 1979); Dawkins (1976); Wilson (1975a); and on readings found in Clutton-Brock and Harvey (1978) and Hunt (1980).

procuring food during the least favourable seasons, and of escaping the attacks of their most dangerous enemies, are the primary conditions which determine the existence both of individuals and of entire species. These conditions will also determine the population of a species; and by a careful consideration of all the circumstances we may be enabled to comprehend, and in some degree to explain, what at first sight appears so inexplicable—the excessive abundance of some species, while others closely allied to them are very rare . . .

Wild cats are prolific and have few enemies; why then are they never as abundant as rabbits? The only intelligible answer is, that their supply of food is more precarious. It appears evident, therefore, that so long as a country remains physically unchanged, the numbers of its animal population cannot materially increase. If one species does so, some others requiring the same kind of food must diminish in proportion. The numbers that die annually must be immense; and as the individual existence of each animal depends upon itself, those that die must be the weakest—the very young, the aged, and the diseased,—while those that prolong their existence can only be the most perfect in health and vigour—those who are best able to obtain food regularly, and avoid their numerous enemies. It is, as we commenced by remarking, "a struggle for existence," in which the weakest and least perfectly organized must always succumb . . . .

Most or perhaps all the variations from the typical form of a species must have some definite effect, however slight, on the habits or capacities of the individuals. Even a change of colour might, by rendering them more or less distinguishable, affect their safety; a greater or less development of hair might modify their habits. More important changes, such as an increase in the power or dimensions of the limbs or any of the external organs, would more or less affect their mode of procuring food or the range of country which they inhabit. It is also evident that most changes would affect, either favourably or adversely, the powers of prolonging existence. An antelope with shorter or weaker legs must necessarily suffer more from the attacks of the feline carnivora; the passenger pigeon with less powerful wings would sooner or later be affected in its powers of procuring a regular supply of food; and in both cases the result must necessarily be a diminution of the population of the modified species. If, on the other hand, any species should produce a variety having slightly increased powers of preserving existence, that variety must inevitably in time acquire a superiority in numbers. These results must follow as surely as old age, intemperance, or scarcity of food produce an increased mortality. In both cases there may be many individual exceptions; but on the average the rule will invariably be found to hold good. All varieties will therefore fall into two classes—those which under the same conditions would never reach the population of the parent species, and those which would in time obtain and keep a numerical superiority. Now, let some alteration of physical conditions occur in the district—a long period of drought, a destruction of vegetation by locusts, the irruption of some new carnivorous animal seeking "pastures new"—any change in fact tending to render existence more difficult to the species in question, and tasking its utmost powers to avoid complete extermination; it is evident that, of all the individuals composing the species, those forming the least numerous and most feebly organized variety would suffer first, and, were the pressure severe, must soon become extinct. The same causes continuing in action, the parent species would next suffer, would gradually diminish in numbers, and with a recurrence of similar unfavourable conditions might also become extinct. The superior variety would then alone remain, and on a return to favourable circumstances would rapidly increase in numbers and occupy the place of the extinct species and variety. (Wallace, 1858/1980, p. 327–332)

In short, species become extinct if they fail in the struggle for existence. They will survive unchanged if they are perfectly suited to their environments. They change (evolve) when some of their members struggle more effectively than others and are therefore able to pass on their genes to more offspring that live longer, while the weak die young and childless and their genes with them. There is no obvious reason to exclude social behavior from the process of natural selection. The ability to find, choose, and keep a mate and to rear offspring with it are abilities needed for the struggle for existence, and so will be subject to selection. When group living confers selective advantage, it will evolve; when the ability to learn quickly and react flexibly to new challenges confers selective advantage, it will evolve.

Two misconceptions about Darwinian theory are especially important for a correct grasp of sociobiology, and they need to be confronted immediately. Each was poetically expressed by Alfred Tennyson in his poem *In Memoriam* (1850) even before the theory of evolution was stated.

First, consider this famous phrase:

Who trusted God was love indeed
  And love Creation's final law—
  Though Nature, red in tooth and claw
With ravine, shrieked against his creed—

"Nature red in tooth and claw" is a famous image seemingly borne out by Wallace's description of the struggle for existence. But the struggle is usually quiet, indirect, and involves no bloodshed. All that really counts in evolution is having offspring that live to maturity. *Any* trait or behavior that serves that end, or, more precisely, that aids one in having more successful offspring than anyone else, confers selective advantage.

An economic example will help (Ghiselin, 1974). Two merchants may provide the same product and the same service at the same price, and so will likely have the same number of customers and the same amount of sales. Yet if merchant A can lower her costs—for example by paying lower rent—she will have more profits and be better off than merchant B. The competition is not direct, not "red in tooth and claw": B is not driven to the wall. Yet A prospers more.

Competition in nature may be similarly indirect and unbloody. Bird A competes with bird B not (necessarily) by attacking it or killing it or depriving it of resources, but in other, more subtle ways. The female (A) may attract a stronger, fitter mate, who is better able to help protect and raise her (and his) offspring. A may be able to lay more eggs than B, have more clutches than B, secure a better nest site than B. These behaviors need not involve direct competition between A and B, but they do confer a selective advantage on A. She will have more of *her* genes present in the next generation, and that is what evolution is all about—the changing frequencies of genes in the total gene pool. Evolutionary success is a gene's frequency rising; failure is its lowering.

The gene leads us to the next important misconception about evolution, one biologists themselves did not shake until the 1960s. Again, Tennyson aptly expressed it:

> Are God and Nature then at a strife,
>   That Nature lends such evil dreams?
>   So careful of the type[2] she seems,
> So careless of the single life.

It is widely believed that natural selection (Nature) acts for the good of the species (the type) not for the individual. But recent analyses show that *group selection*—as this belief is called—is practically impossible.

Nature is filled with behaviors—quite red in tooth and claw—that are clearly detrimental to the species as a whole but do benefit the individual. There is a species of langur (monkey) in which a harem of females mates with, and is dominated by, a single male. Adult males struggle for control of harems, and when a new male ousts and replaces an old harem master he regularly kills all the infant monkeys in the band. Such infanticide can hardly redound to the benefit of the langur species. But it does benefit the new harem master: He has eliminated the offspring of a rival, and he ensures that *his* genes, not someone else's, will continue in the next generation.

His advantage is further served when the former mothers immediately come into estrus—rather than waiting two or three years while they nurse their young—and mate with the conqueror. Thus, the brood he protects is his own.

This example demonstrates the gene-thinking that made sociobiology possible. Dawkins (1976) calls it the *selfish gene theory*. What matters in evolution is not the survival of the species, or even the individual (as we shall see when we get to altruism), but the survival of genes. Samuel Butler, a critic of Darwin, once poked fun at the theory by saying that a chicken was just an egg's way of making more eggs. In modern biology this is now seen as correct, for an organism *is* DNA's way of making more DNA. What struggles for existence according to gene-thinking is individual genes, and they do it not by competing directly, but through organisms, their "survival machines" (Dawkins, 1976) who possess traits and behaviors that phenotypically express the genes composing their genotypes. More than anything else, sociobiology is the application of gene-thinking—and the mathematical models that can be constructed with gene-thinking—to social behavior (Maynard Smith, 1982).

The Claims of Sociobiology

Sociobiology is a very complex field. To understand it we need to discuss and define a few of its central claims and terms.

---

[2]species

Proximate and ultimate causation, or why sugar tastes good   To ask why people like sugar seems inane—it tastes sweet. But *why* does it taste sweet? Several kinds of answers can be given. One might give a phenomenological analysis of the pleasures of sweetness. Then one might explain the experience of sweetness in terms of physiological mechanisms in the tongue and brain. For many purposes these answers are sufficient. But we can still ask, "Why do people have a physiology that makes sugar taste sweet?" The only possible answer is evolutionary—that ancestors who tended to like sugary foods, primarily ripe, vitamin-rich fruits, ate them, and this gave them superior energy to continue the struggle for existence, so that they had more offspring than (say) alkaline-liking rivals. As a result, the gene that expressed itself as "sweetness-liking" so rose in frequency as to become almost universal, driving people to eat not only medically protective apples (an apple a day keeps the doctor away), but also to invent and eat candy bars, to the harm of our teeth.

Consider children at play. What do they do? Run, jump, climb, swing on monkey bars. Why do they do these things? Because they are fun to do. Why are they fun? Because each of these was a survival skill to our hominid ancestors and needed practice. A child of our evolutionary ancestors who did not find them fun would not do them, and would soon be eaten by the first predator that rushed his familial troop. His genes would die, while those of his playful friends would survive—including the one(s) that made running, jumping, climbing, and swinging "fun." Why does orgasm feel good? Because if it did not, we would not have sex (and for males, *could* not have sex) and would not have offspring. A gene for not enjoying orgasm is obviously unfit.

What makes sociobiology of such potential importance is that it not only addresses the behavior of a species, but also reaches deep into its *mentality,* providing new kinds of answers to questions about mind and behavior. To say I like sugar because it is sweet, or orgasm because it feels good, or to run because it is fun, is to assign the *proximate causes* of my behavior or my likings. That is, in each case I describe the immediate causes of my behavior. I explain what I do or like in terms of what I know makes me do or like them. Physiological explanations also cite proximite causes, describing the physiological underpinnings of tasting sweetness, having an orgasm, or running.

But when we explain psychology and physiology in terms of past evolutionary success, we are moving toward what biologists call *ultimate causation.* Here we describe the evolutionary causes of the proximate causes—why my brain has mechanisms for liking sugar, orgasms, or running. Figure 10–1 (from Alcock, 1979) shows the relation of ultimate to proximate causation, including the developmental connection between genes and the phenotypes that express them, and how these phenotypes—the proximate mechanism of physiology and psychology—lead to behaviors that either succeed or fail in the struggle for existence, affecting the gene-frequencies in the next generation.

Now there is nothing wrong or false about proximate causation. It is perfectly true that you like sugar because it is sweet; the physiologist's ex-

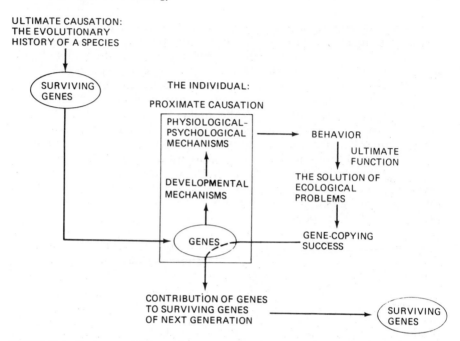

ULTIMATE CAUSATION:
THE EVOLUTIONARY
HISTORY OF A SPECIES

SURVIVING
GENES

THE INDIVIDUAL:

PROXIMATE CAUSATION

PHYSIOLOGICAL–
PSYCHOLOGICAL
MECHANISMS

BEHAVIOR

ULTIMATE
FUNCTION

DEVELOPMENTAL
MECHANISMS

THE SOLUTION OF
ECOLOGICAL
PROBLEMS

GENES

GENE-COPYING
SUCCESS

CONTRIBUTION OF GENES
TO SURVIVING GENES
OF NEXT GENERATION

SURVIVING
GENES

FIGURE 10–1   Proximate and Ultimate Causation of Behavior. Ultimately an animal has within it certain genes because they have survived to the present. These genes regulate the development of the proximate mechanisms of behavior. These mechanisms make possible certain behavioral reponses to environmental events—responses that will determine the number of copies of the individual's genes that are passed to the next generation. The ultimate function of behavior is to meet ecological pressures in such a way that the individual maximizes its gene-copying success.

planation of sweetness is equally true. Neither are sham explanations. Ultimate explanation does not destroy the proximate explanations; it just helps us understand where they came from. Some people think that when sociobiologists attribute altruism to the calculus of kin selection (see below) it turns the love of a parent for its child into a cynical calculation. Nonsense. Love is no less real because it helps us survive. Love is no more destroyed by ultimate explanation in terms of survival than is Chartres Cathedral destroyed by explaining where the stone that built it was quarried.

Inclusive fitness and kin selection   The concept of **fitness** refers to how successful an individual is in passing his or her genes on to the next generation. Traditionally, as in Wallace's classic passage, the measures of fitness has been the number of offspring, since this is the most obvious and direct way of transmitting one's genes. More recently, however, gene-thinking has expanded the older concept of fitness. In gene-thinking we realize that (to speak metaphorically) it is each gene (or nucleotide segment of DNA, see Box 10–1) that seeks to replicate itself, and to increase its frequency in the next generation. Since any individual is genetically related to many people besides one's children, a gene can increase its frequency in the population by changing one's behavior toward one's relatives as a whole. If a

BOX 10–1   *SELFISH DNA?*

Although we like to think of human beings as the most complex creatures in nature, humans do not carry the most DNA—the encoder of genetic information. Frogs, lilies, and lungfish have much more DNA—in the case of the lungfish 42 times as much—than human beings do. Moreover, geneticists have found that in may species as little as 5 percent of the DNA carries instructions for manufacturing a new member of the species.

These findings are rather puzzling and have led to some bizarre speculations inspired by sociobiology. In his book *The Selfish Gene*, Richard Dawkins (1976) forcefully presented the case for sociobiological gene-thinking. What really counts in evolution is the continued survival of the gene, not the individual or the species. Dawkins hinted at the possibility that some DNA might be "hitching a ride" within the genonome, its host organism—replicating itself within the host and being transmitted to the host's offspring without contributing in any functional way to the phenotype of its carrier.

Following up Dawkins' suggestion, Leslie Orgel and Francis Crick (co-discoverer of DNA) (1980), and W. F. Doolittle and Carmen Sapienza (1980) have proposed that the apparently excess DNA carried by most species is, in the title of Orgel's and Crick's paper, "Selfish DNA: The ultimate parasite." They argue that the seemingly useless (at least to the organism) DNA is just that—useless—serving no function beyond its own self-replication, and engaging in "a kind of molecular struggle for existence" within the host organism.

Not surprisingly, these proposals have proved controversial. Other biologists have argued that the "useless" DNA does functionally serve the organism in ways not yet proved. It may function as an editing device separating genetically meaningful DNA units; it may act as a reserve bank of DNA in case of damage to "useful" DNA, or it may take a structural role in holding together a large cell nucleus. In any event, sociobiology has stirred lively controversy not only among social scientists but also among microbiologists.*

*See James Gorman, "The Case of the Selfish DNA," *Discover* June 1981.

gene causes a person to act so as to enhance his or her relatives' fitness, that gene—which is very likely to be present in those relatives—will increase its numbers in the next generation.

Sociobiologists now distinguish the concepts of *individual* fitness and *inclusive fitness*. Individual fitness refers to my genes' level of success in the struggle for existence as measured through my own individual offspring; the more offspring, the higher is the level of individual fitness. Inclusive fitness adds to this a proportion of my fitness measured through my effects on my relatives. To the extent that my genes lead me to help my relatives survive and raise their offspring, I will increase my inclusive fitness. Inclusive fitness *includes* individual fitness, being the measure of my gene's total fitness in the struggle for existence.

Another way of defining inclusive fitness has been suggested by Brown and Brown (1981). As shown in Figure 10–2, we may distinguish

FIGURE 10–2 The inclusive fitness of an individual may be divided into two components, *direct fitness,* which is mediated through the genes in an individual's own offspring, and *indirect fitness,* which is mediated through copies of the same genes in the offspring of other individuals. Similarly, an individual's inclusive fitness is affected by influences from its parents (direct path) and from others (indirect path). These paths converge on the individual, where they are blended and expressed as the individual's direct and indirect fitness. (From Brown & Brown, 1981) Courtesy Chiron Press, Inc.

between *direct* and *indirect fitness pathways.* An individual receives fitness directly from his or her parent and contributes it directly to his or her children. An individual receives fitness indirectly from others, either from kin-selected behaviors or from reciprocity, and contributes it to others, whether relations (kin selection) or nonrelative (reciprocity). The terms *direct* and *indirect* fitness help us see that inclusive fitness includes effects that may not be based on genetic relatedness, but embrace aid or harm done to nonrelatives as well. So inclusive fitness includes the fitness we inherit from relatives (individual fitness and kin-selected fitness) *and* the fitness we accrue from interactions with nonrelatives.

The concept of inclusive fitness leads to the idea of **kin selection,** already inherent in our discussion so far. A gene whose strategy is to enhance only individual fitness, perhaps by causing an individual to want and raise many offspring, is subject to *individual selection*: Whether it succeeds or fails depends on the life and death of its host survival-machine. A gene whose strategy is to cause me to help my relatives—and thereby to help itself replicate through them—is subject to *kin selection*: Whether it succeeds or fails depends less on my own life or death than on the degree to which my sacrifices aid my kin. The logic of kin selection is central to the sociobiological analysis of altruism.

Difficulties and Aims of Human Sociobiology

We are not just rather like animals:
we *are* animals.

Mary Midgley (1978)

Despite the obvious truth of Mary Midgley's statement, there is no doubt that the sociobiology of *homo sapiens* is much more controversial than the sociobiology of other species. As Wilson found out, it is only when sociobiologists touch on human nature that paroxysms of controversy begin. Moreover, acknowledgment of biological roots of human action may be deeply and personally disturbing. A female graduate student and feminist was so enraged after reading Robert Trivers' "Parental Investment and Sexual Selection," for example, that she had herself sterilized (Bingham, 1980).

In addition to working in a swirling sea of controversy, sociobiologists studying human behavior face a more scientific problem: The kinds of data that can be collected on animal behavior are simply unavailable for human beings. The selective breeding experiments of animal behavior genetics are not permissible with humans. Nor are the kind of extended field studies of naturalists possible with our species: No young man or woman about town would tolerate being followed 24 hours a day by a note-taking ethologist; no human family would admit strangers to their most intimate intercourse.

So the sociobiologist is thrown back on analogy, everyday observation, field studies conducted by anthropologists, and speculation. Each of these methods has its drawbacks. Analogy from animals can be useful. Chimpanzees and the other primates are biologically close relatives—very close in the case of the chimpanzee with whom we share 99 percent of our blood factors (Baba, Darga, & Goodman, 1982). So studies of primate societies may be instructive. Although we *are* animals, we are *not* chimpanzees, and extrapolations must be made with care. The same goes for a second kind of animal analogy, from more distant species who are under the same ecological pressures that we are. Bird monogamy may tell us something about human monogamy, but we must be careful in deciding how much.

Everyday observation of ourselves and others is a rich source of human sociobiological data (Box 10–2). Yet our culture is one among many and we must be careful not to take a unique cultural trait as a universal biological condition. Going to other cultures is an important corrective in this connection, but is again of often limited value to sociobiological reasoning. Our knowledge of other cultures comes from anthropologists who collected most of their data before sociobiology came on the scene, and thus had a different set of questions in mind. Hence, important information may be lacking. For example, to test sociobiological hypotheses we would need to know about differential reproduction rates for different members of a studied tribe or village, yet this is the kind of information traditional ethnographies did not report. Only a few recent ethnographies have been carried out to test sociobiological hypotheses directly.

What remains is our most far-ranging but unreliable tool, *speculation*. We must use what data we have, but finally putting it together into a picture of human nature is, at present, as much art as science. Nonetheless, it is important work. The sociobiologist does not wish to show that human beings are prisoners held fast by their genes. Rather, as Richard D. Alexander (1979a) put it:

> The challenge of Darwinism is to find out what our genes have been up to and to make that knowledge widely available as a part of the environment in which each of us develops and lives so that we can decide for ourselves, quite deliberately, to what extent we wish to go along.

BOX 10–2   *A SIMPLE FIELD STUDY IN HUMAN SOCIOBIOLOGY*

Here is an easy-to-carry-out observational study of human beings with results that can be analyzed sociobiologically. This box simply describes what to do; the last box in the chapter discusses the usual results. Please collect your data before looking up the answer.

Go to a place on campus where students are likely to congregate. Then, for about 20 of them—half males and half females—record their sex and how they hold their books, noting particularly which hand is holding the books and whether they are held at the chest or straight at the side. Record your data by making ticks in the following chart:

POSITION OF BOOKS

	LEFT HAND		RIGHT HAND	
	AT CHEST	STRAIGHT	AT CHEST	STRAIGHT
Male				
S e x				
Female				

Although the standard assumption of American psychology has been that people at birth are virtual blank slates, and are, in Skinner's phrase, completely shaped by their environments, evidence has been mounting that many behavior patterns we have taken to be learned do, in fact, possess strong innate components (Bower, 1979; Eibl-Eibesfeldt, 1975; Freedman, 1974; Wells, 1980). Cognitive abilities such as attention (Lumsden & Wilson, 1981), depth perception, form perception, ability to locate objects in space by eye and ear, integration of sensory modalities and face recognition (Bower, 1974) have been shown to be present at birth or at least as early as they can be tested. There is a universal system of basic color categories that exists even in those cultures that have few basic color terms, and cultures acquire these terms in a sequence that correlates with industrialization and recapitulates children's acquisition of color terms (Lumsden & Wilson, 1981).

On the social side, the development of expressive responses such as smiling, laughing, and crying develop the same way in both normal, blind, and deaf-blind infants and children (Eibl-Eibesfeldt, 1975; Freedman, 1974). Cross-cultural analyses reveal universal human patterns of nonverbal expression in such areas as flirting, coyness, eyebrow raising, eating alone, and food-sharing. For example, like chimpanzees and baboons worried about scavengers, humans eating alone—even in civilized restaurants—look up and scan the horizon after every few bites. Food-sharing is used by members of most primitive cultures to foster bonding and allay aggression. A similar if unconscious inclination seems also present in industrialized cultures: Eibl-Eibesfeldt (1975) reports a soldier whose assault on an enemy was forestalled by being reflexively given a piece of bread. So touched was he that he could not kill again. It is even possible that career interests are more influenced by genes than by upbringing (Grotevant, Scarr, & Weinberg, 1978).

Abnormal patterns of behavior may also have genetic bases. Scientists have long searched for a genetic-biochemical basis for such psychoses as schizophrenia, and strong patterns of heritability have emerged from family relationship studies (Wells, 1980). Even lesser disorders such as neuroses may have a biological component. Lumsden and Wilson (1981) suggest that phobias may represent a prepared form of human learning. For example, human fear of snakes is widespread even where wild snakes are never encountered. Chimpanzees also run away from snakes and even hoses in apparent terror. Lemurs, unlike chimpanzees and people, evolved in snake-free regions and find snakes interesting. As Lumsden and Wilson point out, human phobias are most typically evoked by things that would have endangered our early primate ancestors—snakes, spiders, open or closed spaces, heights, thunderstorms—rather than by the real dangers of modern life—guns, knives, electrical sockets, buses.

The most dramatic, if hard to study, evidence for heritability of even the most trivial behaviors comes from studies of twins (see Freedman, 1974), especially the rare and well-publicized (Farber, 1981; Holden, 1980a, 1980b) cases of identical twins reared apart. Striking similarities ranging from dress—one pair of twins reunited only briefly in childhood turned up wearing the same dress—to phobias such as claustrophobia or fear of escalators—turn up among such sets of twins. It is even turning out that separated identical twins may be *more* alike than identical twins reared together, since in the latter case parents and the twins themselves actively try to create distinctive personalities.

While little of this evidence bears directly on the claims of sociobiology, it is nevertheless relevant because it undermines extreme environmentalism. If people are entirely shaped by their environment—by parents, teachers, and culture—then sociobiology could not be true for human beings no matter how true it might be for animals. But evidence of the sort we have briefly reviewed here underscores Midgley's assertion that we *are* animals, possessing partial genetic determination of a wide range of behaviors, attitudes, and personality traits. Moreover—and this is also a necessary prerequisite for sociobiological analysis (Lumsden & Wilson, 1981)—there is evidence for systematic *variation* in many social traits. For example, compared to European-American children, Chinese-American children are calmer, harder to upset, and less noisy in groups (Freedman, 1974). If evolution is correct, isolated breeding populations ought to show differences in behavior, which seems to be indeed what we find.

EXAMPLES OF SOCIOBIOLOGICAL REASONING

Sociobiology has been employed to explain everything from group size to parental care (Wilson, 1975a). In this section we will consider sociobiological explanation in four major areas, moving from accounts of animal behavior to human behavior.

Altruism

Altruism—helping another at some risk to one's self—appears to fly in the face of natural selection. How can there be a gene that puts its survival-machine, and thus itself, at risk of death? If the organism dies, so do its genes, and so it appears quite impossible for natural selection to have favored altruistic, suicidal genes. The answer lies in gene-thinking: The altruist is the tool of a selfish gene. Three gene-thinking analyses of altruism have been offered, of altruism as kin-selected, of reciprocal altruism and mutualism, and of individually selected "altruism."

Altruism and kin-selection   A number of insect species, including the familiar honeybee and the summer house pest, the paper wasp, have evolved what biologists call *eusociality,* a highly organized social structure including a distinct caste of sterile female workers. Such a caste represents the height of altruism, for these workers give up having offspring of their own and toil "for the good of the hive." Altruism of this order was recognized by Darwin himself as a serious challenge to natural selection, and solution of the problem (Hamilton, 1964/1980; Samuelson, 1983; Trivers & Hare, 1976/1980) represented a triumph for gene-thinking.

What was first most suggestive about eusociality was that of the two dozen or so species that display it, all but one (certain termites) are of the order *Hymenoptera,* which possesses a very unusual genetic system called haplodiploidy. In the haplodiploid species the paper wasp (shown in Figure 10–3), a female mates once with a male and stores his sperm inside her body, and then goes on to found a colony. When she fertilizes an egg and deposits it in the nest, it becomes a female; when she deposits an egg *without* fertilizing it, it becomes a male.

The vast majority of living things are like the female wasp: They are *diploid,* possessing two sets of chromosomes, one set from each parent. For simplicity's sake, only two chromosomes, A and B, are considered in Figure 10–3. In the female the pairs of A chromosomes are called A_1 and A_2, the pairs of B chromosomes are B_1 and B_2; thus, the queen carries four chromosomes altogether. Male wasps, however, are *haploid:* Since they develop from an unfertilized egg, they possess only *one* set of chromosomes, not two sets. In Figure 10–3, the male carries only two chromosomes, A' and B'.

When the queen forms an egg from her genotype, taking half the chromosomes, four possible eggs can result, as shown. However, the sperm she carries are all identical—the male must contribute all of his genotype to each sperm, not just half of it as diploid creatures do. This simple fact does odd things to the genetic relatedness of the sisters produced by the queen. Figure 10–3 shows the four possible genotypes that can be formed from

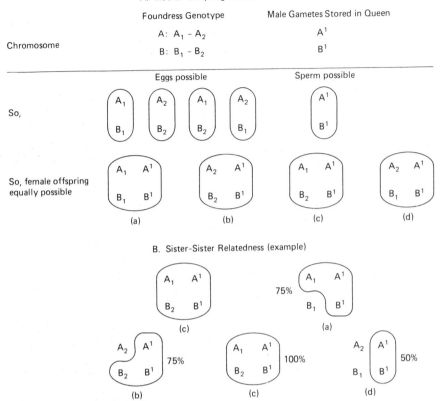

FIGURE 10–3 The Genetics of Haplodiploid Insects (Adapted from Alcock, 1979)

each mating of sperm and egg, and then picks one possible female and measures her degree of relatedness to her sisters. In diploid genetic systems, siblings are related by half their genes; however, in the haplodiploid system all sisters begin with the same genes gotten from the haploid father and *add* some degree of relatedness through their mother. As Figure 10–3 shows, each female is on average 75 percent related to her sisters.

These calculations make possible a **kin-selection** explanation of female sterility in eusocial insects. (But see Hunt, 1980, for other equally sociobiological accounts using individual selection, and West-Eberhard, 1981, for a comparative evaluation.) If a sister has her own offspring, she will be related to them by 50 percent of her genes (just as they are related to the queen). But she is related to her sisters by sharing 75 percent of their genes. Therefore, her genes will do better in the struggle for existence—increasing their numbers in the wasp gene pool—by helping the queen produce other sisters who share 75 percent of their genes, than by having their own offspring, who would share only 50 percent of their genes. In this way kin-selection produces selfish altruism. In sacrificing their own individual fitness by "altruistically" remaining sterile and helping their mother run the colony and raise her offspring, worker wasps (and bees) are really acting in the (selfish) interest of their own genes. Selection acts through kin, specifically sisters in this case, rather than through an individual's own offspring.

Certain interesting features of eusocial insect life may be explained by this model. We all know about drones—useless males who selfishly fritter away their lives (Wodehouse, 1940). Hymenopteran males are true drones, contributing no labor to the colony while aggressively begging for food from the female workers. Kin-selection explains this: Their genetic relatedness to their siblings is only 50 percent—the same as to direct offspring—and so altruism has no special benefits to them. A quantitative test of the hypothesis is possible by looking at the sex ratio of male to female offspring from the mother. In most species under normal conditions there is no reason to prefer having either male or female offspring; you are related to either by 50 percent. However, in a haplodiploid system the living sisters should prefer to produce more sisters than brothers in a ratio of about 3:1. And this appears to be just what happens; either the females manipulate the queen in as yet unknown ways, or they neglect, and so kill, many of their brothers.

The kin-selection explanation of altruism can be, and has been, extended to other species including mammals. It may explain why ground squirrels give predator alarm calls when they are near close relatives but not otherwise, why wild turkeys form brother-brother pairs while looking for mates, and why young male Florida scrub jays often help their parents rear more offspring. In general, kin-selection of altruistic behavior may be invoked whenever we wish to explain a behavior that reduces one's own fitness but enhances that of relatives. Whenever the risk to your own genes is outweighed by the benefit to your genes carried by relatives, then kin-selection may take place.

Reciprocal altruism   Even in the animal world not all altruism is directed at close relatives. Can sociobiology explain the evolution of behavior that immediately benefits neither the individual nor his or her relatives but some total stranger? Perhaps it can (see Trivers, 1971/1980). If one offers aid to another, one likely expects future aid in return. This is **reciprocal altruism**: You scratch my back and I will scratch yours. Reciprocal altruism can evolve whenever individuals, at small cost to themselves, can aid another and expect a great genetic return. In baboon troops a male may enlist the aid of another male to defeat a higher status male and steal his mate. Later, the helper is similarly aided by his co-conspirator. Again, sociobiology says that phenotypic altruism is genetically selfish: I will help you only if I can expect to benefit later on.

The evolution of reciprocal altruism may be an engine of cognitive evolution. Imagine a species that cannot recognize its fellows as distinct individuals. An altruist in such a species would blindly aid whoever asked for aid. Quickly a conniving counter-strategy would evolve to prey upon the saintly sucker: Get aid from the altruist but never return it. Only a smart altruist could avoid extinction by the new egotists. He or she would give aid when called upon, but never to one who had earlier cheated by refusing aid. Mathematical models indicate that the smart, reciprocal altruist would soon become the dominant type (Dawkins, 1976). But the strategy of reciprocal altruism necessitates concomitant cognitive evolution. The reciprocal altruist would need to be able to discern individual differences in appearance; be able to remember each individual and associate that individual with acts of helping or cheating; be able to base a behavioral decision on memory and calculation of a risk/benefit ratio. Thus, evolution of one social trait—altruism—may fuel the evolution of cognitive abilities, and as these grow they may in turn feed back on social development. Perhaps intellect originated in just this way; if so, in humans it has ironically expanded to the point of finding reciprocal altruism cynical, and constructing truly nonselfish systems of ethics.

Reciprocal altruism may be seen as a more specific form of a broader class of mutual helping, *mutualism* (Maynard Smith, 1982a; Wrangham, 1982). Mutualism occurs whenever several individuals cooperate for the immediate benefit of all under circumstances in which no individual can exploit a given situation. So, for example, orb weaver spiders, unable alone to throw a web across a stream to catch the many insects flying above, may cooperate with others in the initial spanning of the stream. Then, each spider builds its own nest. Here, unrelated individuals cooperate in order that each spider may enjoy a rich payoff, which is why the behavior has evolved. Since the mutual cooperation occurs at the same time, controls on cheating are unnecessary, so mutualism is simpler than reciprocal altruism. But it remains truly altruistic; although each spider gains an individual reward (each catches its own prey and does not share) it succeeds by aiding and without exploiting its fellows, as occurs with individually selected "altruism."

Beyond the scope of our introduction to sociobiology lies the sophisticated analysis of altruism using *game theory* (see Box 10–3).

Altruism and individual selection   Finally, it is possible for apparent altruism to be entirely selfish, and to be subject to individual selection. Consider alarm calls in birds. A flock is on the ground eating and a cat stalks up. The first bird to see the cat gives a cry of alarm, and the flock flutters off. The alarm-giver appears to risk calling the cat's attention to itself while "altruistically" warning the flock. But appearances deceive. The caller knows that the flock will take off when it cries (and so the flock benefits), but the caller benefits *even more* because it knows where the predator is and can position itself advantageously in the confusing swarm of birds, and so *increase* its own chances of escape (Alcock, 1979). Altruism in this case is totally selfish: The herd is manipulated by a single member for its own advantage.

Human Altruism

Sociobiologists propose that the forces of natural selection produced human altruism as well as animal altruism. Altruistic behavior can be se-

BOX 10–3   *SOCIOBIOLOGY AND GAME THEORY*

Game theory is a branch of mathematics that has occasionally been applied to psychology; for example, in social psychology's studies of the prisoner's dilemma. Game theory describes the outcomes of interactions between individuals who adopt different strategies in their encounters, and it evaluates the outcomes of each encounter by weighing the relative costs and benefits of adopting each strategy. As is clear already, sociobiology makes extensive use of cost/benefit analysis, and game theory is becoming its most powerful mathematical tool for understanding the strategies genes adopt and the games they play to survive. While the formal refinements of game theory lie well beyond the scope of our book, we will present here a simple and brief analysis of altruism in game theory terms.

Consider a population of organisms, say birds (Dawkins, 1976), who pick lice from each other's heads. We begin with the whole population being *suckers*, who groom any head presented to them—they are completely altruistic. Now imagining we can quantify inclusive fitness, let us assume that the benefit of being groomed is 5 fitness units, and the cost (time lost from foraging or mating while grooming another) is 2 units. Each grooming interaction is beneficial: $5 - 2 = 3$; the *payoff* exceeds the *cost*. However, this happy state of affairs is not an *evolutionarily stable strategy*, or ESS, because a mutant gene may easily arise, creating a new strategy, *cheating*. The *cheat* presents his or her head for grooming and is groomed by suckers, but never grooms in return. The resulting costs and benefits may be summarized in this *payoff matrix*, showing the result of each possible interaction of strategy:

	SUCKER	CHEAT	NET PAYOFF
Sucker	$5 - 2 = 3$	$0 - 2 = -2$	1
Cheat	$5 - 0 = 5$	$0 - 0 = 0$	5

Cheating is a superior strategy, for the cheat gets groomed without ever paying the cost, and the sucker is constantly wasting time grooming cheats. This new pattern is not stable either, because the cheating strategy works too well. Early cheats will flourish among the many suckers, but as cheats multiply (and suckers diminish) the actual payoff of cheating declines, as each cheat finds it hard to get groomed. So the ratio of cheats-to-suckers population may oscillate; pure sucker strategy isn't stable, as a few cheats flourish; pure cheating isn't stable, because then no one gets groomed.

While there may be a stable population ratio of suckers to cheats, this is unlikely, since the optimum strategy, the ESS, is reciprocal altruism; let us call it the *bourgeois* strategy. The bourgeois grooms the heads of those who present themselves—*except* those known to have cheated in the past! We can construct the following payoff matrix, omitting for simplicity's sake the occasional interaction between a new cheat and a bourgeois.

	SUCKER	CHEAT	BOURGEOIS	NET PAYOFF
Sucker	5 − 2 = 3	0 − 2 = −2	5 − 2 = 3	4
Cheat	5 − 0 = 5	0 − 0 = 0	0 − 0 = 0	5
Bourgeois	5 − 2 = 3	0 − 0 = 0	5 − 2 = 3	6

The bourgeois strategy is superior to either cheating or being a sucker, and depending on the actual cost/benefit values, an evolutionarily stable situation should be reached, since no new, superior strategy should arise to displace the bourgeoisie.

Game theory is now being applied to every area of sociobiology—aggressive interactions, altruism, mating strategies, parent-child interactions, population size and so on—and promises to bring mathematical rigor to the field. An introduction to game theory and ESS's may be found in the second edition (not the first) of Barash's *Sociobiology and Behavior* (1982), while the more serious student may see *Evolution and the Theory of Games* by John Maynard Smith (1982b), the pioneer in applying game theory to sociobiology (Maynard Smith, 1982a).

lected in three ways: through kin-selection, through reciprocal altruism, mutualism or reciprocity, and through individual selection.

While readers of this book live in large, impersonal, modern societies, humans evolved—and most people today still live—under very different conditions in which relationship with an extended community of kin was a major factor in determining social success or failure. Such conditions naturally favor kin-selected altruism. The fitness of any individual gene carrier is greatly enhanced by cooperating with relatives in such matters, say, as negotiating a marriage. Conversely, the relative's fitness is also increased because the individual carries some of each relative's genes, which will be increased by the marriage. It pays your genes to help others who carry those genes. The closer blood ties are, the greater altruism is kin-selected, and is simply what we normally call *nepotism*: One's inclusive fitness is enhanced by helping one's relatives. The larger the social organization, the more distant kin ties become, and altruism is less and less kin-selected, but must be based on mutualism and reciprocity—reciprocal altruism.

Studies of traditional cultures support the sociobiological contention that cooperative social interaction is a relatively direct function of degree of genetic relatedness, while conflict splits societies at the weakest links in the chain of relatives. (See van der Berghe & Barash, 1977/1980; Chagnon & Irons, 1979; Chagnon, 1981; Flinn, 1981; and Irons, 1981 for extensive discussions.) To take a simple example, Hames (1979) studied the amount of social interaction between pairs of individuals as a function of their degree of genetic relatedness; this was done among the Ye'kwana of Venezuela's upper Orinoco basin. Hames found a remarkably precise relationship between kinship and amount of interaction, frequency of interaction increasing linearly with degree of relatedness. One's reaction to Hames' finding is likely to be: Well of course, people naturally want to help their relatives, so they live together and must interact more frequently. But remember that sociobiology seeks ultimate causes, to know why sugar tastes sweet and why we "naturally" are fond of our relatives. Hames argues that living together—and, by implication, the desire to live together—is the proximate mechanism by which human kin-selection operates. Only if people live in related groups can they help the genes they share with relatives.

For it is not obvious to reason that we ought to favor our relatives. Selfish egoistic reason would dictate that I ought to treat everyone impersonally as a means to my own gratification: as temporary allies or enemies. Unselfish moral reason would dictate that I ought to treat everyone impersonally as autonomous human beings: each person to be cherished as such and treated equally. But traditional societies—where humans evolved—do not work in these ways. In them people want to help and be helped by their kin, to establish new kin relations as a means to social peace and harmony, and they want to hurt alien kin groups. In these natural preferences we see the hand of natural (kin) selection. People are, by nature, neither egoists nor saints.

This brings us to reciprocal altruism and the problem of mass societies. As the circles of interaction widen from village to tribe and beyond to the nation state and the urban civilization modern Western people live in, ties of kin weaken, and kin-selected altruism becomes irrelevant. Relations with strangers cannot be based on shared genetic interest; they must rest on reciprocal altruism, or reciprocity: I will cooperate with others insofar as I can expect they will cooperate with me.

But, reciprocal altruism encourages cheating, or "negative reciprocity." I take a risk when I help another, and he or she may cheat me by not returning my help. Especially in mass societies when people are likely to interact only once (making it hard to learn who the cheaters are), fraud and deception become serious problems. Just consider commercial transactions. You hand over money at the same time the merchant gives you your purchase: Neither one has to trust the other, for you reciprocate at the same moment. Hence, the merchant's distrust of checks—he or she has learned by experience that, like the empty balloon with which the male hanging fly woos his mate (see below), some people's checks signify nothing of value. Thus, the consumer's distrust of mail-order business, since one entrusts one's money to strangers with no guarantee it will buy anything.

But reciprocity is the only social cement that holds urban society together. Cultural evolution in Western civilization has produced complex mechanisms for enforcing reciprocity: government, police, the law. In the absence of kin ties we bind ourselves with the impersonal ties of rules and regulations. Biological evolution has given us a conscience and guilt (Trivers, 1971/1980). Guilt motivates a cheater to make amends, and restores his or her position in society. A cheater with no guilt, on the other hand, would be ostracized by society; unrepentant cheaters' genes will die with them. The guilty cheater returns and may prosper; his or her guilt-feeling genes survive him or her.

As in the other animals, then, human altruism may be evolved by kin-selection and by the evolution of reciprocal altruism. It may also be produced by pure individual selection. Outspoken biologist Michael Ghiselin (1974) has gone farthest in favoring individual selection, arguing that kin-selection is not operative, even among the hymenoptera, and that reciprocal altruism is a sham. For him, helping others is only an indirect way of helping one's self, and will not happen except when it is in one's own interest.

Besides the theoretical arguments that altruism can be an innate human trait, there is now direct evidence that it is (Pines, 1979). Some infants as young as one year of age, before any appreciable degree of social learning can take place, attempt to console or even help people who are crying or in pain. Differences in altruism at one year persisted in a follow-up study five years later: One-year-old altruists became six-year-old altruists. There was also evidence of parental correlates of baby altruism. Parents who forcefully and emotionally explained how their child had hurt someone had more altruistic children, as did parents who were themselves altruists. It is unclear, however, if these parental behaviors caused the children to be altruistic, or if they simply reinforced a predisposition toward altruism shared by parent and child alike. The early appearance of altruistic behavior, individual differences in altruism, and its temporal stability, all point to some genetic basis for this important human trait.

Aggression

We cannot ignore the fact that aggression is part of animal living—nature *is* sometimes red in tooth and claw. Contrary to the writings of cynical misanthropes, it turns out that animals are at least as guilty of murder, cannibalism, and killing more than they need to eat as are human beings. Nonetheless, most animal aggression is controlled, seldom resulting in death or serious injury to either combatant. Two questions pose themselves: Why do animals fight at all? And why is their aggression so seldom lethal?

Why aggression occurs has a simple sociobiological answer—sometimes it benefits an individual's inclusive fitness. Aggression can enhance fitness in many ways. It is usually males who are aggressive, and their fitness may be improved by fighting for a territory to control and to live off, for one or more females to mate, or for high status in a dominance hierarchy and the access to females that this ensures. Excluding parental discipline and predator-prey aggression most aggression is a form of competition for resources, typically either for scarce natural resources or for a limited supply of females.

Thus success at aggressive competition enhances fitness. The successful aggressor with a good territory and many mates will pass his genes on into the next generation in greater numbers than the vanquished will. If this be so, why is aggression restrained at all? Surely the best strategy would be for a male to kill all his rivals, ensuring that their genes have no hope of survival.

The answer to this apparent puzzle is that aggression always entails *risks*. As with altruism, sociobiology holds that an organism acts as if it calculates the ratio between the benefits of aggression against its costs. To enter an all-out fight to the death is to risk losing everything; even should one win, one might be so damaged that later fitness is reduced. A drive for lethal aggression would be so detrimental to its holders that a gene for it cannot evolve. Moreover, even losers in aggressive interchanges benefit from controlled aggression. If one dies, one's genes die too. But if one loses nonfatally, one can hope to be more successful later.

Aggression exists in nature, therefore, in a kind of compromised state. Aggressiveness enhances fitness, so it has evolved; at the same time too much aggressiveness reduces fitness, so constraints on aggression have evolved. The result is the evolution of a set of behavioral mechanisms that give individuals of many species the capacity to fight, but which limit the aggression to the establishment of competitive superiority—for a territory or for females—without resulting in the death of the loser. In the animal world, nature is red in tooth and claw, but within certain evolutionary constrained boundaries.

Human Aggression

Since Cain slew Abel, aggression has been the dark side of human nature. The men of Homer's *Iliad* seem to enjoy killing and worship the glory to be won in war. The seventeenth-century political philosopher Thomas Hobbes observed that without society—and a strong ruler—human life would be solitary, nasty, brutish, and short. This view of human aggression as an impulse barely checked by repressive civilization was shared after World War I by Sigmund Freud, who had previously rejected it. And, of course, the background to all philosophical and scientific speculation—and no one has gone much beyond speculation—on human aggression is our species' history of murder, torture, war, and genocide.

In the modern era, but before sociobiology, proponents of theories of human aggression have divided into two quarrelsome camps. On one side was the ethological Neo-Freudian view whose scientific spokesman was Konrad Lorenz (1966) and whose able publicist was author and screenwriter Robert Ardrey (1966). Like Freud, Lorenz claimed that aggression was a distinct innate *drive*, a *need* to be aggressive that constantly seeks expression. Unlike Freud, in the ethological perspective the aggressive drive was only a "so-called evil" (the subtitle of Lorenz' book in German), since aggression was recognized to have the adaptive properties discussed earlier. For Lorenz, the problem of human aggression was that the drive was no longer under the control of the mechanisms that in animals constrain it short of murder, a problem multiplied many times by humankind's inventive technology of death. The solution to the problem of aggression was to rechannel aggressiveness into moral equivalents of war—activities that, like space exploration, provide the thrills, glory, heroism, and solidarity of war within a socially constructive context. For Lorenz and his followers, then, aggressiveness was an ineradicable part of human nature, a drive that could not be escaped but could be redirected.

The other side viewed aggression as alien to the human condition (Montague, 1968), a view represented in psychology by the social learning tradition (for example, Bandura & Walters, 1963). Like Lorenz' view, this camp developed in part from psychoanalysis, following Freud's earlier idea that aggression was not an autonomous drive but derived from frustration of other drives such as sex or hunger and from infantile oral-aggressive sexuality. So the Montague camp argued against Lorenz that aggression was a product of culture and not of biology. Through imitation of observed aggression, especially when it was seen to pay off, and reinforcement of aggressive acts, a child was molded by its environment into an aggressive adult. According to these environmentalists, aggression was nothing more than a set of learned skills that could be unlearned by an adult and, of course, not taught to children. A pacific utopia is to be achieved not by redirecting aggression but by refusing to model it and refusing to let it pay; aggression could go the way of the bustle. The policy impact of the social learning account was substantial. A great deal of research in the 1960s and 1970s was done showing that children learned aggressive skills by watching violent television. As a consequence, the amount of killing and maiming on television has declined considerably since *The Untouchables*; today, crime shows are apt to show even a minor villain thrown clear from a flaming car crash in order to keep down their "body counts."

The sociobiological view is, in effect, a compromise between Lorenz' adaptive aggressive drive and social learning's set of learned skills. Rejecting any notion that aggression is an instinctive drive, sociobiology holds that aggression results instead from *competition*. Whenever resources are in limited supply—be they food, space, or mates—aggression becomes an adaptive response. Thus, for the sociobiologist, aggression is an innate set of skills, or an innate disposition to *learn* aggressive skills, which evolved because it has been adaptive in the past. Sociobiology shares with Lorenz the insight that aggression is not a purely gratuitous evil, but shares with the social learners the insight that aggression is a capacity, not a drive, whose learning and manifestation depend on environmental circumstances.

Some anthropological evidence indicates that human aggression occurs for the same reasons as aggression between animals. To begin with (and this is an observation supported by history and observation of our own society) aggression may stem from efforts to establish dominance. People, especially males, struggle to establish power over others in our numerous hierarchical organizations. Status displays, such as joining the country club or buying a Rolls-Royce, are peaceful ways of showing one's superior dominance position. As in animals, human aggression sometimes—but all too rarely—is channeled into ritualized mock combat, as in medieval jousts, when one knight established his superiority over his rivals.

Human aggression and warfare are also caused by resource competition. The Munducurú of Brazil fight frequent wars with their neighbors, wars that appeared quite senseless until fitted to a sociobiological model (Durham, 1976). As were human beings for most of their evolutionary history, the Munducurú are hunter-gatherers who rely on hunting as their primary source of high quality protein. The mere existence of other tribes—in Munducurú the word for *enemy* means all who are not Munducurú—threatens their supply of game. So their propensity for war is adaptive for each and every individual of their tribe by helping assure a plentiful supply of protein. The individual fitness of the best warriors is directly increased through increase in social status and lavish gifts. The most outstanding warrior in a particular battle is by no sociobiological accident called "mother of the peccary": one who increases valued game by killing those who might diminish it. Where women are a scarce resource, as in periods of rapid geographical and population expansion (for example, among the Yanamamö of Brazil and Venezuela) men fight for opportunities to take wives. In short, where some resource is in short supply, aggression occurs, even among groups that are otherwise quite pacific (Eibl-Eibesfeldt, 1975).

Factors that tend to inhibit aggression are also explicable in sociobiological terms. Medieval rulers arranged marriages to make alliances with each other, reducing the likelihood of war between them, a practice pursued by many primitive groups as well. One is less likely to kill kin than to kill strangers, for kin carry one's genes, and their murder would harm one's own inclusive fitness. Reciprocal altruism, too, can check forces pushing toward aggression. Where people and groups of people can cooperate to increase their fitness over what each alone could achieve through aggression, aggression will no longer pay and would be shunned.

Apart from these general tendencies that humans share with other animals, tendencies that lead at us once toward and away from fighting, sociobiologists have considered the unique problem of human aggression. First, however, it should be pointed out that there may not be a special problem of human aggressiveness, despite Lorenz. Human technology makes humans uniquely *efficient* killers, but it does not follow that we are the most aggressive—even if we are the most dangerous—species on earth. Wilson (1975a, 1978) has catalogued among animals brutalities extending to cannibalism. As Wilson (1978, p. 107) observes, "If hamadryas baboons had nuclear weapons they would destroy the world in a week. And alongside ants, which conduct assassinations, skirmishes, and pitched battles as routine business, men are all but tranquilized pacifists."

Nevertheless, human aggression does possess certain unique features. The naked (human) ape is an ill-equipped killer. Our teeth and our claws, or fingernails, are poor offensive weapons set alongside the natural equipment of the lion or wolf. Unfortunately, as Lorenz originally suggested, this means during our early evolution in the pretechnological past it was so unlikely that a man could kill another that we lack the reflexive aggression-inhibiting responses possessed by lions and wolves. So give a human weapon, and death can follow all too readily. It is not surprising, then, that while ritual aggression is common in the rest of the animal kingdom, knightly mock combat occurs but seldom. Human intelligence and our capacity for morality (or at least for moralizing) create the unique human capacity for moralistic aggression (Trivers, 1971/1980). Human history is replete with crusades, massacres, and orgies of execution in the name of a higher moral power, be it God, Allah, the State, or Reason. The suggestion here is not that moral reasons are just rationalizations for innate bloodthirsty behavior. Quite the contrary. Sociobiology says that we are driven not to kill but to be moral, to cooperate with our in-group. Morality is a human imperative that makes us *want* to kill the immoral, the out-group. Morality *causes* aggression; it does not rationalize it.

The main evolutionary roots of human aggression can be traced to our long period spent as technologically primitive hunter-gatherers. Since most of our evolution occurred in this stage, sociobiologists look there for the ecological pressures that created human nature, and these are summarized in Figure 10–4, from Alcock (1979).

As humans moved from the trees to the plains, they began to hunt game and to be exposed to predators who hunted them. Given the poor fighting equipment of the individual human, survival became possible only by cohesive group living and the ability of human beings to cooperate. Now while cooperation is one of our most admirable traits, it also made warfare possible and intensified the human capacity for certain forms of aggres-

FIGURE 10–4   Evolution of the Capacity of Humans for Warfare. The ability to cooperate may have originally evolved because it improved hunting efficiency and defense against nonhuman predators. Later the ability may have been employed in the competition among human bands for good hunting areas and for other limited resources.

sion. *Groups* now competed for resources and resource-rich territory, creating warrior groups and warfare. Sex-based division of labor also occurred, with consequences to be explored later.

Cooperativeness and the tendency to form dominance hierarchies created in people tendencies toward social compliance and obedience toward superiors. The shocking dangers of compliance and obedience have been amply demonstrated by Stanley Milgram's (1974) classic experiments. Milgram has shown that while no one thinks he or she would deliberately injure another person just because a researcher tells that person to, a great many people will, in fact, do so. When told to administer intense electric shocks to a "learner" for failing to learn a paired-associate list, most subjects did so, despite screams of pain from the learner (really a confederate of Milgram's) in the next room. Even when the "learner" was in the same room with the "teacher," and the real subject, (the "teacher") could *see* the agony he was (apparently) inflicting, 40 percent of the subjects nevertheless delivered the maximum shock (450 volts) as ordered; 30 percent did so when they had to hold the "learner" to the shock-delivering electrode.

We see, then, that while the human capacity for aggression is in most ways similar to aggression in the rest of the animal kingdom, special features of our evolutionary ecology have affected how that capacity is directed and used. If this sociobiological analysis is correct, we may be relieved that there is no inherent aggressive drive ineluctably pressing for release, but we must be wary of the human propensities to kill in the name of morality and to kill simply because one has been told to kill. It is because of these propensities to cooperate and obey—not because of aggressive capacity per se—that human history is so often blood-red, from the butchery of the Hundred Years' War to the reign of terror during the French Revolution, to the nightmare of Auschwitz, to the misdirected revenge at My Lai, to the tribal genocide in Idi Amin's Uganda.

Sexual Behavior

Besides being eternally fascinating, sex obviously has something to do with evolutionary fitness. Sex is the essence of individual fitness. Therefore, we must expect the struggle for existence to have strongly shaped the way animals attract mates and reproduce.

The first significant fact about evolution and sexual behavior is that the struggle for existence—or more precisely in this context, the struggle to mate—has fallen much harder on males than females. Studies and experiments on many species from insects to apes have shown that every female has opportunities to mate and produce offspring, but that only some males get such opportunities. In the vast majority of animal species, females represent a limited resource for which males compete. Therefore, male sexual behavior, being under evolutionary pressure, has been more strongly shaped than female behavior.

Once sex itself appeared on earth millions of years ago—for reasons that are still unclear (see Box 10–4)—the basic fact underlying male-female differences emerged. This is the fact that the *parental investment* (Trivers,

BOX 10–4   *WHY SEX?*

As Jacob Bronowski (1973, p. 203) observed, "Most of the world's literature, most of the world's art, is preoccupied with the theme of boy meets girl. We tend to think of this as being a sexual preoccupation that needs no explanation." But it does. Studies show that sexual reproduction, as opposed to the asexual reproduction practiced by many simple plants, insects, and single-celled organisms, exacts enormous cost. The rituals of courtship and mate selection use up time and energy. Competition to reproduce exposes animals to the risk of damage or even death.

Sex is an antisocial force (Wilson, 1975a). The most harmonious societies are the colonial invertebrates such as the jellyfish-like *siphonophorans*. These are complex colonies of genetically identical members descended from a single parent whose altruistic specialization and coordination make them appear at first glance to be a single organism. It may even be not too far-fetched to suggest that each of us is a cooperative colonial society, since each of our cells is genetically identical and therefore 100 percent interested in the survival of every other cell and the whole. Only cancer cells—genetic mutants—reproduce selifshly to the harm of the organism.

Sex introduces conflict into society. Each parent is related to its offspring only by 50 percent, making parent-offspring conflict inevitable. Genetic relations among other members of society range from 50 percent (siblings) to 0 percent (strangers) making altruism problematic. Asexually reproducing species are 100 percent invested in each offspring who are in turn 100 percent invested in their parents and siblings.

Why, then, has sexual reproduction evolved? While this remains the central problem of evolutionary biology (Trivers, 1983), several suggestions have been put forward. Dawkins (1976) has suggested that somehow mutant selfish genes arose which benefited from causing organisms to become sexual. Thus, while sex does indeed *not* serve the interests of all genes, it does serve the interests of a few. Before it was rejected in evolutionary theory, some biologists embraced group selection to explain the origin of sexuality. *Species* benefit from sexual reproduction because the variety it produces—the mixing of genes from mother and father make each indivual unique—gives the species great flexibility in meeting environmental demands. It makes possible the progress of the species (Bronowski, 1973).

An individual-selection theory has been proposed by George C. Williams (1975, 1980). It, too, looks to the high variability that sexual reproduction creates, but finds its benefit in helping individuals ensure their genes' survival. Asexual reproduction exactly duplicates the parent and offspring are therefore best fit to the same environment the parent lived in. But movement or climatic change may so alter the environment that the parent's identical offspring all die, reducing its fitness to zero. Sexual reproduction, however, ensures diversity of offspring, adaptable to varying environments. Williams explains the advantage of sexual reproduction in terms of gambling. One's best chance to win at roulette is to bet many numbers, not by risking one's entire investment on a single outcome. Asexual reproduction is like betting one number; sexual reproduction—producing many unique offspring, each of whom can survive in *some* environment—is like betting many numbers and helps ensure that while fitness may not be 100 percent, it won't be 0 percent either.

But Williams' theory (and a related one proposed by Maynard Smith, 1971, 1978) has been contradicted by recently described data (Bell, 1982). It turns out that asexual creatures predominate in novel or disturbed habitats, while sexual creatures are favored in stable, unchanging ones, the exact reverse of Williams' prediction.

Two theories remain possible, Ghiselin's (1974) "tangled bank" theory, and the "Red Queen" theory favored by Trivers (1983). The tangled bank theory holds that the diversity created by sexual reproduction becomes highly advantageous when intraspecific competition is strong. If individuals are struggling against others of their kind for one set of resources, it would be advantageous to be able to produce many very different offspring who could move out and exploit new ecological niches, rather than compete with closely related conspecifics for the same resource base.

The Red Queen theory sees sexual reproduction as an adaptation to fierce interspecific competition, especially that between predator and prey. If all predators were the same, or all prey the same (as under asexual reproduction) over-specialization would result—the identical predators might become perfectly adapted to killing their identical prey, and wipe them out—or the prey might become perfectly adapted to eluding the predators, and the predators would starve. Sexual reproduction assures diversity of offspring, so that disastrous perfect adaptation is avoided. No matter how efficient predators get, some prey will survive, and no matter how elusive prey get, some predators will be able to catch them. So parents producing many different offspring through sexual reproduction will be more fit than asexually reproducing parents who make Xerox copies of themselves.

Of course it is possible that all the factors suggested may have contributed to the evolution of sexual reproduction, or that it has evolved independently in different places and times for different reasons. However it arose, sex has been on earth for millions of years, and as we shall see, has itself exerted strong selective pressure on sexually reproducing species.*

*Read Graham Bell, *The masterpiece of nature: The evolution and genetics of sexuality.* Berkeley, Calif.: University of California Press, 1982.

1972/1978) of each parent in its offspring is quite radically different. The male gametes (sperm) are small, biologically cheap to produce, highly mobile, and can be made continuously in huge numbers; the sperm in one male human ejaculate are enough to fertilize every woman in North America. The female gamete, or egg, on the other hand, is larger and biologically more expensive to make, since it contains both genetic material and nourishment for the developing organism. The egg is also incapable of movement, and is produced in smaller quantities only at certain periods of the female biological cycle.

Additionally, in mammals the female must bear and nurse her young, a task spared the male. We see, then, that the biological investment of male and female parents in their offspring is vastly different. A male can sire many offspring in many females quickly and cheaply, while a female must invest, especially if a mammal, a great deal of energy and time in each of her young. We can add to this basic difference a further, related fact, that a female knows with certainty that its offspring are her own and must carry her genes, while a male can never know with certainty that "his" offspring truly carry his genes.

Putting all these considerations together we should expect to find—and do find—that evolution has produced very different strategies by which males and females go about the business of reproducing. The most dramatic illustration of this difference, at least in animals, is called the *Coolidge effect,* from the following story (Berment, 1976, pp. 76–77):

> One day the President and Mrs. Coolidge were visiting a government farm. Soon after their arrival they were taken off on separate tours. When Mrs. Coolidge passed the chicken pens she paused to ask the man in charge if the rooster copulates more than once each day. "Dozens of times" was the reply. "Please tell that to the President," Mrs. Coolidge requested. When the President passed the pens and was told about the rooster, he asked, "Same hen every time?" "Oh, no, Mr. President, a different one each time." The President nodded slowly, then said, "Tell that to Mrs. Coolidge."

In a great many mammals, a male will mount a given female only a few times and then lose interest. But if a new female is introduced he mounts her just as enthusiastically as the first. This pattern can be repeated over and over. Males are also remarkably hard to fool into re-mating with an already inseminated female: They have sex indiscriminately but are nonetheless discriminating about the condition of their partners (Symons, 1979). The Coolidge effect is almost absent in females.

This makes a great deal of evolutionary sense given the basic difference between egg and sperm. Once fertilized, a female has nothing to gain by further copulation with any male at all; her genes are now developing (along with the father's) into a new member of the species. For her, further sexual activity is pointless at best and risky at worst. On the male side, further copulation with a female he has just fertilized is pointless for the same reason, and he should lose interest in her; further copulation just wastes time, effort, and sperm, thereby reducing fitness. But it would pay to have sex with new, unfertilized females. Sperm are cheap and continuously produced, so further opportunities for sex with new females should be seized to increase individual fitness by impregnating them. So it is genetically profitable for males, but not for females, to desire and perform sex with many partners. The reproductive strategies of male and female thus shape their mentalities and desires in different directions.

All these differences create two different kinds of selection pressure on the further evolution of sexuality. First, females become for males a desirable resource to control. If a male can collect many females—which he is likely to desire—and impregnate them himself to the exclusion of other males—which he is capable of doing—then his individual fitness will be enhanced and the fitness of others harmed. He will gain in the struggle for existence. Males will therefore compete for possession of females, creating *intrasexual selection:* Males who successfully compete will be selected and their fitness enhanced.

For a female the situation is rather different. A male can have profligate sex with many females whose own fitness may be high or low. But this is of small moment, for *some* of his sperm will impregnate *some* fit females, and so his genes will survive. But a female is putting up a large investment when she copulates, a large investment of biological matter (her eggs) and time and effort in bearing, nursing, and raising the offspring. Should she mate with an unfit male her fitness will be correspondingly harmed. So in the struggle for existence it pays for females to be choosy, to mate only with the fittest available male in order to protect her large (and his small) investment. And females can be choosy because they are a scarce resource. The criteria for their choices create a selection pressure, called by Darwin *sexual selection,* but now called *epigamic selection.* Genes carried by male survival machines that meet female criteria will prosper, while those carried by losers will go extinct. Male appearance and behavior will thus be pushed in the direction of pleasing the female.

In this way is born the strategem and counter-strategem of the war between the sexes. Females set criteria for male fitness, and males try to meet them or deceive females into *thinking* they met them. Females see through the ruses and set new tests; new, craftier deceptions evolve, and so on through an endless and fascinating cycle.

Intrasexual selection   Competition among males (and in a *very* few species, females) has resulted in a number of adaptations that serve each competitor, summarized in Table 10–1 (from Alcock, 1979).

The first set of adaptations help a male compete for access to females. First (A), males, much more than females, are easily aroused and sexually promiscuous; males need not be choosy and need to be ready to seize every opportunity, while females must be more cautious. Second (B), in many group-living species the males fight one another, generally without bloodshed, to establish a *dominance heirarchy,* which runs from the dominant "alpha" male who can defeat everyone else, to a lowest ranking male who defers to everyone else. Dominance expresses itself in reproductive success in the ways listed in Table 10–1:

1   A dominant male may be able to keep away all other males from a female who is receptive (that is, in estrus, or "heat").
2   He may gather unto himself a harem of females for his exclusive use.
3   In social species without harems the dominant male(s) typically have first or exclusive access to the females.
4   In some species, typically birds, dominant males establish territories that are attractive to females because of bountiful resources or some other feature.
5   Dominant males are more attractive to females than the territories of lesser males, and the attracted female(s) will then mate only with him.

TABLE 10–1   Results of Intrasexual Selection on the Evolution of Male Behavior

ADAPTATIONS THAT PLAY A ROLE IN THE COMPETITION TO SECURE COPULATIONS

A.   A low threshold for mating attempts
B.   Dominance behavior (the monopolization of females): the exclusion of other males from:
    1.   The vicinity of a female that is or will become receptive
    2.   A harem of females
    3.   Positions of high status in multimale groups
    4.   Areas with useful resources attractive to females
    5.   Display sites attractive to females
C.   Subordinate behavior (coping with dominant males)
    1.   Submissive behavior and the (temporary) postponement of attempts to reproduce
    2.   Courtship of females only when dominant males are absent or occupied
    3.   Sneak copulations
    4.   Rape

ADAPTATIONS THAT HELP A MALE ENSURE THAT HIS SPERM WILL BE USED BY FE-MALES HE HAS INSEMINATED

A.   Guarding behavior
    1.   Temporary guarding of a recently inseminated female
    2.   Prolonged protection of a female or harem against other males
B.   Behavior that reduces the likelihood that an unguarded female will copulate again
    1.   The insertion of mating plugs in females after copulation
    2.   The use of biochemical or behavioral signals to active mechanisms within the female that reduce her receptivity

ADAPTATIONS THAT LOWER THE REPRODUCTIVE SUCCESS OF COMPETITORS

A.   Sexual interference
    1.   Interruption of another male's courtship
    2.   Female mimicry by males that induces other males to waste time, energy, or sperm
B.   Attempts to injure competitors
    1.   Assault on other males, including homosexual rape
    2.   Assault on mates or offspring of other males

In all these ways males' struggle for dominance aids their reproductive success and therefore increases their individual fitness.

Third (C), subordinate males have strategies open to them that give their genes a chance at survival. As we mentioned earlier in discussing aggression, submitting now in a dominance fight leaves open the possibility of later success as practice perfects competitive abilities and dominant males weaken or die. Or males may try to court (2) or secretly copulate (3) with females when a dominant male is absent or occupied. Finally, there is the possibility of rape, which, contrary to general opinion, is by no means confined to humans (Shields & Shields, 1983).

The second set of male adaptations produced by intrasexual selection has evolved to help a male be sure it is his sperm that fertilize a female's egg, since in many species it is not the first male's whose sperm succeeds, but rather the last male's. Even when this is not the case, it is in a male's interest to increase his certainty of paternity. To accomplish these ends, males can guard their mates (A) either just long enough to ensure insemination (1) or more permanently through monogamous union or harem keeping (2). Other behaviors may be used to keep females from mating again (B). In some species, including the familiar rat, a male inserts a plug in the female after copulation that at once retains his own sperm and excludes others (1). In some species a male may use chemical or behavioral signals that automatically reduce a female's receptivity after mating (2). It appears that male lions do this by gently biting the neck of their mate during copulation, signaling her that she is inseminated.

Finally, there are adaptations that directly lower other males' reproductive success. Males can interfere with other males' courtship or copulations (A,1), perhaps by attacking them *in flagrante*. In a few species, for example, the salamander *Plethodon jordani,* males pretend to be females and induce other males to waste time, effort, and sperm (A,2) to the detriment of their fitness. And, of course, males can turn red in tooth and claw and try to injure each other or each other's mates (B,2), or to kill the offspring of other males, as langurs and lions do. Homosexual rape may be included here (B,1), which takes a particularly bizarre form in an insect species wherein a male may rape another male, depositing his sperm in his victim's genitals, seeing to it that if the victim later mates with a female it will be the rapist's semen and genes that survive, not the poor victim's!

We can summarize the effects of intrasexual selection by saying that most of the evolutionary pressures favor males who are aggressive with each other and their mates, are easily aroused and sexually promiscuous, and who jealously watch over their mates. The sole countervailing pressure is the advantage of monogamy in heightening certainty of paternity. Whether and in what ways these pressures have affected male human sexuality will be explored later in this chapter.

Sexual or epigamic selection   Because of the differences between egg and sperm, female behavior has been very differently affected by evolution. A female must exercise great care in selection of a mate; she must be cautious, willing to test out possible suitors before committing her eggs to his sperm. Table 10–2, based on Trivers (1972/1978) and Alcock (1979), summarizes criteria suggested by sociobiologists, especially Trivers, that females can use in choosing a mate. Perhaps, too, they can select which sex to give birth to; see Box 10–5.

The first set of criteria (I) are used by all females but especially those of the many species in which the male does nothing to help raise his offspring. The most basic question is whether a given male can, in fact, fertilize the female's eggs (A), as indicated by the four listed criteria. Doing this is not always as obvious as it seems. Many insects resemble each other, especially if they are related species or members of a species that practices mimicry. Usually, the male's courtship behavior, which is often highly elaborate and ritualized, indicates *yes* answers to all these questions, so the female can

TABLE 10–2   Criteria Used by Females on Choosing Mates

I.   Criteria used by females of all species, but especially those where males offer little parental care.

    A.   Can he fertilize my eggs?

        1.   Is he of the correct species?
        2.   Is he of the correct sex?
        3.   Is he mature?
        4.   Is he sexually competent?

    B.   What is the quality of his genes?

        1.   Does he show high survival ability?
            (a) by being old
            (b) by possessing a survival handicap
        2.   Can he dominate other males?
            (a) as shown by high dominance ranking
            (b) by fighting well when I incite him

II.   Criteria used by females of species whose males offer parental care.

    A.   What will be the quality of his care?
        1.   Is he able to control needed resources?
        2.   Is he willing to share these resources?
        3.   Is he willing to protect me and my offspring?

Adapted from Trivers (1972) and Alcock (1979)

BOX 10–5   *ALTERING THE SEX RATIO*

Since the typical pattern among animals is for every female to get to mate, perhaps with the same male, but for only a few, dominant males to mate, with many females, why is it that parents generally produce a ratio of male to female offspring of 1:1? It might seem the prudent strategy would be to produce mostly females and let a few males do all the stud work. However, it turns out that under most conditions a sex ratio of 1:1 is the most adaptive for parents to produce. Although a daughter is a safe investment, almost guaranteed to "payoff" in grand-offspring, the *number* of offspring she can have is limited. On the other hand, while a son is a risky investment, since he might not mate at all, the potential payoff is very great, for a dominant harem-master may have large numbers of offspring. It has long been recognized that evolution has in this way produced two counterbalancing forces— toward daughter production as a safe low-payoff strategy and toward son production as a risky but potentially lucrative strategy—that combine to produce the prevailing 1:1 ratio.

However, precisely because having sons or daughters results from different biological strategies, there may very well be times when it would be in parents' interests to try to produce mostly sons or mostly daughters. Trivers and

Willard (1973) have argued this as follows. All females mate successfully with healthy dominant males. Larger, healthier females (and in some social groups, more dominant females) produce larger, healthier offspring than weaker females (and, in the same groups, pass dominance on to their offspring). Therefore, the larger, healthier females should produce more males than females, since a male offspring should do well in the competition for females and produce many grand-offspring. Weaker females, on the other hand, should favor the production of daughters, for even if they are relatively ill-favored, they will still be able to mate and produce at least some offspring. Environmental changes may exert similar pressures. In stressful, risky environments it is better to produce daughters, who need only a few mates to breed successfully, while under favorable conditions the risky bet of a male becomes preferable.

Trivers' and Willard's proposals have been supported. For example, stress causes more males than females to be aborted, exactly as expected. Dramatic support for their line of reasoning comes from certain fishes (for example, Australian wrasses) in whom gender is not fixed. Wrasses live in female harems controlled by one male harem master. If he is removed, the females fight for dominance and the winner changes into a male, becoming the new harem-master. The winner has by becoming dominant won the genetic jackpot, opportunity to beget the maximum number of offspring, and so becomes male to fulfill the possibility. The subordinate wrasses, however, benefit by remaining female. A subordinate male could have no offspring, but as a subordinate female is guaranteed of a few.

While the facts accord with Trivers' and Willards' hypotheses, the proximal mechanisms that might determine sex of offspring remain mysterious. They are not impossible to imagine, however. Males, carriers of the sex-determining chromosomes, might be able to control their output of X and Y sperm. Females might be able to alter the chemical composition of vaginal fluids to favor male, Y, sperm (alkalinity) or female, X, sperm (acidity). Hormones produced during stress might differentially affect male and female embryos. And there is even the possibility that male embryos might "altruistically" tend to abort themselves during stressful times.

then choose among qualified males. Thus, the fact of female choice becomes a pressure on *male* behavior: Male courtship rituals have evolved precisely because of the need to convince females that a male is ready, willing, and able to perform his role.

Next, in order not to waste her precious eggs on an unfit mate, the female must assess her suitor's individual fitness (B). She can ask if he possesses (and thereby his genes ought to possess) high survival ability (B,1). The most obvious measure of fitness is age: A young male is untested while an older male has, by definition, survived. So a female should prefer an older to a younger suitor. A more interesting criterion is possession of a survival handicap. It has been suggested (Zahavi, 1975) that the reason males of some species have evolved apparently useless and even disadvantageous traits is to signal fitness to females. Peacock plumes, for instance, are large and cumbersome and must be at a disadvantage in escaping from predators. But on the other hand, survival despite such a handicap must mean good overall fitness. You would be impressed with anyone's fighting off a shark, but you would be even more impressed if a one-armed person did it. So females may take a particularly large and showy handicap, such as a male peacock's plume, as evidence that he has really outstanding genes. Of course, once females begin to exercise such a choice, selection pressure increases, and males will become even more "handicapped," until, perhaps, the species goes extinct.

Gene quality may also be measured through dominance (B,2). Dominance hierarchies, in those species that have them, provide a direct measure of fitness. Lacking a hierarchy, females might get males to fight each other and pick the winner. Humans are not the only species to play what transactional analysis (Berne, 1964) calls "let's you and him fight." Elephant seal males keep harems; when another male attempts a sneak copulation with a female, she bellows and attracts the harem-master, who fights off the intruder. In this way the female prevents copulation by a low-ranking male and at the same time tests her mate's continued fitness. When mallards are forming their pair bond the female may direct her prospective partner to attack a nearby male, presumably to test his fitness—which sounds positively medieval.

Additional criteria come into play if a female can choose a mate who will invest in his offspring (II). Now she must weigh the quality of his parental care. Can he control resources (A,1) needed by her and her offspring? In territorial species females will prefer males having environmentally rich territories. Will he share resources (A,2)? In many species males give females valuable presents, especially food, to induce them to mate. Finally, can he protect me and my offspring (A,3)? Often these criteria boil down to assessing general genetic fitness, as above.

Two important observations need to be made about this last class of criteria. First, to the degree that males invest in caring for their offspring they risk lowering their fitness by giving up possible copulations with other females. Therefore, to the extent they invest in offspring they must act like females and be choosy about their mates. If, for example, a species is really monogamous, the male has just as much invested—everything—in his offspring as his mate. Both he and she must be equally careful in choosing a partner for life, or even for a breeding season. In a very few species such as doves and giant water bugs this process has gone so far that males invest more in offspring than females do, and the usual roles are reversed, males being cautious and sexually reserved while the females are aggressive and promiscuous. There is even a species of worm that is hermaphroditic, becoming alternately male and female. While it is a male it adopts male strategies of sexual aggression and indiscriminate mating; when it becomes female it adopts the female strategy of "choosiness" and shyness. Such apparent exceptions to the general run of things in fact support Trivers' sociobiological analysis: Sexual behavior depends on the degree of biological investment in offspring. To the degree an individual's investment is large and lasting, the usual "female" strategy will be adopted; to the degree that investment is small and fleeting, the usual "male" strategy will be adopted. Biology blends with economics, as Michael Ghiselin argues in his book *Economy of Nature and the Evolution of Sex* (1974), "a cross between the *Kama Sutra* and the *Wealth of Nations.*"

The second observation about this last class of female criteria is that it gives rise to the strategem and counter-strategem of the war of the sexes, for males may pretend to be more fit than they are. They may share resources only long enough to copulate and then abandon the female; especially if the female can rear her young alone, this becomes an important male option for it frees him to increase his fitness with other females. Fortunately for females, if they *all* require long courtship and monogomous mating, abandonment will not pay, for lengthy courtship reduces male fitness, and monogamy reduces the population of available females. Under these circumstances, deception may arise, as males pretend to be more willing to invest than they are, and females attempt to see through the deceptions, which only calls forth more male cunning—and so on.

Deception is well illustrated by the hanging fly, whose species exhibit a gradation from male sincerity to flattery to fraud. In one species, the male brings a present of food, a blowfly he has caught. She feeds on it during copulation, which enhances her fitness and keeps him from being eaten in the way male praying mantises are. In another (more advanced?) species the male makes the present more attractive by wrapping it in a balloon of silvery webbing. The female unwraps the present, which gives the male a little longer, and feeds. In another species she opens the wrapping and finds a fly already sucked dry—too late, for the male is gone. Finally, in the highest (?) species, the female unwraps her balloon to find . . . nothing!

Mating systems   All these varied factors that play a part in evolving sexuality have resulted in a variety of stable mating systems; they are listed in Table 10–3. The ecology of male investment that gives rise to these systems are summarized in Table 10–4. What Tables 10–3 and 10–4 show— their contents speak for themselves—is the powerful synthesizing power of sociobiology. It allows us to give a useful classification of a complex and varied set of behaviors (mating arrangements) and account for the classification on a few quantifiable principles, primarily the degree of male investment in offspring. Even the unusual case of polyandry fits neatly in place, not as an exception, but as the logical outcome of more male than female investment. Examples are given of each mating system. Where do people fit in?

Human Sexuality[2]

When sociobiologists enter the field of human sexuality, they find well-trodden ground. Because it is such a consuming interest of human beings, sexuality has touched and been touched by every human endeavor

[2]In addition to the standard sociobiological works cited in the animal section, the present account of sexuality draws especially on Symons (1979), Daley and Wilson (1978), and van den Berghe (1979). For views contrary to Symons, see Hrdy (1981). Hrdy (1979) reviewed Symons' book, and Symons (1983) reviewed Hrdy's.

TABLE 10–3   Mating Options of Males and Females (From Alcock, 1979)

Monogamy: an individual mates with one partner per breeding season
Polygyny: individual males may mate with more than one female per breeding season

A.   Parental investment polygyny: males vary in attractiveness to females because of great individual variation in male parental investment

   1.   Resource defense polygyny: males monopolize resources that are useful to females; several females may mate with a male that controls access to superior resources.

   2.   Parental care polygyny: males vary in the quality of direct parental care they offer their progeny; several females may choose a superior parent

B.   Pure dominance polygyny: males vary in dominance status (and, therefore, genetic quality), with several females selecting a high-ranking male

   1.   Harem defense polygyny: males compete for priority of access to groups of females that have formed for nonreproductive reasons (usually for mutual protection against predators)

   2.   Lek polygyny: males compete for high dominance ranking within a group, usually at a traditional display arena (called a *lek*); females mate with the top males

Polyandry: individual females may mate with more than one male per breeding season

A.   Parental investment polyandry: females mate with several males that provide parental investments

   1.   "Prostitution" polyandry: females mate with several males to gain the parental investment benefits offered by their mating partners

   2.   Resource defense polyandry: in cases in which males make a *greater* parental investment per offspring than females, a female may control a resource attractive to more than one male

B.   Pure dominance polyandry: in cases in which the male parental investment per offspring exceeds that of the female, females may compete for dominance positions in female aggregations; high-ranking females may be chosen by more than one male

and institution from literature to religion to science. Social scientific studies on sex and sex roles numbered at least *10,000* by 1975 (Heilbrun, 1981). So virtually anything sociobiologists might propose would be controversial. This is especially so in current American psychology, where there is general resistance to nativist ideas, and where psychological theories are openly used to support the feminist movement, which itself resists imputations of innate psychological sex differences (Bem, 1981). We can here only scout around this fearsome territory, beginning by recalling the typical patterns of sexuality found in other animals.

We have found that the parental investment of males in most species is much less than that of females. Consequently, natural selection has produced males who are aggressive with each other and toward prospective mates, who are easily aroused and sexually promiscuous, and who watch jealously over their mates. Additionally, males are high-variance gambles in the struggle for existence: Many males do not mate at all and are evolutionary failures, while some males are spectacularly successful, siring large numbers of offspring. Females, on the other hand, have been selected to be unaggressive, sexually reserved, and choosy about their mates. Females are

TABLE 10–4   **The Ecology of Mating Systems. Different Mating Systems Reflect Ecological Factors That Determine How Much a Male Can Help His Mate Produce and Rear Offspring and How Much Males of a Species Vary in Their Ability to Assist Their Mates. (From Alcock, 1979)**

MALE ABILITY TO PROVIDE USEFUL SERVICES TO MATE		FEMALE CHOICE	MATING SYSTEM
	Most males offer same medium-to-high assistance	Females prefer unmated males	Monogamy robins, foxes
Males can monopolize useful resources or provide parental care			
↑	Some males offer much more than others	Females prefer superior helpers	Parental investment polygyny redwing blackbird, impala
Ecology of species	Male's parental ability exceeds that of female	Females invest in egg production only, mating with several males	Polyandry stickleback fish, tinamou
↓			
Males cannot provide useful assistance to females	Males compete to demonstrate genetic quality to females or to monopolize group of females	Females choose the competitively superior male	Pure dominance polygyny manakins, elephants

safe but low-paying evolutionary investments: Every female can find a mate, but the number of offspring she may have is small compared to males. We will now consider whether this common pattern fits human beings.

There is no doubt that humans are one of the sexiest species. While we are not as physically prodigous as lions, who may copulate a hundred times a day and require about 3000 copulations to produce a litter of cubs, we invest a great deal of time, thought, and effort in sex and its pursuit, and have a copulation/offspring ratio of about 1000:1 (van den Berghe, 1979). Most species engage in sex with far less frequency, some only once in a lifetime. Moreover, culture has embroidered our physical sexuality with art, religion, and recently, science and technology—making human sexuality unique and pervasive. Nevertheless, because culture has embroidered our animal nature, not altered it, the fundamental animal patterns persist in human sexuality.

Aggressiveness   One of the few generally acknowledged sex differences is that males are inherently more aggressive than females (Maccoby & Jacklin, 1974). The general division of labor in cultures around the world reflects this fact: Men hunt, make weapons, and go to war, while women gather and prepare food. In our own society, violent crime is committed almost exclusively by impoverished young males, those old enough to seek mates but who find themselves denied the usual signs of fitness awarded by our society, namely, education, wealth, status, and prospects for advancement. Among the middle class, competition for women is nonviolent and indirect; among the poor and disenfranchised, nature turns red in tooth and claw, and male youths seek female attention through toughness, *machismo,* and dominance within a male gang (Alexander, 1979).

Viewed sociobiologically, the human pattern makes sense. The young male must fight to become a man, whether through actual physical competition with others, through indirect status-competition, or through the ritualized torture of initiation rites unknown to females (Barash, 1979). Only through competition can males earn females, thus ensuring their fitness, while females need but choose the successful competitor.

The proximate mechanism of male aggressiveness is the male hormone testosterone, produced by the testes. Testosterone creates the male pattern, an energy-consuming, active, and aggression-prone way of life; female animals injected with testosterone become more active and aggressive. But testosterone also contributes to characteristic male vulnerability. By driving the male toward activity and aggression—the basic male fitness strategy—it makes him more likely to be killed (Daly & Wilson, 1978). Males also tend to suffer higher rates of embryonic, fetal, and infantile mortality, and to senesce more rapidly than females (Alexander, Hoogland, Howard, Noonan, & Sherman, 1979).

Contrary to popular beliefs, cultural sex-typing falls more heavily on males than on females, for sexual stereotypes are more rigidly imposed on males. Even contemporary American couples consciously trying to raise their children apart from sexist stereotypes find it easier to do so for girls. The girl playing with a fire truck is applauded; but the boy playing with dolls is often not (Katchadourian, 1979).

Cultural expectation reflects and magnifies the underlying biological reality that males are risk-taking, aggressive people who must struggle for success, for biological fitness. Girls will become women and find mates as a matter of course, so culture need not teach any particular role. These differences are evident even when we determinedly try to change. Contemporary sexual liberation has usually meant women becoming free to act like men—seeking places in business, industry, and the professions, where aggressiveness and risk-taking pay—rather than the other way around. The househusband is much more a curiosity than the female stockbroker.

Sexual arousability   Observation of the contemporary American scene also suggests that human males are, like most males, easily aroused sexually, while human females, like most females, are not. Pornography—manufactured sexual stimulation—is a huge business run by men for men. Sales of everything from *Playboy* to hardcore pornographic magazines run to at least $600 million a year, and are made for men, whether heterosexual or homosexual, while attempts to sell pornography to women of any orientation have proved unsuccessful. There is evidence that the modest success of the one magazine that aims pictures of naked men at women partly results from sales to homosexual men, while lesbians find magazines such as *Playboy* rather silly and puzzle that men enjoy them (Symons, 1979). So the bull market for arousal thrives on men, not women.

Some recent research has suggested that women can be aroused by sexually explicit materials at least as much as men, at least in experimental settings in which subjects view or read erotica and have their arousal measured through self-report or physical monitoring. These results have been taken to cast doubt on traditional stereotypes of the "turned-on" man and "frigid" woman. However, a closer look reveals features that support sociobiological hypotheses.

To begin with, close analysis of one such experiment (Heiman, 1979, re-analyzed by Symons, 1979), showed that men responded more strongly than women to tapes depicting sexual activity. Moreover, men, but not women, responded (at least initially) about as strongly to control tapes—a discussion between a male and female student about choice of college major—as to any explicit tape. Males are clearly more easily and strongly aroused by *any* situation in which sex *might* play a part. Women often complain that on dates any word or gesture meant as general friendliness is taken as expressing sexual interest, a real-life finding well grounded in sociobiology.

Analysis of these studies also shows that the proximate psychological mechanisms of sexual arousal are entirely different in males and females (Money & Erhardt, 1972; Symons, 1979). A man responds directly to the image of the woman photographed or described, and fantasizes about having sex with her. A woman, if aroused at all, is aroused by identifying with a photograph of a naked woman, and imagines herself to be similarly desirable. In erotica with male-female interaction, she is likely again to identify with the woman to learn ways in which she can be arousing and sexually skilled herself. So sexual arousal from erotic literature is possible for both men and women, but the thoughts that connect erotic depiction to actual arousal are not the same in men and women.

Finally, we must remember that only men *seek* arousal through pornography. This is not a cultural artifact created by sleazy adult bookstores that socially inhibited women fear to enter. A recent study (Kenrick, Stringfield, Wagenhals, Dahl, & Ransdell, 1980) called male and female college students and asked if they would volunteer to participate in experiments involving seeing geometric figures, soft-core "loving" erotica, or hard-core "lustful" erotica. Women were less likely than men in every case to volunteer for the erotic experiment, and, when they did choose erotica, they preferred the soft-core description. As the marketplace indicates, men seek arousal while women do not.

All of this suggests that we must make an important distinction between *appetitive* sexuality, or an actual sex drive, and sexual *responsiveness*. Once they are in a sexual situation, women are at least as sexually responsive as men, and perhaps even more so, given the female ability to have multiple orgasms (Hrdy, 1979). Nevertheless, women seem not to have the driven sexual appetite of men; they do not seek out arousal through pornography. There are cultures in which the female orgasm is unknown, indicating that women do not have a drive to seek sexual outlet as men do (Symons, 1979). Again, the proximate mechanism seems to be testosterone. Women who for medical reasons have high levels of this hormone show characteristically male patterns of sexuality, becoming much more sexually aggressive. When treated, such women express relief at being able to return to "normal"—that is, nondriven-sexuality (Money & Erhardt, 1972; Symons, 1979).

Promiscuity   We come naturally, then, to promiscuity, a characteristic male trait in nonhuman animals. There is good evidence that men—whose minimum parental investment is so much less than women's—seek sexual variety. They fantasize about sex with many different women through pornography: No erotic publication contains pictures of just one woman. While adultery rates for men and women may be equalizing, men still have more partners than women do, and they are more likely to have one-night stands; the roving male seeks sex, the female is looking for a better partner. The Coolidge Effect appears to apply to humans. The frequency of intercourse falls off after a couple is married, and wives are often puzzled by male adultery when they are always available to their husbands. Sexual autobiographies suggest that males are readily re-aroused by a new woman shortly after intercourse with another, who may instantaneously be transformed from alluring to repulsive (Symons, 1979). "Swinging" is largely a male-instigated practice, and most frequently involves adding a new woman to a married couple, sometimes a merger of couples, and almost never the addition of a new man (van den Berghe, 1979).

Patterns of homosexual conduct reinforce our picture of this pattern. Indeed, Symons (1979) has suggested that homosexuals represent the "acid test" of theories of sexuality, for in a homosexual encounter male and female strategies will be directly revealed, there being no need to compromise with or manipulate the other sex's strategy. Male homosexuals are quite promiscuous, and even though they desire permanent, stable relationships, they find them difficult to maintain, and often institutionalize sex with another partner outside the relationship. Male homosexuals seek out quick, anonymous, orgasmic encounters, even finding many in one night with multiple partners. The lesbian pattern is quite different. Relationships between couples are more stable and more frequent, there is little compulsive seeking of new partners, and lesbian sex is more extended and does not center on the orgasm (Symons, 1979).

Promiscuity—or rather a tendency toward it—seems to characterize human male sexuality.

Jealousy   While jealousy is clearly an emotion experienced by both men and women, the evidence is that it is a more powerful emotion in men (Daly, Wilson, & Weghorst, 1982). The enraged husband slaying his wife and her lover (and getting off) is well known; the reverse is not. This pattern—the classic double-standard—is found in almost all cultures

(Symons, 1979; Daly, Wilson, & Weghorst, 1982). That males should be especially jealous makes good biological sense. Men can never be certain of paternity, and adultery by their wives (who they know in their hearts can find willing partners) reduces their fitness. So evolution has produced men who feel sexual jealousy and become outraged by their wives' affairs, even while they themselves aim to seduce their neighbor's wife. Male sexual jealousy is perhaps the leading cause of familial assault and murder (Daly, Wilson, & Weghorst, 1982). Women, on the other hand, are certain of maternity, and their fitness is not harmed by any purely sexual liaisons their husbands might have. The natural female fear is being abandoned for another woman, losing valuable male investment in child-rearing. Therefore, jealously has a different, more biologically remote basis in women, and is less purely sexual.

Male uncertainty of paternity and sexual jealously also leads to attempts by men to control female reproduction, just as male animals do. There are practices designed to isolate women from men who are neither husbands nor fathers; they help increase male certainty of paternity and thus have a biological basis not always apparent to the culture, which often views them as "protection" of women. Some such practices are:

> Chinese footbinding. From an early age Chinese girls' feet were tightly bound, preventing proper growth of the foot, resulting in tiny, misshapen feet. Chinese men thought of this as a technique for enhancing women's sexual attractiveness, but it kept women literally hobbled and mostly at home. (Dickemann, 1981).

> Claustration and veiling (*Purdah*). This practice involves the isolation of women from men other than kin or husband, and the covering of their bodies when they do go abroad. The Koran explains this as a means by which women "may be recognized and not annoyed" (Dickemann, 1981), but it serves men's reproductive control of women.

> Surgical procedures such as the sewing up of the vagina (until the husband wants access) or castration of the clitoris. The former is usually recognized as a means of reproductive control, while the latter may be explained, as in the nineteenth century, as a way to prevent masturbation. (Barker-Benfield, 1976).

What all of these practices really accomplish is control of women's reproduction in the interest of male genes.

Female choice   So far we have catalogued differences between men and women on arousability, sex drive, promiscuity, jealousy, and probable degree of reproductive success, focusing on the consequences of minimum male parental investment. Now we look at the consequences of human female parental investment. In our species it is especially large. A woman produces a single protein-rich egg once a month for about 35 years and can have *at most* 20 or so children regardless of how many partners she has. (This is in stark contrast to the male whose cheap sperm may father hundreds of children in many women.) She must then bear the child for nine increasingly difficult months, followed by several more months of nursing.

The child who is born is singularly helpless, needing prolonged care, supervision, and education. Child-rearing would be easier with continuing male interest after marriage.

It is therefore of paramount importance in our species—as in other slowly reproducing species—for females to be choosy about their mates. While modern contraception distinguishes choice of sexual partner from choice of father for one's children, people did not evolve with contraceptives. Alcock (1979) provides a table (Table 10–5) of criteria that women are likely to employ.

The criteria for choice adduced by Alcock are human versions of most of the criteria used by females of other animal species in which males may offer care of offspring. First, it is a cultural universal that close relatives are not suitable mates—Freud's famous incest taboo. There is a good biological basis for it, since it prevents incestuous inbreeding that would likely result in combining recessive lethal genes, reducing fitness of offspring (van den Berghe, 1983). A woman must gauge the willingness of a man to provide parental investment, which may be indicated by his behavior toward her and his general reputation—a uniquely human possession. As with many other animals, it is quite common in all cultures for a man to woo a woman with gifts, especially meat from the hunt in traditional cultures. Such behavior shows, at least on the surface, a willingness to share resources. Of course, human females—like hanging fly females—may find male gifts deceiving. Finally, not only must a man be willing to share resources, but he must also possess resources to share, and a woman must estimate these by judging the quality of his gifts, his wealth, his status, and his intelligence, or as our Victorian ancestors might have called it—his "prospects." Cross-cultural research has confirmed that the sorts of traits listed by Alcock are in fact those used by women and/or their relatives in the choice of a husband. Physical appearance counts for relatively little.

Given the importance of female choice to their individual fitness, we can readily see that it is most adaptive for women to be less arousable than

---

TABLE 10–5 Characteristics of Males that Are of Potential Interest to Females in Selecting Mates

DEGREE OF RELATEDNESS
  Fathers, brothers proscribed relatives not acceptable mates

WILLINGNESS TO PROVIDE PARENTAL INVESTMENT
  Quality of attention given female by suitor
  Gifts given to female by suitor
  Reputation of suitor

ABILITY TO PROVIDE PARENTAL INVESTMENT
  Quality of gifts given to female by suitor
  Resources known to be controlled by male
  Dominance status of male within the society
  Intelligence

men and to largely lack appetitive sexuality. A woman driven by constant stimulation and an autonomous sex urge would be relatively unable to test and evaluate men's fitness. Women find it relatively easy to control their sexual desires with strangers, and this is of great adaptive value. Males, on the other hand, benefit—in ultimate terms—from their constant sexual stimulability and sex drive, for it makes it possible for them to search for and seize opportunities to mate, and so enhance their fitness. Of course, this does not justify their doing so, but it does mean that the tendency is an inherent part of male human nature and must be controlled, not wished away.

What about male choice? From what we have learned about male sexuality, we would expect their criteria to be simple physical attractiveness, which research and cross-cultural studies strongly support. Precisely because men are primed for quick physical arousal, they will judge a woman by her looks, by how arousing she is. Because his minimal parental investment is so low—simple insemination—a man is not likely to evaluate a woman on any deeper criteria. The basic male strategy is the high-risk one: impregnate many women (which he desires to do) and his genes are bound to survive.

The sociobiological result of these differences between men and women is the war between the sexes. A woman evaluates the fitness of a man and tries to get him to invest in her to show whether he will invest in offspring after birth. A man wishes to impress females, trying to act fitter than he is, and to invest just enough in a woman to seduce her but without committing himself and without giving up opportunities to enhance his fitness with other women. Popular songs are full of the battles between the sperm and the egg—the man who professes his love as a tactic of seduction versus the woman who hopes to turn the tactic into a reality.

Changing cultural environment may change the rules of the game. In a strongly monogamous environment, men will act more like women. A long courtship followed by a permanent marriage multiplies the male's actual parental investment many times over his minimal one. So men will be choosy not about whom they bed but whom they wed. They will look for maternal and perhaps economic qualities that will ensure their offspring's fitness. In our culture, to cite another example, men have traditionally sought female approbation through swaggering machismo—advertising their fitness by (at least apparent) toughness. But as the satirists on the TV show *Saturday Night Live* (October 10, 1981) suggest, machismo may now be a losing strategy, and the man who wants to attract the new woman would do well to imitate the sensitivity and emotional vulnerability of Alan Alda.

Sociobiology offers a picture of human sexuality that conforms to the more firmly established sociobiology of nonhuman creatures, that makes sense of our own observation of our everyday lives, and is reasonably supported by cross-cultural data and research results from social psychology. Many may find it an unpleasant picture, preferring to think of differences in sexuality as cultural products, especially of our own "sexist" society. The account is also disturbing in its suggestion that in such an intimate arena men and women are so different that they almost cannot communicate, cannot intuitively understand one another. Nevertheless, if we share our sexuality with the animals, sociobiology likely describes our condition. It will take the resources of humankind's master trait—intelligence—to bridge the gap between man and woman through art, poetry, writing, science, and a determined effort to understand and respect those with whom we share our lives.

Parental Care and Parent-Offspring Conflict

Once mating has occurred and young are born, what happens? In many species the young are left entirely on their own, to fend for themselves or die. This lack of parental care usually occurs in species living in unstable, unpredictable environments, which produces *r-selection*. Species subject to *r*-selection generally adopt a strategy of producing a huge number of offspring all at once (and sometimes only once), and completely neglecting them. Although most will die, enough offspring—the toughest and luckiest—will survive to reproduce.

Degrees of parental care evolve under *K-selection,* which occurs in stable, predictable environments. *K*-selection leads to larger size and longer life, giving parents the capability of extended child care. It leads to smaller brood sizes as animals reproduce many times in a longer life, giving parents a greater investment in each child than under *r*-selection. *K*-selection, therefore, is likely to lead to increased parental care. It may be helped along by a dangerous environment requiring parental protection, and also by the evolution of offspring who are helpless long after birth and who thereby need parental care if they (the holders of the parents' genes) are to survive at all.

Once parental care has evolved, however, it is usually the female who bears the burden of child-rearing. Only in the most strictly monogamous species (a small minority) is child care about equally shared. Otherwise, the male does much less, because his investment is much less. Females *always* have a high investment in their offspring, as we have seen, and for them parental care always pays. Males, however, typically have a lower degree of investment and so typically care less to begin with; furthermore, they are less certain a given child is theirs, taking some of the edge off the desire to care for what may be an imposter. Moreover, in nonmonogamous species, the male's (or females' under polyandry) fitness is better served by begetting more offspring with more females, as in a harem, than by caring extensively for one mate's small brood. Thus, many animal families resemble the lion's pride. The females possess the territory (passed by inheritance through a group of sisters), care for the young, and do all the hunting (although the male of the pride gets to eat first). The male's role is merely looking regal, protecting the pride from occasional harm, and begetting offspring.

Sociobiological analysis can be extended to parent-offspring interactions, as Trivers (1974) has done with his parental investment concept. Attachment—the bond between parent and child—is a much studied phenomenon of human and animal behavior. It must have biological roots because it is so fitness-enhancing. Emotional attachment is the proximate motivator of parental care, and has evolved to protect the parents' investment in their offspring and, of course, the offspring's investment in itself.

Given this, we might expect parent-offspring behavior to be harmonious, which every parent knows is not true. Trivers' analysis suggests why. Certainly a parent has an investment in his or her offspring, for it carries his or her genes—but only 50 percent. A child, on the other hand, has a 100 percent investment in itself. This differential investment means there will be times when the parents' genetic interest and the child's are not identical.

Consider the simple case of weaning. For some period of time, nursing benefits the fitness of both mother and child. But at some point, when the child no longer needs to nurse, the mother's fitness would be better served by having additional offspring. But the offspring continues to benefit from nursing for a longer period, gaining risk-free nourishment and so enhancing fitness. The stage is set for parent-offspring conflict, a process that takes place in three steps in dogs and cats, to cite a familiar example (Wilson, 1975a). In the beginning, the mother initiates nursing and never resists an infant's approach. In the second phase, mother and child initiate feeding about equally often, and occasionally mother rebuffs child. Finally, during weaning the mother resists (often violently) all approaches by the no-longer-quite-an infant.

Trivers' analysis suggests a further point, increasingly (and independently) recognized by developmental psychologits, that contrary to the usual view, the parent-child relationship is not a one-way affair in which the parent molds a passively dependent child. Parents and child differ in their investments in each other and themselves rendering conflict inevitable. Although it appears that the parents have all the power, children are not without resources. Consider the *attachment bond.* Every human parent knows the ineffable joy of an infant's smile, which can wash away anger and resentment; (see Box 10–6). Of course that smile is sweet—for the same reason sugar is sweet. A child can manipulate a parent with that smile and through attachment. Many a parent has been gulled into doing something against his or her better judgment by the cute demeanor and innocent smile of his or her three-year-old! Just as deception and a war of strategem and counter-strategem occurs between the sexes, so does it occur between parent and child. Discussion of the subtler points of Triver's analysis will be discussed later because as Wilson (1975a) suggests, the higher deceit is probably limited to the higher primates and quite possibly to human beings alone.

Families, Parents, and Children

There are two features of *Homo sapiens'* sexuality—specifically, women's sexuality—that, while not entirely unique among animals, have been carried to a high pitch among our species. Women are unusual in experiencing orgasms, and in concealing ovulation, that is, not entering a period known generally as "heat" (technically **estrus**) when they advertise

BOX 10–6   *SURVIVAL OF THE CUTEST*

Which of the pictures of children's heads in Figure 10–5 do you find cuter, more attractive?

FIGURE 10–5
(From Wickler, 1973).

If you are like most people, you chose B2 over B1 and K2 over K1, although this preference pattern is stronger in women than in men (Wickler, 1973). What is interesting is that B1 and K1 are more realistic depictions of children's heads than B2 or K2, which almost never occur. Instead, B2 and K2 conform to what Wickler calls the *infant scheme:* Their large crania simply exaggerate what we find cute in infants with whom we have evolved to fall in love. Just as the female gull is fooled by the larger, fake egg that exaggerates the size of her own eggs, and a man is especially aroused by especially large breasts, so we find this "supernormal" cuteness especially appealing.

Love is the proximate mechanism that binds parents and children, and parents are adaptively disposed to find infantile traits especially attractive, since it intensifies parental investment. Children, of course, learn to manipulate their parents' proclivities, learning to look small and helpless in order to get their way. The lesson has also been learned by stuffed-toy makers and *schlock* artists. Stuffed toys—for whom cuteness is the only survival strategy—uniformly come with absurdly large heads and innocent expressions. There are "artists" who live and thrive by selling cheap pictures and by painting cute children, puppies, and kittens with large heads and impossibly wide eyes in paintings whose cuteness may lapse into nauseousness.

fertility and sexual availability. There is a lively controversy within sociobiology about the significance and possible adaptive value, if any, of these female traits.

The most popular hypothesis, possessing roots in ethology, is the theory that both female orgasm and loss of estrus are adaptations creating a male-female pair-bond, which in turn creates the basic nuclear family (e.g., Wilson, 1978; Barash, 1979; van den Berghe, 1979). According to this reasoning, loss of estrus makes a woman continuously sexually available to a male partner, who then has less need to look elsewhere for sexual satisfaction, creating a bond between him and her. The bond is reciprocated by the woman's deriving pleasure from sex with her partner. Thus is created—so the the pair-bond story goes—the intimate loving attachment between husband and wife that is the rock of the nuclear family, enhancing the fitness of both mother and father.

Consoling as this idea may be, there are good reasons to think it fable rather than fact (Symons, 1979; Hrdy, 1979, 1981). As Wilson pointed out in his book *Sociobiology*—notwithstanding his later belief in the pair-bond theory—sex is a divisive, not a solidifying, force in animal or human society. In the animal world, monogamous species are *hyposexual*—engaging in little sexual activity—a characterization that hardly fits *Homo sapiens*. Primates copulate throughout the sexual cycle and have not developed monogamy (Daniels, 1983). In the vast majority of societies, marriages are arranged on calculations of gain to the partners and (especially the man's) kin group, not on grounds of mutual satisfaction. Finally, in most cultures couples stay together despite quarrels over sexuality (mutual recriminations concerning adultery and abandonment) and when marriages become happy they do so late in life, when sexual fires are dampened. In the general run of human experience, then, it appears that marriage—the pair-bond—is not built on sexuality but endures when it does in spite of sexuality. Human sexuality seems instead to be an adaptation to a cultural environment in which marriage is ubiquitous, the man seeking outside opportunities to increase his fitness and the woman seeking to increase her husband's parental investment.

Unfortunately, although the pair-bond theory may be challenged, sociobiologists do not agree on the origins of the family, the adaptiveness of women's concealment of ovulation, or their ability to have orgasms. Symons (1979) argues that female orgasm is a physiological accident rather than an adaptation, pointing to the fact that unlike the male orgasm it is not necessary to procreation, hence plays no role in fitness and cannot have been selected. In some societies female orgasm is unknown; in most it is highly variable between and within women; and in those societies in which it is expected as normal, it only comes about from men being carefully trained in the arts of love.

Moreover, orgasm is not considered by most Western women to be their favorite sensation—the moment of penetration is. On the other hand, Alexander (1979) thinks that orgasm, through its outward manifestations, is an adaptive signal from the woman to her lover that she finds him sexually satisfying and is unlikely to cuckold him, reassuring his feeling of paternity; Hrdy (1979, 1981) suggests that the capacity to have orgasm makes a woman have many lovers, all of whom may invest in her offspring.

With regard to concealment of ovulation, sociobiological theories are even more at odds (For a thorough review, see Daniels, 1983.) The problem is simple but intractable: When women ceased to go into estrus did they thereby stop advertising their sexual availability, or did they begin to *continuously* advertise their availability? Alexander (Alexander & Noonan, 1979; Alexander, 1979) adopts the former line of reasoning. He argues that by concealing ovulation women enticed men into an extended consortship, for since neither he nor his mate knew when she was fertile, he would have to remain with her to keep inseminating her and guarding against insemination by other males. At the same time, by no longer going into estrus, the woman reassured her mate's sense of paternity by making her less likely to seek or attract adulterous partners during "heat." One might call Alexander's theory the Machiavellian pair-bond based on uncertainty and manipulation.

Symons (1979) and Hrdy (1979), on the other hand, think that women continuously advertise their sexuality, *reducing* their mate's certainty of paternity, since she is always available for sex with another male. Symons offers two scenarios by which loss of estrus might be adaptive and have evolved. In the first, continuously advertising women would be more successful than estrus women in obtaining meat from males to exchange for sex. In the second, continuous availability is adaptive by allowing a woman to be fertilized by presumably fitter males other than her husband. Hrdy (1979) suggests additionally that loss of estrus made it easier for a woman to manipulate men's uncertainty about paternity, entangling them in a web of parental investment, serving her own genetic fitness.

Finally, Daniels (1983) suggests that loss of estrus promotes general social solidarity. Open estrus would constantly incite men to competition not cooperation, and would divert female attention from social tasks such as child-rearing and food gathering.

Whatever the origin of the human family, it is a cross-cultural universal, although it may take on very different forms in different cultures.

Surveys of the world's cultures find that polygyny in some form is the most common marital arrangement (when polygyny is "usual," most men have or want to have two or three wives; when it is "occasional," a few high-status men secure a large number of wives, leaving few women for other men to marry). Monogamy is uncommon, and was quite rare until the coming of religions that impose it as a moral requirement. Polyandry is practically unknown; as among other species it occurs only in rare ecological situations and is viewed by its participants as making the best of a bad deal (van den Berghe, 1979). Humans also display the sexual dimorphism of a mildly polygynous species: Generally speaking, the greater the difference in bodily size between males and females of a given species, the greater is their degree of polygyny, and among humans, men are on average slightly larger than women (Alexander, Hoogland, Howard, Noonan, & Sherman, 1979). If we use data on sexual dimorphism we can calculate that on average men should want about two or three wives, as is the case with "usual" polygynous societies, and in the nominally "monogamous" ones that allow a man to keep concubines. These data, taken together with human hypersexuality, indicate that as far as nature is concerned, human beings are polygynous, not monogamous.

One should remember that this represents the ideal state of affairs for men only, since they, but not women, can increase their fitness by holding many mates, at once gaining women to impregnate and keeping other men from finding wives. Women, on the other hand, are hurt by polygyny, since female fitness declines in polygynous marriages among all species (Daly & Wilson, 1978). Emotionally, too, women prefer monogamy, since in general women see sex as part of a deep, intimate, and loving relationship with another person, not as an end in itself or as superficial recreation (Symons,

1979). Therefore, if we apply human intelligence to the question of marriage systems we may freely disagree with natural selection's production of natural human polygyny, and say that monogamous union based on love, respect, and personal intimacy is the ideal for which we should aim.

At the same time, evidence from utopian experiments indicates that it would be unwise to depart too far from the form of the family as it has naturally evolved. During the heyday of the U. S. counter-culture of the 1960s and early 1970s, various communitarian "families" were established, few of which survive today. Study of their children reveals a dismal record: children neglected, deprived and emotionally stunted, incapable of prolonged attention or making friends (Barash, 1979). A more formal and determined experiment in communal living was undertaken in Israel's kibbutzes. The dedicated, socialist, kibbutzim aimed to abolish sexual discrimination and to replace the nuclear family with the crêche, a child being raised and living with his or her peers and not with the natural parents. Nevertheless, the division of labor within kibbutzes reflected traditional practices; men predominating in primary production jobs and in holding leadership posts, women predominantly in the service occupations and running the children's houses (van den Berghe, 1979). Furthermore, primarily in response to complaints by women, the kibbutzes are returning to more traditional modes of family life and sex-roles (Beit-Hallahmi & Rabin, 1977).

The family is quite flexible in responding to historical-ecological changes. A fascinating suggestion has been made by van den Berghe (1979) that the isolated nuclear family unit found in industrialized societies today is, in fact, a return to the earliest form of the family found among our earliest human ancestors, the hunter-gatherers. Most contemporary cultures lead the lives of settled agriculturalists and pastoralists. In such circumstances the complex networks of human kin studied by anthropologists flourish, and it is possible for a man to have surplus resources and so attract and support many wives. But life for hunter-gatherers is very different. While they may not live a marginal existence—the old picture of the ever-struggling-to-avoid-starvation hunter-gatherer is false—the economy of hunting and gathering simply does not make possible the amassing of resources controlled by one man, meaning that polygyny is seldom possible. Extended families are likewise maladaptive, for as the game moves so must the hunter, and he must not be burdened by large numbers of wives, extended kin, and all of their children. The family of the hunter-gatherer travels light and is stripped to its essentials; man, woman, and a few children.

Modern society, in its own way, makes similar demands on the family. It is extraordinarily expensive to raise—and especially to educate—a child in contemporary society. Extended and costly education is the major form of parental investment today, and few men can afford to educate more than two children, so having multiple wives and their inevitably many children is impossible. Supporting a nonworking wife is difficult, so we find that working wives are becoming more common than not, contributing equally, like her ancient female ancestors, to the viability of her family. Our survival depends not on chasing wandering game, but on chasing jobs, advancement, and educational opportunities, which, like game, may shift about. So the modern family must be ready to move unencumbered by extended kin. Our families, too, are stripped to their essentials: an economically productive man and woman and a small number of children.

Within the family, parent-offspring conflict—even child abuse (Box 10–7)—can be expected to occur. The rudiments of parent-offspring conflict were covered earlier. Those simpler forms of conflict should apply to humans as to other species. But human intelligence increases the sophistication of the conflict. For example, conflict should arise between parents and children over altruism between siblings. A pair of siblings share 50 percent of their genes, which motivates kin-selected altruism between them. But a given child has a 100 percent genetic investment in one's self and will be altruistic only when the benefit to one's brother or sister is at least twice the cost to one's self. But parents are equally (50 percent investment) interested in all their children and will encourage sibling altruism whenever costs and benefits between them are equal. Conflict is inevitable: Parents will emphasize precise sharing and "fairness," treating each sibling equally, while each individual child will want something more than his or her exact fair share (Trivers, 1974/1980). Socialization plays an important proximate role for the parent. Parents and cultures value honesty, fairness, openness, generosity, self-denial, and sharing, and when parents teach these values they are passing their culture on to their children and their children are becoming members of the culture. At the same time, however, the parents are furthering their genetic investment in all their children, because mutual aid and support ensure that all the children will be able to reproduce.

Human Intelligence

What most obviously separates human beings from the other animals is that we study them, not the other way around. Humankind's greatest adaptation is intelligence, which makes us flexible, able to invent and use religion (Box 10–8), culture, science, and technology. It is a natural question, then, to inquire into the evolutionary origins of human intelligence. (For background, see Jerison, 1973, 1982; Hahn, Jensen, & Dudek, 1979).

Speculation on the problem predates ethology and sociobiology, and both groups of scientists have offered a range of hypotheses, but there does seem to be an emerging consensus that the origin and function of intellect is social—to hold society together (Humphrey, 1976). However, the roles of hunting in demanding sophisticated cognition (Jerison, 1982) and diet in changing the chemical functioning of the brain (Blumenberg, 1983) cannot be overlooked. Wilson (1975) and Dawkins (1976) follow Trivers (1971/1978, 1974/1978) in suggesting that intelligence is required to carry out the sophisticated calculations of reciprocal altruism, and engage in the "games" of parental investment strategies and parent-offspring conflict. Alexander (Alexander & Noonan, 1979; Alexander, 1979) argues that intergroup competitiveness created human intelligence, making adaptive

BOX 10–7   *CHILD ABUSE AND EVOLUTION*

Most sociobiological theories about families attempt to understand why families work—why parents and children love each other, how children are socialized, how parent-offspring conflict is mediated. But as we know all too well today, families don't always work; child abuse and neglect are tragically commonplace even among animals. Can sociobiology shed any light on abnormal family patterns? Daly and Wilson (1981) think it can, that patterns of abuse and neglect can be explained in terms of biologically likely variables.

For example, degree of paternal investment in offspring after birth, throughout the animal kingdom, is a function of confidence of paternity. The more a species' behavior or ecology makes it possible for a male to be sure a female's offspring are his, the more likely is he to help raise them. From the standpoint of fitness, this is quite sensible, since raising offspring not your own would injure your own fitness and increase that of someone else. Daly and Wilson present data showing that abuse and neglect are more common between step-parents and children than in intact families, and is more likely perpetrated by men than women. Other factors that vary with child abuse and neglect also are compatible with sociobiological reasoning: Neglect and abuse are more likely when resources are scarce or when the child is abnormal, cases in which a parent may estimate that the reproductive capacity of the child as an adult will be low, making awaiting new times or a new child a reproductively more attractive option. Finally, factors that disrupt mother-child bonding—the proximate cause of maternal love—are likely to lead to later neglect or abuse. Such factors include prematurity or congenital disease, indicators of poor reproductive potential.

Observe that in each case, parents' behavior is adaptive or at least not maladaptive for them. The father who suspects a child is not his own is likely to abandon it and its mother for reproductive success elsewhere. A child whose life is at risk due to malnutrition, disease, prematurity, or defect is a poor reproductive investment. Morally, child abuse and neglect are abhorrent, and we all must strive to eliminate these ills. But to do so, we should first understand them, see that there are explicable causes acting to bring about abuse and neglect, in order to act effectively. Shrinking back in horror and condemnation is unlikely to lead to effective action. For example, an important proximate cause of mother-infant bonding appears to be very early contact—in the first hours after birth—between mother and child. Hospitals should encourage such contact, especially in the case of children born prematurely, who are often kept for days away from mother in an incubator. Similarly, presence at birth of the father may stimulate father-child bonding. We may think such measures trivially obvious—such conclusions are just "natural." The perspective of evolutionary biology lets us see why they *are* natural.

BOX 10–8   *IS RELIGION INNATE?*

Religion is a unique and uinversal part of human life: "The predisposition to religious beliefs is the most complex and powerful force in the human mind and in all probability an ineradicable part of human nature." (Wilson, 1978, p. 176.). It is also quite ancient, as archaeologists have found evidence of rituals said over burials among the remains of the earliest form of *Homo sapiens,* the Neanderthals. The question naturally arises whether dispositions to believe in gods, to construct rituals, and to invent myths is an innate part of human nature.

Along with E. O. Wilson, neurobiologist Eugene d'Aquili thinks so. D'Aquili (1978) argues that because religion has proved adaptive to people to explain what they experience and to see nature whole, we possess an irresistible tendency to postulate unseen forces—gods, demons, angels—lurking behind observed reality. Organized science has restrained this tendency but has not erased it, certainly not in the masses of nonscientists, nor even in the dreams and fantasies of scientists.

Wilson thinks religion serves more social functions. Shared beliefs and rituals cement individuals together into a more adaptive whole, while myths give the universe moral and personal meaning by explaining events as part of a grand cosmic scheme, often featuring warring forces of absolute Good and absolute Evil. Individuals have been shaped by evolution so they can be socialized by religion and culture. People are highly indoctrinable, which serves cohesion and thus the ultimate survival of the genes or the individual members of the groups.

Partisans of religion should take no comfort in finding that religious belief is innate. Since what is believed results from indoctrination, religious faith is predicated less on truth than on effective brainwashing. More seriously, while the sociobiological explanation of religion does not demolish religious belief, it weakens it by reducing God and myth to brain and genes. Finally, as Wilson suggests, science offers a new faith to satisfy human religious needs.

> It presents the human mind with an alternative mythology that until now has always, point for point in zones of conflict, defeated traditional religion. Its narrative form is the epic: the evolution of the universe from the big bang of fifteen billion years ago through the origin of the elements and celestial bodies to the beginnings of life on earth. The evolutionary epic is mythology in the sense that the laws it adduces here and now are believed but can never be definitely proved to form a cause-and-effect continuum from physics to the social sciences, from this world to all other worlds in the visible universe, and backward through time to the beginning of the universe. (Wilson, 1978, p. 200).

Whether science's new mythology will replace traditional religion or religious cults is a question Wilson leaves unanswered. Clearly it is his own faith. But the offer has been made many times since the Enlightenment of the eighteenth century, and there have been few takers. We shall see.

in-group cooperation and altruism, which in turn depend on foresight and calculation. An older line of thinking (summarized by Pfeiffer, 1976) traces intelligence to the demands of big-game hunting with its prizing of male cooperation in the hunt and sexual division of labor. It is also possible that the large human brain resulted from a sudden genetic mutation rather than being the outcome of selection pressures (Blumenberg, 1983). In all cases it is recognized that human intelligence and our upright stance—bipedalism—are intimately related, because it is through tools that our intelligence works most effectively on the environment, and tool use requires free and skillful hands. Figure 10-6 provides a very useful summary of the likely evolution of the human brain and the accompanying human behavior.

The most complete account of bipedalism and the evolution of intelligence is offered by Lovejoy (Lovejoy, 1981; Johansen & Edey, 1981), as it weaves together the above considerations with loss of estrus and a remade pair-bond theory into an impressive multifactor story.

FIGURE 10–6

The point of departure for Lovejoy's theory is the danger of *K*-selection: extinction. Humans are not the most *K*-selected species. The great apes are, as gorillas, for example, bear about one child every five years. While humans have no doubt hastened the extinction of the apes, their low rate of reproduction would probably have brought them to that fate eventually. *K*-selection, in other words, can be carried too far. All the forces in early human evolution were driving us more and more to the extreme of *K*-selection—the need for parental care of children during an extended childhood, which requires increased intelligence and brain development, hence a reduced number of offspring who can only survive within a protective group held together by complex social behaviors, which require intelligence, and so on. Each adaptation was causally linked to each other, being mutually reinforcing, and made us increasingly vulnerable to extreme *K*-selection (see Figure 10-7, from Johansen & Edey, 1981).

According to Lovejoy, bipedalism is the way out of the *K*-selection trap, for it allows people to avoid the extreme childbearing spacing of the great apes. If women bear one child a year, the benefits of *K*-selection are retained with enough *r*-selection to avoid extinction. To do this, women and children had to move around less, using less energy and being less likely to fall out of trees or be eaten by predators. When movement was necessary, bipedalism was useful, for now a woman could carry her helpless infant.

A problem now arises: How can one woman raise several children at once on a smaller resource-base? They needed help, specifically from males. Males could hunt and bring back meat, which requires bipedalism to

FIGURE 10–7 Mutual reinforcement of factors in the early evolution of man.

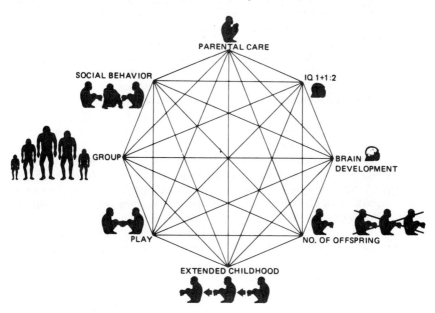

carry the meat, supporting offspring from a large area. They would also have to cooperate, and help rear the increased number of children.

But why should a man do this? Here Lovejoy revives the pair-bond theory. Lovejoy points out that human females have not only lost estrus and begun to sexually advertise continuously, they (and men) also become more *individual-looking* than other animals. The sexual symbols of the human female are not just arousing; they are individuating, too. As Lovejoy says, "The development of stimulating systems that are specific to individuals is called epigamic differentiation. I call it being in love." (Quoted in Johansen & Edey, 1981 p. 334) Moreover, epigamic differentiation emphasizes outward differences in male and female appearance, and Lovejoy (1981) thinks that it is this, not polygyny, that has created human sexual dimorphism.

So it is now possible for a man to fall in love with a distinctively individual woman and *want* (proximate mechanisms) to bring her food and help raise *their* offspring. Pair-bonding also reduces intragroup aggression. As women lose estrus they no longer are periodically provocative to all males, who would start fighting over them. (Daniels, 1983). Now each man has his own private gene-receptacle, as it were. Loss of estrus and pair-bonding also gives subordinate males a better chance of reproduction and a stake in the bond. No longer will dominant males be able to sequester fertile females, since no one knows when women are fertile. And women will be able to choose men who, while not fit through ferocity, are willing to invest a lot in her and her children (Alexander & Noonan, 1979). Additionally, loss of estrus accounts for human hypersexuality as opposed to the hyposexuality of other pair-bonding species. Since a woman does not know when her fertile period is, she must be sexy and prepared for intercourse all the time in order to ensure that copulation will occur when she is fertile. Although Lovejoy does not say so, perhaps this is also an adaptive function of the female orgasm—to motivate continuous sexual activity. Finally, Lovejoy's theory may explain the universal human preference for face-to-face copulation: Only thus can one see, appreciate, and be stimulated by the epigamically differentiated features of one's beloved. Humans copulate as individuals, not just as male and female conspecifics.

Once this complex process is underway—summarized in Figure 10-8—all the various factors will feed back on themselves and each other, so that the push toward bipedalism, social cooperation, intelligence, self-awareness (Box 10-9), and love (epigamic differentiation) will become self-sustaining. Upright posture made tool use possible, and our socially developed intelligence created sophisticated tools in the beginning of technology. Armed with intelligence, tools, and enough r-selection to proliferate, humans quickly spread over the earth's surface and could aim at the stars. Add to this the development of culture, and later the discovery of agriculture (Pfeiffer, 1977), and humankind's enormous success was assured, provided we do not destroy ourselves with our most dangerous tools.

While Lovejoy's proposal is attractive and persuasive, we must remember that like all evolutionary scenarios it is informed speculation, and certain shortcomings should be noted (McHenry, 1982). For example, Lovejoy may be placing the origin of monogamy too early. Most monogamous species show little sexual dimorphism. As we have seen, present-day humans show modest sexual dimorphism and a modest male preference for modest polygyny. But *Australopithecus afarensis*, the species Lovejoy is speculating about, displayed great sexual dimorphism—the males being twice as large as the females—indicating that they were probably strongly polygynous as well. It appears that although *Homo sapiens* is evolving toward monogamy, it is not an ancient trait of our hominid forebears. Similarly, while it is now established that bipedality preceded the development of the human brain, it did so by 2 million years, challenging Lovejoy's thesis that bipedality was an immediate precursor to the explosion of human brain size and intelligence.

Hill (1982) has modified Lovejoy's theory to eliminate the troublesome appeal to an early pair-bond. Hill, too, sees the crucial event as the shift from plant-gathering to predation. Hunting is the most efficient food-gathering strategy, since meat is rich in protein and comes in large, easy-to-carry natural "packages"—carcasses; the need to carry meat would favor bipedality. Hunting would also lead, as Lovejoy argued, to a sexual division of labor, the mates hunting and the females gathering and child-rearing. The males would share their kills with estrus females in return for sex. Such arrangements would lead to group living without pair-bonds, and early human sexual dimorphism would be allowed for. Hill's scenario explains human loss of estrus not as the outcome of pair-bonding, but as an adaptation to male meat sharing. Since males would prefer to share food with and mate with estrus females, a female deception—loss of estrus and continuous sexual availability— would be favored, as then a woman could obtain food at all times.

CONCLUSION

We have now reviewed sociobiology's leading ideas as they are applied to animals and people. With regard to animals, sociobiology has proved relatively uncontroversial; it is only when its principles are extended to human beings that controversy is sparked, and after reviewing sociobiology's research program we will take up a critical evaluation of sociobiology's claims and ideas.

Sociobiology's Research Program

Spelling out the research program of sociobiology is relatively straightforward. Since it is an extension of Neo-Darwinian evolutionary theory to animal and human behavior, its hard core consists of the well-

FIGURE 10–8   These four diagrams, prepared by Owen Lovejoy, illustrate some of the conditions he believes acted in concert to produce a fully erect hominid. Section 1 of each diagram traces the
probable progress of erectness itself. Section 2 refers to epigamic differentiation, the symbols for males and females becoming increasingly individualistic as time goes on, and leading to greater selectivity in sexual pairing. This is reflected in the mating patterns shown in
Section 3, where males at first mate indiscriminately with females but later settle down as
mated partners of specific females. Section 4 deals with the spacing of infants. In Diagram A
there is no overlap, in Diagram B there is a little, and finally, in Diagram D, there are families
of three and four children.

These changes are accompanied by changes in sexual activity (Section 5). The female
menstrual cycle is represented by the long bar, with a portion in the middle representing her
actual period of sexual receptivity. In Diagram A, virtually all sexual activity takes place during estrus. In the subsequent diagrams the period of receptivity increasingly lengthens,
eventuating, in Diagram D, in a condition of continuous sexual receptivity on the part of the
female, entirely independent of her estrus cycle. Meanwhile, kinship relationships are
changing (Section 6). In Diagram A, the only kinship bonds are between a mother and her
children. In Diagram B there is a beginning of a male-female relationship, but no true

established principles of Neo-Darwinian theory and the concepts of modern genetics. To this is added the central theorem of sociobiology: "When
the behavior under study reflects some component of genotype, animals
should behave so as to maximize their inclusive fitness" (Barash, 1977).
The protective belt of hypotheses consists of the specific accounts of how a
given behavior arose and is maintained in a given species. We have examined numerous instances of specific sociobiological analyses, and have seen
that hypothesis testing is a difficult but feasible task, at least for animals.
We have seen how behavioral data can be used to support specific models—
often elegantly mathematical—of animals' behavior from aggression to altruism (Maynard-Smith, 1984).

   Two important points about the power of sociobiology should be recalled. First, despite the fact that it is quite sensitive to species differences in
behavior, the hard-core principles of sociobiology are held to be universal.

bonding. In Diagram C the male is established as a parent, and a family group is formed. In Diagram D there are many such groups.

All these activities take place within (and probably under the influence of) a changing environment (Section 7), where the tropical forest in which quadrupedal apes casually mated and formed no families gradually changes to open woodland and savanna. The circles in the centers of the four diagrams have to do with foraging and movement. The inner circle marks the core area of the group, where females and infants spend their time. The larger circle represents the limit to which males forage. In Diagram A the two circles are nearly the same size, because the female is not being given any food by the male and must do all her own foraging. In Diagram B the male ranges more widely to remove himself from the core area and leave more food for the female—which she must have because she is beginning to have more infants to feed. In Diagram C, this behavior intensifies. The male is now bringing food back to his mate. To do this he ranges still farther, and she can afford to move around less, thus exposing herself to less danger. Diagram D shows the establishment of a true home base, where the mother can leave her infants in the care of aunts or older siblings. Now she is free to range more widely herself. (From Johansen & Edey, 1981).

For example, Triver's theory of parental investment is asserted as applying to all sexually reproducing species, and his hard-core theory leads to specific hypotheses that modify the basic principles of parental investment according to the ecology of each species. Hence, all the diverse mating patterns observed in the wild are explained by combining the concept of parental investment with the ecological circumstances in which animals find themselves. Right or wrong, this theory is an outstanding example of scientific thinking, the precise application of a few general principles to an initially bewildering array of observations.

The other important point to bear in mind is that sociobiology is, at least potentially, not only a theory about behavior. For sociobiology may be able to explain the ultimate causes of a species' *mentality*. This is not readily apparent in talking about animals to whom we ordinarily feel uncomfortable atributing mental states such as wants and desires. However, when we

BOX 10–9 *SELF-AWARENESS, SELF-DECEPTION, AND THE UNCONSCIOUS*

Within our own minds, humankinds' most striking trait is probably our self-awareness. Indeed, the seventeenth-century philosopher Rene Descartes made self-awareness (*Cogito, ergo sum,*" I think, therefore I am") the cornerstone of modern rationalism. Psychologists themselves have debated the importance of human self-awareness. The radical behviorist B. F. Skinner sees it as no more than a collection of socially learned labels for internal sensations and observations of one's own behavior, while humanistic psychologists, such as Carl Rogers and Abraham Maslow, follow Descartes in seeing self-awareness as the *sine qua non* of the human condition.

In the present context, it is interesting to ask if any other animals possess self-awareness. Descartes thought not; he viewed animals as mere deterministic machines, lacking reflection and consciousness. Gordon Gallup (1977) has used mirrors to investigate the question empirically. Monkeys and apes are known to enjoy looking at mirrors and can even use them as tools to solve visual problems. However, they typically respond to a reflection of themselves as an image of a conspecific—they do not perceive them*selves* in the mirror. But since similar self-perception is learned by humans (it does not appear until age two, may never appear in severely retarded persons, and is sometimes lost in schizophrenia) Gallup wondered if perhaps apes and monkeys could learn self-perception.

His first experiment was to place a ten-foot mirror in a cage with wild-born chimpanzees. Initially, they responded to the image as to a conspecific, but after two days their behavior indicated self-recognition. For examples, they groomed parts of the body they could not normally see, they picked their teeth, and they made faces at the mirror. To further test them, Gallup anesthetized the chimps and applied a bright-red, odorless, nonsensitive dye over their foreheads. When they awoke, each chimpanzee clearly showed that it knew the dye was on its own face: They examined the spot in the mirror and touched it repeatedly. When the same procedure was performed with chimpanzees who had never experienced mirrors before, they showed no sign of recognizing the red spot as belonging to themselves. Gallup and others have tried these and similar experiments with virtually all species of monkeys and apes, and they have found that only the great apes—our closest living relations—learn self-perception. Despite hundreds of hours of exposure to mirrors, monkeys and the lesser apes (for example, gibbons) continue to see mirror images as just another conspecific.

If we may take self-perception as a resonable indicator of self-awareness, then, while awareness is not unique to human beings as Descartes suposed, it is limited to the few highest primate species. It also appears that while the great apes may develop self-awareness, they do not do so routinely as humans do. Finally, Gallup's research suggests that as with so much of our nature, the origin of self-awareness is a social phenomenon. Chimpanzees raised in social isolation never learned to perceive themselves in the mirror and never passed the painted forehead test. It seems we must live with others before we can learn to see ourselves.

While we are supremely self-aware, it also appears that humans are supremely self-deceptive. We have already remarked that deception is an important survival strategy, and that the best deceiver is also a self deceiver: One who does not know he or she is being deceptive cannot give oneself away. Alexander (1979) has suggested that concealment of ovulation is a deceptive strategy through which women, by not advertising their fertility, secure long-term male consortship. Moreover, Alexander argues that this strategy is made more effective by self-deception; women themselves do not know when they are fertile, and so cannot accidentally reveal their cycles to men, undoing the effectiveness of no longer advertising ovulation. Lack of self-knowledge in this respect was not inevitable; it is plausible that purely internal sensations of ovulation might remain after external signs were lost. But this did not happen, and Alexander concludes that self-deception about ovulation was adaptive just as was deceiving males.

Alexander has generalized his argument to explain why people are made uncomfortable by sociobiology. According to him, our consciousness (as self-aware as it appears to be) has actually been shaped by evolution to be unaware of the genetic roots of much of our behavior. It would be maladaptive to be too Machiavellian, too coldly calculating, and so our consciousness has made us blissfully unaware of our genetic interests. Daniels (1983) suggests that concealment of ovulation concealed women's genetic self-interests and made it easier for them to devote themselves to their group's interests. Of course, all the while individual genetic interests are molding our behavior and feelings toward their own ends. Daniels points out that devotion to the group actually served genetic self-interest because helping the group survive helped the individual survive. Hence Alexander believes sociobiology has moral value. Only by studying the strategies of our genes can we be made aware enough of them to defeat their ends if we so choose.

A final hypothesis: Could the unconscious—that realm of mind beyond the reach of introspection—have been created by the self-deceptive strategy of the genes described by Alexander?

talk about human beings in sociobiological terms, our discussion soon embraces mental life. The Coolidge Effect only leads us to attribute a *disposition* to enjoy female variety to male animals, but when we turn to male humans we may want to say men *desire* female variety. Such attributions of mentality strike us as uncomfortably presumptuous. We do not like to be told that our most intimate likes and dislikes, desires and schemes, have a merely genetic ultimate causation. Controversy boils to white heat when sociobiologists' claims of what constitutes "natural" mentality run counter to cultural orthodoxies. You should remember, however—and bear it in mind during any discussion about the biological basis of behavior—not to confuse the natural with the good. Polio is natural; vaccination is unnatural.

The Sociobiology Debate

Sociobiology, whatever its final merits prove to be, surely throws new light on human behavior and provides some fascinating accounts of both mundane and unusual features of human life. Above all, it says that there *is* a biologically given human nature apart from society and culture, and that society and culture are shaped by human nature, not just the other way around as environmentalism claims.

Precisely because it challenges some conventional wisdom, however, sociobiology has been fiercely debated.[3] While academic debates do not literally lead to blood in the gutter, the sociobiology debate has come about as close to this as scientists and professors ever come. Numerous papers, books, and symposia have criticized, denounced, praised, or revised sociobiological theory, and the approaches have ranged from technical defenses of group selection to accusations of racism and sexism. We will survey briefly some of this battered terrain, beginning with the most emotion-laden issue: values.

Sociobiology, morality, and politics   The loudest outcries against sociobiology have come from those who find it politically and morally offensive. From the political-scientific left have come charges that sociobiology is just a pseudoscientific apology for the status quo, making competitive capitalism seem right and natural, and justifying racism and sexism. At the other end of the spectrum we find Christian fundamentalists attacking evolution as the cornerstone of secular humanism, which they find a wicked and pernicious doctrine.

Unfortunately, some sociobiologists—most notably Wilson himself—have invited such criticism by their foolish treatment of the relation between evolution and ethics. Wilson has proposed that ethics be taken out of the hands of philosophers and "biologicized," by which he means explaining our ethical judgments as sequences of genetically programmed brain states. Trivers, in a high-school film devoted to sociobiology, similarly maintains that we ought to construct our culture to suit our genes. Both claims are nonsense; both commit what philosophers since David Hume call the "naturalistic fallacy" of deriving an *ought* from an *is*.

Let us take Trivers' point first. Just because something is natural—is innate (the *is*)—it does not follow that it is morally *good* (the *ought*). Smallpox is natural, and we surely do not think it good; its eradication—making smallpox bacterium extinct—is unnatural, and we find it a good worthy of tenacious pursuit. In the case of human behavior, should there turn out to

---

[3]The sociobiology debate has created a vast literature. Good collections of papers include Barlow and Silverberg (1980); Caplan (1978); Gregory, Silvers, and Sutch (1978); Wispé and Thompson (1976); Wyers (1980); Wiegele (1982); and Montague (1980), which must be used with caution as it is an openly negative collection. General reviews may be found in Ruse (1979), which is balanced and comprehensive; Midgley (1978), which is well-written but focuses more on ethology than sociobiology; Sahlins (1976), a hostile attack by an anthropologist; and Singer (1981), which concentrates on ethics. Accounts of the genesis of the controversy—in which we find academia red in tooth and claw—may be found in Bethell (1980), Bingham (1980), Gurin (1976), Keen (1981), and Rosenfeld (1980).

be genes for murder or rape, there is no reason we ought to change our laws (our culture) to tolerate murderers or rapists. Something may be natural but evil, or unnatural and good; that which we morally *ought* to do is clearly separable from what we may want to do. I may be tempted to commit adultery, which is, sociobiologically speaking, quite natural for a male, but I resist the temptation because I believe adultery is morally wrong. Now we should not go too far the other way and say that facts, sociobiological or otherwise, are completely irrelevant to moral reasoning. If certain tendencies that society finds immoral and deserving of control or punishment are, in fact, innate, then perhaps our tactics of control and punishment need to be altered. For example, a male's knowledge of the Coolidge Effect should lead him to accept adulterous impulses as inevitable and natural, so that he can control them calmly and rationally, rather than repressing them as horribly wicked, which is likely to breed neurosis.

Wilson's argument that philosophical ethics is deprived of all force by biological reduction is just preposterous. Mathematics is a human activity carried out by human brains, but this does not mean the principles of mathematics are just biological accidents. To "biologicize" mathematics sounds silly; to "biologicize" ethics is just as silly. The *reasons* of ethics are just as separate from the causal activities of the brains that propounded them as are the reasons of mathematics. This does not make finding sound ethical principles easy, but it does mean we should not look for them in the genome.

As Ruse (1979) remarks, we must save sociobiology from the sociobiologists. Sociobiology cannot *justify* anything, morally speaking. It may suggest that people are naturally competitive, but this does not make capitalism either good or bad. It may suggest there are differences between the reproductive strategies of men and women, but this hardly justifies sexism. It may even challenge it; if women are more naturally concerned with fairness there ought to be more women judges; if they are more naturally nurturant, there out to be more women physicians. As to racism, sociobiologists have rarely suggested there are any racial differences at all, and have certainly never aligned themselves with theories asserting the superiority of one race over another on any trait or behavior.

Those who think evolution undermines morality also commit the naturalistic fallacy, and add to it an egregious misunderstanding of animal nature. Jerry Falwell (*Old Time Gospel Hour* radio broadcast of October 28, 1981) alleges that evolution is morally degrading, for it follows from evolution that we are animals, and that therefore like animals we should just eat, drink, and make merry. Besides confusing *is* and *ought*, this notion rests on a slanderously inaccurate picture of animal nature. Animals eat, but they are never gluttons (except very occasionally in zoos). They drink fluids, but what Rev. Falwell obviously has in mind is strong drink, and animals do not manufacture and consume liquor. And animals do not make merry; they are not irresponsibly hedonistic pleasure seekers. As you know by now, people's stereotypes of what animals are like are shamefully incorrect.

Only humans can "eat, drink and make merry"—it is a unique capacity of our species, and one we indulged long before anyone thought of evolution. Gluttony, drunkenness, and hedonism are not sins that can be justified by evolution. Rather, it is the opposite, since evolution shows that these are unnatural, that they are things we must work at (Roman party-goers, for example, made themselves regurgitate so they could eat more). Evolution poses no threat to human morality.

Genetic determination   Lurking underneath some of the moral and po-litical fears raised by sociobiology is the idea that it implies *genetic determin-ism,* that where biological differences between individuals and sexes exist they are fixed, unchangeable, unmodifiable by the environment; in short, that we cannot do anything about them. Again, the extravagant rhetoric of some sociobiologists—particularly Richard Dawkins—has gotten socio-biology into more trouble than it deserves. Dawkins (1976, p. ix) wrote that, "We are survival machines—robot vehicles blindly programmed to pre-serve the selfish molecules known as genes." Indeed, Dawkins says that ab-solute genetic determinism is true; that we, like all animals, are ignorant robots carrying out the commands of the genes.

This is just silly, and is denied by more sober sociobiologists. Closer to the mark is David Barash's (1979) felicitous phrase "the whisperings within." As Barash explains it, we are not robots but complex creatures compounded of both biology and culture, and what biology provides in the genes are certain insistent whisperings that make us like certain things and want to perform certain behaviors. While Barash thinks we ought to listen to our genes' whispering, he does not think they are commands, and he argues that it is within our power to do other than what they suggest.

Nor does sociobiology undermine free will. Quite the contrary. Symons (1979) revives an argument of William James (1890/1950) to the effect that natural selection has evolved consciousness and free will as adaptive functions of the mind. How else explain the existence of con-sciousness at all? As William James phrased it, " . . . the moment you bring consciousness into the midst, survival ceases to be a mere hypothesis . . . It has now become an imperative decree 'Survival *shall* occur, and therefore organs *must* so work' ." (James, 1890, Vol. 1, p. 141) Consciousness and free will are adaptive products of evolution, and sociobiology may therefore be used to justify them, not to tear them down.

It is on the issue of genetic determinism that sociobiology conflicts with the psychology of learning. Psychologists assumed for many years that animals, including people, are behaviorally a sort of putty to be shaped—Skinner's term—by the environment acting through reinforcement and punishment. However, sociobiology seems to suggest—especially if we read genetic determinism into it—that learning does not accomplish very much, that males grow into men and females into women. We do not just learn these things from the culture that labels us and shapes us because of our socially irrelevant genitalia, as most psychologists believe (see Bem, 1981).

But no sociobiologist, even Dawkins, denies the role of the environ-ment, culture, and learning in determining human behavior. They insist, as all modern geneticists do, that development is not an either-learning-or-genes proposition, but is instead a complex interaction between genetic givens and cultural shaping.

For example, Alexander (1979) maintains that social learning is a proximate mechanism serving adaptive ends. We may illustrate this with the incest taboo. In both animals and humans, close inbreeding is genetically dangerous, and that therefore we ought to have evolved to innately avoid sex and marriage with close relatives. In human beings, social learning may be the proximate mechanism that prevents brother-sister incest.

In traditional Israeli kibbutzes, groups of similar-aged but unrelated children are reared together collectively. Now although it is certainly in the interest of the kibbutz to get these children to marry one another as adults, and there is pressure for them to do so, marriages between such children simply *do not occur,* nor does sex between adolescent age-mates seem to occur. Similarly, in some areas of old China (and sometimes in Taiwan today) there was a practice of contracting marriage between an infant boy and girl, and bringing the girl to grow up with the boy's family. But when the children reached marriage age they usually resisted carrying out the marriage contract.

Clearly this is a form of learning. It appears that boys and girls who grow up together on an intimate, everyday, familial basis *learn* to not feel sexual desire for each other later on. Such learning under normal family circumstances would keep brother-sister incest from happening, and so it is a useful proximate mechanism serving the ultimate end of outbreeding. In both the kibbutz and the Chinese family, the learning misfires, but in so doing reveals itself to us.

So incest avoidance is both genetic *and* learned. Our species is so constructed by evolution to avoid close inbreeding (ultimate cause) by having its members learn (proximate cause) to inhibit sexual desire toward intimate age-mates (van den Berghe, 1983). The species was shaped by evolution, but the particular individual learns to avoid sex with certain other particular individuals. This situation reminds us of the constraints on animal learning recently discovered by psychologists, discussed in Chapter Four. Biology makes certain kinds of learning easier than others, and now we see evidence of the same thing in people. The "whisperings within" may constrain learning, but they do not substitute robotic preprogramming for the flexible and adaptive patterns of learning.

In people, of course, flexibility and learning are most highly developed, as all sociobiologists recognize. The vast majority of human adaptation is cultural; there are no genes for building airplanes, telephones, or computers, or for writing books and attending classes. What we have evolved is an enormous capacity to be flexibly clever. We adapt by what we make, rather than by changing our bodies, and by turning our cleverness on the world itself, making it serve our ends rather than we serve its ends.

The primary vehicle of our flexibility is language and the culture it makes possible. We will see in the next chapter, however, that the human capacity for language, and therefore for culture, has a genetic and biological basis. The ability to learn and the ability to communicate must be embodied in some creature, and that creature is *Homo sapiens,* the product of millions of years of evolution and, so far at least, the most successful survivor on earth.

Misuse of terms   An important class of objections to sociobiology centers on the misleading way in which sociobiologists use certain ordinary words, especially *altruism.* Sociobiologists' treatment of altruism as *really* selfish makes sociobiology repellant to some and perversely fascinating to others. Sociobiologists' rhetoric frequently revels in reducing altruism to selfishness: Dawkins called his book *The Selfish Gene,* and Ghiselin wrote notoriously, "Scratch an altruist and watch a hypocrite bleed."

This, however, is willful equivocation. Sociobiologists define altruism solely in terms of behavior and its genetic outcome. A behavior is "altruistic" if it increases one's inclusive fitness while risking one's individual fitness (kin-selected altruism) or increases one's individual fitness by helping another's (reciprocal altruism). So, Dawkins and Chiselin maintain, altruism is really selfish, because it serves the interests of our genes.

But we ordinarily define altruism not in terms of behavior but in terms of *intention.* We say someone is altruistic if he or she intended to aid another at some risk to one's self. As Midgeley (1978) points out, it would be absurd to say of someone, "He's really selfish—he thinks only of the welfare of his relatives," or "He's really selfish—he thinks only about the welfare of great-grandchildren he hasn't got yet." It is also most unlikely that the bystander who plunges into the water to save a drowning child has calculated that by saving the child one might be helped later on, or that upon pulling the child from the water one would be chagrined to discover he or she had saved a polio victim unlikely to be able to give reciprocal aid in future.

It may be that there are biological reasons for how we feel about our family, our relatives, our descendants, and distressed strangers; but if this is so, altruism has not been destroyed and reduced to conniving Machiavellianism. Our love of friends and family, and our desire to help others, are genuine motives, and when we act on them we are being genuinely altruistic, not secretly selfish.

Uniquely Human: Co-evolution

Sociobiologists and sympathetic social scientists are coming to recognize that understanding human beings requires attention both to cultural factors (which classic animal-based sociobiology naturally overlooked) and biological factors (which traditional psychology overlooked) if it is to be at all adequate. Recently, the notion of cultural-biological co-evolution has been proposed by various authors (Durham, 1978, 1982; Flinn & Alexander, 1982; Lumsden & Wilson, 1981; Ruse, 1979).

Co-evolutionary theory recognizes that natural selection has produced in human beings a creature whose nature is much less constrained by the genes than is that of other animals. Human beings' abilities to learn, to speak, and to build culture have evolved because they have worked in the struggle for existence. Therefore, while *natural* selection has evolved an open and flexible human nature (within broad limits), it has thereby created a new selection pressure, *cultural selection,* which acts on cultural practices, ideas, and institutions. Any given human trait is the joint product of natural selection, which gives us our genetic dispositions, and cultural selection, which gives us our individual ideas and dispositions.

Ruse (1979) offers an informative example of this in the case of sexuality. The fact that a male is sexually aroused by the female form is an obvious (and obviously adaptive) biological disposition. Yet a contemporary Western male will be (if he is typical) especially aroused by large breasts (which may be habitually uncovered in another culture) but unmoved by the bare female ankle (which may have driven his Victorian great-grandfather to feverish lust). Biology and culture meet to determine the concrete mind of the individual in society.

BOX 10–10   *RESULTS OF THE FIELD STUDY*

Perhaps the most important emotional attachment in life is between mother and infant. One component of this emotional bond seems to be based on the mother's heartbeat, since infants can be soothed by recording of the human heart beating at a normal rate, but are disturbed by recordings of a faster heartbeat.

As discussed by Lumsden and Wilson (1981) women unconsciously enhance this effect by holding infants to the left side, near the heart. Studies of mothers carrying infants found that 78 percent of left-handed mothers, and 83 percent of right-handed mothers carried their babies on the left near the heart. These findings have been replicated in non–Western cultures. Men, on the other hand, carry their infants equally on the right and the left. Interesting confirmation of these biases come from Western (Grüsser, 1983) and non-Western art, in which women are shown holding babies on the left while men hold them to either side.

Book-carrying is a possible analogue to baby-carrying, and a study found that 82 percent of male students carried their books held straight along the right side, while 79 percent of female students carried them pressed to the left side by the forearm or clasped to their chest. We hope you got similar results in your study.

A strong mother-infant bond is assuredly adaptive to the genes of both mother and child. For her genes to thrive, the mother (as the primary caretaker) must be emotionally moved to care for a helpless infant who is often troublesome and at times hard even to like. The infant, too, must learn to love its mother, to seek her care and protection if it is to survive.

How the infant is held appears to be one of the many proximate mechanisms that enhance the mutual love of mother and infant child, love which is itself a proximate mechanism ensuring survival of the genes in the next generation. In its turn, the genes have created a bias in women to hold their infants in the optimal way, and the circuit of ultimate and proximate causation is closed.

Co-evolution, however, is more than a simple juxtaposing of biological and social sciences, for it emphasizes the pervasiveness of selection. Natural selection favors genes that promote survival; cultural selection favors ideas, practices, and institutions that promote survival. In either case, the scientist must ask questions new to the social sciences: Whom does culture benefit and how? Cultures that violate selection too wantonly cannot survive. The Shakers refused, on moral grounds, to reproduce, so their moral ideas went extinct. In both the biological and cultural realms, co-evolutionary theory focuses our attention on selection, on how human traits, whatever their source, help or hinder our ability to survive and grow.

Finally, co-evolutionary theory points out that cultural and natural evolution must interact in important ways so that we can never again consider each in isolation. Cultural evolution must ultimately serve reproduction and survival, or the culture will become extinct. Cultural change cannot wander too far from the underlying biological imperatives of human nature. At the same time, once culture is created it imposes new selection pressures on biological evolution. Culture is the most important part of the environment in which humans develop, mate, and raise children. Therefore, cultural pressures for or against aggression, for or against altruism, for or against traditional sex roles, will act on the underlying genotypes and change their relative frequencies. So not only can *Homo sapiens* construct their own social nature, but their own nature as an animal.

SUGGESTED READINGS

The ambitious reader may want to tackle E. O. Wilson's original *Sociobiology* (Harvard University Press, 1975), which is surprisingly readable, especially in its abridged paperback edition, from which the more fearsome mathematics was pruned. Two other lively secondary primers are available—Richard Dawkins' *The Selfish Gene* (Oxford University Press, 1976), which is the most aggressive sociobiology work, and David Barash's *Sociobiology and Behavior* (Eleesevier, 1977, 2nd ed., 1982), which is written with clarity and grace. Finally, students of animal behavior should read John Alcock's *Animal Behavior: An Evolutionary Approach* (Sinauer Associates, 1979), a truly excellent book on which this chapter relied for much of the data on animal behavior. Alcock does a superb job summarizing data and theory for all areas of animal behavior, not just sociobiology. An excellent introduction to human sociobiology is Barash's *The Whisperings Within* (Penguin, 1979).

CHAPTER ELEVEN

THE ORIGIN AND DEVELOPMENT OF LANGUAGE

INTRODUCTION

Whatever else may be unique about the human species, there is no doubt that our most important single possession is language. Language makes possible human culture, creating the co-evolution of biology and society that is uniquely human. We can express and explore ideas and feelings in ways unknown to the animal world. With language we can communicate, entertain, and rhapsodize. Without language we would surely not be human.

But important as language is, is it *special*? Is human language a particular and unique species-specific human trait—as is the opposable thumb—or is language a consequence of other, more general learning and cognitive abilities, and therefore unique to humans (if it is unique) only because our conceptual powers are so highly developed? This question, which is very old but still controversial, will occupy us in this chapter.

Behaviorism and Language

The shared attitude of the behaviorists (see Mowrer, 1954; Skinner, 1957; Osgood, 1963/1967) was that "we neither wish nor require any special theory for language" (Osgood, 1963/1967, p. 110). Language was viewed as just another (albeit complex) behavior to be explained by behavior theoretic principles, and its acquisition explained as a process of classical and/or operant conditioning. For example, Mowrer (1954) described language in terms of classical conditioning. Word meanings are acquired as CS's paired with the objects or actions they designate (US's) with the result that some component of one's reactions to objects and actions come to be elicited by words; this component is the word's "meaning." So when a child meets (and responds, overtly and covertly) to a cat and hears it named "Freya," a classical conditioning paradigm is set up:

B. F. Skinner, on the other hand, described language learning as a process of operant conditioning, as we saw in Chapter 4. Concepts are operant response classes learned under stimulus control through differential reinforcement by the language community.

Although some radical behaviorists still approach language in this way (see Winokur, 1976), what we have already learned about language in earlier chapters suggests that behaviorist accounts of language are implausible at best (Chomsky, 1959). Interestingly, though, whatever their other differences with behaviorists (which cause them to reject conditioning models of cognition and language), cognitive psychologists by and large agree that language is not special, but is just one expression of complex information-processing activities. In this they differ from the followers of Noam Chomsky, the major modern proponent of the idea that language is a unique, species-specific human adaptive organ.

Could Language Be Innate?

Chomsky's thesis   Noam Chomsky calls himself a Cartesian linguist (Chomsky, 1965) because of his stress on language's uniqueness to human beings and its creative power. René Descartes (1596–1650) followed in the older Rationalist philosophical tradition of Plato in maintaining that some of our ideas are **innate.** For example, Descartes maintained that one's idea of God is innate for we know about God without ever having met God. Similarly, many mathematical truths are known without being based on experience. If $A = B$ and $B = C$, we know immediately that $A = C$, and this is an abstract truth not derived from experience. It is an unlearned, *innate* truth. Of course Descartes, like Plato before him, did not think that little babies can do math. Rationalists do allow a role for experience as an activator of innate ideas, a concept quite in keeping with modern genetic thinking.

Unlike Plato, Descartes—and Chomsky—assigned a special role to language. Descartes argued that only human beings think, have ideas to express, and so only human beings have language, which is the expression of thought. Language is therefore specific to the human species, incapable of occurring among animals. A later Cartesian, Julien Offroy de la Mettrie (1709–1751), however, proposed that at least some animals could think and therefore could learn language. Specifically, he sugested teaching language to an ape, making him a "perfect little gentleman." La Mettrie's research proposal was finally carried out some two centuries later, and as we shall see is no less controversial now than when la Mettrie put it forward.

While Chomsky's proposal that language is innate is in the Cartesian tradition (at least he thinks so; for a contrary view see Aarslef, 1982), he views language as even more special than Descartes did. Descartes viewed language as the expression of cognitive processes unique to humans, thereby making language unique to humans. But as la Mettrie's argument shows, if animals can think, however simply, they can possess language, however simple. Chomsky goes much further, proposing that language has all the general properties of an organ of the body (Chomsky, 1976, in following discussion). For Chomsky, then, language is something very specific indeed—the function of an innate language faculty—and not the result of anything else, of learning or cognition, or thinking. Language is an evolved species-specific organ. What argument and evidence does Chomsky offer to support his extreme view?

Chomsky's major contribution to linguistics is his powerful analysis of syntax, transformational grammar. There are several insights from the study of syntax that he brings to bear on formulating the problem of language acquisition.

To begin with, language possesses an invisible structure— **syntax**— that is not given by spoken words themselves, but must be applied by the listener. Ambiguous sentences reveal the workings of the hearer's mind quite nicely. "They are cooking apples" has two meanings depending on how we readers syntactically analyze the sentence. If we treat *cooking* as an adjective, then we understand that those sorts of apples are the sort one cooks with. On the other hand, if we take *cooking* as a verb, we understand that those people are preparing apples to eat. So a sentence is not a set of strung-together words—or CS's or operants—but is organized by an underlying structure. As George Miller, an early collaborator of Chomsky's once noted, word order counts: A Venetian blind is not the same thing as a blind Venetian.

The hidden syntactic structure of language is important to defining the language acquisition problem in two ways. First, since as adults we use syntax to understand sentences, we must have acquired these rules somehow as children. In our society we tend to think we were taught them directly; we all remember boring grammar drills at school and being corrected for certain grammatical errors ("Me and Jimmy went . . ."). However, in preliterate cultures, grammar is not taught. Natives do not know the rules of their own language; it takes an anthropologist months or years to work out the rules. Moreover, even in our own culture children begin to speak in sentences before they go to school and before anyone fusses over their grammar.

The second way that syntax defines the language acquisition problem is more important for Chomsky's thesis. It is the fact that the syntactic structure of the sentences a child hears is not *in the words themselves.* Grammar is an invisible organizer of words into sentences, and somehow children must figure out their language's syntax without direct exposure to it. This suggests that children already know something about grammar, which furnishes a basis for constructing the rules of their individual grammar.

So far, we have only discussed the surface structure of sentences. But as we found in Chapter 7, underneath the surface structure of each sentence lies an even more remote deep structure, and these deep-structure rules must also be learned. Since deep-structure rules are far removed from the words of sentences, learning them is an especially difficult task, and this reinforces the notion that the child must bring to the task of language acquisition more than just an ability to make associations, must possess some innate faculty for constructing linguistic rules.

In tackling this formidable task, the child faces two additional problems also faced by an anthropologist trying to unravel a novel language. First, it is generally the case that given any finite set of sentences that a child has heard—or an anthropologist recorded—up to a given moment, more than one grammar can be written to describe their structures. The anthropologist's problem (and the child's) is to decide which grammar is correct. It would help if certain universal features of all human languages existed to help rule out certain grammars right away as simply impossible. Such universals do, in fact, exist—the agent/object distinction for example—and Chomsky argues that they reflect innately invariant properties of the language faculty, and place constraints on the kinds of grammars the child will construct. Since all speakers of a given language appear to have learned the same rules, even though many rules may be consistent with the data, Chomsky believes that a universal language faculty is at work. At this juncture it should be pointed out that Chomsky does not think that the Chinese child comes prepared to learn Chinese, the French child to learn French, and so on; obviously, this is false. Rather, Chomsky claims that human children come prepared to learn a human language, and the language faculty already knows, in a sense, what human languages are like, setting out of bounds other plausible, but nonhuman syntactic systems.

The second problem shared by the anthropologist and child is that actual speech, what one can listen to and record, is influenced by many factors irrelevant to the grammar of the language. An analogy may be made to hearing a symphony. If a musician records each note as it is played in performance (and does not have the score) what he or she writes down will not be the symphony itself. The performers may be tired, may be unfamiliar with the conductor, may be playing from memory, or may have varying degrees of talent. All these factors, which are irrelevant to the symphony, will lead to mistakes, so that the performance is not a true representation of the symphony, but a distortion of it. And mistakes are inevitable.

In language the situation is similar. Anyone who has read unedited speech, or listened carefully to it, knows that speech is influenced by many extra linguistic factors: memory, change in the point one wanted to make, false starts, hesitations, and so on. Although speakers know the rules of their language, their actual performance—like musicians'—is a distorted embodiment of them. So the anthropologist and child must somehow ignore or correct the errors. Indeed, they must first figure out what is error and what is correct syntax before they can uncover both the surface and deep structures of the language they are confronting. Again, this learning would be greatly facilitated by some preexisting knowledge of human language to be applied to one's specific situation. And the child—who learns most of his or her syntax between ages two and five—does not have the anthropologist's professional training, so that the child's preexisting knowledge must be innate.

Chomsky calls the difference between people's knowledge of their grammar and their actual use of it the **competence/performance distinction,** and we may now formulate the problem of language acquisition as Chomsky sees it.

The problem is to account for the acquisition by a child of linguistic competence in his or her native tongue. Acquisition of language is based on limited exposure to primary linguistic input flawed by deficiencies in adult performance, from which a child between the ages of two and five must nevertheless correctly abstract surface and deep-structure rules without direct teaching. The magnitude of the problem suggests that children are born with a language faculty, or, in more modern terms, a *language acquisition device* (LAD), richly furnished with knowledge of human language in general. This LAD constrains and makes manageable the child's task. Children do not begin to acquire language before 15 months of age or so, and acquisition of a second language in adolescence or adulthood is a markedly different and more difficult process. These facts indicate that there is a critical period in which the LAD is active and during which language acquisition must take place. All of this adds up to the proposal that language is a species-specific human faculty rooted in our biological ancestry.

Criticisms of Chomsky's thesis   Given the controversy surrounding sociobiology, we should not be surprised to learn that Chomsky's nativism has been roundly criticized since it was first proposed in 1959. As with sociobiology, there is even a political dimension to the controversy, except (ironically) in this case the upholder of nativism, Chomsky, is a libertarian socialist (Chomsky, 1980b). He denounces empiricism as a conservative and repressive doctrine, because it justifies a belief by established elites that people can be conditioned to accept any social system at all. Chomsky believes that only a rationalist commitment to an inherent human nature justifies revolution against an unjustly unnatural social order.

Complaints and criticisms concerning Chomsky's proposal have been numerous and varied, ranging from philosophers who just find it unintelligible to psychologists who find it intelligible and interesting, but who cannot reconcile it with the data. For our purposes, two specific points of criticism are important, which in turn raise the fundamental issue of what is learned during language acquisition.

Chomsky makes a great deal of the competence/performance distinctions, and takes his system of transformational grammar to be a reasonable description of adult linguistic competence. But what does this mean? And is it true? Psycholinguistics in the early 1960s took Chomsky to be saying that the syntactic steps that he described as generating deep structures and transforming them into surface structures corresponded to the real psychological steps by which people construct utterances. But this is absurd, since in transformational grammar assignment of words to sentences is a relatively late step, implying that we first pick our sentence-form, and *then* decide what to talk about! Chomsky later explicitly disavowed any identity between his formal grammar and human speech.

The next hypothesis was that the complexity of sentences as measured in formal grammar corresponded to their psychological complexity (Watt, 1970). But this, too, fails. Consider the familiar pair

(1)   Dee is hard to please.
(2)   Dee is eager to please.

Clearly, these sentences are on a par with respect to our ease of understanding them, that is, their psychological complexity. Yet in transformational grammar, (2) derives from the deep structure (roughly) "Dee is eager to please," whereas (1) derives (roughly) from "For anyone to please Dee is hard." Therefore, (1) is a complex derivation from a deep structure, and should be harder to understand, and far more complex than (2) or its own deep structure form. This is clearly not the case.

Hence, it is unclear what connection there is between what people do when speaking and listening, and what Chomsky describes in transformational grammar, what he calls the "competence" that each speaker "knows." Derwing (1973), in a thorough review of the problem, concludes that the only defensible definition of Chomskyan "competence" is that it is a purely formal description of a language with no psychological reality at all.

So we may then ask if children actually acquire linguistic competence in any psychological sense. Many psychologists have argued that they do not, the difference between linguistic grammar and mental grammar (Watt, 1970) being so great that we should concentrate directly on formulating and studying the acquisition and use of the latter.

Now while this argument does not flatly rule out nativism—mental grammar could be innate—the usual alternative offered to Chomsky's rationalism is an empiricist cognitive hypothesis (see Bever, 1970; Eliot, 1981). Behaviorism finds few defenders, but empiricism is common to it and the cognitive approach. What these scientists offer is the view (specifics, of course, vary) that a child possesses certain general cognitive abilities related to perception, learning, reasoning, and so on, that the child can *also* apply to learning language. What is learned on this account is thus neither competence (linguistic grammar) nor even mental grammar, but rather the application of information-processing abilities to the domain of language. Psychologically speaking, then, there is no such thing as grammar at all, only the processing of linguistic information.

One proposal for testing this hypothesis has special relevance to our sociobiological approach to language acquisition: teaching language to apes. Following la Mettrie's research proposal of 1748, the idea is that apes have cognitive abilities and even some form of self-awareness (see Chapter 10), but do not naturally have language. Therefore, if apes could be taught language it would show that general information-processing skills can underlie language acquisition even in humans.

Before examining the fascinating but problematical results of these studies, we should put the whole issue in a sociobiological context by examining the possible evolution of language and communication.

ANIMAL COMMUNICATION

One important question that Chomsky tends to ignore in his rationalist emphasis on human uniqueness is what continuities, if any, exist between human language and animal communication systems. This question is nevertheless important for a sociobiological approach to human language. Ethologists and sociobiologists have closely studied animal communication.

Patterns of Animal Communication

Defining communication   Just defining communication is difficult. Clearly, as I write this I am communicating—I hope!—with the reader. What if I sneeze? Someone who hears me may find out that I have a cold. But have I *communicated* with that person? Or suppose I sneeze deliberately in my wife's presence to let her know I have a cold and so elicit her sympathy; this would seem to be communication, for it is intentional, even if I have not used language. Finally, however, a psychoanalyst might claim an "accidental" sneeze near my wife is really an unconscious but real communication, a reaching out for sympathy that my conscious mind, not wanting to feel dependent, rejects. Much of our nonverbal communication is just like this: unconscious and often beyond our willful control—except, of course, for the actor and poker player.

We must recognize a continuum of communication from verbal language used purposefully to unconscious, nonverbal communication (Figure 11–1). In the case of animals, defining communication is especially problematic since we can assess intention only with difficulty, and are reluctant to attribute intentions to lightning bugs, for example, who not only communicate, but even lie (see Box 11–1). Wilson (1980, p. 90) proposes that "communication is the action on the part of one organism (or cell) that alters the probability pattern of behavior in another organism (or cell) in a fashion adaptive to either one or both of the participants." Unfortunately, this definition is at once too inclusive and too exclusive. It would call "communication" the bright color of a flower that attracts bees to the benefit of both, but few would call this communication by the flower. On the other hand, at least in humans, language communication can be used to the detriment of everyone and the benefit of none, which would mean malicious, spiteful gossip is not communication.

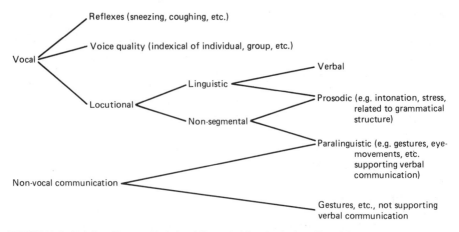

FIGURE 11–1   Relations Between Verbal and Nonverbal Communication. (From Hinde, 1974)

Green and Marler (1979) propose a more formal definition. To count as communication, a signal or set of signals must meet three criteria. First, the signals must be *nonconstant,* that is, emitted only on some occasions. This rules out signals such as coloration or shape, which convey information such as species identity, but are not communication in any useful sense. Second, the signals must be *specialized* to serve a communicative function. Third, there must be *internal processing,* the encoding and decoding of signals. Green's and Marler's criteria seem to formalize our intuitive notion of communication while allowing room for doubtful cases such as the unconscious sneeze.

The best overall definition of communication, then, is to regard it as the emission of one or more signals, which when received (input) and processed by another animal results in some change in behavior or state (output). Signals and responses may be *graded* (Figure 11–2a), that is, lying on a smooth continuum of minimal to maximal intensity. Threat signals are often graded, as an animal increases its ferocity. Or, signals and responses may be *discrete,* having only a preset number of conceivable values with no gradations in between (Figure 11–2b). Human words are discrete signals— each word is a distinct package. In either case, communication may be viewed as a mapping function (Figure 11–2c) that relates signal to behavior (Green & Marler, 1979).

Functions of communication   However we define it, communication serves many important functions in animal life, for species ranging from the slime mold—who reproduce in hard times by emitting a pheremone that gathers a crowd of fellows who temporarily form themselves into a large fruiting body (Gould, 1982)—to human beings. Table 11–1 lists the functions of communication adduced by Wilson (1980) with some examples. One can see that communication is involved in every aspect of animals' lives from birth to death, serving many functions essential to survival. Animal communication must, therefore, have a strong innate component.

BOX 11–1 *DO ANIMALS LIE?*

One thing we learn from sociobiology is to analyze the costs and benefits of different classes of behavior. And nothing costs less than to send a message: Talk is cheap. Since there are obvious benefits to be gained from lying, we might expect to find many cases of deceitful communication in nature, and our expectations are amply confirmed (Barash, 1982). For example, monarch butterflies feed on milkweed plants, which contain a toxin not digested but stored within the butterfly. Birds who eat monarchs get violently ill and, in an example of conditioned food aversion (Chapter 4), avoid eating monarchs thereafter. The distinctive coloring of the monarch signals danger, an honest communication adaptive to both predator and butterfly. But then there is the viceroy butterfly that does not eat milkweed and contains no toxin, but has evolved to look like the monarch. It sends a false message of danger, and since this message is heeded by wary predators, natural selection has favored the viceroy's deceitful coloration. Such mimicry is fairly common among insects, and it was partly his consideration of mimicry in Amazonian insects that put A. R. Wallace onto the theory of evolution.

A particularly interesting form of deceit occurs among fireflies (Gould, 1982). Fireflies' flashing lights serve two adaptive functions. Like monarch butterflies, fireflies contain toxic cardiac glycerides (although they make their own) and the flashing warns predators that they are poisonous. More importantly, firefly males and females locate each other for mating by exchanging coded signals, and each of the many firefly species has its own characteristic code. Females remain stationary as the males fly around flashing. Females—sensing a species' correct flashing pattern in the air—return the males' signals, and the distinctive timing of the return flash lets the male know of an appropriate conspecific female. He lands near her, and perhaps using smell and shape as a final test that she is the correct species, copulates with her.

Females of the species *phutoris versicolor* have learned to lie to their own benefit. After mating with a conspecific male, preparing to bear and hatch offspring, the *photuris* female begins to attract males of other species by mimicing the code of their females. The unwitting male firefly is lured to *photuris* by her deceptive signal and approaches, learning too late that he is going to be a meal, not a mate. Photuris females in this way gain an excellent source of protein for very little work: Talk is cheap.

By the way, you can perform the same trick yourself with a penlight (Gould, 1982). Try various delay times between the offset of a flying (and therefore male) firefly and when you turn on your penlight in return. Some trial and error will give you the right latency, and then you can lure in the male. Of course, you won't smell right and so he won't try to mate with you, or the flashlight.

Fortunately, deceit is not rampant in nature because false signals often exact costs—the liar is found out and his or her fitness reduced. Moreover, natural selection has evolved various reliability signs into many messages (Barash, 1982). For example, the loudness and the low pitch of aggressive roaring among many males—including species as different as Fowler's toad and red deer—correlate well with fighting ability, since a strong male is large and well-muscled. Such correlations help establish truth-in-advertising in the wild kingdom.

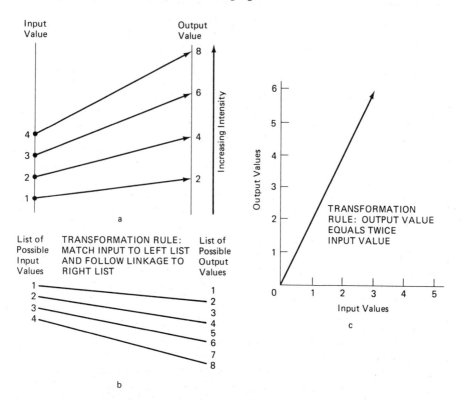

FIGURE 11–2　(a) A Diagram of Relationships Between Input and Output Values That Can Be Achieved Either By (b) A Set of Linkages Between Lists, or (c) A General Rule That Can Be Applied to Determine the Output Given Any Input. The same mapping function that describes (a) can be produced by the separate transformation rules shown in (b) or the general rule pictured in (c). (From Green & Marler, *Handbook of Behavioral Neurobiology*, 1979, p. 88. Plenum Publishers.)

TABLE 11–1　Functions of Communication

Function	Description and Examples
Facilitation and *Imitation*	Behaviors that facilitate group living and cooperation. *Example: Kinopsis* in large-eyed ants, wherein an ant in rapid motion, probably toward prey, attracts other ants.
Contact	Signals that maintain contact between members of a group. *Example*: Under condition of poor visibility (e.g., dense vegetation) South American tapirs emit a short squeal to stay in touch with their herd.
Individual and *Class* *Recognition*	Signals that identify a particular individual and/or his or her (or its) class. *Example*: Pheremones emitted by queens in ant, termite, and bee nests cause workers to act in special ways toward her.
Status Signaling	Signals that communicate the rank of an individual in a status hierarchy. *Example*: Dominant rhesus monkeys walk with head and tail erect, low-ranking males with tail and head drooping.

TABLE 11-1 *(Continued)*

Function	Description and Examples
Begging and Offering of Food	Signals that indicate readiness to share food or that elicit sharing. *Example*: Open mouth gape of baby bird in nest triggers parent placing food in mouth.
Grooming	While it may also serve hygienic functions, *allogrooming*—the grooming of others—can be a social signal. *Example*: Grooming among primates forestalls aggression and reinforces status hierarchies.
Alarm	Signals indicating danger and mobilizing some response *Example*: Alarm calls in birds and ground squirrels.
Distress	Signals indicating that the sender is in trouble. *Example*: Leaf-cutting ants summon help when caught in a cave-in by *stridulating*, emitting a squeak by scraping carapace segments together. And, of course, babies cry.
Assembly and Recruitment	Signals drawing conspecifics closer together and/or recruiting them for a purpose. *Example*: Wolves howl to gather a pack scattered over a patrolled territory.
Leadership	Signals that organize a group behind a leader. *Example*: the "swing step" of a dominant male hamadryas baboon, which induces troop to fall in behind him.
Synchronization of Hatching	Signals inducing a clutch of precocial birds to hatch together. *Example*: click vocalization by chicks in the egg that are most persistent nearest to hatching.
Play Invitation	Signals initiating play. *Example*: the relaxed open-mouth display of the crab-eating monkey.
Threat, Submission, and Appeasement	Signals occurring in connection with aggression. *Example*: the fluffing-up of a cat's fur in the presence of an enemy.
Nest Relief Ceremony	A ceremony occurring between parent birds as they take turns foraging and guarding. *Example*: The male nightjar approaches the nest with a distinctive call returned by the female.
Sexual Behavior	Signals associated with sexual activity, such as courtship rituals. *Example*: See Chapter 10.
Caste Inhibition	*Example*: Queens of advanced social insects emit pheremones inhibiting the development of immature stages into new queens.

Evolution of communication Since communication is so important to individual and group survival, signaling and receiving systems and behaviors are under strong selective pressure (Green & Marler, 1979). On the sending side, an individual must be able to send appropriate and perceivable messages so that natural selection acts on the morphology, behavior, and even cognitive abilities of organisms. For example, signals designed to attract a mate must be locatable, so that the prospective mate can find the signaller. On the other hand, an alarm call should be hard to locate so as not to attract a predator's attention. Thus, selection tends to develop the ability to produce distinctive kinds of calls, and the ability to use each appropriately.

On the receiving side, selection will favor sensory abilities and acuities involved in communication. Thus, any animal's most acute range of sensory discrimination generally coincides with the range of signals. In both cases the simple physical environment—and changes in environment produce evolution—is important, since signals must survive and be received despite noise, obstacles, aquatic thermoclines, and other hazards. So each species' characteristic mode and manner of signalling—chemical, visual, auditory, tactile, or electric—will evolve in accordance with its environment and way of life (Wilson, 1980).

The most important process involved in the evolution of communication is what ethologists call **ritualization** (Wilson, 1980; Hinde, 1974). Ritualization transforms preexisting behaviors unrelated to communication into stereotyped, patterned behaviors that can serve as distinct signals. The process is also called **semanticization** (Wilson, 1980) because the essential change taking place during ritualization is that the behavior acquires *meaning*, and is no longer just a behavior occurring because of some external or internal cause. A ritualized behavior becomes a signal that affects another's behavior rather than one's own.

The three most important sources of ritualized behaviors are *intention movements, displacement activities,* and *autonomic responses* (Hinde, 1974). *Intention movements* are behaviors preparatory to some activity. For example, before a bird takes off, it crouches, pulls its head back, and raises its tail, and most communicative displays in birds are ritualization of these intention movements. *Displacement activities* result from conflicting dispositions or simply appear during unrelated activities. In aggressive interactions, for example, the combatants want to both fight and flee (or at least not fight). So hostile advances may alternate with a nonhostile activity such as pulling at grass. These displacement activities may become ritualized, being selected because they minimize damaging combat, so that aggression may become more a matter of display than fighting. Similar processes can produce courtship displays. Finally, *autonomic responses* may be ritualized into signals. Anger, for example, causes many physiological changes to occur, and the visible ones may become signals of hostility, that is, aggressive displays.

Two Examples: Honeybees and Birds

Nature offers two highly developed forms of communication that approach human language in many respects. One is the **language of the honeybees,** one of the most famous discoveries of ethology, and the other is **birdsong,** long beloved but only recently the object of scientific scrutiny.

The language of the honeybees   That bees can communicate to each other the location of pollen had long been suspected. Aristotle thought that a bee who finds a trove of pollen returns to the hive and recruits her fellows into following her to the pollen site. Early comparative psychology quickly disproved Aristotle's theory. Discoverer bees were marked when they discovered pollen, allowed to return to the hive but captured upon reemergence. Nevertheless, the other workers made straight for the newly found pollen (Gould, 1982). It remained for German ethologist Karl von Frisch to unravel the mystery, showing that bees communicate the location of pollen through a language of dance.

When the bee returns to the hive, she announces her find by dancing in a figure-eight pattern with a waggle in the middle during which the bee shakes rapidly back and forth and gives off a buzzing sound by vibrating her wings (Figure 11–3). Other workers gather around her, touching her, and soon begin to take off for the new food source, locating it with remark-

(a)

(b)

FIGURE 11–3 The Waggle Dance of the Honeybee. As the bee passes through the straight run she vibrates ("waggles") her body laterally, with the greatest movement occurring in the tip of the abdomen and the least in the head. At the conclusion of the straight run, she circles back to about the starting position, as a rule alternately to the left and right. The follower bees acquire the information about the food find during the straight run. In the examples shown here the run indicates a food find 20% to the right of the sun as the bee leaves the nest. If the bee performs the dance outside the hive (a), the straight run of the dance points directly toward the food souce. If she performs a dance inside the hive (b), she orients herself by gravity, and the point directly overhead takes the place of the sun. The angle x (= 20%) is the same for both dances. (From Curtis, 1968).

able accuracy. It is the waggle part of the dance that communicates the location of food. The length of the waggle portion and the rapidity of waggling are graded signals indicating distance to the food site, while the angle of the dance with respect to the sun (if outside) or the gravitational vertical (if within the hive) indicates the direction with respect to the sun along which the food will be found. There are different dialects of honeybee language, so that different species code distance differently into their waggling (Gould, 1982).

Considering the simplicity of the bee's nervous system, all of this is a remarkable—and clearly quite adaptive—achievement. How much it resembles human language is open to debate, however. There is symbolism in that the waggling run represents time (specifically, the effort needed to make the flight; Gould, 1982) and direction to the food, while the quality and the quantity of food are indicated by whether or not dancing occurs at all. The symbolism is abstract in that the object "talked about" is not present, and, partly, arbitrary (like human words) in that distance is marked by dialect-specific waggle-lengths and speeds. Finally, there is some creativity in that a dancer can "say" new things, reporting unique locations.

On the other hand, honeybee language is quite restricted compared to human language (Wilson, 1980). Most importantly, bees can only communicate about one thing: food location. Bees cannot break out of this rigid context and use language in a truly creative way. Their language is *too* preprogrammed and innate to admit any flexibility and creativity. Nonetheless, we should respect the language of the bees as a wonderful example of the subtleties of natural selection.

Birdsong learning   Another remarkable achievement of evolution is *birdsong*, which serves many functions in most bird species: courtship, mate location, establishment of territory, alarms. While lovers of nature and bird enthusiasts have long appreciated birdsong as an art, it is only since World War II that birdsong has been studied scientifically. Research on how birds learn to sing may provide a model for discussing human language acquisition, for we may do experiments on birds that we may not morally perform on children.

W. H. Thorpe and then Peter Marler (see, Marler, 1970; Marler & Peters, 1981) conducted brilliant sets of research showing that birdsong (at least in the species studied by them) is both innate *and* learned. Their conclusions are quite compatible with the constraints on learning findings discussed in Chapter 4. Birdsong is learned, but the learning is prepared and directed so that the right song is learned.

Many experiments have been performed by Thorpe, Marler, and others, but the basic results are summarized in Figure 11-4, from Gould (1982). After hatching, baby birds are reared in isolation, and during the critical period for song-learning, the youngsters are either played tapes of birdsong, or hear nothing. In Case A, the babies heard both their own species' (the white-crowned sparrow) song and that of a related species, the song-sparrow, whose songs are within their vocal capabilities. Then, for many weeks the birds heard nothing (research has shown that exposure after 50 days or so has no effect) and were silent. Then, after 100 days, the

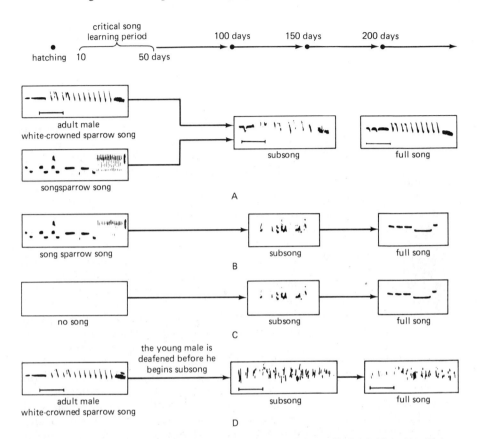

FIGURE 11–4   White-crowned sparrows learn their species' song during a critical period from 10 to 50 days of age. At about 150 days they begin to vocalize and practice making syllable sounds. By 200 days they have developed a stable song which closely matches the song heard during the critical period. The song learning is selective, so that if offered a choice, birds will learn only their own species' song (A); and if offered the wrong song (B) or no song at all (C), the bird will learn nothing and sing only a simple tune. If deafened before he begins to practice (D) the bird will never sing anything melodic while if deafened after the song "crystalizes," subsequent singing is perfect. These visual displays of the songs were made with a sound spectograph, a device which represents frequency on the vertical axis, time on the horizontal axis, and indicates intensity by the darkness of the trace. (Reproduced from *Ethology*, The Mechanisms and Evolution of Behavior, by James L. Gould, by permission of W. W. Norton & Co. Copyright ©1982 by James L. Gould.)

birds break out into their subsong, a sort of practice period preceding appearance of the full song. Case A is analogous to the situation in the wild in that more than one sound is heard, and development is normal.

In Case B only the song-sparrow song is played during the critical period, and we see that the subsong is abnormal, and the full song, while structured, does not resemble the normal song. This case rules out simple imitation as the basis of song-learning, since the white-crowned sparrows do not learn the song-sparrow song.

Case C represents total acoustic isolation, the results of which are identical with hearing the wrong song. Therefore, song-singing is not the result of simple maturation, in which an innate program simply expresses itself at maturity, as in bees.

Finally, Case D reveals the importance of practice and feedback during the subsong phase. Here, the young bird is exposed to the correct song, but is deafened prior to beginning subsong. In this case both subsong and full song are disorganized peeps.

These findings beautifully illustrate the complex and subtle interplay between the innate and the experienced at the base of all learning. Any simply maturational model of birdsong development is untenable. Equally untenable is any behaviorist reinforcement theory, since there is no reinforcement during initial exposure or subsong phases. Nor are the constraints on song learning merely peripheral, being set only by what the bird can hear or the notes it can utter, since songs of physically similar birds of different species are unlearnable.

There must be in species such as the sparrow central constraints on learning. As in humans, bird language is a specialized function of the left hemisphere of the brain, and it is there that natural selection has acted to constrain birdsong learning. It appears that the songbird is born with a template active only during a critical period early in the baby bird's life (Marler, 1970). The template contains a sort of model of the appropriate song of the species. The model is not specified in precise detail, because songbirds develop dialects peculiar to different geographical regions, and young birds can learn any dialect of their song. The template acts as a filter, directing the brain's attention to the biologically important sounds in the helpless infant's environment: its species' song. Sounds of passing 747's, of owls, robins, and other kinds of sparrows are models which, if followed, would lead to an adult male unable to attract a mate. (Females do not sing unless injected with testosterone; their knowledge of the song is adaptive in causing recognition of a true conspecific.) The template thus becomes a model of the correct song against which the adolescent bird can later check his vocalizing during the subsong phase. Feedback checked against the model leads to adjustments and the emergence of full song.

Marler has proposed that birdsong learning is a model for human language acquisition. In a later section we will review evidence bearing on his hypothesis.

CAN CHIMPS READ?

To propose an analogy between songbirds and humans is to do one form of human sociobiology, in approaching humans via a perhaps distant species that, nevertheless, is similar ecologically and functionally. Like human babies, altricial (helpless at birth) bird nestlings are helpless but must anyway learn a sophisticated signalling system essential to later reproductive success. The other kind of analogy one can draw is between humans and their most closely related relatives—primates—especially chimpanzees and gorillas. This is the strategy of the various research teams engaged in teaching language to apes. Their work has proven quite popular, turning up in prime-time TV documentaries and morning news shows. It has also generated heated controversy; the latest claim—by a former believer—is that the apes have only learned a few cute tricks, not language at all, making monkeys out of the investigators.

Ape Language Projects[1]

Early attempts to teach apes language failed. Best known was the charming endeavor by a married pair of psychologists to teach a chimpanzee language by raising it with their own child. This attempt was bound to fail if only because chimps' vocal apparatus is ill suited to language. La Mettrie's challenge to Descartes was not carried out until the 1960s (see Fouts & Rigby, 1980, for a review of early studies) in response to Chomsky's revived Cartesian linguistics. The spirit in which la Mettrie's hypothesis was revived is nicely captured by the title of the first modern project report on ape language (Premack, 1965): "Preparations for Discussing Behaviorism with a Chimpanzee." Interestingly, this project failed because the artificial language Premack devised to get around the vocalization problem involved emitting sounds with a joystick-controlled soundbox worn as a sort of necklace, and was too difficult for Premack's assistants to learn, much less the chimps!

There is no doubt that primates communicate in the wild, both vocally and nonvocally, often sending fairly sophisticated messages. Table 11–2 lists only the alarm calls of the vervet monkey, a small monkey relatively distant from *Homo sapiens*. Notice that the calls name different predators, and even distinguish moving from non-moving predators. Vervet monkeys are therefore able to convey a lot about the location and type of predator, with the ensuing behavior adaptively nuanced as a result.

Experiments with chimpanzees (summarized in Hinde, 1974) demonstrate sophisticated nonvocal communication skills. In one set of experiments individual chimps were shown the location of hidden food and returned to their troop. They were able to lead their companions to the food, usually by adopting a subtle "leader" posture, walk, and glances, causing the others to both follow and move out ahead in the direction of food. Oc-

---

[1]The literature on ape language is vast. There are at least four popular books on the subject, Eugene Linden's *Apes, Men, and Language* (1974; rev. ed. 1981); Ann J. Premack's *Why Chimps Can Read* (1976), which inspired the title for this section of your text; Herbert S. Terrace's *Nim: A Chimpanzee Who Learned Sign Language* (1979); and Eugene Linden's and Francine Patterson's *The Education of Koko* (1982). Linden's books must be read with care, because he over-simplifies Western intellectual history and reads portentous significance into the ape projects.

Scholarly reviews of the projects, sometimes including accounts of earlier twentieth-century work, include Rumbaugh (1980); Fouts and Rigby (1980); Hill (1980); Ristau and Robbins (1982).

Descriptions of the projects by the investigators themselves include Premack (1976); Savage-Rumbaugh, Rumbaugh, and Boysen (1979/1980); Savage-Rumbaugh and Rumbaugh (1980); Gardner and Gardner (1969/1972, 1978/1980, 1980); Terrace, Petitto, Sanders, and Bever (1980); Patterson (1980).

TABLE 11-2 Vervet Monkey Alarm Calls[a]

	UH!	NYOW!	CHUTTER	RRAUP	THREAT ALARM-BARK	CHIRP
Typical stimulus	Minor mammal predator near	Sudden movement of minor predator	Man or venomous snake—but the chutter is structurally different for man and snake	Initial sighting of eagle	Initially and after sighting major predator (leopard, lion, serval, eagle)	After initial sighting of major predator (leopard, eagle)
Typical response of troop members	Become alert, look to predator	Look to predator, sometimes flee	Approach snake and escort at safe distance	Flee from tree-tops and open areas into thickets	Attention and then flight to appropriate cover	Flee from thickets and open areas to branches and canopy

[a]All calls are given by adults of both sexes, except the female "chirp." (From Green & Marler, 1979, p. 132)

casionally, if the others failed to follow, the finder would gesture, whimper, or even pull at them, which Hinde takes as evidence that communication was intentional, not an accidental byproduct of the finder simply returning to the food source.

Even more striking evidence that communication in this setting was intentional was the case of a female who, when she led the troop to food, did not get to eat any of it because she was supplanted by a dominant male. After a while she learned to *not* communicate the location of the food—sitting down away from it and not leading, waiting until she could approach it unseen, or even leading the troop off in the wrong direction and then quickly slipping back to the food.

Several research teams are investigating the acquisition of language by great apes, primarily chimpanzees. Since it is clear chimpanzees and gorillas cannot acquire vocal language, researchers have had to devise nonvocal languages to teach to their subjects. David Premack, after the failure of his soundbox analogue to vocal language, turned to a visual "language" in which chimp and human communicate by placing plastic tokens (roughly equivalent to words) on a board following specified grammatical rules. At the Yerkes Primate Research Center, Georgia, E. S. Savage-Rumbaugh and Duane Rumbaugh use an artificial language called *Yerkish,* in which a chimp "talks" with a computer by pressing symbolic keys—lexigrams—(roughly equal to words) following rules of syntax. The system allows the computer both to "talk" to the chimp, and to provide human-chimp and chimp-chimp interaction.

The best-known projects, however, follow up an old suggestion made by the great primate psychologist Robert Yerkes in the 1920s, using the American sign language of the deaf (Ameslan or ASL) as the medium of communication. The pioneer project was carried out by Beatrice and Allan Gardner at the University of Nevada at Reno with a chimp named Washoe, and they have continued with other subjects. Work with Washoe and others was carried on by Roger Fouts in Kansas, while, in New York, Herbert Terrace and his associates taught ASL to Neam Chimsky (!) or Nim; Francine Patterson in California taught it to a gorilla, Koko. It should be pointed out that in addition to skill and patience, these projects require real courage. Chimps grow up to weigh nearly as much as a large man, are three times as strong, and can—even inadvertently—do real harm to people and property. Many of the projects can only last a few years, until the chimp reaches puberty and becomes a potential danger.

Whatever method was used, the findings of the ape-language projects establish beyond doubt that apes can express themselves symbolically. They can make requests, convey their feelings, and discuss the past. Other experiments have shown that apes can invent new sign or lexigram strings, can name objects, and can communicate about things such as a tool needed to get a piece of food. However, the exact significance of these findings remains unclear and controversial. Have any of the apes learned *language,* not just a new communication system? Can these projects tell us anything about the evolution of human language? How similar is an ape's acquisition of signing (or lexigram use) to the acquisition of language by children?

Controversy

Is it language?   From their inception, the ape language projects pro-voked controversy, primarily over the issue of whether or not what apes acquired was language (it was clearly communication) and, consequently, whether their learning processes were the same as a child's learning lan-guage. Roger Brown (1970), a pioneer in the study of human language ac-quisition (see, Brown, 1973) argued that the Gardner's Washoe did not seem to possess syntax. That is, she constructed utterances out of random aggregations of signs rather than showing any following of word (sign) or-der rules, namely, syntax. This implied the important conclusion that Washoe did not have semantic intentions while signing, but instead just emitted behaviors until reinforcement was forthcoming. Later, Brown (1973) modified his view, conceding that Washoe did have semantic inten-tions, without word order, because of his finding that children learning languages that are less strict about word order than English speak inten-tionally without exhibiting regular syntax.

Bronowski and Bellugi (1970) likewise taxed Washoe for lacking reg-ular word orderings. They tied syntax, and language more generally, to the human ability to build a mental world model by analyzing our experience into fixed objects—named concepts—and synthesizing them together again (in sentences) into a known whole. This mental ability, which gives rise to philosophy and science, they saw Washoe as lacking. Bellugi, like Brown, has subsequently changed her view on the centrality of syntax (Linden, 1981). Bronowski has since died. It is unclear whether any ape possesses the analytic/synthetic skill Bronowski saw as central to human intellect.

Using data from Nim, Terrace et al. (1980) directly investigated the question of rule-governed combination of signs, and concluded that while Nim assembled multisign utterances, there was no evidence there of regu-lar sign-order. They concluded that Nim was just a random sign-generator, emitting signs until they had some desired effect. Similarly, the Yerkes group has tempered earlier claims that its chimps showed syntactic struc-ture in their utterances (Ristau & Robbins, 1982). Since their computer lan-guage requires linear symbol-by-symbol production, it should be ideal for eliciting syntax in apes; in fact, it might produce syntax as an artifact of the experiment. So if there is poor evidence of grammar acquisition in Yerkish, it seems syntax is difficult, perhaps impossible, for chimps to acquire.

The issue of grammar is quite important, for it is syntax that gives human language its infinite expressive and productive powers. Without syntax, only the most rudimentary thoughts or desires can be expressed, and communication must remain tied to an immediate concrete context. With syntax, nuances of expression become possible, and intellect is freed from the immediate and concrete and can soar to the distant and imaginary.

Is it problem solving?   It was not about chimps learning sign language that it was first said "that an animal can think in human ways and can express human ideas in human language" (Hediger, 1981, p. 1). The animal in question was Clever Hans, a horse, who early in the twentieth century fooled many people, including a panel of eminent scientists, and his owner himself, into believing he could do mathematics, think, and understand spoken and written language. It took the clever research of a young psychologist, Oskar Pfungst, to show that in apparently teaching Hans arithmetic and language, his owner had really taught him to attend to subtle, unconscious, nonverbal cues given off by his questioner. Clever Hans should remind us that a very plausible imitation of language is not language itself (Heil, 1982).

Accusations that the linguistic apes were in effect simian Clever Hanses have been raised by Terrace (Terrace, 1979a, 1979b, 1979c, 1982; Terrace, Petitto, Sanders, & Bever, 1979), who argues that the apes did not really learn language, but only to gesture (or arrange plastic tokens, or push computer lexigrams) to satisfy their masters and get things they want. Sebeok and Umiker-Sebeok (1979, 1980; Sebeok, 1980) also make this claim. This new aspect to the ape language controversy has engendered a bitter debate between skeptics and most of the project directors (Benderly, 1980). Indeed, at a conference devoted to the Clever Hans phenomenon with respect to the ape language projects (Sebeok & Rosenthal, 1981) the phrase "witch hunt" was used by Duane Rumbaugh (1981; see also Linden, 1981).

It is no wonder that the accusations provoke bitterness because they are accusations, not of fraud but of self-delusion and foolishness. Such accusations place the ape programs on the same footing as parapsychology, as a suspect science. Skeptics have always explained instances of ESP as consciously or unconsciously deceptive communication, and the inclusion in the Clever Hans conference (Sebeok & Rosenthal, 1981) of papers on deceptive communication in parapsychology seemed to underscore the apes' suspect status.

Unfortunately, evaluating claims of deceptive communication is difficult because of the methodological deficiencies of the various studies (Ristau & Robbins, 1982). In general, the data base from all the projects—save Nim's—is very poor. The Gardners' data (1969/1971) consists of diaries, and one study showed serious errors in recording the apes' signing. The Yerkes project only recorded what the apes punched on their keyboard, but not the possibly cuing activities of the trainers. Sarah, the Premack chimp, was drilled in such a way that she could have functioned by rote-learning of symbol sequences rather than language-rule learning. Most of the famous and persuasive creative utterances of the chimps are merely anecdotal, and open to other interpretations than those given by the investigators, who, of course, wanted the apes to have language. The best known of these events was Washoe's signing "water bird" upon seeing a swan on a river. Advocates of chimp language (for example, Linden, 1981) see this as creative naming—calling the swan a "waterbird." Skeptics see it as two separate signs under distinct stimulus control, "water" (water was present) and "bird."

The only project with adequate records was Terrace's Nim project, where extensive videotapes were made. Terrace for a long time believed Nim had learned language until he started studying the videotapes after the project ended. Among other things, he detected the Clever Hans phenomena, specifically cuing in the form of signs that Nim could imitate. Apparently, Nim's trainers were unaware of their cuing since they expressed surprise on seeing the tapes.

On the other hand, even if Nim were a Clever Hans, it does not follow that all the other apes were too, and of course the other trainers have defended their projects. The best conclusion at present is offered by Ristau and Robbins (1982). While radical skepticism—believing that nothing linguistic was going on in any of the apes—is probably unjustified, there was no doubt a good deal less language than optimists believed. Language remains the major cognitive difference between *Homo sapiens* and other vertebrate species (Fox, 1983).

Conclusion

Chomsky's remarks (1979, 1980a) on the linguistic apes raise the crucial issue: What is language and what is *human* language? For it is not clear that even if the various apes do in fact acquire language that they have acquired anything like human language.

Confounding the two runs all the way through our interpretation of what the apes are doing. Consider interpreting two- and three-word sentences—assuming even that they are sentences—such as "water bird." Children, too, pass through a two-word stage, and we assume that their utterances are simple language. Defenders of the linguistic capacity of apes have said that skeptics apply a double standard, requiring more of the ape than of the child to call these utterances "language." Chomsky's analysis suggests the double standard is not misplaced: We call the children's two-word sentences language in view of what they later will achieve, not by virtue of their present linguistic sophistication, which indeed is no greater than the apes'. Terrace's data support Chomsky's argument, since he found the mean length of Nim's utterances got stuck at three or four words, while children's—even of comparable stages of linguistic experience—continued to grow.

Chomsky points out that no matter how sophisticated ape language may be, there is (at present) no strong reason to see it as incipient human language. It is more likely to be a separate cognitive activity not closely related to normal human language. Chomsky (1979) cites studies in which patients with damage to the language centers of their brains are able to acquire symbol-systems akin to the apes, and whose use of these systems seems much like the use of signing and symbols by the apes. If Chomsky's parallel is valid, it means that the ape language projects may tell us much about ape mentality (Box 11–2), but can offer us little insight into human language.

BOX 11–2   *Do Apes Have a Theory of Mind?*

Premack has lately shifted the focus of his work away from language in apes to an exploration of the ape's mind (Premack, 1983; Premack & Premack, 1982). In doing so he has raised an interesting question—given that apes have minds (cognitive processes): Do they have a theory of mind (Premack & Woodruff, 1978)?

Of course, Premack is not asking if apes do cognitive psychology. People with no knowledge of psychology at all have a folk-theory of mind. Each of us experiences our own beliefs, purposes, desires, and so on, and we attribute these states to others, using them to explain behavior, just as a scientist does. "Bill wrote the check that bounced because he *believed* he had enough money in the bank" is an example of a folk psychology explanation of behavior. What Premack asks is if chimpanzees will spontaneously make similar mental attributions.

He thinks they do. Premack and Woodruff (1978) showed videotapes of people coping with a problem, such as reaching for inaccessible food or escaping from a locked cage, to their symbolizing chimp Sarah, and to four- and three-year-old children. Before the people in the videotape solve their problem, the action was frozen and the subject was shown several still photographs, one of which represented a solution to the problem. Sarah and the four-year-olds (but not the three-year-olds) were able immediately to choose the solution picture. Premack takes these results as indicating attribution of mentality—specifically purpose—to the actor by the subject, because the behavior on tape constitutes a problem with a solution only on the assumption that the actor has a goal in mind; otherwise, it is just random motor activity. Choosing the solution picture only makes sense if Sarah believes that the actor faced a goal-defined problem; hence, she attributes mentality to people, and has a theory of mind.

Limitations to Sarah's theory showed up in another experiment in which the tapes showed a person either watching a box have food placed in it, or not being allowed to watch. In the first case, the person knew where the food was; in the latter, the person had to guess. Sarah was shown photographs of the actor choosing the correct or incorrect box, but her choices between the pictures were not influenced by what had gone before, indicating that she could not distinguish between guessing and knowing by the actor. Instead, if she liked the actor, she selected the one choosing the correct box regardless of what she had seen, but if she did not like the actor, she chose the one choosing the wrong box.

While these experiments are not decisive (see the "Open Peer Commentary" following Premack & Woodruff, 1978), they do open up a new line of research on nonhuman cognitive processes. Regardless of our conclusion regarding apes' narrow linguistic capacity, we must recognize in them reasonably sophisticated cognitive skills. Premack is investigating metacognition—what we know about our own cognition—in apes.

HUMAN LANGUAGE

Evolution of Language

The evolution of language is a venerable field of human speculation (Aarsleff, 1976) that has again become active (Harnad, Steklis, & Lancaster, 1976). Chomsky's nativist thesis, research on the evolution of color names (Box 11–3), the ape-language projects, improved knowledge of the human evolutionary tree (Johanson & Edey, 1981), including studies in paleoneurology, and sociobiology have all come together to revive theories of language origins. We must remember as we proceed, however, that informed speculation is the best we can achieve. Behavior does not fossilize: All we can do is to infer cognitive and linguistic capacities from fossil skeletons, remains of tools, campsites, and art, seasoned with judicious cross-species comparisons. It is most unlikely that any final answers can be forthcoming.

To properly ground ourselves for the exercise, we need to know something about human evolution. Figures 11–6, 11–7, and 11–8 provide sketches of human evolution. Figure 11–6 summarizes the major fossil finds along a time axis, and relates the finds to cultural traditions and geological periods. Figures 11–7 and 11–8 depict one recent and influential attempt to draw a human family tree. Roughly, the picture is that the stem creature from which hominids descended was *Australopithecus afarensis*, living about 3.5 and perhaps as much as 5 million years ago. *Afarensis* gave rise to two distinct lines, the other *Australopethicines*, *africanus*, and *robustus*, which died out about 1 million years ago. The other line began with *Homo habilis* (2 million years), and continued through *Homo erectus* (1.5 million to 1 million years) and finally to *Homo sapiens*. All hominids through *Homo habilis* had small brains, in the case of the *Australopithecines* about the same size as a chimpanzee's, and in *Homo habilis* about 50 percent larger. Around 1.8 million years ago a revolution in brain size occurred when *Homo erectus* appeared, with a brain 2½ times larger than a chimpanzee's; *Homo sapiens'* brain is three times as large (McHenry, 1982). *Homo sapiens* has had two forms, *Homo sapiens neandertalensis* and *Homo sapiens sapiens* (ourselves). While it remains possible that *sapiens sapiens* (Cro-Magnon man) evolved out of Neandertals, the current consensus is that Neandertal is an extinct form replaced by Cro-Magnon. This is a point of some linguistic importance, as we shall find. A final important issue involves the origin date of *sapiens sapiens*. There are a very few apparently *sapiens* forms as early as 300,000 years ago (see the Steinheim skull in Figure 11–5), but some archaeologists dispute these dates and insist that *sapiens sapiens* did not appear until about 40,000 years to 50,000 years ago (Krantz, 1980).

The first reasonable question to ask is when language appeared in human evolution; disagreement on this issue is extreme. The end points are anchored by Montague (1976) and Jaynes (1976b). Montague argues that language must have been well developed by the time of *Homo habilis*, 2 million years B.P. (before present). *Habilis* was the first hominid for whom there is clear-cut evidence of the making of stone tools, which Montague presents as an activity mediated by language. Jaynes denies this, main-

BOX 11–3   *EVOLUTION OF COLOR TERMS*

Languages around the world possess different sets of basic color terms; English has 11, while some "primitive" languages possess as few as two, designating light and dark. This diversity of color names had been taken to support the linguistic relativity hypothesis of Edward Sapir and Benjamin Lee Whorf, which says that each culture (and language) carves up reality into categories unique to itself, and not directly equivalent to any other culture's categories. In the case of color it was held that the visible spectrum forms a continuum divided up by different cultures and named in unique ways.

However, the work of Berlin and Kay (1969) challenges the linguistic relativity hypothesis, and shows that the division of the spectrum into parts is not arbitrary, but is done the same way around the world. Berlin and Kay gave complete sets of color chips to speakers of a wide variety of languages, who categorised them into natural categories and chose the "focal" or ideal color chip for each category. Berlin and Kay found that while there was much disagreement about color category boundaries, there was overwhelming agreement on what were the ideal, focal colors for each category.

Moreover, they found a close relationship between the number of color terms in a language and what colors the subjects named, suggesting an evolutionary sequence from a simple black-white discrimination to the elaborate 11-color list of English. See Figure 11–5.

FIGURE 11–5

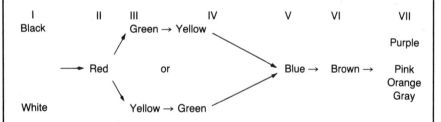

The simplest nomenclature (Stage I) possesses just the two terms, *black* and *white*. Then, in successive stages new color names are added to the basic set one at a time, until Stage VII, when four new terms are added in no special order. Berlin and Kay not only have evidence for a linguistic universal, but also evidence for a universal sequence of linguistic development.

Subsequent work (Ratliff, 1976; Lumsden & Wilson, 1981) has tied the universal color categories to the way the retina and brain process color information. It will be interesting to find out if the development of color names in children parallels the evolution of color terms in language.*

*See B. Berlin and P. Kay. *Basic Color Terms: Their Universality and Evolution.* Berkeley University of California Press, 1969.

YEARS B.C.	GEOLOGICAL PERIODS		CULTURAL TRADITIONS		FOSSIL HOMINIDS
	Europe (Glaciation)	Africa (Pluviation)	Europe	Africa	
15,000		Gamblian III	Magdelenian	Lupemban III	
			Solutrean	Smithfield	
20,000			Proto. Magdelenian		Solo Man Rodesoids
		Gamblian II	Gravettian	Stillbay	Cro-Magnon Combe Capelle
30,000			Perigordian		
	Würm IV	Gamblian I	Chatelperronian	Lupemban I	Florisbad
40,000				Proto-stillbay	
	Würm III				Classic Chappelle-aux-Saints Neanderthal
	Würm II	(Drier)	Mousterian	Sangoan	
	Würm I				Kanjera (?)
		Kanjeran			Progressive Sapiens
100,000	Riss-wurm Interglacial			Fauresmith	Sacco Pastore Enrings-Dorf ?
				Final Acheulean	
200,000			Micoquian		Fontechevade
	Riss	(wetter?)	Mesvinian		Montmaurin
300,000		Interpluvial			Steinheim Swanscumbe
			Tayacian		Rabat Sidi Abderahman Homo Erectus (pithecanthropines)
	Mindel-Riss Interglacial		Acheulean	Acheulean	
500,000			Clactonian		
	Mindel	Kamasian			
600,000					Kromdram Swartkrans
	Günz-Mindel Interglacial	Interpluvial			(Robustus) Sterk Fontein Ternifine Makapan Olduval Bed II Taung Peking Heidelberg
1,000,000			Abbevillian (Chellean)	Chellean	
	Günz	Kagerian			AUSTRALOPITHECINES
1,300,000			Pre-chellean? (Eolithic)	Oldowan	
	Villa-Franchian			(Kafuan?)	Zinjanthropus (Africanus) Homo Hablis (?)
2,000,000					EARLIEST HOMINIDS
	Pliocene				(Australopithecus Afarensis In Africa)
13,000,000					Pre- and Proto-Hominids
	Miocene				Early Generalized Anthropoids . . .possibly split between apes and man (Ramapithecus) ((Dryopithecus)
25,000,000					
	Oligocene				Earliest Anthropoid apes (Aegyptopithecus) Earliest monkeys
36,000,000					
	Eocene				Rapid evolution and spread of modern orders of birds, Lemuroids, Tarsioids (Fossil Tarsioid)
60,000,000					
	Palocene				First Lemuroid Primates; Forerunners of most mammacian orders. (Fossil Lemuroid)
75,000,000					

Vertical labels: PLEISTOCENE; Levalloisian; Aurignacian

THE CENOZOIC ERA

Note: This correlation is merely a consensus, and all classifications are fluid.

FIGURE 11–6 The Evolution of *Homo Sapiens* as Indicated in the Fossil Record. Drawing prepared by, and published with the permission of, Dr. Robert L. Humphreys, George Washington University.

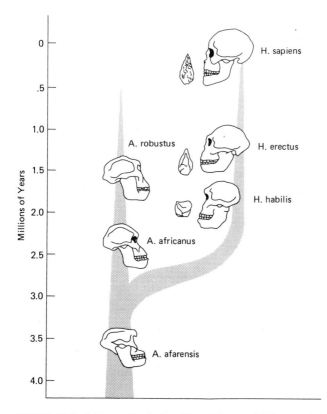

FIGURE 11–7   A Human Family Tree (From Johanson & Edey, 1981). All the *afarensis* fossils can be lumped between four and three million, all the *africanus* ones between 2.7 and 2.2 million, all the *robustus* ones between 2.1 and 1.0, and so on. *Afarensis*, the oldest and most primitive hominid known, was ancestral to all the others. Tools, as the chart indicates, are a *Homo*, not an australopithecine, invention.

taining that tool use can develop quite separately from language. Wild chimpanzees, for example, use simple tools, carefully chosen grass stalks, or small twigs from which they remove the leaves to dig up termites and ants to eat, but have not developed language. Jaynes, therefore, places the evolution of language quite late, beginning as primitive calls at about 70,000 years B.P., and achieving its full development only 8,000 years ago.

Evidence from hominid fossils is equivocal on this issue. Liebermann (1975) has proposed reconstructions of hominid skulls indicating that *only homo sapiens sapiens* could speak, ruling out even the Neandertals from having vocal language; however, his reconstructions are not universally accepted (Harnad et al., 1976). Paleoneurologists have been trying to infer the size and structure of the brain of ancient hominids in order to see if they had brains capable of language, but they cannot reach agreement. Holloway (1976) believes australopithecines had small brains of nevertheless human structure, and suggests they may have had language.

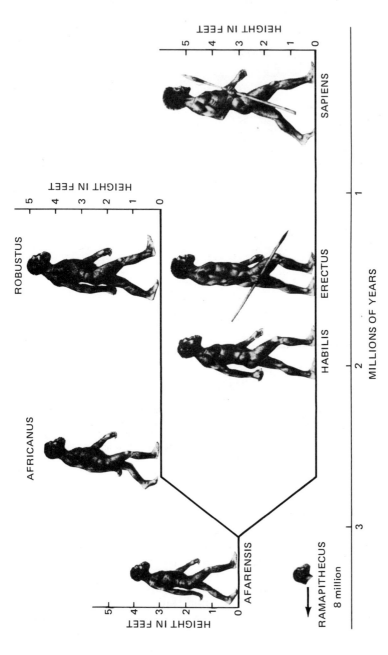

FIGURE 11-8 A Possible Human Family Tree (From Johanson & Edey, 1981). If the family tree on page is turned on its side, and the fossils turned into fleshed-out individuals, they would look like this—maybe. No one can be sure just what any extinct hominid looked like with its skin and hair on. Sizes here are to scale, with *afarensis* about two feet shorter than the average modern human being. *Ramapithecus*, so far known only from teeth, jaws and bits of skull, was smaller yet, perhaps not much more than three feet tall.\ Original reconstruction drawings by artist Jay H. Matternes. Copyright © Jay H. Matternes.

Jerison (1976), on the other hand, is skeptical of the possibility of inferring brain structure from fossil skulls, and on the basis of computations of brain size in relation to body weight argues that australopithecines did not have language, that *Homo erectus* probably did not, and that all *sapiens* forms (including Neandertal) did. More recent finds and analyses tend to support Jerison's conclusions (McHenry, 1982).

Evidence from artifacts—tools, engraved bones and so on—generally supports a date of about 40,000 years B.P. for the final development of language. As with the chimps, the very simple stone tools made by *Homo habilis* probably do not require or imply language, and these tools did not change much for hundreds of thousands of years. However, they do increase greatly in sophistication at about 40,000 years B.P. (Isaac, 1976), and at about the same time and a little earlier there is evidence of symbolic abilities in engraved bones (Marshack, 1972, 1976). Evidence from glottochronology coincides with these dates (Miller, 1981). *Glottochronology*, the study of how languages change, has found that for historical periods languages all change at a fairly steady rate. If this rate is used to extrapolate back in time, vocal language—the first language spoken by human beings—cannot have begun later than 10,000 years B.P. or earlier than 100,000 years, so that the date of 40,000 to 50,000 years B.P. looks like a fair compromise.

So far we have considered only vocal language, but we now come to an important question: Did vocal language develop suddenly, perhaps as a mutation (Myers, 1976), or did it slowly evolve out of some other communication system, whether simian-like cries (Jaynes, 1976b; Marler, 1976) or a preceding gestural language that later shifted to the vocal-auditory channel (Hewes, 1975, 1976; Lamendella, 1976; Steklis & Harnad, 1976; Parker & Gibson, 1979)?

We have already noted that monkeys possess vocal signals such as alarm calls, and there is now evidence that these signals are truly symbolic (Ristau & Robbins, 1982; Snowden, 1983). Vervet monkeys have calls that separately name each major predator they encounter; squirrel monkeys use certain friendly calls only between closely affiliated females; while titi monkeys utter syntactically organized call sequences. One might then hypothesize that such prehominid calls were the raw material out of which natural selection fashioned human language.

However, such a hypothesis encounters difficulties. The major problem is that the neural substrates of human language and monkey calling are radically different. Human language is controlled primarily by the left frontal neo-cortex, while monkey calling is controlled by much older brain systems, particularly the limbic system (Malmi, 1976). Moreover, monkeys show little (Snowden, 1983) or no (Warren & Nonneman, 1976) cerebral lateralization for vocal functions. It is interesting to observe in this context that aphasics—people who have lost language due to damage to the language centers of the cortex—are most likely to retain simple, emotionally charged utterances such as curses (Robinson, 1976) suggesting that their intact limbic system controls monkey-like cries that are not really language any more.

Additionally, the ontogeny of monkey calls is quite different from human language (Snowden, 1983) or even birdsong, it being much more preprogrammed than either. Isolated and deafened monkeys develop mostly normal calls, unlike humans or songbirds. At best, their innate cries are refined by experience to apply to a precisely delimited group of objects, suggesting a process of simple stimulus discrimination learning based on built-in vocalizations.

These considerations do not, of course, completely rule out the possibility that evolution gradually shifted the control of vocalization from the limbic system to the cortex—*encephalization,* as suggested by Jaynes (1976a,b)—but they do point out a large gap between animal and human vocal communication that seems hard for evolution to bridge (Myers, 1976). A popular alternative theory is to seek antecedents of vocal language in gestural language.

Seeking the origin of vocal language in a preceding language of gestures goes back in psychology to psychology's founder, Wilhelm Wundt (Wundt, 1973), and has been revived by the efforts to teach sign language to apes (Hewes, 1975). If human vocal language did not evolve from existing prehominid calls, perhaps it is a specialization of the cognitive abilities that the signing apes use in today's research.

Again, the hypothesis faces difficulties. As we have seen, there is some question about whether or not the signing apes have language or are just gesturing until they get what they want. One important function of language is cooperation, and so far the signing apes seem only to be using signing selfishly. For example, in the last chapter we saw how profoundly food-sharing is ingrained in human nature. It is likely that our hominid ancestors were sharing food as far back as 2 million years ago (Isaac, 1976) and that the cooperation involved in food sharing was one selective force favoring the evolution of language (Parker & Gibson, 1979). The researchers on the Yerkes project have attempted to get apes to use Yerkish to cooperate in getting food and sharing, but have found that food sharing does not happen spontaneously, but must be enforced by humans (Ristau & Robbins, 1982).[2] Therefore, both structurally and functionally we must remain skeptical about ape sign language and its implications for human language acquisition. The similarities are tantalizing, but the differences are always present.

The gesture-language hypotheses also face a problem similar to the encephalization problem of the vocal theorists. Once gesture language arose, why did a shift take place to spoken language? It is easy to see that vocal language is superior—we can talk, but not sign, in the dark and around corners—but evolution is conservative and not teleological. Vocal language may be better, but gesture language may have been good enough for reproductive survival, which is all that counts in evolution. Moreover, why has gesture language so atrophied in humans if it was once so impor-

---

[2]Jane Goodall's chimps, observed at the Gombe Stream Research Center in Tanzania, do share the meat of bushpigs and monkeys they have cooperatively killed. But much haggling and squabbling goes on before the owner will share the kill. As with ape language, there is a low level similarity to humans.

tant? Why do not our monkey and ape relatives show evidence of gesture language?

However language appeared—perhaps throwing rocks had something to do with it (Box 11–4)—there is no doubt that once in existence it has had a powerful effect on the evolution of *Homo sapiens*. Language creates culture, and culture-change, directed and Lamarckian, begins to replace pure evolution as the major mode of human adaptation (Lumsden & Wilson, 1983). Krantz (1980) and Washburn (1981) have reviewed evidence suggesting that language was the major selective factor in the final emergence of *Homo sapiens sapiens* out of *Homo erectus* types, including the Neandertals. Around 40,000 years B.P., many changes appear in human life: More complex tools and more types of tools are manufactured; tools become specialized to particular jobs; the first projectile points (spear and arrow tips) appear in addition to hand tools; use of fire becomes an everyday activity not confined to cold periods; the pace of technological change accelerates; population increases and expands geographically. All these changes are associated with the fossil remains of *Homo sapiens sapiens*. Krantz argues that around 40,000 years ago vocal language—and therefore the human culture it creates—appeared, favoring those anatomical forms (that is, *sapiens sapiens*) that could learn and use vocal language. The result was relatively rapid evolution, over only about 10,000 years, of *Homo erectus* into *Homo sapiens sapiens*, a change marked by the developments reviewed above. Once the evolution of *Homo sapiens sapiens* was complete, language acquisition became an essential task for every human child.

Acquisition of Language[3]

The three major approaches to explaining language acquisition in children are biological, cognitive, and behavioral. The last was largely elim-

---

[3]Back when psychology was the "Science of Mental Life," language acquisition (like language evolution) was an important topic. Although formal studies were not done, many eminent scientists—including Charles Darwin and Wilhelm Wundt—kept "baby diaries"—records of their own children's language acquisition—and they discovered some of the phemonena later recovered by modern research. Extracts from several such diaries (along with some of the pioneering modern studies) may be found in Bar-Adon & Leopold (1971). During the behaviorist era, developmental psycholinguistics lay fallow; the only studies were of vocabulary acquisition, it being assumed that words were the behavioral units of language being learned as classical or operant responses.

Chomsky's nativistic thesis reawakened interest in children's language, and modern developmental psycholinguistics began. It has remained a growth industry ever since. There is so much data available it defies easy summary, and the problem is compounded by the current tendency, evident in the 1983 *Annual Review* by Eve Clark, for psychologists to narrow their research focus to small puzzles, a tendency no doubt inspired by the information-processing approach.

Given these difficulties and our own major concern with theoretical explanation, this section will not attempt to review research findings. The interested reader may find useful summaries in several book-length treatments. McNeil (1970) was the first synthetic treatment, and represents a strong nativist approach. Comprehensive, relatively atheoretical treatments include Dale (1976); Bloom & Lahey (1978), which includes chapters on abnormal language development; and de Villiers & de Villiers (1978). Elliot (1981) is a brief summary from a cognitivist perspective. Finally, Atkinson (1982) provides a broad consideration and evaluation of major approaches to exploring language acquisition.

BOX 11–4 *JUST A STONE'S THROW TO LANGUAGE?*

William Calvin (1982) has recently proposed an unusual basis for the evolution of the large human brain and human language: throwing stones. Apes throw stones with both hands only a short distance and with little accuracy. Humans—especially young males—love to throw things, can do so with great speed and accuracy, over a fair distance, and even invent games that turn on throwing skills. When we find something that a species loves to do and does well, we should suspect that evolution—ultimate causation—has been at work.

Calvin proposes that one-handed stone throwing was an efficient hunting technique for our omnivorous ancestors. While one cannot bring down big game with a rock, it ought to be possible to hunt smaller animals with rocks, later aided by spears, spear throwers, and slings. Once begun, skill in throwing would be quickly selected for, with important consequences for brain development. Stone throwing would tend to enlarge the brain, for accurate throwing requires complex and finely controlled patterns of muscle movement and eye-arm-hand coordination. Since accurate throwing is done with one hand, hemispheric specialization would be favored, and we find that it is males who have the more lateralized brains today. So stone throwing could help create the large, specialized brain of modern *Homo sapiens,* and because throwing is an infinitely improvable skill—faster and more precise throws are always better—it would set off an autocatalytic effect of continuing pressure toward larger, more specialized brains.

Certain broader benefits would accrue as well. The skill of stone throwing would open new niches for exploitation, and would also improve the motor skills needed to make better stone tools. Finally, with respect to language, the neural organization needed for good throwing would require precise sequencing of complex neural firing patterns, precisely what is needed in human language function. Most people are right-handed, the side controlled by the left, linguistic hemisphere. According to Calvin, this is no accident, but arose because we evolved throwing skills in the left hemisphere, whose neural circuitry could then be adapted to the sequential skill of language.

Evolution is normally very slow. One of the puzzles of human evolution is our (relatively) rapid change from ape to human. If Calvin's hypothesis contains any truth it could partially solve this puzzle, because throwing is a single and highly adaptive skill that ramifies in many ways, all of which would push our ancient ancestors in the direction of *Homo sapiens sapiens.**

*See William H. Calvin. *The Throwing Madonna: From Nervous Cells to Hominid Brains.* New York: McGraw-Hill, 1983.

inated as a general explanation by some of the first studies of child language acquisition inspired by Chomsky's revival of the issue.

The behaviorist treats language just like any other behavior, possessing no special properties or biological specialization (Skinner, 1957). Therefore, the behaviorist would expect language—verbal behavior—to be shaped by reinforcement contingencies, perhaps supported by imitation of adult forms. However, both these processes can be ruled out as the sole determiners of language acquisition. Of course, reinforcement and imitation play roles in language acquisition and use—children use language to get what they want, and can only talk about what they have heard about—but they seem to play little role in acquiring syntax.

Studies of parent-child interaction have shown that, aside from a few pet language peeves we all remember, such as "ain't," parents pay more attention to—that is, reinforce or punish—the content of what their children say than to its grammatical form. Moskowitz (1978) reports a charming example of this. A mother hearing her son, Stevie, say, "Tommy fall my truck down," quickly turned to Tommy and asked, "Did you fall Stevie's truck down?" The mother was clearly more concerned about the truth of Stevie's claim, and the moral issues it raised, than with its syntactic correctness. Since this is generally true, it follows, as Brown (1973) points out, that if the contingencies of reinforcement shaped language, we should find ungrammatical but truth-telling adults. Obviously, though, what develops is people who lie with good grammar.

Imitation, too, has been found to be a less important process in language acquisition than most people and psychologists have believed. Bloom, Hood, and Lightbown (1974) showed that there is considerable difference between children in whether or not they imitated utterances they had heard. Some children imitate very little, yet learn language as quickly as their peers who imitate a great deal. More generally, imitation is ruled out by the fact that as children construct their grammatical rules—which, of course, should not exist according to behaviorist theory—they use rules at first that differ from adult rules, and so create utterances that they cannot have heard.

The phenomenon of over-regularization offers a nice example establishing that language is rule-learning, because it requires invoking cognitive structures underlying behavior, and cannot be due to imitation. Language is based on rules, but the rules have exceptions, and children must learn what they are. For example, most verbs in English convert to the past tense by adding the morpheme /-ed/. However, there are many common exceptions to this rule, such as *fall-fell* or *go-went*. As they learn language, children typically first learn both the regular and irregular verbs correctly, and can say, "I went home." Then, however, they formulate the general rule but over-apply it: "I goed home." Now they cannot be imitating *goed*, nor has it been shaped by reinforcement. Instead, the child has induced a general rule and over-generalized it, losing the correct, reinforced form and suddenly emitting a new, deviant form in its place. Later, perhaps after a phase of saying "I wented home," the child learns the exceptions and returns to the correct form, "I went home." (Moskowitz, 1978.)

So it is clear that language acquisition cannot be explained behaviorally. We must invoke inner processes to explain language, and changes in those processes to explain language acquisition. The usual behavioral forces of selective reinforcement and imitation are inadequate to explain language learning. What remains is to try to sort out how much of language acquisition is a unique, species-specific process, and how much is a consequence of broader human intellectual sophistication.

The leading exponent of the view that language is a species-specific biological capacity of *Homo sapiens,* and that much of language acquisition is simply maturation, was Eric Lenneberg (1964, 1965, 1967, 1969). We may list some of the more important reasons Lenneberg adduced in support of his thesis:

1 Humans possess many anatomical specializations related to language use from the shape and placement of the larynx to specialization of language functions in the left hemisphere of the brain. (See Marshall, 1980, for a more recent review.)

2 Damage to certain parts of the brain (in the left hemisphere only) lead to damaged or lost linguistic abilities. Moreover, time of damage during childhood is related to clinical outcome. Damage to the left hemisphere during the first few years of life can be overcome; after puberty it cannot be. Recent research shows Lenneberg to have conceded too much to the environment. Woods (1980) provides evidence of very early left hemisphere specialization for language. Dennis (1980) has found that infants who have their right hemispheres removed at birth develop normal language, while those who lose their left hemispheres have only imperfect (though usable) language all their lives.

3 Language cannot be suppressed. Studies of completely untutored deaf children found that they spontaneously invent sign language to use with each other: Teaching signing to chimps is hard work, but children learn language by themselves (Miller, 1981). On the other hand, language learning cannot be speeded up by more than a few days, as training studies have shown (Moskowitz, 1978).

4 The time of onset and early steps of language learning are universal around the world.

5 The early sequence of language acquisition is closely correlated with motor development, which is known to be due entirely to maturation. Just as children kept swaddled begin to walk at the same time as unswaddled children, Lenneberg reports a baby at the babbling stage who was tracheostomized for six months, and who picked up babbling not where she left off but where she should have been when the tracheostomy was reversed.

6 Language cannot be taught to any other species. Although this claim is controversial, it is not clearly false.

7 Linguistic universals do exist.

8 Certain forms of aphasia (disordered language) are inheritable.

9 Timing of speech onset and onset of speech deficits (if any) are more similar between identical than between fraternal twins.

10 So-called wolf-children denied access to speech until adolescence cannot learn language despite intensive tutoring (Jeffrey, 1980), while similar children discovered at an earlier age can learn language.

11 Language is present in all cultures.

To Lenneberg's list we can add some further considerations:

12 There is a clear difference between learning a second language in adulthood and first language learning. We learn our primary language without think-

ing; most of us struggle through language classes with great difficulty, despite adult cognitive skills and careful instruction. Vocabulary learning provides a dramatic contrast. The adult language learner struggles to master a few new words a week. Without trying, the average six-year-old learns 22 new words a day! As Miller (1981) puts it: "Their minds are like little vacuum pumps designed by nature to suck up words." (p. 119)

13   Both children and adults suffering from aphasia can learn Premack's token "language," indicating that the problem-solving, but not linguistic, parts of their brains are intact (Cromer, 1981).

14   Neonates (12 hours old) show "interactional synchrony" with spoken language (Condon & Sander, 1974; Bower, 1977). When they hear human language—any human language—but not when they hear other sounds, they move their bodies in a regular rhythmic fashion following the sound pattern of what they hear. Speech is clearly a special sound to even the youngest human.

15   Human speech perception is categorical, and there is evidence that these categories are innate. Categorical perception refers to the fact that we perceive a range of stimuli to be the same. For example, the phonemes (*ba*) and (*pa*) differ only in their *voice onset time* (VOT), that is, at what point we begin to vibrate our vocal chords in making the sound. In (*ba*) it is early, in (*pa*) it is late. It is possible to synthesize speech and play subjects sounds differing only in VOT, gradually shifting it from early to late. Figure 11–9 shows that although objectively the synthetic sound slides from (*ba*) to (*pa*) as VOT slowly changes, humans perceive an abrupt shift from (*ba*) to (*pa*), not a slow change.

FIGURE   11–9   Categorical Perception of Speech. Average Identification Scores of Nine Subjects Listening to Seven Steps in a Synthetic Speech, Voice-Onset-Time Continuum. There is a consistent partitioning of the stimulus continuum into the two categories [ba] and [pa]. Stimuli in which laryngeal voicing starts early in the sound are heard as the voiced consonant *b*. Sounds with a later voicing onset are heard as the unvoiced consonant *p*. (From Green & Marler, 1979)

Eimas, Siqueland, Jusczyk, and Vigorito (1971) and Miller and Eimas (1983) showed that prelinguistic infants show the same kind of categorical perception, and they proposed that infants have innate human speech detectors. Subsequent research has shown that some other (but not all) distinctive features are recognized by infants including features not used in their natural language (see Blumenstein, 1980, for a review). On the other hand, nonhuman species perceive categorically, too (Eilers, 1980): Chinchillas, like adult and infant humans, categorically perceive (*ba*) and (*pa*). So the species-specificity of this ability is unclear. Evolution may have incorporated pre–existing perceptual abilities into the human language system.

Taken together, these considerations suggest that human language acquisition is a biologically based, genetically constrained and directed form of learning that takes place during a fixed critical period ending at adolescence. The analogy to birdsong is striking. In both cases language does not simply mature, but requires input and practice that must occur in a certain period of time. In both cases there is a range of languages (or dialects) that may be learned, but certain kinds of languages may not be learned. In both, there is cerebral (left hemisphere) specialization of language function.

The cognitivist counter-proposal is based essentially on negative reasoning: It is not *necessary* to postulate specifically linguistic innate processes and structures (see Atkinson, 1982, for a review). With regard to neurology, it is claimed that hemispheric specialization is really for two broad types of cognitive abilities, linear (left hemisphere) and holistic (right hemisphere) so that language winds up in the left hemisphere by virtue of being a linear processing task (Bever, 1980). With regard to the work on categorical speech perception in infants, the cognitivists maintain that since not all distinctive features are innate, and those that are are not species-specific, there is no linguistic specialization at work (Aslin & Pisoni, 1980). This, by the way, is an objection of limited force, since as Gould (1982) points out, evolution is a great opportunist, and in building language it took advantage of older, preexisting abilities. In general, communication systems show a careful tuning between already present sensory abilities and characteristics of the message (Wilson, 1980).

Most generally it is argued that broad cognitive universals, not specific to language, are what actually give rise to the universal onset and sequencing of language acquisition. Slobin (1973) has proposed seven such universal cognitive operating principles. Table 11–3 lists these, along with examples of the specific linguistic universals that they allegedly cause. The idea is that language is not innate; cognition is, and universal rules of cognition give rise to the universals of language that nativists mistake for purely linguistic entities.

Although the cognitivist hypothesis is the favorite among current psychologists (Moskowitz, 1978; Elkind, 1981), a careful review of their claims (Cromer, 1981) shows it to be flawed. The general problem with the cognitivist approach is oversimplification. It assumes that once a cognitive strategy or concept is acquired it is immediately translated into language. But Cromer argues that the translation is not a trivial automatic affair, and is likely to involve specifically linguistic processes, perhaps innate ones.

TABLE 11–3 Possible Cognitive Universals in the Acquisition of Language

UNIVERSAL OPERATING PRINCIPLE USED BY CHILDREN		UNIVERSALS OF LANGUAGE ACQUISITION (EXAMPLES)	
A.	Pay attention to the ends of words.	A1.	Suffixes are learned sooner than prefixes.
B.	The phonological forms of words can be systematically modified.	B1.	Children's word play.
C.	Pay attention to the order of words and morphemes.	C2.	Word order in child speech reflects word order in the input language.
D.	Avoid interruption or rearrangement of linguistic units.	D4.	The greater the separation between related parts of a sentence, the greater the chance a child will not understand it.
E.	Underlying semantic relations should be marked overtly and clearly.	E4.	When the full form of an expression permits contraction (e.g., I will → I'll), the full form will be learned first.
F.	Avoid exceptions.	F2.	Overregularization of grammatical rules.
G.	The use of grammatical markers should make semantic sense.	G3.	Semantically consistent grammatical rules are acquired early and without error.

Based on Slobin (1973)

On the empirical side, evidence indicates that cognitive and linguistic development can be almost completely decoupled, suggesting separate developmental paths. Cromer cites a study with two subjects in whom such decoupling took place in opposite ways. One subject was a 20-year-old female deprived of language until 12, and who despite intensive instruction had still not acquired language beyond a two-year-old level; nevertheless, her general cognitive ability was much higher, at Piaget's level of concrete operations (7 to 12 years old). Another subject—a child—did poorly on cognitive tests, but spoke using highly complex syntactic constructions. The content of his speech—clearly depending on thinking—was often nonsense, but his grammatical skills were high. In this connection we may again mention the ape language projects, because chimpanzees have (relatively) sophisticated intelligence, but acquire only rudimentary language at best.

One of the major findings making the cognitivist hypothesis attractive has been the discovery of baby talk, or "motherese." Chomsky alleged that children heard only fragmentary, ill-formed utterences, from which only an innate language faculty could extract linguistic competence. However, studies (see Snow, 1972) of parental speech to children showed that it differed from speech to adults, and was in general well formed and framed in short sentences. From this, advocates of cognitivism concluded that children were getting a sort of tutorial in language, and that Chomsky's nativism was unnecessary.

However, Cromer uses a careful study of motherese (Newport, Gleitman, & Gleitman, 1977) to undermine the cognitivist claim (see Wexler & Culicover, 1980; Box 11–5). One immediate problem with the

BOX 11–5   *LEARNABILITY THEORY*

A promising line of investigation of language acquisition has been begun by Kenneth Wexler and Peter Cullicover (1980), called **learnability theory**.

Wexler and Culliover point out that there is a necessary tradeoff between the kinds and power of learning mechanisms invoked to explain language acquisition on the one hand, and constraints on the forms of possible human grammars on the other. Very general—and therefore linguistically weak—learning mechanisms will only be able to learn a small class of highly constrained grammers; that is, specific universal constraints on kinds of human language grammars will have to be innate. On the other hand, if a broad variety of relatively unconstrained grammars exist to be learned, much more (innately) powerful learning mechanisms will have to be invoked.

Earlier work (see Atkinson, 1982 for a simplified account) had proved that even implausibly powerful cognitive mechanisms could not, *in principle*, learn the accepted grammars of human language, or even simplified versions thereof. What Wexler and Cullicover have done is to prove that if language is to be learned at all—as it clearly is—there must exist specific linguistic constraints (innate universals) on the form of possible grammars, and these two researchers offer specific (highly technical) hypotheses as to what these might be.

Wexler and Cullicover have opened a new path to studying language acquisition by focusing our attention on exactly what the child must learn. Once we better understand the dimensions of the task, and the kinds of principles that must be innate, we will be in a much better position to learn from what children and their parents say to one another.

idea that motherese is used to teach children language is that baby talk, motherese, could have other functions than teaching: to express affection (it is used between lovers), to facilitate communication (it is used with foreigners), or to assert power (nurses use it with patients). Against the tutorial view Newport et al. (1977) found that while motherese sentences are short, they are syntactically complex, by some measures more complex than speech between adults. Moreover, the "lessons" seem ill designed to teach syntax. For example, the canonical form of English sentences is a declarative sentence in subject-verb-object word order: 87 percent of adult-adult sentences are of this type; but only 30 percent of sentences directed to children are, there being many more commands and questions. In investigating the influence of motherese or subsequent child speech, Newport et al. (1977) found that motherese affected the acquisition *only* of English-language specific structures, and had no impact on the rate of acquisition of more universal aspects of language.

From their research, Newport and colleagues concluded that the nativist hypothesis could not be rejected. While motherese is real, it seems to play a limited role in language acquisition; and, in general, the details of the kinds of language directed at children seem to have little effect on the course of language acquisition. (Bates, Bretherton, Beeghly-Smith, & McNew, 1982).

CONCLUSION: THE BIOLOGICAL BASIS OF LANGUAGE

Let us reflect once again on the difference between child and chimp. The child learns language naturally, with little or no tutoring and with little visible effort. The chimp is carefully taught by a team of intelligent, dedicated researchers who want very much to succeed and who work as hard as possible to give their subjects language. Yet the chimp—despite such heroic efforts—acquires no more than the simplest language, and perhaps not even that.

Whatever else may be innate, it is quite clear that human children have a powerful *drive* to learn language (Gould, 1982). Even if all the mechanisms of language acquisition should turn out to be those of general intelligence—which, as we have seen is by no means clear—evolution has provided at least this much: To learn human language is one of a child's deepest needs.

Given the evidence we have reviewed in this chapter, concerning the evolution of communication in animals, the mixed results of the ape language projects, the speculations on human language evolution, and the findings on child language acquisition, we can reach a stronger conclusion. We humans swim in a sea of language. It is the key to much of our adaptive success, providing the basis for educating the long-helpless, K-selected infant, for socializing our children, for cooperation, for binding ourselves together in groups and for expressing love for our epigamically differentiated loved ones. Without language we would not be human, and so it is unlikely that evolution—natural selection—did not produce a human language faculty.

SUGGESTED READINGS

The full range of mammalian communication systems from hedgehogs to humans is presented in Roger Peters' *Mammalian Communication* (1980). A good place for the student interested in Chomsky's work to start is with his *Language and Mind* (1968; enlarged ed., 1972). As Footnote 1 explained, there are many popular books on the ape language studies; Herbert Terrace's *Nim* is recently out in a mass-market paperback. There is no easy work on language evolution, but chapters in George Miller's *Language and Speech* (1981) provide an introduction, and *Origins and Evolution of Language and Speech* (Harnad et al., 1976), the proceedings of a conference on the subject, provides a bewildering variety of approaches and speculations. On child language acquisition the standard reference seems to have become Jill and Peter de Villier's *Language Acquisition* (1978), though other works are listed in Footnote 2.

CHAPTER TWELVE
DEVELOPMENT, LEARNING, AND COGNITION

DEFINING DEVELOPMENT

Introduction

That human development is teleological—directed to a final end, mature adulthood—is a commonplace idea reaching back to Aristotle. He envisioned the development of any living being as the unfolding of a preexisting plan of development (called an *entelechy*) that brought an organism from seed to mature plant, from egg to adult bird, from embryo to mature animal, from fetus to mature human being. While this view may be challenged, as we will see in this chapter, it is undeniably comfortable and appealing. Another popular view of development is to divide it into stages, as Shakespeare did (see Box 12–1).

In nineteenth-century Europe—the birthplace of much of psychology—the teleological view of development was particularly strong, and had been extended to include the history of human society. So it was widely believed that just as a human being passes from the simple and primitive thoughts and feelings of infancy to the sophisticated thinking and nuanced emotion of adulthood, so did human societies progress from simple and primitive tribalism to the sophistication of the Western nation state; usually, it was hoped that one stage yet remained: achievement of a harmonious brotherhood of man under a peaceful world government. Karl Marx's theory of history is the best known example of such historicism today;

BOX 12–1 *SHAKESPEARE'S SEVEN AGES OF MAN.*

The idea that the human lifespan may be divided into discrete stages is popular with laymen and developmental psychologists alike. In this passage, William Shakespeare describes a Renaissance stage theory of human life, one rather cynical and misanthropic.

All the world's a stage,
And all the men and women merely players;
They have their exits and their entrances,
And one man in his time plays many parts,
His acts being seven ages. At first the infant,
Mewling and puking in the nurse's arms.
Then the whining schoolboy, with his satchel
And shining morning face, creeping like snail
Unwillingly to school. And then the lover,
Sighing like furnace, with a woeful ballad
Made to his mistress' eyebrow. Then a soldier,
Full of strange oaths, and bearded like the pard,
Jealous in honor, sudden, and quick in quarrel,
Seeking the bubble reputation
Even in the cannon's mouth. And then the justice,
In fair round belly with good capon lined,
With eyes severe and beard of formal cut,
Full of wise saws and modern instances;
And so he plays his part. The sixth age shifts
Into the lean and slippered Pantaloon,
With spectacles on nose, and pouch on side,
His youthful hose, well saved, a world too wide
For his shrunk shank, and his big manly voice,
Turning again toward childish treble, pipes
And whistles in his sound. Last scene of all,
That ends this strange eventful history,
Is second childishness, and mere oblivion,
Sans teeth, sans eyes, sans taste, sans everything.*

*Read *As You Like It*. The quotation is from Act II, scene vii, lines 139–166.

Marx envisioned history as an inevitable progression, beyond the possibility of human intervention, through a series of stages from barbarism to feudalism to capitalism and finally to world socialism, at which point history ends. For Marx the autonomous force underlying historical development was economic change, specifically changes in who owns the means of production characteristic of each stage. Moreover, each system of ownership (save socialism) possesses internal contradictions that ensure its eventual overthrow and replacement by a superior one. History, according to Marx, is the inevitable progress of humankind to economic and social maturity as the logic of economic change unfolds.

Historicism did much to reinforce and preserve the teleological concept of human development, and it is therefore not surprising that shortly after psychology began there appeared in Europe historicist-developmentalist theories of human development. For example, there are interesting parallels between Marx's theory of history and Piaget's and Kohlberg's theories of cognitive and moral development. They propose that cognition and morality develop through fixed sequences of stages such that each stage (save the last) contains inconsistencies that bring about its overthrow and replacement by a more adequate one. Human development is therefore the inevitable progress of a child to cognitive and moral maturity as the logic of development unfolds.

Heinz Werner and Orthogenesis

The theorist who was most emphatic in distinguishing between mere change and true development, and who applied the concept of development to everything from perception to history was Heinz Werner (1890–1964). Werner was educated in Germany, steeped in the German historical-developmental tradition, before fleeing the Nazis and settling in the United States. Werner occupied himself with studying the processes of development from an organismic-teleological perspective as they manifested themselves in children and adults, primitives, and moderns, and in psychotics and normals (Baldwin, 1980; Langer, 1970; Werner, 1978).

Werner was careful to distinguish development from change or growth. Not all change is development, for change may be regressive. Nor is all growth development; a savings account "grows" as interest is added, but this does not constitute development because no qualitative improvement takes place. Werner (1978) borrowed the term **orthogenesis** from embryology and defined development thus:

> It is an orthogenetic principle which states that whenever development occurs it proceeds from a state of relative globality and lack of differentiation to a state of increasing differentiation, articulation, and hierarchic integration. (Werner, 1957, p. 126)

The principle naturally fits embryogenesis perfectly. What begins as a single nonspecialized cell gradually develops into an organism, a collection of specialized cells (differentiation) structurally organized (articulation) into an efficient system under central control (hierarchic integration). Werner thought that the same functional principles of development characterized not only the development of the embryo, but the evolutionary history of a species (phylogenesis), the long-term development of a person (orthogenesis), the short-term development of thinking, emotion, and perception (microgenesis), the development of societies (ethnogenesis), and the development of psychopathology (pathogenesis). While of course the material basis (what develops) in each case is different, Werner believed the orthogenetic principles of development—the teleological drive to differentiation, articulation, and integration—could be found in each case (Langer, 1970).

Werner defined four dimensions—although *vectors* might be a better word—along which development takes place. Development proceeds:

From the *syncretic* to the *discrete*. In syncresis, things that will later be distinguished are jumbled together. For example, synaesthestic perception involves a stimulus in one modality creating experience in another, as when a child might say a dead leaf "smells brown."

From the *diffuse* to the *articulated*. The thought of the young child is diffuse: Concepts are confused, emotions are experienced vaguely, action is haphazard. With development, concept and emotions get sorted out, behaviors become well defined and coordinated.

From *rigidity* to *flexibility*. The child and the traditional tribesman often rigidly adhere to single ways of doing things. With development, behavior becomes more flexible as new problems are met and mastered in new ways.

From *lability* to *stability*. While given processes of thinking may be rigid in childhood, for example, rigid use of a previously successful technique when it might no longer be the best—overall behavior is liabile: haphazard and undirected. For example, facing a new problem a child uses random trial and error rather than systematic testing of possible solutions. With development, behavior and thought become better controlled and stable, making for flexible but coordinated responses to challenges.

Werner's experiments and his more detailed theory of *how* development proceeds have had only limited influence on psychology; nevertheless, he has nicely separated the concept of development from other kinds of change and has offered a definition of development we can use to distinguish developmentalists from learning theorists. The other theoreticians of this chapter will all share Werner's general organismic, inner-directed view of human development, even though their theories will be otherwise quite different.

COGNITIVE DEVELOPMENT

There are two areas where the development *vs* learning controversy has been most hotly debated. One of them is cognitive development, where the leading developmentalist theory is Jean Piaget's genetic epistemology, which has been attacked by non-developmentalists of all theoretical persuasions.

Genetic Epistemology

Piaget as philosopher   Jean Piaget was one of the towering psychological theorists of the twentieth century, yet his ideas are often misunderstood and misrepresented. One reason for this is that Piaget represents the European developmentalist tradition alluded to already. Specifically, he belongs in what Blumenthal (1980), following Brett (1912) calls the Leibnizian (European) tradition in philosophy. Gottfried Leibniz (1646–1716) described the mind as an active entity, developing itself through inner-directed principles toward ever-greater perfection. The Leibnizian tradition stands in contrast to the English, Lockean, empiricist tradition that depicts the mind as quite passive, building up knowledge by receiving and copying sense impressions as if it were clay to be molded (compare Skinner's term "shaping"). Since Americans are raised in the empiricist tradition, it is hardly surprising that Piaget's theory may strike us as odd and incomprehensible.

The other most serious reason for misunderstanding Piaget is even less often acknowledged, and it is that in an important sense Piaget—despite collecting data and theorizing about cognition—was not a psychologist at all. He called what he did **genetic epistemology,** the study of the origins (genesis) of knowledge (epistemology), specifically in child development. But the term *epistemology* needs closer attention, because it was Piaget's concerns as an epistemologist that led to his developmentalism.

Epistemology is the branch of philosophy concerned with knowledge—what it is and how we acquire it. Naively, we think that knowledge is true belief; I can say I *know* that George Washington was the first President because it is true. But this cannot be all that knowledge is. On an American history test you might be asked, "Who was the third President?", and be unable to remember. So you recall the name of the only President after Washington and before Lincoln you can remember, namely, Jefferson, and write that down. The answer happens to be correct, but we would not say that you knew Jefferson was the third President even though you expressed the true belief that he was. Philosophers concede that knowledge is more than simply true belief, but what that "more" is remains elusive. Some have even given up the quest altogether and asserted that there is no knowledge, only workable beliefs that may nevertheless eventually be proven wrong. This was the view of the Scottish philosopher David Hume and the American philosopher and psychologist William James, so it is part of Americans' intellectual heritage.

Piaget, however, is among those philosphers who have not given up the quest, and he proposes his genetic epistemology as an answer to this central problem of epistemology. One old candidate (going back to Plato) for what is needed to make true belief knowledge is *provable certainty.* To count as knowledge, something must have the character of a mathematical or logical theorem—it can be proven true by deductive logic (see Chapter 9).

Manifestly, any generalization from experience cannot have this characteristic of provable certainty, as David Hume showed in the eighteenth century. No matter how confident I may be that all swans are white from having examined 2000 of them, I must realize that I could be wrong, that the 2001*st* swan may be some other color. Therefore, while experience may yield up true beliefs, it cannot yield up knowledge.

Another move in the search for knowledge was tried by many thinkers from Plato down to the present. It is to claim that human knowledge is *innate.* So, for example, the eighteenth-century Scottish philosopher Thomas Reid (1710–1796) held that humans possess God-given beliefs and cognitive processes, which, since God made us in His image, cannot be mistaken. These, therefore, constitute knowledge.

However, in light of modern evolutionary theory such a comfortable nativism is no longer convincing. Whatever human propensities and abilities may be innate (Chapter 10), they were selected by the nondirective happenstances of natural and sexual selection. They are not necessarily true; had our ancient ecology been different, our human nature would be different. In a sense, innate ideas are not very different from ideas drawn from experience—useful, but the product of whatever experience our ancestors had and therefore not certain, not knowledge.

Now none of this need bother a psychologist; he or she can study what's innate and what's learned without caring whether our beliefs are ultimately true or not. In this the psychologist would resemble Hume or James. But Piaget, even as a teenager, wanted certainty, and his genetic epistemology is in his view a third way to knowledge through development rather than through learning or heredity.

Piaget proposes that cognitive development unfolds in much the way a logical argument unfolds, step by step in a logically necessary sequence of stages and substages. The child's cognitive structures might be regarded at any moment as a set of logical premises. Experience provides information that children can use to make deductions from their premises, resulting in a new set of premises or logical structures, from which further deductions are made in the light of experience, and so on until an adequate set of structures is achieved that can deal effectively and creatively with the environment.

If Piaget is correct, then the making of deduction after deduction from given cognitive structures, or premises, has the character of a logical argument, moving step by step to a provably certain conclusion. In short, cognitive development is the construction of knowledge. We see, then, that it is his epistemological concerns that led Piaget to postulate autonomous developmental forces beside maturation (nativism) and experience (empiricism), and it is these concerns, together with his inheritance of the Leibnizian tradition, that can make him so hard to understand.

The process of development[1] Piaget's area of earliest interest and university training was biology, so he brought a strong biological, adaptationist influence to developmental psychology, in addition to his philosophical aims. In fact, his goal was to make epistemology a science along biological lines. He viewed intelligence—cognitive structures and processes—as an

---

[1]The following discussion of Piaget's theory is based primarily on the following sources: Piaget (1963, 1965, 1967a, 1967b, 1969, 1970a, 1970b, 1971a, 1971b, 1971c, 1972, 1973, 1976); Piaget and Inhelder (1969a, 1969b, 1969c, 1971, 1973); Inhelder and Piaget (1958). Secondary sources consulted include Elkind and Flavell (1969); Baldwin (1980), Furth (1969). An interesting attempt to picture Piaget as a learning theorist is Gallagher and Reid (1981). A good single source for reading Piaget is Gruber and Voneche (1977), which contains extracts from Piaget's leading work over his entire lifetime, together with thoughtful and insightful commentary.

organ of biological adaptation like the hand or the eye. The only unique thing about intelligence as an adaptation is that it is mental and behavioral rather than morphological. Intelligence, especially human intelligence, is the most powerful organ of adaptation there is, and we reflected on its evolutionary origins in Chapter Ten. Piaget is concerned with the evolution of intelligence in the individual child as he or she attains mature cognition, perfect adaptation to the environment, and certain knowledge.

Piaget draws a sharp and significant distinction between physical (or *empirical*) and *logico-mathematical* knowledge, which correspond to *learning* and *development* respectively (see Figure 12–1). Empirical knowledge has to do with facts—knowledge of the outside world—and how we represent them internally, which Piaget calls *figurativity*. Logico-mathematical knowledge has to do with our actions on the world or its internal representations, which Piaget calls *operativity* in an unconscious echo of Skinner's coinage "operant." Both Piaget and Skinner thereby emphasize an organism's activity and study how it operates on the world it lives in.

The source of empirical knowledge is experienced objects. As we perceive and interact with the objects in our environment we learn about them through *perception* and the cognitive process of **empirical abstraction,** which gives rise to concepts. For example, a child meets many small furry animals and must learn to group them into distinct conceptual categories such as dog, cat, and gerbil. Each class will have features in common with the others—dogs, cats, and gerbils are all furry; all of them eat, drink, and move; many are brown. Other features distinguish each class from the others. Dogs chase cats and cats chase gerbils; dogs bark, cats meow, and gerbils (occasionally) squeak. What the child does is to abstract from each particular animal the features that define its class, and so builds up a concept of DOG, of CAT, of GERBIL. This process Piaget calls *empirical* (sometimes *physical*) *abstraction,* because it is an abstraction from the perceived physical world. The child is also able to represent the world internally, both as memory of his particular experiences (for example, an image of a pet gerbil) and as concepts representing general classes (what gerbils are). Developing representations is an *internalization* of one's experience, and the representations themselves are called *schemas*. This represents *learning* for Piaget.

Now while this kind of knowledge is important, useful, and adaptive, it is less important than logico-mathematical knowledge to Piaget. To begin with, it falls short of the universality Piaget seeks in true knowledge. Indian children learn about *dacoits, dhotis,* and Krishna, while American children learn about muggers, suits, and Jehova: Empirical knowledge—facts—are culture-specific and particular. More importantly, facts are meaningless and unlearnable without actions and cognitive processes, and these change over time while objects do not. To an infant, a gerbil is an interesting moving object; to a six-year-old it is a beloved pet coming from a mysterious place called Mongolia; to a biology student a gerbil is a member of the class of rodents along with mice and rats, with certain unique properties resulting from its evolution in a specific ecological niche. So Piaget rejects the copy theory; concepts and schemas are not simply given by experience im-

PROCESSES OF TRANSFORMATION

TYPE OF CHANGE	TYPE OF KNOWLEDGE	SOURCE	TYPE OF ABSTRACTION	BEHAVIORAL BASIS	MENTALIZATION PROCESS	MENTAL UNITS	PROCESS OF CHANGE
Learning Field of Figurativity	Empirical	Objects	Empirical	Perception	Internalization	Schemas (Representations, Concepts)	Learning
Development Field of Operativity	Logico-mathematical	Actions	Reflective	Schemes (Abstracted actions)	Interiorization	Operations (Mental actions)	Assimilation Accommodation Equilibration

Figure 12-1. Processes and Units of Learning and Development in Piaget's Theory. Terms *internalization* and *interiorization* are Furth's (1969) Clarifications of Piaget's French Usage.

pressing itself on a child, but depend on the child's preexisting and changing cognitive structures. Piaget's work has concentrated on these cognitive structures that he believes are human universals that pass through an invariant sequence of development.

Cognitive structures comprise human logico-mathematical knowledge and are rooted in action rather than the perception of objects. Piaget tells a story about a mathematician friend of his who, as a child, had a great insight one day playing with pebbles. The boy found that if he lined up ten pebbles in a row, he had ten; if he changed the line to a circle, still ten; to a square, still ten. He discovered what Piaget calls *conservation of number,* that no matter how a group of objects is arranged, their number remains the same. This piece of knowledge is logico-mathematical knowledge, and it is far more general and certain than empirical knowledge, for it is capable of proof and applies to pebbles, rocks, bricks, children, *dacoits,* U. S. Senators, and stars.

Naturally, the boy was gaining empirical knowledge about the pebbles, too. He had schemas (images) of the pebbles he was using, and doubtless had a schema (concept) of the PEBBLE, abstracting away the features common to all pebbles. But the generalization about conservation of number did not derive from the pebbles, since the same insight could have come from playing with leaves, Lego pieces, toy soldiers or pieces of candy. Piaget maintains that logico-mathematical knowledge is an abstraction, called **reflective abstraction,** from a child's actions. The young mathematician could have arranged pebbles, leaves, Lego pieces the same way, and what would be the same in each case, and therefore abstractable as a generalization, is the acts of arranging and counting, getting the same number in each configuration. Again, observe that the actions, like conservation of number, are quite general, applying to any countable objects, and operative on the world. Logico-mathematical knowledge is operative knowledge and constitutes an organ of adaptation, because it is able to deal effectively with virtually every concrete situation and is not limited to any given context or culture.

Reflective abstraction creates two units of operative intelligence corresponding to sensori-motor, or behavioral, and mental intelligence, respectively; these units are the *scheme* and the *operation.* Schemes are sensori-motor ways of knowing the world by direct perception or action. Attentive looking or grasping qualify as schemes. Schemes are rather like Skinnerian operants, in that they are defined by their consequences or purposes, not by their topography. Thus, schemes, like operants, are not specific muscle movements but are purposive actions. Piaget (1963) describes an incident involving his infant daughter, Jacqueline, that illustrates how schemes are to be understood. Piaget arranged a mobile over her crib and tied one end of a string to the mobile and taped the other end to her right arm. Like all infants, Jacqueline would wiggle; she discovered that her wiggling would jerk the mobile about, which she found fascinating. After a great deal of trial and error she learned to move the mobile just by pulling on the string with her right arm. Piaget then taped the string to the left arm. If Jacqueline had acquired only a specific muscular response, she would have had to relearn it with her left arm. However, she immediately began to use her left arm to work the mobile, showing that she had learned something more general and goal-defined, namely, a scheme.

Schemes provide the original behavioral foundations of later mental actions. Schemes operate on immediately given physical objects; objects are internalized into mental schemas, and as such they are subject to mental action by *interiorized* schemes, called *operations*. For example, infants "classify" objects by what can be done to them—that is, what schemes apply to them. Some objects can be sucked on, others hit, some picked up, and so on. This constitutes a primitive, sensory-motor sort of classification of objects into overlapping classes. Piaget believes that this sensory-motor "classification" becomes interiorized and more general, providing the cognitive structures underlying classification of objects under conceptual heads in later childhood and adulthood. As he does with all thought, Piaget thus views classification as action—mental action—whereby objects are actively sorted into groups; classes are not given by nature and imposed on a passive organism.

The adaptive virtue of operations as opposed to schemes—and therefore the source of the evolutionary advantage—is that they make possible mental trial-and-error learning, enhancing adaptive coping. At the sensorimotor level one can only act and then discover—perhaps to one's great, even fatal cost—that the act was unwise. Operations encourage prudence, because one can try out a line of action (operations) on one's mental world (schemas), estimating its likelihood of success or failure. Piaget calls this the *precorrection of errors* made possible by operational thought.

Individual schemes and operations develop because of two processes, **assimilation** and **accommodation**. Assimilation and accommodation come into play when a child (or adult) encounters a new object or situation requiring adaptive mastery. Piagetian organisms, being active learners, seek out new learning opportunities, boldly going where they have not been before. *Assimilation* refers to the organism bringing a new object, concept, or situation within the competence of its schemes or operations. An infant coming across a keyring for the first time (infants find them fascinating) fumbles with it for a while until it can securely grasp it, rattle it, and pass it from hand to hand (all schemes). This process may take days, and to the Piagetian-informed parent is fascinating to watch. When all these things can be done smoothly and competently, the object is assimilated to the schemes and will soon become boring.

At a more mature level, you fumbled with the concept "parental investment" until you mastered it (we hope), thereby assimilating it to your operations. Neither you nor the baby was unchanged during all of this. The infant's schemes were tested and refined by the encounter with the keyring, improving its adaptive fit to the environment and better equipping it for future challenges. Encountering "parental investment" tested and refined your intellectual operations, improving your adaptive fit to your academic environment, and better equipping you for future challenges whether in psychology or in marriage. A change to schemes and operations taking place during an adaptive learning encounter Piaget calls *ac-*

commodation, which always takes place alongside assimilation. In fact, Piaget maintains that while we can conceptually separate them, assimilation and accommodation are inextricably intertwined in the actual development of infant, child, and adult.

There is one final developmental process, shown in Figure 12–1, **equilibration**. Equilibration is the master *developmental* process, lying behind assimilation and accommodation and being responsible for transitions between Piaget's well-known stages of cognitive development. As with evolution, so with development for Piaget: He needs to find a motor to move both forward. In evolution, the orthodox motor (Chapter Ten) of the Neo-Darwinians is the struggle for existence and natural selection. In development, the common alternatives are maturation, espoused by nativists (Piaget calls them *preformationists*) or the environment, which simply shapes the organism through learning, according to empiricists and behaviorists.

We have seen that for Skinner the process of learning is the same as the process of evolution, selection by the environment among random variations emitted by organisms. Piaget agrees that evolution and development (not learning) are based on the same process, but seeks, as usual, a *via media* between learning and maturation, proposing a basic process quite different from Skinner's: *equilibration* (Piaget, 1971a, 1978). Equilibration refers to what Piaget also calls the *auto-regulation* of behavior and behavior change. He maintains with Lamarck that organisms do not just respond passively to a selecting environment, but actively strive to improve their adaptation. They seek not just an adequate level of adaptation, but the best adaptation possible (Flanagan, 1983). Auto-regulation (a term Piaget in his last works preferred to equilibration; Furth, 1981) captures what Piaget means— organisms regulate their own behavior, their own adaptive fit; it is not blindly imposed on them by either environment (as empiricists argue) or genes (as maturationists say).

Cognitive development is driven by equilibration: assimilation and accommodation, reflective abstraction, and interiorization are all processes that alter the child's understanding, schemes, and operations in search of superior logico-mathematical knowledge, which uses the facts and concepts gleaned from experience. Therefore, equilibration and its various processes of logico-mathematical development are far more important than learning in accounting for intellectual development; from first to last it is equilibration that shapes perception, concept formation, and behavior. Auto-regulation is also responsible for the general restructuring of logico-mathematical knowledge that occurs three times in a child's life. Piaget believes that logico-mathematical knowledge can be described as a set of logical structures of schemes and/or operations, and that these structures are assembled in distinct ways at different points in cognitive development, moving from immediate, context-bound knowledge to abstract, context-free creative knowledge. Each structured ensemble of logico-mathematical structures defines a distinct *stage* in cognitive development.

Stages of development   Thinking of development in terms of *stages,* as Shakespeare did, is quite common, occurring in all the developmentalists surveyed in this chapter. The intuitive appeal of stages is evident in our common-sense usage: We divide life into infancy, childhood, adolescence, adulthood, and old age. However, we mean by these things no more than convenient descriptions—"the terrible twos"—and do not take them to be real entities in any fundamental sense. But Piaget does; his stages are proposed as psychological realities, not convenient sketches of age-typical behavior. See Table 12–1. You may investigate stages of development by doing the simple experiment described in Box 12–2.

Piaget has offered various criteria for defining true stages, and they have been usefully assembled by Pinard and Laurendeau (1969), Brainerd (1978a,b), and Flanagan (1983):

1   Each stage must be *qualitatively different and more complex* from the previous stage. Piaget maintains that the growth of knowledge is more than the slow accumulation of facts and skills, but that the *way* children think at a given stage is qualitatively different from other stages. So at IIB there is a logic of functions, at IIIB a logic of classes, and at IV a logic of propositions.

2   Each stage is *more adequate,* that is, more adaptive, than the previous one.

3   The stages must follow each other in an ordered sequence such that
   a   the sequence is *culturally universal*
   b   it occurs in the *same order* for everyone
   c   all normal children *reach the last stage*
   d   there is *never regression* from á higher to a lower stage.

4   Each stage subsumes and integrates the abilities of the previous stage. The stages thus form a *hierarchy* such that formal operations includes and reintegrates concrete operations, which includes and reintegrates functional and sensori-motor structures. Abilities from earlier stages are not lost or erased, therefore, but take a new place in the higher form of intelligence.

5   Each stage's schemes and operations form a *structured whole.* The schemes and operations do not exist simply as a collection of loosely connected parts but are integrated into a larger, overall structure, that is, the logic of classes or the logic of propositions.

Taken together, Piaget's claims assert that the development of intelligence is not a continuous process of growth, but is marked by leaps from one mode of knowing to a distinct, more adequate one, and that these leaps are made by all individuals in all cultures without backward steps. While development is thus not continuous, it is cumulative, since the structures of earlier stages are not abolished by later ones, but are restructured into a new and more adaptive way of knowing.

Piaget on memory   Since memory is a form of learning and since memory is the psychological function most studied by cognitive scientists (Chapters 5 and 6), it will be useful to consider Piaget's recent research on memory (Piaget & Inhelder, 1973). Piaget, like the schema theorists discussed in Chapter 8, believed memory to be a constructive process, dependent on the operative level of the child. Piaget argues that what is stored in memory depends on a child's stage of cognitive development, so that memory for an early event can actually improve with age. This aspect of Piaget's theory of

TABLE 12–1 Piaget's Stages of Intellectual Development

I. SENSORI-MOTOR INTELLIGENCE (0 TO 24 MOS.)

Adaptation is "practical," oriented to the here and now, based on behavioral schemes only—few if any mental representations present. Interiorization, coordination, and enriching of sensori-motor schemes provide basis for operational thought. Six substages:

1 *Modification of innate reflexes* (0 to 1 mos.)   Initially fixed S-R reflexes become adaptive schemes as they assimilate objects and accommodate reality.

2 *Acquisition of new habits* (1 to 4 mos.)   First new schemes, *primary circular reactions,* learned. Child discovers some behavior centering on its own body that has interesting effects (for example sucking a thumb) and it learns to reinstate it.

3 *Secondary circular reactions* (4 to 10 mos.)   Reinstatement of interesting effect taking place in outside world (for example, Jacqueline and the mobile). First signs of *object concept;* for example, child will now continue to track the trajectory of a previously visible, now occluded, object.

4 *Coordination of secondary schemes* (4 to 12 mos.)   First indication of true intentional intelligence and first step toward general knowledge. Infant can now detach an old scheme from its familar context (for example, hitting things to see them move or hear them make noise) and use it as a means to a more remote end (for example, striking an obstacle to the grasping of an interesting object). Object concept much more developed: Child will now search for a vanished object, showing it now knows that objects continue to exist even when they cannot be sensed.

5 *Tertiary circular reactions* (12 to 18 mos.)   Secondary circular reactions with systematic variation to explore the effect of behavior on the world instead of just repeating an old effect, as before. New schemes invented on the spot to solve problems instead of use of older scheme in new context.

6 *Beginnings of thought* (18 to 24 mos.)   Transition to next major stage as semiotic function—the ability to represent mentally—begins to appear. Insightful problem solution—the result of the precorrection of errors—now possible as solutions are first tried mentally before being translated into behavior. Full development of the object concept as child can now infer location of a hidden object from witnessing a series of both visible and invisible displacements.

II PREOPERATIONAL INTELLIGENCE (2 TO 7 YRS.)

With the acquisition of the semiotic function (marked by appearance of delayed imitation, symbolic play (pretending), drawing, mental images, and above all by language acquisition) real thinking, the manipulation of a mental world (Box 12–3) begins. During this period, schemes are interiorized into operations as concrete operational intelligence is constructed. Two substages.

A *Preconceptual* (2 to 4 yrs.)   Interiorization of schemes just beginning, so that a child can do many things in reality but not with representations. For example, a four-year-old may be able to navigate a path between its house and nursery school, but be unable to tell anyone else how to do it, even with the aid of a realistic map on which are set the principle landmarks.

B *Intuitive,* or *Functional* (5 to 7 yrs.)   Operations beginning to appear but are not yet integrated and coordinated into an overall logical structure. Child intuitively understands certain functional relations but fails tests of deeper understanding. For example, shown a nail driven into a board with a string running around it at right angles such as this:

The child understands that if one pulls on the end of string at A, the distance B-C will shorten and vice-versa, i.e., that lengths A-C and B-C are functionally (inversely) related. But this understanding is not fully coordinated, for the child will deny that the total length of the string A-C is unchanged by moving the string around the nail. Child does not yet *conserve* length.

TABLE 12-1 *(Continued)*

III CONCRETE OPERATIONAL INTELLIGENCE (7 TO 12 YRS.)

Appearance of logically integrated thought. The logic at this stage is the logic of classes, similar to formal syllogistic logic. That is, the child can reason about logically defined classes defined over *objects* (hence, *concrete* operational), and can represent (and internally manipulate) concrete, familiar, objects competently and adaptively, so errors are precorrected. Two substages.

A (8 to 9 yrs.)   Operations coordinated into a logical system. Onset best marked by the first appearance of the *conservations,* the knowledge that physical quantities do not change despite changes in appearance. An example is conservation of amount, or continuous quantity. A child is shown two identical glasses filled with identical amounts of water, A_1 and A_2, and an empty vessel B, much narrower but taller than A. The water in A_2 is poured into B, and the child is asked if there is still the same amount in A_1 and B. At IIA, the child denies this, claiming B has more because it's taller. At IIB the child may answer correctly but be unable to justify its response, even though it does conserve the water's identity, recognizing that the water in B is the same water that was in A_2; it was merely poured. At IIIA, the child can justify its response.

B (10 to 12 yrs.)   Continuation of the consolidation of concrete operations into an equilibrated system; more conservations mastered. Limitations to concrete logic can be seen. Most importantly, the child cannot think *hypothetically* about all the things that might be done in a given situation so that they might be explored systematically. For example, given a set of clear liquid chemicals and told that some combination of them will produce a yellow color, the child proceeds haphazardly, combining pairs of chemicals at random (never trying three), so that even if the solution is achieved, it likely cannot be explained or repeated. Possibility is still subordinate to reality.

IV FORMAL OPERATIONAL INTELLIGENCE (12 YRS. ON)

Operations become yet more abstract and formal, dealing not with objects at all but with formally stated relations or hypotheses. The logic of this stage is *propositional* logic, in which what is understood and manipulated are not classes of objects (concepts) but whole statements or propositions. The power of this stage is that in language—propositions—one can state anything, whether true or false, real or imaginary, so that reality becomes just an instantiation of one among many possible worlds. Einstein's elevator (Box 12–4) is an excellent example of formal thinking at its best. Adolescents' involvement with novel political systems, utopias, and their identity crises are partly the outcome of formal operational thinking, as the teenager is both exhilarated and confused by what he or she and society may be, and angry and resentful of what he or she and society are. Reality becomes subordinate to possibility, and the imagined possible gleams like utopia from the future. But remember, u-topia means "no-where."

Substages are not clearly marked, but around 12 years the child shows the ability to think hypothetically. In the chemical combination task the subject of formal operations will work systematically through all possible combinations, keeping records of what was done as all possibilities are exhausted. He or she will be able to explain his or her strategy and repeat the solution if asked. There is now a great deal of evidence, some of it reviewed in the chapter (9) on Thinking, that for most (perhaps all) people, formal operational thinking remains more an occasionally reached ideal than an everyday actuality, manifesting itself only in familiar domains, but not everyday in every decision. This may be just as well, since weighing all possible *pros* and *cons* of every decision is probably not adaptive. It is said that the great philosopher Immanuel Kant—a formal operational reasoner, surely—took so long to weigh the *pros* and *cons* of marriage that by the time he decided to propose, his intended was already wed!

One final note on Piaget's stages. The ages given are approximations only, and are not to be taken as norms in any sense. There will be wide individual variation from child to child in the speed with which the stages are traversed. What matters to Piaget is the invariant sequence of the stages, not their age of acquisition.

BOX 12–2   *TILTING A BOTTLE: PROCEDURE*

One interesting pencil-and-paper Piagetian task that is easily done is his water-level problem.

Draw a picture of a table from a side view, with a glass on it, as shown in Figure 12-2.

FIGURE 12–2

Now draw a bottle or pitcher pouring water into the glass, and be sure to show some water remaining in the bottle or pitcher. Collect as many as possible such drawings from friends and classmates before reading Box 12–4, which discusses the usual results.

BOX 12–3   *COGNITION AND REPRESENTATION*

The crucial development that defines the preoperational stage and sets off true cognition from sensory-motor intelligence is the appearance of mental *representations*. What the child acquires is the ability to represent the world internally and to manipulate images and concepts rather than real objects.

We take representational ability for granted; thus, it is hard to grasp its significance. A simple problem, however, should help sharpen our understanding. Answer this question before going on: How many windows do you have at home?

Almost invariably, people answer this question by walking through a mental image of their houses and counting the windows. The number is not filed away in long-term memory (LTM)—even people who repeat this task after a few weeks must reimage and recount. Rather, we depend on our ability to represent our surroundings and to act on that representation in ways similar to action in the world.

Whether or not animals possess mental representations and the means to use them is a hotly debated question (Beck, 1983; Galef, 1983), but cognitive scientists agree with Piaget that an essential feature—for them *the* essential feature—of the human mind is this power to make the real imaginary, to alter the world in imagination, ultimately transcending the limits of ordinary experience (see Box 12–4).

BOX 12–4 *EINSTEIN'S ELEVATOR*

When formal operations are achieved anything becomes possible. Piaget emphasizes that the great power of formal operational thought lies in how it subordinates reality to possibility. While most of us may make little use of this power, merely imagining pleasant things that cannot be, in a genius with scientific discipline it may build possible worlds that turn out, however unlikely to common sense, to be our world. The finest example is the vivid imagination of Albert Einstein. Einstein obtained many of his insights through *Gedankenexperimenten* (thought-experiments): imaginary worlds created in his mind rigorously manipulated to produce deep insights into the nature of reality.

In one of his famous thought-experiments, Einstein imagined an elevator in empty space, drawn upward by an imaginary genie pulling a rope of infinite length at a constant acceleration producing a downward force of 1_g (i.e., 1 gravity, equal to the force of gravity at the earth's surface).

A person standing in Einstein's elevator would be unable to tell if he or she were at rest in the earth's surface or under 1_g acceleration in empty space. Reasoning that if two forces have the same observable effects they are really the same force, Einstein concluded that gravity and the force exerted by acceleration were the same, and he derived a stunning prediction from his imaginary elevator.

The elevator is moving through space at a constant acceleration. Imagine now a hole cut in the side of the elevator through which we shine a beam of light. Since the elevator is moving, what happens, as seen by the person shooting the beam of light at time 1 (t_1) is shown in Figure 12-3.

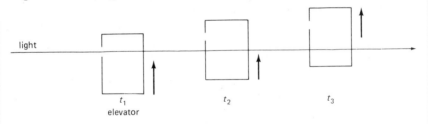

FIGURE 12–3

That is, the person sees a straight beam of light enter the elevator and strike the other side at a point some distance down from the point opposite the entry hole. It is just as if someone threw a ball into the open front driver's window of a moving car—it wouldn't pass out the passenger's window, but land in the back seat.

However, the elevator's passenger sees what is shown in Figure 12-4.

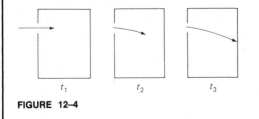

FIGURE 12–4

369

Relative to his or her perspective the light has taken a curved path, as the thrown ball would to the car's occupants.

Now, if accelerational force and gravity are the same force, and since light bends for a viewer influenced by accelerational force, it should also bend in the presence of gravity. Of course the bending in our illustrations is much exaggerated—light is very fast—but Einstein's proposition can be tested by looking at light rays from distant stars as they pass near the Sun and through its strong gravitational field. Such observations have been made, and they accord well with Einstein's precise mathematical predictions.

Even without the mathematics, we can appreciate—and marvel at—Einstein's disciplined but playful use of formal operational thought. In accord with simple assumptions, he imagined a conceptually possible (if practically impossible), little universe from which he drew a strong, counterintuitive proposition that was brought back to the actual world and proved. Einstein himself always explained his mind in terms of visualizing possible worlds, not in terms of mathematical equations; they came later and tidied up and made rigorous insights achieved in thought-experiments.*

*Read Albert Einstein and Leopold Infeld, *The Evolution of Physics*. New York: Simon & Schuster, 1954.

memory contrasts with the schema view, which locates the constructive—and in the research always distorting—process at the time the memory is laid down, with little or no modification, and certainly no improvement, occurring during storage. But Piaget sees the child as developing increasingly accurate cognitive structures that affect both perception and memory storage, resulting in the possibility that memory traces may improve along with schemes and operations.

A simple example concerns **seriation**. In a seriation task, a child is given a number of sticks of slightly different lengths and is asked to arrange them in a row stairstep fashion, being shown a set of already seriated sticks as an example, removed before the child begins. The task defeats the IIA (preconceptual) child, who is likely to sort them into "tall ones" and "short ones." At IIB (intuitive) the child typically constructs the series in a laborious manner, comparing sticks in a fumbling pair-wise fashion, making many mistakes before getting it right. The concrete operational child solves the problem efficiently, choosing the longest stick remaining unseriated and putting it next to the longer ones already chosen.

An especially elegant strategy was revealed by a concrete operational child in a film made by Piaget himself (*Piaget on Piaget*): The youngster held the sticks loosely upright resting on the table in her left fist, and then chose the tallest among them, set it down, chose the next tallest, and so on until done. The incident nicely illustrates the power of concrete operations to structure a problem and precorrect errors.

In their study of memory, Piaget and Inhelder showed children of different ages a set of already seriated sticks, took it away, and asked the subjects to draw what they had seen. (In order to verify that their findings did not result from poor drawing skills, Piaget and Inhelder showed that other children of matching ages could copy a seriated display left before

Stage   Construction or memory drawing

FIGURE 12–5   Stages in the Development of Seriation Behavior and Memory. (Adapted from *Memory and Intelligence* by Jean Piaget and Barbel Inkelder. ©1973 by Basic Books Inc., Publishers. Reprinted by permission of the publisher.)

them.) They found that children created drawings that reflected what they would be expected to do on the seriation task given their age. More surprisingly—even to Piaget and Inhelder—they found that as the children were retested at later ages, their drawings from memory improved, resulting finally in an accurate drawing of the seriated array seen months before. Figure 12-5 shows typical results, which have largely been confirmed by American replications (Liben, 1977).

The example, and Piaget's work on memory generally, illustrates the Piagetian view of all experience, including learning. Experience must, of course, affect a child, but experience is assimilated to existing schemes and/or operations, so that what a child can learn at a given time is conditioned by his or her operative stage. Ultimately, accommodation and equilibration change the child to more effectively fit reality, but this cannot be done all at once. The child can understand and learn from only experience that is at or just ahead of his or her cognitive stage, assimilating anything else in a form that can be understood. Again we find that Piaget's is a truly developmental theory, because development leads learning, and the latter can only be effective within bounds set by the former. (See Box 12-5).

Criticisms of Genetic Epistemology

Piaget's genetic epistemology has naturally attracted a great deal of criticism, ranging from accusations of poor design and sloppy methodology (Gruen, 1966) to findings that his formulation of symbolic logic is inad-

BOX 12–5   *TILTING A BOTTLE: RESULTS*

When Piaget asked children to do a task similar to that described in Box 12–3, he reported results as shown in Figure 12-6.

Stage	Age	Drawing

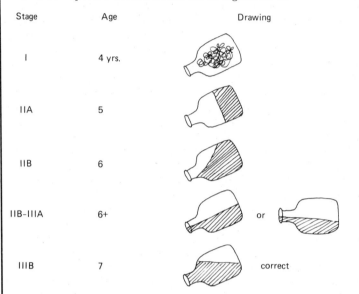

FIGURE 12–6   From "Television as a Moral Teacher" by Robert M. Liebert and Rita Wicks Poulos in MORAL DEVELOPMENT AND BEHAVIOR ED. by Thomas Lickona. Copyright ©1976 by Holt, Rinehart and Winston, CBS College Publishing.

Interestingly, however, when groups of adults are given this problem (having been a subject once, one of us (THL) has done this as a class demonstration for years) few of them get it right. Although no one gives the preschooler's response (Stage I), their responses cover Piaget's entire range of drawings, the most common being the IIB drawing and the IIB–IIIA drawings, the latter being possible, but not certainly, correct.

Piaget interpreted his results as reflecting *decentration*, the increasing ability of children to consider an ever larger frame of reference for their activities. The young child of five focuses (*centers*) narrowly on the bottle itself, defines the frame of reference for water level as the sides of the bottle, and maintains the familiar right-angle relationship of water surface and bottle side of a bottle standing up, even when the child is drawing a tilted bottle. This centration only gradually breaks up through intermediate stages, as the child realizes that something happens to the water's surface, but cannot yet grasp the correct frame of reference. That frame of reference is the surface of the earth: Water responds to gravity and so maintains a surface parallel to the ground whatever the orientation of the bottle.

If your results are typical, you caught many subjects' cognitive processes napping. Clearly a moment's reflection would reveal the absurdity of one's response to an adult who drew a Stage II drawing, but it appears that when they are not careful, people lapse back into earlier forms of thought. Such findings suggest again that real-world reasoning is a mixed bag of hunches, fancies, and misconceptions tainting a larger set of correct information processed in a rather haphazard fashion.*

*Read Jean Piaget and Bärbel Inhelder, *The Child's Conception of Space*. New York: Norton, 1967 (Originally published, 1948.)

equate (Parsons, 1960). Here, we will focus on attacks on Piaget's stage concept of development. Followers of Piaget have termed it a "key" part of the overall theory (Pinard & Laurendeau, 1969), and stage-thinking is characteristic of developmentalists generally. The central developmental force of equilibration is closely tied to the stages, since stage transitions come about because of equilibration, not learning. The postulation of real, explanatory stages is therefore perhaps the major issue that separates developmentalists from nondevelopmentalists.

Beginning with the simpler and more testable criteria, those concerning the ordered sequence of stages, we find that the empirical evidence is mixed. Criteria 3a and 3b from the list of criteria defining a true stage theory say the stage sequence must be culturally universal, and most cross-cultural Piagetian research indicates that children do pass through the stages up through concrete operations in the same sequence, with the speed of acquisition varying from culture to culture, usually as a function of degree of Westernization (Dasen, 1972). However, reaching the stage of formal operations is *not* a cross-culturally universal achievement, and the findings we discussed in Chapter 9 (Thinking) suggest that formal operations are not routinely used even by scientists. Therefore, criterion 3c is not met, formal operations remaining an ideal to be aimed at, rather than a realistically achievable goal. Criterion 3d states there must be no regression from a higher stage to a lower. Temporary regression has been observed by Inhelder, Bovet, and Sinclair (1974) in experiments challenging the thought of early concrete operational children, by replicators of Piaget's memory studies (Liben, 1977), and suggested by a cross-sectional study of acquisition of conservation of liquid problems (Leahey, 1977). While permanent regression would be a serious blow to Piaget's theory, temporary regressions may be only a sign of confused thought during the restructuring of cognitive structures taking place at stage transitions. On the other hand, an information-processing perspective could see temporary regressions as similar to overgeneralization phenomena in language acquisition when learning a new rule leads to apparent loss of mastery of irregular forms. So regression could be the result of an incremental learning process and not a mark of stage boundaries. On the whole, data regarding criterion 3 is equivocal, offering neither clear support nor disproof of Piaget's stage hypothesis.

Criterion 2 claims that each stage is more adequate than the previous one. This criterion is more philosophical than empirical, and seems uncontroversial (Flanagan, 1983). Piaget's stages are so constituted that if they are real, clearly formal operations are more adequate—more adaptive—than concrete operations, which in turn is better than preoperational thinking, which in turn, is an advance over sensory-motor intelligence.

The remaining criteria—that the stages are *qualitatively different* (1), that they form a *hierarchy* (4), and that each stage's structures form a *structured whole* (5)—are much more difficult to test and have been the subject of much controversy (Brainerd, 1978b, and subsequent commentary). Most observers agree that taken together, these criteria suggest that stages should appear relatively abruptly, as equilibration restructures thinking according to a new logic now applied to all experience. Three lines of research have been brought to bear on this empirical prediction: training studies, studies modifying the content of the standard Piagetian tasks, and studies of horizontal *decalages*, differences in the ages at which the same children master closely related cognitive tasks.

When Piaget attracted the attention of American psychologists during the cognitive revolution of the 1960s, they asked him a question that had not arisen during decades of research in Europe. The "American question," as Piaget called it, was: "How can we make the stages go faster?" Besides illustrating the American character, this question raises important issues about the unity of the stages (criterion 5) and the reality of equilibration. For if mastery of some Piagetian task (for example, conservation of liquid) can be taught, it would undermine the concept of stages as structured wholes—only a single task is mastered—and support a learning as opposed to an equilibration account of development. Success in training would also suggest that various cognitive skills are learned piecemeal rather than appearing as part of an overall stage change.

For both practical and theoretical reasons, therefore, studies attempting to train children on Piagetian tasks became very popular (Brainerd & Allen, 1971) and were even carried out at Geneva by Inhelder and her colleagues (Inhelder, et al., 1974). Overall, the studies show that a wide variety of techniques can be used to turn preoperational into operational reasoners for some skill area in a short period of time. However, interpreting these findings is difficult, since the results may be assimilated to Piagetian theory, and because there may be differences between trained and untrained children despite superficial similarities (Cromer, 1981).

Consider the classic training experiment by Smedslund (1961), who trained children on *conservation of weight*. In the standard Piagetian form, a child is shown two identical balls of clay that the child acknowledges to be of the same weight. Then one ball is transformed, typically by rolling it into a sausage, and the question is repeated. The preoperational subject will now deny equality of weight, usually claiming that the sausage shape is lighter because longer, even when the child can pick up the pieces. The concrete operational child conserves weight, pointing out that the experimenter only altered the appearance of the clay, not its weight.

Smedslund pretested children on the standard task and then put the nonconservers through a training phase in which he used a balance to demonstrate several times that weight is unaffected by shape, the two pieces of clay remaining equal in weight before and after transformation. The nonconservers came to say that weight remains unchanged in the standard task. Smedslund now repeated the standard task with all subjects, except he secretly removed some clay during the transformation and used the balance to show a difference in weight. Smedslund found that trained conservers quickly reverted to nonconservation, concluding that sometimes weight *does* change when shape is changed. Natural conservers, on the other hand, stood their ground, insisting that weight *must* remain the same and that the experimenter must have somehow cheated.

Smedlund's results suggest that even if a training program appears to be successful, it may have had only a surface effect, engaging a child's verbal agreement but leaving untouched the deeper cognitive processes that change with development. Inhelder et al. (1974) argue, and provide data to show, that training can be successful only when, first the child is nearing stage transition anyway, and second, when it induces cognitive conflict by challenging the child's preoperational understanding. By creating disequilibrium, equilibration is brought into play, and the child is accelerated into operational structures. Therefore, the successful training studies can be explained as the creation of superficial verbal change or acceleration of a deeper change already underway.

Another empirical difficulty for the unified stage hypothesis is that different methods of assessment from those of Piaget's often find Piagetian concepts at much earlier ages than the standard tasks. For example, early studies by Leahey and Gildenhorn (1969) and Gelman (1972) used conjuring techniques to violate conservation rules. Leahey and Gildenhorn showed that children as young as three were surprised that an experimenter could pour a large glass of milk into a smaller one and that the experimenter could turn six coins into 14. The children put these feats down to magical powers (the experimenter had a magic wand), which indicates that some sense of conservation of amount and number was present, even if it did not show up on standard tasks. Gelman found that very young children who failed ordinary number conservation tasks could detect when one penny was secretly removed from a small collection of coins (three or four), causing them to unfairly lose a game played with the experimenter, which indicates a sense of number conservation with small, but not large, arrays. There is now a large amount of data demonstrating similar effects for many Piagetian concepts (Gelman, 1978, 1983). Critics take such findings to indicate that concrete operational cognitive abilities are present very early in a child's life and grow slowly and incrementally, Piaget's apparently discrete stages being artifacts of his particular measurement tasks (Gelman, 1978; Donaldson, 1978). While these studies showed that some abilities appear much earlier than Piaget thought, other investigators found that adults do not understand some things they should (see Box 12–6).

This problem is linked to the broader and most serious one of what Genevans call *horizontal decalages*, or differences in the age of acquisition of behaviors supposedly depending on the same operational structures. A well-established *decalage* involves the conservations, all of which depend on

BOX 12–6   *INTUITIVE PHYSICS*

As children, most of us tied something heavy to a string, twirled it around our heads, and then let it go. How much do we actually *understand* about such a familiar bit of physics? Even if we learn to hit a target with our primitive sling, do we grasp the principles underlying our behavior? Figure 12-7 shows a man twirling a ball on a string and releasing it when the ball is at point *A*. Which path shown will the ball subsequently take, Path 1 or Path 2?

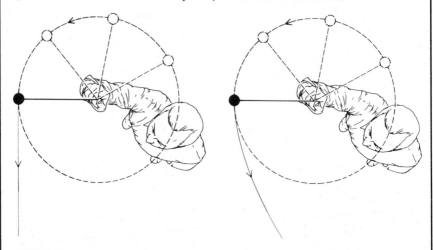

FIGURE 12–7   From "Intuitive Physics" *Scientific American* by Mc Closkey, Copyright ©1983. By Scientific American, Inc. All rights reserved.

Michael McCloskey (1983) asked college students this and other questions testing their intuitive knowledge of physics, specifically concerning the laws of objects in motion. Fifty-one percent correctly chose Path 1; 30 percent incorrectly chose Path 2, and 19 percent made other errors. Path 1 is correct because according to Newton's laws of motion an object once set in motion will continue in a straight line unless acted on by an outside force. As long as it is held, the string acts as such a force and the ball moves in a circle. When the string is released its constraining force vanishes and the ball moves in a straight line. Path 2 would be expected from medieval impetus theory, which held that the circular motion would persist after the string was released, resulting in a curved trajectory. In other experiments, McCloskey found that many, sometimes most, of his well-educated subjects' intuitive physics was closer to medieval natural philosophy than to modern physics. Even having passed physics courses did little to alter students' folk beliefs.

Such findings pose a special problem for Piagetian theory, especially its account of formal operations. For here are familiar situations (every child has spun objects on a string, thrown and caught balls, and dropped objects while moving, providing rich opportunities for accommodation, assimilation, and reflective abstraction), yet conscious understanding of such activities is weak.

They may be done—sensory-motorically—very well, even brilliantly as by sports stars, yet they are reflectively known very poorly.

In Piagetian terms, McCloskey's results provide further evidence that formal operations are not a universal achievement. Piaget has always held that at earlier stages consciousness knows only the products of cognitive operations, not the operations themselves. Here we see how hard it is for people to understaṇd what they may do very well, and conscious understanding is a formal operational achievement.

More broadly, we again are reminded of the surprising gulf between behavior and insight. Much of what we do is learned effortlessly and without tuition. Yet being able to explain what we do, to understand it consciously, requires great effort, the insights of genius and deliberate education. And it is disappointing to the professor and scientist to find that years of education leave many young people back in the Middle Ages, behind Newton and far behind Einstein.*

*Read Michael McCloskey, Intuitive physics. *Scientific American*, April 1983, 248, (4) 122–130.

concrete operational structures, according to Piaget. Table 12–2 shows the sequence of acquisition—stretching over at least five years—for several physical quantity conservations. Observe that all the tasks have the same structure: quantity A and A' are established as equal, the shape of A' is changed, and the subject B asked if the quantity is still the same. Conservation of substance and weight are especially similar, yet appear about three years apart. Even slight changes in the material used can change the child's response from nonconservation to conservation (Uzgiris, 1964).

Decalage can also appear across related tasks using the same materials. For example, Leahey (1977) tested the same children in grades N through 2 on four liquid conservation tasks: (1) the standard task; (2) a variant in which the vessel into which one of the first glasses is poured is covered with a sheath that keeps the child from seeing the new water level; (3) a level-prediction task in which the child is shown a glass of liquid and an empty glass of a different shape (for example, narrower and taller) and is asked how high the liquid will go if poured into the empty glass; and (4) a level-prediction task in which two differently shaped empty glasses are provided, and the child is told to fill each with the same amount from a large pitcher. In (3) and (4) the question is not accuracy of prediction but simply an indication that the level should be different in the direction appropriate to the shapes of the glasses. There was a regular sequence of ages at which the tasks were mastered from (3) to (4) to (2) to (1) across the entire age range.

The existence of *decalages* such as these suggests that cognitive development is not a very stagelike affair, proceeding, instead, in an incremental, but still orderly, way. Many critics of Piaget's stage concept have simply concluded that his stages should be taken as descriptive only, and that equilibration is unnecessary and is in any case a mysterious force (Brainerd, 1974a, 1974b, 1978a, 1978b; Flavell, 1971, 1977; Flavell & Wohlwill, 1969;

TABLE 12–2   *Decalage* in the Development of Physical Quantity Conservation
Problems

	APPROXIMATE AGE REQUIRED	TASK DESCRIPTION
1	6	*Conservation of discontinuous quanty* Child fills two identical vessels with the same number of discrete objects, such as marbles; experimenter pours contents of one glass into a differently shaped one and asks if contents still same in amount.
2	6½	*Conservation of substance* Child shown two identical balls of clay that he or she acknowledges to be the same in amount (or they are adjusted); experimenter transforms one ball into a sausage and asks if there is still just as much clay in each piece.
3	7	*Conservation of continuous quanty* Same as (1) except begin with vessels identically filled with a liquid.
4	9 to 10	*Conservation of weight* Same as (2) except questions concern weight of clay pieces.
5	10 to 11 (some data indicate concept not present in all college freshmen)	*Conservation of volume.* Begin with identical glasses of liquid and balls of clay. First ball placed in a glass; liquid level rises. Second ball deformed; subject asked (1) if deformed piece placed in glass how high will liquid rise? and (2) do the two pieces take up same amount of space?

Toulmin, 1971; Macnamara, 1976). Some neo-Piagetians have backed away from the stage hypothesis, asserting that while invariant sequence in the acquisition is an important part of Piaget's theory, the existence of large comprehensive stages is not (Gruber & Voneche, 1977), or have moved toward an information-processing view of cognitive development (Cellerier, 1972; Inhelder, 1972). Whatever the fate of Piaget's stages, however, the general question of the existence of stages is not resolved as yet (Flavell, 1982; Cairns & Valsiner, 1984). Simply because one stage theory is mistaken, it does not follow that there are no stages to be found. The notion is still an attractive one, especially for developmental psychologists who wish to clearly separate themselves from traditional students of learning.

Although Piaget's theory is resilient and capable—through revising accommodation—to assimilate a fair amount of challenging data and criticism (Beilin, 1980), it is now commanding less interest from developmental researchers. In particular, alternative accounts of cognitive development based on traditional, nondevelopmentalist principles of learning and cognition are being proposed, and we will briefly examine some examples.

Alternatives To Genetic Epistemology

Neo-Hullian behaviorism   One approach to cognitive development by traditional learning theorists derives from the work of followers of Clark Hull. Within the tradition of mediational behaviorism (Staats, 1964, 1975) such neo-behaviorists accept Hull's S-R framework, but elaborate on it by considering the existence and influence of covert, mediating s-r processes that take place in the brain and intervene between a received stimulus (S) and an overt response (R). One of the most widely cited studies in experimental child psychology concerns human discrimination learning and how it develops.

Hull's foremost pupil, Kenneth Spence, intensively studied animal discrimination learning, but unlike Hull, he suspected that his theory of animal discrimination learning might not apply to human beings because of our verbal abilities. Some of Spence's students, especially Howard and Tracy Kendler, set out to investigate Spence's hunch.

Consider the discrimination problem pictured in Figure 12-8. We may require an organism to discriminate the simuli shown under Preshift Training, rewarding responses (say, bar-pressing) only to the stimuli marked "+", and not those marked "−". Soon the organism will only press the bar when (+) stimuli are present and not otherwise. This is so far only simple discrimination learning as described earlier. After this initial learning, we then change the contingencies of reinforcement as shown under Postshift Training in one of two ways, each without informing the organism of the change, but simply requiring a new discrimination to be learned. In either case the reinforced responses are marked (+); the nonreinforced ones marked (−). The point of the experiment is to find out which kind of shift in contingencies will be more easily learned.

FIGURE 12–8 Discrimination Shift Learning Experiment Involving a Comparison Between a Reversal and a Nonreversal Shift. For each pair of stimuli, plus (1) indicates reinforcement follows a response to that stimulus; Minus (−) indicates nonreinforcement.

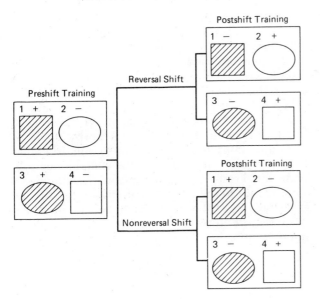

According to Hull's theory, as modified by Spence, what the learner acquires during preshift training is a set of S-R associations. The learner must learn to bar-press (R) to stimuli 1 and 3, but not to bar-press (−R) to stimuli 2 and 4. Four S-R habits are learned: (1) $S_1{\rightarrow}R$; (2) $S_2{\rightarrow}-R$; (3) $S_2{\rightarrow}R$; (4) $S_4{\rightarrow}-R$. Given these four habits, a learner should find the extradimensional shift easier. For in an extradimensional shift two habits are still correct, (1) $S_1{\rightarrow}R$ and (2) $S_2{\rightarrow}-R$, while two habits must be unlearned and replaced: (3) $S_3{\rightarrow}R$ is incorrect and must be replaced by $S_3{\rightarrow}-R$, and (4) $S{\rightarrow}-R$ is incorrect and must be replaced by $S_4{\rightarrow}R$. In a reversal shift, however, all the earlier habits must be unlearned and replaced with new ones.

Research on this problem revealed an interesting pattern. Animals in a discrimination shift procedure behaved as predicted by the simple S-R model, finding nonreversal shifts easier than reversal shifts. However, college students responded to the shifts the opposite way, preferring reversal to nonreversal shifts. Further, when children were the subjects, it was found that the younger the child the more he or she behaved according to S-R theory, that is, like animals. These findings present an anomaly for Hullian theory. Hull's laws of S-R learning were found not to be the same across different species or even across members of the same species at different ages.

Howard and Tracy Kendler (1962) proposed a mediational analysis of these findings. They suggested that the usual S-R laws, now called *single-stage* S-R laws, applied to animal learning, but that humans possess central and developing cognitive processes—including, most importantly, language—that modify the laws of learning. These central responses *mediate* between environmental stimuli and overt response. According to this model, an environmental stimulus elicits a central, covert symbolic response: $S{\rightarrow}r$. This central response has covert stimulus properties: $r{\rightarrow}s$. These stimulus properties then control overt behavior: $s{\rightarrow}R$. Thus, any cognitively mediated behavior is an associative chain of stimulus-response events some of which are covert: $S{\rightarrow}r{\rightarrow}s{\rightarrow}R$. It is assumed that central responses ($r{\rightarrow}s$) obey the same behavioral laws as overt responses ($S{\rightarrow}R$). According to this scheme, the brain functions like the body, only covertly.

The mediational apparatus may be used to explain the apparently anomalous behavior of the college students. The adult subject makes a mediational response (r) to the stimuli to be discriminated. We may regard these responses as implicit labels for the stimuli that categorize them according to the two stimulus dimensions defining the four stimuli. In Figure 12–3, two dimensions, brightness and shape, define the stimuli. The subject learns to make the mediational response "brightness" to the stimuli, because this is the dimension relevant to the preshift training where stippled figures are reinforced and white ones are not. The mediational association $r_{brightness} - s_{brightness}$ controls the terminal overt response: to press the lever when black stimuli are present. We may write what is learned as follows in S-R language.

$$S \rightarrow r \xrightarrow{\hspace{2cm}} s \xrightarrow{\hspace{2cm}} R$$

brightness   brightness   black (press lever)

What happens after each possible shift? In the reversal shift, brightness is still the relevant stimulus dimension, so the mediational response is correct, and all the subject must learn is a new terminal response, pressing the lever when the white stimuli are present:

$$S \rightarrow r \xrightarrow{\hspace{2cm}} s \xrightarrow{\hspace{2cm}} R$$

brightness   brightness   white (press lever)

However, when the shift is a nonreversal one, the terminal responses are wrong and the mediational response must learn the S-R chain:

$$S \rightarrow r \xrightarrow{\hspace{1cm}} s \xrightarrow{\hspace{1cm}} R$$

shape   shape   circle (press lever)

There is more to learn in the nonreversal shift, and so it naturally takes longer.

In general the Neo-Hullian regards development as the accumulation of learning. Human cognitive development is different from animal learning because human beings possess symbolic, mediating responses; nevertheless, mediators follow the usual laws of conditioning, and the development of thinking can be explained as the learning of a large number of mediating s-r connections. This theory posits no stages and has no need to invoke a developmental force such as equilibration. Developing from an infant to an adult is a matter of acquiring mediational responses and then piling them up.

Radical behaviorism   The radical behaviorist approach to cognitive development is a staightforward application of the principles of operant learning reviewed in Chapter 4 (see Bijou & Baer, 1968; Bijou, 1976). No special principles of development are invoked; no explanatory stages are postulated. The child is viewed as an organism emitting responses that are shaped by reinforcement contingencies into the behaviors characteristic of the adult in the child's culture. From the standpoint of the experimental analysis of behavior, developmental psychology scarcely exists, since the developmental psychologist is simply a behavior analyst who has chosen to study children instead of animals or adults.

Information processing   Since the early 1970s—Farnham-Diggory (1972) provides a useful starting point—information-processing concepts have been applied to cognitive development as cognitive science extended its influence over human experimental psychology. While as yet there is no generally accepted theory of development from this perspective (though Kail

Kail and Bisanz (1982) provide a beginning), two lines of research have been pursued by cognitive scientists writing information-processing accounts of Piagetian problems (Boden, 1978) and studying the development of standard information-processing topics such as memory (Kail, 1979).

As an example of the former approach (rethinking Piaget) we may take the work of Klahr and Wallace (1973, 1976) on the development of conservation. They view conservation as the induction of general rules—statements of conservations—reflecting what is learned about the invariance of physical properties despite apparent transformations.

Klahr and Wallace endow the young information processor with three **quantification operators** whose operations provide the data base for learning conservation rules. The first operator is *subitizing*, which applies only to very small arrays of discrete objects, never more than four. Subjects presented with such small displays just see without counting that there are 1, 2, 3, or 4 objects, even with very brief display times. The next quantification operator is *counting*, applicable in principle to any array of discrete objects, but under time limitation abandoned in favor of the third operator, *estimation*: No one tries to count the beans in a jar of jelly beans. Estimation also applies to continuous quanties, such as liquid amount, which cannot be quantified by subitizing or counting.

In each of its domains, conservation rule learning develops in the following manner. The child quantifies an array (for example, two rows of six jelly beans each, by counting), sees one altered, as in the usual Piagetian task, and quantifies again, getting the same result. Eventually, repeated experience leads to rule induction: Number (or whatever attribute is at issue) remains invariant despite changes in appearance. The motivation for forming conservation rules is *economy of processing*. Simply knowing that a property is conserved eliminates the need for constant quantifications and comparisons.

The rule-learning approach easily explains some of the data—particularly the *decalages*—so troublesome for Piaget. Since development is seen as gradual (the slow accumulation of conservation rules) there is no reason to be troubled by an absence of sharp stage boundaries. Moreover, the observed *decalages* fit well with the theory. Subitizing is the most primitive quantification operator, possessed before counting is taught, and we found that very young children conserve small arrays but not larger ones. At the other extreme, a quantity like *volume* is very hard to estimate and is the last conservation learned, while more tangible, estimatable quanties such as *weight* form a middle ground between number and volume.

However, the Klahr-Wallace theory faces difficulties. For example, estimation operators are quite inaccurate even in adults (Leahey, 1978), so that for liquid amount, for example, the same amount is estimated differently depending on the shape of the glass. If so, in the nonconserver the estimator would usually produce different estimates of the same amount in different vessels leading a child to conclude that conservation does *not* hold. Nevertheless, the information-processing approach has provided usefully detailed analyses of the skills underlying various Piagetian problems and has been extended to new domains (Klahr, 1980).

The second kind of research done in cognitive development by information processors is to watch children doing the same things researchers get adults to do: remember, pay attention, comprehend, and so on (Cairns & Valsiner, 1984). The picture that emerges is rather undevelopmental: Children are incompetent adults. That is, they possess (to use the computer metaphor quite strongly) all the wiring of the adult computer, but have yet to learn the control strategies to use it efficiently. To take a simple example, young (preoperational) children have short memory spans, about three or four items, because they have not learned to rehearse. If they are taught how, their memory spans leap up to the usual adult level—six or seven items. The short-term storage capacity of the adult was there, but was not being used (Hagen, 1972).

One aspect of information processing that was first investigated by child psychologists is **metacognition** (Flavell, 1979), particularly *metamemory* (Flavell & Wellman, 1977; Cavanaugh & Perlmutter, 1982). All of us have ideas, whether right or wrong, about how we think and remember. For example, college students know they remember telephone numbers by rehearsal long before they have taken Psychology 101. Similarly, we each have beliefs about how we solve problems or study for tests, and about what sorts of games or puzzles we are good at. Since these beliefs are beliefs *about* cognition and memory, they count as *meta*cognitition and *meta*memory. Obviously, metacognition develops. Young children who do not rehearse cannot believe they rehearse, and it probably takes some later experience with rehearsing when the skill develops before they can articulate the knowledge of what they are doing when remembering a list of words or numbers.

Studies of metamemory suggest again that the basic structure of the human information processor is innate and that cognitive development is mostly a matter of accumulating experience in long-term memory organizing and drawing generalizations from it, and learning how to use it effectively. This suggests slow, gradual development rather than stages punctuated by qualitative shifts in mode of thought.

Nevertheless, even without stages and equilibration to worry about, the greatest challenge facing the cognitive scientist studying development is how the processor changes at all. It is easy to write a simulation of the age 4 nonconserver and of the age 10 conserver; it is very much harder to get model 1 to change by itself into model 2, as the developing child does.

A sketch of an answer—it is no more than a sketch—has been essayed by Kail and Bisanz (1982). Figure 12-9 schematizes their proposed *transitional system*. As we learned in earlier chapters, the major bottleneck in human information processing is the limited amount of attentional resources we have to allocate to different tasks. In the view of Kail and Bisanz, cognitive development is driven by dealing with this bottleneck, through maturational growth in total amount of resources (as the brain matures), or through increased availability of resources within an unchanging capacity as mental processes that were once conscious become unconscious and automatic—*automatized*—reducing their demand for attention.

Increased availability of attentional resources both facilitates and is made possible by **knowledge modification processes**. These are the agents

FIGURE 12–9   Factors in Cognitive Development According to Information-processing Theory. (After Kail & Bisanz, 1982, Academic Press)

of cognitive development, and they consist of two main operations; first, adding or deleting memory nodes and connections (representations) in LTM, or control processes; and second, stregthening or weakening connections in LTM. Change is abetted by the *performance monitors* that detect *inconsistencies* to be eliminated, such as believing whales are fishes while knowing they are warm blooded and nurse live-born young, or *regularities* that can be more simply handled, (as when a conservation rule is induced based on observed regularities in quantification operations), in the Klahr and Wallace model of conservation.

While there is a residual Piagetian flavor to the model—the inconsistency detector is likened to equilibration—it is clear that the information-processing approach is far less developmentalist than genetic epistemology, though more developmentalist than radical behaviorism. There are no stages, no large-scale cognitive reorganization of thinking. In this view, children learn about the world—that is, store information—gradually and piecemeal, and equally gradually learn and sort out efficient information-processing strategies. It is likely, too, that the information-processing theory will make less universalist claims that Piaget. Beyond having to deal with roughly the same laws of nature all around the world, there is no reason to think that any two people, much less any two cultures, will arrive at the same information stored in LTM and the same strategies for dealing with it. There are bound to be many individual and cultural differences in information processing, and discovering what they are should prove most interesting (Laboratory of Comparative Human Cognition, 1979).

PERSONAL AND MORAL DEVELOPMENT

Although several of the most important developmentalist theories— Freud's, Erikson's, and Kohlberg's—fall somewhat outside the range of learning and cognition, they merit some attention precisely because they challenge standard notions of behavioral and cognitive learning. And, of course, we must remember that much of what a person learns in the course of development has to do with feelings, attitudes, and values, problems that ultimately even information-processing psychology will have to cope with. In this section we will briefly review the most important developmental theories in this area, and then contrast them with an influential and heuristically successful nondevelopmentalist alternative—*social learning theory.*

Personality Development: Psychoanalysis

Sigmund Freud and biogenesis[2]   Freud proposed a theory of development based on a concept that we know today to be false. It was, however, extremely popular in Freud's time, and some people still unwittingly believe it: Ernst Haeckel's biogenetic law. Haeckel was the leading nineteenth-century exponent of evolutionary theory in Germany, and his biogenetic law is based on Lamarck's theory of evolution in which species improve over time by accumulating favorably acquired traits learned by each generation. The biogenetic law stated that, "Ontogeny [the development of an individual] is a short and quick repetition, or recapitulation of Phylogeny [the evolution of a species] . . ." (quoted by Flanagan, 1981). Haeckel's law is (falsely) appealing because embryos do seem to pass through stages in which they resemble "lower" evolutionary forms. So a developing human embryo goes through a phase when it resembles a fish, then a lizard, then a lower mammal, and at the earliest stages of embryonic development different mammals resemble each other very closely, reflecting shared common ancestors, and resemble each other less at later stages of development, reflecting their ancestor's branching off the evolutionary tree (Sulloway, 1979). Haeckel also proposed that the units of heredity carry "unconscious memories" of the experiences of past ancestors; Freud took up this idea, turning it into a general theory of personality development that is very biological and maturational in character.

---

[2]The importance of childhood and concepts of development are so important to psychoanalysis that they lie explicitly or implicitly in almost every line Freud wrote, but he never sat down and wrote on development per se. Certain works are, nevertheless, somewhat more developmental in their concerns than others, and these are: *Three Essays on the Theory of Sexuality, The Ego and the Id,* "Some Psychological Consequences of the Anatomical Distinction Between the Sexes," *A General Introduction to Psychoanalysis* (Chapters 20 to 23), *Civilization and Its Discontents* (Chapter 8), and *Outline of Psychoanalysis* (Chapters 3, 5, 7). Sigmund's daughter, Anna, became a great psychoanalyst in her own right, and prepared a work, *Psychoanalysis for Teachers and Parents,* which provides the sort of child-rearing tutoring her father seldom offered. She was also the major force behind the development of child analysis, and every year a new volume in the series *The Psychoanalytic Study of the Child* appears, containing papers on various aspects of developmental psychoanalysis.

Useful secondary sources include Rapaport (1960) and Talbott (1982) who review the analytic and neoanalytic approach to development, and Loevinger and Knoll (1983), who review the most recent data.

Finally, one should consult Frank Sulloway's tremendous *Freud: Biologist of the Mind* for a detailed study of Freud as a Lamarckian, biological developmentalist.

As is well known, Freud proposed a stage theory of human development (see Figure 12–10), and he viewed the stages as the biogenetic unfolding of the past phylogenetic history of the human species. Freud is quite explicit on this. Speaking of the first (oral) stage of development and the attachment to the mother brought about by the infant's gratification at mother's breast, he wrote, "In all this the phylogenetic foundation has so much the upper hand over personal accidental experiences that it makes no difference whether a child has really sucked at the breast of has been brought up on the bottle . . . In both cases the child's development takes the same path . . ." (Freud, 1949, pp. 45–46).

The developmental recapitulation of the past is not unilineal and free from conflict. On the contrary, it is full of storm and stress because alongside innate instinctual development there is innate moral development, providing inherent disgust and shame over the perverse sexual desires of developing libido (Freud, 1962; Rapaport, 1960). To use modern terms, all that individual experience can do is act on an organism prepared to learn certain things at specific critical periods of development, but the basic course of development is set by biology.

Freud thought of sexuality not as a single instinct aiming at reproduction, but as a collection of component instincts rooted in different erotogenic zones that must pass through a complex developmental sequence before they fuse—at least in the normal human—into adult reproductive sexuality. Freud believed that a biological timetable, repeating the phylogeny of the past, activated each erotogenic zone in a fixed, universal sequence, and he defined each stage around the erotogenic zone dominant at that period. Each stage recreates in the individual a mode of life from the distant evolutionary past. For example, the oral stage recreates the mode of life of simple asexual organisms that feed by constant ingestion of food into an opening designed for the purpose, a sort of mouth.

The first two stages of development are the **oral** and the **anal,** and are referred to as the pregenital phases in which development is the same for males and females. Sexuality—by which Freud meant the getting of any sort of physical pleasure—is centered first on the oral erotogenic zone, the mouth, and then the anal erotogenic zone, the anus, as the child gets pleasure from sucking (of which Freud took a very different view than did Piaget; see Box 12–7) and biting (especially the mother's nipple and one's own fingers) and then withholding and releasing feces. Sexuality is also said to be narcissistic, as the child gratifies itself and no other. During these phases the child develops a deep primary attachment to its mother as the one who feeds, pleases, and consoles.

The next stage is the **phallic** stage, Freud's msot controversial, in which the development of boys and girls takes different paths. The boy's path is the less troublesome one, though not lacking for conflict from both innate moral factors and social demands. Biogenetic development activates the penis as the dominant erotogenic zone, and, in a still narcissistic way, the boy begins to masturbate. At the same time the first stirrings of genital sexuality appear, and sexual desire is aroused toward mother, already loved as caretaker and comforter Any such union would be incestuous,

	ERIKSON			FREUD	PIAGET
APPROXIMATE AGE	ZONE AND MODE	CRISIS	INSTITUTION		
Infancy 0–2	Oral-sensory	Basic trust vs. mistrust	Religion	Oral	Sensory-motor
Early childhood 2–3	Muscular-anal	Autonomy vs. shame and doubt	Law	Anal	Preoperational
Middle childhood 3–6	Locomotor-genital	Initiative vs. guilt	Economics	Phallic	
Late childhood 6–12	Latency	Industry vs. Inferiority	Technology	Latency	Concrete operational
Adolescence 12–18	Puberty and Adolescence	Identity vs. role confusion	Ideology and Aristocracy	Genital	Formal operational
Youth 18–25	Young adulthood	Intimacy vs. isolation	[Courtship]		
Adult & middle-age 25–65	Adulthood	Generativity vs. stagnation	[Education]		
65–	Maturity	Ego integrity vs despair	[?]		

FIGURE 12-10 Three Stage Theories

BOX 12–7   *THUMBSUCKING: SEX OR COGNITION?*

One of the fascinating things in comparing two psychological theories is to watch two great theorists treat the same phenomenon. Both Freud (1962) and Piaget (1963) describe and explain thumbsucking in their own ways.

Freud regarded thumbsucking as the classic example of pregenital autoerotic behavior. The mouth is an erotogenic zone, and sucking at mother's breast gives the child sensuous joy as well as nutriment. In adulthood, the sexual nature of the mouth is revealed in kissing, and the importance one attaches to kissing is a function of the kind of oral stimulation received as a child. Certain adult behaviors concerning the mouth, such as overeating or undereating, drinking, and sucking, are traceable to the oral stage.

Like Freud, Piaget observed how children repeatedly suck their thumbs, but he saw in it not sexual development but cognitive development. Thumbsucking requires motor and hand-eye coordination, and a distinction between self and outside world. Specifically, thumbsucking is a *primary circular reaction* (see Table 12–1). It also expresses *functional assimilation*, the tendency to repeat a sensori-motor sequence until it is mastered.

Who is right? Should parents be dismayed by their infant's autoerotism or elated by the infant's cognitive progress? Obviously, both explanations may be correct at the same time; we may accept Freud's description of the motive for thumbsucking and Piaget's description of the cognitive skill needed to satisfy the motive. But parents are advised to follow Piaget. Contrary to some earlier views, thumbsucking does no dental harm, and its little sensuous pleasure seems harmless enough. Moreover, knowing Piaget and his theory enriches the experience of being a parent, and it provides daily pleasures as parents watch as their child acquires new skills and gradually masters itself and its world.

and innate factors and society's incest taboo engender feelings of guilt in the young child. According to Freud, the imagined punishment is loss of his penis, castration, reinforced by discovering that girls do not—as the boy had egocentrically assumed—have penises, and perhaps by actual parental threats of castration, probably made to discourage masturbation. The tremendous resulting *castration anxiety* smashes the Oedipus complex—the boy's desire for his mother and fear and hatred of the father as a rival for her—bringing on latency, which is also a biogenetic recapitulation of the ice age, during which sexuality dampens down.

At puberty, biological development reawakens sexuality in the genital stage, and all the component instincts come together under command of reproductive sexuality, which seeks out a new partner for love, affection, and child rearing. In abnormal individuals, in whom the Oedipus complex is repressed instead of smashed, puberty brings on either abnormal sexual behavior, such as homosexuality or fetishisms, neurosis, or a narcissistic inability to love another.

The developmental path of females is less certain and is strewn with obstacles. The chief problem they face is that unlike boys they must abandon their initial attachment to mother and redirect it to father. Since adult choice of a partner to an extent repeats the choice of childhood, the turning of the young girl from mother to father is crucial to the development of her sexuality, and it greatly complicates her sexual development.

For reasons that remain unclear, Freud rejected the obvious biological hypothesis, held by many scientists today, that heterosexuality or homosexuality is innate (Sulloway, 1979). Instead, he advanced the following' rather more complicated, less plausible hypothesis (Freud, 1950), which perhaps says more about the Victorian estimation of women than about child development.

Castration anxiety—what destroys the male Oedipus complex—is the event that triggers it in the female. When she discovers that her clitoris—activated by maturation—is a poor imitation of a male's penis, she is at once overwhelmed by **penis envy,** desiring to have one and coveting it in all boys. She feels that she herself has been castrated and, blaming her mother for her mutilation, transfers her affections to her father, which take on a sexual tone with her first genital sexuality. But her desire and love are tinged with envy of her father's possession of a penis, so she feels inferior to him in a way a boy never does toward his mother during his Oedipal phase.

Observe now that there is no force to smash a girl's Oedipus complex; it can only be repressed, with unfortunate implications for her adult personality. A woman is more likely to become neurotic than a man, and can find true happiness only in submission to a patriarchal husband, reliving her Oedipal fantasies. Latency is entered more slowly, as ontogeny recapitulates phylogeny, and incest taboos repress her incestuous desires.

One more difficult transition lies ahead, however. At puberty, genital sexuality reawakens, but the girl must renounce her clitoral sexuality, as it is an imitation of male genital sexuality, and find sexual satisfaction in her vagina. Indeed, Freud (1962) went so far as to say that sexual drive—*libido*—is inherently masculine, so that any woman who retains her clitoris as her adult sexual zone is necessarily abnormal. If she can achieve this second transformation of her sexual life, penis envy will become a desire to bear a child, particularly a male child, fulfilling indirectly her old longing.

For both men and women, the Oedipal period is the most important one. Difficulties at this stage lead later to full-blown neuroses, psychoses, or sexual aberrations—true mental illnesses. Difficulties at pregenital stages lead only to less severe character disorders such as narcissism. The stage is also crucial to the formation of a person's internal moral agent, the **super-ego.** Especially in the boy, the Oedipus complex strengthens identification with the same-sex parent—he wants to be like his father because his father already possesses mother and because he fears him as the enforcer of moral law. A girl's relations with each parent are a good deal more ambivalent—and the child *introjects,* or takes into itself the values of the parent. Again, Freud also offers a Lamarckian explanation of morality, arguing that the superego is a residue of moral prohibitions—especially that against incest—laid down in the ancestral past:

> One gets an impression from civilized children that the constructions of these (moral) dams is a product of education, and no doubt education has much to do with it. But in reality this development is organically determined and fixed by heredity, and it can occasionallly occur without any help at all from education. (Freud, 1962, pp. 43–44).

In closing our discussion of Freud's stage theory of personality development, we should be careful not to interpet his scheme too rigidly. He was aware of *decalages* in the development of the sexual instincts. He said that the stages often "overlap" and may even occur "alongside" one another, and that the process of fusion of instincts under a genital organization begins in the phallic stage and is only completed at puberty. Therefore, as with Piaget's stages, the divisions between psychosexual stages should be seen as fuzzy, not sharp and distinct, and the ages shown in Figure 12–5 read as rough approximations only.

Erik Erikson and epigenesis   Freud had many followers, and one of them, Erik Erikson, turned Freud's theory of psychosexual development into a broader perspective on *psychosocial* development (Erikson, 1963). Like Piaget, Erikson describes his theory as one of **epigenesis,** although following Freud he takes a stronger biological position than Piaget:

> [T]his evolutionary principle of epigenesis . . . governs the unfolding before birth of the organic basis for all behavior and continues after birth to govern the unfolding of an individual's social potentialities in the successive encounters of impulse systems and cultural realities. (Erikson, 1939, pp. 131–132; quoted in Rapaport, 1960, p. 217).

While Lamarckianism and biogenesis have had to be abandoned, Erikson retains Freud's belief that development is an unfolding of given potential, which qualifies him as a true developmentalist.

Erikson's proposed stage sequence is also given in Figure 12–5, and will be briefly summarized. The first five stages—of childhood—build closely on Freud's foundations, but the remaining stages break new ground in proposing for the first time that development does not stop at puberty, a recognition at long last fully realized in the new field of life-span developmental psychology. Erikson defines his stages (at least the first five) around erotogenic zones, and their major modes of functioning, the latter in addition to Freud's narrower perspective (Rapaport, 1960). Associated with each stage is a crisis, the happy resolution of which leads to a personality strength, and the unhappy resolution of which leads to a weakness. Finally, reflecting Erikson's larger social concerns, each strength-weakness pair has associated with it a societal institution that embodies and expresses it in adult life.

The first stage is the **oral-sensory,** primarily a stage of dependence and passivity in which the child simply ingests food (through the mouth) and information (through the senses). The crisis concerns trust versus mistrust: The helpless infant learns either that the world is basically a good place that meets his or her needs, something one can trust, or that it is a hostile, dangerous place, deserving mistrust. As with all the stages, resolving the crisis involves setting a proper balance between the poles defined by it. Here, for example, while one will clearly be happier if one trusts the world, some level of mistrust is required to avoid its real dangers. The basic attitudes of trust or mistrust will be found in a culture's *religion,* which paints a picture of the universe as benign or malignant.

The next stage is the **muscular-anal,** in which children gain control of their large muscles. The prototype is control of the anal sphincters, and the child's learning to hold on or let go of its feces. Toilet training invokes the first serious conflict between the child's impulses and society's rules, and it defines the period's crisis of autonomy, of feeling that I can manage myself, versus shame and doubt, of feeling that I am ashamed of my failures and am riddled with doubts about self-control. The parallel institution is, naturally enough, *law,* the body of rules a society imposes on its citizens. Again, it is a favorable ratio of traits that is ideal; autonomy is important, but there are things we can do that we ought not to do, and a sense of shame over them is morally appropriate.

Morality is also involved in the third stage, the **locomotor- genital.** As the child learns to control fine muscle movements, the child can seize the *initiative* to carry out plans and pursue ambitions. On the other hand, some ambitions are evil, too coercive of others, to be right, and so the balance to initiative is *guilt,* an internalized voice of right and wrong, the super ego. The institutional embodiment of initiative is economics, referring not to the "dismal science," but to a given society's means of production in which ambitions may be realized.

As with Freud, the anatomical differences between the sexes now separate the developmental paths of boys and girls. In keeping with his genitals, the boy develops an active, thrusting, aggressive kind of initiative; in keeping with her genitals, the girl is more passive and receptive. In support of his idea, Erikson noted how differently boys and girls play with blocks at this stage. The boy builds tall towers—often too tall—and enjoys toppling them. The girl builds shorter, more open structures, the action coming as people and animals intrude into the defined space.

Latency is seen more positively by Erikson than by Freud. Precisely because it is mostly devoid of sexuality, Freud thought it a stage in which little of psychosexual consequence could happen. But from his psychosocial viewpoint, Erikson sees it as an important stage, the one in which education begins, and in simpler cultures is usually completed. The crisis is between *industry,* learning to become a productive member of society, versus *inferiority,* feeling worthless and unproductive. Technology, in the sense of the productive skills and tools a culture has, is the institution that embodies the crisis.

In the stage of **puberty and adolescence,** we find Erikson's best-known crisis, the *identity crisis,* between identity, a sense of self and purpose, of knowing who one is and what to do with one's life, *versus* role confusion, in which one is confused about one's identity and one's future. As the wider world opens out before the adolescent, questioning—perhaps confusion—sets in as the child becomes an adult who must function independently. Our society seems to have special trouble handling this stage, partly because there are so many roles available, and partly because our extended education imposes a prolonged moratorium on growing up, awkwardly trapping adolescents between childhood and adulthood. Consider that if one is going to be a professional, such as a doctor, lawyer, or scientist, education involves four years of college, four to six years of graduate school, and perhaps a year of postdoctoral training. So young men or women may be nearing age 30 by the time they are really on their own. The institutions related to the identity crisis are *ideology* and *aristocracy*. Ideologies are often popular with adolescents, since they appear to answer all questions and provide a framework for living. Aristocracy also helps define the self as commitment to a well-defined in-group. High schools are collections of cliques and lonely outsiders, each clique defining itself as special and superior. Aristocracy and ideology may merge in political activity, as adolescents may commit themselves to a cause pursued by a cadre of like-minded friends.

Young adulthood brings the task of forming a family, of establishing a deep relation of *intimacy* with another person, or of remaining in the cold *isolation* of oneself. While Erikson is not explicit on the issue, it seems likely that the relevant social institution is *courtship,* the social practices that bring men and women together as couples. In many cultures, courtship is well defined, even ritualistic. In modern America—perhaps due to the length of education—there are few rules, and many young adults have trouble forming a soundly intimate relationship, as our divorce rate suggests.

The longest state is **adulthood,** in which one achieves *generativity*—achieving ambitions and rearing children—or falls into *stagnation,* accomplishing nothing of real worth. The broad task and institution here is *education,* although Erikson again is not explicit. Ideally, one is producing something valuable to leave to the next generation while socializing children into their culture.

Finally, with **maturity** one faces death. One looks back on one's life with a sense of ego-integrity, if one's life is whole, and was well spent, or of despair, if one has failed and wishes to start again. Erikson specifies no embodying institution, and the question mark contained in Figure 12–5 suggests that we may have no institution concerned with the mature. As longevity increases in the Western world (when Social Security was enacted the life expectancy past retirement was but two years) older people seem to be at a loss about what to do, and society at a loss about how to cope with this new kind of citizen. Society now faces the task of formulating institutions and practices to integrate the mature with the rest of society and to prevent boredom and despair being part of their later years.

Conclusions   While both Freud's and Erikson's theories of development have their attractions and have exerted undeniable influence on psychology and society (Box 12–8), neither is entirely satisfactory. Freud's ac-

BOX 12–8   *IS NARCISSISM THE DISORDER OF OUR TIMES?*

The classic neurotic of Freud's time—the hysteric (conversion-reaction)—is virtually unknown today. Rather, analysts are seeing more and more patients with a certain character disorder, *narcissism.* Narcissism does not mean self-love in the sense of glorifying one's self, of thinking well of one's self, but a more passive involvment with one's self—seeing one's self as the natural center of the universe, seeing others as mirrors of one's self or tools of self-gratification, and a reveling in one's experience without commitment to others or to real action. The narcissist is the opposite of the vain, ambitious person, for ambition accomplishes something. The narcissist typically entertains grandiose fantasies about being famous or powerful (but the emphasis is on *being*) and no ambitious path of action is undertaken or prepared for. In Freudian terms, the narcissist is stuck in infancy, when everything was done for one, and all one's needs were met: One was then the center of the universe and had to do nothing to earn that place.

Culture critics Richard Sennett (1977) and Christopher Lasch (1978) contend that narcissism is the disorder of our age; in Freud's time everyone was at least a little neurotic; today, everyone is at least a little narcissistic. In Lasch's phrase, we live in a *culture of narcissism.*

Just looking at ourselves seems to confirm these critics' conclusion. People are tied up in projecting the right image—choosing the right designer clothes, driving the right car, joining the right clubs—rather than in objective accomplishment. People cultivate their bodies at spas and health clubs, their personalities at "growth" seminars and "personal development" workshops. Modern therapy suggests sharing feelings, not thoughts. In advertising, praise is conveyed when an actor says he or she "feels good" about a product. In one ad, a woman wishes she "felt better" about her laxative, not that she had a more *effective* one. In TV and movies what counts is expressing one's feelings, in having feelings, not in doing something or having thoughts.

Politics well reveals contemporary narcissism. The narcissist cannot separate attitude from action, feeling from accomplishment. And we citizens, sharing in this syndrome, wonder how an apparently good man such as President Reagan can pursue policies that seem to hurt so many. And if we oppose him we may force ourselves to believe he is insincere, or a dupe of more sinister interests. Such thinking betrays our own narcissism—*being* good must lead to *doing* good, and we have all too often elected deeply sincere people, good, honest people who just do not accomplish anything.

While the portrait drawn by Lasch and Sennett may be too harsh (Battan, 1983), there is truth in it. One unfortunate legacy of psychoanalysis is its focus on the self and its emotions, on our inner lives instead of on what we do. So in our age, as in the ancient Hellenistic world, we have turned from a confusing burdensome world that seems to offer us little to accomplish, and turn inward, making ourselves our egocentric life-work of art.*

*Read Christopher Lasch, *The Culture of Narcissism: American Life in an Age of Diminishing Expectations,* New York: Norton, 1978.

count of development is, of course, seriously undermined by the fact that Lamarckianism and biogenesis are wrong. Yet without ontogeny recapitulating phylogeny there is nothing to make development go. Erikson, while avoiding the explicit mistake of citing biogenesis, winds up with a mysterious epigenesis, or "unfolding," of innate potential. Certainly, the claim for a biological basis for development weakens after the locomotor-genital stage, and individual circumstance and cultural influence loom much larger as determinants of development. Erikson has also been accused of being too optimistic, idealistic, even Pollyanna-ish, missing the darker, tragic side of life that Freud limned so well (Roazen, 1976). For example, Paul Roazen asks why maturity should be quiet resignation to the inevitable, isolated detachment, or *ataraxia,* as the Greeks called it. More productive might be anger at past mistakes, an attempt to remedy them or at least to teach others not to repeat them. Finally, while Freud's theory is impressive (if wrong) by being quite detailed, Erikson seems to get by with liberal sentiments and scientific hand wavings, offering a vision of development, not a theory of it (Roazen, 1976).

Moral Development: Lawrence Kohlberg

One of Freud's legacies to psychology was his treatment of morality as part of emotional and personality development. His focus on the feelings associated with morality, especially shame and guilt, has continued to be the focus of even anti–Freudian developmental psychologists. But as almost any philosopher of ethics would remind us, morality has a strong intellectual element, at the very least in weighing moral ends and calculating the best means to them. Influenced more by Piaget than Freud, Lawrence Kohlberg has redressed the imbalance—indeed, has probably gone too far—by offering a cognitive developmental view of moral development.

One of Piaget's methods for investigating children's levels of moral understanding was to present them with a little moral anecdote and then ask the child questions about it. So the child might be told that while helping her parents prepare for a party, Sarah inadvertently broke a dozen records, while in a contrasting case Becky broke one record while playing in a closet she knew was forbidden to her. Subjects are asked which child had done the naughtier deed, which should be punished more, and why? Up until about age nine, children, in Piaget's terms, are **moral realists,** weighing right and wrong solely in relation to the objective damage done. So in the story above, Sarah is more in the wrong and more to be punished because she broke more records than Becky. After about age nine, children become **moral relativists,** judging actions more in relation to the virtue of the intent behind them. The moral relativist reverses the judgment of the moral realist, recognizing that Sarah was trying to be helpful, breaking the records out of clumsiness only, and condemning Becky's willful flouting of a clear rule, however slight the actual damage.

Beginning in 1958, Kohlberg (1958, 1971, 1976; Kohlberg & Kramer, 1969; Rosen, 1980) has developed the Piagetian cognitive-developmental approach to morality into an articulate theory of moral development, including the assessment of stage of moral reasoning, a theory of stage-change, and plans for improving individuals' moral judgments.

Kohlberg's assessment instrument—revised several times since 1958—is a more structured form of Piaget's clinical method. A child (or adult) is presented with a series of dilemmas turning on a moral issue (for example, is it right for a poor man to steal a rapaciously priced drug in order to save his dying wife?) and has to choose and defend a particular course of action, or condemn its opposite. These dilemmas are meant to measure a person's moral *reasoning* only, and not *his* likely moral *behavior* (all the subjects studied by Kohlberg in 1958 and his continuing longitudinal study are *male*, a point of some later importance). Kohlberg is interested in the structure of moral thinking, and as we shall soon find, the same style of moral reasoning may yield different prescriptions for moral action; data surveyed by Blasi (1980) indicate at best a modest relationship between Kohlberg's stage and moral behavior.

What has emerged from the application of this scale to a great many subjects in several cultures is a multistage theory of the development of moral reasoning rather more complex than Piaget's. Kohlberg has proposed somewhat different stage sequences in different publications over the years, and Table 12–3 shows every stage ever proposed, whether or not Kohlberg is presently committed to it. There are three *levels* of morality, divided into two or three substages each. Empirically, the preconventional levels are found in childhood, the conventional levels in most adults, and postconventional levels in a few superior men and women. The table speaks pretty well for itself, so we will comment only upon certain difficult points.

The ambiguous connection between moral reasoning and behavior exists at all stages, but may be easily illustrated at Stage 3. With regard to whether a drug may morally be stolen to save a spouse's life, a Stage 3 subject may reason his or her way to either answer. A person at this stage measures right and wrong against conventional social stereotypes of correct behavior (for example, a Nice Girl does not kiss on the first date), and there is often more than one stereotype available. In this dilemma, if we evaluate the "thief" against the stereotype of the Good Citizen, we must condemn that person because Good Citizens do not lie, cheat, steal, or swindle. On the other hand, if we evaluate the person against the stereotype of the Good Husband, we will hold him in the right, since the Good Husband loves, protects, and cares for his wife. Because behavior is variable while the structure of reasoning is the same, Kohlberg has chosen to study the development of the former only.

Positing a Stage 4½ (sometimes called 4B) was an awkward step forced on Kohlberg by the depth of his commitment to the cognitive-developmental research program. One of the hard-core assumptions of Piaget's stage theory was that cognitive development proceeds universally through a fixed series of stages showing no regression from an attained higher stage to a lower one. (Having just read Freud's theory, the alert reader may detect a whiff of the biogenetic law.) However, in following Kohlberg's initial adolescent sample (Kohlberg, 1958) into their thirties,

TABLE 12–3   Definition of Moral Stages

I.   PRECONVENTIONAL LEVEL

At this level the child is responsive to cultural rules and labels of good and bad, right or wrong, but interprets these labels in terms of either the physical or the hedonistic consequences of action (punishment, reward, exchange of favors), or in terms of the physical power of those who enuciate the rules and labels. The level is divided into the following two stages:

STAGE 1: *The punishment and obedience orientation.* The physical consequences of action determine its goodness or badness regardless of the human meaning or value of these consequences. Avoidance of punishment and unquestioning deference to power are valued in their own right, not in terms of respect for underlying moral order supported by punishment and authority (the latter being Stage 4).

STAGE 2: *The instrument relativist orientation.* Right action consists of that which instrumentally satisfies one's own needs and occasionally the needs of others. Human relations are viewed in terms like those of the market place. Elements of fairness, of reciprocity, and of equal sharing are present, but they are always interpreted in a physical, pragmatic way. Reciprocity is a matter of "you scratch my back and I'll scratch yours," not of loyalty, gratitude, or justice.

II.   CONVENTIONAL LEVEL

At this level, maintaining the expectations of the individual's family, group, or nation is perceived as valuable in its own right, regardless of immediate and obvious consequences. The attitude is not only one of *conformity* to personal expectations and social order, but of loyalty to it, of actively *maintaining,* supporting, and justifying the order, and of identifying with the persons or group involved in it. At this level, there are the following three stages:

STAGE 3: *The interpersonal concordance or "good boy–nice girl" orientation.* Good behavior is that which pleases or helps others and is approved by them. There is much conformity to stereotypical images of what is majority or "natural" behavior. Behavior is frequently judged by intention—"he means well" becomes important for the first time. One earns approval by being "nice."

STAGE 4: *The "law and order" orientation.* There is orientation toward authority, fixed rules, and the maintenance of the social order. Right behavior consists of doing one's duty, showing respect for authority, and maintaining the given social order for its own sake.

STAGE 4½: *Ethical egoistic orientation.* Apparent Stage 2 reasoning by previously conventional Stage 4 person. Argues that all moral judgments are relative, there there are no moral absolutes, and that moral judgments are primarily emotional, not rational. Moral terms such as "duty" are dismissed as meaningless. Represents breaking up of conventional morality in preparation for Stage 5.

III.   POSTCONVENTIONAL, AUTONOMOUS, OR PRINCIPLED LEVEL

At this level, there is a clear effort to define moral values and principles that have validity and application apart from the authority of the groups or persons holding these principles, and apart from the individual's own identification with these groups. This level again has three stages:

TABLE 12–3 *(Continued)*

STAGE 5: *The social-contract legalistic orientation,* generally with utilitarian over-tones. Right action tends to be defined in terms of general individual rights and standards, which have been critically examined and agreed upon by the whole society. There is a clear awareness of the relativism of personal values and opinions and a corresponding emphasis upon procedural rules for reaching consensus. Aside from what is constitution-ally and democratically agreed upon, the right is a matter of personal "values" and "opin-ion." The result is an emphasis upon the "legal point of view," but with an emphasis upon the possibility of changing law in terms of rational considerations of social utility (rather than freezing it in terms of Stage 4 "law and order"). Outside the legal realm, free agree-ment and contract is the binding element of obligation. This is the "official" morality of the American government and Constitution.

[STAGE 6: *The universal ethical principle orientation.* Right is defined by the decision of conscience in accord with self-chosen ethical principles appealing to logical comprehen-siveness, universality, and consistency. These principles are abstract and ethical (the Golden Rule, the categorical imperative); they are not concrete moral rules like the Ten Commandments. At heart, these are universal principles of *justice,* of the *reciprocity* and *equality* of human *rights,* and of respect for the dignity of human beings as *individual per-sons.* The Declaration of Independence is at Stage 6.]

[STAGE 7: *The cosmic-transcendental orientation.* Shift from humanistic reasoning of previous stages to religious, transcendental intuition. Right and wrong not defined in terms of human need or dignity, but in terms of an infinite, trans-human perspective of absolute right and wrong.]

Source: Kohlberg (1971) except for descriptions of Stages 4½ and 7, which are based primarily on Kohlberg & Kramer (1969) and Rosen (1980). Stages in brackets (6 and 7) are hypothetical only, since no one studied by Kohlberg has achieved them. See text for discussion.

Kohlberg and Kramer (1969) found evidence that many subjects who had initially tested as solid Stage 4 or even Stage 5 now seemed to reason at Stage 2!

Now common sense would fully expect this, for it often happens that youthful idealism, nurtured in the hothouse of high school, gives way to a more practical outlook upon contact with adult life. Jerry Rubin, Yippee leader and one of the noisiest of the Chicago 7, for example, wound up working on Wall Street. It is, however, entirely at odds with the cognitive-developmental paradigm. Unwilling to abandon the fixed-stage concept, Kohlberg denied that any of his subjects regressed, undergoing instead what he is pleased to call *retrogression* (Kohlberg & Kramer, 1969).

Kohlberg argues that the subjects he tested had never really achieved Stage 4 or Stage 5 to begin with, and that their seeming to do so was a fail-ing of the initial test instrument, not cognitive-developmental theory. Kohlberg's most recent scoring system has been revised to correct those al-leged errors. Stage 4½ represents a transitional stage between conventional and postconventional thinking, resulting from the breaking up of rigid, social-oriented conventional morality preparatory to the individual-rights centered philosophy of Stage 5. But in the meantime, there is an apparent return to egoism and a questioning of all absolutes. Kohlberg defends his view by pointing out that unlike real Stage 2 subjects, the Stage 4½ subjects still understand Stages 3 and 4, and can reason at those levels if asked to do so.

Kohlberg's rethinking of his scoring procedures has also had the startling effect—to anyone who has read about the theory before—of eliminating Stage 6. It remains an ideal to be aimed at, and perhaps has been achieved by great minds such as Thomas Jefferson, author of the Declaration of Independence (and a slave-owner), but it no longer is the achievement of any of Kohlberg's subjects.

Even more remote, therefore, is Stage 7, once proposed in a paper on moral development in the elderly (Rosen, 1980). In Stages 1 through 5, right and wrong can be grounded in secular, purely human terms, ranging from simple pain and pleasure through social rules to the notion of the freely chosen contract. However, Stage 6 posits rules that transcend human experience, social rules, or contracts, which may be used to strike the latter. It appears difficult to justify such principles without appealing to some moral dimension outside human life and society, a more cosmic perspective, and it is this that is found at Stage 7. However, since no one (or practically no one) reaches Stage 6, the question of reaching Stage 7 seems to be moot.

Finally, with regard to the facilitation of moral development, Kohlberg has advanced an equilibration account of moral development and its improvement. Various studies by Kohlberg and others (see Turiel, 1973) have found that if presented with an array of answers to a moral dilemma, subjects typically choose as the best answer that from one stage beyond their own stage. If, as cognitive developmental theory maintains, development is a process of successive equilibrations in resolution of cognitive conflict, this finding suggests that the best way to foster moral development is quite simple: promote discussions of moral issues. Any sufficiently heterogeneous group (a high school class, for example) will have members at almost all levels (save the first and the last), so that a person at Stage X will give arguments of that stage that will help another at Stage $X-1$ move up, and will be exposed to arguments at Stage $X+1$, advancing his or her own development. Teaching teachers and counselors how to foster moral growth is now a major activity at Harvard, where Kohlberg regularly conducts seminars and workshops in moral development and education.

Kohlberg's theory is well known and influential. Every text in introductory or developmental psychology discusses it at least briefly. Questions on teacher competence exams concerning ways to foster morality are based on the theory. Nevertheless, Kohlberg's work has serious deficiencies and some vocal detractors (for reviews see Kurtines & Greif, 1974; Flanagan, 1983).

To begin with, as a cognitive-developmental theory closely modeled on Piaget's, it faces all the difficulties of the latter, such as the problem of *decalage*. A subject's responses to Kohlberg's instrument may scatter over three or more stages, making it hard to determine the subject's "dominant" stage (Kurtines & Greif, 1974).

Two special problems within the cognitive-developmental framework arise for Kohlberg's theory as compared with Piaget's. First, Kohlberg runs up against the intuitive and reasonable idea that development of reasoning about morals is different from development of reasoning about physical concepts (Flanagan, 1982a, 1982b). Every child everywhere grows up in the same physical universe—the laws of motion, matter, and mathematics are indifferent to a culture's beliefs. But not every child grows up in the same moral world. Each culture and subculture has its own values, religious beliefs, notioᴜs of justice, and procedures for righting wrongs; there is no underlying physical reality common to everyone in this domain. So our astonishment at Kohlberg's claim of universality and the data he offers to support it may be so great to make us doubt his test and his theory rather than doubt our belief that human cultures are morally heterogeneous.

The other problem faced by Kohlberg more than by Piaget is his claim that the final stage in his hierarchy is the most adequate. Whether or not Piaget has correctly described the most adequate form of scientific reasoning with his model of formal operations, at least it is easy to decide what kind of reasoning is more adequate when dealing with physical concepts: Which level of reasoning gives the better scientific answers, concrete or formal operations? Clearly, formal operations are more scientifically adequate. Kohlberg, however, has to claim that Stage 6 (or the newly combined Stage 5–6) is the most *morally* adequate stage.

That is, unlike the sociobiologist often wrongly accused of it, Kohlberg is trying, in his own words, "to commit the naturalistic fallacy and get away with it" (Kohlberg, 1971 p. 151). The incoherence of moving from "is" to "ought" is easily found in Kohlberg's theory. For years he argued that Stage 6 was clearly the highest form of morality but now says that almost no one reaches that stage, so now there is no "is" on which to base the "ought." And what about Stage 7? Furthermore, how can we assess any claim that the last stage is morally best? Kohlberg likes to point to a convergence between his Stage 6 and philosopher John Rawls' book *A Theory of Justice*. This, however, is just an appeal to authority that settles nothing. Another well-regarded Harvard philosopher is Robert Nozick, whose ethical theory *Anarchy, State, and Utopia* is libertarian, and looks like Stage 2.

Difficulties of claiming moral superiority for a given stage are pointed out by two arguments having a rather sociobiological air about them (unintended by their proponents). Consider the following moral problem. A mother is on the shore watching her child and a stranger's child rowing a boat out on the lake. Suddenly, the boat capsizes and the helpless children are flipped into the water. The mother can save only *one* child. She swims out and saves the stranger's child, justifying her action with the clear Stage 6 assertion that all human lives are of equal value, so she flipped a coin saying, "Heads my child, tails the other child." Tails came up and she saved the other child. (Flanagan, 1983). How do we feel about the mother and her actions? Flanagan and the people he has queried on this problem felt strongly that the mother did the wrong thing and that they would feel very strange around such a person.

What our example reveals is an important limitation on Kohlberg's theory; there is more to morality than the impersonal equal distribution of justice. In particular, it suggests that Kohlberg's highest stages represent the best way to administer justice in a particular social world, specifically our own modern, industrialized, impersonal West (Flanagan, 1983). In Chapter Ten we saw how modern society is quite unlike the societies that shaped human evolution and in which most people still live. In those societies, kinship still plays the most important role in regulating human affairs, and certain contemporary problems can be traced to the breakdown of kin ties. Our example reveals that kinship still plays a role in our concepts of right and wrong. Stages 5 and 6 describe right and wrong in a society of strangers—but not all human beings are unrelated strangers.

The second sociobiological-sounding difficulty concerns the consistent finding that women always score lower than men on Kohlberg's scale. Now while Freud would have expected this finding, it seems extraordinarily unlikely that women are really less moral than men. One of Kohlberg's own students, Carol Gilligan (1977, 1979, 1982), has argued that Kohlberg's scale—based on the initial testing and continued following of 84 males—is sex-biased. She argues that men's concepts of morality focus on stern, abstract principles of justice rationally arrived at, whereas women are more attuned to personal relationships, to feelings, and to the unique context of particular moral problems. Gilligan states:

> Whereas the rights conception of morality that informs Kohlberg's principled level (Stages Five and Six) is geared to arriving at an objectively fair or just resolution to the moral dilemmas to which "all rational men can agree," the responsibility conception focuses instead on the limitations of any particular resolution and describes the conflicts that remain . . . a woman in her thirties . . . says that her guiding principle in making moral decisions has to do with "responsibility and caring about yourself and others, not just a principle that once you take hold of, you settle (the moral problem)." The principle put into practice is still going to leave you with conflict. (Gilligan, 1977, p. 482)

We can detect in this contrast of male and female moral styles the same sorts of sex differences surveyed in Chapter 10. From the earliest days, girls are more alert to emotional expression and nuances of feeling than are boys, and in women and men this carries through to a wide range of differences, including, we now find, differing conceptions of morality and justice. We should not conclude that women are less (or more) moral than men but that, to borrow Gilligan's phrase, they speak "in a different voice" about moral issues. If it is correct that much of human violence is instigated or at least abetted by moral imperialism—crusades against those labeled "evil"—as Alexander suggested (Chapter 10), then a voice of compassion and feeling is one that is well heeded. Impersonal abstract justice easily becomes persecution; morality erected on intimate personal ties does not.

Of the various deficiencies that mark Kohlberg's cognitive-developmental theory of moral development, the one that troubles most psychologists is its indifference to behavior. Partially, this concern is motivated by the general dominance of behaviorism, for no theory that fails to explain behavior is seriously scientific to a behaviorist. But there is a larger concern. Surely we ought to be concerned with behavior; a sophisticated terrorist can sound awfully Stage 6, acting in the name of higher morality against crass imperialists. What practical good is high moral reasoning if it does little to reduce crime and war? Concern with moral behavior and its causes has characterized the major alternative to both psychoanalysis and cognitive-developmentalism, namely, social learning theory.

Alternative: Social Learning Theory

In sharp contrast to Kohlberg's developmentalism, **social learning theory** views personality and morality as learned, part of the overall socialization of children. Social learning theory began some decades ago as an attempt to marry what were then seen as the artful insights of psychoanalysis with the scientific rigor of behaviorism (Dollard, Doob, Miller, Mowrer, & Sears, 1939; Dollard & Miller, 1950; Miller & Dollard, 1941; Whiting & Child, 1953). Over the years social learning theory has changed, moving away from its Freudian roots and becoming, along with the rest of psychology, more cognitive (Mischel & Mischel, 1976; Bandura, 1982). Nevertheless, despite these changes and despite often strong disagreement among its proponents on theoretical details (Graham, 1972), the social learning perspective maintains its emphasis on moral behavior and learning. In this section we will focus on the living and lively controversy (Wren, 1982, and following papers) between social learning and cognitive developmental theories of morality.

Two aspects of the psychoanalytic approach to moral socialization have been retained down to the present and, more specifically, distinguish it from Kohlberg's approach. One of these is paying more attention to the affective side of morality—feelings of anxiety, shame, and guilt—than to the cognitive (although recent work by Bandura, 1974, 1978, 1982 certainly does not neglect cognition). The other is attentiveness to parental and social role models as sources of moral values and behavior.

From a dynamic psychoanalytic perspective, conscience is built on feelings of shame, guilt, and moral rightness that are internalizations of parental punishment and reward. This accords well with any behavioral perspective, which holds that since moral behavior *is* behavior, it must follow the usual laws of punishment and reinforcement. Morality, therefore, consists in learning to inhibit actions that are punished, and to perform those that are rewarded. So, for example, Aronfreed (1976) reports that children punished for choosing the more attractive of a series of toys quickly learn not to choose them. Furthermore in keeping with the standard laws of learning, this inhibition, or resistance to temptation, generalizes best to a test situation when the child is alone, if the punishment is delivered immediately after the "wrong" choice, rather than delayed. An inner moral agent—a conscience—is formed as the child internalizes moral rules and learns to regulate its own behavior rather than having to receive actual rewards and punishments (Aronfreed, 1976; Mischel & Mischel, 1976). That both *cognition* and *affect* are part of internal moral regulation is indicated by Aronfreed's (1976) further finding that punishment delivered with a plausible rationale was more effective in inducing later resistance to temptation than punishment alone.

Freud and the other psychoanalysts placed great stress on *identification* as a source of morality. Children identify with their parents first because they depend on them to meet their needs (anaclitic identification) and then because they fear them as punishing agents (identification with the aggressor); the latter is especially strong in boys' Oedipal period. Identification leads to imitation of the parents and the adoption (introjection) of the parents' values.

While learning theorists play down the role of identification in socialization and speak of *imitation* as a direct behavioral copying of a model (Bandura, 1967), and while they disagree over whether imitation is a spontaneously occurring natural process relatively independent of reinforcement (Bandura, 1974), or is itself something that must be learned through shaping (Gewirtz & Stingle, 1968), they all agree with Freud that parents and others provide models of moral behavior from which their children learn right and wrong (Miller & Dollard, 1941; Bandura & Walters, 1963; Bandura, 1967; Rushton, 1982a & 1982b).

Figure 12–11 (Liebert & Poulos, 1976) illustrates how most social learning theorists regard the process of imitation, modeling, or observational learning, as it is variously called. The first of the three stages in modeling is simply *exposure* (I) to the model, seeing some behavior occur. The second stage, *acquisition*, may (IIA) or may not (IIB), take place in a given instance. According to more cognitively oriented learning theorists (see Bandura, 1974), acquisition depends on having paid attention to the model and on constructing an internal representation of the behavior that serves as a template for later imitation.

If the template is acquired, then it may (IIIA,B) or may not (IIIC) affect behavior. This is the phase of *acceptance*. Various factors may lead to nonimitation, such as the degree of identification (or lack thereof) the child feels with the actor (Eron, 1982). If imitation does occur, it may be *imitative* (IIIA) or *counter-imitative* (IIIB). Imitative effects include *direct imitation* of the modeled behavior or *disinibition* of similar behaviors. Counter-imitative effects include *direct counter-imitation* and *inhibition* of similar behaviors. Again, various factors determine whether an actor's behavior is imitated or counter-imitated, but the most important seems to be the consequences following that behavior. If the actor is rewarded, imitation is more likely; if punished, counter-imitation is more likely; but the effect is weaker (Bandura & Walters, 1963; Liebert & Poulos, 1976).

One particularly interesting source of models intensively studied by social learning theorists is one Freud did not have to worry about: the mass media, especially television (Liebert & Poulos, 1976; Roberts & Bachen, 1981; Eron, 1982). Television and movies provide a wide range of possible models to imitate for good or ill from characters such as Hawkeye and Captain Kirk to J. R. Ewing and Darth Vader. Social-learning theorists have investigated whether films as well as parents *can* influence behavior, and whether what children actually see on television *does* influence their behavior.

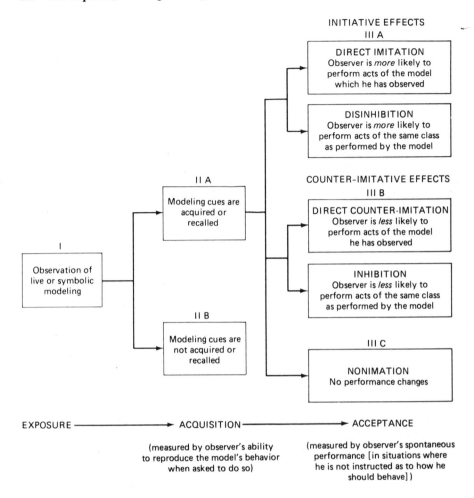

FIGURE 12–11 Schematic Presentation of the Stages of Observational Learning. (From Liebert & Poulos, 1976)

Beginning with the work of Bandura and his colleagues around 1960 (see Bandura, Ross, & Ross, 1961), the answer to the first question is quite clear. Laboratory experiments soon showed that viewing films or video can have dramatic impact on children's behavior. If children see an adult or another child being aggressive, especially if the actor is rewarded or not punished, children will later act aggressively in remarkably similar ways (Bandura, 1967).

While the results are not as dramatically unequivocal, it also appears that children's behavior is, in fact, affected by their exposure to real television, which is many hours each day. Most field research has focused on television violence, asking if it leads to increased levels of aggression or toleration for aggression in children (Eron, 1982) or even adults (Roberts &

Bachen, 1981). The consensus of researchers is that it does (APA *Monitor,* 1983). Of particular concern is the self-reinforcing nature of aggressiveness and television watching: Children proven to be aggressive watch more violent television (Eron, 1982).

Fortunately, recent research (Eron, 1982) indicates that fairly simple tutorial techniques, such as explaining to children the nature of television production, can reduce the negative effects of violent programs. Moreover, it has also been found that TV programs can be morally beneficial. Children who view shows stressing cooperation and helping show more altruism than others (Liebert & Poulos, 1976).

Social-learning theory's stress on morality as learned and on understanding the determinants of moral learning and behavior naturally leads it to be much more relativistic than Kohlberg's theory at all levels—cultural, familial, and situational. Kohlberg's theory posits a universal sequence of stages of moral development cutting across cultures and families, and it maintains that people should be reasonably consistent, showing judgment and behavior consistent with their stage of moral development across the situations they find themselves in.

By contrast, social-learning theorists view morality as relative. Different cultures have different values and practices, so that people in different cultures espouse different moralities (Whiting & Child, 1953; Garbarino & Bronfenbrenner, 1976). Since parents have different child-rearing practices, different effects on moral learning should occur. For example, parents who use love-withdrawal rather than physical punishment as a discipline technique produce more moral children (Hoffman & Saltzstein, 1967; Hoffman, 1976, 1979), and this is particularly true of those who are authoritative—firm, but giving explanations of their actions—as opposed to authoritarian or permissive parents (Baumrind, 1971).

Finally, since social-learning theory focuses on the environmental determinants of behavior, social learning theorists expect moral behavior to be situation-specific rather than consistent across situations. An especially distressing example of the situational specificity of morality is an experiment by Haney, Banks, and Zimbardo (1973). They built a simulated prison in the basement of the psychology department at Stanford University, and chose a group of male students to be either "prisoners" or "guards" for several weeks in this pretend prison. The subjects were screened for emotional stability and assigned randomly as "prisoners" or "guards." The researchers were shocked to discover that very quickly the "guards" became guards—brutal, domineering, and inhumane—and the "prisoners" became prisoners—fearful yet hostile, prepared to riot and rebel, or to go into depressive withdrawal. So vicious did the situation become that the experiment was ended very early. This study and others (see Milgram, 1974) seem to show that morality—indeed, perhaps personality—is not a permanent, enduring part of an individual, but a momentary product of his or her surroundings.

In the social-learning view, then, actual moral behavior and reasoning are relative indeed. They are relative to the culture in which you grow up, the family that raises you, and the circumstances in which you find yourself. Philosophically, right and wrong may be universal—indifferent to culture, family, and circumstance—but psychologically they are not. Kohlberg perhaps catches people's understanding that morality ought to be universal, applicable to all men and women everywhere. Every stage offers some general, universal guide to right behavior, though in each case the guide is grounded differently. Yet in the actual world we fall short, as social-learning theory demonstrates; morality, in fact, is relative. Kohlberg and social-learning theory fall on the two sides of the is-ought dichotomy, Kohlberg studying what people think ought to be right and wrong, social-learning theory studying people being right and wrong.

CONCLUSION: A BIOLOGICAL SYNTHESIS

Having surveyed conflicting developmentalist and learning theories in a number of areas, let us step back and view them from the modern biological perspective developed over the last two chapters. With the exception of Freud, whose Lamarckian biogenesis is now known to be incorrect, the theorists we surveyed, whether developmentalist or learning, share a general hostility to biological, nativistic explanations of learning and development. However, their rejection of biology rests on a familiar misconception of genetics, namely, the belief that if a behavior, trait, or developmental sequence is innate, it is rigid, inflexible and uninfluenced by the environment. Piaget, for example, labels nativism "preformationism" and claims, with regard to Chomsky's linguistic nativism, that if Chomsky were correct, children would talk at birth.

However, as we learned in Chapter 10, such a characterization of nativism is a caricature. Modern biology and genetics recognize that genes and environment interact—that behavior can be both innate *and* learned at the same time. What genes provide is a direction for development, not a mechanical series of steps. The evolutionary biologist C. H. Waddington (see, for example, 1968) calls the direction-giving of the genes **canalization**. Canalization keeps development on a normal course, responding to environmental challenges—assuming an environment within a broad normal range.

One of the problems learning theory faces is that people are everywhere much the same, within limits, indicating that learning neglects some unifying force behind development. Developmentalists, of course, postulate a unifying, direction-giving force, such as Werner's orthogenesis or Piaget's equilibration. Unfortunately for developmentalists, such forces seem rather mysterious and metaphysical to most psychologists, who remain committed to some learning theory, today usually of a cognitive sort.

But biology and the concept of canalization provides a new way to look at development, a way that recognizes the role of learning and experience, but explains the direction of development without positing any unusual causal force. Some psychologists began to take a biological approach to development at about the same time Wilson was propounding *Sociobiology* (Chevalier-Skolnikoff & Poirier, 1977; Fishbein, 1976; Freedman, 1974; Hinde, 1974; Scarr-Salapatek, 1976; Smith, 1974), and the approach is gaining acceptance as a force in developmental psychology (Siegler, 1983). Two recent contributions are especially relevant to the present chapter: Parker's and Gibson's (1979) neobiogenetic account of Piaget's stages of cognitive development, and Keil's (1981) new general theory of cognitive development.

As shown in Table 12–4, Parker and Gibson integrate Piaget's stages of development (Column 1) with comparative studies of intelligence in our simian relatives (Columns 2 to 4) and the likely course of evolution of the early hominids, our distant ancestors (Column 5). As you can see, as we move from simple simians through the monkeys and to our closest relatives, the great apes (chimpanzees and gorillas), higher levels of sensory-motor intelligence are obtained, until with the apes, early preoperational, representational intelligence is achieved. It is the symbolic capacity of the apes that has made it possible for some of them to learn to communicate, as we saw in the last chapter. The evolution of early human ancestors reflects a similar increase in cognitive capacity, ultimately moving past the achievements of the apes to human preoperational intelligence marked by the distinctive human traits of tool manufacture, the building of shelters, and throwing stones as a hunting tactic. If Parker's and Gibson's proposed evolutionary sequence is correct, then a new biogenesis may be proposed: that human cognitive development—ontogenesis—recapitulates the phylogeny of human evolution.

Descriptively, Parker's and Gibson's neo-biogenesis seems plausible, and is nicely supported by the comparative data and the independent findings of archaeologists and anthropologists reviewed earlier. Does this mean we must resurrect Haeckel's old Lamarckian biogenetic Law? Fortunately not. For Keil (1981) has provided a new biological framework for understanding cognitive development that can integrate Parker's and Gibson's proposal with current nativistic thinking.

In the last chapter we discussed the similar arguments of Chomsky and Wexler and Cullicover with regard to language acquisition. They argued that learning language is such a vast and potentially infinite task that we cannot explain the relative ease and rapidity with which children do learn language without positing innately given constraints on the human language acquisition device. Keil applies the same reasoning to cognitive development: The immensity of the task and the ease and universality of children's cognitive development force on us the recognition that there must be native constraints on the course of intellectual growth.

Keil offers a quotation from the American philosopher Charles Sanders Peirce (1839–1914), who first proposed the constraints approach, nicely summarizing its basic argument:

> Suppose a being from some remote part of the universe, where the conditions of existence are inconceivably different from ours, to be presented with a United States Census Report which is for us a mine of valuable inductions, so vast as almost to give that epithet a new signification. He begins, perhaps, by comparing the ratio of indebtedness to deaths by consumption in counties

whose names begin with different letters of the alphabet. It is safe to say that he would find the ratio everywhere the same, and thus his inquiry would lead to nothing. The stranger to this planet might go on for some time asking inductive questions that the Census would faithfully answer without learning anything except that certain conditions were independent of others . . . . Nature is a far vaster and less clearly arranged repertoire of facts than a census report; and if men had not come to it with special aptitudes for guessing right, it may well be doubted whether in the ten or twenty thousand years that they may have existed their greatest mind would have attained the amount of knowledge which is actually possessed by the lowest idiot. But, in point of fact, not man merely, but all animals derive by inheritance (presumably by natural selection) . . . classes of ideas which adapt them to their environment.

Side by side, then, with the well established proposition that all knowledge is based on experience, and that science is only advanced by the experimental verifications of theories, we have to place this other equally important truth, that all human knowledge, up to the highest flights of science, is but the development of our inborn animal instincts. (Keil, 1981, p. 199)

There is nothing very mysterious about Keil's argument that cognitive ontogeny is subject to innate constraints, for it, along with the language-learning constraints theory of Chomsky and Wexler and Cullicover, is simply an extension of well-established views in sociobiology and animal learning applied to human beings. In Chapter 4 we saw that animal learning is constrained—some things are easy for a given species to learn, others difficult. It is important to see that the idea of modern nativism departs from the stereotypical view of innate behaviors as rigidly preprogrammed. Conditioned nausea is both learned, since experience is needed to learn what causes illness, and innate, since rats, by virtue of their evolution, learn to avoid poisonous foods by taste cues, while birds, by virtue of their evolution, learn to avoid them by visual cues.

A human case discussed in Chapter 10 may be usefully recalled now, the case of incest taboos. Freud, in his Lamarckian biogenetic way, viewed the incest taboo in a child as a racial memory from the ancient past. Social-learning theorists reject all nativism; they argue that incest avoidance is a learned behavior based on direct punishment of incipient incestuous acts and modeling (negative imitation) when others are seen to be punished for incest. In a modern biological account, both views are partly correct. As we learned in Chapter 10, avoidance of inbreeding is a widespread animal behavior firmly based on consideration of fitness. So there is a likely genetic basis for incest avoidance, but not Freud's Lamarckian one. At the same time we found that incest avoidance is a learned phenomenon—we must *learn* with whom sexual relations must not take place. More specifically, it appears that humans are prepared to learn not to feel lust for the constant age-mates of childhood.

Keil deploys similar arguments to explain cognitive development. In discussing Piaget's theory we considered the problem of *decalage,* the frequent finding of apparently continuous development instead of stages. In a constraints view, this makes sense, for we would expect constrained knowl-

TABLE 12–4 Primary Adaptive Functions of Primate Intelligence, by Grade Levels. (From Parker & Gibson, 1979)

KIND OF INTELLIGENCE	PROSIMIAN	OLD-WORLD MONKEY	GREAT APE	EARLY HOMONID
Sensorimotor intelligence *Stages 1 & 2* Simple prehension, hand-mouth coordination	manual prey catching, branch-clinging, climbing-by-grasping			
Stage 3 Hand-eye coordination Secondary circular reactions		manual foraging	object play for tool use	same
Stage 4 Coordination and application of manual schemes on single objects		manual food preparation and cleaning, manual grooming		
Stage 5 *Object permanence* Object-object coordination, trial-and-error investigation of object prop. (tertiary circular reactions), discovery of new means (tool use)		food location, memory (?)	same trial-and-error discovery of tool use for extractive foraging on embedded foods	same same

Stage 6	imitative learning of tool-use traditions	same
Deferred imitation of novel schemes		
Mental representation of images of actions	search for new embedded foods, insightful tool-use	same
Preoperational intelligence		
Symbolic subperiod		
Topological preconcepts of enclosure and proximity	search for rare embedded foods	same, plus shelter-construction
Make-believe games		practice of subsistence roles
		tool manufacture, tool use in butchery, shelter-construction
Intuitive subperiod		
Euclidean and projective preconcepts of straight line and angle		shelter-construction
Classification and seriation		food division
1 to 1 correspondence		practice in shelter-construction and tool manufacture
Construction games		
Aimed-throwing games		practice for aimed-throwing in hunting and defense

From C. Parker and K. Gibson, *Behavioral and Brain Science* (1979), Vol. 2. Cambridge University Press.

edge to apply to at first narrow and then increasingly wider domains. We may take *number development* as an example. Like language, number and counting systems possess universal properties, likely reflecting underlying cognitive regularities, that is, *constraints,* as in the case of language (Keil, 1981). In this chapter we saw that contrary to Piaget's stage notion, Gelman (see 1978) demonstrated numerical competence with small arrays of objects in children as young as 30 months old. This suggests that all human beings at every age possess shared cognitive skills—given innately—and that these develop with experience, applying to larger sets of data and more and more problems. As with language or incest taboo learning, experience interacts with biological constraints to produce human knowledge.

Keil's constraints view is compatible with, and integrates, all the diverse approaches reviewed in this chapter. If outmoded ideas about evolution and genetics can be discarded, developmentalists and cognitive-learning theorists may be reconciled. Human knowledge, personality, and even morality (remember the sociobiology of altruism) are both innate *and* learned; they develop through universal patterns set by genetic constraints within which learning acts to produce each individual's path of development.

SUGGESTED READINGS

The best general survey of theories of development is Alfred Baldwin's *Theories of Child Development,* 2nd ed., 1980. There is no single account of the new biological view, so the interested reader must consult the references in the text, especially Parker and Gibson (1979) and Keil (1981).

REFERENCES

AARSLEFF, H. (1976). An outline of language origin theories since the Renaissance. In Harnad, Stelkis, & Lancaster.

AARSLEFF, H. (1982). The history of linguistics and professor Chomsky. In H. Aarsleff, *From Locke to Saussure*. Minneapolis: University of Minnesota Press.

ABELSON, R. P. (1981). Psychological status of the script concept. *American Psychologist, 36,* 715–729.

ADAMS, J. L. (1976). *Conceptual blockbusting*. San Francisco: San Francisco Book Company.

ADAMS, M. J., & COLLINS, A. (1979). A schema-theoretic view of reading. In R.O. Freedle (Ed.), *New directions in discourse processing*. Norwood, NJ: Ablex.

ALBA, J. W., & HASHER, L. (1983). Is memory schematic? *Psychological Bulletin, 93,* 203–231.

ALCOCK, J. (1979). *Animal behavior* (2nd ed.). Sunderland, MA: Sinauer Associates.

ALESANDRINI, K. L. (1983). Strategies that influence memory for advertising communications. In R.J. Harris (Ed.), *Information processing research in advertising*. Hillsdale, NJ: Lawrence Erlbaum.

ALEXANDER, R. D. (1979). *Darwinism and human affairs*. Seattle: University of Washington Press.

ALEXANDER, R. D. (1979). Sexuality and sociality in humans and other primates. In Katchadourian.

ALEXANDER, R. D., HOOGLAND, J. L., HOWARD, R. D., NOONAN, K. M., & SHERMAN, P. W. (1979). Sexual dimorphisms and breeding systems in pinnipeds, ungulates, primates, and humans. In Chagnon & Irons.

ALEXANDER, R. D., and NOONAN, K. M. (1979). Concealment of ovulation, parental care, and human social evolution. In Chagnon & Irons.

ALEXANDER, R. D., & TINKLE, D. (Eds.) (1982). *Natural selection and social behavior*. New York: Chiron Press.

ALLEN, E. et al. (1975). Against sociobiology. Reprinted in Caplan (1978).

AMAN, R. (1982). Interlingual taboos in advertising: How not to name your product. In H. DiPietro (Ed.), *Linguistics and the professions.* Norwood, NJ: Ablex.

AMERICAN PSYCHIATRIC ASSOCIATION. (1980). *Diagnostic and statistical manual of neural disorders* (3rd ed.). Washington, DC: American Psychiatric Association.

AMSEL, A. (1958). The role of frustrative nonreward in noncontinuous reward situations. *Psychological Bulletin, 55,* 102–119.

AMSEL, A. (1962). Frustrative nonreward in partial reinforcement and discrimination learning. *Psychological Review, 69,* 306–328.

AMSEL, A. (1967). Partial reinforcement effects on vigor and persistence. In K. W. Spence & J. T. Spence (Eds.), *The psychology of learning and motivation* (Vol. 1). New York: Academic Press.

ANDERSON, B. F. (1980). *The complete thinker.* Englewood Cliffs, NJ: Prentice-Hall.

ANDERSON, J. R. (1976). *Language, memory, and thought.* Hillsdale, NJ: Lawrence Erlbaum Associates.

ANDERSON, J. R. (1980). *Cognitive psychology and its implications.* San Francisco: W. H. Freeman & Company Publishers.

ANDERSON, J. R., & BOWER, G. H. (1973). *Human associative memory.* Washington, DC: Winston.

ANDERSON, N. H. (1981). *Foundations of information integration theory.* New York: Academic Press.

ANDERSON, R. C., & ORTONY, A. (1975). On putting apples into bottles—a problem of polysemy. *Cognitive Psychology, 7,* 167–180.

ANDERSON, R. C., & PICHERT, J. W. (1978). Recall of previously unrecallable information following a shift in perspective. *Journal of Verbal Learning and Verbal Behavior, 17,* 1–12.

APA (1983). *Monitor.* Caution: TV on. Letter from 43 psychologists and communications researchers. APA *Monitor,* May *14*(5), p. 4.

D'AQUILI, E. G. (1978). The neurobiological bases of myth and concepts of deity. *Zygon, 13,* 257–275.

ARDREY, R. (1966). *The territorial imperative.* New York: Atheneum.

ARKES, H. R., & HARKNESS, A. R. (1980). The effect of making a diagnosis on subsequent recognition of symptoms. *Journal of Experimental Psychology: Human Learning and Memory, 6,* 568–575.

ARONFREED, J. (1976). Moral development from the standpoint of a general psychological theory. In Lickona.

ASLIN, R. N., & PISONI, D. B. (1980). Some developmental processes in speech perception. In Yeni-Komshian, et al.

ATKINSON, M. (1982). *Explanations in the study of child language development.* Cambridge, UK: Cambridge University Press.

ATKINSON, R. C. (1975). Mnemotechnics in second-language learning. *American Psychologist, 30,* 821–828.

ATKINSON, R. C., & RAUGH, M. R. (1975). An application of the mnemonic keyword method to the acquisition of Russian vocabulary. *Journal of Experimental Psychology: Human learning and memory, 104,* 126–133.

ATKINSON, R. C., & SHIFFRIN, R. M. (1968). Human memory: A proposed system and its control processes. In K. Spence and J. Spence (Eds.), *The psychology of learning and motivation* (Vol. 2). New York: Academic Press.

AZRIN, N. H., HOLZ, W., ULRICH, R., & GOLDIAMOND, I. (1961). The control of the content of conversation through reinforcement. *Journal of the Experimental Analysis of Behavior, 4,* 25–30.

BABA, M. L., DARGA, L., & GOODMAN, M. (1982). Recent advances in molecular evolution of the primates. In A. Chiarelli & R. Corruccini (Eds.), *Advanced views in primate biology.* Berlin: Springer-Verlag.

BADDELEY, A. D. (1978). The trouble with levels: A reexamination of Craik and Lockhart's framework for memory research. *Psychological Review, 85,* 139–152.

BADDELEY, A. D. (1982). Domains of recollection. *Psychological Review, 89,* 708–729.

BAETENS BEARDSMORE, H. (1982). *Bilingualism: Basic principles.* Clevedon, UK: Tieto.

BALDWIN, A. (1980). *Theories of child development* (2nd ed.). New York: John Wiley.

BALTES, P. B., REESE, H. W., & LIPSITT, L. P. (1980). Life-span developmental psychology. *Annual Review of Psychology, 31,* 65–110.

BANDURA, A. (1967). The role of modeling processes in personality development. In W. Hartup (Ed.), *The young child: Reviews of research.* Washington, DC: National Association for Education of Young Children.

BANDURA, A. (1974). Behavior theory and the models of man. *American Psychologist, 29,* 859–869.

BANDURA, A. (1978). The self-system in reciprocal determinism. *American Psychologist, 33,* 344–358.

BANDURA, A. (1982). Self-efficacy mechanism in human agency. *American Psychologist, 37,* 122–147.

BANDURA, A., ROSS, D., & ROSS, S. (1961). Transmission of aggression through imitation of aggressive models. *Journal of Abnormal and Social Psychology, 63,* 575–582.

BANDURA, A., & WALTERS, R. (1963). *Social learning and personality development.* New York: Holt, Rinehart & Winston.

BAR-ADON, A., & LEOPOLD, W. F. (Eds.), (1971). *Child language: A book of readings.* Englewood Cliffs, NJ: Prentice-Hall.

BARASH, D. (1979). *The whisperings within.* New York: Penguin.

BARASH, D. P. (1977). *Sociobiology and behavior* (1st ed.). New York: Elsevier.

BARASH, D. P. (1982). *Sociobiology and behavior* (2nd ed.). New York: Elsevier.

BARKER-BENFIELD, G. J. (1976). *The horrors of the half-known life.* New York: Harper Colophon.

BARLOW, G. W., & SILVERBERG, J. (Eds.) (1980). *Sociobiology: Beyond nature/nurture?* Boulder, CO: Westview Press (AAAS Selected Symposium 35.)

BARON, A., KAUFMAN, A., & STAUBER, K. (1969). Effects of instructions and reinforcement-feedback on human operant behavior maintained by fixed-internal reinforcement. *Journal of the Experimental Analysis of Behavior, 12,* 701–712.

BARSALOU, L. S. (1983). Ad hoc categories. *Memory and Cognition, 11,* 211–227.

BARTLETT, F. C. (1932). *Remembering: A study in experimental and social psychology.* London: Cambridge University Press.

BASTIAN, J., EIMAS, P. D., & LIBERMAN, A. M. (1961). Identification and discrimination of a phonemic contrast induced by silent interval. *Journal of the Acoustical Society of America, 33,* 842.

BATES, E., BRETHERTON, I., BEEGHLY-SMITH, M., & McNEW, S. (1982). Social bases of language development: A reassessment. In H. W. Reese & L. P. Lipsitt (Eds.), *Advances in child development and behavior* (Vol. 16). New York: Academic Press.

BATTAN, J. F. (1983). The "new narcissism" in 20th–century America: The shadow and substance of social change. *Journal of Social History, 17,* 199–220.

BAUMRIND, D. (1971). Harmonious parents and their preschool children. *Developmental psychology, 4,* 63–72.

BECK, B. (April 10, 1983). Tools and intelligence. Paper presented at the Second National Zoological Park Symposium, Animal Intelligence, Washington, DC.

BEGG, I., & PAIVIO, A. (1969). Concreteness and imagery in sentence meaning. *Journal of Verbal Learning and Verbal Behavior, 8,* 821–827.

BEILIN, H. (1980). Piaget's theory: Refinement, rejection, or revision? In R. H. Kluwe & H. Spada (Eds.), *Developmental models of thinking.* New York: Academic Press.

BEIT-HALLAHMI, B., & RABIN, A. (1977). The kibbutz as a social experiment and as child-rearing laboratory. *American Psychologist, 32,* 532–541.

BEM, S. L. (1981). Gender schema theory: A cognitive account of sex typing. *Psychological Review, 88,* 354–364.

BENDERLY, B. L. (July-August 1980). The great ape debate. *Science 80, 1*(5), 60–65.

BERLIN, B., & KAY, P. (1969). *Basic color terms: Their universality and evolution.* Berkeley: University of California Press.

BERMANT, G. (1976). Sexual behavior: Hard times with the Coolidge Effect. In M. Siegel & H. Zigler (Eds.), *Psychological research: The inside story.* New York: Harper & Row.

BERNE, E. (1964). *Games people play.* New York: Grove Press.

BETHELL, T. (December 1980). Burning darwin to save marx. *Harper's, 257* (1543), 31–38, 91–92.

BEVER, T. G. (1970). The cognitive basis for linguistic structures. In Hayes.

BEVER, T. G. (1980). Broca and Lashley were right: Cerebral dominance is an accident of growth. In Caplan.

BEYTH-MAROM, R., & LICHTENSTEIN, S. (1984). *An elementary approach to thinking under uncertainty.* Hillsdale, NJ: Lawrence Erlbaum.

BIJOU, S. (1976). *Child development: The basic stage of early childhood.* Englewood Cliffs, NJ: Prentice-Hall.

BIJOU, S., & BAER, D. M. (1968). *Child development: Readings in behavior analysis.* New York: Appleton-Century-Crofts.

BINGHAM, R. (March/April 1980). Trivers in Jamaica. *Science 80,* 1 (*3*), 56–67.

BLACK, A., COTT, A., & PAVLOSKI, R. (1977). The operant learning theory approach to biofeedback training. In G. Schwartz & J. Beatty (Eds.), *Biofeedback: theory and research.* New York: Academic Press.

BLANCHARD, E., & EPSTEIN, L. (1978). *A biofeedback primer.* Reading, MA: Addison-Wesley.

BLASI, A. (1980). Bridging moral cognition and moral action. *Psychological Bulletin, 88,* 1–45.

BLOCK, N. (Ed.). (1981). *Imagery.* Cambridge, MA: MIT Press.

BLODGETT, H. S. (1929). The effect of the introduction of reward upon the maze performance of rats. *University of California Publications in Psychology, 4,* 113–134.

BLOOM, L. (Ed.). (1978). *Readings in language development.* New York: John Wiley.

BLOOM, L., HOOD, L., & LIGHTBOWN, P. (1974). Imitation in language development: If, when, and why. *Cognitive Psychology, 6,* 380–420. Reprinted in Bloom (1978).

BLOOM, L., & LAHEY, M. (1978). *Language development and language disorders.* New York: John Wiley.

BLUMENBERG, B. (1983). The evolution of the advanced hominid brain. *Current Anthropology, 24,* 589–623.

BLUMENFELD, W. S., BLUMENFELD, E. R., & TERRELL, S. A. (1978, August). Readability of source and explanatory materials associated with the Medicare program. Paper presented at meeting of the American Psychological Association, Toronto.

BLUMENSTEIN, S. E. (1980). Speech perception: An overview. In Yeni-Komshian et al.

BLUMENTHAL, A. (1980). Wilhelm Wundt and early American psychology: A clash of cultures. In R. W. Rieber (Ed.), *Wilhelm Wundt and the making of a scientific psychology.* New York: Plenum.

BODEN, M. A. (1978). Artificial intelligence and Piagetian theory. *Synthese, 38,* 389–414.

BOLLES, R. C. (1971). Species-specific defense reactions. In R.F. Brush (Ed.), *Aversive learning and conditioning.* New York: Academic Press.

BOLLES, R. C. (1975). Learning, motivation and cognition. In W. K. Estes (Ed.), *Handbook of learning and cognitive processes* (Vol. 1). Hillsdale, NJ.: Lawrence Erlbaum.

BOWER, G. H. (1981). Mood and memory. *American Psychologist, 36,* 129–148.

BOWER, G. H., BLACK, J. B., & TURNER, T. J. (1979). Scripts in memory for text. *Cognitive psychology, 11,* 177–220.

BOWER, G. H., KARLIN, M. B., & DUECK, A. (1975). Comprehension and memory for pictures. *Memory and Cognition, 3,* 216–220.

BOWER, T. G. R. (1974). *Development in infancy.* San Francisco: W. H. Freeman Publishers.

BOWER, T. G. R. (1977). *A primer of infant development.* San Francisco: W. H. Freeman.

BOWER, T. G. R. (1979). *Human development.* San Francisco: W. H. Freeman.

BRAINERD, C. J. (1974a). Neo-Piagetian training experiments revisited: Is there any support for the cognitive-developmental stage hypotheses? *Cognition, 2,* 349–376.

BRAINERD, C. J. (1974b, June). Structures of the whole: Is there any glue to hold the concrete-operational 'stage' together? Paper presented at the annual meeting of the Canadian Psychological Association, Windsor, Ontario.

BRAINERD, C. J. (1978a). *Piaget's theory of intelligence.* Englewood Cliffs, NJ: Prentice-Hall.

BRAINERD, C. J. (1978b). The stage question in cognitive developmental theory. *Behavioral and brain sciences, 1,* 173–213.

BRAINERD, C. J., & ALLEN, T. W. (1971). Experimental inductions of the conservation of 'first order' quantitative invariants. *Psychological Bulletin, 75,* 125–144.

BRANCH, M. (1977). On the role of 'memory' in the analysis of behavior. *Journal of the Experimental Analysis of Behavior, 28,* 171–179.

BRANSFORD, J. D. (1978). *Human cognition.* Belmont, CA: Wadsworth.

BRANSFORD, J. D., & FRANKS, J. J. (1971). The abstraction of linguistic ideas, *Cognitive psychology, 2,* 331–350.

BRANSFORD, J. D., & JOHNSON, M. K. (1972). Contextual prerequisites for understanding: Some investigations of comprehension and recall. *Journal of Verbal Learning and Verbal Behavior, 11,* 717–726.

BRANSFORD, J. D., & JOHNSON, M. K. (1973). Considerations of some problems of comprehension. In W. Chase (Ed.), *Visual information processing.* New York: Academic Press.

BRANSFORD, J. D., & McCARRELL, N. S. (1974). A cognitive approach to comprehension: Some thoughts about understanding what it means to comprehend. In W. B. Weimer, & D. S. Palermo (Eds.), *Cognition and the symbolic processes.* Hillsdale, NJ: Lawrence Erlbaum.

BRELAND, K., & BRELAND, M. (1961/1972). The misbehavior of organisms. In Seligman & Hager.

BRETT, G. S. (1912). *A history of psychology* (Vol. 2). London: Allen.

BREWER, W. F. (1977). Memory for the pragmatic implications of sentences. *Memory and Cognition, 5,* 673–678.

BREWER, W. F. (1974). There is no convincing evidence for operant or classical conditioning in adult humans. In W. Weimer and D. Palermo (Eds.), *Cognition and the symbolic processes.* Hillsdale, NJ: Lawrence Erlbaum.

BREWER, W. F., & HARRIS, R. J. (1974). Memory for deictic elements in sentences. *Journal of Verbal Learning and Verbal Behavior, 13,* 321–327.

BREWER, W. F., & NAKAMURA, G. V. (1984). The nature and functions of schemas. In R. S. Wyer & T. K. Srull (Eds.), *Handbook of social cognition.* Hillsdale, NJ: Lawrence Erlbaum.

BRITTON, B. K., & TESSER, A. (1982). Effects of prior knowledge on use of cognitive capacity in three complex cognitive tasks. *Journal of Verbal Learning and Verbal Behavior, 21,* 421–436.

BRITTON, J., BURGESS, T., MARTIN, N., MacLEOD, A., & ROSEN, H. (1975). *The development of writing abilities (11–18).* London: Macmillan Education.

BROADBENT, D. (1958). *Perception and communication.* New York: Pergamon Press.

BRONOWSKI, J. (1973). *The ascent of man.* Boston: Little, Brown.

BRONOWSKI, J., & BELLUGI, U. (1970). Language, name, and concept. *Science, 168,* 669–673. Reprinted in Sebeok & Umiker-Sebeok (1980).

BROWN, J. A. (1958). Some tests of the decay theory of immediate memory. *Quarterly Journal of Experimental Psychology, 10,* 12–21.

BROWN, J. L., & BROWN, E. R. (1982). Kin selection and individual selection in babblers. In Alexander & Tinkle.

BROWN, P. C., & JENKINS, H. M. (1968). Autoshaping of the pigeon's key peck. *Journal of the Experimental Analysis of Behavior, 11,* 1–8.

BROWN, R. (1970). The first sentences of child and chimpanzee. In *Psycholinguistics: Selected papers.* New York: Free Press. Reprinted in T. A. Sebeok & J. Umiker-Sebeok (1980).

BROWN, R. (1973). *A first language.* Cambridge, MA: Harvard University Press.

BRUNO, K. J., & HARRIS, R. J. (1980). The effect of repetition on the discrimination of asserted and implied claims in advertising. *Applied psycholinguistics, 1,* 307–321.

BRYANT, P. (1974). *Perception and understanding in young children.* New York: Basic Books.

BUCKHOUT, R. (1974). Eyewitness testimony. *Scientific American, 231(6), 23–31.*

CAIRNS, R. B. & VALSINER, J. (1984). Child psychology. *Annual Review of Psychology, 35,* 553–577.

CALFEE, R. C., CHAPMAN, R. S., & VENEZKY, R. L. (1972). How a child needs to think to learn to read. In L. W. Gregg (Ed.), *Cognition in learning and memory.* New York: John Wiley.

CALVIN, W. H. (1982). Did throwing stones shape hominid brain evolution? *Ethology and Sociobiology, 3,* 115–124.

CAMPBELL, D. T. (1975). On the conflicts between biological and social evolution and between psychology and moral tradition. *American Psychologist, 30,* 1103–1126.

CANTOR, N., & MISCHEL, W. (1977). Traits as prototypes: Effects on recognition memory. *Journal of Personality and Social Psychology, 35,* 38–48.

CAPALDI, E. J. (1966). Partial reinforcement: An hypothesis of sequential effects. *Psychological Review, 73,* 459–477.

CAPALDI, E. J. (1971). Memory and learning: A sequential viewpoint. In W. Honig & P. James (Eds.), *Animal memory.* New York: Academic Press.

CAPLAN, A. L. (1978). *The sociobiology debate.* New York: Harper Colophon.

CAPLAN, D. (Ed.). (1980). *Biological studies of mental processes.* Cambridge, MA: MIT Press.

CARRELL, P. L. (1983). Background knowledge in second language comprehension. *Language Learning and Communication, 2,* 25–33.

CASSON, R. W. (1983). Schemata in cognitive anthropology. *Annual Review of Anthropology, 12,* 429–462.

CAVANAUGH, J. C., & PERLMUTTER, M. (1982). Metamemory: A critical examination. *Child Development, 53,* 11–28.

CELLERIER, G. (1972). Information processing tendencies in recent experiments in cognitive learning—theoretical implication. In Farnham-Diggory.

CHAGNON, N. A. (1980). Kin-selection theory, kinship, marriage and fitness among the Yanomamö Indians. In Barlow & Silverberg.

CHAGNON, N. A. (1981). Terminological kinship, genealogical relatedness and village fissioning among the Yanomamö Indians. In Alexander & Tinkle.

CHAGNON, N. A., & IRONS, W. (Eds.) (1979). *Evolutionary biology and human social behavior.* North Scituate, MA: Duxbury Press.

CHAPMAN, L. J., & CHAPMAN, J. P. (1967). Genesis of popular, but erroneous diagnostic observations. *Journal of Abnormal Psychology, 72,* 193–204.

CHAPMAN, L. J., & CHAPMAN, J. P. (1969). Illusory correlation as an obstacle to the use of valid diagnostic signs. *Journal of Abnormal Psychology, 74,* 271–280.

CHARROW, R. P., & CHARROW, V. R. (1979). Making legal language understandable: A psycholinguistic study of jury instructions. *Columbia Law Review, 79,* 1306–1374.

CHARROW, V. R. (1982). Linguistic theory and the study of legal and bureaucratic language. In L. K. Obler & L. Menn (Eds.), *Exceptional language and linguistics.* New York: Academic Press.

CHEVALIER-SKOLNIKOFF, S., & POIRIER, F. (Eds.). (1977). *Primate bio-social development.* New York: Garland.

CHIESI, H. L., SPILICH, G. J., & VOSS, J. F. (1979). Acquisition of domain-related information in relation to high and low domain knowledge. *Journal of Verbal Learning and Verbal Behavior, 18,* 257–273.

CHOMSKY, N. (1957). *Syntactic structures.* The Hague: Mouton.

CHOMSKY, N. (1965a). *Aspects of the theory of syntax.* Cambridge, MA: MIT Press.

CHOMSKY, N. (1959). Review of Skinner's *Verbal Behavior. Language, 35,* 26–58. Reprinted in Jakobovits & Miron, (1967).

CHOMSKY, N. (1965b). *Cartesian linguistics.* Cambridge, MA: MIT Press.

CHOMSKY, N. (1972). *Language and mind* (Enlarged ed.). New York: Harcout Brace Jovanovich.

CHOMSKY, N. (1976). On the nature of language. In S. R. Harnad, H. D. Steklis, & J. Lancaster.

CHOMSKY, N. (1979). Human language and other semiotic systems. *Semiotica,* 31–44. Reprinted in Sebeok & Umiker-Sebeok, 1980(a).

CHOMSKY, N. (1980b). *Rules and representations.* New York: Columbia University Press.

CLARK, E. V., & HECHT, B. F. (1983). Comprehension, production and language acquisition. *Annual Review of Psychology, 34,* 325–350.

CLARK, H. H. (1977). Inferences in comprehension. In D. Laberge & S. J. Samuels (Eds.), *Basic processes in reading: Perception and comprehension.* Hillsdale, NJ: Lawrence Erlbaum.

CLARK, H. H., & CLARK, E. V. (1977). *Psychology and language.* New York: Harcourt Brace Jovanovich.

CLARK, H. H., & HAVILAND, S. E. (1977). Comprehension and the given-new contract. In R.O. Freedle (Ed.), *Discourse production and comprehension.* Norwood, NJ: Ablex.

CLIFFORD, B. R., & LLOYD-BOSTOCK, S. (Eds.). (1983). *Evaluating witness evidence: Recent psychological research and new perspectives.* Chichester, UK: John Wiley.

CLONINGER, C. R., & YOKOYAMA, S. (1981). The channeling of social behavior. Review of C. Lumsden & E. O. Wilson, *Genes, mind, and culture. Science, 213,* 749–751.

CLUTTON-BROCK, T. H., & HARVEY, P. H. (Eds.). (1978). *Readings in Sociobiology.* San Francisco: W. H. Freeman.

COHEN, D. (1979). *J. B. Watson.* London: Routledge & Kegan Paul.

COLLINS, A. M., & LOFTUS, E. F. (1975). A spreading-activation theory of semantic processing. *Psychological Review, 82,* 407–428.

COLLINS, A. M., & QUILLIAN, M. R. (1969). Retrieval time from semantic memory. *Journal of Verbal Learning and Verbal Behavior, 8,* 240–247.

COLLINS, A., WARNOCK, E. H., AIELLO, N., & MILLER, M. L. (1975). Reasoning from incomplete knowledge. In D. Bobrow & A. Collins (Eds.), *Representation and understanding: Studies in cognitive science.* New York: Academic Press.

CONDON, W. S., & SANDER, L. (1974). Neonate movement is synchronized with adult speech: Interactional participation and language acquisition. *Science, 183,* 99–101.

CONLEY, J. M., O'BARR, W. M., & LIND, E. A. (1978). The power of language: Presentation style in the courtroom. *Duke Law Journal,* 1375–1399.

COOPER, L. A., & SHEPARD, R. N. (1973). Chronometric studies of the rotation of mental images. In W.G. Chase (Ed.), *Visual information processing.* New York: Academic Press.

CORBETT, A. T., & DOSHER, B. A. (1978). Instrument inferences in sentence encoding. *Journal of Verbal Learning and Verbal Behavior, 17,* 479–491.

CORCORAN, D.W. (1967). Acoustic factors in proofreading. *Nature, 214,* 851.

COTTON, J. W. (1955). On making predictions from Hull's theory. *Psychological Review, 62,* 303–314.

COWAN, P. A. (1978). *Piaget with feeling.* New York: Holt, Rinehart & Winston.

COX, J. R., & GRIGGS, R. A. (1982). The effects of experience on performance in Wason's selection task. *Memory and Cognition, 10,* 496–502.

CRAIK, F. I. M. (1979). Human memory. *Annual Review of Psychology, 30,* 63–102.

CRAIK, F. I. M., & LOCKHART, R. S. (1972). Levels of processing: A framework for memory research. *Journal of Verbal Learning and Verbal Behavior, 11,* 671–684.

CRAIK, F. I. M., & TULVING, E. (1975). Depth of processing and the retention of words in episodic memory. *Journal of Experimental Psychology: General, 104,* 268–294.

CROMER, R. F. (1974). The development of language and cognition: The cognition hypothesis. In B. Foss (Ed.), *New perspectives in child development.* Baltimore: Penguin.

CROMER, R. F. (1981). Reconceptualizing language acquisition and cognitive development. In R. L. Schiefelbusch & D. D. Bricker (Eds.), *Early language: Acquisition and intervention.* Baltimore: University Park Press.

DALE, P. S. (1976). *Language development* (2nd ed.). New York: Holt, Rinehart & Winston.

DALY, M., & WILSON, M. (1978). *Sex, evolution and behavior: Adaptations for reproduction.* North Scituate, MA: Duxbury Press.

DALY, M., & WILSON, M. (1982). Abuse and neglect of children in evolutionary perspective. In Alexander and Tinkle.

DALY, M., WILSON, M., & WEGHORST, S. (1982). Male sexual jealousy. *Ethology and Sociobiology, 3,* 11–27.

DANIELS, D. (1983). The evolution of concealed ovulation and self-deception. *Ethology and Sociobiology, 4,* 69–87.

DARWIN, C. (1965). *The expression of emotion in man and animals* (1872). Chicago: University of Chicago Press.

DARWIN, C. J., TURVEY, M. T., & CROWDER, R. G. (1972). The auditory analogue of the Sperling partial report procedure: Evidence for brief auditory storage. *Cognitive Psychology, 3,* 225–267.

DASEN, P. R. (1972). Cross-cultural Piagetian research: A summary. *Journal of Cross-Cultural Psychology, 3,* 23–39. Reprinted in J. Berry & P. Dazen (Eds.), *Culture and cognition: Readings in cross-cultural psychology.* London: Methuen, 1974.

DAVIS, H., & HURWITZ, H. (Eds.). (1977). *Operant-Pavlovian interactions.* Hillsdale, NJ: Lawrence Erlbaum.

DAVY, J. (1981, Sunday, August 30). What if Darwin were wrong? *Washington Post,* pp. C1; C3.

DAWKINS, R. (1976). *The selfish gene.* New York: Oxford University Press.

D'AZEVEDO, W. L. (1962). Uses of the past in Gola discourse. *Journal of African History, 3,* 11–34.

DE GROOT, A. D. (1965). *Thought and choice in chess.* The Hague: Mouton.

DELGADO, J. (1969). *Physical control of the mind.* New York: Harper & Row.

DELGADO, J. (1976). New orientations in brain stimulation in man. In A. Wauquier & E. Rolls (Eds.), *Brain-stimulation reward.* Amsterdam: North Holland.

DENNIS, M. (1980). Language acquisition in a single hemisphere: Semantic organization. In Caplan.

DERWING, B. L. (1973). *Transformational grammar as a theory of language acquisition.* Cambridge, UK: At University Press.

DEUTSCH, J. A. (1956). The inadequacy of the Hullian derivations of reasoning and latent learning. *Psychological Review, 63,* 389–399.

DE VILLIERS, J. G., & DE VILLIERS, P. A. (1978). *Language acquisition.* Cambridge, MA: Harvard University Press.

DEWSBURY, D. A. (1981). Effects of novelty on copulatory behavior: The Coolidge Effect and related phenonmona. *Psychological Bulletin, 89,* 464–482.

DICKEMANN, M. (1982). Paternal confidence and dowry competition: A biocultural analysis of Purdah. In Alexander & Tinkle.

DOHERTY, M. E., MYNATT, C. R., TWENEY, R. D, & SCHIAVO, M. D. (1979). Pseudodiagnosticity. Reprinted in Tweney, Doherty, & Mynatt, (1981).

DOLLARD J., DOOB, L., MILLER, N., MOWREY, O., & SEARS, R. (1939). *Frustration and aggression.* New Haven: Yale University Press.

DOLLARD J., & MILLER, N. (1950). *Personality and psychotherapy.* New York: McGraw-Hill.

DOMJON, M. (1980). Ingestional aversion learning: Unique and general processes. *Advances in the study of behavior* (Vol. 11). New York: Academic Press.

DONALDSON, M. (1978). *Children's minds.* New York: Norton.

DONDERS, F. C. (1969). Over de snelheid van psychische processen. Onderzoekingen gedaan in het Psychologish Laboratorium der Utrechtsche Hoogeschool: 1868–69. Tweede Reeks, II, 92–120. In W. G. Koster (Ed. and trans.), Attention and performance II. *Acta Psychologica, 30,* 412–431.

DOOLING, D. J., & LACHMAN, R. (1971). Effects of comprehension on retention of prose. *Journal of Experimental Psychology, 88,* 216–222.

DOOLING, D. J., & MULLET, R. L. (1973). Locus of thematic effects in retention of prose. *Journal of Experimental Psychology, 97,* 404–406.

DOOLITTLE, W., & SAPIENZA, C. (1980). Selfish genes, the phenotype paradigm and gene evolution. *Nature, 284,* 601–603.

DURHAM, W. H. (1976). Resource competition and human aggression. *Quarterly Review of Biology, 51,* 385–415.

DURHAM, W. H. (1978). Toward a coevolutionary theory of human biology and culture. In Caplan.

DURHAM, W. H. (1982). Interactions of genetic and cultural evolution: Models and examples. *Human Ecology, 10,* 289–323.

EBBINGHAUS, H. (1964). *Memory* (1885). New York: Dover.

EDWARDS, B. (1979). *Drawing on the right side of the brain.* Los Angeles: J.P. Tarcher, Inc.

EIBL-EIBESFELDT, I. (1975). *Ethology* (2nd ed.). New York: Holt, Rinehart & Winston.

EILERS, R. E. (1980). Infant speech perception: History and mystery. In Yeni-Komshian et al.

EIMAS, P. D., SIQUELAND, J. R., JUSCZYK, P., & VIGORITO, J. (1971). Speech perception in infants. *Science, 171,* 303–306.

ELIOT, A. J. (1981). *Child language.* New York: Cambridge University Press.

ELKIND, D. (1981). Recent research in cognitive and language development. In L. T. Benjamin (Ed.), *The G. Stanley Hall lecture series* (Vol. 1). Washington, DC: American Psychological Association.

ELKIND, D., & FLAVELL, J. H. (1969). *Studies in cognitive development.* New York: Oxford University Press.

ERIKSON, E. (1939). Observations on Sioux education. *Journal of Psychology, 7,* 101–156.

ERIKSON, E. H. (1963). *Childhood and society* (2nd ed.). New York: Norton.

ERICKSON, B., LIND, R. A., JOHNSON, B. C., & O'BARR, W. M. (1978). Speech style and impression formation in a court setting: The effects of 'powerful' and 'powerless' speech. *Journal of Experimental Social Psychology, 14,* 266–279.

ERON, L. (1982). Parent-child interaction, television violence, and aggression of children. *American Psychologist, 37,* 197–211.

ESTES, W. K. (1950). Toward a statistical theory of learning. *Psychological Review, 57,* 94–107.

ESTES, W. K. (1972). Reinforcement in human behavior. *American Scientist, 60,* 723–729.

ESTES, W. K., KOCH, S., MacCORQUODALE, K., MEEHL, P., MUELLER, C. G., SCHOENFELD, W. N., & VERPLANCK, W. S. (1954). *Modern learning theory.* New York: Appleton-Century-Crofts.

EVANS, J. ST. B. T. (1982). *The psychology of deductive reasoning.* London: Routledge & Kegan Paul.

EVANS, J. ST. B. T., & WASON, P. C. (1976). Rationalization in a reasoning task. *British Journal of Psychology, 67,* 470 100.

FALK, J. L. (1961). Production of polydipsia in normal rats by an intermittent food schedule. *Science, 133*, 195–196.

FALK, J. L. (1971). The nature and determinants of adjunctive behavior. *Physiology and Behavior, 6*, 577–588.

FALK, J. L. (1981). The environmental generation of excessive behavior. In S. J. Mule (Ed.), *Behavior in excess*. New York: Free Press.

FALLON, J. J., JR., ALLEN, J. D., & BUTLER, J. A. (1979). Assessment of adjunctive behaviors in humans using a stringent control procedure. *Physiology and Behavior, 22*, 1089–1092.

FARB, P. (1978). *Humankind*. Boston: Houghton Mifflin.

FARBER, S. (1981, January). Telltale behavior of twins. *Psychology Today, 15* (1) 58–62, 79–80.

FARNHAM-DIGGORY, S. (Ed.) (1972). *Information processing in children*. New York: Academic Press.

FEDIGAN, L. M. (1982). *Primate paradigms: Sex roles and social bonds*. Montreal: Eden Press.

FERSTER, C. B., & SKINNER, B. F. (1957). *Schedules of reinforcement*. Englewood Cliffs, NJ: Prentice-Hall.

FIELDING, G., & EVERED, C. (1980). The influence of patient's speech upon doctors: The diagnostic interview. In R. N. St. Clair & H. Giles (Eds.), *The social and psychological contexts of language*. Hillsdale, NJ: Lawrence Erlbaum.

FILLMORE, C. J. (1968). The case for case. In E. Bach & R. Harms (Eds.), *Universals in linguistic theory*. New York: Holt, Rinehart & Winston.

FILLMORE, C. J. (1971). Verbs of judging: An exercise in semantic description. In C. J. Fillmore & D. T. Langendoen (Eds.), *Studies in linguistic semantics*. New York: Holt, Rinehart & Winston.

FISCHHOFF, B. (1975). Hindsight ≠ foresight: The effect of outcome knowledge on judgment under uncertainty. *Journal of Experimental Psychology: Human Perception and Performance, 1*, 288–299.

FISCHHOFF, B. (1977). Perceived informativeness of facts. *Journal of Experimental Psychology: Human Perception and Performance, 3*, 349–358.

FISCHHOFF, B., & BEYTH, R. (1975). 'I knew it would happen'—Remembered probabilities of once-future things. *Organizational Behavior and Human Performance, 13*, 1–16.

FISHBEIN, H. D. (1976). *Evolution, development and children's learning*. Santa Monica, CA: Goodyear.

FLANAGAN, O. J. (1981, June 12). The Freud-Lamarck connections: The philosophical foundations of the penis-envy hypothesis. Paper presented at Cheiron XIII, River Falls, WI.

FLANAGAN, O. (1982a). Virtue, sex and gender: Some philosophical reflections on the moral psychology debate. *Ethics, 92*, 499–512.

FLANAGAN, O. (1982b). A reply to Lawrence Kohlberg. *Ethics, 92*, 529–532.

FLANAGAN, O. (1982c). Moral structures? *Philosophy of the Social Sciences, 12*, 255–270.

FLANAGAN, O. (1983). *The sciences of the mind*. Cambridge, MA: MIT Press.

FLAVELL, J. H. (1971). Stage related properties of cognitive development. *Cognitive Psychology, 2*, 421–453.

FLAVELL, J. H. (1977). *Cognitive development*. Englewood Cliffs, NJ: Prentice-Hall.

FLAVELL, J. H. (1979). Metacognition and cognitive monitoring. A new area of cognitive-developmental inquiry. *American Psychologist, 34*, 906–911.

FLAVELL, J. H. (1982). On cognitive development. *Child Development, 53*, 1–10.

FLAVELL, J. H., & WELLMAN, H. M. (1977). Metamemory. In R. Kail & J. Hogen (Eds.), *Perspectives on the development of memory and cognition*. Hillsdale, NJ: Lawrence Erlbaum.

FLAVELL, J. H., & WOHLWILL, J. (1969). Formal and functional aspects of cognitive development. In Elkind & Flavell.

FLINN, M. (1982). Uterine *vs.* agnatic kinship variability and associated cousin marriage preferences: An evolutionary biological analysis. In Alexander & Tinkle.

FLINN, M. V., & ALEXANDER, R. D. (1982). Culture theory: The developing synthesis from biology. *Human Ecology, 10*, 383–400.

FOSS, D. J., & HAKES, D. T. (1978). *Psycholinguistics*. Englewood Cliffs, NJ: Prentice-Hall.

FOUTS, R. S., & RIGBY, R. L. (1980). Man-chimpanzee communication. In Sebeok & Umiker-Sebeok.

FOX, J. L. (1983). Debate on learning theory is shifting. *Science, 222*, 1219–1222.

FREDERIKSEN, C. H., & DOMINIC, J. F. (Eds.). (1981). *Writing: Process, development, and communication*. Hillsdale, NJ: Lawrence Erlbaum.

FREEDMAN, D. G. (1974). *Human infancy: A biological perspective*, Hillsdale, NJ: Lawrence Erlbaum.

FREUD, S. (1920). *Beyond the pleasure principle.* New York: Norton, 1961.

FREUD, S. (1949). *An outline of psychoanalysis* (Rev. ed.). (1940). New York: Norton.

FREUD, S. (1950). A note upon the 'Mystic-Writing Pad' (1925). *Collected Papers* (Vol. V). London: The Hogarth Press.

FREUD, S. (1950). Some psychological consequences of the anatomical distinction between the sexes (1925). *Collected Papers* (Vol. V).

FREUD, S. (1952). *A general introduction to psychoanalysis* (1920). New York: Washington Square Press.

FREUD, S. (1954). *Project for a scientific psychology* (1895). Reprinted in S. Freud, *The Origins of Psychoanalysis.* New York: Basic Books.

FREUD, S. (1954). Letter 52 (6/12/1896). Reprinted in S. Freud, *The Origins of Psychoanalysis.* New York: Basic Books.

FREUD, A. (1979). *Psycho-analysis for teachers and parents.* (1935). New York: Norton.

FREUD, S. (1962). *Three essays on the theory of sexuality* (6th ed.) (1925). New York: Basic Books.

FREUD, S. (1962). *The ego and the id* (1923). New York: Norton.(1962).

FREUD, S. (1962). *Civilization and its discontents* (1930). New York: Norton.

FREUD, S. (1965). *The interpretation of dreams* (1900). New York: Avon.

FREUD, S., & BREUER, J. (1966). *Studies on hysteria* (1895). New York: Avon.

FURTH, H. G. (1969). *Piaget and knowledge: Theoretical foundations.* Englewood Cliffs, NJ: Prentice-Hall, (2nd ed.). Chicago: University of Chicago Press, 1981.

GALEF, B. (1983, April 10). Tradition and social learning in animals. Paper presented at the second National Zoological Park Symposium, Animal intelligence, Washington, DC.

GALIZIO, M. (1979). Contingency-shaped and rule-governed behavior: Instructional control of human loss avoidance. *Journal of the Experimental Analysis of Behavior, 31*, 53–70.

GALLAGHER, J. M., & REID, D. K. (1981). *The learning theory of Piaget and Inhelder.* Monterey, CA: Brooks/Cole.

GALLUP, G. G. (1977). Self-recognition in primates: A comparison approach to the bidirectional properties of consciousness. *American Psychologist, 32*, 329–338.

GARBARINO, J., & BROFENBRENNER, U. (1976). The socialization of moral judgment and behavior in cross-cultural perspective. In Lickona.

GARCIA, J. (1981). Tilting at the windmills of academe. *American Psychologist, 36*, 149–158.

GARCIA, J., CLARKE, J., & HANKINS W. (1973). Natural responses to schedule rewards. In P. Bateson & P. Klopfer (Eds.), *Perspectives in ethology.* New York: Plenum.(1973).

GARCIA, J., McGOWAN, B., & GREEN, K. (1972). Biological constraints on conditioning. In Seligman & Hager.

GARDNER, B. T., & GARDNER, R. A. (1980b). Two comparative psychologists look at language acquisition. In Nelson.

GARDNER, R. A., & GARDNER, B. T. (1969). Teaching sign language to a chimpanzee. *Science, 165*, 664–672. Reprinted in Seligmann & Hager, 1972.

GARDNER, R. A., & GARDNER, B. T. (1980a). Comparative psychology and language acquisition. In Sebeok & Umiker-Sebeok.

GEIS, M. L. (1982). *The language of television advertising.* New York: Academic Press.

GELMAN, R. (1972). The nature and development of early number concepts. In H. Reese (Ed.), *Advances in child development and behavior* (Vol. 7.). New York: Academic Press.

GELMAN, R. (1978). Cognitive development. *Annual Review of Psychology*, Vol. 29.

GELMAN, R. (1983). Recent trends in cognitive development. In G. Scherrer & A. M. Rogers (Eds.), *The G. Stanley Hall Lecture Series*, Vol. 3. Washington, DC: *American Psychological Association.*

GENTNER, D., & COLLINS, A. (1981). Studies of inference from lack of knowledge. *Memory & Cognition, 9*, 434–443.

GEWIRTZ, J. L., & STINGLE, K. (1968). Learning of generalized imitation as the basis for identification. *Psychological Review, 75*, 374–397.

GHISELIN, M. (1974). *The economy of nature and the evolution of sex.* Berkeley: University of California Press.

GIBSON, E. J., BISHOP, C., SCHIFF, W., & SMITH, J. (1964). Comparison of meaningfulness and pronounceability as grouping principles in the perception and retention of verbal material. *Journal of Experimental Psychology, 67*, 173–182.

GIBSON, E. J., & LEVIN, H. (1975). *The psychology of reading*. Cambridge, MA: MIT Press.
GILLIGAN, C. (1977). In a different voice: Women's conception of self and morality. *Harvard Educational Review, 47*, 481–517.
GILLIGAN, C. (1979). Woman's place in man's life cycle. *Harvard Educational Review, 59*, 431–446.
GILLIGAN, C. (1982). *In a different voice*. Cambridge, MA: Harvard University Press.
GINSBERG, A. (1954). Does Hullian theory provide the adequate foundations for a comprehensive theory of human behavior? *Journal of General Psychology, 51*, 301–330.
GITTELMAN-KLEIN, R., KLEIN, D. F., ABIKOFF, H., KATZ, S., GLOISTEN, A. C., & KATES, W. (1976). Relative efficacy of methylphenidate and behavior modification in hyperkinetic children: An interim report. *Journal of Abnormal Child Psychology, 4*, 361–379.
GLENN, C. G. (1978). The role of episodic structure and story length in children's recall of simple stories. *Journal of Verbal Learning and Verbal Behavior, 17*, 229–247.
GLUCKSBERG, S., & DANKS, J. H. (1975). *Experimental psycholinguistics*. Hillsdale, NJ: Lawrence Erlbaum.
GOLDING, E. (1981, April). The effect of past experience on problem solving. Paper presented at the annual conference of the British Psychological Society, Surrey University.
GOUGH, P. B., & COSKY, M. J. (1977). One second of reading again. In N. J. Castellan, D. G. Pisoni, & G. R. Potts (Eds.), *Cognitive theory* (Vol. II). Hillsdale, NJ: Lawrence Erlbaum.
GOULD, J. E., & GOULD, C. (1981, May). The instinct to learn. *Science 81, 2*, 44–50.
GOULD, J. L. (1982). *Ethology*. New York: Norton.
GOULD, P., & WHITE, R. (1974). *Mental maps*. Harmondsworth, UK: Penguin.
GRAHAM, D. (1972). *Moral learning and development: Theory and research*. New York: Wiley-Interscience.
GREEN, S., & MARLER, P. (1979). The analysis of animal communication. In P. Marler & J. G. Vandenbergh (Eds.), *Handbook of Behavioral Neurobiology* (Vol. 3): *Social behavior and communication*. New York: Plenum.
GREENSPOON, J. (1955). The reinforcing effect of two spoken sounds on the frequency of two responses. *American Journal of Psychology, 68*, 409–416.
GREENWALD, A. G. (1981). Self and memory. In G. H. Bower (Ed.), *The psychology of learning and motivation* (Vol. 15). New York: Academic Press.
GREGG, L., & STEINBERG, E. (Eds.). (1980). *Cognitive processes in writing*. Hillsdale, NJ: Lawrence Erlbaum.
GREGORY, M. S., SILVERS, A., & SUTCH, D. (Eds.). (1978). *Sociobiology and human nature*. San Francisco: Jossey-Bass.
GRICE, J. P. (1975). Logic and conversation. In P. Cole & J. L. Morgan (Eds.). *Syntax and semantics III: Speech acts*. New York: Academic Press.
GRIGGS, R. A. (1983). The role of problem content in the selection task and THOG problem. In J. St. B. T. Evans (Ed.), *Thinking and reasoning: Psychological approaches*. London: Routledge & Kegan Paul.
GRIGGS, R. A., & COX, J. R. (1982). The elusive thematic materials effect in Wason's selection task. *British Journal of Psychology, 73*, 407–420.
GRIGGS, R. A., & COX, J. R. (1983). The effect of problem content on strategies in Wason's selection task. *Quarterly Journal of Experimental Psychology, 35*, 519–534.
GROSJEAN, F. (1982). *Life with two languages*. Cambridge, MA: Harvard University Press.
GROTEVANT, H., SCARR, S., & WEINBERG, R. (1978, March). Are career interests inheritable? *Psychology Today, 11* (10) 88–90.
GRUBER, H. E., & VONECHE, J. J. (Eds.). (1977). *The essential Piaget*. New York: Basic Books.
GRUEN, G. E. (1966). Note on conservation! Methodological and definitional considerations. *Child Development, 37*, 977–983. Reprinted in Sigel & Hooper (1968).
GRÜSSER, O.- J. (1983). Mother–child holding patterns in Western art: A developmental study. *Ethology and Sociobiology, 4*, 89–94.
GURIN, J. (1976). Is society hereditary? *Harvard Magazine, 79* (2), 21–25.
GUTHRIE, E. R. (1930). Conditioning as a principle of learning. *Psychological Review, 37*, 412–428.
GUTHRIE, E. R. (1933). Association as a function of the time-interval. *Psychological Review, 40*, 355–367.
GUTHRIE, E. R. (1934). Reward and punishment. *Psychological Review, 41*, 450–460.
GUTHRIE, E. R. (1939). The effect of outcome on learning. *Psychological Review, 46*, 480–484.

GUTHRIE, E. R. (1940). Association and the law of effect. *Psychological Review, 47,* 127-148.

GUTHRIE, E. R. (1952). *The psychology of learning* (2nd ed.). New York: Harper & Row.

GUTHRIE, E. R., & HORTON, G. (1946). *Cats in a puzzle box.* New York: Rinehart Press.

HABER, R. N. (1979). Twenty years of haunting eidetic images: Where's the ghost? *Behavioral and Brain Sciences, 2,* 583–594.

HAGEN, J. W. (1972). Strategies for remembering. In Farnham-Diggory.

HAHN, M., JENSEN, C., & DUDEL, B. (Eds.). (1979). *The development and evolution of brain size: Behavioral implications.* New York: Academic Press.

HALEY, A. (1976). *Roots.* New York: Doubleday.

HAMES, R. B. (1979). Relatedness and interaction among the Ye'kwana: A preliminary analysis. In Chagnon & Irons.

HAMILTON, D. L., KATZ, L. B., & LEIRER, V. O. (1980). Organizational processes in impression formation. In R. Hastie, T. Ostrom, E. Ebbesen, R. Wyer, D. Hamilton, & D. Carlston (Eds.), *Person memory.* Hillsdale, NJ: Lawrence Erlbaum.

HAMILTON, W. D. (1964). The genetic evolution of social behaviour. Reprinted in Caplan (1978) and Hunt (1980).

HAMM, R. J., PORTER, J. H., & KAEMPF, G. L. (1981). Stimulus generalization of schedule-induced polydipsia. *Journal of the Experimental Analysis of Behavior, 36,* 93–99.

HANEY, C., BANKS, C., & ZIMBARDO, P. (1973). Interpersonal dynamics in a simulated prison. *International Journal of Criminology and Penology, 1,* 69–97.

HARNAD, S. R., STEKLIS, H., & LANCASTER, J. (1976). *Origins and evolution of language and speech.* Annals of the New York Academy of Sciences (Vol. 280). New York: The New York Academy of Sciences.

HARRIS, B. (1979). What ever happened to Little Albert? *American Psychologist, 34,* 151–160.

HARRIS, R. J. (1974). Memory and comprehension of implications and inferences of complex sentences. *Journal of Verbal Learning and Verbal Behavior, 13,* 626–637.

HARRIS, R. J. (1977a). The comprehension of pragmatic implications in advertising. *Journal of Applied Psychology, 62,* 603–608.

HARRIS, R. J. (1977b). The teacher as actor. *Teaching of Psychology, 4.* 185–187.

HARRIS, R. J. (1978). The effect of jury size and judge's instructions on memory for pragmatic implications from courtroom testimony. *Bulletin of the Psychonomic Society, 11,* 129–132.

HARRIS, R. J., & MONACO, G. E. (1978). Psychology of pragmatic implication: Information processing between the lines. *Journal of Experimental Psychology: General, 107,* 1–22.

HARRIS, R. J. (1981). Inferences in information processing. In G. H. Bower (Ed.), *The psychology of learning and motivation* (Vol. 15). New York: Academic Press.

HARRIS, R. J., DUBITSKY, T. M., & THOMPSON, S. (1979). Learning to identify deceptive truths in advertising. In J. H. Leigh & C. R. Martin, Jr. (Eds.), *Current issues and research in advertising.* Ann Arbor: University of Michigan Graduate School of Business Administration, Division of Research, 1979.

HARRIS, R. J., LAHEY, M. A., & MARSALEK, F. (1980). Metaphors and images: Rating, reporting, and remembering. In R. P. Honeck & R. R. Hoffman (Eds.), *Cognition and figurative language.* Hillsdale, NJ: Lawrence Erlbaum.

HARRIS, R. J. (Ed.) (1983). *Information processing research in advertising.* Hillsdale, NJ: Lawrence Erlbaum.

HARRIS, R. J. (1982, January). The use of student journals in teaching psychology. ERIC Clearinghouse on Higher Education, *Resources in Education,* #ED206223.

HARRIS, R. J., DUBITSKY, T. M., CONNIZZO, J. F., LETCHER, L. E., & ELLERMAN, C. S. (1981). Training consumers about misleading advertising: Transfer of training and effects of specialized knowledge. In J. H. Leigh & C. R. Martin, Jr. (Eds.), *Current issues and research in advertising.* Ann Arbor: University of Michigan Graduate School of Business Administration, Division of Research, 1981.

HARRIS, R. J., TESKE, R. R., & GINNS, M. J. (1975). Memory for pragmatic implications from courtroom testimony. *Bulletin of the Psychonomic Society, 6,* 494–496.

HARRIS, R. J., DUBITSKY, T. M., & BRUNO, K. J. (1983). Psycholinguistic studies of misleading advertising. In R. J. Harris (Ed.), *Information processing research in advertising.* Hillsdale, NJ: Lawrence Erlbaum.

HARRIS, R. J., & LEE, D. J. (1983, November). *The effects of cultural schemata on cognitive processing.* Paper presented at Psychonomic Society, San Diego, CA.

HASTIE, R. (1983). Social inference. *Annual Review of Psychology, 34,* 511–542.

HASTIE, R., & KUMAR, P. A. (1979). Person memory. Personality traits as organizing principles in memory for behaviors. *Journal of Personality and Social Psychology, 37,* 25–38.

HAVILAND, S. E., & CLARK, H. H. (1974). What's new? Acquiring new information as a process of comprehension. *Journal of Verbal Learning and Verbal Behavior, 13,* 512–521.

HAYES, J. R. (Ed.). (1970). *Cognition and the development of language.* New York: John Wiley.

HAYES, J. R. (1978). *Cognitive psychology.* Homewood, IL: Dorsey Press.

HEAD, H. (1920). *Studies in neurology.* Oxford: Oxford University Press.

HEARST, E. (1975). The classical-instrumental distinction: Reflexes, voluntary behavior, and categories of associative learning. In W. K. Estes (Ed.), *Handbook of learning and cognitive processes* (Vol. 2.). Hillsdale, NJ: Lawrence Erlbaum.

HEDIGER, H. K. P. (1981). The clever Hans Phenomenon from an animal psychologist's point of view. In Sebeok & Rosenthal.

HEIL, J. (1982). Speechless brutes. *Philosophy and Phenomenological Research, 42,* 400–406.

HEILBRUN, A. B. (1981). *Human sex-role behavior.* New York: Pergamon Press.

HEIMAN, J. R. (1975, April). The physiology of erotica: Women's sexual arousal. *Psychology Today, 8,* 90–94.

HEWES, G. W. (1975, August 30).The evolutionary significance of pongid sign language acquisition. Paper presented at the Annual Meeting of the American Psychological Association, Chicago.

HEWES, G. W. (1976). The current status of the gestural theory of language origin. In Harnad et al.

HILGARD, E., & BOWER, G. (1975). *Theories of learning* (4th ed.). Englewood Cliffs, NJ: Prentice-Hall.

HILL, J. H. (1980). Apes and language. In Sebeok & Umiker-Sebeok.

HILL, K. (1982). Hunting and human evolution. *Journal of Human Evolution, 11,* 521–544.

HINDE, R., & STEVENSON-HINDE, J. (Eds.). (1973). *Constraints on learning:* New York: Academic Press.

HINDE, R. A. (1970). *Animal behavior* (2d ed.). New York: McGraw-Hill.

HINDE, R. A. (1974). *Biological basis of human social behaviour.* New York: McGraw-Hill.

HINELINE, P. (1981). The several roles of stimuli in negative reinforcement. In P. Harzen & M. Zeiler (Eds.). *Advances in analysis of behaviour* (Vol. 2). Chichester, UK: John Wiley.

HIRST, W. (1982). The amnesic syndrome: Descriptions and explanations. *Psychological Bulletin, 91,* 435–460.

HOFFMAN, M. (1976). Empathy, role-taking, guilt and development of altruistic motives. In Lickona.

HOFFMAN, M. (1979). Development of moral thought, feeling and behavior. *American Psychologist, 34,* 958–966.

HOFFMAN, M., & SALTZSTEIN, H. (1967). Parent discipline and the child's moral development. *Journal of Personality and Social Psychology, 5,* 45–57.

HOGEN, R., & SCHROEDER, D. (1981, July). Seven biases in psychology. *Psychology Today, 15,* 8–10, 12, 14.

HOLBROOK, M. B. (1978). Beyond attitude structure: Toward the informational determinants of attitude. *Journal of Marketing Research, 15,* 545–556.

HOLDEN, C. (1980a). Identical twins reared apart. *Science, 207,* 1323–1328.

HOLDEN, C. (1980b, November). Twins reunited. *Science 80, 1* (7) 1–8, 54–59.

HOLLIS, K. L. (1982). Pavlovian conditioning of signal-centered action patterns and autonomic behavior: A biological analysis of function. In J. Rosenblatt, R. Hinde, C. Beer, and M.-C. Busnel (Eds.) *Advances in the study of behavior,* (Vol. 12). New York: Academic.

HOLLOWAY, R. L. (1976). Paleoneurological evidence for language origins. In Harnad et al.

HOSCH, H. M., BECK, E. L., & McINTYRE, P. (1980). Influence of expert testimony regarding eyewitness accuracy on jury decisions. *Law and Human Behavior, 4,* 287–295.

HOWARD, D. V. (1983). *Cognitive psychology: Memory, language, and thought.* New York: Macmillan Publishing Co.

HOWE, M. J. A. (1983). *Introduction to the psychology of memory.* New York: Harper & Row.

HRDY, S. B. (1979). The evolution of human sexuality: The latest word and the last. *Quarterly Review of Biology, 54,* 309–314.

HRDY, S. B. (1981). *The woman that never evolved.* Cambridge, MA: Harvard University Press.

HUBEL, D. H., & WIESEL, T. N. (1962). Receptive fields, binocular interaction, and functional architecture in the cat's visual cortex. *Journal of Physiology, 160,* 106–154.

HUBEL, D. H., & WIESEL, T. N. (1968). Receptive fields and functional architecture of monkey striate cortex. *Journal of Physiology, 195,* 215–243.

HULL, C. L. (1930a). Simple trial-error learning: A study in psychological theory. *Psychological Review, 37,* 241–256.

HULL, C. L. (1930b). Knowledge and purpose as habit mechanisms. *Psychological Review, 37,* 511–525.

HULL, C. L. (1931). Goal attraction and directing ideas concerned as habit phenomena. *Psychological Review, 38,* 478–506.

HULL, C. L. (1934). The concept of the habit-family hierarchy and maze learning. *Psychological Review, 41,* 33–54; 134–152.

HULL, C. L. (1937). Mind, mechanism and adaptive behavior. *Psychological Review, 44,* 1–32.

HULL, C. L. (1943). *Principles of behavior.* New York: Appleton-Century.

HULL, C. L. (1952). *A behavior system.* New Haven, CT: Yale University Press.

HULL, C. L., FELSINGER, J., GLADSTONE, I., & YAMAGUCHI, H. (1947). A proposed quantification of habit strength. *Psychological Review, 54,* 237–254.

HULSE, S., FOWLER, H., & HONIG, W. (Eds.). (1978). *Cognitive processes in animal behavior.* Hillsdale, NJ: Lawrence Erlbaum.

HUMPHREY, G. (1968). Personal communication.

HUMPHREYS, L. G. (1939). Acquisition and extinction of verbal expectations in a situation analogous to conditioning. *Journal of Experimental Psychology, 25,* 294–301.

HUMPHREY, N. K. (1976). The social function of intellect. In P. P. G. Bateson & R. A. Hinde (Eds.), *Growing points in ethology.* Cambridge, UK: Cambridge University Press.

HUNT, J. H. (Ed.) (1980). *Selected readings in sociobiology.* New York: McGraw-Hill.

HYDE, J. S. (1981). How large are cognitive gender differences? *American Psychologist, 36,* 892–901.

INHELDER, B., & PIAGET, J. (1958). *The growth of logical thinking.* New York: Basic Books.

INHELDER, B. (1972). Information processing tendencies in recent experiments in cognitive learning-empirical studies. In Farnham-Diggory.

INHELDER, B., SINCLAIR, H., & BOVET, M. (1974). *Learning and the development of cognition.* Cambridge, MA: Harvard University Press.

IRONS, W. (1982). Why lineage exogamy? In Alexander & Tinkle.

ISAAC, G. L. (1976). Stages of cultural elaboration in the pleistocene: Possible archaeological indication of the development of language capabilities. In Harnad et al.

JAKOBOVITS, L. A., & MIRON, M. S. (Eds.). (1967). *Readings in the psychology of language.* Englewood Cliffs, NJ: Prentice-Hall.

JAMES, W. (1890). *The principles of psychology* (Vols. 1 & 2). New York: Henry Holt.

JANIS, I. (1980). The influence of television on personal decision making. In S. B. Withey & R. P. Abeles (Eds.), *Television and social behavior: Beyond violence and children.* Hillsdale, NJ: Lawrence Erlbaum.

JAYNES, J. (1976a). *The origin of consciousness in the breakdown of the bicameral mind.* Boston: Houghton Mifflin.

JAYNES, J. (1976b). The evolution of language in the late Pleistocene. In Harnad et al.

JEFFREY, W. E. (1980). The developing brain and child development. In M. C. Wittrock (Ed.) *The brain and psychology.* New York: Academic Press.

JENKINS, J. M. (1970). Sequential organization in schedules of reinforcement. In W. N. Schoenfeld (Ed.), *The theory of reinforcement schedules.* New York: Appleton-Century-Crofts.

JERISON, H. J. (1973). *Evolution of the brain and intelligence.* New York: Academic Press.

JERISON, H. J. (1976). The paleoneurology of language. In Harnad et al.

JERISON, H. J. (1982). The evolution of biological intelligence. In R. J. Sternberg (Ed.) *Handbook of human intelligence.* Cambridge, UK: Cambridge University Press.

JOHANSON, D. C., & EDEY, M. A. (1981). *Lucy: The beginnings of humankind.* New York: Warner Books.

JOHNSON, M. K., BRANSFORD, J. D., & SOLOMON, S. K. (1973). Memory for tacit implications of sentences. *Journal of Experimental Psychology, 98,* 203–205.

JOHNSON, M. K., DOLL, T. J., BRANSFORD, J. D., & LAPINSKI, R. J. (1974). Context effects in sentence memory. *Journal of Experimental Psychology, 103,* 358–360.

JOHNSON-LAIRD, P. N., & TRIDGELL, J. (1972). When negation is easier than affirmation. *Quarterly Journal of Experimental Psychology, 84,* 87–91.

JOHNSTON, T. (1981). Contrasting approaches to a theory of learning. *Behavioral and Brain Sciences, 4,* 125–139; Open Peer Commentary 139–161; reply, 161–169; references 169–173.

JONES, D. M. (1979). Stress and memory. In M. M. Gruneberg & P. E. Morris (Eds.), *Applied problems in memory.* London: Academic Press.

KAHNEMAN, D. (1973). *Attention and effort.* Englewood Cliffs, NJ: Prentice-Hall.

KAHNEMAN, D., & TVERSKY, A. (1973). On the psychology of prediction. *Psychological Review, 80,* 232–251.

KAHNEMAN, D., SLOVIC, P., & TVERSKY, A. (Eds.). (1982). *Judgment under uncertainty: Heuristics and biases.* Cambridge UK: Cambridge University Press.

KAHNEMAN, D., & TVERSKY, A. (1982). The simulation heuristic. In Kahneman, D., Slovic, P., & Tversky, A. (Eds.), *Judgment under uncertainty: Heuristics and biases.* Cambridge, UK: Cambridge University Press.

KAIL, R. (1979). *The development of memory in children.* San Francisco: W. H. Freeman.

KAIL, R., & BISANZ, J. (1982). Information processing and cognitive development. In H. W. Reese (Ed.), *Advances in child behavior and development.* New York: Academic Press.

KAMIN, L. (1968). Attention-like processes in classical conditioning. In M. Jones (Ed.), *Miami Symposium on the prediction of behavior: Aversive stimulation.* Miami, FL: University of Miami Press.

KAMIN, L. (1969). Predictability, surprise, attention, and conditioning. In R. Church and B. Campbell (Eds.), *Punishment and aversive behaviors.* New York: Appleton-Century-Crofts.

KANT, I. (1963). *Critique of pure reason.* London: Macmillan. (Originally published, 1781.)

KASPRZYK, D., MONTANO, D. E., & LOFTUS, E. F. (1975). Effect of leading questions on jurors' verdicts. *Jurimetrics Journal, 16,* 48–51.

KATCHADOURIAN, H. A. (Ed.). (1979). *Human sexuality: A comparative and developmental perspective.* Berkeley: University of California Press.

KEEN, S. (1981, February). Eros and Alley Ooop: An interview with Donald Symons. *Psychology Today, 15,* (2), 52–61.

KEENAN, J. M., MACWHINNEY, B., & MAYHEW, D. (1977). Pragmatics in memory: A study of natural conversation. *Journal of Verbal Learning and Verbal Behavior, 16,* 549–560.

KEIL, F. C. (1981). Constraints on knowledge and cognitive development. *Psychological Review, 88,* 197–227.

KENDLER, H., & KENDLER, T. S. (1962). Vertical and horizontal processes in problem solving. *Psychological Review, 69,* 1–16. Reprinted in R. Harper (Ed.), *The cognitive processes: Readings.* Englewood Cliffs, NJ: Prentice-Hall, 1964, and Staats (1964).

KENNEDY, A. (1973). Decision latencies to thematic and nonthematic distractors in prose. *Journal of Experimental Psychology, 98,* 432–434.

KENRICK, D. T., STRINGFIELD, D. O., WAGENHALS, W. L., DAHL, R. H., & RANSDELL, H. J. (1980). Sex differences, andrognyny, and approach responses to erotica: A new variation on the old volunteer problem. *Journal of Personality and Social Psychology, 38,* 317–524.

KERN, L., MIRELS, H. L., & HINSHAW, V. G. (1983). Scientist's understanding of propositional logic: An experimental investigation. *Social Studies of Science, 13,* 131–146.

KESS, J. F. (1976). *Psycholinguistics: Introductory perspectives.* New York: Academic Press.

KIERAS, D. (1978). Beyond pictures and words: Alternative information-processing models for imagery effects in verbal memory. *Psychological Bulletin, 85,* 532–554.

KIMBLE, G. A. (1961). *Hilgard and Marquis' conditioning and learning* (2nd ed.). New York: Appleton-Century-Crofts.

KINTSCH, W. (1974). *The representation of meaning in memory.* Hillsdale, NJ: Lawrence Erlbaum.

KINTSCH, W. (1977). On comprehending stories. In P. Carpenter & M. Just (Eds.), *Cognitive processes in comprehension.* Hillsdale, NJ: Lawrence Erlbaum.

KINTSCH, W., & BATES, E. (1977). Recognition memory for statements from a classroom lecture. *Journal of Experimental Psychology: Human Learning and Memory, 3,* 150–159.

KINTSCH, W., & VIPOND, D. (1979). Reading comprehension and readability in educational practice and psychological theory. In L. G. Nilsson (Ed.), *Perspectives on memory research*. Hillsdale, NJ: Lawrence Erlbaum.

KIPARSKY, P., & KIPARSKY, C. (1970). Fact. In M. Bierwisch & K. Heidolph (Eds.), *Progress in linguistics*. The Hague: Mouton.

KLAHR, D. (1980). Information-processing models of intellectual development. In R. H. Kluwe & H. Spada (Eds.), *Developmental models of thinking*. New York: Academic Press.

KLAHR, D., & WALLACE, J. G. (1973). The role of quantification operators in the development of conservation of quantity. *Cognitive Psychology, 4*, 301–327.

KLAHR, D., & WALLACE, J. G. (1976). *Cognitive development: An information-processing view*. Hillsdale, NJ: Lawrence Erlbaum.

KLATZKY, R. L. (1980). *Human memory: Structures and processes* (2nd Ed.). San Francisco: Freeman.

KNAUTH, P. (1972). *The north woods*. New York: Time-Life Books.

KOCH, S. (1951). Theoretical psychology, 1950: An overview. *Psychological Review, 58*, 295–301.

KOCH, S. (1954). Clark L. Hull. In W. K. Estes et al., *Modern learning theory*. New York: Appleton-Century-Crofts.

KOHLBERG, L. (1958). The development of modes of thinking and choice in the years 10 to 16. Unpublished doctoral dissertation, University of Chicago.

KOHLBERG, L. (1971). From is to ought: How to commit the naturalistic fallacy and get away with it in the study of moral development. In T. Mishel (Ed.), *Cognitive development and epistemology*. New York: Academic Press.

KOHLBERG, L. (1976). Moral stages and moralization: The cognitive-developmental approach. In T. Lickona (Ed.), *Moral development and behavior*. New York: Holt, Rinehart and Winston.

KOHLBERG, L., & KRAMER, R. (1976). Continuities and discontinuities in childhood and adult moral development. *Human Development*, 1969, 12, 93–120. Reprinted in N. Endler, L. Bolter, & H. Osser (Eds.), *Contemporary issues in developmental psychology* (2nd ed.). New York: Holt, Rinehart and Winston.

KOLERS, P. (1972). Experiments in reading. *Scientific American, 227(1)*, 84–91.

KOZMINSKY, E. (1977). Altering comprehension: The effect of biasing titles on text comprehension. *Memory & Cognition, 5*, 482–490.

KRANTZ, G. S. (1980). Sapienization and speech. *Current Anthropology, 21*, 773–779.

KRECHEVSKY, I. (1932). Hypotheses in rats. *Psychological Review, 49*, 516–532.

KUHN, T. S. (1970). *The structure of scientific revolutions* (Rev. ed.). Chicago: University of Chicago Press.

KURTINES, W., & GREIF, E. (1974). The development of moral thought: Review and evaluation of Kohlberg's approach. *Psychological Bulletin, 81*, 453–470.

Laboratory of Comparative Human Cognition. (1979). The cross-cultural psychology's challenges to our ideas of children and development. *American Psychologist, 34*, 827–834.

LACHMAN, R. L., LACHMAN, J.M., & BUTTERFIELD, E. C. (1979). *Cognitive psychology and information processing*. Hillsdale, NJ: Lawrence Erlbaum.

LAKATOS, I. (1970). Criticism and the methodology of scientific research programmes. In I. Lakatos & A. Musgrave (Eds.), *Criticisms and the Growth of Knowledge*. Cambridge, UK: Cambridge University Press.

LAMENDELLA, J. T. (1976). Relations between the ontogeny and phylogeny of language: A neorecapitulationist view. In Harnad et al.

LANGER, J. (1970). Werner's comparative organismic theory. In P. Mussen (Ed.), *Carmichael's Manual of Child Psychology* (3rd ed., Vol. 1). New York: John Wiley.

LASCH, C. (1978). *The culture of narcissism: American life in an age of diminishing expectations*. New York: Norton.

LAVINE, L.O. (1972). The development of perception of writing in pre-reading children: A cross-cultural study. Unpublished doctoral dissertation, Department of Human Development, Cornell University.

LAZARUS, R. (1977). A cognitive analysis of biofeedback control. In G. Schwartz & J. Beatty (Eds.), *Biofeedback: Theory and research*. New York: Academic Press.

LEAHEY, T., & GILDENHORN, A. (1969). Assessment of class inclusion and conservation of continuous quantity by magical illusions. Unpublished manuscript.

LEAHEY, T. H., & WAGMAN, M. (1974). The modification of fallacious reasoning with implication. *Journal of General Psychology, 91,* 277–285.

LEAHEY, T. H. (1977a). Training reasoning with implication. *Journal of General Psychology, 96,* 63–73.

LEAHEY, T. H. (1977b). The effect of sentential and abstract rules on implicational reasoning and judgment. *Journal of General Psychology, 97,* 185–191.

LEAHEY, T. H. (1977). The development of conservation abilities: An intertask analysis of continuous quantity. *Merrill-Palmer Quarterly of Behavior and Development, 23,* 215–225.

LEAHEY, T. H. (1978). Adult strategies in two conservation related tasks. *Journal of General Psychology, 98,* 133–143.

LEAHEY, T. H. (1979). A cognitive reanalysis of anagram solution set learning. *Journal of General Psychology, 100,* 133–141.

LEAHEY, T. H. (1980a). *A history of psychology.* Englewood Cliffs, NJ: Prentice-Hall.

LEAHEY, T. H. (1980b). The myth of operationism. *Journal of Mind and Behavior, 1,* 127–143.

LEAHEY, T. H. (1980b). A chronometric analysis of simple deductive reasoning. *Journal of General Psychology, 102,* 225–232.

LEAHEY, T. H., & LEAHEY, G. (1983). *Psychology's occult doubles: Psychology and the problem of pseudoscience.* Chicago: Nelson-Hall.

LEAKEY, R. E., & LEWIN, R. *People of the lake.* Garden City, NY: Anchor Press/Doubleday.

LEE, W. (1971). *Decision theory and human behavior.* New York: John Wiley.

LENNEBERG, E. H. (1964). A biological perspective of language. In E. Lenneberg (Ed.), *New directions in the study of language.* Cambridge, MA: MIT Press.

LENNEBERG, E. H. (1965). The natural history of language. In G. Miller & F. Smith (Eds.), *The genesis of language.* Cambridge, MA: MIT Press.

LENNEBERG, E. H. (1967). *Biological foundations of language.* New York: John Wiley.

LENNEBERG, E. H. (1972). On explaining language. *Science, 1969, 164,* 635–643. Reprinted in Seligman & Hager.

LEPPER, M., & GREENE, D. (EDS.). (1978). *The hidden costs of reward.* Hillsdale, NJ: Erlbaum.

LE ROY LADURIE, E. (1978). *Montaillou: The promised land of error.* New York: George Braziller.

LEVINE, F. J., & TAPP, J.L. (1973). The psychology of criminal identification: The gap from *Wade* to *Kirby. University of Pennsylvania Law Review, 121,* 1079–1131.

LEWIN, R. (1981). Do jumping genes make evolutionary leaps? *Science, 213,* 634–636.

LEWIS, D. J. (1979). Psychobiology of active and inactive memory. *Psychological Review, 86,* 1054–1083.

LIBEN, L. S. (1977). Memory from a cognitive developmental perspective: A theoretical and empirical review. In W. F. Overton & J. M. Gallagher (Eds.), *Knowledge and development* (Vol. 1, *Advances in research and theory*). New York: Plenum.

LIBERMAN, A. M., HARRIS, K. S., EIMAS, P. D., LISKER, L., & BASTIAN, J. (1961). An effect of learning on speech perception: The discrimination of durations of silence with and without phonemic significance. *Language and Speech, 4,* 175–195.

LICKONA, T. (ED.) (1976). *Moral development and behavior.* New York: Holt, Rinehart and Winston.

LIEBERMAN, P. (1975). *On the origins of language.* New York: Macmillan.

LIEBERT, R., & POULOS, R. (1976). Television as a moral teacher. In Lickona.

LIEBERT, D. E. (1979). Television advertising and values. In B. Logan & K. Moody (Eds.), *Television awareness training.* New York: Media Action Research Center.

LIEBERT, J., & WICKS-NELSON, R. (1981). *Developmental psychology* (3rd ed.). Englewood Cliffs, NJ: Prentice-Hall.

LIMBER, J. (1980). Language in child and chimp? *American Psychologist, 1977, 32,* 280–295. Reprinted in Sebeok & Umiker-Sebeok.

LINDE, C., & LABOV, W. (1975). Spatial networks as a site for the study of language and thought. *Language, 51,* 924–939.

LINDEN, E. (1981). *Apes, men, and language* (Rev. ed.). New York: Penguin.

LINDSAY, P. H., & NORMAN, D. A. (1977). *Human information processing* (2nd ed.). New York: Academic Press.

LINGLE, J. H., GEVA, N., OSTROM, T. M., LEIPPE, M. R., & BAUMGARDNER, M.H. (1979). Thematic effects of person judgments on impression formation. *Journal of Personality and Social Psychology, 37,* 674–687.

LIPTON, J. P. (1977). On the psychology of eyewitness testimony. *Journal of Applied Psychology, 62,* 90–95.

LLOYD, B., & ARCHER, S. (EDS.). (1976). *Exploring sex differences.* New York: Academic Press.

LOCKHART, R. S., & CRAIK, F. I. M. (1978). "Levels of processing": A reply to Eysenck. *British Journal of Psychology, 69,* 171–175.

LOEVINGER, J., & KNOLL, E. (1983). Personality: Stages, traits, and the self. *Annual Review of Psychology,* Vol.34.

LOFTUS, E. F. (1979). *Eyewitness testimony.* Cambridge, MA: Harvard University Press.

LOFTUS, E. F. (1980a). Impact of expert testimony on the unreliability of eyewitness identification. *Journal of Applied Psychology, 65,* 9–15.

LOFTUS, E. F. (1980b). *Memory.* Reading, MA: Addison-Wesley.

LOFTUS, E. F., & BURNS, T. E. (1982). Mental shock can produce retrograde amnesia. *Memory & Cognition, 10,* 318–323.

LOFTUS, E. F., & LOFTUS, G. R. (1980). On the permanence of stored information in the human brain. *American Psychologist, 35,* 409–420.

LOFTUS, E. F., MILLER, D. G., & BURNS, H. J. (1978). Semantic integration of verbal information into a visual memory. *Journal of Experimental Psychology: Human Learning and Memory, 4,* 19–31.

LOFTUS, E. F., & PALMER, J. C. (1974). Reconstruction of automobile destruction: An example of the interaction between language and memory. *Journal of Verbal Learning and Verbal Behavior, 13,* 585–589.

LORENZ, K. (1966). *On aggression.* New York: Harcourt Brace Jovanovich.

LOVEJOY, C. O. (1981). The origin of man. *Science, 211,* 341–350.

LUBEK, I., & APFELBAUM, E. (1981). The hidden injuries of classical conditioning: An historical and psychological look at editorial taste in taste-aversion learning. Paper presented at the Annual Meeting of the Cheiron Society, River Falls, WI, June 10–13.

LUMSDEN, C. J., & WILSON, E. O. (1981). *Genes, mind, and culture.* Cambridge, MA: Harvard University Press.

LUMSDEN, C., & WILSON, E. O. (1983). The dawn of intelligence. *The Sciences, 23* (2, March/April), 22–31.

LURIA, A.R. (1968). *The mind of a mnemonist.* New York: Basic Books.

LYNCH, K. (1960). *The image of the city.* Cambridge MA: M.I.T. and Harvard University Press.

LYONS, J. (1970). *Noam Chomsky.* New York: Viking Press.

MACCOBY, C. E., & JACKLIN, C. N. (1974). *The psychology of sex differences* (2 Vols.). Stanford, CA: Stanford University Press.

MACCORQUODALE, K., & MEEHL, P. (1954). Edward C. Tolman. In W. K. Estes et al., *Modern learning theory.* Appleton-Century-Crofts.

MACFARLANE, D. A. (1930). The role of kinesthesis in maze learning. *University of California Publications in Psychology, 4,* 277–305.

MACKINTOSH, N. J. (1978). Cognitive or associative theories of conditioning: Implications of an analysis of blocking. In S. Hulse, H. Fowler, and W. Honig (Eds.), *Cognitive processes in animal behavior.* Hillsdale, NJ: Lawrence Erlbaum.

MACNAMARA, J. (1976). Stomachs assimilate and accommodate, don't they? *Canadian Psychological Review, 17,* 167–173.

MACWHINNEY, B., KEENAN, J. M., & REINKE, P. (1982). The role of arousal in memory for conversation. *Memory & Cognition, 10,* 308–317.

MAHONEY, M. J., & DEMONBREUN, B. G. (1981). Problem solving bias in scientists (1978). Reprinted in Tweney, Doherty, & Mynatt.

MAIER, S. (1970). Failure to escape traumatic shock: Incompatible skeletal responses or learned helplessness? *Learning and Motivation, 1,* 157–170.

MAIER, S., & SELIGMAN, M. (1976). Learned helplessness: Theory and evidence. *Journal of Experimental Psychology: General, 105,* 3–46.

MALCOLM, N. (1964). Behaviorism as a philosophy of psychology. In T. W. Wann (Ed.), *Behaviorism and phenomenology.* Chicago: University of Chicago Press.

MALMI, W. A. (1976). Chimpanzees and language evolution. In Harnad et al.

MALTZMAN, I. (1955). Thinking: From a behavioristic point of view. *Psychological Review, 66,* 367–386.

MALTZMAN, I. (1977). Orienting in classical conditioning and generalization of the galvanic skin response to words: An overview. *Journal of Experimental Psychology: General, 106,* 111–119.

MALTZMAN, I. (1979). Orienting reflexes and significance: A reply to O'Gorman. *Psychophysiology, 16,* 274–282.

MALTZMAN, I., & MORRISETT, L. (1952). Different strengths of set in the solution of anagrams. *Journal of Experimental Psychology, 44,* 242–246.

MALTZMAN, I., & MORRISETT, L. (1953a). The effects of single and compound classes of anagrams on set solutions. *Journal of Experimental Psychology, 45,* 345–350.

MALTZMAN, I., & MORRISETT, L. (1953b). Effects of task instructions on solutions of different classes of anagrams. *Journal of Experimental Psychology, 45,* 351–354.

MALTZMAN, I., RASKIN, D., AND WOLFF, C. (1979). Latent inhibition of the GSR conditioned to words. *Physiological Psychology, 7,* 193–203.

MAREK, G.R. (1975). *Toscanini.* London: Vision Press.

MARKUS, H. (1980). The self in thought and memory. In D. M. Wegner & R. R. Vallecker (Eds.), *The self in social psychology.* London: Oxford University Press.

MARLER, P. (1970). A comparative approach to vocal learning: Song development in white-crowned sparrows. *Journal of Comparative and Physiological Psychology, 71,* 1–25. Reprinted in Seligman & Hager (1972).

MARLER, P. (1976). An ethological theory of the origin of vocal learning. In Harnad et al.

MARLER, P., & PETERS, S. (1981). Sparrows learn adult song and more from memory. *Science, 213,* 780–782.

MARSHACK, A. (1972). *The roots of civilization.* New York: McGraw-Hill.

MARSHACK, A. (1976). Some implications of the Paleolithic symbolic evidence for the origin of language. In Harnad et al.

MARSHALL, J. C. (1980). On the biology of language acquisition. In Caplan.

MARSCHARK, M., & PAIVIO, A. (1977). Integrative processing of concrete and abstract sentences. *Journal of Verbal Learning and Verbal Behavior, 16,* 217–231.

MARTLEW, M. (ED.). (1983). *The psychology of written language: A developmental approach.* New York: John Wiley.

MASSON, M. E. J. (1979). Context and inferential cuing of sentence recall. *Journal of Verbal Learning and Verbal Behavior, 18,* 173–186.

MATLIN, M. (1983). *Cognition.* New York: Holt, Rinehart & Winston.

MAY, R. (1980). *Sex and fantasy.* New York: Norton.

MAYER, R. F. (1983). *Thinking, problem solving, cognition.* San Francisco: W. H. Freeman & Co.

MAYNARD SMITH, J. (1971). What use is sex? *Journal of Theoretical Biology, 1971, 30,* 319–335.

MAYNARD SMITH, J. (1978). *The evolution of sex.* London: Cambridge University Press.

MAYNARD SMITH, J. (1982a). The evolution of social behaviour: A classification of models. In King's College Sociobiology Group (Eds.), *Current problems in sociobiology.* Cambridge, UK: Cambridge University Press.

MAYNARD SMITH, J. (1982b). *Evolution and the theory of games.* Cambridge, UK: Cambridge University Press.

MAYNARD SMITH, J. (1984). Game theory and the evolution of behavior. *Behavioral and Brain Sciences, 1,* 95–126.

MCCALL, R. B. (1977). Challenges to a science of developmental psychology. *Child Development, 48,* 333–344.

MCCLOSKEY, M., & EGETH, H. E. (1983). Eyewitness identification: What can a psychologist tell a jury? *American Psychologist, 38,* 550–563.

MCHENRY, H. M. (1982). The pattern of human evolution: Studies on bipedalism, mastication and encephalization. *Annual Review of Anthropology, 11,* 151–173.

MCKOON, G., & RATLIFF, R. (1981). The comprehension processes and memory structures involved in instrumental reference. *Journal of Verbal Learning and Verbal Behavior, 20,* 671–682.

MCNAMARA, H., LONG, J., & WIKE, E. (1956). Learning without response under two conditions of external cues. *Journal of Comparative and Physiological Psychology, 49,* 477–480.

MCNEIL, D. (1970). *The acquisition of language.* New York: Harper & Row.

MEDIN, D., ROBERTS, W., & DAVIS, R. (EDS.). (1976). *Processes of animal memory.* Hillsdale, NJ: Lawrence Erlbaum.

MEYER, D. E., SCHVANEVELDT, R. W., & RUDDY, M. G. (1974). Loci of contextual effects on visual word recognition. In P. Rabbitt & S. Dornic (Eds.), *Attention and performance V.* New York: Academic Press.

MIDGLEY, M. (1978). *Beast and man.* Ithaca, NY: Cornell University Press.

MILGRAM, S. (1974). *Obedience to authority.* New York: Harper & Row.

MILLER, G. A. (1956). The magical number, seven, plus or minus two: Some limits on our capacity for processing information. *Psychological Review, 63,* 81–97.

MILLER, G. (1981). *Language and speech.* San Francisco: Freeman.

MILLER, J. L., & EIMAS, P. D. (1983). Studies on the categorization of speech by infants. *Cognition, 13,* 135–165.

MILLER, N. (1969). Learning of visceral and glandular responses. *Science, 163,* 434–445.

MILLER, N. E., & DOLLARD, J. (1941). *Social learning and imitation.* New Haven: Yale University Press.

MISCHEL, T. (1971). *Cognitive development and epistemology.* New York: Academic Press.

MISCHEL, W., & MISCHEL, H. (1976). A cognitive social learning approach to morality and self-regulation. In Lickona.

MITROFF, I. (1974). Scientists and confirmation bias. Reprinted in Tweney, Doherty, & Mynatt (1981).

MOATES, D. R., & SCHUMACHER, G. M. (1980). *An introduction to cognitive psychology.* Belmont, CA: Wadsworth, 1980.

MODGIL, S., & MODGIL, C. (Eds.). (1982). *Jean Piaget: Consensus and controversy.* London: Holt, Rinehart & Winston.

MONEY, J., & ERHARDT, A. (1972). *Man & woman: Boy & girl.* Baltimore: The Johns Hopkins University Press.

MONTAGUE, A. (1976). Toolmaking, hunting, and the origin of language. In Harnad et al. (1976).

MONTAGUE, A. (ED.). (1980). *Sociobiology examined.* New York: Oxford University Press.

MONTAGUE, M. F. A. (ED.). (1968). *Man and aggression.* London: Oxford University Press.

MORRIS, C. D., STEIN, B. S., & BRANSFORD, J. D. (1979). Prerequisites for the utilization of knowledge in the recall of prose passages. *Journal of Experimental Psychology: Human Learning and Memory, 5,* 253–261.

MOSKOWITZ, B. A. (1978). The acquisition of language. *Scientific American, November, 239,* 92–108.

MOWRER, O. H. (1954). The psychologist looks at language. *American Psychologist, 9,* 660–694. Reprinted in Jakobovits & Miron (1967).

MUELLER, C., & SCHOENFELD, W. (1954). Edwin R. Guthrie. In W. K. Estes et al., *Modern learning theory.* New York: Appleton-Century-Crofts.

MÜNSTERBERG, H. (1908). *On the witness stand.* New York: Boardman.

MYERS, R. E. (1976). Comparative neurology of vocalization and speech: Proof of a dichotomy. In Harnad et al.

MYNATT, C. R., DOHERTY, M. E., & TWENEY, R. D. (1981). A simulated research environment (1978). Reprinted in Tweney, Doherty, & Mynatt.

NEISSER, U. (ED.). (1982). *Memory observed.* San Francisco: W. H. Freeman & Company Publishers.

NELSON, K. E. (Ed.). (1980). *Children's language* (Vol. 2). New York: Gardner Press.

NEWELL, A., & SIMON, H. (1972). *Human problem solving.* Englewood Cliffs, NJ: Prentice-Hall.

NEWPORT, E. L., GLEITMAN, H., & GLEITMAN, L. R. (1977). Mother, I'd rather do it myself: Some effects and non-effects of maternal speech style. In C. Snow & C. A. Ferguson (Eds.), *Talking to children: Language input and acquisition.* Cambridge, UK: Cambridge University Press.

NICKERSON, R. S., & ADAMS, M. J. (1979). Long-term memory for a common object. *Cognitive Psychology, 10,* 287–307.

NISBETT, R. E., & ROSS, L. (1980). *Human inference: Strategies and shortcomings in social judgment.* Englewood Cliffs, NJ: Prentice-Hall.

NORMAN, D. A. & RUMELHART, D. E. (1975). *Explorations in cognition.* San Francisco: W. H. Freeman & Company Publishers.

O'BARR, W. M. (1982). *Linguistic evidence: Language, power, and strategy in the courtroom.* New York: Academic Press.

OBRIST, P., SUTTERER, J., & HOWARD, J. (1972). Preparatory cardiac changes: A psychobiological approach. In A. Black and W. Prokasy (Eds.), *Classical conditioning II.* New York: Appleton-Century-Crofts.

O'KEEFE, J., & NADEL, L. (1974). Maps in the brain. *New Scientist, 62,* 749–751.

O'KEEFE, J., & NADEL, L. (1978). *The hippocampus as a cognitive map.* Oxford, UK: Clarendon Press.

O'KEEFE, J., & NADEL, L. (1979). Précis of The hippocampus as a cognitive map. *The Behavioral and Brain Sciences, 2,* 487–533.

OLDS, J., & MILNER, P. (1954). Positive reinforcement produced by electrical stimulation of the septal area and other regions of rat brain. *Journal of Comparative and Physiological Psychology, 47,* 419–427.

OLDS, J. (196^). Differentiation of reward systems in the brain by self-stimulation techniques. In E. Ramey & D. O'Doherty (Eds.), *Electrical studies on the unanesthetized brain.* New York: Paul B. Hueber.

ORGEL, L., & CRICK, F. (1980). Selfish DNA: The ultimate parasite. *Nature, 284,* 604–607.

OSGOOD, C. E. (1963). On understanding and creating sentences. *American Psychologist, 18,* 735–751. Reprinted in Jakobovits & Miron (1967).

OWENS, J., BOWER, G. H., & BLACK, J. B. (1979). The 'soap opera' effect in story recall. *Memory & Cognition, 7,* 185–191.

PAIVIO, A. (1971). *Imagery and verbal processes.* New York: Holt, Rinehart, & Winston.

PAIVIO, A. (1975). Coding distinctions and repetition effects in memory. In G. H. Bower (Ed.), *The psychology of learning and motivation* (Vol. 9). New York: Academic Press.

PAIVIO, A., & BEGG, I. (1981). *Psychology of language.* Englewood Cliffs, NJ: Prentice-Hall.

PARKER, S. T., & GIBSON, K. R. (1979). A developmental model for the evolution of language and intelligence. *Behavioral and Brain Sciences, 2,* 367–408.

PARSONS, C. (1960). Inhelder's and Piaget's the growth of logical thinking II: A logician's view. *British Journal of Psychology, 51,* 75–84.

PATTERSON, F. (1980). Innovative uses of language by a gorilla: A case study. In Nelson.

PATTERSON, F., & LINDEN, E. (1982). *The education of Koko.* New York: Holt, Rinehart & Winston.

PATTERSON, T. E., & MCCLURE, R. D. (1976). *The unseeing eye: The myth of television power in national politics.* New York: Putnam's.

PAVLOV, I. P. (1928). *Lectures on conditioned reflexes* (Vol. 1). London: Lawrence and Wishart.

PAVLOV, I. P. (1941). *Conditioned reflexes and psychiatry (Lectures on conditioned reflexes)* (Vol. 2). London: Lawrence and Wishart.

PAVLOV, I. P. (1927). *Conditioned reflexes.* New York: Dover.

PENDERY, M., & MALTZMAN, I. (1977). Instructions and the orienting reflex in "semantic conditioning" of the galvanic skin response in an innocuous situation. *Journal of Experimental Psychology: General, 106,* 120–140.

PENFIELD, W., & ROBERTS, L. (1959). *Speech and brain mechanisms.* Princeton, NJ: Princeton University Press.

PENFIELD, W. (1969). Consciousness, memory, and man's conditioned reflexes. In K. Pribram (Ed.), *On the biology of learning.* New York: Harcourt Brace Jovanovich.

PETERS, R. (1980). *Mammalian communication.* Monterey, CA: Brooks/Cole.

PETERSON, L. R., & PETERSON, M. (1959). Short-term retention of individual items. *Journal of Experimental Psychology, 58,* 193–198.

PFEIFFER, J. E. (1976). *The emergence of man.* New York: Harper & Row.

PFEIFFER, J. E. (1977). *The emergence of society.* New York: McGraw-Hill.

PIAGET, J. (1963). *The origins of intelligence in children* (1952). New York: Norton.

PIAGET, J. (1965). *The child's conception of number* (1941). New York: Norton.

PIAGET, J. (1967a). Cognitions and conservations: Review of J. S. Bruner et al., *Studies in cognitive growth. Contemporary Psychology, 12,* 530–533.

PIAGET, J. (1967b). *Six psychological studies* (1964). New York: Random House.

PIAGET, J. (1969). *Psychology of intelligence* (1947). Totowa, NJ: Littlefield, Adams.

PIAGET, J. (1970a). *Genetic epistemology.* New York: Norton.

PIAGET, J., & INHELDER, B. (1969a). Intellectual operations and their development. In P. Fraisse & J. Piaget (Eds.), *Experimental Psychology: Its scope and method* (Vol. VII, *Intelligence*) (1963). London: Routledge & Kegan Paul.

PIAGET, J., & INHELDER, B. (1969b). Mental images. In P. Fraisse & J. Piaget (Eds.), *Experimental Psychology: Its scope and method* (Vol. VII, *Intelligence*) (1963). London: Routledge & Kegan Paul.

PIAGET, J., & INHELDER, B. (1969c). *The psychology of the child* (1966). New York: Basic Books.

PIAGET, J. (1970b). Piaget's theory. In P. H. Mussen (Ed.), *Carmichael's manual of child psychology* (3rd ed., Vol. 1.) New York: John Wiley.

PIAGET, J. (1971a). *Biology and knowledge* (1967). Chicago: University of Chicago Press.

PIAGET, J. (1971b). *Psychology and epistemology*. New York: Viking.

PIAGET, J. (1971c). *Structuralism* (1968). London: Routledge & Kegan Paul.

PIAGET, J. (1972). *The principles of genetic epistemology* (1970). London: Routledge & Kegan Paul.

PIAGET, J. (1973). *The child and reality* (1972). New York: Grossman, 1973.

PIAGET, J. (1976). *The grasp of consciousness* (1974). Cambridge, MA: Harvard University Press.

PIAGET, J. (1978). *Behavior and evolution* (1976). New York: Pantheon.

PIAGET, J., & INHELDER, B. (1971). *Mental imagery in the child* (1966). New York: Basic Books.

PIAGET, J., & INHELDER, B. (1973). *Memory and intelligence* (1968). London: Routledge & Kegan Paul.

PICHERT, J. W ., & ANDERSON, R. C. (1977). Taking different perspectives on a story. *Journal of Educational Psychology, 69,* 309–315.

PINARD, J., & LAURENDEAU, M. (1969). 'Stage' in Piaget's cognitive-developmental theory: Exegesis of a concept. In Elkind & Flavell.

PINES, M. (1979). Good samaritans at age two? *Psychology Today,* June, 13 (1), 66–77.

PLOTKIN, H. C., & ODLING-SMEE, F. J. (1979). Learning, change, and evolution. *Advances in the study of behavior* (Vol. 10). New York: Academic Press.

PORTER, J. H., & ALLEN, J. (1977). Schedule-induced polydipsia contrast in the rat. *Animal Learning and Behavior, 5,* 184–192.

POSTMAN, L., & SASSENRATH, J. (1961). The automatic action of verbal rewards and punishments. *Journal of General Psychology, 65,* 109–136.

PREMACK, A. J. (1976). *Why chimps can read.* New York: Harper Colophon.

PREMACK, D. (1959). Toward empirical behavior laws: I. Positive reinforcement. *Psychological Review, 66,* 219–233.

PREMACK, D. (1962). Reversibility of the reinforcement relation. *Science, 136,* 255–257.

PREMACK, D. (1965a). Preparations for discussing behaviorism with a chimpanzee. In Smith & Miller.

PREMACK, D. (1965b). Reinforcement theory. In M. R. Jones (Ed.), *Nebraska Symposium on Motivation:* Lincoln, NB.: University of Nebraska Press.

PREMACK, D., & WOODRUFF, G. (1978). Does the chimpanzee have a theory of mind? *Behavioral and Brain Sciences, 1,* 515–526.

PREMACK, D., & PREMACK, A. J. (1982). *The mind of an ape.* New York: Norton.

PREMACK, D. (1983). Animal cognition. *Annual Review of Psychology* (Vol. 34). Palo Alto, CA: Annual Reviews, Inc.

PRESTON, I. L. (1975). *The great American blow-up: Puffery in advertising and selling.* Madison: University of Wisconsin Press.

PRESTON, I. L. (1977). The FTC's use of puffery and other selling claims made 'by implication.' *Journal of Business Research, 5,* 155–181.

PRESTON, I. L. (1980). Researchers at the Federal Trade Commission—Peril and Promise. In J. H. Leigh & C. R. Martin, Jr. (Eds.), *Current issues and research in advertising 1980.* Ann Arbor: University of Michigan Graduate School of Business Administration, Division of Research.

PRIBRAM, K., & GILL, M. (1976). *Freud's 'Project' reassessed.* New York: Basic Books.

PROKASY, W. (ED.). (1965). *Classical conditioning.* New York: Appleton-Century-Crofts.

RAPAPORT, D. (1960). Psychoanalysis as a developmental psychology. In B. Kaplan & S. Wapner (Eds), *Perspectives in psychological theory.* New York: International Universities Press.

RATLIFF, F. (1976). On the psychophysiological bases of universal color terms. *Proceedings of the American Philosophical Society, 120,* 311–330.

REESE, H. W., & OVERTON, W. F. (1970). Models of development and theories of development. In L. R. Goulet & P. B. Baltes (Eds.), *Life span developmental psychology.* New York: Academic Press.

REICHER, G. M. (1969). Perceptual recognition as a function of meaningfulness of stimulus material. *Journal of Experimental Psychology, 81,* 275–280.

REITMAN, J. S. (1971). Mechanisms of forgetting in short-term memory. *Cognitive Psychology, 2,* 185–105.

REITMAN, J. S. (1974). Without surreptitious rehearsal, information in short-term memory decays. *Journal of Verbal Learning and Verbal Behavior, 13,* 365–377.

RESCORLA, R. (1968). Probability of shock in the presence of CS in fear conditioning. *Journal of Comparative and Physiological Psychology, 56,* 1–5.

RESCORLA, R. (1975). Pavlovian excitatory and inhibitory conditioning. In W. K. Estes (Ed.), *Handbook of learning and cognitive processes,* (Vol. 2). Hillsdale, NJ: Lawrence Erlbaum.

RESCORLA, R. (1978). Some implications of a cognitive perspective on Pavlovian conditioning. In S. 'Iulse, H. Fowler, & W. Honig (Eds.), *Cognitive processes in animal behavior.* Hillsdale, NJ: Lawrence Erlbaum.

RESCORLA, R. (1980). Simultaneous and successive associations in sensory preconditioning. *Journal of Experimental Psychology: Animal Behavior Processes, 6,* 207–216.

RESCORLA, R., & WAGNER, A. (1972). A theory of Pavlovian conditioning: Variations in the effectiveness of reinforcement and nonreinforcement. In A. Black and W. Prokasy (Eds.), *Classical conditioning II.* New York: Appleton-Century-Crofts.

REYNOLDS, A. G., & FLAGG, P. W. (1983). *Cognitive psychology* (2nd ed.). Boston: Little, Brown.

RIECHMANN, P. F., & COSTE, E. L. (1980). Mental imagery and the comprehension of figurative language: Is there a relationship? In R. P. Honeck & R. R. Hoffman (Eds.), *Cognition and figurative language.* Hillsdale, NJ: Lawrence Erlbaum.

RISTAU, C. A., & ROBBINS, D. (1982). Language in the great apes: A critical review. In J. S. Rosenblatt, R. A. Hinde, C. Beer, & M. C. Busnel (Eds.), *Advances in the study of behavior* (Vol. 12). New York: Academic Press.

ROAZEN, P. (1976). *Erik H. Erikson: The power and limits of a vision.* New York: Free Press.

ROBBINS, D. (1980). Mathematical learning theory: W. K. Estes and stimulus sampling. In G. Gazda & R. Corsini (Eds.), *Theories of learning.* Itasca, IL: F. E. Peacock.

ROBERTS, D., & BACHEN, C. (1981). Mass communication effects. *Annual Review of Psychology, 32,* 307–356.

ROBINSON, B. W. (1976). Limbic influences on human speech. In Harnad et al.

ROEDIGER, H. L. (1980). Memory metaphors in cognitive psychology. *Memory & Cognition, 8,* 231–246.

ROGERS, T. B. (1981). A model of the self as an aspect of the human information processing system. In N. Cantor & J. F. Kihlstrom (Eds.), *Cognition, social interaction and personality.* Hillsdale, NJ: Lawrence Erlbaum.

ROSEN, H. (1980). *The development of sociomoral knowledge.* New York: Columbia University Press.

ROSENBERG, A. (1980). *Sociobiology and the preemption of social science.* Baltimore: The Johns Hopkins University Press.

ROSENFELD, A. (1980). Sociobiology stirs a controversy over the limits of science. *Smithsonian,* September, 73–80.

ROSS, M., & SICOLY, F. (1979). Egocentric biases in availability and attribution. *Journal of Personality and Social Psychology, 37,* 322–336.

ROTFELD, H. J., & PRESTON, I. L. (1981). The potential impact of research on advertising law. *Journal of Advertising Research, 21*(2), 9–18.

ROTHBART, M., FULERO, S., JENSEN, C., HOWARD, J., & BIRRELL, P. (1978). From individual to group impressions: Availability heuristics in stereotype formation. *Journal of Experimental Social Psychology, 14,* 237–255.

ROTHBART, M., EVANS, M., & FULERO, S. (1979). Recall for confirming events: Memory processes and the maintenance of social stereotypes. *Journal of Experimental Social Psychology, 15,* 343–355.

ROZIN, P., & KALAT, J. (1971). Specific hungers and poison avoidance as adaptive specializations of learning. *Psychological Review, 78,* 459–486.

ROZIN, P., & KALAT, J. (1972). Learning as a situation-specific adaptation. In Seligman & Hager.

ROZIN, P. (1976). The evolution of intelligence and access to the cognitive unconscious. In J. Sprague & A. Epstein (Eds.), *Progress in Psychobiology and Physiological Psychology* (Vol. 6). New York: Academic Press.

ROZIN, P. (1977). The significance of learning mechanisms in food selection: Some biology, psychology, and sociology of science. In L. M. Barker, M. R. Best, & M. Domjan (Eds.), *Learning mechanisms in food selection.* Waco, TX.: Baylor University Press.

RUBENSTEIN, H., LEWIS, S. S., & RUBENSTEIN, M. A. (1971). Evidence for phonemic recoding in visual word recognition. *Journal of Verbal Learning and Verbal Behavior, 10,* 645–657.

RUMBAUGH, D. M. (1980). Language behavior of apes. In Sebeok & Umiker-Sebeok.

RUMBAUGH, D. M. (1981). Who feeds clever Hans? In Sebeok & Rosenthal.

RUMELHART, D. E. (1980). Schemata: The building blocks of cognition. In R. Spiro, B. C. Bruce, & W. F. Brewer (Eds.), *Theoretical issues in reading comprehension.* Hillsdale, NJ: Lawrence Erlbaum.

RUSE, M. (1979). *Sociobiology, sense or nonsense? (Episteme,* Vol. 8.). Dordrecht, Holland: D. Reidel.

RUSHTON, J. (1982a). Altruism and society: A social learning perspective. *Ethics, 92,* 425–446.

RUSHTON, J. (1982b). Moral cognition, behaviorism and social learning theory. *Ethics, 92,* 459–467.

SAHLINS, M. D. (1976). *The use and abuse of biology.* Ann Arbor: University of Michigan Press.

SAMELSON, F. (1980). Little Albert, Cyril Burt's twins, and the need for a critical science. *American Psychologist, 35,* 619–625.

SAMUELSON, P. A. (1983). Complete genetic models for altruism, kin-selection and like-gene selection. *Journal of Social and Biological Structures, 6,* 3–15.

SAVAGE-RUMBAUGH, E. S., RUMBAUGH, D. M., & BOYSEN, S. (1980a). Linguistically mediated tool use and exchange by chimpanzees. In Sebeok & Umiker-Sebeok.

SAVAGE-RUMBAUGH, E. S., & RUMBAUGH, D. M. (1980b). Language analogue project, phase II: Theory and tactics. In Nelson.

SCHANK, R. C., & ABELSON, R. P. (1977). *Scripts, plans, goals, and understanding.* Hillsdale, NJ: Lawrence Erlbaum.

SCARR-SALAPATEK, S. (1976). An evolutionary perspective on infant intelligence. In M. Lewis (Ed.), *Origins of intelligence.* New York: Plenum.

SCHATZ, C. (1954). The role of context in the perception of stops. *Language, 30,* 47–56.

SCHEFFLER, I. (1967). *Science and subjectivity.* Indianapolis: Bobbs-Merrill.

SCHNEIDER, W., & SHIFFRIN, R. M. (1977). Controlled and automatic human information processing: I. Detection, search, and attention. *Psychological Review, 84,* 1–66.

SCHRANK, J. (1977). *Analyzing advertising claims.* Palatine, IL: The Learning Seed Company.

SCHWARTZ, B. (1978). *Psychology of learning and behavior.* New York: Norton.

SCHWARTZ, B. (1982). Reinforcement-induced behavioral stereotyping: How not to teach people to discover rules. *Journal of Experimental Psychology: General, 111,* 23–59.

SEAMON, J. G. (1980). *Memory & cognition.* New York: Oxford University Press.

SEBEOK, T. A. (1980). Looking in the destination for what should have been sought in the source. In Sebeok & Umiker-Sebeok.

SEBEOK, T. A., & ROSENTHAL, R. (Eds.). (1981). *The clever Hans phenomenon. Annals of the New York Academy of Sciences* (Vol. 364). New York: New York Academy of Sciences.

SEBEOK, T. A., & UMIKER-SEBEOK, J. (1979). Performing animals: Secrets of the trade. *Psychology Today,* November, *13* (6), 78–91.

SEBEOK, T. A., & UMIKER-SEBEOK, J. (Eds.). (1980). *Speaking of apes: A critical anthology of two-way communication with man.* New York: Plenum.

SECHENOV, I. M. (1965). *Reflexes of the Brain* (1863). Partially reprinted in R. Herrnstein and E. Boring (Eds.), *A source book in the history of psychology.* Cambridge, MA: Harvard University Press.

SELIGMAN, M. (1975). *Helplessness.* San Francisco: W. H. Freeman & Company Publishers.

SELIGMAN, M. E. P., & HAGER, J. L. (EDS.). (1972). *Biological boundaries of learning.* New York: Appleton-Century-Crofts.

SELIGMAN, M., & JOHNSTON, J. (1973). Cognitive theory of avoidance learning. In F. McGuigan & D. Lumsden (Eds.), *Contemporary approaches to conditioning and learning.* Washington, DC: Winston.

SEM-JACOBSEN, C. (1976). Electrical stimulation and self-stimulation in man with chronic implanted electrodes. Interpretation and pitfall of results. In A. Wauquier & E. Rolls (Eds.), Brain-stimulation reward. Amsterdam: North-Holland.

SENNETT, R. (1977). *The fall of public man: On the social psychology of capitalism.* New York: Vintage.

SEWARD, J. P., & LEVY, N. (1949). Sign learning as a factor in extinction. *Journal of Experimental Psychology, 39,* 660–668.

SEWARD, J. P., & SEWARD, G. (1980). *Sex differences: Mental and tempermental.* Lexington, MA: Lexington Books.

SHAPERE, D. (1964). The structure of scientific revolutions. *Philosophical Review, 73,* 384–394.

SHEPARD, R. N. (1978). The mental image. *American Psychologist, 33,* 125–137.

SHEPARD, R. N., & METZLER, J. (1971). Mental rotation of three-dimensional objects. *Science, 171,* 701–703.

SHEPARD, R. N., & FENG, C. A. (1972). A chronometric study of mental paper folding. *Cognitive Psychology, 3,* 228–243.

SHERMAN, J. A. (1978). *Sex-related cognitive differences.* Springfield, IL: Chas. C Thomas.

SHETTLEWORTH, S. (1972). *Constraints on learning: Advances in the study of behavior* (Vol. 4). New York: Academic Press.

SHIELDS, W. M., & SHIELDS, L. M. (1983). Forcible rape: An evolutionary perspective. *Ethology and Sociobiology, 4,* 115–136.

SHIFFRIN, R. M. (1973). Information persistence in short-term memory. *Journal of Experimental Psychology, 100,* 39–49.

SHIFFRIN, R. M., & SCHNEIDER, W. (1977). Controlled and automatic human information processing: II. Perceptual learning, automatic attending, and a general theory. *Psychological Review, 84,* 127–190.

SHIMP, C. P. (1976). Organization in memory and behavior. *Journal of the Experimental Analysis of Behavior, 26,* 113–130.

SHIMP, T. A. (1979). Social-psychological (mis)representations in television advertising. *Journal of Consumer Affairs, 13,* 28–40.

SHIMP, T. A. (1983). Evaluative verbal content and deception in advertising: A critical review. In R.J. Harris (Ed.), *Information processing research in advertising.* Hillsdale, NJ: Lawrence Erlbaum.

SHUY, R. W. (1981). Toward a developmental theory of writing. In C. H. Frederiksen & J. F. Dominic (Eds.), *Writing: Process, development, and communication.* Hillsdale, NJ: Lawrence Erlbaum.

SHUY, R. W., & LARKIN, D. (1978). Linguistic consideration in the simplification/classification of insurance policy language. *Discourse Processes, 1,* 305–321.

SIEGLER, R. S. (1983). Five generalizations about cognitive development. *American Psychologist, 38,* 263–277.

SIEGLER, R. S., & ROBINSON, M. (1982). The development of numerical understandings. In H. W. Reese & L. P. Lipsitt (Eds.), *Advances in child development and behavior* (Vol. 16). New York: Academic Press.

SIGEL, E. E., & HOOPER, F. H. (Eds.). (1968). *Logical thinking in children.* London: Holt, Rinehart & Winston.

SINGER, M. (1979). Processes of inference during sentence encoding. *Memory & Cognition, 7,* 192–200.

SINGER, M. (1981). Verifying the assertions and implications of language. *Journal of Verbal Learning and Verbal Behavior, 20,* 46–60.

SINGER, P. (1981). *The expanding circle.* New York: Farrar, Straus & Giroux.

SINGULAR, S. (1982). A memory for all seasonings. *Psychology Today,* October, 16(10), 54–63.

SKINNER, B. F. (1931). The concept of reflex in the description of behavior. *Journal of General Psychology, 5,* 427–458.

SKINNER, B. F. (1938). *Behavior of organisms.* Englewood Cliffs, NJ: Prentice-Hall.

SKINNER, B. F. (1948a). 'Superstition' in the pigeon. *Journal of Experimental Psychology, 38,* 168–172.

SKINNER, B. F. (1948b). *Walden II.* New York: Macmillan.

SKINNER, B. F. (1950). Are theories of learning necessary? *Psychological Review, 57,* 193–216.

SKINNER, B. F. (1957). *Verbal behavior.* Englewood Cliffs, NJ: Prentice-Hall.

SKINNER, B. F. (1961). A case history in scientific method (1956). Reprinted in *Cumulative Record* (3rd ed.) Englewood Cliffs, N.J.: Prentice-Hall.

SKINNER, B. F. (1961). Pigeons in a pelican (1960). Reprinted in *Cumulative Record* (3rd ed.). Englewood Cliffs, NJ: Prentice-Hall.

SKINNER, B. F. (1969). *Contingencies of reinforcement.* Englewood Cliffs, NJ: Prentice-Hall.

SKINNER, B. F. (1972). *Beyond freedom and dignity.* New York: Bantam.

SKINNER, B. F. (1972). A critique of psychoanalytic concepts and theories (1954). Reprinted in *Cumulative Record* (3rd ed.). Englewood Cliffs, N.J.: Prentice-Hall.

SKINNER, B. F. (1974). *About behaviorism.* New York: Knopf.

SKINNER, B. F. (1976). *Particulars of my life.* New York: Knopf.

SLOBIN, D. I. (1973). Cognitive prerequisites for the development of grammar. In C. A. Ferguson & D. I. Slobin (Eds.), *Studies of child language development.* New York: Holt, Rinehart & Winston.

SLOVIC, P., & LICHTENSTEIN, S. (1971). Comparison of Bayesian and regression approaches to the study of information processing in judgment. *Organizational Behavior and Human Performance, 6,* 649–744.

SLOVIC, P., & FISCHHOFF, B. (1977). On the psychology of experimental surprises. *Journal of Experimental Psychology: Human Perception and Performance, 3,* 544–551.

SLOVIC, P., FISCHHOFF, B., & LICHTENSTEIN, S. (1982). Facts versus fears: Understanding perceived risk. In Kahneman, D., Slovic, P., & Tversky, A. (Eds.), *Judgment under uncertainty: Heuristics and biases.* Cambridge UK: Cambridge University Press.

SMEDSLUND, J. (1968). The acquisition of conservation of substance and weight in children, I–VI. *Scandinavian Journal of Psychology, 2,* 11–210. I, III, V, & VI reprinted in Sigel & Hooper.

SMITH, E. E., SHOBEN, E. J., & RIPS, L. J. (1974). Structure and process in semantic memory: A featural model for semantic decisions. *Psychological Review, 81,* 214–241.

SMITH, F., & MILLER, G. (1965). *The genesis of language.* Cambridge, MA: MIT Press.

SMITH, E. E. (1978). Theories of semantic memory. In W. K. Estes (Ed.), *Handbook of learning and cognitive processes* (Vol. 6). Hillsdale, NJ: Lawrence Erlbaum.

SMITH, P. (1974). Ethological methods. In B. Foss (Ed.), *New perspective in child development.* Baltimore: Penguin.

SNOW, C. E. (1978). Mother's speech to children learning language. *Child Development, 43,* 549–565. Reprinted in C. Bloom.

SNOWDEN, C. T. (1983). Ethology comparative psychology and animal behavior. *Annual Review of Psychology* (Vol. 34). Palo Alto, CA: Annual Reviews.

SNYDER, M., TANKE, E. D., & BERSCHEID, E. (1977). Social perception and interpersonal behavior: On the self-fulfilling nature of social stereotypes. *Journal of Personality and Social Psychology, 35,* 656–666.

SNYDER, M., & URANOWITZ, S. W. (1978). Reconstructing the past: Some cognitive consequences of person perception. *Journal of Personality and Social Psychology, 36,* 941–950.

SOLANTO, M., & KATKIN, E. (1979). Classical EDR conditioning using a truly random control and subjects differing in electrodermal lability level. *Bulletin of the Psychonomic Society, 14,* 49–52.

SOLOMON, R. (1964). Punishment. *American Psychologist, 19,* 239–253.

SPELKE, E., HIRST, W., & NEISSER, U. (1976). Skills of divided attention. *Cognition, 4,* 215–230.

SPENCE, K. (1944). The nature of theory construction in contemporary psychology. *Psychological Review, 51,* 47–68.

SPENCE, K. (1956). *Behavior theory and conditioning.* New Haven, CT: Yale University Press.

SPENCER, H. (1897). *Principles of psychology* (3rd ed.) (1855). New York: Appleton & Co.

SPERLING, G. A. (1960). The information available in brief visual presentation. *Psychological Monographs, 74,* Whole No. 498.

SPILICH, G. J., VESONDER, G. T., CHIESI, H. L., & VOSS, J. F. (1979). Text processing of domain-related information for individuals with high and low domain knowledge. *Journal of Verbal Learning and Verbal Behavior, 18,* 275–290.

SPIRO, R. J. (1980). Constructive processes in prose comprehension and recall. In R. J. Spiro, B. C. Bruce, & W. F. Brewer (Eds.), *Theoretical issues in reading comprehension.* Hillsdale, NJ: Lawrence Erlbaum.

STAATS, A. (Ed.). (1964). *Human learning.* New York: Holt, Rinehart & Winston.

STAATS, A. (1975). *Social behaviorism.* Homewood, IL.: Dorsey.

STADDON, J. (1975). Learning as adaptation. In W. K. Estes (Ed.), *Handbook of learning and cognitive processes* (Vol. 2). Hillsdale, NJ: Lawrence Erlbaum.

STADDON, J. (1977). Schedule-induced behavior. In W. Honig & J. Staddon (Eds.), *Handbook of operant behavior.* Englewood Cliffs, NJ: Prentice-Hall.

STADDON, J., & SIMMELHAG, V. (1971). The 'superstition' experiment: A reexamination of its implications for the principles of adaptive behavior. *Psychological Review, 78,* 3–43.

STEBBING, G. L., & AYALA, F. J. (1981). Is a new evolutionary synthesis necessary? *Science, 213,* 967–971.

STEKLIS, H. D., & HARNAD, S. R. (1976). From hand to mouth: Some critical stages in the evolution of language. In Harnad et al.

STRATTON, G. M. (1917). The mnemonic feat of the 'Shass Pollak.' *Psychological Review, 24,* 244–247.

STROMEYER, C. F. (1970). Eidetikers. *Psychology Today,* November, 76–80.

STROMEYER, C. F., & PSOTKA, J. (1970). The detailed texture of eidetic images. *Nature, 225,* 346–349.

SULIN, R. A., & DOOLING, D. J. (1974). Intrusion of a thematic idea in retention of prose. *Journal of Experimental Psychology, 103,* 255–262.

SULLOWAY, F. J. (1979). *Freud: Biologist of the mind.* New York: Basic Books.

SYMONS, D. (1979). *The evolution of human sexuality.* New York: Oxford University Press.

SYMONS, D. (1983). Another woman that never evolved. *Quarterly Review of Biology, 57,* 297–300.

TALBOTT, J. A. (1982). Development. In S. Gilman (Ed.), *Introducing psychoanalytic theory.* New York: Brunner/Mazel.

TART, C. (1975). *Learning to use extrasensory perception.* Chicago: University of Chicago Press.

TAYLOR, S. E. (1982). The availability bias in social perception and interaction. In Kahneman, D., Slovic, P., & Tversky, A. (Eds.), *Judgment under uncertainty: Heuristics and biases.* Cambridge, UK: Cambridge University Press.

TAYLOR, S. E., & CROCKER, J. (1981). Schematic bases of social information processing. In E. T. Higgins, C. P. Herman, & M. P. Zanna (Eds.), *Social cognition: The Ontario Symposium* (Vol. 1). Hillsdale, NJ: Lawrence Erlbaum.

TERRACE, H. (1963a). Discrimination learning with and without errors. *Journal of the Experimental Analysis of Behavior, 6,* 1–27.

TERRACE, H.(1963b). Errorless transfer of a discrimination across two continua. *Journal of the Experimental Analysis of Behavior, 6,* 223–232.

TERRACE, H. S. (1979a). *Nim: A chimpanzee who learned sign language.* New York: Washington Square Press.

TERRACE, H. S. (1979b). How Nim Chimpsky changed my mind. *Psychology Today,* November, *13* (6), 65–76.

TERRACE, H. S. (1979c). Is problem-solving language? *Journal of the Experimental Analysis of Behavior, 31,* 161–175.

TERRACE, H. S. (1982). Why Koko can't talk. *The Sciences,* December, 22(9), 8–10.

TERRACE, H. S., PETITTO, L. A., SANDERS, R. J., & BEVER, T. G. (1979). Can an ape create a sentence? *Science, 206,* 891–902.

TERRACE, H. S., PETITTO, L. A., SANDERS, R. J., & BEVER, T. G. (1980). On the grammatical capacity of apes. In Nelson.

THISTLETHWAITE, D. (1951). A critical review of latent learning and related experiments. *Psychological Bulletin 48,* 97–129.

THOMPSON, C. P. (1982). Memory for unique personal events: The roommate study. *Memory & Cognition, 10,* 324–332.

THOMPSON, C. P. (1983). *Memory for unique personal events: Some implications of the personal schema.* Unpublished manuscript.

THOMSON, D. M., & TULVING, E. (1970). Associative encoding and retrieval: weak and strong cues. *Journal of Experimental Psychology, 86,* 255–262.

THOMSON, R. H. (1930). An experimental study of memory as influenced by feeling tone. *Journal of Experimental Psychology, 13,* 462–467.

THORNDIKE, E. L. (1965). *Animal intelligence* (1911). New York: Hafner Press.

THORNDIKE, E. L. (1968). *Human learning* (1928–1929). New York: Johnson Reprint Corp.

THORNDIKE, L. (1923–1958). *History of magic and experimental science* (8 Vols.). New York: Columbia University Press.

THORNDYKE, P. W., & HAYES-ROTH, B. (1982). Differences in spatial knowledge acquired from maps and navigation. *Cognitive Psychology, 14,* 560–589.

TIGER, L. (1979). *Optimism: The biology of hope.* New York: Touchstone.

TINBERGEN, N.(1951/1972). The innate disposition to learn. In Seligman & Hager.

TOLMAN, E. C., & HONZIK. (1930). 'Insight' in rats. *University of California Publications in Psychology, 4,* 215–232.

TOLMAN, E. C. (1933). Sign-gestalt or conditioned reflex? *Psychological Review, 40,* 391–411.

TOLMAN, E. C. (1938). The determiners of behavior at a choice point. *Psychological Review, 45,* 1–41.

TOLMAN, E. C. (1948). Cognitive maps in rats and men. *Psychological Review, 55,* 189–208.

TOLMAN, E. C. (1959). Principles of purposive behaviorism. In S. Koch (Ed.) *Psychology: A study of a science* (Vol. 2). New York: McGraw-Hill.

TOLMAN, E. C. (1967). *Purposive behavior in animals and men.* New York: Irvington. (Originally published, 1932).

TOLMAN, E. C., HALL, C. S., & BRETNALL, E. P. (1932). A disproof of the law of effect and a substitution of the laws of emphasis, motivation, and disruption. *Journal of Experimental Psychology, 15,* 601–614.

TOULMIN, S. (1971). The concept of 'stages' in cognitive development. In Mischel.

TOULMIN, S. (1972). *Human understanding* (Vol. I). *The collective use and education of concepts.* Princeton, NJ: Princeton University Press.

TREISMAN, A. M. (1964). Monitoring and storage of irrelevant messages in selective attention. *Journal of Verbal Learning and Verbal Behavior, 3,* 449–459.

TRIVERS, R. L. (1983). The evolution of sex. Review of G. Bell, *The masterpiece of nature: The evolution and genetics of sexuality. Quarterly Review of Biology, 58,* 62–67.

TRIVERS, R. L., & HARE, H. (1976). Haplodiploidy and the evolution of social insects. Reprinted in Hunt (1980).

TRIVERS, R. L., & WILLARD, D. E. (1973). Natural selection of parental ability to vary the sex ratio of offspring. *Science, 179,* 90–92.

TRIVERS, R. L. (1971). The evolution of reciprocal altruism. Reprinted in Clutton-Brock & Harvey (1978); Hunt (1980); and Caplan (1980).

TRIVERS, R. L. (1972). Prenatal investment and sexual selection. Reprinted in Clutton-Brock & Harvey (1978).

TRIVERS, R. L. (1974). Parent-offspring conflict. Reprinted in Clutton-Brock & Harvey (1978); and Hunt (1980).

TURIEL, B. (1973). Adolescent conflict in the development of moral principles. In R. L. Solso (Ed.), *Contemporary issues in cognitive psychology.* Washington, DC: V. H. Winston.

TVERSKY, A., & KAHNEMAN, D. (1973). Availability: A heuristic for judging frequency and probability. *Cognitive Psychology, 5,* 207–232.

TVERSKY, A., & KAHNEMAN, D. (1974). Judgment under uncertainty: Heuristics and biases. *Science, 185,* 1124–1131.

TVERSKY, A., & KAHNEMAN, D. (1981). The law of small numbers (1971). Reprinted in Tweney, Doherty & Mynatt.

TULVING, E. (1972). Episodic and semantic memory. In E. Tulving & W. Donaldson (Eds.), *Organization and memory.* New York: Academic Press.

TULVING, E., & THOMSON, D. M. (1973). Encoding specificity and retrieval processes in episodic memory. *Psychological Review, 80,* 352–373.

TWENEY, R. D., DOHERTY, M. E., & MYNATT, C. R. (EDS.). (1981). *On scientific thinking.* New York: Columbia University Press.

UMIKER-SEBEOK, J., & SEBEOK, T. A. (1980). Introduction: Questioning apes. In Sebeok & Umiker-Sebeok.

UZGIRIS, I. C. (1968). Situational generality of conservation. *Child Development,* 1964, *35,* 831–841. Reprinted in Sigel & Hooper.

VAN DEN BERGHE, P. (1979). *Human family systems: An evolutionary view.* New York: Elsevier.

VAN DEN BERGHE, P. (1983). Human inbreeding avoidance: Culture in nature. *The Behavioral and Brain Sciences, 6,* 91–124.

VAN DEN BERGHE, P., & BARASH, D. (1977). Inclusive fitness and human family structure. In Hunt (1980).

VERPLANCK, W. (1955). The control of the content of conversation: Reinforcement of statements of opinion. *Journal of Abnormal and Social Psychology, 51,* 668–676.

VOEKS, V. (1950). Formalization and clarification of a theory of learning. *Journal of Psychology, 30,* 341–363.

VOEKS, V. (1954). Acquisition of S-R connections: A test of Hull's and Guthrie's theories. *Journal of Experimental Psychology, 47,* 137–147.

WADDINGTON, C. H. (1968). The theory of evolution today. In A. Koestler & J. R. Smythies (Eds.), *Beyond reductionism.* New York: Macmillan.

WAGNER, A. (1978). Expectancies and the priming of STM. In S. Hulse, H. Fowler, and W. Honig (Eds.), *Cognitive processes in animal behavior.* Hillsdale, NJ: Lawrence Erlbaum.

WALLACE, A. R. (1980). On the tendency of species to depart indefinitely from the original type. Reprinted in A. C. Brackman, *A delicate arrangement.* New York: Times Books. (Originally published, 1858.)

WARREN, J. M., & NONNEMAN, A. J. (1976). The search in cerebral dominance in monkeys. In Harnad et al.

WARREN, W. H., NICHOLAS, D. W., & TRABASSO, T. (1979). Event chains and inferences in understanding narratives. In R. O. Freedle (Ed.), *New directions in discourse processing.* Norwood, NJ: Ablex.

WASER, P. M., & WILEY, R. H. (1979). Mechanisms and evolution of spacing in animals. In P. Marler & J. G. Vanderbergh (Eds.), *Handbook of behavioral neurobiology* (Vol. 3): *Social behavior and communication.* New York: Plenum.

WASHBURN, S. L. (1981). Language and the fossil record. *Anthropology UCLA, 7,* 231–238.

WASON, P. C. (1965). The context of plausible denial. *Journal of Verbal Learning and Verbal Behavior, 4,* 7–11.

WASON, P. C., & JOHNSON-LAIRD, P. N. (1972). *Psychology of reasoning.* Cambridge, MA: Harvard University Press.

WASSERMAN, E., NELSON, K., & LAREW, M. (1980). Memory for sequences of stimuli and responses. *Journal of the Experimental Analysis of Behavior, 34,* 49–60.

WATSON, J. (1930). *Behaviorism.* New York: Norton.

WATSON, J., & RAYNER, R. (1920). Conditioned emotional reactions. *Journal of Experimental Psychology, 3,* 1–14.

WATT, W. C. (1970). On two hypotheses concerning psycholinguistics. In Hayes.

WEINER, H. (1970). Instructional control of human operant responding during extinction following fixed-ratio conditioning. *Journal of the Experimental Analysis of Behavior, 13,* 391–394.

WEINER, S. L. & GOODENOUGH, D. R. (1977). A move toward a psychology of conversation. In R. O. Freedle (Eds.), *Discourse production and comprehension.* Norwood, NJ: Ablex.

WELLS, B. W. P. (1980). *Personality and heredity.* London: Longman.

WELLS, G. L., LINDSAY, R. C. L., & TOUSIGNANT, J. P. (1980). Effects of expert psychological advice on human performance in judging the validity of eyewitness testimony. *Law and Human Behavior, 4,* 275–285.

WELLS, G. L., & LOFTUS, E. F. (EDS.). (1983). *Eyewitness testimony: psychological perspectives.* New York: Cambridge University Press.

WERNER, H. (1957). The concept of development from a comparative and organismic point of view. In D. Harris (Ed.) *The concept of development.* Minneapolis, MN: University of Minnesota Press.

WERNER, H. (1978). *Developmental processes* (2 Vols.). S. S. Barten & M. B. Franklin (Eds.). New York: International Universities Press.

WEST-EBERHARD, M. J. (1982). Intragroup selection and the evolution of insect societies. In Alexander and Tinkle.

WEXLER, K., & CULICOVER, P. W. (1980). *Formal principles of language acquisition.* Cambridge, MA: MIT Press.

WHEELER, D. D. (1970). Processes in word recognition. *Cognitive Psychology, 1,* 59–85.

WHITEMAN, M. F. (Ed.). (1981). *Variation in writing: Functional and linguistic-cultural differences.* Hillsdale, NJ: Lawrence Erlbaum.

WHITING, J., & CHILD, I. (1953). *Child training and personality.* New Haven: Yale University Press.

WICKENS, D. (1938). The transference of conditioned excitation and conditioned inhibition from one muscle group to the antagonistic muscle group. *Journal of Experimental Psychology 22,* 101–123.

WICKLER, W. (1973). *The sexual code,* Garden City, NY: Anchor Books.

WIEGALE, T. (ED.) (1982). *Biology and the social sciences: An emerging revolution.* Boulder, CO: Westview Press.

WILCOXON, H., DRAGOIN, E., & KRAL, P. (1972). Illness-induced aversion in rats & quail. In Seligman & Hager.

WILLIAMS, G. C. (1980). Kin selection and the paradox of sexuality. In Barlow and Silverberg.

WILSON, E. O. (1975). *Sociobiology*. Cambridge, MA: Harvard University Press.

WILSON, E. O. (1975a). *Sociobiology: The new synthesis* (abridged ed.). Cambridge MA: Harvard University Press, 1980.

WILSON, E. O. (1975b). For sociobiology. Reprinted in Caplan (1978).

WILSON, E. O. (1979). *On human nature*. New York: Bantam Books.

WILSON, E. O. (1980). *Sociobiology: The new synthesis* (Abridged ed.). Cambridge, MA: Harvard University Press. (Originally published, 1975).

WINGFIELD, A., & BYRNES, D. L. (1981). *The psychology of human memory*. New York: Academic Press.

WINOKUR, S. (1976). *A primer of verbal behavior: An operant view*. Englewood Cliffs, NJ: Prentice-Hall.

WISPE, L. (Ed.). (1978). *Altruism, sympathy and helping*. New York: Academic Press.

WISPE, L. G., & THOMPSON, J. N. (EDS.). (1976). The war between the words: Biological *vs.* social evolution and some related issues. *American Psychologist, 31,* 341–384.

WITKIN, H. A., & GOODENOUGH, D. R. (1981). *Cognitive styles: Essence and origins. Psychological Issues,* Monograph 51. New York: International Universities Press.

WODEHOUSE, P. G. (1940). *Eggs, beans, and crumpets*. New York: Doubleday, Doran.

WOLF, T. (1976). A cognitive model of musical sight-reading. *Journal of Psycholinguistic Research, 5, 143–171.*

WOLL, S. B., WEEKS, D. G., FRAPS, C. L., PENDERGRASS, J., & VANDERPLAS, M.A. (1980). Role of sentence context in the encoding of trait descriptors. *Journal of Personality and Social Psychology, 39,* 59–68.

WOLL, S., & YOPP, H. (1978). The role of context and inference in the comprehension of social action. *Journal of Experimental Social Psychology, 14,* 351–362.

WOODRUFF, D. S. (1983). A review of aging and cognitive processes. *Research on Aging, 5,* 139–153.

WOODS, B. T. (1980). Observations on the neurological basis for initial language acquisition. In Caplan.

WRANGHAM, R. W. (1982). Mutualism, kinship and social evolution. In King's College Sociobiology Group (Eds.), *Current problems in sociobiology*. Cambridge, UK: Cambridge University Press.

WREN, T. (1982). Social learning theory, self-regulation and morality. *Ethics, 92,* 409–424.

WUNDT, W. (1973). *The language of gestures*. The Hague: Mouton.

WYER, R. S., & CARLSTON, D. A. (EDS.). (1979). *Social cognition, inference, and attribution*. Hillsdale, NJ: Lawrence Erlbaum.

WYERS, E. J., ADLER, H. E., CARPEN, K., CHISZAR, D., DEMAREST, J., FLANAGAN, O. J., VON GLASERSFELD, E., GLICKMAN, S. E., MASON, W. A., MENZEL, E. W., & TOBACH, E. (1980). The sociobiological challenge to psychology: on the proposal to 'cannibalize' comparative psychology. *American Psychologist 35,* 955–979.

YATES, A. (1980). *Biofeedback and the modification of behavior*. New York: Plenum.

YATES, F. (1966). *The art of memory*. Chicago: University of Chicago Press.

YARMEY, A. D. (1979). *The psychology of eyewitness testimony*. New York: Free Press.

YENI-KOMSHIAN, G. H., KAVANAUGH, J. F., & FERGUSON, C. A. (EDS.). (1980). *Child phonology* (Vol. 2): *Perception*. New York: Academic Press.

YERKES, R., & MORGULIS, S. (1909). The method of Pavlov in animal psychology. *Psychological Bulletin, , 257–273.*

YOUNG, J. (1970). *Mind, brain and adaptation in the nineteenth century*. Oxford: Oxford University Press.

YOUNG, R. M. (1976). *Seriation by children: An artificial intelligence analysis of a Piagetian task*. Basel, Switzerland: Birkhouser.

ZAHAVI, A. (1975). Mate selection—a selection for a handicap. *Journal of Theoretical Biology, 53,* 205–214.

ZECHMEISTER, E. B., & NYBERG, S. E. (1982). *Human memory*. Monterey, CA: Brooks/Cole.

INDEX